Human Learning

David L. Horton
University of Maryland

Thomas W. Turnage
Iowa State University

Prentice-Hall, Inc., Englewood Cliffs, New Jersey

Library of Congress Cataloging in Publication Data

HORTON, DAVID L.
    Human learning. See slip.

    (Prentice-Hall series in experimental psychology)
    Bibliography: p. 451–484.
    Includes index.
    1. Learning, Psychology of.   I. Turnage, Thomas W.,
(date)   joint author.   II. Title.
LB1051.H7895   153.1'5   75-25655
ISBN   0-13-445312-3

Prentice-Hall Series in Experimental Psychology
James J. Jenkins, Editor

Prentice-Hall International, Inc., *London*
Prentice-Hall of Australia, Pty. Ltd., *Sydney*
Prentice-Hall of Canada, Ltd., *Toronto*
Prentice-Hall of India Private Limited, *New Delhi*
Prentice-Hall of Japan, Inc., *Tokyo*
Prentice-Hall of Southeast Asia (Pte.) Ltd., *Singapore*

To

Darlene
Janet
Christopher
Jackie
Leslie
T. J.

Contents

v

CONCLUDING REMARKS

Preface

SEVERAL YEARS AGO James J. Jenkins approached us about the possibility of writing a textbook on human learning for Prentice-Hall. We all agreed on the need for a general text, because the field has expanded and changed quite remarkably over the past two decades. However, the very nature of these developments made us hesitant about accepting the task. No text reasonably could cover the entire field, and diverse changes still are occurring at a rapid rate. Nevertheless, we decided to make the attempt.

Our first problem was to limit our coverage in an appropriate and manageable way. For the most part we chose to emphasize verbal behavior, since it is in the realm of verbal and linguistic skills that the behavior of man is most readily distinguished from that of other organisms. Within the area of verbal behavior both learning and memory have been emphasized. We also wanted to provide coverage of the main theoretical-empirical orientations that have characterized recent work in human learning.

The first chapter introduces the text and human learning in general. Part I (Chapters 2, 3, 4, and 5) deals traditionally with human learning and memory and emphasizes the learning and retention of associations. Part II (Chapters 6, 7, and 8) covers the still developing views of human learning and memory in which man is characterized as an active coder, storer, organizer, and retriever of streams of input information. Part III (Chapters 9, 10, 11, and 12), which emphasizes the rule-governed nature of man, focuses on learning and memory in humans as reflected in man's use of language and concepts. Our conclusion, Chapter 13, reviews the major trends noted in the preceding chapters. In addition, Chapters 2 through 12 each contain a conclusion section on its respective subject.

We present a broad cross section of the theory and evidence that has been attained over much of the present century, with emphasis on recent developments. The three main parts of the book deal with relatively coherent approachs to human learning. However, the reader should note that not every chapter or subsection within a given part is equally congruent with the approach characterizing that part. This situation arises most noticeably in Chapter 8 (Part II) and Chapter 12 (Part III). It occurs because we have provided a historical perspective for each chapter. Since the approaches of Parts II and III are relatively recent, a certain incongruence may occur when important background material that is more traditional is contained in one of their chapters. Throughout we provide references both to historical and contemporary material for the student interested in reading further on a given topic.

We are indebted to many colleagues, students, and former teachers for whatever virtues this text may have. We are particularly grateful to James J. Jenkins for his comments, suggestions, and encouragement. We also thank Larry L. Jacoby for his most helpful suggestions on several chapters. Many graduate students at Maryland and Iowa State have read, criticized, and thereby improved the contents of the book. We acknowledge our debt to David L. Imhoff for his assistance in proofreading the manuscript and in checking numerous details. Several secretaries assisted in typing, but only Ruth Crovo worked on the many revisions and typed the entire final manuscript. We also owe a great deal to all those colleagues whose research and theorizing contributed to the contents of this text. Finally, we wish to thank our families, friends, and students for putting up with us while this book was being written.

David L. Horton

Thomas W. Turnage

Introduction

1

Historical Review and Perspective

IN A CERTAIN SENSE virtually everything the mature human organism does, or is capable of doing, can be viewed as a result of learning. In fact, this proposition seems so obvious that it is almost trivial to restate it except to indicate why learning has been of recognized importance throughout the history of psychology. During the period that preceded the beginnings of experimental psychology, such philosophers as Descartes, Hume, Kant, and Locke devoted considerable attention to the nature of learning and to the role it plays in man's psychological development. This concern with learning reached a position of paramount importance in experimental psychology in the first half of the twentieth century, during the Behavioristic Era. Despite this long history of systematic importance, however, a number of issues concerning the nature of learning have yet to be resolved.

Let us consider what the term *learning* means. For most people the concept of learning is one that applies in a wide variety of situations and that describes much of everyone's daily activities. We commonly recognize the role of learning during our formal education, from the beginning of elementary school through college and postgraduate training. This not only includes course information but also the more abstract activities that are involved in "learning to think and reason" as well as "learning to remember" what we have learned. Our learning experiences are not limited to the classroom, however.

We are continuously involved in learning. The young child must learn to identify objects correctly. He must learn such various skills as walking,

3

talking, and even how to tie a shoelace. As the child grows older he learns to play games and how to participate in various sports. He learns to ride a bicycle and, later, to drive a car. Throughout the developmental period the individual learns a variety of social skills as well as the attitudes and prejudices that characterize social interaction with others. Even for the adult learning continues to be a daily experience. The adult must learn his job, how to care for his home and family, and the adjustments required to live in a changing world. Nor is learning always associated with improvement or utility. Many of us acquire various tics or mannerisms that have no apparent utility. When we acquire the behaviors associated with the psychoses or neuroses, certainly no improvement is implied.

When the term *learning* is applied to these situations, it becomes clear what sense is intended when someone says that almost everything the mature human does can be regarded as a result of learning. The sense implies that learning refers to the entire set of *acquired* behaviors. Thus viewed, learning becomes virtually synonymous with any reasonably permanent changes in behavior, whether or not these changes are due to inborn characteristics, maturational processes, or the experiences of the organism. This use of the term makes it equally appropriate to say that a child *learns* to see or to walk or to swim or to speak his native language. That is, the emphasis is on a change in behavior and not on the reasons for the change. Such a definition turns out to be quite unsatisfactory for the psychologist.

Psychologists have known for some time that it is necessary to make a distinction between learning and performance. Performance is what the organism does, and from performance we can infer that learning has taken place. But obviously not everything that is learned will necessarily be demonstrated in performance. The man who is not hungry does not go to a restaurant even though he knows the location. When a child does not make his bed it does not necessarily mean that he does not know how to make it. At the very least the organism must be motivated to perform before learning can be inferred from performance. There are certain changes in behavior, however, that would not be considered results of learning. These include transient changes such as those resulting from intoxication or fatigue as well as more permanent behavior changes that might be due, for example, to injury or long-term exposure to drugs.

Although the preceding characterization of learning can be useful, and is perhaps the most precise we can offer, it still is not the type of definition most popular in psychology. More traditional definitions of learning, which still are widely employed today, not only emphasize relatively permanent changes in behavior but also stress that these changes must occur as a result of experience or practice. By implication, definitions of this type focus on the causal role of experience in learning. For example, learning to operate a typewriter or learning to play a piano requires lengthy experience and practice. An infant, however, would obviously not profit as much from practice as would an adult. Thus definitions of learning in terms of practice tend to separate the effects of experience from those effects associated with the genetic background or developmental stage of the organism.

What Is Learned? Hilgard and Bower (1966), in their definition of learning, emphasize that those changes in activity that result from maturation or native response tendencies should not be viewed as a result of learning. By native response tendencies they mean *reflexes* such as pupillary constriction to light, *tropisms* such as a moth flying into a flame, and at least some aspects of *instincts* such as the nest-building activities of birds. Although such definitions are entirely appropriate, considerable difficulty arises when we try to separate the contributions of these various causal factors or when we try to specify just *what* is learned.

Let us briefly consider some of the complexities involved in attempting to separate the effects of experience from those effects more closely connected with the structure of the organism. Before the contribution of experience can be specified, we need to know much more than we do about the structure of the organism. We need to know how man's sensory, perceptual, and cognitive systems operate—how they interact, how they naturally develop, and how they may be modified through experience. This is obviously a complex task, but without such knowledge it will be difficult to specify *what* is learned or what experience contributes to the process of learning. For example, do children discover the "sounds of speech" through experience with language, or do they acquire these sounds as a result of biological and developmental factors that determine the way speech sounds are processed? In either case, experience with language is necessary, but until more is known about the perception of speech it will not be possible to specify the precise contribution made by experience.

A somewhat similar example involves the act of walking, a skill that every normal child acquires in a relatively short time. Most psychologists consider this activity to be primarily the result of maturation. Yet some experience is necessary, and experience may be important in mastering the finer details of walking, such as those that differentiate the gait of a very young child from that of a somewhat older child. But in acquiring the gross skill of walking no special training is necessary, nor does special training seem to provide any long-lasting advantage. The point here, as in the preceding example, is that although experience is necessary for learning, it is not clear what experience contributes to learning. Does the child learn to put one foot in front of the other as a result of experience? Or does this pattern of movements naturally occur once a firm footing is provided? Perhaps experience simply provides the young child with an opportunity to adjust to the way this motor system is designed to function without contributing a great deal to the specific actions involved. Although walking may be a rather trivial example of the problem of isolating the contributions of experience, the problem is one that arises in virtually any example of acquired knowledge or skill.

The preceding discussion of the concept of learning illustrates some of the problems involved in defining *learning*. We can offer no easy solutions to these problems. In the remaining sections of this chapter we shall review some of the more important concepts of learning from a historical point of view. Our focus will be on the way such basic questions as "What is learning?" and "What is learned?" have been treated. We shall also refer to specific developments in the history of learning that are pertinent to material presented in subsequent chapters. No attempt will be made to provide a systematic review of earlier periods or specific schools of thought—such reviews can be found elsewhere (cf. Boring, 1950; Woodworth and Sheehan, 1964).

THE PRE-BEHAVIORISTIC ERA

The Philosophical Period

Historically speaking, questions about the process of learning have been basically concerned with the way an organism profits from experience and the conditions under which those profits are greatest. According to philosophers in the tradition of British associationism, when the organism is man, the "mind" comes to be "furnished" with ideas as a result of experience. For John Locke, one of the leading British philosophers, ideas were the basic units of the mind, the items of knowledge. When we analyze the contents of immediate consciousness, we find that the basic elements are ideas and that these ideas are acquired through experience. Most ideas are acquired through direct sensory experience with external objects and qualities. According to Locke, ideas acquired in this way are represented in the mind by such concepts as man, army, motion, yellow, hard, cold, bitter, and loud. This is basically an *empiricistic* position, since it states that without experience the "mind" would be void of ideas. In other words, learning is totally dependent upon experience.

Locke also suggested that there was an internal sense, involving the process of reflection, by which the mind obtains knowledge about the sources of its ideas and about its own operations. The ideas acquired in this way are represented by such concepts as perceiving, thinking, doubting, reasoning, and believing. Thus the basic units of learning, according to Locke, were ideas, and the process of learning involved experience with various aspects of the external world as well as experience with various aspects of the mind through the process of reflection. The particular theory of learning favored by Locke was *associationism*. Ideas were seen as basic elements which became organized in the mind through associations resulting from such factors as temporal or spatial contiguity of experience, frequency of experience, and similarity of experience. This theory of association, which had been in existence since the days of Aristotle, was further developed by eighteenth- and nineteenth-century British philosophers, such as James Mill and John Stuart Mill. These philosophers placed particular emphasis on the way simple ideas could be combined to form more complex ideas. As we shall see, this notion of combining elements to form more complex units had considerable influence on psychological thought in later periods.

The eighteenth-century philosopher Immanuel Kant took exception to the general position of Locke and the other associationists that the mind was a passive tablet upon which experience was written. In contrast to their *empiricist* viewpoint, Kant reestablished the earlier philosophical conception of *innate* operations of the mind. According to Kant, objects that occur together in our perception do so not because they are closely related in space or time (the associationists' principle of contiguity) but because the mind must react to them in that way. For Kant, the notions of space and time were a priori intuitions and were not part of the external, objective world. Objects in themselves are not temporally or spatially related but are naturally put in temporal or spatial order because of these intuitions. He also stated that certain categories of understanding, such as unity, totality, reality, existence, necessity, and cause-effect, were not acquired through experience but also represented innate ways of structuring experience. Kant's assertion that the mind has innate (unlearned) ways in which it organizes incoming information is a *nativistic* position. To some extent it avoids many of the questions concerning what is learned by reducing the systematic importance of learning through an emphasis on complex "prewired" conceptualizations.

Despite the obvious disagreements between the historical "nativist" and "empiricist" positions, there were certain areas of overlap with respect to the studying of learning. The most obvious area of agreement concerns the view that ideas constitute the basic units, that is, *what* is learned. Both positions focus on "impressions of the mind," some or all of which may be dependent on experience for initial learning. Of course, there was a divergence of opinion about the relative importance of learning. But early nativists and empiricists generally agreed that self-observation of one's mental activities was a perfectly valid way of studying the ideational and sensory events, irrespective of how the items of consciousness were incorporated into the mind.

The Structuralist Period

The points of disagreement between the nativist and empiricist positions provided theoretical issues that have persisted well into the twentieth century. In the latter part of the nineteenth century, however, the points of agreement between these positions provided the cornerstone of the newly founded experimental psychology. The exact beginning date for the new psychology is not critical for our purposes, although it is usually given as 1879 when Wilhelm Wundt founded the experimental laboratory at Leipzig. The psychology developed by Wundt and his associates came to be known as *structuralism,* since the major emphasis was on the structure of the mind.

According to Wundt, the subject matter of psychology was restricted to the immediate phenomena of conscious experience, and the approach to follow in studying these phenomena was one that would afford direct contact with experience. An intimate part of the new psychology was the emphasis upon self-observation under specified experimental conditions. In fact this approach to experimentation, which is better known as *trained introspection,* became so intimate a part of structuralism that many psychologists refer to this era as the *introspectionistic* period.

As Wundt saw it, the problem for psychology was the analysis of conscious processes into elements and the establishment of laws governing the connection of these elements. Locke's notion of an inner sense of reflection was rejected. Wundt, however, did hold to the view that psychology is concerned both with "outer experience," which refers to the perception of objects, and with "inner experience," which refers to the consciously subjective experience of feeling. While altering Locke's view of basic elements, the *what* of learning, from mere ideas to sensations, images, and feelings, the structuralists still accepted the British associationists' view of learning. Simple elements were acquired through experience and were combined into more complex units by means of classical laws of association such as contiguity, similarity, and frequency. The task of the trained introspectionist was, therefore, the analysis of conscious experience into its basic elements and the synthesis of basic elements into more complex wholes.

Although structuralism had considerable influence on psychology well into the twentieth century, a number of philosophical and experimental difficulties soon arose with the introspective study of consciousness. For example, the work of the psychoanalyst Sigmund Freud came to public attention around the turn of the century. His work suggested that a considerable portion of mental content, and by implication much of what is learned, was unconscious. Freud's general thesis was that the study of unconscious processes was essential to understanding the psychological nature of man. Therefore it seemed that other, nonintrospective, techniques would have to be developed for the study of such mental phenomena, since self-observation was clearly an inadequate procedure for studying the unconscious.

As it turned out, similar perplexities became evident even in the study of apparently conscious processes. In Bavaria the work of psychologists associated with the *Würzburg* school indicated, contrary to previous opinion, that much of our everyday mental activity involves *imageless* thought. For example, a person might lift two weights and judge which was heavier. There was usually no lack of conscious contents such as sensations and images, but introspection typically failed to reveal any clear-cut process of judgment. The judgments were made and were usually correct, but the person making the judgments did not know how they came to mind. Such results appeared to contradict the widely held belief that the laws of thought were consistent with the laws of logic. On the contrary it seemed, according to introspection, that unconscious and hence irrational trains of thought could lead to rational solution of problems. The implication that much of thinking and learning was devoid of imagery or conscious content was momentous for scientists whose major assumption had been that the analysis of such processes depends on the introspective study of images and ideas.

It thus became evident around the turn of the century that some operations of the mind were, in a most exasperating manner, just out of view of the prying eye of inward reflection. The inescapable implication for the study of human learning was that either new methods would have to be developed or the science of psychology would have to be restricted to the conscious components of mental life. To follow the latter course would greatly limit the domain of study with the adult human, and the domain would be almost nonexistent with the young child or the nonverbal lower organism. One consequence of these considerations, at least in part, was the development in the United States of the so-called *functionalist* school of psychology. The functionalists accepted the basic premises of structural psychology, but they also provided additions to them. Not only was trained introspection an acceptable psychological method but so also was direct observation of the behavior of other organisms.

The functionalists, influenced by the Darwinian theory of evolution, sought to study the *adaptive functions* of mental processes and behavior, not just their structure. Since their approach made room for introspective analysis as well as the study of nonverbal organisms, the functionalists provided some continuity between the developing field of comparative psychology and the psychology of structuralists such as Wundt. This continuity, which lasted only a short time, was shattered by the advent of behaviorism. Before turning to this development we shall consider the contributions of another prominent psychologist who was active during the structuralist period.

The Study of Human Learning. Even before introspective psychology was well established, Hermann Ebbinghaus, a German scholar, began a series of systematic studies of higher mental functions that was to influence the psychology of human learning for more than half a century. Ebbinghaus was to accomplish this by an *objective* attack on one of the most important strongholds of the human mind, according to the philosophical tradition of his day—the process of memory. He specifically recognized that memory was a complex, multifaceted process and that such factors as individual differences as well as variations in content, meaning, attention, interest, practice, defects in knowledge, and time all played a role in the memorial process.

Ebbinghaus (1885) divided memory into three separate classes. One class of memories included those that could be *called back* into consciousness even though such memories were accompanied by other images into the light of consciousness. That is, during the attempt to recall a particular experience, other memories are recollected which may be totally unrelated to the memory in question. A second class included those images and ideas that "spontaneously" return to consciousness, which we then recognize as characterizing a previously experienced mental state. As with the preceding class of memories, careful observation convinced Ebbinghaus that these processes were regular, not random, and that they could be described by the laws of association. The third class of memories was composed of unconscious mental events. In a manner reminiscent of Freud's later writings, Ebbinghaus stated that "most of these experiences remain concealed from consciousness and yet produce an effect which is significant and which authenticates their previous existence" (1885, p. 2).

Ebbinghaus was mainly influenced by the British associationists and the psychophysics of Gustav Fechner (1860). From the British philosophers he adopted the view that contents of the mind, and hence memory, could be described in terms of the principles of association. From Fechner he accepted the importance of systematic measurement in the study of mental phenomena. Although Ebbinghaus did not employ Fechner's methods as such, since they were not appropriate to his particular interests, he did invent new techniques that emphasized precise measurement. Thus Ebbinghaus adopted the empiricist-associationist view of learning while rejecting the introspective method as the only approach to the study of learning and memory.

Ebbinghaus was interested in examining the *acquisition* and *retention* of associations in the laboratory, in contrast to previous methods that took associations already in the mind and then attempted to infer how such associations had come about. To do this, however, he needed a unit that was relatively free of prior associations or at least low in associational content. He therefore invented nonsense syllables, combinations of letters that had no obvious linguistic meaning. He then asked questions such as the following.

1. How does repetition of material influence the subsequent recall of a series of nonsense syllables?
2. How many syllables can be recalled after one presentation? (In moddern terms this would be called the *immediate memory span.*)
3. Is strict contiguity necessary for associations to develop between items, or do associations form between items that are temporarily separated?
4. Does reordering of the items in a previously learned serial list (*method of derived lists*) have any effect on the learning of the new list?

Ebbinghaus's measure of retention and transfer is called a *savings score,* and it is based on the time taken to learn an original list compared with the time taken to relearn the same list (as in retention) or to learn a different list (as in transfer). In contrast to the introspective method, this measure provides public, not private, information and in principle allows for the reflection of both conscious and unconscious memorial processes.

Ebbinghaus provided a systematic, objective approach to the study of human learning and memory at a time when experimental psychology was just beginning. His approach to the study of memory anticipated the methodological orientation of the subsequent behavioristic period. A careful reading of his classic work on memory, however, indicates that he did not reject mental phenomena as proper objects for psychological study, as did the behaviorists. Thus, while providing an objective base for mentalistic psychology, Ebbinghaus also introduced a methodological framework that was quite compatible with the behavioristic psychology of the twentieth century and that characterized much of the study of human learning and memory for over fifty years.

THE BEHAVIORISTIC PERIOD

According to Thomas Kuhn (1962), certain shifts in direction and goals—*scientific revolutions*—periodically occur in the development of a science. These revolutions involve changes in pretheoretical orientations that have major implications for both the kinds of theory and the type of methodology that will be considered. Such changes occurred in psychology with the advent of behaviorism, whose major pretheoretical views included the assertion that mental events were not proper objects for psychologists to study. Instead, the focus was on behavior. Subjective reports stemming from introspective analysis were disclaimed in favor of objective behavioral measures. An effort was made to shift psychology from a science of mental life to a science of behavior, and, for a while at least, man became mindless in the eyes of the behaviorist.

The motivations and reasons for the behavioristic revolution involved both content and methods. We noted previously that a considerable restriction in the domain of psychology was implied by the structuralist orientation. This emphasis on the introspective analysis of conscious mental states left little room in psychology for the study of nonverbal organisms or unconscious processes. Even the functionalists, who were more flexible on this point, thought animal psychologists should translate observed behavior into the vague terms of inferred consciousness. This constraint was objectionable to many comparative psychologists and particularly to John B. Watson. In submitting his proposal for a new "objective psychology," Watson (1913) argued that the study of behavior itself was both interesting and important and that psychology should not be restricted to the study of mental phenomena.

Watson also pointed out the notorious inconsistency of experimental reports obtained by means of introspection. He noted that such inconsistencies were typically attributed to the inadequate training of observers, whereas similar discrepancies in the natural sciences of chemistry and physics would be attributed to differences in the experimental conditions. In addition, most psychologists in the United States considered the introspective method to have failed at Würzburg.

As an alternative to introspective psychology, Watson proposed a strictly objective psychology in which human and animal behavior were to receive equal emphasis and in which neither mental states nor introspective reports had any place. Watson proposed to define psychology as a science of behavior whose orientation centered upon procedures for investigating the conditions that influence behavior.

As is typical with revolutions in science, the behavioristic revolution was accompanied by major changes in the methods for experimentation. In large part these methods were derived from the work of Pavlov (1927) and Thorndike (1898). Although neither of these pioneers in animal learning was actually part of the behavioristic movement, their methods and theoretical formulations were to have a profound influence on the psychology of learning.

Pavlov and the Conditioned Reflex

Ivan Petrovich Pavlov, the eminent Russian physiologist, was awarded the Nobel Prize in 1904 for his work on the digestive glands. However, it was not this work that made Pavlov an important theorist in psychology, but rather his later investigations of something he had observed during the original experimental program.

What Pavlov noted was that the dogs he was using in his experiments salivated not only to food placed in their mouths, a natural response if the dog was hungry, but also to the sight of the food dish or at the sound of the approaching attendant who brought the food. Now, perhaps common sense would tell one that the dog "naturally" would learn to associate the various stimuli accompanying food with the food itself, and let it go at that. On the other hand, if one were as ingenious as Pavlov, one might perceive this as an important scientific observation with a number of intriguing, sophisticated implications:

1. To the extent that the salivary response could be associated with previously neutral stimulus events, it involved higher cortical activity rather than an unlearned reflex. Therefore it presumably reflected "higher nervous activity" of one form or another.
2. It was a readily measurable response, not a covert response whose detection depended on the unreliable methods of introspection previously used by psychologists.
3. The systematic investigation of such a *conditioned response* provided a means of developing a true physiology of the cerebral hemispheres in their natural state, i.e., without surgical intervention.

The development of a physiology of the cerebral hemispheres was of great importance to Pavlov. Not only was he aware of the meager state of physiological knowledge concerning the hemispheres but he also seemed somewhat chagrined by the observation that the "study" of the hemispheres had been relegated to another discipline, which he perceived to be somewhat less than scientific—namely, psychology. Pavlov recognized that the cerebral hemispheres were of unquestioned importance in man, and even in the dog they subserved extremely complicated activities such as watching, hunting and other duties that dogs had been taught for centuries. In fact, the almost complete dependence of these activities on the cerebral hemispheres in the dog made this organism particularly suitable for study.

Pavlov realized that extrapolation of data from lower animals to man's mind was risky business. However, he also believed that the more complicated higher activity in man rested on the same physiological foundations as those found in dogs and other animals. In this regard, Pavlov believed that he had discovered a method that offered much hope in the understanding and treatment of psychological disturbances, and also a method for ferreting out subtle relationships between the *conscious* and *unconscious* process of the mind. For example, Pavlov believed his experiments indicated that diverse units of neural activity could become unconsciously interrelated during the conditioning process. He suggested that although the actual synthesizing activity involved might never enter our field of consciousness, such synthesis could nevertheless take place. Under favorable conditions the results of this synthesis might enter the field of consciousness as an already formed link, thus seeming to originate spontaneously.

Pavlov's Conditioning System. In demonstrating the learning of a conditioned response, Pavlov placed the dog in a restraining device, presented the dog with some neutral stimulus such as the sound of a metronome, and then immediately placed meat powder directly into the dog's mouth. The sound of the metronome is the *conditioned stimulus* (CS), the meat powder is the *unconditioned stimulus* (US), and salivation to the meat powder in the mouth is the *unconditioned reponse* (UR). If the dog comes to salivate to the CS before the meat powder is presented, or if he salivates to the CS when the meat powder is omitted on a given trial, such salivation is called the *conditioned response* (CR). Thus the demonstration of salivation to both the sound of the metronome and the meat powder is an empirical example of a conditioned reflex.

The very fact that conditioning could be demonstrated convinced Pavlov of the existence of an important brain state of *excitation*. In addition, he supposed that there was a corresponding brain state of *inhibition*. This state was suggested by the finding that a CR could be disrupted by extraneous stimuli such as a sudden noise or that the continued presentation of the CS without the US led to a diminution of the CR. Therefore, he theorized that there were two opposed brain states, excitation and inhibition, which were the basic processes of conditioning. These master concepts or balancing processes began to be incorporated systematically into emerging *psychological* learning theories, especially those following in the behavioristic tradition. The subsequent use of these concepts by behaviorists, who emphasized only observables, was somewhat paradoxical, since they were originally viewed as physiological processes mostly by analogy (cf. Woodworth and Sheehan, 1964).

Pavlov and his associates also noticed that the development of every conditioned response seemed to be accompanied by what was called a "period of generalization." Thus, if the CS was a tone of a given frequency, tones of other frequencies spontaneously acquired the properties of a CS. The CR to these other tones varied in strength as a function of the difference in frequency between the tone in question and the original CS. The development of such "accessory reflexes," named *generalization of stimuli* by Pavlov, is illustrated in Figure 1.1. This finding had a great deal of significance for Pavlov's conditioning system as well as for theoretical models of learning that were to be built on conditioning principles.

Pavlov interpreted the fact of generalization of stimuli as having obvious biological significance for the animal's survival. As an example, he noted that natural stimuli that have survival value for an organism are not constant but range over a set of values. Thus the defensive flight of the zebra when it hears the roar of the lioness may be triggered over wide variations in pitch, strength, and timbre of the roar. On the other hand, constant flight to any sound, the extreme of generalization, would have little survival value and would soon exhaust the zebra completely. There-

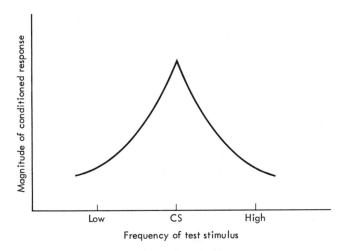

Figure 1.1 Illustration of a generalization gradient following conditioning to one particular stimulus (the CS).

fore, the organism must be reasonably accurate in *discrimination of stimuli* as well.

The question next considered is how the organism comes to make appropriate and relatively precise discriminations among stimuli varying in degrees of "significance." Pavlov discussed two general methods of experimentation. The first of these involved presentation of the CS (tone) with the US (meat powder) numerous times. The second involved presentation of two or more stimuli (tones), with only one of these (the CS) being accompanied by the US. Thus, the CS was contrasted with the other stimuli that were never accompanied by the US. As it turned out, the first method was very inefficient. Even though the CS was paired with the US over a thousand times, the dog never achieved an absolute discrimination. The second method, however, the *method of contrast,* was quite efficient and produced precise and rapid discriminations in the dog.

A classic demonstration of the use of the method of contrast was performed in Pavlov's laboratory by Shenger-Krestovnikova. This demonstration had a number of exciting implications, both for Pavlov's general theoretical model and for specific conceptualizations of conditioning factors in pathological disturbances. In this experiment a circle was projected on a screen in front of the dog, and this CS was always followed by feeding. After the salivary reflex (CR) had been firmly established to the circle, differentiation training was begun with the CS remaining the circle and the contrasted stimulus being an ellipse. Presentation of the ellipse, of course, was never followed by food. Differentiation of the circle and the ellipse was quickly established. Then the shape of the ellipse was changed by stages until it slowly began to approximate the circle, with discrimination training continuing throughout. Finally, when the ellipse was very close to the circle in shape, the dog failed to develop a discrimination, even after three weeks of training. Clearly, the limit of the dog's discrimination capacity had been reached, which was to be expected at some point. Other interesting aspects of the experiment, however, which had not been anticipated, seemed to have relevance to pathological disturbances of personality.

As differentiation training proceeded unsuccessfully over the last three weeks of the experiment, discrimination behavior began to deteriorate until it finally disappeared altogether. Meanwhile the dog's general behavior underwent a series of bizarre changes. The dog, which had previously been a calm animal, tore at the restraining apparatus and began to squeal and wriggle about. At the beginning of the day, the dog began to bark violently as it was being taken into the experimental room. In short, as Pavlov describes the situation, the animal presented all the symptoms of *acute neurosis.* It was obvious to him that under certain conditions the clashing of excitation with inhibition could lead to a pathological disturbance of the nervous system. We are not to conclude from this example, however, that all discrimination training led to such unusual behavior, since it did not in most instances. But Pavlov did find that under unusually stressful circumstances, the antagonistic processes of inhibition and excitation could literally be placed "out of balance," with the result being a pathological state.

Thorndike and the Law of Effect

Pavlov (1927) notes that he was influenced not only by Darwin's theory of evolution, which suggested a sound basis for a comparative physiology of behavior, but also by the work of the American psychologist Edward Lee Thorndike (1874–1949). Pavlov explicitly recognizes Thorndike's work as preceding his own, but the theoretical focus of the two scientists was somewhat different. The basic processes in Pavlov's system could be characterized as the *law of excitation* and the *law of inhibition,* whereas the most basic principle in Thorndike's system was the *law of effect.* This principle held that action that leads immediately to pleasure becomes habit, whereas action that leads to pain does not become habit.

Philosophical Origins of the Law of Effect. Boring (1950) notes that at the turn of the eighteenth century the great motivational theory was *hedonism,* the theory that *human* behavior arises out of the interaction of a desire to gain pleasure and to avoid pain. In a sense this was the culmination of various streams of philosophical and religious thought that characterized the whys and wherefores of man's behavior as involving the fact that, corporeally and biologically, man is gratified by pleasure and grieved by pain.

Boring notes that Troland had distinguished three varieties of hedonism—hedonism of the present, hedonism of the past, and hedonism of the future. He states that it was the hedonism of the future that Freud took as the major determinant of purpose and motive, whereas the behavioristic psychologists rejected the future and looked to the past for the determinants of behavior. Thus it seems historically and philosophically appropriate to find a formalization of hedonistic principles in theories of human learning such as that of Thorndike. In a sense the advent of such theorizing could be described as involving a posthedonistic view of man, extended by Darwinian principles to a similar view of animals.

Thorndike's Learning System. Thorndike's theoretical system was described in his doctoral dissertation (1898), *Animal Intelligence: An Experimental Study of the Associative Process in Animals.* For studying the course of learning and problem solving in his various animal subjects, Thorndike developed the puzzle box. An animal confined in this apparatus could release itself *if* it performed some simple act like pulling a cord. In general, not only would the animal release itself, it could also get to food placed just outside the puzzle box. Thorndike's general procedure was to place the subject in the box and then carefully observe the behavior of the animal as it attempted to master the problem. The basic theoretical structure of Thorndike's system seems to be best characterized by citing him directly:

> When put into the box the cat would show signs of discomfort and an impulse to escape from confinement (not a reaction to the sight of food, but only a blind attempt to escape). It tries to squeeze through any opening; it claws and bites at the bars and wire; it thrusts its paws out through any opening and claws at everything it reaches; it continues its efforts when it strikes anything loose and shaky; it may claw at things within the box. *It does not pay very much attention to the food outside,* but seems simply to strive instinctively to escape confinement . . .
> Whether the impulse to struggle be due to an instinctive reaction to confinement or to an association, it is likely to succeed in letting the cat out of the box. The cat that is clawing all over the box in her *impulsive* struggle will *probably* claw the string or loop or button so as to open the door. And *gradually* all the other nonsuccessful impulses will be stamped out and the particular impulse leading to the successful act will be stamped in by the resulting pleasure until, after many trials, the cat will, when put in the box, immediately claw the loop or button in a definite way (Thorndike, 1898, pp. 13 ff., italics added).

And there we have the Thorndikian doctrine of "learning by trial and error," with no purpose or foresight postulated as a supporting mechanism. There was only the "stamping in" of successful responses or impulses and the "stamping out" of unsuccessful ones. Furthermore, the gradual decrease in the time required to get out of the box indicated "the absence of reasoning . . . the wearing smooth of a path in the brain, not the decision of a rational consciousness" (1898, p. 45). Thus the core of Thorndike's theory was the automatic strengthening of specific connections to action, without intervening conscious influence. Insight was not denied by Thorndike, especially in humans, but it was not awarded a special place in the theoretical scheme of things. In fact, it was to be best understood by the same associative laws that applied to "trial-and-error situations"—for example, an experienced cat behaved "insightfully" in the box. Thorndike apparently left it to others to specify, if they could, the manner in which habit and insight are related.

Like Pavlov, Thorndike perceived the laws of learning to be applicable to humans, as was made clear by a subsequent period of some thirty years of research and writing in the area of educational psychology. Thorndike believed that although the simple semimechanical laws revealed in animal learning were much more complex in the advanced stages of human learning, they were nevertheless fundamental laws of human learning as well. He went on to state that there was nothing magical or unique in man's nature that would result in his behaving in an unpredictable way when confronted with a new situation. Indeed, he argued that nowhere is the bondage of prior habit more clearly revealed than when a new situation appears.

In its original form the law of effect, as stated by Thorndike, was symmetrical. Rewards stamped in connections between stimuli and responses, and punishment stamped them out. In work with human subjects, Thorndike equated reward with symbolic reinforcement, as when telling a subject his response was *right*. Symbolic punishment, then, might involve telling a subject his response was *wrong*. A series of studies with human subjects, however, convinced him that although the effect of reward was the stamping in of responses, the effect of punishment was clearly *not* the stamping out of responses (Thorndike, 1932). He revised his position with respect to punishment, leaving the asymmetrical law of effect as the basic concept of his learning theory.

Critical support of this law, from Thorndike's point of view, was the demonstration in human learning of the *spread of effect*. These experiments indicated that the influence of reward acts not only on rewarded responses but also on other responses occurring in close proximity. The closer a response was to one that was rewarded, the stronger the spread of effect. This appeared to be the case even with incorrect responses. Critics of Thorndike's position were quick to look for flaws in the experiments demonstrating the spread of effect, since general acceptance of its validity meant that blind, automatic, and unconscious learning might be basic to human knowledge.

Thorndike's studies of trial-and-error learning, including the law of effect, had a number of exciting and important implications for the form a comprehensive theory of human learning might take. In fact, the trial-and-error situation, which is better known as the instrumental conditioning paradigm, has provided the primary context for investigating the influence of reinforcement.

Conditioning and Learning

The theoretical and empirical contributions of Pavlov and Thorndike had a profound influence on the development of psychology during the first half of the twentieth century. Watson's view of learning was largely based on Pavlov's work in classical conditioning, and the theoretical offerings of most psychologists during the early part of the behavioristic period were substantially influenced by the discoveries made in both classical and instrumental conditioning. It was not until the early 1930s, however, that the psychology of learning became almost synonymous with conditioning.

From the early 1930s to the early 1950s learning theory was almost exclusively based upon concepts derived from instrumental and classical conditioning. One of the major theorists during this so-called neobehaviorist period was Clark L. Hull (1884–1952). The key concept in Hull's theory of learning was *habit,* and the strength of a habit was viewed as being a direct function of the number of times a contiguous stimulus and response had been followed by reinforcement. Pavlov's learning situation, the *classical conditioning* paradigm, was seen as a special instance of habit being strengthened by the successive application of a reinforcer (food) correlated with the pairing of a stimulus (the CS) and a response (the CR). Thorndike's learning situation, the *trial-and-error* paradigm, could be understood in the same manner—the subject makes a response in the presence of some stimulus, and *if* this event is correlated with reinforcement, *then* there is an automatic increment in habit strength. In Hull's system *what the organism learned* was a stimulus-response association called a "habit," and the major conditions of learning were the contiguity of stimulus and response events and reinforcement. In fact, reinforcement was so important in Hull's theory that it was assumed that learning could not take place without it (cf. Hull, 1952).

Other prominent theorists of this period were less inclined to agree with Hull concerning the primary importance of reinforcement. Edwin R. Guthrie (1886–1959) argued that contiguity alone was sufficient for learning, although he shared Hull's view of what is learned, namely, stimulus-response associations. Edward C. Tolman (1886–1959), while also advocating a behavioristic orientation, took issue with Hull on several points. Tolman held that there were various types of learning and that one important type was what has been referred to as stimulus-stimulus learning, or what leads to what. For example, in Pavlov's experiment the dog learns that one stimulus (the CS) is a sign of another stimulus (the food) that is to follow. It does not learn a stimulus-response connection. Even in the instrumental situation, where a response must occur before the second stimulus (the food) can be obtained, Tolman often emphasized stimulus-stimulus learning rather than stimulus-response learning. The learning of such stimulus-stimulus relationships did not, in his view, require reinforcement, although reward could serve to emphasize the relationship for the subject.

Despite disagreements concerning the role of reinforcement as well as other learning principles, most theorists of this period were in substantial accord concerning the basic aspects of learning and the central importance of instrumental and classical conditioning. This agreement on the importance of conditioning principles, regardless of theoretical persuasion on other matters, is clearly exemplified in the position taken by B. F. Skinner. Skinner raised strenuous objection to much of the theorizing about the process of learning while basing his system almost exclusively on the facts of instrumental learning. In fact, this general emphasis on the conditioning paradigms too often resulted in a situation in which there was no clear disentanglement of the paradigm for experimentation from the structure of theory. The major theoretical concepts employed arose for the most part from those used to describe conditioning, and the view was widely held, at least implicitly, that if an organism can learn in a conditioning situation, learning *must* be based on conditioning principles.

As for the general concept of learning, the emphasis on psychology as a science of behavior clearly implied that mentalistic terms and concepts were to be avoided. It is not surprising to find that learning was defined as ". . . a change in performance which occurs under the conditions of practice" in one of the major textbooks on human learning (McGeoch and Irion, 1952). That is, apart from the distinction between learning and performance, the term *learning* was intended to mean little more than what the objective, public observations of performance indicated. There was fairly general agreement that associations between stimuli and responses constituted what the organism learned, and complicated behaviors such as problem solving or transfer to novel situations were presumably the result of combining associations that had been acquired previously by the organism.

Behaviorism and Human Learning. The major impetus for the behavioristic movement came from animal psychologists, and it was not until well after Watson's initial proposals concerning the nature of psychology that the field of human learning was materially influenced by behavioristic views. During the early part of the twentieth century most of the work in human learning and memory followed the initial lines introduced by Ebbinghaus and developed subsequently by others. Despite this methodological orientation's compatibility with behaviorism, it was not until the 1930s that psychologists concerned with human learning abandoned mentalistic concepts in favor of a more behavioral approach. Even then, most investigators of human learning followed a sort of neofunctionalist tradition. While rejecting the mentalistic orientations of classic functionalism in favor of more objective concepts, these psychologists continued the search for functional relationships that describe stimulus and response events. These neofunctionalists did not see themselves as followers of either the early behaviorist or the neobehaviorist tradition. Despite this view, however, there was little to differentiate human-learning psychologists from those more explicitly committed to behavioristic concepts of learning.

The advent of behaviorism constituted a dramatic change in psychology as well as in the field of human learning. These changes, in many ways, could be termed the behavioristic revolution. Yet, as we look back on the transition from introspective psychology to behaviorism, we are struck by the many similarities in viewpoints which are too often ignored. Despite the profound shift in subject matter, from a concern with conscious mental states to a concern for behavioral analysis, and the rejection of the method of introspection in favor of more objective procedures, there were far less dramatic changes in the concept of learning. The behaviorists, like the structuralists, generally accepted the empiricist-associationist view of learning handed down from British associationism. That is, learning was said to depend almost exclusively on experience, and the laws of learning were essentially the laws of association, albeit refined, that had been part of psychology in one form or another since Aristotle. Of course the units of analysis, the what of learning, changed from bonds involving images and ideas to bonds between stimuli and responses, but in many other ways the general view of learning changed very little. As complex ideas were composed of simple ideas for the structuralists and British associationists, so complex habits were made up of elementary habits for the behaviorists. From Locke to Watson to Hull learning was viewed as a unitary, completely general process involving one set of machinery, one operation, one mechanism.

CONTEMPORARY VIEWS OF LEARNING

There has been a major emphasis on the role of experience in learning throughout the history of experimental psychology. It was not that the behaviorists and their predecessors denied the importance of constitutional factors but rather that they placed such a heavy emphasis on experience that the study of hereditary factors tended to be neglected. Nevertheless, certain evidence has focused attention on the importance of constitutional factors and the interaction of these factors with experience. Much of this evidence comes from the *ethologists,* who emphasize the innate aspects of

behavior and study animals in their natural habitat in order to avoid artifacts that might be introduced in a laboratory situation. One particularly
germane finding concerns *imprinting* (Lorenz, 1937).

Innate Mechanisms and Learning.   The phenomenon of imprinting
is most strongly demonstrated in birds such as ducks, geese, or chickens.
It was discovered as an answer to the question: How is it that the newborn
members of a species learn to follow their mother? Imprinting occurs
during a very short period of time, usually within a few hours after hatch-
ing, and does not take place at all—or takes place only very weakly—outside of this *critical period*. Young birds will also imprint on mother substi-
tutes within a certain range characterized by movement, vocalization, and
size, including the human experimenter crawling on hands and knees. Lorenz
claimed that imprinting is quite unlike associative learning in that the
learning can occur only during a short period in the young bird's life, and,
once established, it is both permanent and nontransferable. Some questions
have been raised concerning such absolute, sharp differences. Nevertheless,
the work on imprinting, together with other ethological studies involving
such phenomena as nest building in birds and courtship sequences, strongly
suggests innate behavior patterns that may be "triggered" in specific and
limited situations. The importance of such findings in refuting a theory of
learning that emphasizes completely general learning principles—and hence
principles that are relatively independent of the organism's biological
makeup—cannot be taken lightly.

Although much of the detailed experimental work demonstrating the
importance of innate factors on learning has involved animal subjects,
there is increasing evidence for such effects in the human. For instance,
human infants only two days old may already show preferential attention
to certain complex visual stimuli (Hershenson, 1964). This is much too
early an age to invoke explanations based on complex learning experiences.
In addition, shape constancy—the ability to perceive the correct shape of
objects despite rotation of position—has been reported in infants only two
months old (Bower, 1966), which is long before they can move around
well enough to explore their visual world. That learning of this kind is at
least partially dependent upon experience is suggested by the work of
Hubel and Wiesel (1962, 1963). They demonstrated that newborn kittens
have innate mechanisms for detecting the slope of lines. But they also
showed that if the kitten is prevented from receiving normal visual stimulation for the first two months of life, the specialized cells involved are
no longer excitable. Just how much stimulation is required is not clear,
but some visual experience of a reasonably normal variety is necessary.

The importance of verbal behavior and language in the psychology
of human learning has stimulated considerable interest in the study of
language acquisition. Particular language experience would seem to be

paramount here, but recent studies suggest that certain aspects of language acquisition in the child may also depend in very important ways upon innate (unlearned) processes. Careful analysis of the phonetic and grammatical competence displayed in the language of very young children, up to age four or five, makes it difficult if not impossible to view language in accordance with traditional accounts of learning. Contemporary investigators of human learning are forced to consider the possibility that some mental processes either are innate or depend upon innate ways of processing and organizing incoming information.

The Nature of Learning

When we turn our attention from these issues to the characterization of learning itself we see related changes in outlook. These changes are less in the direction of specifying what learning is and more in the direction of raising questions about learning that have been ignored previously. When contemporary psychologists refer to learning, they place considerably less emphasis on the *unique* role of experience. Instead, they tend to view learning as the result of a complex interaction of experience and biological structure.

Contemporary psychologists also seem less inclined to adopt a unitary view of the learning process. That is, they are less inclined to believe that any single, completely general process governs all learning. Instead of holding to one mechanism for learning, as the associationists did, it is now possible to talk about special purpose mental equipment perhaps at the service of more general machinery. Thus it is possible to talk about theories for separate parts. For example, imprinting can be viewed as a kind of learning dependent on experience only at a particular time and relevant to a highly limited set of inputs and a particular set of responses. A related development concerns the interest in *generative* theories such as those proposed by Chomsky (1957, 1965) and others to account for human language. That is, an important shift has occurred toward greater concern with the generation of behavior from basic information and rules as opposed to its piece-by-piece assembly in chains.

Modern views of human learning are therefore generally more mentalistic and nativistic in tone than psychology has seen for some time. This is not to imply any direct return to eighteenth-century thought on these matters. Rather, the intent is to indicate that there is a greater willingness to view behavior as the result of complex mental processes in conjunction with prior experience and current stimulation. This shift in attitude also carries the implication that psychology is "about" these mental processes in a more important sense than it is "about" behavior, a view that bordered on the heretical not too many years ago. Thus, although not all psychologists subscribe to this view, there appears to be a trend in which greater effort is being made to map the cognitive capacities of the organism, with less attention being paid to the discovery of experimentally produced regularities in chains of behavioral output.

OUTLINE OF THE TEXT

The main objective of this textbook is to provide a comprehensive review of the major phenomena and theories of human learning, memory, and language that have characterized this area of psychological inquiry in recent years. The text is divided into three sections, each of which deals with a different approach to the study of human learning. All three sections focus on verbal behavior, since what most obviously separates man from other animals is his verbal and linguistic skills. It is also in the realm of verbal behavior that traditional approaches, such as those reviewed in the present chapter, have met the greatest difficulties in attempting to account for learning, memory, and other cognitive phenomena.

The chapters in Part I (2, 3, 4, and 5) deal primarily with the traditional *learning approach*—the focus is mainly on principles of learning and their application. The learning approach has been intimately related to the phenomena of conditioning and the extension of conditioning principles to more complex learning situations. Even in Chapter 5, which deals with forgetting, considerable emphasis is placed on principles derived from the conditioning situation. Although Part I is basically concerned with the strengthening and weakening of supposed connections or associations between stimulus and response events, we shall also see indications of the complexities that arise in human behavior and that have led psychologists to consider additional or alternative approaches to the study of human learning.

Part II consists of three chapters (6, 7, and 8). In this section the emphasis is on "the flow of information" in the organism. This theme stems from the so-called *information-processing approach* to the study of human behavior, which was given considerable impetus in the 1950s by the work of a British psychologist, Donald A. Broadbent. The information-processing approach is a neutral sort of neofunctionalist approach in which the emphasis is on attempting to describe the passage of information in the organism from input to output. Historically speaking, this approach has been closely tied to an analogy with computer models. The focus here is on the storage and retrieval of information. The processes that underlie attention and memory play a major role in the information-processing approach, but there is considerably less emphasis on learning in the traditional sense.

Part III consists of four chapters (9, 10, 11, and 12). Human learning is approached here through an *analysis of structures,* particularly those that characterize human language. This approach owes much to the work of Noam Chomsky, a linguist, and it is most clearly exemplified in Chapters 9, 10, and 11. Psychologists employing this approach have paid close attention to the phonological, grammatical, and semantic structure of language. Here the effort has been to develop theoretical accounts that consider both the structure of language and the nature of human performance. Chapter 12 deals with concepts and rules in human learning. The relationship to the structural approach is less clear in this chapter, although we shall see signs of this approach exemplified in the more recent experimental and theoretical work in the area.

The final chapter (13) represents a review and overview of the material discussed previously. In this chapter we present a brief resumé of those changes in theory and experimental strategy that appear to be of major importance in human learning.

I

The Learning Approach

2

Human Learning and Conditioning

As INDICATED IN CHAPTER 1, both Pavlov and Thorndike supposed that conditioning principles studied in lower animals would generalize to human behavior. This possibility raised a number of important philosophical and psychological questions concerning the nature of man. One classical view-point, which sprang in part from the work of the early French philosopher René Descartes (1596–1650), was that humans enjoyed free will, reason, and purpose while animals were blind, mechanical brutes.

According to Descartes, man had a free soul or mind, but a mechanically operated body. Therefore, a dual set of principles had to be considered in accounting for both man's physical and man's psychological nature. One set of mechanistic principles, compatible with the laws of physics, might explain the operation of man's body; and these principles might be generally applied to the bodies of both man and animals. Unlike animals, however, man had a soul or mind, and a unique set of principles had to be considered with respect to man's psychological nature.

On an overall basis, then, the mind-body distinction denied on logical grounds the view that common principles of mind could operate across the intellectual chasm between rational man and irrational beast. Pavlov's assertion that the nervous systems of man and other animals rested on the same foundations and Thorndike's belief that man and lower animals had the same characteristic form of learning were in direct opposition to this dualistic point of view. We may therefore ask why the ideas and works of Pavlov and Thorndike were so influential in psychology during the early part of the twentieth century. Two major factors seem to have been involved.

First, the weighty influence of associationistic theories had persisted well into the nineteenth century. Such systems emphasized the association of events occurring contiguously during an individual's life span as a major determinant of learning. This viewpoint was of course quite compatible with the conditioning theories presented by Thorndike and by Pavlov. Second, and perhaps more important, the advent of evolutionary biology, especially as proposed in the nineteenth century by the English naturalist Charles Darwin (1809–82), seemed to place man and lower animals firmly on a common continuum with respect to *both* mind and body. Thus the conditioning models of learning could be seen as arriving at a rather propitious moment in the history of psychology as well as being most consistent with the general picture of evolutionary biology. Let us turn to this second source of influence.

Darwin (1859) suggested that *all* living organisms evolved from common ancestors over extraordinarily long periods of time. A basic principle in this evolution was the process of *natural selection*. That is, only those organisms who are equipped to survive in their environments are likely to survive. They are also likely to have offspring with adaptive characteristics of a similar nature to propagate the species. Other species succumb to their own weaknesses, or lack of adaptability, and become extinct in the evolutionary process. Darwin's work also clearly implied that both man and animals were on common physical and psychological continua. In a sense Darwin's (1872) contention that the curling of the human lips in a sneer was a remnant of the rage response in some carnivorous ancestor forced man to pay more than lip service to his common biological heritage in considering his own psychology along with that of other animals.

Primitive biological factors in human behavior were also being emphasized in the work of the founder of psychoanalysis, Sigmund Freud (1856–1939), who was to have a powerful influence on psychological thought in the beginning of the twentieth century. Freud suggested that the deepest wellsprings of man's psychological activity might be unconscious and biological in origin. He indicated that inherent in living matter are certain biological drives that lead to inevitable developmental sequences and predictable patterns of psychological adjustment. Thus, it appeared that the mind was no longer free. On the contrary, events in the psychological world were to be viewed as determined in just as lawful a manner as those in the physical world (cf. Freud, 1938).

The Law of Natural Selection. Although the main thrust of evolutionary biology was toward an elucidation of biological factors in the structure and behavior of animals, which explicitly included man, our concern here is with its implications for the selection of adaptive behaviors. The biologist Herbert Spencer Jennings (1868–1947) noted that both individual selection and natural selection work toward the same ends. The former involves selection among the various acts of a given individual; the latter involves selection among the acts of different individuals. The acts selected in each case are adaptive reactions, whether they occur in simple one-celled organisms or in complicated multicelled organisms.

Jennings (1906) illustrated these views by supposing that any organism has an action system that leads to typical acts in the presence of noxious stimulation. Consider, for example, the reaction in an extremely simple organism, *Stentor roeseli,* which usually attaches itself to bits of debris in marshy pools. This organism gathers food by means of small currents of water, produced by the beating of rows of fine cilia, which propel food particles toward the organism's mouth. Now, when a noxious stimulus, such as a heavy concentration of india ink, is placed next to the *Stentor,* what happens? At first the organism simply continues with its normal activities. After a while, however, the *Stentor* bends slightly as if attempting to continue normal activities while avoiding the stream of noxious stimulation. If this reaction proves unsuccessful, more vigorous bending activities may occur in an attempt to avoid the ink. Finally, if all prior actions are ineffective, the organism may give up normal activities, detach itself, and move away. If only the last action is effective, the organism may perform this reaction immediately when the noxious stimulation occurs again because the adaptive reaction had been fixed by "the law of the readier resolution of physiological states." Since the sequence of behaviors involved suggests that the *Stentor* "tries" different actions until it finds one that provides "relief," Jennings saw the process as being analogous to trial-and-error learning in higher animals. He did not mean to suggest, however, that the organism was being motivated by some purpose or aim. Based on his observations, he merely assumed that since the animal's behavior might vary in the presence of the same stimulus due to past experience, some change in the animal had to be postulated to account for the observed differences in behavior.

The emphasis on selection of adaptive behaviors by Jennings and others was also reflected in the systematic development of conditioning principles. Theorists perceived Darwin's concept of natural selection as applying not only to survival of the fittest organisms but also to selection of the fittest responses, that is, the responses that helped the organism to survive by finding food and avoiding dangerous situations. In the main, then, at the turn of the twentieth century the major assumptions of learning theorists appeared to be that gross discontinuities in learning mechanisms would not be expected across the entire animal continuum and that the most general laws of learning were probably founded on basic associationistic ideas which could be formally incorporated under conditioning principles. We shall now consider some of the most basic principles of association theory.

CONDITIONING: GENERAL PRINCIPLES

The Principle of Contiguity

At least since the time of British associationism the belief that spatial or temporal contiguity was a necessary condition for learning has been widely accepted in psychology. This primary principle of contiguity was based on the historical assumption, shared by both scientists and laymen, that cause-and-effect relationships may be inferred from the repeated observation that some event, *A,* is *immediately* followed by another event, *B*.

Although the essential correctness of the contiguity principle has rarely been questioned, immediate contiguity is not always required for events to become associated. When immediate contiguity is not required, the observer usually looks to other causal events that mediate the interplay of the events in question. Thus Pavlov (1927) found it necessary to postulate an unobservable *stimulus trace* to account for the conditioning that occurs with intervals as long as sixty seconds between the offset of some signal (e.g., a light) and the onset of a second signal (e.g., food) in classical conditioning. In fact, most theorists have found it necessary at one time or another to postulate mediating mechanisms to bridge such gaps in time and space. Before turning to that issue, however, let us examine some of the early work on the role of contiguity in conditioning.

Thorndike's (1913) analysis of the principle of contiguity focused on the *direct* strengthening of connections between situations (stimuli) and actions (responses) as a function of repetition rather than on a single contiguous occurrence per se. The general principle he investigated was the *law of exercise*. In a subsequent form the law of exercise was divided into two sublaws—the *law of use* and the *law of disuse*. The law of use was essentially a restatement of the general law of exercise (and of contiguity); the law of disuse stated that connections between stimuli and responses diminished in strength over time unless they were practiced (cf. Hilgard and Bower, 1966).

A review of some concepts introduced by Ebbinghaus (1885) indicates quite clearly that he and Thorndike were in close agreement concerning these basic laws. In addition, the laws of use and disuse seem to be what one would expect on the basis of common sense, although subsequent researchers have offered several theoretical and empirical reasons to doubt the complete validity of these laws as well as our common sense. It is important to note that Ebbinghaus and Thorndike were among the first to bring systematic empirical evidence to bear on these associative principles despite their having been accepted, in one form or another, since the time of Aristotle.

The Law of Use

During the early part of the twentieth century Thorndike conducted a number of investigations dealing with various aspects of human learning. Much of this work has been reviewed by Postman (1962) in a paper that serves as a basic reference for this discussion. Let us first look at one of Thorndike's most frequently cited experiments in which he attempted to assess the systematic influence of repetitions per se on learning.

Thorndike (1932) constructed a list of word-number pairs in which some pairs (e.g., building-99) occurred more often than others.[1] Repetitions of the same pair were scattered throughout the list. The list was then read to two groups of subjects, with one group being told to "pay close attention" to the list while the other group was told to merely "stay awake and listen." Figure 2.1 shows the number of correct digits given when the words were presented in a subsequent recall test. As can be seen, recall increased as a function of the number of times a word-number pair was presented. This result appears to provide direct support for the law of use and, of itself, may seem almost trivial.

The situation in this experiment becomes more complicated, however, when other aspects of the experiment are considered. For example, Figure 2.1 also shows that subjects who had been instructed to pay close attention apparently learned more than those subjects who were only instructed to stay awake and listen, although both groups profited by repetition of the pairs. Thus effects other than pure frequency of presentation, such as *attention* and *set,* also have to be included, and these considerations turn out to be difficult to deal with in traditional associationistic terms.

A second limitation of the law of use was also illustrated in this experiment. Consider a sequence of pairs that might have been read aloud to a particular subject: building-99, answer-40, and so on. Following presentation of the pairs the subject was asked to indicate which numbers came just after certain words and which words came just after certain numbers. As we noted previously, some pairs were repeated more often than others. In addition, there were variations in the frequency with which particular words followed particular numbers. Now according to the law of use, associative strength between temporally adjacent numbers and words should increase with repetition in the same manner as it does with word-number pairs. The subjects in this experiment, however, rarely gave responses such as "answer" when numbers such as "99" were presented, even in cases

[1] In such a situation, one usually designates the first member of the pair as the *stimulus* term and the second member as the *response* term. The stimulus and response terms, of course, can be other than the word-number pairs being considered here.

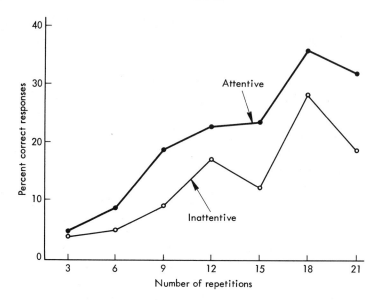

**Figure 2.1   The effects of repetition of stimulus-response pairs
and of attention on recall. Original data from Thorndike, 1932.**
(After Postman, 1962.)

where they had been contiguously presented quite often. Thus, not only
was the law of use modified by attentional factors, it also appeared to be
dependent upon some principle of *belongingness*. The subjects were somehow set, perhaps through instructions, to perceive certain contiguous items
as belonging in pairs (e.g., building-99) but not others (e.g., 99-answer).

When viewed in its entirety, therefore, Thorndike's study appeared
to raise as many questions as it answered. Support was obtained for the
law of use (or frequency), but in what sense does "paying close attention"
during learning strengthen associations over and above pure repetition?
And what is "belongingness" in terms of an association theory? Although
answers to such questions might be given, it is doubtful that a completely
acceptable answer could be stated in terms of associationistic bonds and
the law of use, which were the major factors in Thorndike's theory.

Another well-known experiment performed by Thorndike and his
associates (cf. Thorndike, 1932) raised several questions concerning
the validity of the law of use. In this experiment, subjects were blindfolded
and instructed to draw a four-inch line with one quick movement. The
subjects were not told how accurate they were. The subjects continued to
follow these instructions until more than two thousand lines had been
drawn over a period of twelve experimental sessions. Although the results
of this study were somewhat complicated, there were a number of important
findings.

First, there was no consistent increase in the accuracy of the subjects' responses, although this might be expected since no feedback was given concerning accuracy. Second, the length of line drawn most frequently by a given subject at the beginning of the experiment was not the most frequent length drawn at the end of the experiment. Thus there was no increase in accuracy of responding and there was no evidence that the initial and, presumably, stronger responses persisted over the course of the experiment.

Although it may not be immediately apparent, such results present a number of difficulties for a strict application of the law of use. For example, if we invoke the old associationist concept that responses that have just been practiced are very strong, as a result of both frequency and recency, we would have to predict that the subject would respond in a stereotyped manner throughout the experiment and that he would only solve the problem if the initial responses were correct. Therefore, the finding that responses were variable, not stereotyped, posed an important problem for a strict application of the law of use and suggested the need for additional explanatory mechanisms. The one given greatest emphasis by Thorndike, and subsequently by behaviorists, involved the effect of rewards in selectively strengthening responses.

The Law of Effect

Thorndike's experiments on human learning raised a number of theoretical and logical problems concerning the law of use. In his work with lower animals, however, the role of reward was given considerable emphasis. Thus it was quite natural for him to extend these studies to include an investigation of the effects of symbolic reward and punishment in human learning. Thorndike assumed that telling a subject that a particular response was "correct" would be rewarding in that the subject would do nothing to avoid repeating that response and, in fact, would try to reproduce it on the next appropriate occasion. Correspondingly, telling someone that a response was "wrong" would be punishing in that the subject would do nothing to repeat the response and would often actively avoid it. Thorndike formally adopted such definitions to supplement the law of use under the general rubric of the *law of effect*. This law held that reward strengthens stimulus-response connections, whereas punishment weakens such connections.

In a typical experiment that Thorndike (1932) used to demonstrate the law of effect, subjects were asked to make judgments about line lengths with respect to a comparison line. The subjects in one condition of the experiment were "reinforced" for every response. The symbolic cue "right" was given after a correct response, and the cue "wrong" was given after an incorrect response. No information was provided concerning the direction or magnitude of an error when one occurred. In the control condition, "no reinforcement" in terms of reward or punishment was provided. The data presented in Figure 2.2 show the effect of "reinforcement" over the several training sessions. Evidently use (i.e., repetition) without either reward or punishment leads to very little improvement.

In another experiment by Thorndike (1932) the subjects were given a series of two hundred Spanish words. As each word was presented, the subject had to select the English word that had the same meaning from a set of five alternatives. When the subject was correct the experimenter said "right," and when he was incorrect the experimenter punished him by saying "wrong." The series of words was repeated on successive days until twelve or more repetitions of each Spanish word had been presented. Thorndike then examined the effects of saying "right" or "wrong" on the likelihood of repeating a particular response. What he found was that reward (saying "right") increased the probability of repeating a response, but punishment (saying "wrong") neither increased nor decreased it. The

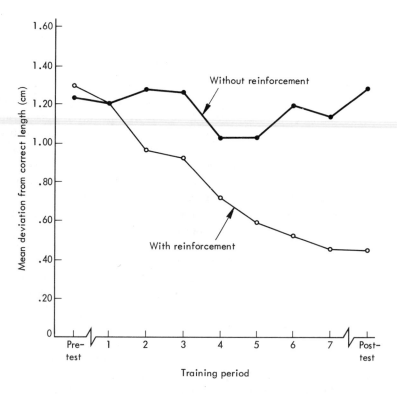

Figure 2.2   The effects of practice with and without reinforcement on judgments of length.
Original data from Thorndike, 1932. (After Postman, 1962.)

asymmetrical effects of reward and punishment observed in experiments such as this led Thorndike to revise his original statement of the law of effect. The revised law, which has been called the *truncated law of effect,* held that rewards always strengthen connections, whereas punishment has little or no effect on the strength of connections.

Despite the revision in the law of effect, Thorndike still considered it a master principle in his system. The "traditionally" central law of contiguity as well as its derivatives, the law of frequency and the sublaws of use and disuse, were consequently relegated to a minor position. Since Thorndike minimized the role of awareness in his discussion of the principles of human learning, we should not be misled by his concern with symbolic rewards and punishments into believing that he assigned a primary role to awareness or ideation in mediating the effects of reinforcement. On the contrary, Thorndike's theory minimized the role of the informative influence of rewards or the expectation of rewards and emphasized the automatic strengthening of stimulus-response bonds. On an overall basis, then, his system is best understood in terms of the principles of repetition (use) and reward (effect).

The Spread of Effect.   Considering the apparently radical nature of his theory, one can imagine the delight with which Thorndike must have greeted data suggesting that there was in fact a mechanical, automatic effect of reinforcement which not only strengthened stimulus-response bonds directly involved in the reinforcement process but also spread to other stimulus-response connections not so obviously involved. A characteristic experiment to illustrate this so-called spread of effect is cited by Hilgard and Bower (1966).

Subjects in this experiment were asked to state a number from one to ten following the presentation of each word in a long series of words. The experimenter called each response "right" or "wrong," depending on a prearranged schedule of rewards or punishments. But the lists Thorndike used were so long that subjects could not remember on a specific trial just what had been done on the preceding trial. After a number of such trials the responses given by each subject were examined to determine the number of times each response was given to each stimulus word. The data indicated that not only were the rewarded stimulus-response bonds "stamped in," but those responses occurring close in time to reward responses were strengthened.

Figure 2.3 summarizes the essential features of the spread of effect in graphic form. It can be seen there that the effect of reward spreads to adjacent responses in direct proportion to their distance from reward responses. Unfortunately, a number of methodological problems have to be dealt with before convincing theoretical conclusions can be drawn concerning the meaning of this empirical spread of effect. Many of these issues

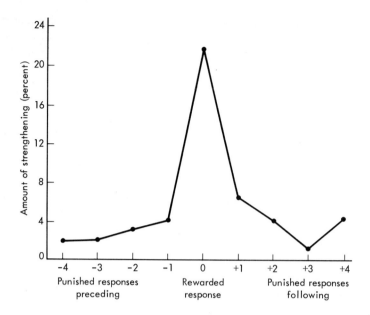

Figure 2.3 The spread of effect reported by Thorndike (1933) in which punished responses adjacent to a rewarded response are strengthened as a function of distance from reward. *(After Postman, 1962.)*

have been discussed in detail elsewhere (cf. Hilgard and Bower, 1966; Postman, 1962). For our purposes it will suffice to note the following point.

Subjects do not choose the digits that they give as responses in the typical spread-of-effect experiment entirely at random. Instead, they are likely to show strong biases against repeating the same digit or else to evidence habits toward repeating short strings of digits. As a consequence, it is difficult to determine whether the repetition of a digit that was adjacent to a rewarded digit, but was not itself rewarded, reflects a spread of effect or merely systematic guessing habits on the part of the subject. In any case, the spread of effect was considered to constitute impressive evidence of blind, automatic "stamping in" of responses by proponents of strict conditioning views of learning in humans. Insight and understanding, according to such a viewpoint, were not basic either to animal or to human learning, although the mechanical law of effect was basic to both.

Insight: Process or Product?

A major theoretical issue raised by Thorndike's emphasis on the automatic and inevitable consequences of reward concerned the role of awareness or insight in human learning. Thorndike and others did not deny that something akin to insight or awareness pervaded much of human activity. The issue that remained, however, was whether insight involved a *process* that facilitated learning or a *product* that resulted from learning. Perhaps this distinction can be clarified by referring to a series of studies by the German psychologist W. Köhler.

About 1913 Köhler began a series of studies on apes which appeared to demonstrate an important role for insight in problem-solving situations, contrary to Thorndike's findings (Köhler, 1925). Basically, Köhler argued that Thorndike's subjects only failed to show insight, and showed trial-and-error behavior instead, because they were placed in a situation in which insight was not "encouraged." According to Köhler, the problems for Thorndike's cats were unnatural and stupid and, as a result, so was the cat's behavior. Köhler argued that under more appropriate and less artificial circumstances, insight in the form of novel solutions (unpracticed) to problems would be quite common in animals, and by implication in humans as well.

As support for his views, Köhler described the problem-solving behavior of apes in situations that were more or less natural for them. His most famous example was that of the ape Sultan, who appropriately joined two short sticks together to make a longer one to snare food that was just out of reach when he used either of the shorter sticks. Sultan's ability to repeat the solution without difficulty was taken as evidence that the original solution was not a random affair. This was not to say that such insightful solutions might not be facilitated by random behavior, but rather that such random behavior was likely to involve an intelligent groping toward problem solution and not a blind thrashing about, as Thorndike had implied.

Both Thorndike and Köhler used the terms "trial and error" or "insight" to describe the flow of behavior they observed under their own particular experimental conditions. Thorndike's cats typically showed a slow, steady decrease in the amount of time taken on each successive trial to escape from the puzzle box. This suggested to Thorndike that problem solution occurred as a function of past experience and prior success. In contrast, Köhler's apes often showed a sudden solution to the problems given to them. Such rapid, novel solutions suggested to Köhler that problem solving involved "insight" or "Aha!" experiences.

At the descriptive level, the differences between the views of Thorndike and those of Köhler seemed to arise from differences in the rate at which the probability of problem solution went from 0.00 to 1.00. Figure 2.4 illustrates this relationship in terms of a transition rate that is slow and orderly (Thorndike) in contrast to one involving a sudden, one-trial shift (Köhler). The findings illustrated here are important because they relate not only to the general question of insight in learning but also to the issue of whether learning occurs on an incremental or on an all-or-none basis.

Despite the apparent conflict between the findings of Thorndike and

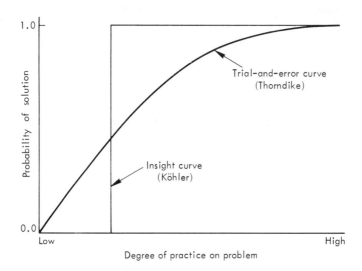

**Figure 2.4 Theoretical curves illustrating the relationship be-
tween speed of problem solution and degree of prior practice.
According to trial-and-error theory, solution speed gradually
increases with practice; whereas according to insight theory,
it increases on an all-or-none basis, independent of practice.**

those of Köhler, both of their interpretations were cast in a different light
by later experimental work. For instance, Birch (1945) showed that even
simple problems requiring minimal stick manipulation by apes were not
solved very rapidly unless the animals had had some prior experience with
the sticks. Given such experience, there was a dramatic increase in the
number of rapid solutions. These findings suggest that prior experiences
may have played a role in both Thorndike's and Köhler's experiments.

Unlike Birch, who reared his apes in controlled captivity, Köhler
gathered his apes from the jungle where they may have used sticks in some
instrumental fashion. Thus Köhler's apes may have had considerably more
prior experience with the "stick" problem than he believed. On the other
hand, Thorndike's cats may not have had prior experiences with puzzle
boxes. This is suggested by the observation that a plotting of solution times
for cats with considerable practice in the puzzle box often showed learning
curves that were insightful, not incremental, in form (cf. Postman, 1962).

Learning curves characteristic of "insight" or "trial-and-error" performance may therefore actually reflect differences in prior experience on
the part of the subjects. When the subject has little prior experience with
the problem at hand, learning may seem incremental. But with a great deal
of relevant experience, learning may take on an "insightful" appearance.
Of course the notion that prior learning can result in subsequent behavior
that appears "insightful" is quite compatible with Thorndike's general views.

Insight would merely reflect the transfer of old habits to new situations. Unfortunately, for a stimulus-response theorist, examples of insight generated out of past habits are not easily explained in terms of behavioristic concepts. This problem is clearly exemplified by Harlow's (1949) work on *learning sets*.

Development of Learning Sets.   It has been observed that as subjects solve successive discrimination problems, they often show a systematic gradual improvement in the rate at which the problems are solved. Harlow (1949) has described such improvement in terms of *learning sets* and has suggested that the gradual increase in rate of learning reflects a continuity between simple examples of discrimination learning and complicated examples of insightful behavior. In a sense, then, insight grows out of habit.

Harlow reports the results of several experiments using both children and monkeys to support his concept. The experimental task typically consisted of requiring the subject (child or monkey) to pick up one of two stimulus objects differing in several characteristics. The task was arranged so that when the subject chose the correct stimulus, it found a reward underneath. If the incorrect stimulus was chosen, there was no reward. Since the positions (left-right) of the stimulus objects were alternated at random, the subjects were required to solve the discrimination problems on the basis of characteristics of the objects and not their location.

Once the subject was well trained on a particular discrimination, as indicated by the consistent choice of the correct stimulus, a new pair of stimulus-objects was presented. Again, only the choice of one of these was rewarded. The experimental question was how rapidly the subject would solve each new problem in the series. In one study with monkeys, Harlow employed 344 different discrimination problems, each represented by a new pair of stimuli. The subjects had six learning trials on each problem before the next pair of stimuli was presented.

Harlow found that learning curves over the six trials of each problem tended to be gradual in form for the first 150 discrimination problems. But after considerable experience with different problems (about 250), the learning curves reflected a sudden solution. At this point in training, the subject was likely to choose a stimulus at random on the *first* trial of a new problem, since there was no information as yet on which to base a choice. After the first trial, however, whether the choice made was correct or not, the subject seemed to "know" which stimulus was correct. Such behavior seems both insightful and a direct function of prior experience with problems having the same abstract solution. The general form of the solution in this case was "if one stimulus is not correct, the other one is correct." Harlow's monkeys learned this solution quite slowly, but this did not mean that it was based on the transfer of stimulus-response bonds.

According to Harlow, one thing the learning set studies show is how a subject is "released from Thorndikian bondage." Harlow points out that even after a monkey has been exposed to all the problems, it is doubtful that he possesses 344 habits, bonds, or connections. The monkey might well respond at a chance level were he exposed to any one of the problems again. The monkey does have a *generalized* solution to any comparable discrimination problem, which he can demonstrate with the greatest of ease. This solution is not based on common *physical* stimuli, since each new problem involves a new pair of stimuli. In fact, it is not clear whether any behavioristic conception can be used to explain the acquired solution. Before we can consider that problem, it will necessary to examine other aspects of the development of behavioristic learning theories.

CONDITIONING: BASIC CONCEPTS AND PHENOMENA

It was noted in Chapter 1 that the period from 1930 to 1950 was marked by the rapid development of learning theory along behavioristic lines. The major theorists of this period (e.g., Guthrie, Hull, Skinner, Spence, Tolman) were all influenced by Pavlov's and Thorndike's work on classical and instrumental conditioning. Thus a common base existed in terms of methods and procedures as well as in terms of basic concepts and principles. Apart from a general acceptance of associations as the units of learning, the most widely shared principles were those of generalization and discrimination. It was around these principles that most theories of this period were developed. Of course, there were differences of opinion, but the areas of agreement were substantial. Therefore, we shall now consider the common features in method and theory that characterized the development of behavioristic theories of learning.

Conditioning Procedures

Classical Conditioning. The sequence of events in classical conditioning typically involves the presentation of a conditioned stimulus (CS), such as salivation, followed by presentation of an unconditioned stimulus (US), such as food. The US is defined as a stimulus that reliably elicits some measurable response, such as salivation, and this response to the US is called an unconditioned response (UR). Prior to training, the CS does not elicit the same responses as the US, although subjects typically attend to the CS. In this situation, classical conditioning is said to occur to the extent that the UR, originally made to the US, comes to be elicited by the CS. When a response such as salivation comes to be elicited by the CS as a result of training, it is called a conditioned response (CR). A commonplace illustration in humans might be the salivary response that occurs when we are hungry and someone says, "Dinner is served." Obviously, the call to dinner (CS) is not mistaken for the dinner (US) itself. Nevertheless, if we are very hungry our mouths may "water" at the thought of food.

The major procedural variations in classical conditioning involve the temporal spacing of the CS and the US. When the time of onset for the CS and the US is the same, the arrangement is called *simultaneous* conditioning. When the onset of the CS follows the onset of the US, the procedure is called *backward* conditioning. Neither of these procedures is very effective in producing a CR. In general, classical conditioning is most likely to be demonstrated when the CS slightly precedes the US.

Two important procedural variations in classical conditioning are those of *delayed* and *trace* conditioning. In delayed conditioning, the CS occurs before the US and is still present when the US is presented. When the temporal interval between the onset of the CS and the onset of the US is fairly long, say thirty seconds, the occurrence of the CR is often delayed somewhat. In trace conditioning, the CS is presented and removed before the US occurs. Since the CS is not actually present at the same time as the US, successful trace conditioning is presumed to involve some residue or "trace" of the CS. Thus a mother's recent call of "Dinner!" may still be ringing in her child's head when he actually begins to eat. It should be clear that as the interval between onset of the CS and onset of the US becomes more extended (with either delayed or trace procedures), conditioning becomes more difficult.[2]

Once classical conditioning has occurred, it can be modified by simply presenting the CS a number of times without presenting the US. This defines the procedure for carrying out *experimental extinction*. During extinction, the subject typically shows a decrease in the frequency and amplitude of the CR. But if a period of time is allowed to intervene following extinction training, and there is a subsequent presentation of the CS, the subject may show an increase in the strength of the CR relative to the last extinction trial. This phenomenon is called *spontaneous recovery*. As the name implies, it refers to an increase in the strength of the CS–CR connection without interpolated pairings of the CS with the US. Spontaneous recovery never seems to be complete in the sense that the CR does not recover to its preextinction strength.

In the classical situation the active participation of the subject is not required for either the CS or the US to be presented. Once the experimental procedure has been determined, it is in no way modified by what the subject actually does or does not do. Let us contrast this situation with that which takes place in instrumental conditioning.

[2] See Kimble (1961) for a more detailed discussion of classical conditioning procedures and related experimental findings.

Instrumental Conditioning.   For expository purposes, it is most convenient to view the sequence of events in *instrumental conditioning as beginning with a response by the subject.* If reward is a consequence of this response, then the subject is likely to produce that response again. One reference experiment for such a procedure is the "cat-in-the-box" experiment by Thorndike, which was discussed in Chapter 1. It will be recalled that in this experiment a hungry cat was placed in a cage from which it could escape by pulling a latch. If the cat made this response, it was released and could eat the food placed outside the cage. When placed back in the cage, the cat was likely to repeat those responses leading to the food reward. Thus the cat's behavior was *instrumental* in securing reward.

A second reference experiment which allows for a more refined analysis of the instrumental conditioning situation was provided by Skinner (1938). In this experiment a hungry rat was placed in a small closed chamber and was rewarded automatically, in the form of food pellets, whenever it pressed a bar. In both reference experiments, instrumental conditioning is said to have occurred to the extent that the critical response leading to reward increases in probability of occurrence. An increase in probability of occurrence is often assessed by a measure such as response frequency per unit of time or response latency.

When the instrumental response no longer produces a reward, the subject is said to be under *extinction* training. Such training results in a decrease in response probability, and, as in classical conditioning, spontaneous recovery may also occur over time. In fact, most of the major phenomena found with classical conditioning techniques have close parallels in the instrumental conditioning paradigm. These common phenomena include stimulus generalization and discrimination.

In contrast to classical conditioning, the sequence of events in instrumental conditioning is highly dependent upon the active participation of the subject. If the subject does not respond in the instrumental situation, or if he responds in a manner that is not rewarded, the operations required for instrumental conditioning are not completed. The subject in classical conditioning situations, however, has no control over stimulus presentation. The US is presented according to schedule whether or not any response to the CS has taken place.

In any extended description of instrumental conditioning, many variations in technique may be considered. For example, a learned reward might be used instead of food, as when a bar press produces a light previously associated with food, rather than the food itself. In another variation a food reinforcer might be given for every sixth bar press instead of for each single bar press (cf. Ferster and Skinner, 1957). Despite all the procedural variations that have been used and the alternate classifications schemes for these techniques that might be employed, there are two major threads in common. First, the behavior of the subject is instrumental in procuring reinforcement, which includes acquiring rewards, avoiding the loss of rewards, and avoiding or escaping from noxious stimulation such as shock. Second, the focus of experimental inquiry is on change in response probability (e.g., number of bar presses) as a function of variations in patterns, amounts, or timing of reinforcement. As used here, the term *reinforcement* refers to a wide variety of stimulus conditions, all of which lead to an increase in the probability that a given response will reappear in the same situation.

With the preceding discussion of conditioning procedures as general background, we now turn to a consideration of the principles of generalization and discrimination. These principles are central to theories of conditioning and learning and have played a major role in the further development of such theories.

Stimulus Generalization

In our previous discussion of the work of Pavlov in Chapter 1, we noted that the principle of stimulus generalization refers to the observation that responses occurring in the presence the CS may also occur in the presence of other stimuli that are similar to the CS. Thus the dog who has learned to salivate to a low tone that is always followed by food may also salivate to higher tones that have never been paired with food. Pavlov noted such spontaneous generalization of responses in animals, and it is not surprising to find related evidence for systematic generalization functions with human subjects. For example, Hovland (1937) was able to show generalization of a conditioned "emotional" response (galvanic skin response, or GSR) based on the pairing of a tone (the CS) with shock (the US). Figure 2.5 shows the empirical relationships that were observed. Keep in mind that the subjects never experienced shock paired with any tone except for the single tone labeled 0 in the figure.

Many subsequent investigations have demonstrated stimulus generalization gradients for humans in both classical and instrumental conditioning situations. Although it is undoubtedly a reliable phenomenon, these studies also indicate that the precise form of the stimulus generalization gradient varies as a function of subjects, method of measurement, response measured, stimulus dimension, and a host of other factors. Thus it is not appropriate to speak of *the* stimulus generalization gradient, since there is no single form. Nevertheless, the empirical fact that stimulus generalization occurs in so many situations encouraged stimulus-response theorists to conjecture about models in which such transfer to novel situations might be predicted.

The most refined and influential treatment of generalization during this period was that offered by Clark L. Hull (1939). The basic concepts

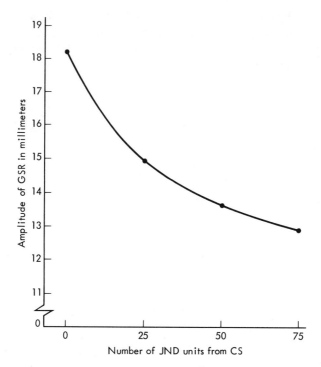

Figure 2.5   Stimulus generalization gradient for the galvanic skin response (GSR) previously conditioned to a tone of 1,000 cycles per second.
(After Hovland, 1937.)

offered by Hull involved generalization through *partial stimulus identity; primary generalization,* or *irradiation;* and *secondary,* or *mediated, generalization.* Generalization based on partial identity between a training stimulus and a test stimulus is illustrated by the dog who salivates to a circle presented alone as well as to the same circle with a cross inside it. Primary generalization, or what Pavlov called irradiation, is illustrated in the studies by both Pavlov and Hovland discussed previously. The essential feature of primary generalization is that the training and test stimuli lie on the same physical dimension, for example, sounds that vary only in frequency or only in loudness.

Secondary, or mediated, generalization is used to explain generalization across different physical dimensions and relies on *response-produced* cues, developed through the learning process, as mediating links. For example, human subjects conditioned to give a GSR to a *blue light* that is paired with shock also give a GSR to the word *blue,* even though the word was never paired with shock (cf. Kimble, 1961; Osgood, 1953). Obviously, something other than physical similarities between the light and word stimuli must be mediating the generalization observed. Perhaps it has to do with the fact that the subject gives the same implicit verbal *response,* "blue," to both stimuli. But, if so, how could this concept of transfer on the basis of common *responses* be made consistent with explanations of generalization based on common stimuli?

One explanation of such generalization based on common stimulus components was developed by Hull (1939) and expanded by others (cf. Osgood, 1953). The basic argument requires one to consider that every response a subject makes to a stimulus produces, in turn, characteristic stimuli of its own. If a rat moves down a maze and makes a right turn, that right-turn response leads to external stimuli associated with the next section of the maze (e.g., a light) and produces internal stimuli associated with activity in muscle receptors and general changes in body orientation. These internal, covert stimuli which result from the act of responding have been called proprioceptive stimuli, and although they are internal and covert, they are still supposed to have the same general properties as overt stimuli, such as a light. As a more theoretically relevant term, however, we will use *response-produced stimuli* to describe those stimuli that are characteristic of specific internal response sequences.

We can now see how a formal stimulus analysis of generalization could be maintained even when generalization occurs to two physically dissimilar stimuli as long as they *have a common response.* It is this common response to physically different stimuli that, through its characteristic *response-produced stimuli,* provides the common physical dimension for stimulus generalization in this analysis. Suppose a blue light was repeatedly paired with shock, after which the word *blue* was presented alone. A subject in such an experiment might respond to the word as if he had been shocked because both the light and the word give rise to a common set of internal stimuli. In this situation generalization occurs, rather than complete stimulus substitution (i.e., the subject does not completely confuse the blue light with the word *blue*), because there are always other responses that are *not* common to both stimuli. As a result, response-produced stimulation from these other response sources "dilutes" the physical similarity of the two stimuli in question.

Hull also assumed that responses could occur implicitly and fractionally such that the stimulus consequences of these implicit responses would also be implicit and fractional. That is, once a response had been associated with a stimulus, on subsequent occasions of stimulus presentation the response could occur in a sufficiently reduced form so as not to disrupt ongoing activity. Quite naturally it was assumed that the stimuli associated with such lightweight responses would also occur in highly reduced form. Thus the rat running down the maze for food might "anticipate" the last right turn before the goal box in terms of an implicit, minute anticipatory right turn. The resulting response-produced stimulation could then act as a continuing spur to action without disrupting the running sequence in progress.

For students of human learning the great significance of Hull's work on generalization, particularly with respect to implicit responding, was that it stimulated renewed interest both in the study of basic mediational processes (cf. Horton and Kjeldergaard, 1961) and in the study of semantic generalization (cf. Cofer and Foley, 1942; Osgood, 1953). In the case of semantic generalization several theories based on Hull's work were advanced to explain word to word or word to object generalization that could not be accounted for on the basis of partial stimulus identity or primary generalization.

Discrimination

The process of discrimination, like that of generalization, seems to be involved in most learning situations. In addition, the concepts of discrimination and generalization are highly interrelated. At the level of observation, stimulus discrimination refers to a restriction in the range of stimulus generalization. Alternatively, a failure of discrimination corresponds to an increase in generalization.

Examples of discrimination are plentiful in the experimental literature. Even Pavlov's finding that a previously conditioned dog would salivate in the presence of the CS, but not in its absence, represents a gross form of discrimination. Some authorities claim that discrimination of this sort is basic to all learning (cf. Kimble, 1961). A finer form of discrimination is illustrated by the observation that once conditioning has taken place, an organism will not respond to all stimuli of the same class as the CS (all tones), but only to a restricted set of them. This observation leads to the question of how sharp a discrimination is possible in conditioning situations.

In Chapter 1 we saw an example using the method of contrast in which one stimulus (a circle) was always paired with food while another stimulus (an ellipse) was never paired with food. Initially the dog easily made the required discrimination. That is, it salivated only in the presence of the circle. As the ellipse was slowly changed toward the shape of the circle, however, a point was reached beyond which the dog could no longer discriminate between the two stimuli. This observation shows that both discrimination and generalization are influenced by the sensory-perceptual capabilities of the organism.

The theoretical concepts of generalization and discrimination were developed and refined in the context of the investigations of classical and instrumental conditioning. In both situations these concepts appeared so basic to accounts of learning that they provided the foundation for most theoretical efforts during the behavioristic period. The centrality of generalization and discrimination in theories of learning is well illustrated in the statement of the *two-factor hypothesis* advanced by Spence in the 1930s.

GENERALIZATION-DISCRIMINATION THEORY

The two-factor hypothesis developed by Spence (1936, 1937) was based on the assumption that the laws of conditioning might provide a source of deductive principles that would apply to much of learned behavior. This assumption was also common to most other theoretical efforts of this period (cf. Osgood, 1953). Thus Spence's main interest was in precisely formulating a theory from basic conditioning principles that would explain not only discrimination learning but also more complex forms of higher-order activity.

We can illustrate the form of Spence's theory by considering a situation in which an organism is learning a discrimination based on size. Suppose there are two stimuli and the larger of the two is positive (leads to reward) while the smaller is negative (does not lead to reward). According to Spence, when the organism approaches the positive stimulus and is rewarded. there is a tendency *automatically* instilled in the organism to repeat the approach response when this stimulus is presented again. There is also an immediate *generalization* of this approach tendency to other stimuli that are physically similar to the positive stimulus.

A second assumption is that when the organism approaches the negative stimulus and is not rewarded, there is a tendency *automatically* instilled in the organism to avoid the negative stimulus as well as other stimuli that are physically similar to it. The results of these generalized tendencies to approach the positive stimulus and avoid the negative stimulus can be described in the form of generalization gradients for excitation (approach) and inhibition (avoidance). These generalization gradients are illustrated in the upper panel of Figure 2.6. Notice that the amount of excitation is greatest for the positive stimulus (B), whereas the amount of inhibition is greatest for the negative stimulus (A).

In predicting the organism's overall tendency to either approach or avoid stimuli of various sizes, Spence assumed that the two gradients of excitation and inhibition would summate algebraically. That is, the values for the avoidance tendency (inhibition) would be subtracted from the values for the approach tendency (excitation) to produce the net tendency to approach or avoid any particular stimulus along the size dimension. The resulting "net" tendency to approach or avoid any particular stimulus is shown in the lower panel of Figure 2.6.

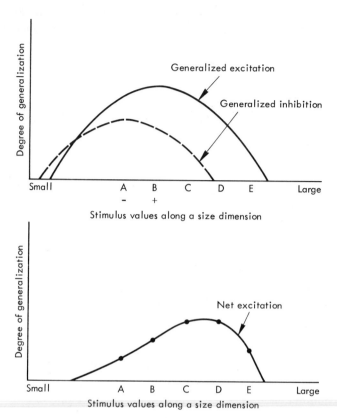

Figure 2.6   Theoretical generalization curves for excitation and
inhibition (upper panel) when responses to stimulus B are rewarded during discrimination training while responses to stimulus A are not. The total tendency to respond to any given
stimulus (net excitation) is obtained by subtracing inhibition
from excitation for each stimulus value (lower panel). See text
for further explanation.
(*After Spence, 1937.*)

Predictions of the Two-Factor Model

In applying the concepts illustrated in Figure 2.6, it should be noted
that the height of the gradient for excitation is greater than that for inhibition, and that both gradients are symmetrical and convex in shape. These
considerations represent rather explicit assumptions of Spence's model of
discrimination learning, and violation of these assumptions could lead to
inaccurate predictions. In any event, one of the main predictions of Spence's
model is that a discrimination will be formed. This prediction, which represents no small accomplishment, is also illustrated in Figure 2.6. Here

we see that the "net excitation" (excitation minus inhibition) is greater for the positive stimulus (B) than it is for the negative stimulus (A).

Now let us examine some of the more complicated predictions based on the two-factor model. Consider that an organism has already acquired a discrimination between the stimuli A and B, as illustrated in Figure 2.6. The organism is then tested on a different pair of stimuli, such as B and C. As illustrated in Figure 2.6, the model predicts that transposition will occur in this situation and that the organism will respond to C, even though B was the positive stimulus during prior training. This prediction is indicated by the greater "net excitation" for C than for B. Since Spence's model was based *only* on the *absolute physical* characteristics of stimuli, this prediction is important. Notice it says that the organism will appear to transpose or generalize a relationship, such as "choose the larger stimulus," at least up to a point.

Two other predictions based on this model can be noted briefly. First, the model predicts that a discrimination, once acquired, will be difficult to reverse. That is, following training in which B is the positive stimulus and A is the negative stimulus, it should be difficult to acquire a discrimination in which A is positive and B is negative. A second prediction concerns the "net excitatory gradient" which results from discrimination training. As illustrated in Figure 2.6, if B is the positive stimulus and A is the negative stimulus, the net excitatory gradient will be asymmetrical in shape and displaced toward the upper end (larger) of the size dimension. As noted in our discussion of transposition, one consequence of the displacement is that the net tendency to approach certain stimuli (such as C) will be greater than the net tendency to approach the stimulus (B) that was positive during training.

Many experimental observations with lower animals seem to be in general agreement with these, and other, predictions derived from Spence's model (cf. Kimble, 1961). The predicted displacement of the net excitatory gradient, which more recently has been called "peak shift," has been observed in the pigeon (Hanson, 1959), and Spence's predictions concerning transposition have been largely confirmed with other animals. Our concern here, however, is with the success of the model in human learning situations.

Two-Factor Theory and Human Learning

One view of learning holds that it always involves discrimination in one form or another. The criterion of learning is assumed to involve an increase in the probability of occurrence of some response in the presence of some stimulus (positive) but not in the presence of other stimuli (negative). Let us consider what the two-factor model says about this conceptualization in the context of an actual learning experiment.

Gynther (1957) performed an experiment in which human subjects were conditioned to give an eyeblink response (CR) to a light (CS) by pairing it with a puff of air (US) to the eye. The learning curve for this group of subjects given "regular conditioning" trials is shown in Figure 2.7 (upper curve). As can be seen, there is an orderly increase in the percentage of CRs given by these subjects over the course of training. To interpret these results in terms of Spence's discrimination learning theory, however, we would need more information. We would need to know how many CRs these subjects gave to both the positive stimulus (light) and the negative stimulus (no light).

The point is clarified by considering a second group of subjects in Gynther's study who were given discrimination training. For these subjects the positive stimulus (light) was followed by an airpuff, but the negative stimulus (a different light) was never followed by an airpuff. The two learning curves for this group are also shown in Figure 2.7 (lower curves). One of these curves shows responses to the positive stimulus, and the other shows responses to the negative stimulus.

The three learning curves in Figure 2.7, taken together, illustrate two important facts. First, the overall level of responding to the positive

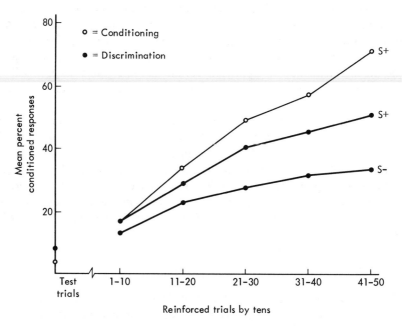

Figure 2.7 Performance in eyeblink conditioning as a function of discrimination training and regular conditioning.
(After Gynther, 1957.)

stimulus is lower in the group given discrimination training than in the group given regular conditioning training. This observation is somewhat surprising, since the experimental procedures ensured that the positive stimulus was presented, and followed by an airpuff, an equal number of times in both groups. Second, the number of CRs given in the presence of *both* the positive and the negative stimulus increased across trials. It might be expected that a decrease in CRs to the negative stimulus should occur across trials rather than an increase.

According to Spence's two-factor model, these apparently surprising results can be explained in a rather straightforward manner. For those subjects given discrimination training, responding to the positive stimulus would be depressed by generalization of inhibition from the negative stimulus. Correspondingly, responding to the negative stimulus would increase over trials because of generalization of excitation from the positive stimulus. Taken in combination, these considerations can explain the increase in responding over trials to the negative stimulus and the reduced level of responding to the positive stimulus in the group given discrimination training.

Spence's theory also suggests that the subjects given regular conditioning training have acquired a discrimination. In effect, these subjects have learned "to blink when the light is on but not when it is off." But the generalization of excitation and inhibition would be greatly reduced in this situation because the positive (light) and negative (no light) stimuli are very dissimilar physically. In this way, Spence's model applies not only to situations explicitly involving discrimination learning but to more ordinary learning situations as well.

Two-Factor Theory and Transposition.   There is evidence to support Spence's general predictions concerning transposition in lower organisms. Although Riley (1958) has pointed out some problems with the definition of the stimulus in such a model, it also appears to predict that transposition will "break down" when the test stimuli are very different from the original training stimuli. This prediction can be illustrated using Figure 2.6. Suppose *A* and *B* were the original training stimuli, with *B* being the positive stimulus. When subjects are subsequently tested on *B* and *C* (near transposition test) they respond in an apparently relational manner by choosing *C*. With stimuli like *D* and *E* (far transposition test), however, relational responding "breaks down"—the net excitatory gradient shows a stronger approach tendency for *D* than for *E*.

The prediction that transposition will "break down" is important for Spence's model. It is important because many nonbehavioristic explanations of transposition assume that the organism learns and operates on the basis of a conceptual relationship such as "choose the larger stimulus." But if this relational view is correct, it is difficult to see why the organism should ever "change its mind," as Spence's theory predicts. Now let us see how well these alternative points of view explain transposition with humans.

Kuenne (1946) studied transposition in children between about three and six years of age. When a near transposition test was employed in which the test stimuli were close in size to the original training stimuli, she found that the children responded in a clearly relational manner which did not vary with age. This observation is consistent with both Spence's predictions and those emphasizing conceptual explanations. Very different results were obtained with a far transposition test in which the test stimuli differed considerably in size from the training stimuli. In this situation the older, more verbal children continued to respond in a relational manner, but the younger, less verbal children showed a "breakdown" in transposition performance. The results for the younger children were consistent with Spence's two-factor model, but the results for the older children were not.

The fact that older children failed to show the predicted "breakdown" in transposition performance on the far transposition test presented a criti- training stimuli and the test stimuli gave rise to some *common* internal responding on the basis of some abstract relationship among the stimuli and not on the basis of absolute physical characteristics of the stimuli. For instance, Kuenne found that her older and more verbal subjects were likely to verbalize the relationship on which they were trained. That is, they could often describe the correct rule for responding in terms like "choose the larger one." In contrast, the younger and less verbal subjects appeared to be more "stimulus bound," and therefore they responded more directly to the physical characteristics of the stimuli.

Several attempts have been made to rescue two-factor theory from embarrassments such as that presented by Kuenne's findings. Most of these efforts have been based on Hull's (1939) concept of secondary, or mediated, generalization. The basic argument is that the older subjects in Kuenne's experiment continued to respond relationally because both the training stimuli and the test stimuli gave rise to some *common* internal response. This internal response, which could be verbal in nature, automatically gave rise to internal stimuli that mediated the same overt response (e.g., "choose the larger stimulus") when either the training stimuli or the test stimuli were presented. Of course there was no need to invoke this explanation for the younger children, since their performance was consistent with predictions from the two-factor model. A similar proposal, offered to account for related aspects of concept learning (cf. Kendler and Kendler, 1959), will be discussed in Chapter 12.

Two-Factor Theory and Mediation.   Mediational factors of the sort discussed here have often been invoked to explain the performance of older subjects. Such explanations have been particularly popular when there was a need to explain semantic relationships between words or between words and objects (cf. Cofer and Foley, 1942; Osgood, 1953). The use of mediational explanations for results such as Kuenne's, however, represents a clear extension of the original Hullian concept. That is, Hull (1939) proposed the concept of secondary, or mediated, generalization to explain observed relationships among stimuli that lie on different physical dimensions. This concept is clearly appropriate for words or words and objects where several dimensions of meaning may be involved, but the stimuli Kuenne used differed on only a single dimension (size). In this situation the observed relationships were to be explained on the basis of primary generalization.

Grice and Davis (1958) have shown that mediational concepts can be applied to explain relationships among stimuli that differ on a single dimension. The stimuli used in their study consisted of three tones which differed in frequency. The tone of intermediate frequency served as the CS for conditioning an eyeblink response, with an airpuff as the US. At various points during training, generalization tests were administered using either the high or the low tone. Neither of these test stimuli was ever paired with the airpuff.

The adult subjects used in this experiment were also required to make a manual response—push or pull a lever—whenever one of the three tones was sounded. Different manual responses were made to the test stimuli, but one of these was always the same as the response made to the CS. For example, one subject might *push* the lever when either the low or the intermediate tone was sounded, but *pull* the lever when the high tone was sounded. This procedure was designed to make those stimuli sharing the same manual response more similar and to exaggerate differences between stimuli leading to different manual responses.

The results of this experiment showed that when the same manual response was made to both a test tone and the CS, more eyeblinks were given to the test tone than when the manual response to it differed from that made to the CS. These findings suggest that the presence of a common manual response makes stimuli more alike (mediated equivalence), whereas the presence of different manual responses makes them less alike (mediated distinctiveness).

The results of the Grice and Davis study suggests a role for mediational interpretations even when stimuli differ only along one dimension. Of course, it is not clear whether the introduction of mediators in this situation served to alter the shape of the usual generalization gradient or to relocate stimuli on some abstract dimension of similarity. If we assume, along with Spence, that generalization gradients are usually symmetrical, then Figure 2.8 serves to illustrate how they might be altered when mediators are introduced. Alternatively, it might be argued that the generalization gradient is not changed, but rather that the stimuli themselves are

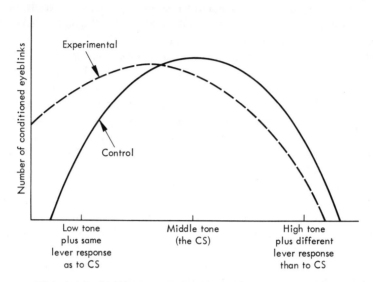

Figure 2.8 Idealized generalization curves suggested by the work of Grice and Davis (1958). Note symmetry of the simple generalization curve (control) and the asymmetry of the mediated generalization curve (experimental). See text for further explanation.

relocated either closer to, or farther from, the CS. In either case, successful application of generalization-discrimination theory requires careful specification of both the generalization gradient and the stimulus before predictions of behavior can be made. Let us consider this problem in more detail.

The Problem of Stimulus Specification

The problem of stimulus specification has continued to plague behavioristic stimulus-response theories. Specifying what the stimulus is in any particular situation was once referred to as the *only* problem in psychology (cf. Stevens, 1951). The difficulty here for a stimulus-response theory is contained in the basic assumption that *some* stimulus is required for *every* response. Therefore, to the extent that the stimulus cannot be specified in a given situation, it is not possible to predict which response will occur. In short, an adequate definition of *the* stimulus is a prerequisite to testing any theory that invokes concepts such as stimulus generalization and, therefore, stimulus similarity and dissimilarity.

The problem of stimulus specification was illustrated in our discussion of learning sets, where Harlow's monkeys demonstrated an ability to solve successive discrimination problems after one trial, even though each new problem involved a new pair of stimuli. Another example was Kuenne's study of transposition in children. In this case some children seemed to respond to the physical character of the stimuli, and others based their responses on abstract relations among stimuli.

Mediational theories attempt to resolve some of these problems by suggesting that mediators can make stimuli that are grossly different at the physical level (e.g., a blue light vs. the word *blue*) more alike, and stimuli that are alike at the physical level (e.g., base ball and baseball) quite dissimilar. Such attempts have been only partially successful, however, because of the difficulty of specifying either the stimulus that is being responded to or the relationship between that stimulus and other stimuli.

CONCLUSION

As we have seen, the notion that general associative principles might apply to the behavior of both humans and nonhumans was consistent with views of *evolutionary biology* as expressed in the work of both Darwin and Jennings. The emphasis on adaptive behavior as a means by which an *individual organism* survives was congruent with the concept of the law of effect as a means by which an *individual response* might survive. The concepts embodied in such a point of view were also compatible with the theories of Pavlov and of Thorndike, and by the 1930s the classical and instrumental conditioning paradigms were viewed by some theorists as providing a basis for a synthesis of the principles of evolution and associative learning. In addition, it was presumed that such a synthesis would permit psychology to become a truly objective science of behavior.

The result of this attempted synthesis was that the introspective analysis of mental events gave way to a functional analysis of behavior. The basic view was that behavior was presumed to be controlled in a systematic, mechanical way by the master principles of contiguity and reinforcement. More complex processes, such as insight, were assumed either to be directly understood in terms of these basic conditioning principles or in terms of processes that could be derived from these principles. Objections were raised to these assertions, particularly by psychologists who looked to innate laws of organization as providing the cornerstone for understanding insightful behavior. The behaviorists, however, were quite successful, for some time, in offering experiment after experiment to support the general validity of the stimulus-response model.

By the middle of the twentieth century a number of cracks in the armor of stimulus-response psychology became apparent. Rewards might "stamp in" responses, but punishment did not seem to "stamp out" responses. Attention seemed to influence learning, but it was not clear what attention involved or how it might be dealt with in stimulus-response terms. The verbal human was also a problem for the behaviorist. He "talked" too much, and in doing so supplied himself with a variety of potential mechanisms which were difficult to capture in purely behavioristic terms. This led to the realization that an expansion of the theoretical concept of mediated generalization would be required to keep stimulus-response theories viable. Yet, at the same time, this would require the behaviorist to lean quite heavily on "unobservables" in his analysis of behavior. It also raised the question of how much would be gained theoretically by substituting the notion of "implicit stimulus-response acts" for "ideas of the mind."

It was also becoming clear that even nonverbal organisms could generalize abstract solutions to learning problems and that these solutions were difficult to understand in terms of conditioned habits or associations. Some felt that learning theories in general would soon have to be released from both "Thorndikian bondage" and "Pavlovian inhibition." Yet we must raise the question of how firmly bound theorists ever were to these ideas. Certainly it would be an exaggeration to claim that Pavlov and Thorndike, or even Watson, did not recognize the "leap of faith" involved in the assumption that conditioning principles would generalize completely from simple well-controlled laboratory situations to the complex world outside. Perhaps the greatest strength of these theories was that they were explicit enough to be boldly stated, tested, and found wanting.

The beginnings of behavioristic psychology were based on a combination of conditioning models and associative principles which were characterized in terms of stimulus-response conceptions. To deal with much of human behavior, including such phenomena as transposition and problem solving, the behaviorist was forced to depend heavily on the concepts of generalization and discrimination. These concepts, particularly in the mediational framework in which they were often cast, required a precise specification of the stimulus to which the organism was responding. This turned out to be a difficult task and one that resulted in numerous theoretical problems. The consequences of these problems for stimulus-response theory will be considered in greater detail in subsequent chapters. In the next chapter we turn to some of the practical applications that stemmed, at least initially, from behavioristic concepts.

3

Conditioning
and Behavior
Technology

IN CHAPTER 2 WE CONSIDERED theoretical explanations of human learning that were derived from studies of both classical and instrumental conditioning. Such explanations encounter considerable difficulty when attempting to account for many aspects of human behavior. The reliability of certain relationships observed in conditioning situations has been impressive, however. The very reliability of these relationships has fostered the development of an interest in conditioning principles per se and in a technology of behavior. In this chapter we shall review the main features of this development.

Let us first distinguish between the *theoretical* and *empirical* laws of effect. The empirical law of effect refers to the observation that responses can be made to occur with greater probabilities if they are followed by reward. The empirical law is neutral as to why this happens—it only states that it does happen. In contrast, the theoretical law of effect involves abstract explanations of the observation, which may include stimulus-response contiguity, reinforcement due to reduction of drives, and so forth. Although there has been considerable controversy concerning the theoretical law, most psychologists accept the empirical law in one form or another.

Within the context of the empirical law, the present chapter will focus on two main topics. The first, *conditioning in humans* from the earliest beginnings of life to adulthood, will be mainly concerned with examples of conditioning and not with explanations of why it occurs or how general a phenomenon it may be. The second, *behavior technology,* will discuss the application of conditioning principles in practical situations. Again, our purpose is to survey some examples of such applications without going into the theoretical issues too deeply.

CONDITIONING IN HUMANS

Conditioning Before Birth?

What is the earliest age at which conditioning principles can be successfully applied? There are no widely accepted answers to this question, but there is some evidence that conditioning can occur before birth. This is not to assert that complex learning occurs *in utero,* but rather to indicate that the unborn child is probably not without "habit" during its nine-month tenure in the womb.

The possibility of conditioning in the womb should not be particularly startling. Certainly the unborn infant is exposed to various stimuli that might qualify as a CS, a US, or a reward of some sort. The womb may not always be dark, particularly if the mother stands unclothed in a strong light; and the womb may also be a rather noisy place. Internal sources of sound include the mother's heartbeat and her intestinal rumblings. External sources of sound come from street noises, loud conversations, music, and so on. By eight and one-half weeks the fetus is probably capable of responding to tactile stimuli, and by birth it has reasonably well developed visual and auditory systems (cf. Watson and Lowrey, 1954). In short, the developing fetus is bathed in stimulation from various forms of physical energy and is affected by various types of metabolic activity. Therefore, conditioning might occur in the womb under appropriate circumstances.

Classical Conditioning Before Birth.   Few formal studies of classical conditioning *in utero* seem to have been reported, but there are scattered examples in the literature. An often cited study is that of Spelt (1938), who attempted to condition fetuses between six and one-half and eight and one-half months of age. His technique was to apply tactile vibration to the abdomen of the mother as the CS, with a very loud noise as the US. Movement of the fetus to the noise (UR) was measured by a tambour placed on the mother's abdomen. Spelt found that after a number of CS-US pairings, fetal movement occurred to the CS alone. These findings, however, have not been unanimously accepted as a firm example of fetal conditioning. It has been suggested that the loud noise employed may have made the fetus so "jumpy" that it would respond to any detectable stimulus with movement. In any case, we should not assume that such conditioning would have any great consequences in the overall learning picture for the developing human.

Instrumental Conditioning Before Birth. Studies of instrumental conditioning *in utero* are even rarer than those of classical conditioning. However, a study by De Snoo (1937), cited by Deutsch (1960), seems interpretable as a special instance of instrumental conditioning. De Snoo was concerned that some of his pregnant patients were too heavy, apparently because the amniotic fluid surrounding their fetuses was not being metabolized (drunk) at a desirable rate. To modify these conditions, De Snoo made the fluid more "tasty" by injecting saccharine into the amniotic sac. The success of this stratagem was evidenced by an increased rate of intake of the fluid by the fetuses, as indicated by urine analyses performed on the mothers, and (we presume) by a decrease in the mothers' weights. It does not seem too whimsical to interpret this as a special case of instrumental conditioning under the empirical law of effect. That is, a response (drinking) was rewarded and, hence, increased in probability, as a result of increasing the "sweetness" of the amniotic fluid.

Conditioning in the Infant

The evidence for both classical and instrumental conditioning in the newborn infant is somewhat more plentiful than for such learning in the fetus. Casual observations would also appear to support this assumption. For example, infants appear to use crying behavior in an instrumental fashion to attract the attention of adults to their needs. There also seems to be an element of instrumental conditioning involved in the social interactions that occur between parent and infant. The infant smiles (response), the parent tickles her (reward), and the incidence of smiling by the infant increases. The parent may also smile in turn (response), and the infant may reciprocate with a "gurgle" or a "coo" (reward). Thus, both parent and child may be mutually reinforcing many of the behaviors supporting the social interaction between them. Elements of classical conditioning also seem to be involved in the behavior of infants. For instance, the parent, especially the mother, may come to serve as CS paired with the occurrence of very pleasant USs such as feedings, cuddlings, and diaper changes. But these uncontrolled observations may be somewhat misleading at times, as we shall see.

Classical Conditioning in the Infant. Studies of infants using classical conditioning techniques are somewhat rare for a number of reasons. Infants must be handled with great care, the stimuli to which they are exposed must be of mild intensities, and the duration of the conditioning sessions must be brief (Bijou and Baer, 1967). Nevertheless, there are some very persuasive demonstrations of the classical conditioning of infants in the literature.

An early study of Marquis (1941) suggests that a special type of classical conditioning may occur as a function of the normal feeding activities of the infant. In Marquis's study, infants fed on a three-hour schedule for the preceding eight days were shifted to a four-hour schedule on the ninth day. As a result their activity level between the third and fourth hour on the critical ninth day was substantially higher than that of a comparison group placed on a four-hour schedule at birth. These findings are shown in Figure 3.1.

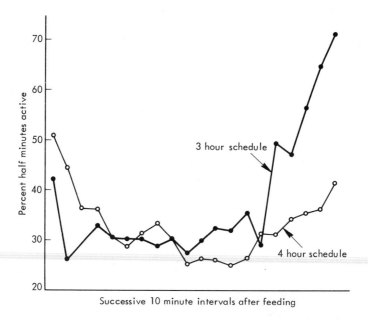

Figure 3.1 **Comparison of three- and four-hour groups on Day IX, when the three-hour group changed to a four-hour schedule. Average of morning and afternoon periods for all subjects.**
(From Marquis, 1941.)

The data in Figure 3.1 seem comparable with those of Pavlov (1927) with respect to *temporal conditioning* in the dog. In Pavlov's experiment a dog was given food every thirteenth minute. Then, any one feeding might be omitted. On these critical trials, despite the omission of food, a secretion of saliva with concomitant alimentary motor reactions occurred. The *duration of time* had somehow or other acquired the properties of a CS. This general experimental paradigm has become known as *temporal conditioning,* and many a parent can attest that it appears to occur with some regularity in the hungry infant.

Classical conditioning of infants with a more explicit CS has also been demonstrated. In one study Lipsitt and Kaye (1964) used a tone as the CS and the insertion of a nipple into the infant's mouth as the US for eliciting sucking reponses. The infants involved were less than five days old. Conditioning of the sucking response occurred, since the infants in the experimental group (CS-US paired) showed more sucking responses to the CS than did a control group (CS and US never paired) of infants. Russian scientists have also reported success in using classical conditioning techniques for discrimination training of infants around three months of age.

Instrumental Conditioning in the Infant. A number of studies show that instrumental conditioning also occurs in infants under well-controlled circumstances. Siqueland and Lipsitt (1966) were able to manipulate head-turning responses in infants less than five days of age by using a dextrose-water solution as a reinforcer. They also presented evidence of an acquired stimulus discrimination. In this situation, turning of the head in the presence of one auditory stimulus was rewarded, but the same response in the presence of a different auditory stimulus was not.

The fact that exploratory behavior starts to appear in infants at about three-months of age has also been used to investigate instrumental conditioning with such subjects. Rheingold, Stanley, and Cooley (1962) used an experimental crib in which infants could manipulate the presentation of visual and auditory stimuli by making appropriate motor responses. Their data suggested that such responding could be controlled by using such stimuli as rewards. Apparently, then, changing patterns of light and sound can serve as rewards in instrumental conditioning situations with relatively young infants.

Haugan (1970) has added an interesting dimension to such studies by investigating the relative efficiency of various types of reinforcers (i.e., food, touch, adult vocalizations) with infants ranging from three to six months of age. Her data suggest that adult vocal imitation (e.g., if the infant said "da," the experimenter said "da") was significantly more effective as a reinforcer in increasing infant vocalization than either food or touch with these subjects. Such findings are especially interesting in light of current speculation that language acquisition, which requires the infant to pay special attention to auditory inputs, may follow developmental sequences determined in great part by biological factors (Lenneberg, 1967).

As we noted earlier, casual observations may lead to erroneous impressions of the role of conditioning in the behavior of infants. For example, conditioning theorists sometimes assume that affectional motive systems in humans are based on more primitive drives, such as those for food and water. Since the mother furnishes the infant with these biological essentials, it has been suggested that the mother comes to be a "lovable CS" because of her close "association" with the alleviation of biological tensions. But Harlow and Suomi (1970) provide experimental evidence that (with monkeys at least) an infant's attachment to its mother is primarily based on tactual stimulation (body contact) and may have less to do with the role of the breast or the bottle as a potential US than was previously thought. The point is sharpened when we note that the act of nursing provides both the opportunity for conditioning based on drive reduction of the drives for hunger and thirst and the opportunity for intimate body contact between mother and infant. Therefore, controlled observations are required to separate the effects of these two variables.

Another cautionary note to consider in conditioning of infants is that often such conditioning is obtained only with great effort under rigorous experimental circumstances. Even then, the resulting conditioned responses may be short lived in infants less than two months of age (White, 1971). Demonstrations of conditioning in infants do have important practical implications, however. For example, they provide (1) techniques for studying the sensory capacity of the developing, nonverbal human (e.g., as with discrimination training); (2) information concerning the importance of conditioning (or other forms of learning) in shaping the infant's psychological world; and (3) technical tools for modifying the behavior of infants, which can be very useful in a short-term therapeutic situation.

At this point a general comment about theory should be made, even though we are focusing on applied aspects of conditioning. As more refined experimental techniques have provided a better understanding of the developing human's abilities, it has become clear that the infant's world is not a blooming, buzzing, confusion. Instead, it may be characterized by more *unlearned* perceptual organization than has been recognized in the past (cf. Fantz, 1963; Hershenson, 1964). Such findings should give us considerable theoretical pause with respect to any general assumption that the infant "has learned all it knows" on the basis of past experience.

Conditioning Beyond Infancy

A number of conditioning studies have been performed using children, young adults, and older adults. Some of these studies involved comparisons of conditioning between younger and older human subjects. Others compared humans with organisms such as monkeys and dogs with respect to the conditioning process. It should not be surprising that the general picture that emerges is that both the *species* of the organism and the *age* of the human subject are important variables to consider in the general conditioning process. Humans, however, may not be "unique" in some instances where it might have been anticipated they would be. For example, some conditioned responses (e.g., eyeblink CRs) in such diverse subjects as the human, the monkey, and the dog may share a common "voluntary" component, rather than being automatic reflexlike CRs (cf. Kimble, 1961).

Humans are unique with respect to their extensive language ability, and this factor is important in studies of human conditioning. For example, the kind of *verbal instructions* given to subjects can affect the overall level of classical conditioning, even when the conditioned response is not completely under voluntary control (Kimble, 1961; Norris and Grant, 1948). Similarly, in instrumental conditioning the response rate may be increased dramatically when the subject is able to verbalize what he is being rewarded for doing. For example, suppose an experimenter required subjects to say individual words continuously and then applied a social reward, saying "Mmm-hmm," whenever a subject mentioned a plural noun. It has been shown that the frequency of plural nouns increases in this situation (cf. Greenspoon, 1955; Verplanck 1955). If the subject could verbalize the contingency being reinforced by the experimenter, the rate would probably increase even more (cf. Dulany, 1968). This leads, however, to the general questions of whether or not the mature human can ever be automatically conditioned.

Conditioning Without Awareness. Verbal factors complicate interpretations of the conditioning process in a number of ways. Verbal behavior can provide complex mediating mechanisms, including self-instructions, as to how to behave in a conditioning situation. One interesting question is whether humans can be conditioned to give some response without being consciously aware of the reward contingencies involved. Here *awareness* is usually defined in terms of the subject's ability to verbalize the relationship between a response and some subsequent reward. Sometimes verbal behavior itself is what the experimenter wishes to condition.

Two general techniques related to instrumental conditioning have been widely employed in studies of verbal conditioning. The first is exemplified in the study by Greenspoon (1955) cited above, in which subjects were rewarded for emitting plural words. With this technique the experimenter decides to reward some particular *class* of responses (e.g., plural nouns). Usually, the subject is already emitting examples of this class (e.g., *trees*) at a relatively low rate, and conditioning is said to have occurred when the number of emitted examples from this class increases as a function of reward.

A second major technique involves rewarding one or more members of a limited set of response alternatives available to the subject. This technique is exemplified in a study by Taffel (1955). Here a subject was presented with a series of cards. Written on each of these cards was a simple verb (e.g., *ran*) and the six pronouns *I, we, you, he, she, they.* The subject's task was to form a sentence beginning with one of the pronouns and using the verb. Whenever the subject used, say, the personal pronouns *I* or *we,* the experimenter would say "Good." As an apparent result of this social reward, there was an increase in the frequency of use of the two personal pronouns, relative to the use of the other pronouns. It has also been shown that extinction training (removal of the reward following conditioning) results in a decrease in frequency of previously rewarded members of such a response class.

As with other conditioning paradigms, the verbal conditioning approach has raised a number of thorny theoretical questions. In spite of this, the procedures involved (or closely related variations) have been used in a number of practical situations. Verbal conditioning techniques have been used to modify verbal behavior in therapeutic situations and to analyze the susceptibility of different classes of responses to the influence of social rewards (cf. Kanfer, 1968).

Generally speaking, the empirical facts of verbal conditioning illustrated above are noncontroversial. The interpretation of the facts, however, especially insofar as they suggest conditioning of humans without awareness, is highly controversial. This controversy arises, in large part, because it often appears that it is only when the subject "understands" the relationship between the response and the reward that conditioning can be demonstrated. But the interpretation of this observation is still open to question. For example, a subject might increase his output of plural nouns *because* he realizes that the experimenter is saying "Mmm-hmm" when he makes that particular type of response. On the other hand, the subject may actually be conditioned without awareness first and *then* become aware of the contingencies involved after the fact. In addition, the interview procedures used after the conditioning experiment to determine if subjects were aware of the reward contingencies may in themselves generate an awareness of the contingencies.

Because of various methodological problems, as well as the difficulty of defining what "awareness" is, these general theoretical issues have not been resolved (cf. Dulany, 1968; Kanfer, 1968; Postman, 1962). There is a close relationship, however, between these issues and those raised by the trial-and-error versus insightful learning issue discussed in Chapter 2.

BEHAVIOR TECHNOLOGY

Our preceding discussion of conditioning situations has generally involved descriptions of rather simple laboratory examples. We shall now consider applications of conditioning principles to human behavior outside the laboratory proper. In doing so, it will be necessary to be more specific in defining certain terms and procedures.

Generally speaking, behavior modification refers to the use of classical or instrumental conditioning techniques to alter behavior patterns. The use of such techniques involves gaining control of behavior in order to accomplish such goals as the following:

1. Improve the well-being of the patient (*behavior therapy*)
2. Exert social control over groups or individuals by appropriate distribution of rewards (*contingency management*)
3. Train animals to substitute for men or machines (*biotechnology*)
4. Improve the efficiency of learning (*programmed learning*)

These examples are far from exhaustive, but they do indicate the wide range of application of conditioning principles in a technological sense.

Behavior Therapy

When conditioning principles are used to improve the psychological well-being of a patient, the technique is broadly classified as a form of behavior therapy. One reason often given for using behavior therapy is that traditional forms of psychotherapy, which often require intense verbal communication between patient and therapist, are obviously not practical for some patients. For example, how could such therapy be employed with a patient who has completely withdrawn into a severe psychotic state?

Another reason given for using behavior therapy instead of traditional psychotherapy is that the principles underlying conditioning have been more carefully evaluated by experimentation and are more efficient than those underlying the other methods. There is also the blunt assertion that conventional psychotherapy does not "work," whereas behavior therapy does (cf. Eysenck, 1961; Wolpe and Lazarus, 1968). Conventional forms of psychotherapy stem from philosophical assumptions that hold that the successful therapist must deal with ideas, will, personality (e.g., the psychoanalytic approach of Freud). In contrast, the behavior therapy orientation stresses the importance of dealing directly with behavior, as contrasted to mind. The following example may clarify this point.

Classical Conditioning and Therapy. Consider the following hypothetical case. A transvestite is being treated for his emotional dependence on wearing women's clothing for sexual arousal. Treatment by conventional therapy might involve extensive exploration of the patient's background and early developmental history. Treatment by behavior therapy is more direct. It might require the patient to watch slides of himself in various types of dresses while punishing shock is being delivered to his fingers. It might also require him to listen to his own recorded voice describing the objects of his fetish at the same time. The trick, the behavioral therapist might say, is to condition an aversive response to the wearing of women's clothing so that it has a negative, not a positive, association for the patient. In a complementary manner, the shock might be withheld and the sound of the patient's voice describing his fetish might be replaced with soothing music anytime a slide depicting the patient in male attire was presented.

The trick here, of course, is to condition a pleasant emotional response (such as relief) to the wearing of men's clothing. Many related examples of such treatment procedures have been described in the literature (cf. Kushner, 1965; Raymond, 1956).

Aversion therapy has also been used to treat alcoholism. In general, alcoholism seems to involve complex physiological-psychological factors, including an emotional dependence that is difficult for the therapist to deal with at a rational or cognitive level. In such instances the therapist might treat part of the problem by pairing the sight, taste, and smell of alcohol (the CS) with some drug (the US) that produces nausea and vomiting when taken in combination with alcohol. The aim, of course, is to condition as many aversive responses as possible to the various stimuli associated with the patient's drinking behavior. Some success with such techniques has been reported (cf. Davidson, 1974). Parenthetically, Pavlov (1927) noted that a dog developed conditioned nauseous responses to the sight of a needle that had been used to administer a drug at levels sufficient to induce vomiting.

Phobias, or irrational fears, have also been treated by classical conditioning techniques. In one basic approach, *systematic desensitization therapy* (cf. Wolpe, 1958, 1962), emotional responses to stimuli are attenuated by repeatedly exposing the patient to them gradually. For example, suppose a subject has an irrational fear of snakes. At the beginning of therapy the subject might be asked to think about snakes. Then he might be shown a picture of a snake. This might be followed by the gradual introduction of a harmless snake in a cage. Finally the patient might be required to handle the snake.

Wolpe (1962) describes desensitization training in terms of a systematic deconditioning of anxiety responses along a stimulus dimension. Presumably the "gradual approach" permits the repeated elicitation and experimental extinction of emotional responses associated with phobia-related stimuli without producing overpowering anxiety. Wolpe also notes that systematic desensitization is not restricted to treatment of classical phobias. It can be used in almost any situation in which individuals are disturbed by stimulus situations with no objective threat.

There are rather explicit assumptions in behavior therapy concerning the central role of classical conditioning in emotional behavior. Pavlov (1927) noted that emotional responses could be elicited in dogs by classical conditioning and that these aberrations suggested a comparison with certain forms of neurosis in man. Correspondingly, one of the most influential studies of learned fear was made in terms of a classical conditioning model by Watson and Rayner (1920). In this study a child was allowed to play with a white rat, which was not a fear-producing stimulus at the beginning of the experiment. As the child reached for the rat, the experimenter made a loud noise, which was already a fear-producing stimulus for the child. As expected, the child shrank back. After several pairings of the CS (rat) and the US (loud noise), emotional responses described as "fear" occurred to other white objects such as mittens, fur coats, and rabbits.

The Watson-Rayner experiment certainly suggests that irrational fears may develop on the basis of classical conditioning principles, presumably on the basis of simple contiguity of the two stimuli. Although there was no reason to believe that the short-term conditioning session used by Watson and Rayner produced permanent effects in their young subject, we can see in principle how an unreasonable fear of white-coated physicians, vendors, or street cleaners might trouble him as an adult. Mowrer (1960) has also suggested that such human emotions as "hope," "fear," "disappointment," and "relief" can all be understood in terms of a basic conditioning model. If emotional behavior does intimately involve classical conditioning, it should not be surprising to find that therapies such as desensitization training or aversion therapy are sometimes effective. However, we now turn to forms of behavior that seem much more "voluntary" and much less automatic.

Instrumental (Operant) Conditioning and Therapy. Some of the most systematic applications of conditioning principles to the control of human behavior derive from the work of Skinner, his students, and his associates (cf. Skinner, 1938; Ferster and Skinner, 1957; Ferster, Culbertson, and Boren, 1975). The techniques utilized are closely related to instrumental conditioning, but they have come to be identified under the specialized title of *operant conditioning.*

An *operant* is defined as some bit of behavior an organism "spontaneously" produces. For example, a rat may run around in a cage or press a lever without any obvious reason for doing so. A pigeon may unexpectedly flutter its wings or peck somewhat "aimlessly" at a spot in its coop. An infant may lift its hand or coo, even though no object is at hand or no other human is present. A woman may idly scratch her ear, but not necessarily because it itches. A psychotic child may bang his head on the floor until it is bloody. In all these cases no particular stimulus seems to elicit these responses automatically. The organism just seems "inclined" to make them.

In operant conditioning the frequency or rate of such operants is supposedly modified by the appropriate reinforcement contingencies. If the bar press, wing flutter, coo, ear scratch, or what have you, results in something rewarding to the subject (e.g., food, warmth, money, companionship, attention), the response is likely to be repeated. In operant conditioning terminology the terms *reinforcement* and *reinforcer* are both used. *Reinforcer* refers to some stimulus (e.g., food); *reinforcement* refers to the operation of presenting a reinforcer (e.g., presenting food). In brief, then, operant conditioning involves making some reinforcement operation contingent on some operant's occurrence.

An important assumption in operant technology is that behavior, whether adaptive or not, is subject to management by appropriate reinforcement contingencies. Some of these contingencies may be deliberate and controlled, but much of our everyday behavior is molded by accidental, unplanned contingencies. For example, we may avoid walking under a ladder if a paint can fell on us the last time we did so. We may continue to wear our favorite suit every time we fly, if the airplane did not crash the last time we did so. A given bit of behavior does not have to be reinforced every time it occurs to be persistent. In other words, there is no reason to believe that frequent behaviors in the real world are supported by regular, uniform schedules of reinforcement. On the contrary, the most persistent behavior is likely to be supported on some *intermittent* schedule.

Suppose a pigeon is trained to peck for grain and is given access to grain for every peck on a continuous basis. Once pecking is established at a rapid rate, the grain is permanently withheld. In this case the pigeon is likely to give up pecking quite soon. On the other hand, if the pigeon had been trained so that a peck led to grain on an intermittent basis, pecking would persist at a relatively high rate for some time, even though grain was no longer available. One factor that may underlie this somewhat paradoxical observation is the relative ease of discriminating between acquisition and extinction following continuous as opposed to intermittent reinforcement. The introduction of extinction procedures after prior training with continuous reinforcement is much more noticeable than when the prior training has been supported on an intermittent schedule with responses being reinforced only occasionally. In other words, intermittent reinforcement is not merely a falling short of the ideal of continuous reinforcement, it is presumed to be the only way in which many significant features of behavior can be explained (cf. Ferster and Skinner, 1957).

A favorite illustration of the influence of intermittent reinforcement in humans is that of the gambler playing slot machines. The "payoff" for each response of placing money in the machine is very intermittent and irregular. Yet almost anyone who has ever observed such gambling will attest that both the *rate* and the *duration* of the level-pressing operant being emitted by the human is impressive. The operant technologist explains that the behavior observed here can be understood in terms of the same principles that apply, say, to the durable pecking behavior of pigeons trained on some intermittent schedule of reward. Perhaps this explains the use of the word *pigeon* to designate a dupe or an easy mark. It may also help explain why the "gambling habit" is so difficult to treat if it becomes a serious psychological problem.

In the application of operant technology to the treatment of psychological problems, the therapist is usually concerned with identifying the reinforcement contingencies that are supporting undesirable behaviors (operants). For example, a mother wishes to train her child not to scream at her. The technologist reviews the home situation and discovers the following. When the child calls the mother softly, she does not come. When the child screams, the mother comes running. The screaming has been reinforced by the mother's coming to the child. The technologist might advise the mother to come *only when* the child is calling her softly. In other words, the mother would be advised to become a *contingency manager*. A special kind of discrimination training is involved in this example. The child would be reinforced for soft vocalizations, but not for loud ones.

There are many operant conditioning techniques, but the two most widely used in behavior therapy are those based on *extinction* and *incompatible response training*. The example of the screaming child involved both extinction and incompatible response training—the loud response was never to be reinforced (extinction training), but the soft response was to be reinforced. Since a soft and a loud response given at the same time would be incompatible, this is a special case of an incompatible response method. Another example of an incompatible response method of treatment is provided by Ayllon (1963) in dealing with a patient who wore an excessive amount of clothing.

This patient might dress herself with a multitude of undergarments, dresses, sweaters, and so on. In addition, she often carried a large bundle of clothing. Instead of treatment involving an analysis of the patient's motivational background, the treatment described by Ayllon was more immediate and direct. The patient was required to shed a certain amount of weight daily (in terms of taking off clothing) in order to obtain her meals. Each day the weight requirement became more stringent, and the patient's behavior changed dramatically. At the beginning of the therapy, she gradually discarded her bundles and handbags. Then she began to shed her numerous pairs of stockings. Finally she would weigh in with only a dress, undergarments, a pair of stockings, and light shoes. In addition, the improvement in her physical appearance due to normal dressing behavior apparently made her more socially acceptable to others in the hospital and to her parents. This resulting social reinforcement (e.g., attention) also helped to maintain the incompatible response of dressing with a moderate, rather than an excessive, amount of clothing.

How Effective Is Behavior Therapy?   Behavior therapy has been reported to have varying degrees of effectiveness in the treatment of catatonic schizophrenia, a severe psychosis; (Isaacs, Thomas, and Goldiamond, 1960); stuttering (Rickard and Mundy, 1965); juvenile delinquency (Schwitzgebel, 1967; Davidson and Seidman, 1974); smoking (Lando, 1975); general disturbances of children (Ferster and Simmons, 1966); and in a number of other therapeutic situations involving the treatment of psychological problems. Some behavior therapists have been so bold as to suggest, on the basis of such successful accounts, that the traditional therapist may have trouble justifying both his methods and his fees. On the other hand, there is not enough evidence to show that behavior therapy is the answer to all problems of behavior disorders. Motivation in some sense ultimately must be considered, since the effectiveness of a reinforcement seems to depend on the human's "willingness" to emit an operant and to "want" a particular reinforcer. For example, it probably is difficult to condition hungry children to do their homework with turnips as a potential reinforcer. In addition, the effectiveness of generally reliable reinforcers in maintaining behavior *may* vary with the biological development (age) of the child as well as with his unique conditioning history. Even so, these considerations do not invalidate the impressive technology that has been derived from conditioning principles for application in the treatment of the behaviorally (or psychologically) disturbed. Of course drug therapy and other nonpsychological methods of treatment often are important parts of the general form of treatment in many extreme cases of behavior disorders.

Traditional therapists (e.g., Freudians) often stress internal psychological forces as the root cause of psychological malfunctions. The patient's behavior is considered only a symptom of the underlying problem, and changing the behavior is not considered a solution to the patient's real problem. In contrast, the behavior therapist stresses the importance of dealing *only* with external, observable responses, without inferences about "deeper" psychological factors. The behavior *is* the problem from this point of view. There seems to be some validity for both positions. Behavior technology does seem effective in controlling some aspects of behavior, but a case can be made that such behaviors are more a reflection of ideas, intentions, or attitudes than of highly specific actions that are controlled through reinforcement. In a sense, behavior itself is an abstraction; and even an operant may be technically defined as a *class* of responses rather than a specific, single bit of behavior (cf. Catania, 1968).

Contingency Management and Social Control

Behavior technology has also been applied to the management of social behavior of humans. Some have found such possibilities potentially disastrous (cf. Huxley, 1946; Orwell, 1949). Others have indicated this is the only way man can survive (cf. Skinner, 1971). Let us consider some specific examples of behavior technology.

Classroom Control. "Spare the rod and spoil the child." This old adage is directly contrary to basic principles applied by behavior technologists to maintain control of behavior in the classroom. Experimental evidence suggests that punishment is not effective in many situations, and good management practices should take this into account. For example, children might be given points for each period of time they remained quiet in the classroom. These points, in turn, might be traded for such things as more free time during recess and access to a hobby shop.

Bijou, Birnbrauer, Kidder, and Tague (1966) have applied these basic techniques to "shape" desirable classroom behaviors in retarded children by reinforcing correct answers with approving remarks and ignoring incorrect answers (extinction). In addition, cooperative social behavior was reinforced by giving points that could be exchanged for money. It was thought that strengthening of those behaviors relevant to general cooperation between student and teacher would provide an appropriate background for the teaching of specific academic behaviors (e.g., reading and writing).

Social Control of Groups.　Gericke (1965) describes a plan for the use of conditioning procedures to increase the incidence of desirable behaviors, and reduce the incidence of undesirable behaviors, in a hospital situation. Behaviors that were considered to be desirable included maintaining personal hygiene and seeking entrance into a therapy group. Tokens, which could be used for entry to an elegant dining facility, were given as behavior reinforcers. Gericke indicates that the techniques employed were generally effective as reflected by desirable changes in the personal and social habits of the patients.

One of the most dramatic applications of conditioning principles to the control of groups is illustrated in Schein's (1956) review of situations faced by American prisoners of war who were held by the Chinese during the Korean conflict. Schein notes that the Chinese created a controlled prison environment in which rewards (e.g., extra food, medicine, special privileges) were given for "correct behaviors" (e.g., collaboration, informing on others), whereas punishments (e.g., decrease in food, threats) were given for "incorrect behaviors." In addition, the Chinese always *paced* their demands and required some level of *participation* by the prisoners. (Other techniques used are not pertinent to our present discussion.)

According to Schein, the basic intent in this situation was to produce changes in the prisoners that would be lasting and self-sustaining. How successful the program was is debatable. It did appear that behavior could be quite effectively controlled within the prison system by such behavioral techniques, even to the extent of "shaping" some prisoners to make false confessions and to question their political beliefs overtly. Yet there seems to be little evidence that the behavior controls instituted were generally self-sustaining after the prisoners left their controlled environment (cf. Schein, 1956). Perhaps a more concentrated behavior technology program might have been more effective; perhaps not. The potential for the control and "rehabilitation" of prisoners in any situation suggested by such an enterprise is both interesting and disturbing.

Biotechnology

Animals have long been trained to perform various kinds of services for man. Donkeys are trained to pull carts. Horses are trained to both tolerate and transport us as riders. Dogs are trained to guard us, herd our livestock, and be companions for our children. Various animals have been trained as circus performers to entertain us. These are useful services, and behavior technology can undoubtedly make both the animals and our training techniques more efficient (cf. Breland and Breland, 1951, 1966).

Animals have also served as subjects in basic experimental situations to answer complex questions that may or may not relate to the learning process directly. The steady pecking behavior that can be maintained in a pigeon on intermittent schedules of reinforcement is well suited to the detailed study of the psychological effects of drugs on behavior over a long period of time (cf. Dews, 1955; Herrnstein and Morse, 1956). Some of these effects are relevant to drug-related behavior in man. Other experimental uses of animals conditioned to perform certain tasks have relevance to questions of sensory capacity in humans and so on. In short, animals have performed a variety of important functions for man, from feeding him to assisting him to become healthier both psychologically and physically. Animals can also be used to alleviate man's boredom in tasks that need to be performed but cannot yet be done reliably by machines. A demonstration reported by Verhave (1966) is a case in point.

Verhave notes that pigeons trained through behavior technology are ideally suited for many operations involving quality control of commercial products. To demonstrate this, Verhave trained pigeons to detect defective capsules on an assembly line in a pharmaceutical company. The basic techniques involved reinforcing the bird for pecking in the presence of a defective capsule (e.g., an empty one), but not in the presence of a good one. The pigeons were able to discriminate accurately, as determined by their pecking behavior, with 99 percent accuracy within one week of daily discrimination training. Even though there was no question about the feasibility of using the highly reliable pigeon inspectors, they were not employed by the company after the experiment primarily because of public relations considerations. Verhave suggests rather wryly that the company did not want its products viewed as being "for the birds."

Numerous additional examples could be given of ways in which animals have been trained to perform services for man. As for conditioning principles used to train these behaviors in animals, it should be noted that the basic principles applied to the training of animals are the same as those used in programmed instruction.

Programmed Learning

One of the more far-reaching applications of behavior technology is in programmed learning or programmed instruction. Developments within this area have enabled psychologists to refute the often-heard criticism that they have nothing practical to say about learning or how to learn. There are many forms of programmed learning, which range from programmed textbooks and teaching machines to elaborate forms of computer-assisted instruction. All of these procedures have decided advantages over many aspects of classroom instruction provided by the most well intentioned teachers.

The advantages of programmed-learning techniques are perhaps best illustrated by considering some things the classroom teacher cannot usually accomplish. In a large class, when the time period is limited, the teacher cannot provide (1) individualized instruction for each pupil, (2) immediate feedback in the form of knowledge of results, (3) immediate corrections for incorrect answers, (4) instruction at the level of specific behaviors for each child, or (5) a patient and cheerful attitude at all times. These factors, however, may be much more important to the child's efficiency in learning and sense of well-being in the classroom than are ability grouping of pupils or up-to-date classrooms. To a large extent, all of these factors can be taken into account in carefully programmed learning techniques (cf. Skinner, 1961).

The development of techniques for programmed learning can be traced far back in the history of psychology, but the contemporary popularity of the approach is largely due to the work of behavior technologists. The principles that behavior technologists have emphasized are taken from the conditioning laboratory. These principles are extremely simple, but they have proved to be of value in teaching both animals (biotechnology) and humans.

To begin with, behavior technologists emphasize the notion that behavior is shaped by its own consequences and that it is shaped most effectively when those consequences are immediate. In other words, reinforcement is most effective when it follows a particular response without delay. This principle is based on well-established observations. For example, a pigeon will learn to peck a key more rapidly if the reward provided for that response is given immediately rather than delayed a short time.

This principle could be applied in teaching children to spell. Suppose a child is learning to spell the word *man*. If he or she presses the typewriter keys for *m, a,* and *n,* in that order, a picture of a man might be presented immediately or a recorded voice might immediately say "correct." This principle *of immediate feedback* for either correct or incorrect responses is found in most forms of programmed learning. It should be noted, however, that contemporary conceptions of programmed learning emphasize the "guidance" function of feedback and not some automatic strengthening of connections or habits. In any case, the principle appears to be an important one in most learning situations.

A second principle emphasized by behavior technologists, *successive approximations,* is also based on observations from the conditioning laboratory. For example, pigeons are usually taught to peck keys in the laboratory by means of successive approximations to the desired response. At first any response that might facilitate key pecking, such as turning to face the key, is immediately reinforced. Then a closer approximation to the final response, such as raising the head near the key, is required before the reward is provided. Eventually the pigeon may be taken through a series of such steps until the key peck itself becomes the reinforced response.

Various techniques can be used to provide successive approximations with humans. For example, in teaching a student to memorize an entire poem, learning might proceed one line at a time until the poem was learned. Alternatively, the student might begin by reading the entire poem, which would be presented on a screen before him. Then only part of the poem might be presented, with the student having to supply the rest. Finally the entire poem might be faded out so that the student would have to supply it without any written props.

The procedures illustrated with both the pigeon and the student are designed to give rise to responses that can be reinforced immediately. In this way the learner is taken through a series of stages until the desired behavior occurs. The requirement of a response before a reward is given is consistent with an educational philosophy that says a student must be more than a passive receiver of information. He must also be an initiator of action and be directly involved in the learning process. If it is true that we learn by "doing," then programmed learning techniques should help the student learn more efficiently. Figure 3.2 shows a student at work on a teaching machine.

The principle of successive approximations, or behavior shaping, is closely related to the concept of optimal programming of educational material. Many workers in this field believe that it is the emphasis on optimal steps in planning a program that is critical to its success. It is not so much that successive stages are involved in a program as it is what the stages are that determines its effectiveness. In teaching arithmetic solutions to children, it is important that they understand each stage of explanation. And the steps that may be optimal for some pupils may not be optimal for others. To be effective, programmed learning must be designed flexibly enough to provide optimal steps for all learners.

Optimizing the Instructional Process. Different learning programs and different forms of programmed instruction can be devised for different

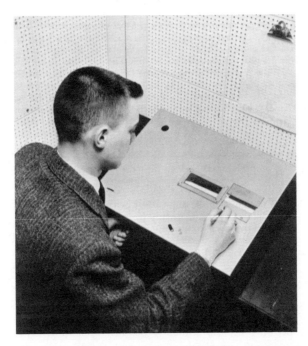

Figure 3.2 Student at work on a teaching machine. One frame of material is partly visible in the left-hand window. The student writes his response on a strip of paper exposed at the right. He then lifts a lever with his left hand, advancing his written response under a transparent cover and uncovering the correct response in the upper corner of the frame. If he is correct, he moves the lever to the right, punching a hole alongside the response he has called correct and altering the machine so that that frame will not appear again when he goes through the series a second time. A new frame appears when the lever is returned to its starting position.
(From Skinner, 1953.)

purposes. A wide range of subject matter can be imparted to students so long as the basic principles of good programming are taken into account, such as individual differences among learners and the most efficient sequencing of materials. The learner should be allowed to move at his own pace and should be given rapid feedback concerning his performance. The sequence of instruction should be coherent with an opportunity to review errors and correct them in a logical order. Given these technically complex restrictions, a computer could undoubtedly be useful in an *educational setting*.

Atkinson (1974) has attempted to link basic work in memory and cognition to designing optimal procedures for teaching reading to first- through third-grade children. A basic element of this effort is computer-assisted instruction (CAI).

A student in the program uses a teletypewriter with an audio headset which is connected to a computer system at another location. On a given day, instruction might begin with the student typing R (for reading) and his first name. The program replies with the student's last name and finds his place from the preceding study period. The computer can be programmed not only to recall this information but to maintain a complete record of a student's entire curriculum for analysis by the programmer. Such a monumental task would obviously be impossible for a teacher in the classroom with many students. When assisted by the computer, however, the task is reduced to quite manageable proportions, and the teacher can attend to other instructional matters.

Atkinson gives the following example of a particular exercise (sight-recognition) with his CAI program. The program types PEN, and the student hears "Type pen." The student then types PEN as a response to the program's request. The computer then reinforces this correct response with the symbol + as well as a verbal "Great!" If the student was wrong and typed PON, the program would respond with / / / PEN on the teletypewriter and with a "No, pen" on the audio headset. Every so often the program gives an enthusiastic "That's fabulous" or a cheering and clapping of hands, depending on the student's performance that day.

On the basis of experimental data and a student's past level of performance and achievement, attempts are made to predict end-of-the-year test scores and to maximize the most effective use of the total time available for the various students involved. Atkinson suggests that the costs involved in CAI are quite acceptable, based on present evaluations of the project. One would certainly have to grant the general validity of such teaching methods, since they take into account well-established learning principles, the needs of individual students, the aims of the teacher, the overall efficiency of the group, and educational costs.

CONCLUSION

We began this chapter by reviewing several examples of both instrumental and classical conditioning in humans. At the youngest ages such demonstrations are relatively rare, but there is some evidence for conditioning prior to birth and during infancy. The theoretical importance of these demonstrations is open to question, but they do tell us something about the organization of the young human's perceptual world. In addition, the successful application of conditioning techniques suggests ways for investigating sensory capacities and simple learning at these early ages.

Demonstrations of conditioning are quite commonplace in the adult. A major issue here is whether such conditioned responses can be established without the subject's being consciously aware of the reinforcement contingencies. This issue is likely to be raised in demonstrations of instrumental conditioning. It has also stimulated a great deal of research, although clear-cut answers have not been forthcoming. In many cases awareness of the reinforcement contingency appears to be necessary for conditioning to occur. Even in these instances it is not always clear whether awareness developed during the conditioning session or during subsequent interviews with the experimental subject.

Most of the chapter reviewed examples of the application of conditioning principles in practical situations. As we have seen, illustrations of behavior technology are quite common in therapeutic settings, in the training of animals, in gaining social control over others, and in educational settings. In all these situations behavior technology can claim a degree of success. Of course this success does not necessarily imply that the tacit assumptions that behavior technologists bring to these situations are necessarily correct.

The central feature of behavior technology is the principle of reinforcement, or the law of effect. The application of this principle to the control of behavior is as old as the history of man. Every human being is familiar with the use of reward to accomplish various objectives. This is not to deny that behavior technologists have taught us a great deal about the effective use of reward and especially about how to use or not use punishment. But this does not mean that rewards have the automatic consequences that behavior technologists often attribute to them. Reward certainly provides an effective means of guiding behavior, and when one organism controls those rewards that are crucial to the survival of another organism, the effect of rewards can be powerful indeed. Let us consider some of the difficulties encountered in attempting to evaluate one aspect of the influence of reward on human behavior.

When we focus on human behavior, and particularly on the way in which undesirable behaviors come to be maintained, certain problems of interpretation become clear. The behavior technologist often assumes that such behavior is supported by intermittent reinforcement contingencies arising in an uncontrolled environment. However, it is far from clear how behaviors such as head banging in an autistic child or compulsive eating in the obese ever come to be supported on these schedules. In the laboratory it is often found that behavior must be "shaped" with great care under continuous reinforcement before it can be brought under the control of some intermittent schedule (cf. Ferster and Skinner, 1957). Surely we would not claim that behaviors such as head banging or compulsive eating are carefully shaped from continuous to intermittent reinforcement schedules by parents, friends, or others in a person's environment. What, then, is the basis for assuming that such undesirable behaviors are supported by schedules of intermittent reinforcement?

The emphasis on the role of intermittent schedules of reward comes from the general observation that naturally occurring behaviors are almost never reinforced continuously in the "real world" and from the laboratory observation that extinction is much more difficult when responses are maintained on an intermittent schedule. There is little argument concerning the everyday observation. However, the laboratory observation may occur because it is easier to recognize that a rule generated by continuous reinforcement (e.g., "I am rewarded every time I respond") has been changed than it is to notice that a rule generated by intermittent reinforcement (e.g., "If I respond, I will be rewarded sometimes") has been altered. That is, behavior in the laboratory may be harder to extinguish following intermittent reinforcement because it is more difficult to notice that "the rules of the game" have been changed and not because behaviors maintained in this manner are somehow stronger.

In the remaining chapters of this text we shall have other occasions to examine rule-governed behaviors. We shall also examine the explanatory value of conditioning principles in various contexts ranging from associative learning to memory and language. For the present it is sufficient to note that principles derived from the conditioning laboratory have provided the basis for practical work that may be of considerable value to man long after their theoretical significance has come to an end.

4

Associative Learning

THIS CHAPTER FOCUSES on associative learning in humans and particularly on the learning of verbal materials. The experimental paradigms to be considered here, the serial and paired-associate paradigms, have formed the primary basis for accounts of associative learning in humans since the days of Ebbinghaus. As seems appropriate in the light of historical developments, we begin the chapter with a discussion of his work.

Ebbinghaus's studies of associative learning were greatly influenced by the philosophical tradition of his time. This tradition stemmed rather directly from the speculations of the British associationists. In the discussion of associations these philosophers placed particular emphasis on verbal materials and on language. Although "ideas" were considered to be the basic units of thought, "words" were often equated with "ideas" in their discussions. This emphasis on units of language arose because the association of words seemed to be so clear. The flavor of associative conceptions as well as the identification of words with the units of thought can be seen in the following quotation from Hobbes:

> The cause of the coherence . . . of one conception to another, is their first coherence . . . at the time when they are produced by sense: as for example, from St. Andrew the mind runneth to St. Peter, because their names are read together; from St. Peter to a stone, for the same cause; from stone to foundation, because we see them together; and for the same cause, from foundation to church, and from church to people, and

from people to tumult: and according to this example, the mind may run
from almost anything to anything (Hobbes, 1651).

It is clear from this quotation that units of language played a major
role in the speculations of the associationists. It is also clear that the fundamental law of association was contiguity of experience. Both of these factors influenced Ebbinghaus's studies of human learning and memory. Of
course the units that Ebbinghaus employed were nonsense syllables and
not words. He chose these units for study because, unlike words, they appeared to be relatively free of prior associations. We might point out a
paradox here that arises from the use of verbal materials. That is, the
fundamental principles of association were supposed to be completely general and applicable across all species. Yet they were first tested, and later
developed, in the species specific context (i.e., human) of verbal material.

The experimental task employed by Ebbinghaus was that of serial
learning in which he served as the only subject. The task consisted of learning lists of nonsense syllables in a serial order. The nonsense syllables consisted of consonant-vowel-consonant (CVC) combinations, all of which
could be pronounced as if they were words. Within this context Ebbinghaus
carried out a number of important experiments concerning learning and
memory. Before turning to his findings, however, let us consider the serial
task and methods for serial learning in more detail.

SERIAL LEARNING: METHODS AND EARLY FINDINGS

In addition to its utility in studying associative processes, serial learning was of interest to psychologists for the deceptively simple reason that
much of human behavior involves sequential patterns that occur in time.
This is perhaps most obvious in speech production and in other motor activities such as swimming, riding a bicycle, or tying a shoelace. Therefore it
was widely assumed that understanding the manner in which serial learning
takes place would provide a great deal of information concerning psychological processes that also take place in time. For example, it was believed
that such higher-order mental processes as thinking and problem solving
involve complex serial organization and that the study of serial learning
would go a long way toward revealing the nature of the complex organization. Such hypotheses were supported by indications that certain neurological and pathological disorders are characterized by defects in the ability
to perform sequential patterns. In such cases timing defects occur, such as
perseveration of responses that were appropriate in the past, but are not at
present, and anticipation of responses that will be appropriate in the future.
but are not at present. Since these classes of error also occur in serial learning with "normal" human subjects, it is not difficult to see why psychologists
became interested in the laws that govern serial learning.

Methods of Serial Learning

Consider a series of verbal units represented by the letters *A, B, C, D, E, F, G*. A subject is presented with these units one at a time and is instructed to learn the series in order. This is the type of task introduced by Ebbinghaus (1885) and referred to as serial learning. Actually, serial learning refers to a variety of procedures, all of which focus on the learning of units in some specified order. For example, a procedure that has been widely employed is the *method of serial anticipation*. Here the subject is presented with unit *A*, and his task is to give unit *B* before it is presented to him. Then, when unit *B* is presented, his task is to anticipate unit *C*, and so on through the entire list. The items are usually presented at a fairly rapid rate, say one every two seconds, and the learning task is complete when the subject can anticipate each item in the list without error.

A variation on this procedure is called the *method of serial recall*. In this situation the subject sees the entire list, one item at a time, and then recalls the entire list in serial order. Both presentation and recall may be paced by requiring the subject to give only one item every few seconds. In addition, the subject may be required to start at the beginning of the list (forward recall) or at the end of the list (backward recall). The recall method approximates the procedure Ebbinghaus employed in his pioneering studies, but certain differences do exist. For example, although Ebbinghaus studied the list one item at a time, paced by the tick of a metronome, the entire list was before him at all times. This is sometimes called the *method of complete presentation*. Furthermore, he studied the list until he thought he "knew it by heart" and then recalled the list in an unpaced manner. These differences in procedure may explain certain discrepancies between the findings reported by Ebbinghaus and those obtained by contemporary investigators.

One apparent advantage of the more recent methods of serial learning is that they permit the experimenter to time the exposure of each item in the series precisely. This, of course, is important to a stimulus-response analysis of serial learning, according to which each item serves both as a response to the preceding item and as a stimulus for the subsequent item in the series. Thus, with the exception of the first and last items in the list, each item is assumed to perform a *double function* in that it is both a stimulus and a response.

Actually, this double-function characteristic of serial learning is one of the reasons why serial tasks declined in popularity during the behavioristic period. For instance, if an investigator wanted to manipulate characteristics of the stimulus and response terms independently, such as their degree of similarity, this could not be done adequately in the serial task due to the double-function character of the items. Any change in a particular item influences its relationship to both the preceding item and the item that follows it. Thus serial methods gave way to other methods, particularly to the paired-associate method, when the focus was on basic aspects of the associative process and where it was desirable to manipulate stimulus and response events independently. However, it would be well for us to continue our discussion of serial learning before turning our attention to other methods.

Ebbinghaus's Findings

Ebbinghaus's studies of associations were mainly influenced by the philosophy of British associationism. According to the British associationists, all laws of association could be reduced to a single principle, the *law of contiguity*. That is, things that are experienced together tend to become associated. Of course, other factors were thought to be important, but contiguity was the sine qua non and other laws had to be derived from this basic law. Thus it was of some importance for Ebbinghaus to discover contiguity to be a matter of "more-or-less" rather than "all-or-none," since he found that associations were apparently formed not only between adjacent items in a series (e.g., *A-B, B-C*) but between items lying farther apart (*A-C, B-E,* etc.).

Types of Association. In his experimental investigations Ebbinghaus reported evidence of at least three classes of association that may be found in serial learning: (1) immediately successive forward associations, such as *A-B* and *B-C,* following the learning of a list like *A, B, C, D, E, F, G, H;* (2) immediately successive backward associations, such as *B-A* and *C-B;* and (3) associations between items that are not immediately adjacent, such as *A-C* or *B-E.* These nonadjacent associations, which may also be either forward or backward, are called *remote associations,* and the degree of remoteness can be stipulated in terms of the number of intervening items. Thus adjacent items such as *A-B* have zero degrees of remoteness, and separated items such as *A-D* have two degrees of remoteness, since there are two intervening items, *B* and *C.* Ebbinghaus found that the strength of these remote associations displayed quite lawful characteristics, and many of the techniques he employed were designed to probe the origin and nature of such associations.

The basic approach that Ebbinghaus employed in the study of remote associations involved the *method of derived lists.* First he would learn a serial list of nonsense syllables, which we will represent as *A, B, C, D, E, F, G,* and *H.* Following this the syllables would be rearranged in the desired degree of remoteness and the new list would be learned. For example, a derived list of one degree of remoteness would be *A, C, E, G, B, D, F,* and *H.*

Ebbinghaus reasoned that if remote associations were formed during original learning, it should take less time to learn the derived list than it took to learn the original list. Furthermore, the stronger the remote associations, the greater the reduction in time to learn the derived list. He indexed the strength of remote associations in terms of a *savings score,* the percentage reduction in time taken to learn the derived list relative to the time taken to learn the original list. For example, if twelve hundred seconds were required for original learning and eight hundred seconds for learning the derived list, then $\dfrac{1,200-800}{1,200}$ would represent the savings score. Expressed as a percentage, this would be 33 percent savings. The results of one of Ebbinghaus's experiments based on these savings scores are given in Table 4.1. The table shows that the percentage saved decreased

Table 4.1 Percentage of savings as a function of degree of remoteness in derived list studies.

Degree of remoteness	Time for original learning (sec.)	Time for relearning (sec.)	Percent savings
0	1,266	844	33.3
1	1,275	1,138	10.8
2	1,260	1,171	7.0
3	1,260	1,186	5.8
7	1,268	1,227	3.3
Random	1,261	1,255	0.5

(AFTER EBBINGHAUS, 1885.)

as the degree of remoteness increased, although a slight amount of savings was obtained even when the derived list was a random rearrangement of the original list.

Despite considerable controversy about their meaning, for many years these findings were taken to indicate that the strength of associations decreased as a simple function of the degree of remoteness between items. This was important at the time for two basic reasons. First, Ebbinghaus had demonstrated the possibility of investigating memorial relationships in systematic, straightforward ways. Second, his results suggested that the basic law of association, the law of contiguity, applied in a "more-or-less" rather than an "all-or-none" manner. This point was particularly important for those who were interested in the span of consciousness because it suggested that associations were formed not only between adjacent items, which the learner consciously attempted to do, but also between nonadjacent items without the conscious deliberation of the learner.

Frequency of Repetition. A principle that has been closely linked to that of contiguity in the history of associationism is the principle of repetition, or frequency. That is, if contiguity of events is the basic associative

principle, then the frequency with which the same events have been experienced contiguously should also influence degree of learning and retention. Ebbinghaus investigated the effect of frequency using lists of sixteen
CVC syllables. A particular list was read once and was then repeated various times. Twenty-four hours after this practice phase the list was learned
"to the point of the first possible reproduction of the series." By comparing
the time taken to learn the list after varying amounts of practice, Ebbinghaus was able to determine the amount of time saved for each repetition.
The results of this experiment are shown in Table 4.2.

Table 4.2 Relationship between frequency of repetition and time
to learn.

Number of repetitions	Time to learn after 24 hours	Savings in seconds	Average savings for each repetition
0	1,270		
8	1,167	103	12.9
16	1,078	192	12.0
24	975	295	12.3
32	863	407	12.7
42	697	573	13.6
53	585	685	12.9
64	454	816	12.8

(AFTER EBBINGHAUS, 1885.)

As the data in Table 4.2 indicate, increasing the number of repetitions during practice results in a steady decrease in the time required to
learn the list twenty-four hours later. When the list is only read once (zero
repetitions), the time required to learn the list twenty-four hours later is
comparable with the time required to learn sixteen-syllable lists "by heart"
in other experiments (see Table 4.1). Thus, little of anything learned
through a single reading is retained after twenty-four hours. With each
increase in the number of repetitions, however, a substantial savings is
obtained. Since Ebbinghaus was the first investigator to systematically
study this relationship between frequency and memory, we have labeled
the observed relationship "Ebbinghaus's axiom."

A second finding of interest in this experiment concerns the influence
of more repetitions than the number required to learn the list. This is typically called the effect of *overlearning*. On the basis of comparisons with
other experiments reported by Ebbinghaus, it appears likely that he required
around thirty repetitions to learn a sixteen-syllable list. Therefore the results
for those conditions involving more than thirty repetitions constitute evidence of a substantial overlearning effect. In fact, Ebbinghaus's data suggest that the amount saved per repetition beyond thirty repetitions is just

as great as the amount saved per repetition up to thirty repetitions. That is, in Ebbinghaus's experiment the amount saved per repetition was almost constant across all repetition conditions.

The findings Ebbinghaus reported concerning the effects of frequency of repetition, including the consequences of overlearning, were to have a profound influence on the development of associationistic thought. In the early part of the twentieth century, findings such as these provided the foundation for Thorndike's "law of exercise" as well as for the common belief that "practice makes perfect." Somewhat later, during the behavioristic period, the emphasis changed from frequency of contiguous events to frequency of reward, but even here findings such as those reported by Ebbinghaus played a major role.

In addition to the study of associative principles, the experiments conducted by Ebbinghaus were designed to investigate many practical aspects of learning and retention. In fact, his entire approach to experimental investigation was to emphasize "the objective conditions of life." Let us now turn to some of these more practical experiments.

The Temporal Course of Retention. It is well known that people forget things they have learned and, generally speaking, that the amount forgotten varies with the time since original learning. Ebbinghaus was the first individual to systematically study the course of retention over time. To do this he learned lists of thirteen CVC syllables and then relearned the same lists after intervals of time which varied from twenty minutes to thirty-one days. By comparing the time taken for original learning with the time taken for relearning, he was able to determine the percentage of savings and by implication the amount of forgetting. As the data in Table 4.3 indicate,

Table 4.3   Retention as a function of time since original learning.

Delay interval	Percent savings	Percent forgotten
20 minutes	58.2	41.8
1 hour	44.2	55.8
9 hours	35.8	64.2
1 day	33.7	66.3
2 days	27.8	72.2
6 days	25.4	74.6
31 days	21.1	78.9

(AFTER EBBINGHAUS, 1885.)

forgetting increased from around 40 percent after twenty minutes to nearly 80 percent after thirty-one days.

Amount of Material. Everyone knows that it is easier to learn a small amount of material than it is to learn a large amount of material. The exact relationship between the amount of material and the time required to learn it, however, is often difficult to specify. Ebbinghaus investigated this relationship by determining the number of readings required to achieve a criterion of one correct recitation of a list. With lists no longer than seven items, only a single reading was required. Miller (1956) has shown that seven is a good estimate of the number of items we can hold in *immediate memory*. Beyond lists of seven items, Ebbinghaus found that many readings were required. With lists of only ten items, thirteen readings were required; and with lists as long as thirty-six syllables, fifty-five readings were required before the list could be recited correctly. Thus the cost in terms of time is greatly increased when more items are added to the list to be learned.

Summary of Ebbinghaus's Work.   The various findings reported by Ebbinghaus (1885) provided the empirical basis for the study of human learning and for the development of association theory. His observations concerning the effects of frequency, amount of material, and overlearning have been generally confirmed by other investigators using a variety of experimental procedures (cf. McGeoch and Irion, 1952). A similar remark can be made about his findings concerning the temporal course of forgetting. Although Ebbinghaus's findings concerning remote associations were to become the subject of considerable controversy, they did suggest that associations were formed by relatively automatic processes that did not require the conscious efforts of the learner. Thus Ebbinghaus presented data that suggested that serial learning was much more complex than might have been expected and that this task might offer a primary tool by which scientists could investigate the main stream of human "cognitive" activities. We shall return to contemporary evaluations of these findings, but first we shall examine one of the most reliable outcomes of serial learning.

The Serial Position Curve

Subjects sometimes give responses in serial learning before they are correct (anticipation errors) as well as after the point at which they were correct (perseveration errors). Early in the list, errors of anticipation are more likely; late in the list, perseveration errors are more likely. Since both types of error could be expected to occur in the middle of the list, we might expect that the overall error rate would be greater in the middle than it is at either end. This turns out to be precisely the situation.

The observation of a bowed serial position curve could be readily explained by associationists who accepted Ebbinghaus's findings. They would argue that a combination of forward and backward remote associations could easily produce more errors in the middle of the list. But for many theorists following in the behavioristic tradition, this observation posed a theoretical problem. The problem arose because these theorists based their theories on the studies of classical conditioning and therefore rejected the possibility of backward associations. This interpretation rested on the failures to obtain backward conditioning in the classical conditioning situation. Before we consider the attempts by such theorists to explain the serial position curve, let us consider the phenomenon a bit more carefully.

The serial position curve is most reliably found when the following conditions apply:

1. The method of serial anticipation is used in learning.
2. The materials being learned have no serial organization due to prior usage, as might be the case if words from an ordinary sentence or an alphabetical list were presented in serial order.
3. The average number of correct responses over a number of learning trials, usually to a criterion of one errorless trial, is plotted as a function of an item's position in the list.

The serial position curve in Figure 4.1 indicates that the fewest correct responses occur in learning at a point just beyond the middle of the list. The largest number of correct responses occurs at the beginning of the list, and the next largest at the end of the list. Thus we see what is often called a primacy-recency effect to indicate the relative ease in learning the initial (primacy) and terminal (recency) items, an outcome that can be demonstrated over a variety of experimental conditions.

Despite the reliability of the serial position curve, its nature is not well understood. The earlier behavioristic theories (Lepley, 1934; Hull, 1935) explained the serial position curve by emphasizing a close congruence between the conditioning mechanisms of excitation and inhibition and those mechanisms assumed to underlie the process of serial learning. These theories attributed the shape of the serial position curve to the influence of inhibitory tendencies developed during learning, the result of which was to suppress the learning of items toward the middle of the list. That is, in addition to forward associations between adjacent items, forward associations also develop among nonadjacent items, and since more of these remote associations span the middle of the list rather than the ends of the list, the middle items are more interfered with or inhibited.

These theoretical accounts are discussed in detail elsewhere (cf. McGeoch and Irion, 1952). For our purposes it is sufficient to point out that although these theories do account for the general form of the serial position curve, they fail to account for several specific factors. Even the most elaborate form of this type of theory, which was offered by Hull and several collaborators in 1940, fails to satisfactorily explain the serial position effect (cf. McCrary and Hunter, 1953).

In more recent years attempts to explain the serial position curve have shifted away from an emphasis on either remote associations or ex-

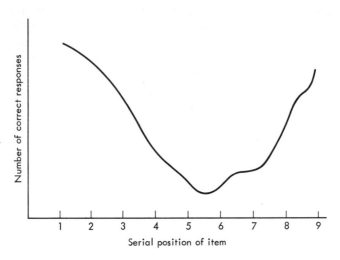

Figure 4.1   A typical serial position curve.

tensions of unidirectional conditioning models that depend only on forward associations. A more empirical account of the serial position curve, and its skewed or asymmetrical form, has been offered by Ribback and Underwood (1950). They assumed that serial learning proceeded in a forward direction from the first item and in a backward direction from the last item. By demonstrating that learning was more rapid in the forward as opposed to the backward direction, the asymmetry of the serial position curve was accounted for. Although such an explanation seems entirely plausible, recent studies suggest that ordinal characteristics of the materials may be the critical factor in producing the position effect and that it is not due to serial learning per se.

Ebenholtz (1966) had subjects learn *pairs* composed of common words as responses, and the digits one through ten as stimuli. Even though the pairs were presented in a random order on each trial, a serial position curve was found. Irrespective of where they appeared in the list of pairs, the pairs having stimuli at the ends of the number series (1 2, 9, and 10) were learned faster than the other pairs. Similar results were obtained when nonsense syllables were used as responses instead of words. But when the digits were used as responses and the nonsense syllables as stimuli, no position curve was obtained. Apparently, the subjects must be responding directly to the ordinal character of the stimuli for the position effect to occur. Studies by Murdock (1960) and Jensen (1962a) also indicate a serial position effect in tasks other than serial learning so long as the task is one in which the subjects can respond to ordinal features in the set.

If the general ordinal character of the task is what determines the serial position effect, then it should be possible to manipulate the anchors for the position effect in serial learning. In fact, this has been demonstrated. Studies by Glanzer and Peters (1962) and Glanzer and Dolinsky (1965) have shown that the gap that typically occurs between the last item on one trial and the first item on the next trial establishes these items as anchor points. They have also shown that the first item continues to serve as the anchor point even when list repetitions involve no gaps (i.e., a continuous loop) beyond presentation of the initial item. This anchor on the initial item often holds in preference to some other item on which subjects had been pretrained. In addition, the anchor points in the serial list are readily shifted by appropriate instructions to the subjects. These findings are quite congruent with the well-established "von Restorff effect," which shows that a unique item in a series of otherwise homogeneous items will be correctly anticipated more often than items surrounding it (von Restorff, 1933). Although the presence of anchor items appears to be a critical factor in producing serial position effects, the mere fact of anchor items does not explain these effects or their asymmetrical form in serial learning.

Deese and Hulse (1967) suggest that the asymmetry may be due in part to the uniqueness of the first item. Subjects typically know what the first and last items are very early in learning, and they rarely give the first item in any position but the initial one. The last item, however, may be given several places in the series. The subjects know what the last item is but are not sure where it goes. Deese and Hulse suggest that the serial position effect "can be described as the combined result of isolation of the end items, intralist confusion within the middle, and a general imbalance in learning in favor of the beginning of the list." They believe that the imbalance may simply be a matter of uncertainty concerning the location of the terminal items.

Although Deese and Hulse recognized the superficiality of their explanation, it seems to be as satisfactory as any offered thus far. Some highly imaginative and quantitative theories of the position effect have been advanced (cf. Atkinson, 1957; Feigenbaum and Simon, 1962), but they do not add much more to our understanding of serial learning. We shall have more to say about serial learning later in this chapter, but first let us consider some views of associative learning that derive from the study of paired-associate learning.

PAIRED-ASSOCIATE LEARNING: METHODS AND THEORY

In the typical paired-associate (PA) task the subject is asked to learn a list of paired items. When the *anticipation* method is used, the stimulus item is presented alone followed by presentation of both members of the pair. For example, if the stimulus term is *wagon* and the response term is *dinner,* the arrangement would appear as

wagon

wagon dinner

The subject's task is to anticipate the response term before the pair is presented. Then the next stimulus is presented followed by that pair and so on until all pairs have been exposed. A trial consists of each pair being presented once in this manner. On subsequent trials the pairs are presented in different orders to avoid the possibility of subjects' learning the responses as a series rather than by actually learning the pairs. Each stimulus and pair is presented for a fixed amount of time, say two seconds, and the response may consist of either spelling or pronouncing the response term. Of course the PA task can be used with nonverbal responses, but verbal materials are generally employed.

The *recall method* of PA learning involves an alternation of study and test trials. During study trials each pair is presented but no responses are required from the subject. The subsequent test trial involves presentation of only the stimulus terms, and each time a new stimulus is presented the subject is to give the response with which it was paired. Feedback concerning correct responding is withheld until the next study trial. Surprisingly, such a delay produces no decrement in learning, and often it is even advantageous (cf. Battig and Brackett, 1961). Remember that developers of programmed instruction have assumed that immediate knowledge of results is particularly beneficial to learning. In any case, the recall and anticipation methods of PA learning are comparable in terms of response requirements and timing conditions, and learning typically continues to some criterion of mastery, such as one or two errorless trials.

Early Views of PA Learning

The PA method has certain advantages over the serial learning method for an associative analysis of learning. In the PA situation there is a clear separation of stimulus and response elements, which makes it possible to manipulate these terms independently. According to association theory, the basic elements of PA learning were seen as the stimulus and response events. Contiguous presentation of these events would lead to development of an association. The more frequently the two events were experienced contiguously, the stronger the association between them would become. Thus the association between each stimulus and its paired response was viewed as *what* is learned, and the PA situation was seen as an ideal one for investigating the nature of associative learning.

Advocates of theories based on the study of conditioning saw in the PA situation an opportunity to extend stimulus-response principles developed within conditioning paradigms to more complex situations (cf. Battig, 1968). In addition to the concepts of stimulus and response, these theorists saw the knowledge of results that follows a correct anticipation as an instance of reinforcement. This superficial similarity between the elements of PA learning and those characteristic of conditioning paradigms led various investigators to view PA learning in terms of a rather straightforward extension of conditioning. With such an analogy in mind, it is not surprising that much of the research on PA learning in the 1940s and 1950s was directed toward this goal.

During this period the most influential of the theories based on conditioning principles was that offered by Eleanor Gibson (1940). Her theory held that principles established in the conditioning laboratory would also apply in other forms of associative learning, particularly in PA learning. The major emphasis was on establishing discrimination among the items to be learned, and the conditioning principle used to specify differences in learning or discrimination was stimulus generalization.

Some years ago Underwood (1961) evaluated this theory in the light of current developments. Apart from noting certain inadequacies at the empirical level, he concluded that it has very limited usefulness: "To a large extent, the flow of research and the new ways of viewing phenomena have left the theory behind."

In a general review Battig (1968) has also noted several inadequacies in theoretical accounts of PA learning based on conditioning principles. We have seen that immediate knowledge of results (i.e., reinforcement) does not have the facilitatory effect in PA learning that it does in instrumental conditioning. Also, Goss (1965) has shown that following "reinforced" training (stimulus and response terms presented) associations acquired in the PA task do not diminish in strength with repeated "nonreinforced" presentations (stimulus terms only). This finding raises serious questions concerning the descriptive adequacy of the concept of extinction in the PA situation. For these and other reasons, concepts of PA learning have changed quite radically in recent years.

Contemporary Views of PA Learning

Underwood and Schulz (1960) offered an analysis of PA learning that has had considerable influence on the nature of research in this area. Their analysis derived from an extensive investigation of PA learning which occurred over a period of several years. These studies were intended to determine the influence of a single variable, *meaningfulness,* on learning.

Interest in the study of meaningfulness stems from a simple and obvious fact of learning. As Underwood and Schulz point out, lists containing such items as *gjx* and *qzb* take much longer to learn than lists containing such items as *cat* and *IBM*. Although this does not surprise anyone, it is difficult to explain on the basis of traditional associative principles. That is, traditional associative accounts emphasize the role of contiguity and frequency in the development of associations. Conditioning models add an emphasis on reinforcement. But nowhere in these theoretical approaches does one find any reference to meaningfulness. Therefore Underwood and Schulz set out to attempt to understand the role of meaningfulness in associative learning.

It may be somewhat misleading to refer to meaningfulness as a single variable. As the concept is employed by Underwood and Schulz (1960), meaningfulness actually refers to several important variables, which they view as having been derived from a common base:

1. *Association value.* Although nonsense syllables had been used in learning studies since the time of Ebbinghaus, the first systematic attempt to order them along a dimension of meaningfulness was carried out by Glaze in 1928. Since that time several investigators have conducted similar projects (e.g., Hull, 1933; Witmer, 1935). One of the earliest attempts at scaling the association value of nonsense syllables is that of Krueger (1934).

   Krueger presented subjects with 2,183 CVC combinations. Each syllable was spelled twice by the experimenter, requiring about four seconds on the average. The subject wrote the syllable as it was spelled and also indicated the idea aroused by the syllable. Those syllables yielding the greatest frequency of response were designated as having 100 percent association value. The value assigned to the other syllables was based on a percentage of this frequency. Thus if an association value of 100 percent was assigned to syllables responded to by 200 out of 250 subjects, then syllables responded to by 100 subjects would be assigned a value of 50 percent.

   A more recent and very comprehensive scaling of meaningfulness or association value was provided by Archer (1960). He examined most of the CVC combinations that are possible in the alphabet. As each syllable was presented, the subjects were told to ask themselves the following questions: Is it a word? Does it sound like a word? Does it remind me of a word? Could I use it in a sentence? The subjects were told to respond yes if they could answer at least one question in the affirmative and no if the answer to all questions was negative. Association value was indexed by the percentage of subjects making yes responses.

2. *Meaningfulness (m).* In 1952 Noble offered a procedure for scaling actual words based on a somewhat different view of meaningfulness. Noble presented single words to his subjects and asked them to write down as many other words as the stimulus word brought to mind. The subjects were given sixty seconds to respond to each word, and the *m-value* of each word was indexed by the average number of responses made to it by the subjects.

   A major difficulty with Noble's procedure is that subjects tend to respond to other responses already given rather than to the stimulus word. For example, if the stimulus is *large* and the responses are *heavy, light, dark,* and *deep,* there would be clear evidence of such response chaining. Noble offered criteria for eliminating these and other inappropriate responses, although the criteria are difficult to employ consistently.

A modified version of *m* was offered by Noble, Stockwell, and Pryor (1957), which could be used with both meaningful and nonsense units. Subjects were asked to rate the number of things or ideas a given item made them think of along a five-point scale, ranging from *none* to *very many.* When nonsense syllables are scaled in this way, *m*-values correlate .90 with the *association values* determined by Krueger. Of course, not all methods of scaling yield such high intercorrelations.

3. *Familiarity.* Perhaps the most obvious index of meaningfulness is familiarity. Familiarity, or acquaintance, has long been viewed as an important factor in learning (cf. Robinson, 1932) and one in which degree of familiarity and not number of associations is the critical factor. Noble (1953) employed a five-point rating scale, ranging from *never* to *very often,* to evaluate previous contact or familiarity with words. As with the case of rated *m,* the median scale value of each item is its score on familiarity. When familiarity in this sense is correlated with Noble's *m*-values, the number of associations produced in 60 seconds, the correlation is .92 (Noble, 1953).

4. *Pronunciability.* Yet another factor related to learning is the ease of pronouncing an item. Noble (1953) employed a nine-point rating scale for evaluating this factor, ranging from *easy* to *hard.* Ratings of pronunciability were found to correlate .78 with rated *m*-values for nonsense syllables.

The problem Underwood and Schulz faced was whether or not one of these highly correlated factors was more basic than the others. Was there some underlying factor responsible for all the various indices, some factor that might or might not be assessed by one of the scaling procedures discussed here? Their conclusion, based on theoretical and empirical considerations, was that *frequency of experience* with units is the fundamental antecedent condition and that frequency of experience gives rise to the phenomena exhibited by the scaling procedures previously discussed. Thus Underwood and Schulz in a sense revived Thorndike's law of exercise by emphasizing the importance of frequency, a major factor in classical associationism (cf. Robinson, 1932) but one whose importance was reduced during the 1940s and 1950s when frequency of reward became the major consideration.

This renewed emphasis on frequency or experience as the underlying factor was not shared by all investigators. For example, Noble (1963) argued that familiarity is produced by frequency of experience, whereas meaningfulness is a consequence of both frequency and the number of associations elicited by an item. Nevertheless, the conclusion reached by Underwood and Schulz, to the effect that all the scaling procedures were indices of meaningfulness (designated M) and that M was due mainly to frequency of experience, had considerable influence on their analysis of associative learning.

A Two-Stage Model.   According to Underwood and Schulz, associative learning of either a serial or a PA list can be divided into two stages. The first stage is called *response learning,* or *response recall,* and it occurs temporally prior to the second stage, which is called the *associative,* or *hook-up,* stage. During response learning the subject must learn to recall the responses—that is, make them available for the associative stage. The response-learning phase involves learning which items are responses and integrating or encoding new items, such as nonsense syllables that the subject may not have experienced previously. Once a response has been learned in this sense, the second or associative stage can proceed. Although these stages are referred to as first and second, it is clear that they may overlap in time. For example, both stages may be completed for some pairs before the first stage is completed for the other pairs in a list, or some degree of associative strength may be developed between a stimulus and a response even though response learning is not complete.

It is during the response-learning phase that M has its primary influence. The basic position taken on the role of frequency or M is contained in Underwood and Schulz's statement of the *spew hypothesis:* "The order of availability of verbal units is directly related to the frequency with which these units have been experienced. Other things being equal, therefore, the more frequently a verbal unit has been experienced, the more quickly will this become a response in a new associative connection" (p. 86). Thus they see frequency per se as influencing only the response-learning stage, a view that they point out is in essential agreement with the earlier position of Thorndike (1932).

Certain theoretical and empirical factors led Underwood and Schulz to conclude that the effects of M were mainly on response learning. They reviewed a series of experiments (see their Chapter 3) in which stimulus and response M were varied. In general, the results of those experiments indicated that although both stimulus and response M influenced rate of learning, the magnitude of the effect was greater for response M than for stimulus M. An illustration of the effect of stimulus and response meaningfulness can be found in a study by Cieutat, Stockwell, and Noble (1958). These investigators examined the effects of stimulus and response meaningfulness in four conditions (high-high, high-low, low-high, and low-low). Figure 4.2 shows that the list with high M stimuli and high M responses is learned most rapidly. Conversely, the list with low M stimuli and low M

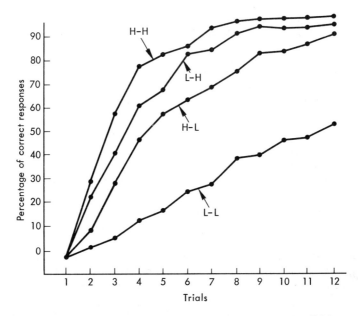

Figure 4.2 Acquisition curves for paired nonsense syllables as a function of combination of high (H) and low (L) stimulus and response M.
(Estimated from Cieutat, Stockwell, and Noble, 1958.)

responses is the most difficult to learn. By comparing the results for these conditions with those for the other two conditions, it is clear that stimulus M has less of an effect on learning than response M.

A second consideration concerning the role of meaningfulness (M) involves the *associative probability hypothesis*. According to this hypothesis, the greater the M value of the items in a PA list, the more rapidly learning will take place. For example, if the stimulus and response terms are both of high M, thus eliciting a greater number of associates, the probability should be greater that associates of these items will link up in either a direct or an indirect manner. A direct link would occur when one of the associates to a stimulus term actually was the response term (e.g., table-chair). An indirect link would involve a common associate to both the stimulus and response terms (e.g., justice-peace-war), although a longer chain of mediating links could be involved.

Although the associative probability hypothesis has some appeal, Underwood and Schulz rejected it for several reasons. First, there is the observation that increasing the number of associates to a stimulus via laboratory training also increases the difficulty of forming an association between that stimulus and a new response (e.g., Bugelski, 1948). That is, increasing the number of associates to a stimulus item would appear to have both facilitative and interfering consequences in subsequent learning. This has been referred to as the *associative probability paradox.*

The second reason for rejecting the associative probability hypothesis is that although there is clear evidence for linking stimuli and responses by direct association, the evidence is much less convincing when the associative links are remote (Russell and Storms, 1955). Consider the case where a nonsense syllable is first associated with the word *justice* and then with the word *war*. Presumably the second association could be accomplished through an indirect chain of associative links (e.g., nonsense syllable → *justice* → *peace* → *war*). The evidence for such associative pathways is not overly impressive, however. For these and other reasons, Underwood and Schulz concluded that the fundamental basis for M was frequency of experience and that it had its major influence on response learning.

A Three-Stage Model. McGuire (1961) offered an analysis of PA learning that was quite similar to that of Underwood and Schulz. This theory actually preceded the Underwood and Schulz theory, since it was contained in McGuire's doctoral thesis (1954), but it was not published until some years later. McGuire proposed a three-stage analysis of associative learning. The first stage consisted of associating to each stimulus a mediating, stimulus-producing response. This response was viewed as a partial representation of the stimulus term sufficient to differentiate it from other stimuli in the list. In more contemporary terms this might be called a *coding response*. The other stages were comparable with the associative and response-learning stages of Underwood and Schulz. The associative stage in McGuire's model, however, involved connections between the stimulus properties of the mediating or coding response and the actual response term. No doubt this rather ingenious analysis would have had substantial influence had it not been for the delayed publication.

Nominal and Functional Stimuli. McGuire's mediating response is similar in some ways to Underwood's (1963) subsequent concept of a functional stimulus. The actual distinction Underwood drew was between the *nominal stimulus,* what is presented to the subject, and the *functional stimulus,* the characteristics of the stimulus that the subject actually uses. He suggests that *selection* of the functional stimulus may involve an active process in that the subject deliberately chooses certain characteristics of the stimulus as the cue. For example, in a study by Mattocks (cf. Underwood, 1963), subjects learned a PA list in which the stimuli were trigrams of very low meaningfulness and the responses were common three-letter words. Systematic questioning of the subjects following learning revealed that only the first letter of the trigram served as the functional stimulus in most cases.

Jenkins (1963) has confirmed the findings of Mattocks. In this experiment subjects learned a PA list in which the stimuli were trigrams and the responses were single digits. After the list was learned, the letters of the trigrams were divided into three groups according to the position they held in the trigrams. These letters were then shown to the subjects one at a time, and the subjects attempted to recall the appropriate digits. The number of correct responses was greater than chance for all three positions in the trigram. However, correct responses were greatest for the first-letter position and lowest for the middle-letter position.

Postman and Greenbloom (1967) reported an experiment very similar to that of Jenkins (1963). Although the general procedure was comparable in these studies, two important differences should be noted. Postman and Greenbloom used two sets of trigrams. One set was easy to pronounce and the other was difficult to pronounce. During the critical test the single letters were presented, and dashes appeared in place of the missing letters. When difficult-to-pronounce trigrams were used as stimuli, their results indicated that stimulus selection was largely limited to the first letter of the trigram. Little evidence for stimulus selection was found with easy-to-pronounce trigrams. Postman and Greenbloom interpreted this latter finding to mean that stimulus selection take place only among functionally discrete units.

The distinction between the nominal and the functional stimulus is well illustrated in a study by Underwood, Ham, and Ekstrand (1962). In this experiment subjects first learned a PA list composed of seven difficult trigrams as stimuli and single digits as responses. The stimuli had many letters in common (i.e., high interstimulus similarity) so that it would be difficult to use a single letter as a functional stimulus. In addition, the trigrams were presented on colored backgrounds which were easily differentiated (e.g., blue, red, brown). Learning was carried to a criterion of one errorless trial, and transfer tests were given immediately following learning.

During transfer the control group just continued to practice the original list. A second group also did this, but now only the background colors were used as stimuli. That is, the trigrams were omitted, but the color-digit pairs were the same as in original learning. For the third group the trigram-digit pairs were maintained as in original learning, but the background colors were omitted. These groups were designated TC-TC (control group), TC-C (colors alone as transfer stimuli), and TC-T (trigrams alone as transfer stimuli). The results shown in the left panel of Figure 4.3 indicate that color alone was a completely effective stimulus. The group with only colors as stimuli in transfer performed just as well as did the control group. However, the trigrams also were effective stimuli for at least some subjects, since transfer was not zero on the trigram-digit pairs, although it was considerably less than in the other conditions. These data suggest that when the nominal stimulus consists of two or more distinct classes of units the unit of highest meaningfulness is more likely to be used

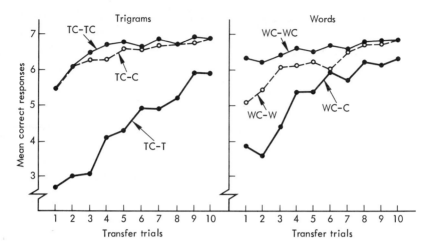

Figure 4.3   Acquisition curves on the ten transfer trials.
(From Underwood, Ham, and Ekstrand, 1962.)

as the functional stimulus (cf. Underwood, 1963). As the right panel of Figure 4.3 indicates, when highly meaningful three-letter words appear on colored backgrounds they are more likely to be chosen as functional stimuli than are the background colors.

A subsequent study by Jenkins and Bailey (1964) indicates that the relationship between the nominal and the functional stimuli can be quite complex. Their experiment involved a replication of the nonsense syllable part of the Underwood, Ham, and Ekstrand (1962) study, with the addition of a group of subjects that learned a transfer list composed of color names as stimuli and digits as responses. The results of this study indicated that color names were just as effective as the actual colored backgrounds that appeared in original learning. In all other respects the results were the same as in the previous experiment. Thus, a cue not present in the original stimulus compound (color name) can serve as a functional stimulus. Of course it may be that the color name only served to remind subjects of the actual color, but in any case the complexity of the relation between nominal and functional stimuli is apparent.

It is difficult to overestimate the importance of the distinction between nominal and functional stimuli in associative learning. Although Underwood's distinction is somewhat similar to McGuire's, the differences turn out to be of greater significance. McGuire's mediating, stimulus-producing response was viewed as a partial representation of the stimulus term itself. This notion is reminiscent of Hull's (1952) or Osgood's (1953) use of implicit mediating responses, the stimulus consequences of which served to bridge or mediate other overt responses. Underwood's concept of the functional stimulus, however, whether intentionally or unintentionally, does not require that it serve as a representation of the nominal stimulus per se, and there is the implication that the functional stimulus need not bear any particularly close relationship to the nominal stimulus. In addition, the concept of functional stimuli carries the implication of an active process of *stimulus selection* or coding, which has fundamentally changed the discussion of learning and memory.

PAIRED-ASSOCIATE LEARNING: SOME THEORETICAL ISSUES

Major theoretical issues have been raised regarding some of the basic concepts of associative theory that have been developed in the PA context. Two issues that have stimulated much research and theoretical controversy involve *backward associations* and *all-or-none learning*.

Backward Associations. It has long been known that after acquiring an association between two items such as *A* and *B,* subjects can produce *B* when *A* is presented alone (forward association) and can produce *A* when *B* is presented alone (backward association). For many years such backward associations were dismissed as artifacts of the learning or retention process. The major reason for rejecting backward associations as "true" associations was that backward conditioning in the classical conditioning situation was thought to be slight or nonexistent (cf. Kimble, 1961). As we noted earlier, theories of PA learning in the 1940s and 1950s were dominated by the conditioning point of view. For theorists who believed in a unitary set of learning mechanisms, it was inconceivable that "true" backward associations could exist in the PA situation and not in the classical conditioning situation. Nevertheless, there was considerable evidence for backward associations in PA learning and this evidence required explanation.

One common explanation stated that backward associations could be attributed to implicit rehearsal during learning. That is, if the subject rehearses a pair several times during presentation (e.g., *A-B, A-B, A-B*), a temporal contiguity exists between both the stimulus and response terms in a forward direction and the response and stimulus terms in a forward direction. Such a view of backward associations was quite compatible with a conditioning analysis of associative learning.

Other explanations of backward associations included the view that when a given response term is presented during the retention test, the subject simply recalls stimuli covertly until he remembers the one that was paired with the response term in question. In fact, it was not so long ago that backward associations were simply dismissed as a form of "incidental learning" (Feldman and Underwood, 1957).

Theoretical interest in backward associations really began when their influence was demonstrated in various transfer situations. For example, consider a subject who learns one PA list, call it the *A-B* list, followed by another list called the *B-C* list. If both forward (*A-B*) and backward (*B-A*) associations were formed during original learning, then learning of the second (*B-C*) list should be interfered with by the previously acquired backward associations. That is, backward associations from *B* to *A* which are formed during original learning should interfere with the subsequent learning of *B-C* pairs. This result was obtained by both Harcum (1953) and Murdock (1958). If backward associations were artifacts of the learning or retention process, such interference effects would be unlikely. In addition, it has been shown that backward associations have facilitating as well as interfering effects. Horton and Kjeldergaard (1961) demonstrated that after learning two PA lists like those mentioned above (*A-B, B-C*), the learning of a third list (*C-A*) was facilitated. According to their mediational interpretation, the facilitation was due to backward associative chains (*C-B-A*) that were made possible by the formation of backward associations during prior list learning.

Interesting though these findings may be, the major impetus in advancing the study of backward associations came from the principle of "associative symmetry" proposed by Asch and Ebenholtz (1962). This principle states that "there are no conditions that will produce an association between *a* and *b* without producing an association of equal strength between *b* and *a*" (p. 136). But how does one reconcile this statement with the finding that across a variety of situations, performance in the forward direction is superior to performance in the backward direction? Of course there are exceptions (cf. Ekstrand, 1966), but the results of most studies favor forward performance.

Asch and Ebenholtz (1962) explain this apparent asymmetry in terms of differential availability of the stimulus and response items. That is, in PA learning the response terms are subject to what Underwood and Schulz call the response learning, or response recall, stage, which makes these items available for recall. In tests of backward association following PA learning, however, it is the stimulus terms from the PA list that have to be recalled, and they have not been subjected to response learning because they are always presented in the PA task. As a result, stimulus items should be less available for recall than response items, and performance in the forward direction would therefore be superior.

If theories of PA learning such as that of Underwood and Schulz (1960) are correct, the explanation offered by Asch and Ebenholtz appears quite sound. In addition, it is supported by the frequent observation that recall of stimulus items is inferior to recall of response items following PA learning (Asch and Ebenholtz, 1962; Battig, Brown, and Nelson, 1963; Newman and Gray, 1964). This observation has led several investigators to attempt to equate the availability of stimulus and response terms. For example, Asch and Ebenholtz (1962) had subjects learn both the stimulus and response terms prior to PA learning by the *method of free recall*. This procedure involves alternating item presentation and recall trials. During presentation the items are shown individually and in a random order. The order of items is different on each presentation trial. On recall trials the subject recalls as many items as possible in any order, hence the name *free recall*. Typically, presentation and recall trials continue until the subject can recall all of the items on a single trial. Asch and Ebenholtz used this procedure prior to PA learning. Despite this training, however, in two of three experiments they reported that performance following PA learning was superior in the forward direction, thus supporting asymmetry.

Although the studies of Asch and Ebenholtz do not appear to favor the symmetry principle, certain difficulties should be pointed out in any attempt to equate the availability of stimulus and response items. The first is a matter of the criterion for equal availability. How does one ensure that one set of items is just as available as another set? The free-recall procedure used by Asch and Ebenholtz resulted in all items being learned, but there is no obvious way to determine whether the items to be used as the stimulus and response terms in the subsequent PA task were learned equally well. Furthermore, the use of any prefamiliarization procedure may bias subsequent PA learning. For example, free recall may result in associations being established among the items that could interfere with PA learning (Horowitz and Larsen, 1963).

A somewhat more direct approach for equating the availability of stimuli and responses involves having some stimuli serve as responses in other pairs in the list. Thus one pair might be *A-B,* another *D-A,* and another *B-C.* In this way response learning for items such as *A* and *B* could be equated. Horowitz, Brown, and Weissbluth (1964) had subjects practice on a six-pair list of this type after which they were instructed to give two free associations to each item. Naturally, those items that served only as responses were given more frequently than items that served only as stimuli. However, items such as *A* were given as responses to *B* just as often as items such as *B* were given as responses to *A*. This study certainly supports the view that pairs are learned as a unit and that differences in forward and backward performances are due to the technique of training. During practice one item may be made more available for recall because it has been practiced as an overt response.

The issue concerning associative symmetry is far from being settled. As Ekstrand (1966) points out in his extensive review of this literature, several studies appear to support the symmetry principle (e.g., Houston, 1964) and several others do not. For example, it would appear that the use of a double-function PA list in which every item serves as both a stimulus term in one pair and a response term in another pair (i.e., *A-B, B-C, C-D, D-E,* etc.) would equate the availability of items and provide a reasonable test of the symmetry principle. But recall following the learning of just such a list still favors performance in the forward direction (Battig and Koppenaal, 1965).

No matter how the symmetry-asymmetry issue is eventually resolved, it will undoubtedly have important implications for traditional views of associative learning. Asch (1968) has argued that if the symmetry principle turns out to be correct, stimulus-response conceptions of associative learning will have to be abandoned. He views an association as involving a central process in which both terms entering into an association have identical roles. Asch suggests that this conception "renders untenable the distinction between stimulus and response."

Whether or not Asch is correct about the nature of an association, his arguments cannot be ignored. As he suggests, it may be that the discrepancies we have noted in empirical findings are due to learning-performance differences. That is, what is learned may be an association between two elements of equal status, and the asymmetry that is often found is actually a reflection of performance factors such as differential availability of items. If this is so, many psychologists may have to revise their views of the relationship between learning and performance in that certain factors thought to be important to learning may be strictly performance factors which have little or no influence on learning per se.

All-or-None Learning.   Still another matter of concern to students of human learning in recent years is whether associative strength develops gradually or reaches some maximum on a single trial. The traditional view of learning is that associative strength develops gradually. Whether this is discussed in terms of a law of exercise (e.g., Thorndike, 1913) or some version of reinforcement theory (e.g., Hull, 1943; Skinner, 1938), it has usually been assumed that increments are added to associative strength on each trial or with each reward. This view can be traced back to classical associationism. We noted earlier that Ebbinghaus discovered the law of contiguity to be a matter of "more-or-less" and not "all-or-none." His findings suggested that associative strength varies as a function of the degree of remoteness of the items in a serial list. The farther apart two items are, the weaker is the association between them. The concept of associative strength has been pervasive in the history of associative thought, and the very idea of strength implies a gradual nature of learning. The incremental view of learning also appears to be exemplified in the typical learning curve which shows improvement in performance across trials or practice sessions.

Despite the long history of the incremental viewpoint in associative conceptions, not all psychologists agree with this view of learning. Some argue instead that learning is an all-or-none affair. The basic issue here is whether associative strength increases by successive increments as a function of practice or changes from zero to some maximum strength on a single trial. Either view is consistent with the improvement in performance across trials that is usually found in the learning of a PA list. On the incremental hypothesis each trial increases the strength of associations, whereas according to the all-or-none principle each trial provides an opportunity for new associations, not previously formed, to be established on a single trial.

One of the earliest advocates of an all-or-none view of learning was E. R. Guthrie (1935). Like most other theorists of his time, Guthrie saw learning as the formation of stimulus-response connections. But whereas other theorists defined responses in terms of their environmental consequences (e.g., whatever actions accomplish some desired effect), for him responses were the individual muscle *movements* of the organism. A response such as bar pressing would be seen as involving several movements or responses by Guthrie; others would see it as a single response. Where the performance curve for individual subjects indicated improvement across trials, Guthrie would attribute this to the acquisition of an *act* involving several responses, each of which was fully learned on some particular trial. Thus the acquisition of *acts* could take many trials even though the stimulus-response associations were learned on an all-or-none basis.

Guthrie's views concerning all-or-none learning had no great impact on other theorists of his day, who continued to subscribe to an incremental view of learning. This was particularly the case among students of human learning. Perhaps among the more obvious reasons for neglecting all-or-none views of learning is the well-established fact, which can be traced back to the work of Ebbinghaus, that overlearning leads to improved retention. That is, all-or-none theories typically maintain that maximum associative strength is established on a single trial and, therefore, continued practice beyond this point (i.e., overlearning) should have no effect on retention. Rock (1957) has avoided this problem by taking the position that trials prior to the first correct response have no effect on associative strength but trials following a correct response may in some way fixate such responses. This has been called a "some-or-none" hypothesis (Postman, 1963).

Rock's experiments (Rock, 1957; Rock and Heimer, 1959) involved what is known as the *dropout method*. This procedure is in contrast to conventional PA methods in which learning of a prescribed set of pairs is continued to some criterion of mastery. With the dropout method only those pairs on which the subject was correct are retained on subsequent trials; incorrect pairs are replaced with new, previously unseen, pairs. The rationale underlying this procedure is that only when the subject is correct can anything be learned. Incorrect pairs involve no learning, and it should make no difference whether or not such pairs are replaced with new pairs on the next trial. Of course it should still take several trials to learn the entire list because only a limited number of pairs can be learned on each trial. According to Rock, therefore, learning by the dropout method should take no longer than learning by conventional PA methods. Alternatively, if the incremental view is correct, some learning will occur on each trial, even for incorrect pairs, with a resulting advantage for conventional PA learning. Rock's data showed almost no difference in rate of learning under the two methods, thus supporting his hypothesis.

The theoretical significance of Rock's findings prompted numerous challenges by other investigators (e.g., Battig, 1962; Postman, 1962; Underwood, Rehula, and Keppel, 1962). Most of these challenges centered on possible defects in his method, the most obvious of which was pair selection. By pair selection in this situation we mean that those pairs a subject gets correct on a given trial may be intrinsically easier to learn than the pairs he does not get correct. If the incorrect pairs are reasonably difficult, it also seems likely that they may be replaced by pairs that are somewhat easier to learn. Continuing this process across a series of trials may thus result in a set of pairs that are considerably easier to learn than the initial set. If this were the case, Rock's dropout group could have learned a list that was easier than the initial list learned by the conventional PA group. That this was at least partly the case is indicated by the observation that when difficult pairs are replaced by even more difficult pairs it takes longer to learn the changing list (Postman, 1962).

A more convincing test of the pair selection view was provided by Underwood, Rehula, and Keppel (1962). They repeated Rock's experiment, but with the addition of a group of subjects who learned the lists on which the dropout subjects reached criterion (i.e., the terminal lists). The results of this study were complicated, but they clearly revealed pair selection. For example, in the dropout condition the terminal lists were shown to be easier than the initial lists. When the initial lists are easy, hence replacement pairs for dropout subjects should be more difficult, the subjects learning initial lists by conventional methods reach criterion faster than subjects learning by the dropout method.

The major importance of findings such as those reviewed here, as well as others discussed elsewhere (cf. Postman, 1963), is to indicate that Rock's experiments do not support the conclusions he based on them. This does not imply that the all-or-none hypothesis is necessarily incorrect. What it does tell us is that the dropout procedure does not provide an adequate situation in which to evaluate the hypothesis. The dropout procedure is too open to the influence of extraneous factors, such as pair selection, to warrant any firm conclusions to be drawn concerning all-or-none learning.

A second experimental procedure was developed by Estes (1960) to evaluate the all-or-none hypothesis. Consider first a situation involving PA learning by the recall method, with a single presentation of the pairs followed by two test-trials in succession. Estes uses the term *reinforcement* to refer to presentation of the pairs. This is therefore called the RTT method because a single reinforcement (R) is followed by two tests (TT). Now imagine the very unlikely situation of two subjects learning a single pair by this method, and for the moment ignore possible individual differences in learning ability among the subjects. On the first test-trial let us assume the proportion of correct responses is .50. That is, one subject is correct and the other is not. At this point the theoretical question of the meaning of this proportion is raised.

An all-or-none interpretation would say that associative strength is maximum (1.0) for the subject who was correct and zero for the other subject. On the other hand, an incremental interpretation might lead us to argue that associative strength was .50 for both subjects—one simply happened to be correct while the other was not. Since we have assumed that the subjects do not differ in learning ability, it is no more unreasonable to assume that associative strength is .50 for both subjects than it is to assume that associative strength is 1.0 for one subject and zero for the other. If the two subjects are equal in learning ability and equally motivated and attentive, traditional association theory leads us to predict that the increment in strength from a single exposure will be the same for both subjects. According to this account, some chance factor is responsible for the difference in performance. In any event the second test-trial is used to differentiate between these interpretations.

If the incremental assumption is correct, both subjects are equally likely to be correct on the second test. If they have learned to an equal degree prior to the second test, the probability of a correct response following an incorrect response should be equal to the probability of two correct responses in succession. The all-or-none hypothesis, however, states that no learning occurs prior to the first correct response. Therefore the probability of a correct response following an incorrect response should be zero, and unless there is forgetting between test-trials, the probability of two correct responses in succession should be 1.0. This analysis can easily be extended to the usual PA situation involving multiple pairs and several subjects.

An experiment based on the preceding rationale was reported by Estes, Hopkins, and Crothers (1960). They used lists consisting of eight pairs in which the stimuli were consonant syllables and the responses were the digits one through eight. Averaging across subjects and lists, 49 percent of the first-test responses were correct. The results obtained on the critical second test are given in Table 4.4.

We can see that the value of 9 percent for an incorrect response followed by a correct response is quite in accord with an all-or-none view. If the subjects merely guessed the responses on all pairs, they would have a probability of one in eight, or 12.5 percent of being correct by chance.

Table 4.4   Percentage of correct and incorrect responses on the second test.

Correct on 1—Correct on 2	71%
Correct on 1—Incorrect on 2	29%
Incorrect on 1—Correct on 2	9%
Incorrect on 1—Incorrect on 2	91%

(ESTES, HOPKINS, AND CROTHERS, 1960.)

But some pairs were learned prior to the second test and the remaining pairs on which subjects might have guessed is smaller, hence the probability of being correct by chance on the second trial is higher than 12.5 percent. Just how much higher is difficult to say, since all correct responses on the first test cannot be attributed to learning. In any event, the 9 percent value is well within even the most conservative estimation of chance effects.

The second value of interest in Table 4.4 is that for two correct responses in succession. All-or-none theory leads to the prediction that this probability should be unity (1.0). This assumes no forgetting between test-trials and no shrinkage in correct responses because of the possibility that some responses were correct on the first test due to guessing and therefore do not reflect learned responses. Although it does not appear likely that these factors could explain the relatively large percentage of responses (29 percent) that were incorrect on the first test, the results cannot be viewed as being too far out of line with predictions derived from an all-or-none hypothesis. On the basis of these comparisons and somewhat more complicated ones, Estes (1960) concluded that all-or-none theory was supported.

Several criticisms have been raised concerning the RTT studies and the all-or-none hypothesis advanced by Estes (1960). Underwood and Keppel (1962) have emphasized the fact that at least one empirical finding is not in accord with the theory. The all-or-none theory states that all responses correct on test one should be correct on test two. We have seen that the discrepancy between the predicted value (100 percent) and the obtained value (71 percent) can be at least partially attributed to forgetting between test-trials, but Estes's theory neglects this possibility. Of greater importance, however, is the experimental finding that pairs on which errors are made on the initial test are more difficult than pairs that are correct (Underwood and Keppel, 1962). The difficulty of these pairs may be responsible for the subsequent low percentage of correct responses (9 percent) on the second test. If pairs more comparable in difficulty with those that were correct initially had been used, the outcome might have been less supportive of the all-or-none hypothesis.

Postman (1963) has reviewed much of the evidence concerning the

Estes et al. studies and concludes that there are compelling reasons for questioning the generality of the findings. He reports studies from his own laboratories using the RTT method which appear to support an incremental interpretation. Following Underwood and Keppel (1962), Postman also notes the failure of most versions of all-or-none theory, Estes's included, to deal effectively with the well-established improvement in retention following overlearning.

What are we to conclude from this array of empirical and theoretical discrepancies? Is the all-or-none or the incremental position better supported by the data? The picture is made even less clear when we examine the contending theories more carefully. Restle (1965) has examined various types of learning theories and concludes that several are capable of explaining all-or-none learning. Even versions of the incremental hypothesis can account for all-or-none learning through certain assumptions concerning threshold levels required before correct responses will occur (also see Underwood and Keppel, 1962). Evidently, empirical demonstrations of all-or-none learning cannot resolve the theoretical issue.

Restle also points out that several versions of the all-or-none hypothesis make quite different claims about learning. He suggests that the view that all learning takes place on this basis is almost certainly wrong. But it would still be possible to argue that learning is all-or-none in some situations or under certain conditions. For example, if a subject is presented with a task that involves several levels of difficulty or several stages, perhaps each one is learned on an all-or-none basis, but this would not be the case for the task as a whole. Thus it appears that numerous theoretical possibilities exist for utilizing various components of all-or-none and incremental theory.

Let us conclude this discussion by taking note of what G. A. Miller (1963) calls *junk box theories* of all-or-none learning. The analogy is to how you find something in a junk box, but let us quote Miller directly on this approach:

> You look in, and if it is something you have put there recently, you find it near the top. If you don't see it, you shove things around a bit. Notice that you may not find it even when it is there. Or, if there are several identical items in the box, you may find what you want very quickly. Thus, it makes perfectly good sense to talk about a retrieval probability different from 0 or 1, even though the item's presence in the box is an all-or-none affair. And it makes equally good sense to talk about variations in the search time, or latency, required to find something (p. 324).

Eimas and Zeaman (1963), using a PA task similar to that of Estes et al. (1960), have shown decreases in the reaction time for responses after the trial on which they were first correct. This finding agrees with Miller's description. The aspect of Miller's description that we wish to emphasize, however, is the distinction between "learning" something and "remembering" what was learned. In a later chapter we shall refer to this as the difference between *storage* and *retrieval*, a distinction widely employed in information-processing accounts of memory. What we want to emphasize here is that, in agreement with Miller, it is perfectly plausible to consider different theories for storage and retrieval. For example, storage could be viewed as an all-or-none affair, whereas retrieval, consistent with the findings of Eimas and Zeaman, may operate on an incremental basis.

SERIAL LEARNING REVISITED

We began this chapter with a discussion of Ebbinghaus's findings and the implications of these findings for a theory of associations. Many of the general implications of his experimental results, such as the importance of frequency of repetition, the effect of overlearning, and the temporal course of retention, are still widely accepted. These findings provided the empirical cornerstone for the development of association theory in the twentieth century. Ebbinghaus, however, carried out his experiments using serial learning procedures and in the context of classical associative concepts that focused on mental events as the subject matter of psychology. In contrast, the development of association theory since Ebbinghaus's time has taken place mainly in the PA context and largely under the influence of behavioristic thought. In view of these differences in both orientation and procedure, it is not surprising to find that certain of Ebbinghaus's findings have been called into question in recent years.

As we have seen, Ebbinghaus's position concerning backward associations was challenged in the 1930s by theorists attempting to explain the serial position curve according to unidirectional conditioning principles. Of course, subsequent investigations appear to have reestablished the notion of backward associations; in addition, the serial position effect was not an important factor in Ebbinghaus's view of associations. Recently, however, two other issues have been raised—remote associations and the nature of the stimulus in serial learning. Examination of these issues has called into question the overall adequacy of associative explanations.

Remote Associations

In their classic textbook on the psychology of human learning, McGeoch and Irion (1952) devoted almost fifteen pages to remote associations. They discussed at some length the original Ebbinghaus studies as well as a great deal of other evidence for remote associations. Although numerous methodological problems were noted in these studies, McGeoch and Irion apparently considered the learning of remote associations to be an important and fundamental part of serial learning.

The recent challenge to the "doctrine of remote associations" arose within the context of a more general reevaluation of several aspects of serial learning, and it has involved a number of methodological issues. For example, Ebbinghaus learned serial lists by the method of whole-list presentation, whereas most recent studies have involved serial anticipation learning. A major characteristic of the anticipation method is that it prevents the subject from looking back and forth over the list, thereby forming associations between nonadjacent items.

A second problem in those experiments conducted by Ebbinghaus involves the method of measurement. In his investigation of remote associations, Ebbinghaus employed the method of derived lists and the savings score. The savings score indicated that it took less time to learn the derived list than it did to learn the original list, and, on this basis, Ebbinghaus concluded that remote associations had been formed. It should also be recalled that the percentage saved was greater for a list of one to seven degrees of remoteness than it was for the random order derived list, which simply involved a random reordering of the items.

According to contemporary views of association theory, there are two problems with these procedures. First, we cannot be certain just what the savings score indicates. That is, Ebbinghaus used nonsense syllables which require considerable response learning, and any savings obtained in learning a derived list composed of the same syllables could easily reflect the prior completion of response learning. The second problem relates to the difference in savings score found between, say, a one-degree derived list (10.8 percent) and the random order list (0.5 percent). The argument here is that associations between adjacent items developed in original learning should interfere with the subsequent learning of any derived list. Since the amount of response learning accomplished prior to derived list learning should be comparable in the two cases mentioned, we cannot determine whether the difference in savings should be attributed to the carry-over of remote associations in the one-degree derived list condition, associative interference in the random order condition, or to both factors. It is certainly possible that considerable interference would be expected when going from original learning to the learning of the same items in a random order, whereas less interference might occur in the one-degree derived list condition.

A study in which the preceding methodological problems were taken into account was reported by Hakes, James, and Young (1964). Their study involved the method of serial anticipation. After learning a list of adjectives in a prescribed order, the subjects in the experimental conditions learned derived lists of one, two, or three degrees of remoteness. Performance on the derived list was compared with that of a control group which learned two unrelated lists. The results were quite surprising. In marked contrast to Ebbinghaus's findings, negative transfer was obtained in all experimental conditions, although significant negative transfer was only found with the one-degree derived list. Thus the condition in which Ebbinghaus obtained greatest positive transfer was the one that yielded the most negative transfer for Hakes, James, and Young. How are we to interpret the discrepancies in these studies? Are they due to the methodological factors discussed previously, or is there some other explanation?

Battig and Lawrence (1967) reported an experiment that suggests that these differences may be due to the method of learning. Their study involved having subjects learn a serial list and then relearn the same list of items in reverse order. Half of the subjects learned by the anticipation method while the other half learned by the recall method. The results indicated positive transfer when the recall method was used, as Ebbinghaus found, but no transfer was obtained with the anticipation method. Although remote associations were not involved in this study, the results suggest that the positive transfer reported by Ebbinghaus may have been due to learning by the recall method or at least a variant of this method.

A second possible explanation for these differences, based on the perception of list patterning, was suggested by Slamecka (1964). In a series of derived list experiments, this investigator provided evidence that suggested that positive transfer may depend on whether the subject perceives the relationship between the original and derived lists. If the relationship is perceived, positive transfer will be found. Since Ebbinghaus was his own subject, it could be argued that despite efforts to avoid it, he was more cognizant of the relationship between lists than naive subjects who have not participated in other learning experiments of this type. This hypothesis may also explain the mixed transfer effects reported by Young, Hakes, and Hicks (1965). Using one-degree derived lists, these investigators found positive transfer with relatively short lists (eight items), but negative transfer with somewhat longer lists (twelve or sixteen items). The discrepancy could be due to a greater ease in perceiving list relationships when the original and derived lists are fairly short.

Slamecka's explanation of derived list findings may also account for the results of the Battig and Lawrence (1967) study. In the recall method the entire list is presented before recall is attempted, and this may provide the subject with a greater opportunity to perceive the relationship between the original and the reversed list than the subject has with the anticipation method. Thus it appears possible that *perception of list patterning* did play a role in this experiment even though no direct tests for remote associations were involved.

Slamecka's explanation seems to account for a variety of otherwise conflicting results. In general, where perception of list patterning is likely, evidence of a positive effect of remote associations is also found. When the perception of list patterning is unlikely or very difficult, no transfer or negative transfer is the typical outcome. But it is difficult to see how associative principles could be used to explain the perception of list patterning. Principles such as contiguity and frequency imply that associations are impressed upon a passive organism. In addition, Ebbinghaus's discovery of remote associations was thought to imply that these associations were formed without the conscious deliberation of the learner. On the other hand, perception of list patterning implies both an active and a conscious process in learning derived lists. If this explanation of derived list findings turns out to be adequate, it would appear to pose problems for association theory. In the next section we shall see that even more significant problems for association theory have arisen from other studies of serial learning.

The Stimulus in Serial Learning

During the 1940s and 1950s the development of association theory was greatly influenced by the stimulus-response analysis that derived from the study of conditioning. One consequence was that psychologists began to talk about serial learning in terms of the *chaining hypothesis*. According to this hypothesis, each item in the serial list serves as a response to the preceding item and a stimulus for the following item. Thus serial learning was thought to involve the formation of a series of stimulus-response associations that link the items of the list to one another. Most investigators have viewed the chaining hypothesis as a statement of Ebbinghaus's position. But it seems likely that, following the classical associationists, he conceived of associations as providing cognitive information concerning *what goes with what,* without any division of stimulus and response functions. Certainly the terms *stimulus* and *response* appear nowhere in his monograph (Ebbinghaus, 1885). The chaining hypothesis, however, does represent the view of serial learning most widely accepted until recent years and the view that is more germane to our discussion.

Evidence Concerning Chaining. The initial attempts to evaluate the chaining hypothesis employed an experimental procedure in which serial learning was either preceded or followed by PA learning. According to this hypothesis, a subject learning a serial list such as *A, B, C, D, E, F* should find it easy to learn a subsequent PA list composed of pairs such as *A-B, C-D, E-F,* since the same associations are involved in both lists. Similarly, it should be easy to learn the serial list after the PA list has been learned. The results, however, have been rather perplexing. Let us consider PA to serial transfer first.

Although moderate positive transfer has been found quite consistently in PA to serial transfer (e.g., Primoff, 1938; Young, 1959), the amount of transfer is considerably less than the 100 percent that the chaining hypothesis would lead us to expect. Jensen (1962b) has suggested that this absence of 100 percent transfer is due to a difference in the strategies employed in serial and PA learning even though both tasks formally have common associative elements. He views the stimulus items as providing a *cue* function in PA learning, whereas the items of the serial list are seen as responses to be integrated in sequence with little in the way of a *cue* function being involved. At present there is little data with which to evaluate Jensen's hypothesis.

A different situation exists with respect to investigations of serial to PA transfer. In general, transfer frequently is not found, and when it is found, the amount is slight and usually confined to the early trials. Let us examine this task in more detail. Suppose a subject learns a serial list such as *A, B, C, D, E, F* to a criterion of one errorless trial. He could then be transferred to either a single-function (*A-B, C-D, E-F*) or a double-function (*A-B, B-C, C-D*) PA list. Alternatively, the PA list could be *A-D, D-G*, and so on, if the investigator wanted to determine the amount of interference that might arise following serial learning of associations such as *A-B, B-C*.

Young (1959, 1961), in a series of studies, tested all three of these cases. In each, transfer was evaluated in comparison with a control condition involving PA learning of entirely new items. His findings showed no transfer at all in the test of interference, and in the other cases slight positive transfer was obtained on the early trials but not on the number of trials to learn the entire list. Thus Young's experiments provide little support for the chaining hypothesis.

Although Young's experiments do not support the traditional view of serial learning, certain methodological issues need to be raised. One of these involves the method of measurement. Psychologists have typically found that trials-to-criterion measures are insensitive indicators of transfer in the PA situation. This is likely to be true because the number of trials required to learn the entire list is dependent on learning the most difficult pair. If one of the PA pairs is very difficult or was poorly learned in the initial task, it might take considerable time to learn the entire list of pairs and little positive transfer would be found. On the other hand, positive transfer on the initial trials of PA learning could be due to the subjects' performance on one or two pairs and need not be a reflection of what was learned during serial acquisition.

Direct tests of these alternatives are extremely difficult, although some support for the use of the initial trials procedure has been provided by Postman and Stark (1967). Their study, which was quite complex, showed reliable differences in PA performance when facilitation and interference conditions were compared. That is, when the PA list was composed of pairs presumably learned during serial acquisition, the subjects did better on the early trials than they did when the PA list was made up of pairs designed to produce interference. This findings was interpreted as an indication that associative transfer had taken place even though overall performance in the facilitation condition was not much better than it was in the control condition.

A second aspect of the Postman and Stark experiment also deserves some attention. Half of their subjects in each condition were told about the relationship between the serial and the PA list. Most importantly, subjects in the facilitation condition were told that their PA list was composed of pairs of adjacent items taken from the serial list. When this was done, reliable differences were found among the facilitation, control, and interference conditions, as would be predicted by the chaining hypothesis. Similar findings were reported by Stark (1968).

These studies show that the experimental tests of the chaining hypothesis have produced decidedly mixed results. Despite some support for the traditional view of serial learning, the amount of serial to PA transfer is considerably less than should be expected. The most convincing support for the chaining hypothesis comes from the work of Postman and Stark. Their findings, however, best agree with predictions derived from the chaining hypothesis when the subjects are told about the list relationships. This observation reminds us of Slamecka's perception of list-patterning results. Again we find the influence of a factor that has little or no status in association theory. We must conclude that support for the chaining hypothesis, at least as a complete account of serial learning, is quite marginal.

Alternatives to Chaining.   Once the chaining hypothesis had been seriously questioned, psychologists began to consider alternative explanations. Most of the alternatives suggested were based on the same stimulus-response concept of learning that led to the development of the chaining hypothesis. That is, most of the alternatives assumed that there *must* be some specific stimulus for every response and some specific response for every stimulus. These alternatives differ from the chaining hypothesis only by assuming that the functional stimulus for each item in the serial list is something other than the immediately preceding item. One view is that the functional stimulus is a compound of several preceding items, not just the one that immediately precedes the item in question. This *compound stimulus hypothesis* has not stood up well in experimental tests (cf. Young, 1962). Another possibility, and the most serious alternative to chaining, is the *ordinal position hypothesis*. According to this view, the functional stimulus in serial learning is the position the item holds in the list. The stimulus for each item is not influenced by other items in the list but only depends on its location. A rather ingenious test of this hypothesis was provided by Young (1962).

Young had his subjects learn a serial list, after which they learned a second serial order of the same items. In this second, or transfer, list, half of the items held the same ordinal position as in the initial list while the remaining items changed position. According to the ordinal position hypothesis, it was expected that items holding the same position (S items) would be learned faster than items holding different positions (D items) because the S items involved the same associations between position and item that were acquired during original learning. This is just what was found. But some support for chaining hypothesis was also provided in that the list containing both S and D items was not learned as quickly as a control list of new items. The point here is that according to the chaining view, the associations between adjacent items formed during original learning should interfere with learning of the transfer list, since the adjacent items are different.

In a study similar to Young's, the superiority of S over D items was confirmed, and both were learned more rapidly than control items (Ebenholtz, 1963). Since Ebenholtz used nonsense syllables and Young used meaningful material, the discrepancy in performance on control items could be attributed to differences in response learning. It may be that performance on control items, relative to S and D items, can be shifted around by varying the meaningfulness of these items and hence the amount of response learning that is required. The results of both of these studies can be viewed as supporting the ordinal position hypothesis, although considerable doubt remains as to whether the facilitation obtained with S items is as great as might be expected.

The lack of clear support for either the *chaining* view or the *ordinal* view has led some investigators to suggest that the functional stimulus may vary with the part of the list that is being learned. For example, chaining could be more important in the middle of the list, whereas position cues play a greater role at the ends (Keppel and Saufley, 1964) or vice versa (cf. Young, 1968). Still others have suggested that not only may different cues be involved in different parts of the list but the cues may change during the course of learning even within the same part of the list (Battig, Brown, and Schild, 1964).

A Nonassociative Alternative.   Evidently there is no lack of alternative hypotheses concerning the functional stimulus in serial learning, and some empirical support has been found for each of them. Perhaps this very fact suggests an alternative interpretation which has received little consideration thus far.

It may be that in the course of serial learning the subject acquires considerable knowledge about the organization of the serial list. This knowledge may include position information, both in an absolute sense and relative to other items, as well as information about which items precede or follow which other items in the list. The emphasis here is on acquiring information about the serial list and not on the formation of associations between stimulus and response events. Certainly the weak support for the various hypotheses considered previously tends to support such an interpretation.

Further support for this interpretation is provided by studies involving serial learning with constant and variable starting points. Keppel (1964) has shown that if a serial list begins at a different point on each trial, it is more difficult to learn than a list that always begins with the same item. If, as Keppel contends, the ordinal cues are reduced or eliminated when starting points are varied, the very fact that the list is learned suggests the operation of other cues. That such cues include knowledge of the preceding item is suggested by the finding of positive transfer on an appropriate PA task following the learning of a variable starting point serial list (Shuell and Keppel, 1967).

Findings such as these support the view that multiple sets of cues may be employed in serial learning and that the subject uses those cues that are available. An interesting stage analysis of serial learning has been suggested by Voss (1968, 1969). Based on a series of experiments, his analysis indicates that subjects first try to learn the items in the list. This is essentially the Underwood and Schulz response-learning stage, and, as in PA learning, not all items are learned at the same rate. The initial items are learned first, followed by the end and middle items in that order. In fact, Voss (1969) suggests that the order in which the items are learned over trials may be a major factor contributing to the shape of the serial position curve.

Once an item is learned, the next step is to place it along a temporal or spatial dimension. Thus the serial list is viewed as a perceptual dimension, which is quite consistent with contemporary views of serial position effects discussed earlier. Instead of a functional stimulus, Voss suggests a complex of cues which includes the subject's knowledge of the *relative* list location of an item as well as the cue property of the preceding item.

Now let us return to the question of what the various transfer studies dealing with serial learning indicate. Voss (1968) has suggested that the rather small transfer effects found in the serial to PA situation are quite understandable, since only some of the cues employed in serial learning are provided in subsequent PA tasks. A somewhat different interpretation of these experiments has been provided by Horton and Turnage (1970). They assume that the result of serial learning is to provide the subject with an ordered set of items that do not elicit one another as a chain of associates. This rather neutral view is quite compatible with the analysis of serial learning offered by Voss. The interesting part of the position stated by Horton and Turnage, however, concerns the subsequent transfer task and what they call the *search hypothesis*.

According to the search hypothesis, if the subject is given a transfer task composed of the items from a previously learned serial list, he may actively search his memory of the list and attempt to apply this information to the performance requirements of the transfer task. The information may include knowledge of adjacent items as well as position within the list. If the subject recognizes that the serial information will be helpful and if he has sufficient time to search through his memory of the serial list, positive transfer can be expected. The importance of these factors is suggested by the increased positive transfer that is obtained when subjects are told of the relationship between serial and PA lists (Postman and Stark, 1967) and when more time is given to anticipate the response in the PA task (Heaps, Greene, and Cheney, 1968). To the extent that these conditions are not met, however, the result may be no transfer or even negative transfer (Horton and Turnage, 1970). Thus the kind of transfer found may depend on a number of factors that are related to both serial learning and the strategies that subjects employ during the transfer task.

At the present time there is not enough evidence to evaluate such views. These interpretations of serial learning and the transfer studies designed to test various hypotheses about serial learning are quite promising, however. They certainly lead away from traditional associative explanations which emphasize the formation of associations that become activated whenever the appropriate stimulus events are again presented. Instead they suggest that the learner is simply acquiring information and that the use of this information in the future depends on the comparability of cues in the original and transfer tasks. In addition, the extent to which information acquired during serial learning can be used in subsequent transfer tasks seems to depend on the subject's perceiving the relationship between the tasks and having sufficient opportunity to make use of that knowledge.

CONCLUSION

In this chapter we have considered the study of associative learning in humans, with emphasis on the learning of verbal materials. The chapter began with a review of Ebbinghaus's investigation of the principles of classical association theory. It was noted that many of his findings were of major importance for the development of association theory in the twentieth century. Our major topic involved tracing the development of association theory through the behavioristic period to more contemporary views. During the behavioristic period we noted that emphasis was placed on stimulus-response concepts and on the principle of reward. Both of these factors served to shift the emphasis in studies of associative learning from the paradigm for serial learning to the paired-associate paradigm.

In recent years we began to observe changes in associative theory which moved away from the position of classical associationism. Psychologists began to talk about the meaningfulness of verbal units and about the learning of responses in addition to the learning of associations. They also began to consider functional stimuli that might be only remotely related to the stimuli originally presented to the learner. The studies of backward association challenged the assumption of a unitary set of principles that governed all learning. These investigations also challenged the view that associations were necessarily connections between independent stimulus and response events. The studies of all-or-none learning also questioned the traditional view that all learning could be described in terms of an incremental process. Although it became clear that there were many problems with the all-or-none assumption, the investigation of this assumption began to suggest an important distinction between the storage of information (learning) and the retrieval of information from storage (remembering). In subsequent chapters the importance of this distinction will be made clear.

The chapter also reviewed more contemporary studies of serial learning. Although several problems for association theory have arisen in the context of paired-associate learning, the problems posed are nowhere as great as those that have arisen in the more recent studies of serial learning. Traditional concepts of the functional stimulus and remote associations have not stood up well to experimental testing. The same conclusion applies to all hypotheses that require a stimulus for every response and a response for every stimulus. Both in this discussion and in the earlier discussion of the serial position curve, it was noted that the explanations that were best supported involved assumptions that were not associative. These explanations emphasized such factors as locating items along a perceptual dimension, perceiving the pattern of list relationships, and, in general, taking an active rather than a passive view of the role of the learner.

Several basic assumptions of association theory can be seriously questioned. Considerable evidence indicates that the human organism is not a passive receiver of information that can be subsequently elicited from him by presentation of an appropriate stimulus. Instead, the human organism is seen as an active seeker and organizer of new information.

Apart from certain details of the theory itself, the assumption most directly called into question is that all learning is based on a unified set of principles. This assumption is challenged by the failure of principles developed within the paired-associate context to apply in the context of serial learning or serial to paired-associate transfer. It is also challenged by the comparison of findings concerning backward associations in the paired-associate and classical conditioning situations. Of course, we saw in the preceding chapters that conditioning principles often fail to apply when verbal behavior or language is at issue. In any case, it appears that association theory is either inadequate or simply does not apply to all learning situations. In the next chapter we shall consider the extent to which association theory provides an adequate account of forgetting.

5

Forgetting

SEVERAL OF THE MORE INTRIGUING questions about the nature of forgetting arise because our memory often fails. It is doubtful whether theories
of memory would ever have evolved if we did not forget. Failures of
memory are quite common, and such failures raise a basic question. Does
forgetting reflect the actual loss of some event from memory (a storage
failure), or does it indicate suppression of the event due to some sort of
interplay with other memories (a retrieval failure)? A commonplace example of forgetting may serve to clarify this distinction between storage
and retrieval failures in memory.

How often have you found yourself unable to recall a name that
goes with a familiar face? You may struggle without success to find the
elusive name when you want to remember it. Yet it may suddenly pop
into your mind at some later time when you are no longer thinking about
it. Such observations suggest that a major difficulty in certain cases of
forgetting is with the retrieval of information that is appropriately stored
in memory but is momentarily inaccessible to our active search.

Conceptions of the forgetting process stated in terms of the blocking
of ideas or events in memory have been suggested for more than a hundred years. For instance, the philosopher-psychologist Herbart (1776–
1841) held that the composition of consciousness at any particular moment
is the result of the interplay of many ideas. One idea may suppress
another without completely destroying it. Freud, the noted psychoanalyst,
also spoke of the blocking rather than the obliteration of ideas in memory.

In his view, recorded events persisted throughout the life of an individual, but memory for such events might be thrust into the unconscious or made unavailable for recall in other ways.

Many of the most influential behavioristic psychologists appeared to agree with the general concept that once an event had been recorded in memory, there was no mechanism for obliterating it. Previously acquired habits (memories) might be unavailable for recall because such factors as competing habits prevented them from being reflected in performance (retrieved). Forgetting in these instances was not attributed to the actual destruction of habits. Instead it was seen as the result of changes in other factors which reduced the probability of a given habit being "activated" and, hence, available for recall.

Certainly not all theories of memory, behavioristic or otherwise, have assumed that forgetting simply reflects difficulties in retrieval. Some theorists have suggested that memories actually fade with time, becoming weaker and weaker copies of the originals until they are completely obliterated. Such memory failures would obviously be attributed to storage factors and not to problems of retrieval.

In an early review of conceptions of memory, Ebbinghaus (1885) discussed the possibility that events in memory may weaken over time if they are not practiced in some way. He also suggested that forgotten ideas might be brought to consciousness on the basis of the laws of association. In some instances inaccessible memories may "remain concealed from consciousness, yet produce an effect which is significant and which authenticates their previous existence." In other instances inaccessible memories may simply weaken over time due to lack of practice and leave no trace of their prior existence. In short, one process of forgetting might involve associational webs; the other, a passive decay over time.

Beginning with Ebbinghaus, then, we can trace two general streams of thought in experimental psychology concerning the most profitable way to characterize the processes of forgetting. One of these has emphasized modification or destruction of the event in memory (storage failure); the other has emphasized a blocking of memories by other memories or mechanisms of memory (retrieval failure). Still a third approach has emphasized *both* storage and retrieval failures to explain the observed complexities of memory. Let us consider these alternatives in terms of general assumptions about forgetting.

GENERAL THEORETICAL POSITIONS

Trace Theory

One influential approach to the study of memory has emphasized the construct of dynamic memory traces to explain both the success and the failure of memory. In general, trace theories place a heavy emphasis on changes in memory storage over time. A basic contention is that the effects of learning or practice persist in the form of a memory trace after active practice has ceased. This trace can then be modified over time by internal, *autonomous* events if the trace is not disrupted or interfered with for some (unspecified) period of time. Forgetting might then be explained in terms of changes in the stored representation of the original memory. At least three different varieties of such internal modification have been suggested.

In the first instance, a memory trace may strengthen or "set" over time spontaneously, and little forgetting would result. This *consolidation hypothesis* might explain why certain old memories remain vivid and sharp, even though they have not been practiced recently. It has also been used to explain the observation that temporal spacing of learning trials (distributed practice) may result in more efficient learning than when the trials are bunched close together in time (massed practice). In such cases the distribution of practice method supposedly provides time for the memory trace to consolidate before the next input, and hence it facilitates learning (cf. Müller and Pilzecker, 1900).

In the second instance, a memory trace is assumed to change spontaneously, but quite lawfully, to a form determined by *Gestalt*[1] laws of *compact organization*. Examples of such effects are provided by subjects who recall asymmetrical figures as being more symmetrical or who remember a circle with a small gap in it as being completely closed (cf. Wulf, 1922). This version of trace theory has been difficult to evaluate because of a number of methodological and theoretical problems, and as a result it has been somewhat dormant in recent years (cf. Riley, 1962).

In the third instance, a memory trace may decay spontaneously over time. This *trace decay hypothesis* provides an explanation for the rapidity with which we often forget materials to which we have been only briefly exposed and which are not rehearsed. This aspect of trace theory has been important in theoretical distinctions between temporary and relatively permanent memory systems (see Chapter 6).

Support for the notion of trace decay comes from the common observation that memories *appear* to weaken over time if they are not practiced. In this sense, trace theory is closely related to Thorndike's law of disuse (see Chapter 2). The concept of decay, however, has most often been employed in theories that are directly opposed to stimulus-response theories such as Thorndike's. The trace decay hypothesis also has been strengthened by analogies between psychological views of memory traces and physiological interpretations of neural activity (Hebb, 1949). For example, the short-term reverberating neural activity presumed to underlie

[1] Some 114 different *Gestalt* (organizational) principles have been identified, but these probably reduce to about 12 basic ones (cf. Boring, 1950).

immediate memory weakens over time in a manner consistent with trace decay theory.

Interference Theory

A second major approach to the analysis of forgetting emphasizes the static nature of memory traces in contrast to their autonomous enhancement or decay. According to this view, forgetting involves difficulties in retrieval rather than in storage. Since these difficulties in retrieving memories are often cast in terms of competition or interference among habits, the resulting explanations of forgetting are usually called interference theories.

Interference explanations of forgetting often begin by assuming that competing habits or associations have already been learned. For example, suppose that A is some stimulus that has previously been associated with two incompatible responses, B and C. Let us also suppose that only one of these associations, say A-C, can be recalled on a particular test of retention. According to interference theory, the failure to recall A-B does not mean that it has been totally forgotten or even modified while in storage. Instead, the A-B association is temporarily unavailable, or difficult to retrieve, because it has suffered response competition from the A-C association.

In an attempt to describe the processes that characterize forgetting, interference theorists have examined two main sources of interference. One of these sources has been identified with the period *between* storage and retrieval; the other involves the period *before* storage has taken place. In both situations, however, forgetting is thought to result from interference between old memories already in storage and new memories coming into storage. When old memories are displaced by new memories, theorists attribute forgetting to *retroactive* processes. In contrast, the displacement of new memories by older memories is explained on the basis of *proactive* processes.

A Choice Among Theories

Although both trace and interference principles could be employed to account for many aspects of forgetting, interference explanations have usually been preferred. One reason for this was that interference theory, with its emphasis on stimulus-response associations, was more compatible with behavioristic accounts of learning. A more important consideration, however, was that interference theory seemed better equipped than trace theory to offer a precise analysis of forgetting. Trace theorists explained forgetting on the basis of autonomous changes that took place over time. In such accounts, little emphasis was placed on the nature of to-be-remembered material or relationships between it and other learned material.

Only the temporal pattern of such experiences was stressed. In contrast, interference theorists emphasized relationships between competing habits. According to this view, forgetting should be influenced by such factors as similarity between competing habits and not by the spacing of events in time.

Interference theory was developed within the framework of associative learning principles. Therefore, the basic principles of interference theory were supposed to account for both the success of memory in learning and the failures of memory in forgetting. In contrast, trace theory mainly focused on failures of memory. Given this situation, once a major role for factors such as similarity was demonstrated in both learning and retention, a theory that incorporated these factors was seen as providing a more adequate account of forgetting.

If we consider an ordinary learning situation in the laboratory, it is not difficult to see why similarity was so important. In such a situation, each trial consists of repeating the same events or inputs that were presented on the preceding trial. That is, inputs on each successive trial are of maximum similarity, and in this way similarity leads to improved retention. Even with only two trials, repeating the same inputs improves retention. Now consider a situation involving two inputs that are not identical. If we ask for recall of the first input after the second one has been presented, retention will be poorer than when the two inputs are identical. As might be expected, accuracy of recall in this situation depends on the similarity between the two inputs.

The actual effects of similarity in both learning and retention can be quite complex, and they vary somewhat depending on the experimental situation (cf. Ellis, 1965; Keppel, 1968). Since details concerning similarity effects are not of great consequence for the subsequent discussion, it is not our intention to review them at this point. It is important to understand, however, that the demonstrated role of similarity factors seemed to support interference theories of forgetting.

Interference explanations of forgetting have generally been preferred to explanations based on trace theory. The main focus in this chapter will therefore be on the development of major concepts and principles of interference theory. However, we shall return to a consideration of some aspects of trace theory in the next chapter. Let us begin the discussion of interference theory by contrasting certain aspects of trace and interference explanations.

RETROACTIVE INTERFERENCE AND FORGETTING

Forgetting that is related to events occurring after storage but prior to retrieval is often attributed by interference theorists to retroactive processes. The basic assumption here is that old memories in storage are interfered with by new memories that are being crowded into storage.

Since this type of explanation also appeals to commonsense views of forgetting, interference theorists placed a heavy emphasis on some form of retroactive process.

According to a general retroactive interpretation, forgetting depends directly on those activities that are interpolated between the learning of some task and a subsequent retention test. When a great deal of interpolated activity takes place, retention will be poorer than when little interpolated activity takes place. This view leads to the prediction that no forgetting would be observed if an individual was totally isolated from potential sources of interference immediately after learning. In contrast, a trace decay theory would predict that some forgetting should still occur in this situation. Only approximate tests of these opposed predictions can be carried out, since it is not possible to completely isolate an individual. Although even approximate tests provide little basis for choosing among theories, it is instructive to consider a few examples of them.

In reviewing early retention studies involving lower organisms (e.g., rats, goldfish, and cockroaches), Osgood (1953) refers to cases in which retention of prior learning was tested following periods of relatively high or low interpolated activity. The results of these experiments were generally consistent with expectations derived from interference theory. Retention was better when interpolated activity was curtailed than when it was not. Of course these findings are also consistent with a trace theory that permits the interpretation that interpolated activity can disrupt memory traces from prior inputs by preventing consolidation.

In the case of human memory, the most frequently cited of these early experiments is one reported by Jenkins and Dallenbach (1924). In this experiment two subjects were given retention tests for previously learned verbal material following intervals during which they were either asleep or awake. The results of this study also supported interference interpretations. Both subjects showed better retention following the interval in which they were asleep than following the interval in which they were awake.

A complicating factor arising in both these human and infrahuman studies of retention is that some forgetting occurs even in the most "inactive" conditions. This might suggest that trace decay was also involved in the observed forgetting. An interference theorist could of course argue that such forgetting occurred because the subjects were not totally isolated from sources of interference. In the case of human subjects, dream activity could be said to provide ample opportunity for interference to occur. We cannot be certain that this explanation, even if true, would rule out any possibility of trace decay. Studies of this type are of little help in the evaluation of trace and interference principles.

Forgetting and Retroaction. Before proceeding with the discussion of retroactive interference, it is important to note the manner in which the studies just mentioned can be characterized in terms of a more comprehensive retroaction paradigm. Consider two groups of subjects, one of which is called the experimental group and the other the control group. Both groups learn Task 1 and are subsequently tested for recall of Task 1. The critical difference between these conditions is that the experimental group engages in other activity during the retention interval (learns Task 2) while the control group does not.

Conditions	Task 1 (learn)	Task 2 (learn)	Task 1 (recall)
Experimental	Yes	Yes	Yes
Control	Yes	No	Yes

The activity interpolated between learning and recall is of course critical to any retroaction model, and a systematic analysis of the effects of such interpolated activity can be made by comparing recall scores for the experimental and control subjects. If the experimental group recalls Task 1 more poorly than the control group, *retroactive interference* has been demonstrated. Interpolated activity does not inevitably produce forgetting, however. The experimental group may recall Task 1 better than the control group. In this case, *retroactive facilitation* has been demonstrated. As we shall see later on, such facilitating effects may occur when Task 2 is similar to Task 1. Finally, it should be noted that if the experimental and control groups do not differ in terms of recall, no retroactive effects have been demonstrated.

When conceptualized in this manner, the retroaction paradigm constitutes a situation in which the full range of facilitating and interfering effects of interpolated activity can be evaluated. Therefore, retroaction does not necessarily imply forgetting. It should also be noted that the retroaction paradigm is theoretically neutral with respect to the trace and interference positions. Even when retroactive interference occurs, there is no necessary implication concerning alternative theoretical interpretations. Both theories can explain why control subjects may show better recall than experimental subjects. But when similarity relationships between the original and interpolated tasks are shown to differentially influence recall, interference explanations seem more plausible (cf. Keppel, 1968). The formal analysis of forgetting in terms of retroactive effects has been so closely identified with interference theory that the term *retroaction* has become almost synonymous with *interference*.

Two-Factor Retroaction Theory

Early interference theories of forgetting were essentially single-factor theories based on the principle of *response competition*. Consider a situation in which the learning of one task *(A-B)* is followed by other learning activities *(A-C)* and subsequent recall of the original task *(A-B)*. Any forgetting observed in this situation is explained in terms of the displacement of correct responses *(B)* by incorrect, competing responses *(C)* which became associated with the common stimuli *(A)* during interpolated learning.

Single-factor theories of response competition also contained the assumption that the learning of new associations *(A-C)* in no way altered the strength of previously learned associations *(A-B)*. In other words this assumption, which has been called the *independence hypothesis* (Barnes and Underwood, 1959), implied that competition between responses *(B and C)* at the time of recall was the only cause of forgetting. Interference theorists soon realized that such a simple concept of forgetting would have to be modified to account for various experimental findings.

In a now classic study Melton and Irwin (1940) demonstrated the importance of factors other than response competition. They required subjects to learn a serial list of nonsense syllables for a constant number of trials as the original learning task. After original learning, various groups of subjects were given an interpolated learning task involving the same type of material. The number of interpolated learning trials for the various groups ranged from zero (control condition for assessing retroaction effects) to forty. Finally, all groups were required to recall the original list. By comparing the performance of the control group with that of the other groups, a measure of *total* retroactive interference was obtained. The influence of response competition was assessed by recording the number of times that responses from the interpolated list were intruded during recall.

The main results of the Melton and Irwin study are shown in Figure 5.1. As can be seen, total retroactive interference increased rather systematically as a function of the number of interpolated learning trials. But the amount of this interference that could be attributed to response competition, as indexed by the number of intrusions, clearly declined after about ten interpolated trials. Thus response competition could not explain all the interference observed, and, in fact, the contribution of response competition appeared to *decrease* just when it should have been greatest.

By subtracting the interference attributable to response competition from the total retroactive interference observed, Melton and Irwin obtained an index of interference due to some other factor or factors. These investigators considered the possibility that this other factor (called factor X) might involve the *unlearning* or extinction of original list associations during learning of the interpolated list. When the number of interpolated learning trials was small, both unlearning and response competition would lead to forgetting. As the number of interpolated trials increased, however, forgetting would be mainly attributed to unlearning and little response competition would be expected.

Certain problems of interpretation arose in connection with the concept of unlearning. Nevertheless, unlearning became an increasingly popular

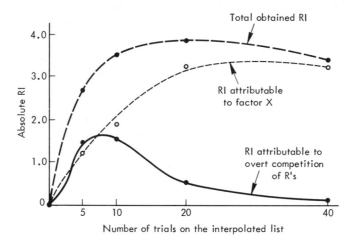

Figure 5.1 Relationship between amount of retroactive inter-ference (RI) and degree of interpolated learning.
(After Melton and Irwin, 1940.)

concept in interference theory, and by the 1960s its importance in ex-planations of forgetting was rarely questioned. With the development of unlearning as a basic concept, interference theory shifted from a one-factor to a two-factor model. Instead of explaining forgetting solely on the basis of response competition, both unlearning and response competition played a major role.

Other Retroaction Paradigms.   In the preceding discussion reference was made to the *A-B, A-C* form of the retroaction paradigm. This arrange-ment of materials, which involves associating each stimulus with two different responses, has been widely used in studies of interference effects. Several other arrangements are possible, however. Different stimuli are associated with the same response in the *A-B, C-B* paradigm. In most investigations of interference effects, the items associated with the common stimulus or response terms are unrelated to each other. These items would of course be related in various degrees when similarity effects were being studied.

Each of these other arrangements for the retroaction paradigm has been important in the investigation of certain retroaction effects. In addi-tion, these paradigm arrangements, as well as others not mentioned, can be employed in studies of proaction as well. It is not necessary to consider them here, however, because the basic principles of interference theory have been mainly developed and tested using the *A-B, A-C* arrangement referred to previously. For other purposes, and in other contexts, these alternative arrangements have been of considerable importance.

A Problem for Retroaction

Two-factor explanations of forgetting based on retroactive processes were able to provide accounts of a wide range of experimental findings. At the same time, however, the theory also had difficulty providing accounts of some rather basic observations obtained in the laboratory. To illustrate this point, let us recall the findings reported by Ebbinghaus in his classic studies of retention of verbal material over time. When nonsense syllables were employed, a typical result was about 55 percent forgetting after one hour, more than 65 percent forgetting after twenty-four hours, and almost 80 percent forgetting after thirty-one days. In contrast to the rapid forgetting of nonsense material, Ebbinghaus experienced little difficulty in recalling meaningful material. Stanzas from Byron's "Don Juan" were remembered quite well after intervals of twenty-four hours.

Such observations are difficult to explain solely on the basis of retroactive processes. The problem arises because a theory of retroactive interference proposes to explain any observed forgetting on the basis of events occurring *between* learning and the subsequent retention test. Yet it is difficult to argue convincingly that the everyday activities that Ebbinghaus engaged in during the retention intervals would be likely to produce extensive forgetting of nonsense syllables and little forgetting of meaningful material, at the same time. These observations became even more puzzling in view of the assumption that nonsense syllables are relatively "isolated" from everyday language experiences and are therefore less likely to be interfered with by them.

Interference During Storage.   In an important analysis of findings such as those just mentioned, Underwood (1957) reviewed some thirty years of research dealing with the forgetting of verbal material. In support of Ebbinghaus, he noted that nonsense materials are often forgotten quite rapidly. Across a variety of situations, the forgetting of nonsense materials reached a level of about 75 percent within twenty-four hours. Underwood also noted, however, that there appeared to be a systematic relationship, in the studies reviewed, between retention level and prior laboratory learning experiences. The more lists a subject had learned prior to the list being tested, the poorer was his retention of the tested list. This relationship is presented in Figure 5.2.

As the results in Figure 5.2 indicate, the amount of forgetting shown by a subject with no prior laboratory learning experience was closer to 25 percent than to 75 percent. With the highly practiced subject, who had learned ten or more lists, the situation was essentially reversed. It should be recalled that Ebbinghaus was also a highly practiced subject. The comparability between the performance of Ebbinghaus and that of these

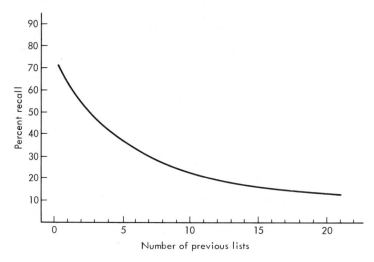

Figure 5.2   Recall over twenty-four hours as a function of number of previous lists learned.
(After Underwood, 1957.)

other highly practiced subjects suggests that prior testing in the laboratory was a major cause of forgetting by these subjects. Therefore the classic Ebbinghaus curve of retention may only be representative of forgetting when subjects are exposed to large amounts of interference from previously learned tasks.

PROACTIVE INTERFERENCE AND FORGETTING

The analysis of forgetting provided by Underwood (1957) is based on a proactive interference paradigm. This paradigm is used to explain retention that is systematically related to events that occur *prior* to the learning of a particular task. When forgetting occurs in a proactive situation, the usual explanation involves several steps or stages. First, it is assumed that previously acquired information or habits make it difficult to learn new material. As a result of this interference, the old information is somehow suppressed so that the new information can be learned. The suppression of the old information or habits, however, only continues *during* new learning. Once new learning is completed, the old information gradually recovers in strength and interferes with subsequent recall of the newly learned material.

The paradigm for proactive interference is also closely identified with interference theories of forgetting. As in retroaction, however, the proactive interference paradigm can be considered as a special case of proactive effects in general. To illustrate this point, consider two groups of subjects, one of which is called the experimental group and the other the control group. Both groups learn Task 2 and are subsequently tested for recall of Task 2. Prior to the learning of Task 2, however, the experimental group learns another task (Task 1) while the control group does not.

Conditions	Task 1 (learn)	Task 2 (learn)	Task 2 (recall)
Experimental	Yes	Yes	Yes
Control	No	Yes	Yes

Comparisons between recall levels in the experimental and control conditions indicate the type of proactive effect observed. When the experimental group recalls Task 2 better than the control group, *proactive facilitation* has been demonstrated. But if superior recall is found for the control group, *proactive interference* is indicated. When the two groups do not differ in recall, no proactive effects have been demonstrated. Within the context of a proactive interference situation, let us reconsider the relationship between retention and amount of prior learning which was reported by Underwood (1957). In terms of proactive effects, it is not difficult to explain why prior learning of several lists would produce extensive forgetting of a subsequently learned list. As the number of prior lists increased, there would be more and more old information in memory to compete with recall of the newly learned list. This analysis obviously does not apply to the 25 percent forgetting actually shown by subjects with no prior learning experience in the laboratory.

Underwood (1957) has provided an interesting account of the forgetting shown by subjects naive to the laboratory situation. He began by assuming about a 10 percent error in most estimates of the amount of forgetting. We shall not consider the basis for this estimate, except to note that methodological considerations concerning the degree of original learning were involved. In any case, this reduced the amount of forgetting for unpracticed subjects to be explained from 25 percent to 15 percent. Underwood suggested that the remaining forgetting might be explained on the basis of proactive interference from everyday language habits which the subject brings to the laboratory situation.

Prior Language Habits and Forgetting

The general notion that prior language habits can influence the learning and retention of new material has a certain appeal to common sense. It explicitly recognizes that subjects are not "blank tablets," even when they are engaged in rote learning. In addition, the assumption rests on rather firm grounds in terms of the subject's experiences. Both the duration and the multitude of learning experiences that the subject brings to a laboratory learning situation are vastly greater than those that occur between learning and recall in the laboratory.

Underwood and Postman (1960) have provided an account of the way in which prior language habits could produce forgetting of verbal materials in the laboratory. The assumed process of forgetting can be conveniently represented in terms of an *A-B, A-C* interference paradigm. In this instance *A-B* is some preexperimental association learned outside the laboratory, and *A-C* is an association to be learned in the laboratory. Underwood and Postman assumed that during the learning of *A-C,* the subject is required to unlearn or extinguish *A-B*. For example, "doctor-lawyer" (*A-B*) is a strong association in the language because of previous usage. Thus if a subject were required to learn "doctor-starch" (*A-C*), which is a relatively weak association, he would have to unlearn the "doctor-lawyer" sequence. But since *B* is a strong, well-practiced association to *A* in the subject's language, it may recover in strength over time and compete with *C* at the time of recall. To the extent that *B* is dominant at recall, forgetting of *C* will occur.

The Underwood and Postman explanation of forgetting emphasizes *response competition* at the time of recall. The competition is between associations learned in the laboratory and strong, natural language associations that were unlearned during laboratory learning. These natural language associations were presumed to spontaneously recover in strength during the retention interval and to compete with associations learned in the laboratory during the retention test. On the basis of these principles Underwood and Postman (1960) derived two general hypotheses concerning the forgetting of verbal materials that occurs in the laboratory: *letter-sequence interference* and *unit-sequence interference*.

Letter-Sequence Interference.   The notion of letter-sequence interference was based on an assumed competition between *A-B* and *A-C* associations involving letters. For example, a subject might recall the sequence *xyz* when *xzy* was correct because *xyz* is a common sequence in the alphabet. The basic idea was that when letter combinations to be learned in the laboratory represent unlikely sequences in the language, the combinations learned in the laboratory would be difficult to recall. Common sequences in the language should of course be easy to recall in the laboratory setting.

Estimates of the frequency of occurrence of various letter combinations in the language can be obtained by counting letter sequences in representative material. Normative data generated in this manner indicate, for example, that the sequence *"g-o"* is more common than the sequence *"g-v"* (Underwood and Schulz, 1960). This should not be too surprising, since the sequence *"g-o"* forms a common word and occurs frequently as part of other familiar words (e.g., *go*ing, e*go*, for*go*tten, *go*od). It would be expected that letter-sequence interference would be quite minimal for this particular sequence, which appears to be a well-integrated language unit.

Unit-Sequence Interference.   As letter combinations begin to approximate frequent items in the language, such as words, unit-sequence effects come into play. For instance, the learning of a sequence like "doctor-starch" (*A-C*) might be interfered with by a more common sequence in the language like "doctor-lawyer" (*A-B*). During *A-C* learning, the *A-B* association would be unlearned, but it would recover in strength during the retention interval to compete with *A-C* at the time of recall. Similarly, the unit-sequence hypothesis can be used to explain difficulties in recalling longer sequences of material. Consider a sequence that might be learned in the laboratory, such as *butterfly-stomach-insect-flower-bird*. Presumably, each of these words is more strongly associated with some other word in the language than it is with the word that follows it in the sequence. These stronger associations, then, could be expected to disrupt recall of the experimental sequence learned in the laboratory.

Meaningfulness and Interference.   The Underwood and Postman theory challenges the traditional assumption that meaningfulness of material favors retention. This is important, since it is difficult for interference theory, in general, to explain the common finding that meaningful verbal material is usually better recalled than meaningless material.[2] The difficulty arises because meaningful items are richer in associations than meaningless items and should suffer more from associative interference over time than meaningless items. Let us see how the Underwood and Postman theory deals with this problem.

We have noted that unit-sequence interference comes into play as sequences of letters begin to constitute units in the language such as words. This source of interference increases thereafter and reaches a maximum for words that occur with high frequency in the language. Since the frequency of occurrence of items and their meaningfulness are directly related (cf. Noble, 1961; Underwood and Schulz, 1960), the entire dimension for letter-sequence and unit-sequence interference can also be conceptualized in terms of the classical dimension of meaningfulness (Underwood and Postman, 1960). Thus, large amounts of interference should occur for items at both the low end (letter-sequence interference) and the high end

---

[2] This may be somewhat misleading, since the problem of equating degree of original learning is present in all retention studies in which the meaningfulness variable is manipulated. When this methodological problem is taken into account, meaningfulness per se seems to have little effect on retention (cf. Underwood, 1964). In other words, the finding that meaningfulness favors retention can often be explained more parsimoniously by referring to "Ebbinghaus's axiom." Meaningful material is usually better learned and, therefore, better retained. This suggests that the facilitatory effects of meaningfulness are more directly on the storage (learning) stage than on the recall (retrieval) stage.

(unit-sequence interference) of this continuum, whereas interference in recall should be minimal somewhere toward the middle of the meaningfulness dimension. This suggests that there should be little difference in forgetting for items from the extremes of the meaningfulness (frequency) dimension and that meaningfulness and probability of recall should be related by an inverted U-shaped function (see Figure 5.3).

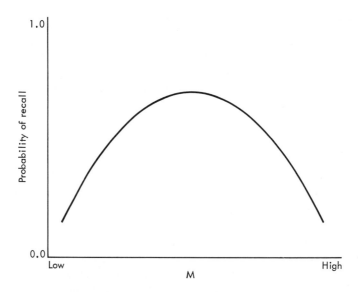

Figure 5.3 Probability of recall as a function of frequency of prior experience (M) with verbal materials according to the Underwood and Postman (1960) theory.

In an early test of some of these predictions, Underwood and Postman (1960) compared the serial learning and recall of high- and low-frequency units composed of three letters. Some of the high-frequency units were words (e.g., *age, was*) and some were nonwords (e.g., *ati, sho*). Correspondingly, some of the low-frequency items were words (e.g., *ado, wry*) and some were not (e.g., *dop, hok*). Recall scores for these various types of items failed to show that meaningfulness and forgetting were directly related, confirming some of the Underwood and Postman predictions. The traditional assumption that meaningfulness directly favors retention was not supported. However, other predicted relationships between meaningfulness and retention were not obtained. Such findings would have made their theoretical explanations much more compelling.

As it turned out, failures to find *any* relationship between meaningfulness and forgetting became a weakness, rather than a strength, of the Underwood and Postman theory. The theory predicts that forgetting of unit sequences (words) should increase with meaningfulness, whereas forgetting of letter sequences (nonwords) should be inversely related to meaningfulness. A number of studies, however, have indicated that degree of learning was about the only variable involved in any substantial way in retention (Turnage and McCullough, 1968; Underwood and Ekstrand, 1966; Underwood and Keppel, 1963).

A few studies did seem to support some of the predictions of interference theory concerning meaningfulness effects (e.g., Saba and Turnage, 1973; Turnage, 1967), but even in these investigations it was not clear whether unlearning and spontaneous recovery of *A-B* associations played any important role. For example, Turnage and Steinmetz (1971) found an inverted U-function relating meaningfulness and recall in a short-term memory situation that appeared in direct accord with interference predictions. But various association tests administered during the experiments failed to reveal any evidence for competition and unlearning with respect to *A-B* associations. On the contrary, their association data suggested that the "psychological segregation" of *A-B* and *A-C* associations was remarkably complete.

BASIC CONCEPTS OF TWO-FACTOR THEORY

In the preceding sections we have described the basic concepts employed in two-factor explanations of retroactive and proactive interference. In both of these situations, accounts of forgetting have centered on the notions of response competition, unlearning of associations, and spontaneous recovery of previously unlearned associations. Generally speaking, variations in the observed level of proactive and retroactive interference have been consistent with predictions based on these concepts (cf. Keppel, 1968). However, a question has arisen concerning the operation of specific explanatory mechanisms. This problem was noted in attempts to explain the influence of prior language habits on forgetting. Since much of the difficulty seems to revolve about the assumptions of unlearning and spontaneous recovery, let us consider these concepts in more detail.

Unlearning and Spontaneous Recovery

A cornerstone of interference theory has rested on the presumed "fate" of competing associations during learning. A general assumption of the theory has been that *A-B* associations are unlearned during the acquisition of *A-C* associations. In retroactive situations the *A-B* associations were those acquired during original learning; in proactive situations the *A-B* associations were presumed to be those that the subject brought with him to the laboratory. In either case, these *A-B* associations were thought to be unlearned when *A-C* associations were acquired. These unlearned associations were also thought to spontaneously recover in strength after *A-C* learning was completed.

The concept of unlearning, or extinction of associations, was borrowed from conditioning theories that assumed that extinction was based on a *temporary* inhibition of specific habits. Because of the temporary character of the inhibitory process, Pavlov (1927) predicted that conditioned responses that had been extinguished would spontaneously recover in strength without further training, given enough time. Hull (1943, 1952) also suggested that dissipation of this transitory inhibition would permit some spontaneous recovery over time.

Although the concepts of conditioning theory had considerable influence in the early analysis of verbal behavior, the unlearning hypothesis is most closely identified with Melton and Irwin (1940). These investigators employed the concept of unlearning in their analysis of the factors responsible for retroactive interference. The possibility that verbal associations would be subject to both unlearning and spontaneous recovery was also recognized by Underwood (1948) and Briggs (1954).

In the study reported by Briggs (1954), stimuli (*A*) common to both lists in an *A-B, A-C* retroaction paradigm were presented during retention tests. In contrast to the procedure of asking for recall of the first-list responses (*B*), Briggs asked his subjects to report the first response (*B* or *C*) that came to mind. This procedure has been called the method of *modified free recall* (MFR). The results of this study indicated that *B* responses decreased in frequency of recall as the number of *A-C* learning trials was increased. Since more *A-C* learning should lead to greater extinction of associations, these findings supported the unlearning hypothesis.

In the same experiment, Briggs also compared the retention of *A-B* and *A-C* associations at retention intervals of various lengths. These comparisons showed some evidence for spontaneous recovery of first-list (*B*) responses with longer retention intervals. A basic problem of interpretation arises in this experiment because the subjects were asked to recall *only* the first response that came to mind. With shorter retention intervals, recall of more *C* responses did not require that *B* responses had been forgotten or unlearned. With long retention intervals, recall of *B* responses did not necessarily mean that they had recovered in strength. Thus, although the results of Briggs's (1954) study were encouraging, more direct evidence of both unlearning and spontaneous recovery was required.

In a further analysis of unlearning, Barnes and Underwood (1959) again used the *A-B, A-C* paradigm in a study of retroactive interference. But instead of asking their subjects to report only the first response that came to mind, these investigators asked for recall of responses from both the original (*A-B*) and interpolated (*A-C*) lists. This modification of the MFR technique has been designated as MMFR. Presumably this procedure overcomes the problem of distinguishing between the effects of unlearning and response competition. The rationale was that if both responses were available, both should be recalled. Response competition would only act to determine which response was given first. If a particular first-list response was not recalled, however, it was thought to have been unlearned.

Using the MMFR procedure, Barnes and Underwood noted that recall of first-list (B) responses gradually decreased as the number of interpolated $(A-C)$ learning trials was increased. This observation was clearly in line with the unlearning hypothesis. On the basis of this result, Barnes and Underwood suggested that nearly all of the retroactive interference observed immediately after interpolated $(A-C)$ learning could be attributed to unlearning of the first-list $(A-B)$ associations during interpolated learning.

The study by Barnes and Underwood (1959) did not provide any evidence concerning the spontaneous recovery of unlearned associations over time. When their results were considered along with those of Briggs (1954), however, such a recovery process seemed to be a strong possibility. Thus the concepts of unlearning and spontaneous recovery became firmly established in two-factor theories of forgetting.

With the MMFR task apparently providing a way of separating the effects of unlearning from those of response competition, the door was opened to a further development of interference theory. For example, McGovern (1964) extended interference theory to account for competition and unlearning effects for both forward and backward associations. Despite successes in this direction, problems soon arose in the attempt to confirm specific theoretical predictions. We saw an illustration of this in our discussion of the influence of prior language habits. Although forgetting was observed, it was difficult to demonstrate that this was due to unlearning and spontaneous recovery.

Related evidence concerning the processes of unlearning and spontaneous recovery came from comparisons of forgetting in the proactive and retroactive paradigms. It will be recalled that forgetting in the retroactive paradigm was thought to be due to both unlearning of first-list $(A-B)$ associations and response competition. In contrast, only response competition was thought to produce forgetting in the proactive situation. These considerations suggested that when retention was tested *immediately* after interpolated learning, retroactive interference should be greater than proactive interference. In fact, in an $A-B$, $A-C$ paradigm, little proactive interference should occur on an immediate retention test because the competing responses from the $A-B$ list would not have recovered from unlearning.

The available evidence shows that retroactive interference is greater than proactive interference on an immediate test, as two-factor theory predicts. This observation would be expected on commonsense grounds, since recall of what has just been learned should be better than recall of previously learned material. But there is evidence of more proactive interference on such a retention test (cf. Koppenaal, 1963) than two-factor theory would predict. This leads to questions about the "purity" of MMFR as an index of unlearning. Let us now turn to another prediction based on two-factor theory concerning differences in proactive and retroactive interference on a *delayed* retention test.

When a retention test is administered some time after the completion of interpolated learning, several factors need to be considered. With such a delayed test, the *A-B* associations that were unlearned during *A-C* learning would have had an opportunity to recover in strength. As a result, less forgetting should occur in the retroactive paradigm relative to an immediate retention test, because the subject is attempting to recall these *A-B* associations. In the proactive situation, however, forgetting should increase because the *A-B* associations are more available to compete with the *A-C* associations that the subject is attempting to recall. The general form of these predictions is shown in Figure 5.4.

The evidence concerning the predicted convergence of retroactive and proactive interference on a delayed retention test is somewhat mixed. The expected convergence does, in fact, occur. In most cases, however, this results from a relative, rather than an absolute, decrease in retroactive interference (cf. Keppel, 1968). Forgetting increases over time in both the proactive and retroactive situations, but proactive interference increases

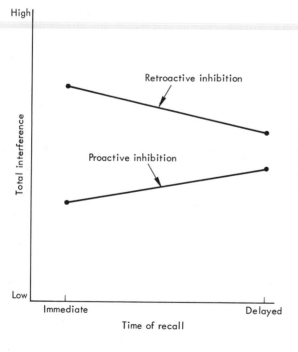

Figure 5.4 Predicted changes over time in proactive and retroaction interference according to a two-factor theory of forgetting.

by a larger amount. In other words, more forgetting occurs in the situation (proaction) in which there is more to forget. The observations in delayed retention support some predictions based on two-factor theory, but important details of these predictions are not supported.

By early 1960s interference theorists found themselves in a somewhat awkward position. As Postman (1961) pointed out in an extensive review, the available data generally supported a two-factor theory of interference based on the unlearning of specific associations and response competition. He suggested that these concepts could be extended to include preexperimental associations as sources of forgetting. There also were repeated failures in the attempt to predict various experimental outcomes, and these failures required a reconsideration of some of the concepts of interference theory.

Unlearning Reexamined

Since the strongest underpinnings of interference theory have been derived from studies of retroactive interference, it is ironic that this same paradigm may have provided evidence that has put the handwriting on the wall for traditional interference theory (Tulving and Madigan, 1970). In a series of studies involving the retroaction paradigm, Postman and his associates (Postman and Stark, 1969; Postman, Stark, and Fraser, 1968) have rejected the assumption that unlearning of specific associations occurs during interpolated learning. Instead, they concluded that the main effect of interpolated learning is to somehow suppress first-list $(A\text{-}B)$ responses.

The evidence supporting this conclusion comes from retroaction studies in which retention was tested by presenting both the stimulus and response terms from the first list to the subjects. Under these conditions, subjects have little difficulty pairing the stimulus (A) and response (B) terms correctly. That is, in comparison with the appropriate control condition, there is no evidence of retroactive interference when both the stimulus and response terms are available to the subjects. This observation suggests that first-list associations are not unlearned during interpolated learning. The observation also implies that the retroactive interference found when responses must be recalled, as in an MMFR test, is due to some sort of response suppression effect. Once the response terms have been provided, however, no retroactive interference is observed.

The introduction of a response suppression factor in explanations of retroactive interference has decided implications for interference theory. Of course if the suppression is not complete, response competition is still a potential source of forgetting. But if unlearning really does not take place neither does spontaneous recovery, and this requires a drastic revision in traditional accounts of both proactive and retroactive interference. In addition, it is most difficult to explain the suppression of an entire *set* of responses on the basis of the associative principles usually subscribed to by interference theorists.

Postman et al. (1968, 1969) suggest an explanation of response suppression based on the so-called selector mechanism described by Underwood and Schulz (1960). The operation of this mechanism seems to be reflected in the tendency of subjects to restrict their responses in most verbal learning situations to items from the list currently being learned. One consequence of this tendency is to reduce interference from prior language habits or from previously learned lists. Postman and his associates suggest that just such a mechanism can explain the suppression of a set of previously learned responses. Such a mechanism is not readily understood on the basis of traditional associative principles. Therefore, the use of a concept like the selector mechanism may require changes in the nature of explanations of forgetting.

A Paradox for Interference Theory

As we have seen, several experimental observations are decidedly contrary to predictions based on interference theory. Although these findings did not doom the theory, they have made life difficult for the theorist who wanted to explain forgetting in terms of relatively pure associative principles. Some of the problems faced by interference theory may relate to associative concepts other than those already mentioned in this chapter. Let us briefly examine a few of these concepts.

A basic ambiguity that arises within the context of interference theory involves the prediction of both interfering and facilitating effects on the basis of the same principles. For example, we noted in Chapter 4 that rates of learning are directly related to the meaningfulness (frequency) of verbal material. This relationship is not easily predicted from the assumptions of interference theory. Although the larger number of associates to highly meaningful items might be expected to interfere with new learning, these same associates might also link up with associates to other items and facilitate learning. Underwood and Schultz (1960) have referred to these conflicting predictions as the *associative probability paradox*.

The very fact that associative principles lead to predictions of both facilitating and interfering effects at the same time causes obvious problems for the theorist. Any outcome can be explained after the fact, but it is difficult to make predictions with any confidence. Postman (1963) has considered the possibility that this complex of facilitating and interfering factors may also interact so as to effectively mask expected effects associated with the unit-sequence hypothesis. This suggestion has in turn led to various attempts to disentangle the opposed factors, but the results have not been overly successful from the standpoint of interference theory (cf. Saba and Turnage, 1973).

The Mediation Hypothesis

An interesting illustration related to the associative probability paradox concerns the possibility of mediation effects. It will be recalled that preexperimental associations *may* facilitate new learning and retention under some circumstances. One instance of this occurs when preexperimental associations provide *mediators* for the learning of experimental associations. For example, a pair of words like "justice-war" might be easy to learn because the common associate "peace" serves as a mediator (i.e., justice-peace-war).

Another situation in which a mediational interpretation has been invoked is in the explanation of similarity effects in transfer. For example, suppose subjects learn a set of pairs such as "gex-table" followed by another set such as "gex-chair," and retroactive facilitation is observed in recall of the "gex-table" list. Presumably these results are found because the associative similarity between *table* and *chair,* which the subject has previously learned outside the laboratory, sets up a mediational chain (e.g., gex-table-chair), which facilitates learning of the "gex-chair" list. As we have seen, however, a situation in which two different responses are associated to the same stimulus should also lead to interference effects.

Postman (1961) attempted to resolve these conflicting predictions by considering the possibility that *mediation* was the basic process and *unlearning* was a derived process. His suggestion was that with high response similarity, as in "gex-table," "gex-chair," the mediational chain would be strengthened and this would result in facilitation. With low response similarity, however, as in "gex-table," "gex-zebra," the tendency to mediate would lead to errors and this should result in unlearning of the mediating association.

Consider an experimental situation in which subjects learn a list of *A-B* pairs followed by a list of *A-C* pairs. Also assume that the items are low-frequency English words and that both the stimulus and response terms are unrelated. According to interference theory, the *A-B* associations should be unlearned during *A-C* learning in this situation. Yet, if these subjects are subsequently given *B-C* pairs to learn, they do learn the *B-C* pairs faster than do appropriate control subjects (cf. Horton and Kjeldergaard, 1961). The mediational interpretation is that *B-C* learning is facilitated by the previously acquired *A-B* and *A-C* associations (e.g., *B-A-C*). According to interference theory, however, the link between *B* and *A* in the mediational chain should have been unlearned before the *B-C* pairs were presented.

Such mediational effects have been found in various situations involving materials of high and low meaningfulness as well as high and low similarity (cf. Kjeldergaard, 1968). For this reason, most attempts to resolve the conflict between mediation and interference principles (cf. Post-man, 1961) have not been convincing. But in view of the evidence suggest-ing that response suppression, not unlearning, is a major factor in the retroactive situation, some resolution may be possible. For example, in the *A-B, A-C, B-C* mediation paradigm described above, the suppressed first-list responses (*B*) would serve as stimuli during *B-C* learning. Because these suppressed items are made available, there would be no disruption of the mediational chain (*B-A-C*). In an *A-B, B-C, A-C* mediation para-digm, it could also be argued that the suppressed responses might function as mediators, even though they could not be recalled overtly.

SOME OTHER FACTORS
INFLUENCING TRANSFER AND RETENTION

There are several factors whose influence on transfer and retention should be considered briefly. One of these factors is *similarity*. Earlier in this chapter it was noted that the dominant position achieved by inter-ference theory was due, in part, to the apparent ability of the theory to provide an account of the effects of similarity of materials. Let us begin this section by examining these effects.

Similarity and Transfer

According to Osgood (1949), the classic position of interference theory is that "the greater the similarity, the greater the interference." As Osgood notes, however, when carried to a logical extreme this assump-tion comes into direct conflict with the optimum conditions for learning. It is common knowledge that if you practice the *same* material over and over again (maximum similarity), you are likely to remember it better.

We have discussed the effects of repetition on retention in terms of "Ebbinghaus's axiom." It should be clear that such repetition effects are related to repeated trials with identical materials, as in a standard learn-ing situation. In this case there is positive transfer from trial to trial (which is another way of describing the standard learning curve), and retention usually increases as a direct function of the number of trials. But if we take the classic position of interference theory seriously, *ordi-nary learning* becomes both the *theoretical* condition for maximum inter-ference and the *practical* condition for maximum facilitation. Osgood (1949) referred to this as the *similarity paradox*.

The basis for the similarity paradox is most clearly illustrated when serial learning is involved in testing transfer from Task 1 to Task 2. In this situation, similarity refers to the relationship between items holding the same position in the original list and the transfer list. The typical

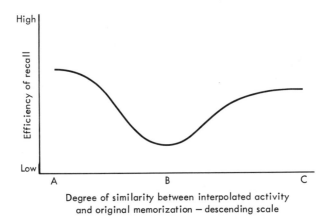

Figure 5.5 Skaggs-Robinson hypothesis relating similarity and efficiency of recall.
(After Robinson, 1927.)

transfer function obtained in such tests is described by the *Skaggs-Robinson hypothesis*. As Figure 5.5 indicates, transfer is maximum when the items are identical (maximum similarity), it begins to decline as similarity decreases, and finally it increases as the items become more dissimilar (cf. Robinson, 1927).

Assuming we have a clear definition of similarity, the Skaggs-Robinson hypothesis suggests a potential resolution of the similarity paradox. When the relationship between the items in Task 1 and Task 2 is at the lower end of the similarity dimension, increasing similarity does appear to result in increasing interference. Of course, the Skaggs-Robinson hypothesis does not indicate whether the interference is absolute (i.e., negative transfer and retroactive interference) or simply relative in comparison with other points on the similarity dimension. With materials ranging from the middle to the high end of the similarity dimension, however, increasing similarity leads to increasing facilitation. This observation is more in accord with our knowledge about the optimum conditions for learning.

A very different function relating similarity and transfer is found when both the original learning and the transfer task involve paired-associate lists. In this case we can consider similarity relationships for the stimulus and response terms separately. As shown in Figure 5.6, when stimuli are identical in Tasks 1 and 2 while responses vary, increasing response similarity leads to positive transfer. A similar relationship holds when responses are identical and stimuli vary across Tasks 1 and 2. These relationships have been well documented when transfer is measured in terms of Task 2 learning (cf. Martin, 1965; Underwood, 1966). When transfer is measured by retention tests (either proactive or retroactive

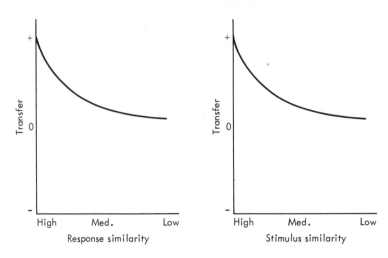

Figure 5.6 Transfer as a function of degree of stimulus or response similarity when the other member of the pair is identical in original learning and transfer tasks.

paradigms) the relationships are less clear, although the general shape of the functions appears to hold (cf. Keppel, 1968).

The findings illustrated in Figure 5.6 suggest that the similarity paradox does not arise in paired-associate learning. When paired-associate tasks are used in both original learning and transfer, increasing similarity usually leads to improved performance. This observation suggests that particular characteristics of the serial and paired-associate tasks are responsible for the differences in the similarity relationships. The different outcomes could be due to different functional stimuli in the two situations or to the possibility that associative learning is less important in the serial situation than it is in the paired-associate situation (see Chapter 4).

Task Differences

Differences between the serial and paired-associate tasks appear to be responsible for differences in observed similarity effects. This observation is consistent with the fact that task differences often lead to discrepant findings and that transfer is usually greatest when training and testing conditions are highly similar (cf. Ellis, 1965). But even when the training conditions are very similar, different outcomes may be seen in retention depending on the retention test used.

An early example of the way different retention tests can influence the forgetting function was reported by Luh (1922). In this experiment subjects learned a list of nonsense syllables by the serial anticipation method. Following learning, retention was measured by various methods, including recognition, recall, and relearning. Figure 5.7 shows the reten-

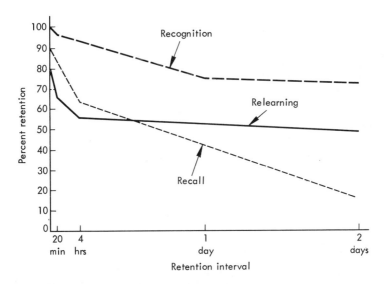

Figure 5.7   Comparisons of several measures of retention over various time intervals.
(After Luh, 1922.)

tion function over time that was obtained with each type of retention test. Recognition (identifying items presented in the correct sequence) appears to yield the highest estimates of retention, followed by relearning (the method used by Ebbinghaus), and then by recall (which requires remembering both the list items and their order in the list). Thus each method appears to be measuring something a little different, and different retention functions are obtained as a result. Whether such observed differences in retention indicate a differential sensitivity of the measures employed or a more fundamental difference in the nature of retrieval, task differences are evidently important in studies of retention.

General Transfer Effects

General factors also influence transfer and retention. For example, Harlow's (1949) work on the development of learning sets (see Chapter 2) showed that continuing experience with *conceptually* similar problems could produce sudden solutions and, therefore, substantial positive transfer, even though the task elements were physically dissimilar. An equally well established, but considerably less dramatic, phenomenon involves continued improvement in performance with a series of tasks *qua* tasks, even when there is little or no relationship between them. Two general types of such transfer effects have been distinguished: (1) *warm-up* and (2) *learning to learn*.

Warm-up is typically defined as the development of a set that maximizes the subject's efficiency in learning. The concept is derived from studies of motor learning. In the case of learning verbal materials, it usually refers to the development of appropriate postural adjustments and rhythm for responding that are required for the task at hand. Warm-up effects are thought to develop and to decline rather rapidly, possibly being lost (forgotten?) soon after an experimental session. In contrast, *learning-to-learn* effects seem to be more enduring. They are usually defined as the acquisition of various skills, such as learning to organize or mediate, which facilitate the learning of new tasks. In any given situation it is often difficult to disentangle the effects of warm-up and of learning-to-learn, but both are important in studies of transfer and retention.

CONCLUSION

This chapter has endeavored to describe and to trace the development of basic concepts and principles employed in interference theories of forgetting. To accomplish this objective it was necessary to introduce the retroactive and proactive interference paradigms, which have provided much of the evidence on which these concepts were based. We saw that early interference theory emphasized response competition as the main source of forgetting but that it was soon modified to include unlearning as a second explanatory concept. The notion of unlearning was borrowed from conditioning theory but was largely developed in laboratory studies of retroactive interference. This concept was also extended to aid in explaining forgetting in laboratory situations on the basis of previously acquired natural language habits.

Two-factor theory can be used to account for many aspects of forgetting. At the same time, however, many specific predictions based on the theory have been difficult to confirm, especially unlearning and the related concept of spontaneous recovery of unlearned associations. In both proactive and retroactive situations it has been difficult to obtain clear evidence concerning the operation of unlearning and spontaneous recovery. In addition, interference theory has suffered from the fact that many of its basic associative concepts give rise to conflicting predictions. For these reasons, a reassessment of interference theory has been taking place.

In discussing current trends in interference theory, and theories of memory in general, it is necessary to go beyond the scope of the present chapter. In part, this is due to the close relationship between associative principles of interference and associative principles of learning. Therefore, some trends noted in Chapter 4 apply to concepts of memory as well. Other trends concerning memory go beyond traditional associative concepts, however.

In recent years proponents of interference theory have begun to stress a thorough reconsideration of the theory's weaker propositions concerning unlearning, spontaneous recovery, and associative strength (cf. Postman, Stark, and Fraser, 1968). At the same time a greater emphasis has been placed on observed relationships such as the influence of frequency of repetition on item availability (cf. Underwood and Schulz, 1960; Underwood and Freund, 1970). Overall, this represents a greater focus on response availability in both learning and retention and less emphasis on associational processes. In the traditional stimulus-response scheme of things, this reflects an interference theory that has, temporarily at least, lost its hyphen. As a case in point, Underwood (1969) notes that a viable theory of memory must consider various attributes of memory, only some of which may be associational in the traditional stimulus-response meaning of the word.

In a broader context, the modern look in theories of memory is to consider other than associative connections in explaining the observed relationship indicating that the probability of some response, *B,* in the presence of some stimulus, *A,* increases as a function of repeated pairing. It is now believed that "Ebbinghaus's axiom" may reflect a *number* of diverse psychological processes and mechanisms. In short, the venerable laws of *contiguity* and *repetition* continue to be important aspects of theories of learning and memory, but contemporary psychologists are more likely to view them as empirical rather than as theoretical laws. No one seriously questions the reliable observation indicating that recall improves with overlearning, but many question the interpretation that such improvement is due to increases in associative strength between stimuli and responses.

Alternative interpretations of "Ebbinghaus's axiom" suggest the possibility that the effect of repetition is to (1) reorganize the materials to be recalled into more efficiently stored "chunks" of information; (2) provide alternative routes for retrieving materials from memory; (3) afford time to find mnemonic devices for efficient retrieval of materials from memory; (4) encourage the transmission of items held in a temporary memory store into a more reliable long-term store (cf. Hebb, 1949; Melton, 1963, 1970; Miller, 1956). Practice does seem to make perfect, but the question remains as to what "perfect" implies in the domain of memory.

Trace theory had been almost dormant for a variety of theoretical and methodological reasons (cf. Postman, 1961; Riley, 1962) prior to the mid-1950s. Then a number of findings began to emerge which suggested that there might be *more than one kind* of forgetting, with interference principles applying in one special instance and trace principles in the other. Theorists began to suspect that there was a long-term memory system, which more or less followed the basic principles advocated by interference theorists, as well as a short-term memory system, which involved the rapid decay of unstable traces that were not influenced by associative interference. It was also suggested that one effect of repetition in learning situations was to transfer information from the short-term system to the long-term system. Thus, trace theory was revived with a vengeance, and in such a way as to offer a challenge to the interference theorist who asserted that there was only one set of laws (associative) for the entire domain of memory.

II

The Information-Processing Approach

6

Multiprocess Views of Memory

As WE HAVE SEEN in the preceding chapters, learning theorists in the behavioristic tradition emphasized stimulus-response associations as the monolithic building blocks of learning and memory. The storage of events in memory in the form of associations was viewed as a natural and continuous development of the basic acquisition process. Stable, well-established memories were viewed as the result of numerous repetitions of stimulus-response events, with the stronger associations being those repeated most often. Once formed, all such associations were assumed to be permanent, even though they were subject to retrieval failure due to associative interference. Thus habits and memories were all viewed as cut from the same fabric by the same pair of scissors.

Early trace theorists also viewed learning and memory in terms of a common set of principles. To be sure, some memories might be more compact, organized, consolidated, or decayed than other memories. All memories, however, were subject to the influence of common trace mechanisms. Historically, the more systematic versions of trace theory have been closely associated with *Gestalt* psychology and have assumed that trace systems are organized under the laws of compact organization. That is, traces were assumed to develop properties of stability, compactness, regularity, simplicity, and so on insofar as prevailing conditions would allow. These general concepts of trace dynamics focused on systematic changes in organization of traces over time (cf. Hilgard and Bower, 1975).

Initial versions of both trace and interference analyses of memory assumed, implicitly at least, that a *single-process* theory was tenable. Both theoretical approaches involved the assumption that all events in memory were acquired, stored, and retrieved according to a single, all-encompassing set of principles. The major theoretical question was *which* universal set (trace or association?) could more appropriately deal with the facts of memory.

As various facts about memory began to accumulate from clinical, biological, and experimental sources, it became increasingly difficult for any theorist to hold to a single-process analysis of memory. Things appeared much too complicated for that. Collectively considered, the data indicated that human memory might involve (1) at least two qualitatively different systems, with one operating according to some version of trace theory and the other according to some version of association theory; (2) distinct storage and retrieval processes at both the physiological and the psychological level; and (3) complex coding of events in terms of both physical attributes (e.g., visual vs. auditory) and psychological attributes (e.g., semantic content). Given these considerations, it was to be expected that theorists would begin to develop complex models of memory based on the explicit assumption that memory was not a unitary process.

DUAL-PROCESS THEORY OF MEMORY

One of the most influential statements of multiprocessing in memory was the two-factor model outlined by Hebb (1949). Hebb's concept of memory involved two distinct processes. The first process, often referred to as short-term memory (STM), was assumed to involve a transient, unstable trace of very recent events. This trace was carried by some form of reverberating neural circuitry that lasted very briefly. The second process, often referred to as long-term memory (LTM), was thought to involve some relatively permanent structural change in the nervous system that might emerge from the transient short-term trace. Hebb's two-factor interpretation of memory advanced an important theoretical concept concerning memory. That is, memory might involve two distinctly different storage states. In one state, memory for an event might eventually fade if it were not transferred to the next state. In the next state, the memory for an event was more or less permanent. A number of important questions were raised by Hebb's theory concerning (1) the biological foundation of the two-factor model, (2) whether or not the central nervous system could be permanently modified in the manner suggested by a concept of LTM, and (3) the manner in which the unstable STM trace gets converted into a more permanent structural representation in LTM.

Biological Evidence

There is evidence for some rather refined distinctions between STM and LTM processing at the physiological level. For example, it is suspected that there are specialized areas in the brain (hippocampus) that subserve consolidation of STM traces (cf. Hydén, 1970; Milner, 1970) and that large molecules such as ribonucleic acid (RNA) may provide the biochemical basis of LTM. These physiological-biochemical theories are complex and controversial, but it should be noted that many investigators do not expect to find "the" memory engram. That is, they do not expect to find a memory localized in a particular place in the brain. Instead, they believe that a rather complex biochemical *system* may be involved (cf. Gurowitz, 1969). Such a viewpoint is consistent with considerable psychological evidence that makes it appear unlikely that memory can be completely localized in places as specific as a single cell containing modified memory molecules. Brain lesion and brain damage studies suggest that a substantial amount of cortex can be removed without distinct consequences on behavioral measures or intelligence test performance (cf. Hebb, 1949). If a memory engram does exist, it must exist in more than one place for a given memory, and it is not completely clear how biochemical theories would deal with this particular theoretical difficulty (cf. Hydén, 1970). At a more molar level, clinical observations of patients suffering from memory deficits associated with damage to the central nervous system continue to suggest that different physiological mechanisms are involved in supporting immediate memory as compared with more permanent memory.

Clinical Evidence

Some support of two-factor theory arises from observations of patients with brain damage suffering memory deficits with time-related features. For example, in some patients with progressive brain disease, recent memories may be disturbed considerably, but older memories may be relatively unaffected. An early analysis of such disturbances led to the formation of the so-called law of regression (Ribot, 1887). In effect, this law stated that somehow or other older memories were more consolidated or insulated against disruption than were newer memories.[1]

[1] Related principles were also emerging from early laboratory studies with normal subjects. For example, *Jost's laws* (cf. Woodworth and Schlosberg, 1954) which were stated in 1897, suggested that memories (like good wine) improved with age. One of these laws stated that for two memories of equal strength, but of different ages, the older would enjoy a greater increment in strength with an additional practice trial. The second of these two laws held that if two memories were of the same strength, the older would weaken less rapidly over time.

Although the law of regression by itself does not necessarily require a consideration of STM versus LTM storage, it does clearly indicate the possibility that newer memories are carried in an unstable system, whereas older memories have been "consolidated" into a more stable system. Of greater relevance to this distinction are data from studies of memory defects associated with *amnesias*. Our major focus here will be on *retrograde* amnesia and *anterograde* amnesia, both of which involve memory defects with a temporal gradient.

In retrograde amnesia the patient may have great difficulty recalling very recent events (in STM?) but little difficulty recalling events that occurred in the remote past (in LTM?). For example, a victim of an automobile accident might not be able to recall where she was a few hours before the accident but might be able to recall the name of the salesman from whom she purchased her automobile some two years ago. The overall temporal gradient of memory loss in such cases contrasts sharply with the temporal gradients in more familiar examples of forgetting. This in turn suggests that old memories may be more resistant to disruption because they have consolidated over time.[2] The temporal gradient of forgetting in retrograde amnesia is not a pristine one, however. Patients frequently report "islands" of memory that extend beyond the gap of immediate memory, and they may also "recapture" lost memories of events that occurred close to the temporal point of trauma. In other words, there may be a shrinkage of the temporal range of forgetting which was observed immediately following the original memory disturbance, and retrieval of "lost" memories may then take place. Even so, there does seem to be a limit to shrinkage, and in the final stages of retrograde amnesia some immediate memories may be irretrievable because they are permanently lost from storage (cf. Russell and Nathan, 1946; Williams, 1969). These observations concerning characteristics of retrograde amnesia suggest, then, that some events may be forgotten because they are temporarily unavailable but others may be forgotten because they have been obliterated.

Whereas retrograde amnesia refers to difficulties in remembering events occurring prior to the trauma, *anterograde amnesia* refers to memory difficulties with events that occur *subsequent* to the trauma. The patient may have difficulty learning new information, such as his physician's name, or in recalling recently experienced events. One interesting case history was reported by Milner (1970). She describes a patient called H. M. who

---

[2] Coons and Miller (1960) have suggested a possible artifact in this regard. When a recent memory appears to be erased, it is more likely that this will be noticed because there are fewer of them. Old memories, however, may be erased with equal probability, but the loss may not be as readily detected because there are so many of them. This could make it appear that new memories are more susceptible to disruption than older memories.

underwent surgery involving an area of the brain (hippocampus) that is thought to serve some sort of consolidation function in the normal learning process:

Although H. M. shows some retrograde amnesia for events occurring prior to surgery, the important aspect of his memory deficit is anterograde in form. This is reflected in his failure to show long-term retention for most ongoing events. For example, H. M. appears to have difficulty in remembering the surroundings of the house where he has lived the past six years and in recalling the names of regular visitors if he meets them on the street. In more formal test situations, H. M. does not appear to have difficulty in registering new information, and he can maintain such information for short periods of time by constant verbal rehearsal. However, he has great difficulty in storing this information over long periods of time, when verbal rehearsal can no longer bridge the delay. This suggests that H. M. suffers from a disruption of the normal consolidation process such that new memories "fade" before they can be formed in long-term storage.

Some evidence reported by Milner suggests that relatively long-term storage of motor activities as contrasted to verbal activities is not as seriously affected in H. M. Thus there may be more than one kind of memory store and, in addition, different mechanisms of storage and retrieval for different kinds of events (e.g., verbal vs. motor).

There is also evidence for multiple storage and processing in memory deriving from studies of *aphasias*. In general, aphasias refer to disturbances in verbal communication due to circumscribed cerebral lesions (Hecaen, 1969). More specifically, aphasias may involve disorders in speaking, writing, or reading a language, and they may also be differential across sensory modalities. For example, with *sensory aphasia* there may be disturbances in the ability to understand the meaning of language as heard or in the ability to understand the meaning of language as read. With other forms of aphasia, the problem may be with verbal, syntactical, nominal, or semantic aspects of language. In fact, aphasias are sometimes viewed as impairments of the formal language code at different levels of verbal performance.

The clinical data from memory impairments involved in disorders such as amnesias or aphasias seem to suggest that information correctly perceived and stored at one time may be permanently lost from store or become inaccessible for varying lengths of time. Such memory impairments may involve (1) loss of some parts of an experience, but not others; (2) an inability to recall recent events, but not more temporally remote ones; and (3) selective memory disturbances with respect to sensory mode of input or retrieval.

The negative implications of such clinical observations of memory disorders for a general, single-process theory of memory are considerable. Unfortunately, a problem inherent in the clinical situation always clouds theoretical interpretations of phenomena such as amnesias or aphasias. If a particular event is not accessible in memory, it is not clear whether the problem is one of storage loss or of retrieval failure. This problem emphasizes the need to turn to laboratory situations in which it is possible to institute tighter controls with respect to disentangling storage and retrieval difficulties in memory losses.

Experimental Evidence

Although a scattering of evidence obtained in the earlier part of the twentieth century indicated that immediate memory for events presented on a single trial was far from perfect, little importance was attached to this fact until the late 1950s. Two sets of studies were then published (Brown, 1958; Peterson and Peterson, 1959) which set off a chain of reactions at both the experimental and the theoretical level. These investigations both indicated a decrement in the retention of subspan materials in normal subjects over very short intervals of time. Only the Peterson and Peterson study, however, was concerned with the course of short-term retention over time.

Short-Term Memory. The Peterson and Peterson study was concerned with the recallability of consonant trigrams (e.g., *xjr*) over retention intervals that ranged from three to eighteen seconds. These stimulus events are well within the span of immediate memory when no delay in recall is required or when subjects are allowed to rehearse the items prior to recall. But in this study each trial consisted of the experimenter's spelling a given trigram aloud, followed immediately by a spoken three-digit number (e.g., 309). The subject was instructed to count backward by threes or fours from the number presented until a light was flashed in front of him. At this point the subject attempted to recall the trigram. A total of forty-eight different consonant trigrams were presented and tested in this manner. The results of this experiment, as shown in Figure 6.1, indicated some forgetting after only three seconds of counting backward and a retention function that dropped from 90 percent correct to less than 10 percent correct over the eighteen-second interval.

The findings reported by Peterson and Peterson (1959) contained several important implications. First, there was the possibility that the forgetting observed in this short-term memory (STM) task might reflect the transient memory trace previously suggested by Hebb (1949). Brown (1958, 1959) had also suggested that material in STM would fade away over time unless some effort, such as rehearsal, was made to retain it. But Peterson and Peterson employed the task of counting backward follow-

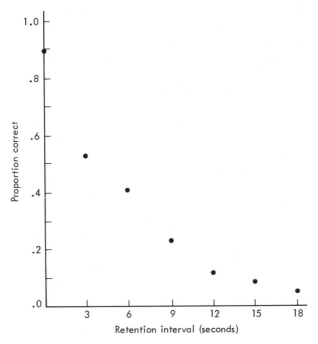

Figure 6.1 Proportion of correct recall of consonant trigrams as a function of retention interval.
(After Peterson and Peterson, 1959.)

ing presentation of the trigram to prevent just such rehearsal. And since numbers and letters are quite dissimilar, it seemed unlikely that retroactive interference could be called on to explain the retention losses observed.

There also was little reason at that time to believe that associative interference of the proactive variety was an important factor in producing the observed forgetting. This possibility posed a particular problem for interference theory, since each subject was exposed to many items and proactive interference from earlier items would be expected to influence the recall of later items. Thus one-factor theorists of the stimulus-response tradition were faced with major theoretical difficulties. The concept of a rapidly fading memory trace was difficult enough to deal with, since stimulus-response theory did not provide for rapid decay. This problem was further compounded by the observation that associative effects, which formed the backbone of interference theory, did not appear to operate in STM. Certainly the potent effects of repeated testing demonstrated for long-term memory (LTM) should also be expected in STM.

The broad implications of the studies reported by Brown and the Petersons were soon to lead to an intensive investigation of STM. The question of whether STM and LTM obeyed the same set of psychological laws was to become a major issue. The historical controversy between trace and interference theorists now began to shift in focus, with trace theorists conceding that associative effects might be major determinants of forgetting in LTM while maintaining the importance of trace concepts in STM.

Melton (1963) summarized some major contentions regarding the theoretical differences between STM and LTM as follows:

1. STM involves activity traces; LTM is based upon structural changes.
2. STM involves autonomous changes over time; LTM involves irreversible, nondecaying structures.
3. STM has a fixed capacity that is subject to overload; LTM is virtually infinite in capacity.

SHORT-TERM MEMORY AND DUAL PROCESSING

The apparent absence of proactive interference effects in the Peterson and Peterson (1959) experiments posed a particular problem for interference theory. Since little retroactive interference was thought to be produced by the activity used to prevent rehearsal in the STM task, it appeared that an interference theory based on retroactive and proactive interference would not be capable of accounting for the very rapid forgetting observed in studies of STM.

Interference in STM

In a response to the implication that STM may involve processes different from those characteristic of LTM, Keppel and Underwood (1962) conducted a series of experiments designed to evaluate the role of proactive interference in STM. These experiments closely followed the procedures employed by Peterson and Peterson (1959), and the results indicated that retention of single items over an eighteen-second retention interval did decrease as a function of the number of *prior* items on which the subjects had been tested. The data from one of their experiments are given in Figure 6.2.

The findings reported by Keppel and Underwood were consistent with the known effects of proactive interference in LTM and suggested that such interference effects contribute to forgetting in both LTM and STM. A similar outcome was reported by Murdock (1961), but this investigator also noted that proactive interference in STM first increases and then decreases as a function of the number of prior items. Although the reports of Keppel and Underwood (1962) as well as Murdock (1961) appear to contradict the findings of Peterson and Peterson with regard to

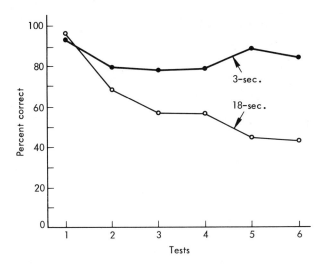

Figure 6.2   Retention as a function of number of prior syllables tested and length of the retention interval.
(After Keppel and Underwood, 1962.)

interference effects, the issue is still not fully resolved. In addition, the claim that STM and LTM involve the same processes has been challenged by other studies of STM.

Intraunit Interference.   Melton (1963) has identified another potential source of interference in STM, *intraunit interference*. This concept is based upon competition between the elements that make up the to-be-remembered units. The more elements a given unit contains, the greater the expected intraunit interference. In discussing this concept, Melton drew upon Murdock's (1961) extension of the Peterson and Peterson investigation. The test items in Murdock's study consisted of consonant trigrams, highly familiar single words, and triads of familiar but unrelated words. The results indicated that single words were much less susceptible to forgetting than consonant trigrams and that a retention function much like the one reported by Peterson and Peterson was obtained for both consonant trigrams and triads of unrelated words.

If it is assumed that a single familiar word consists of a single element, or one *chunk* of information, whereas consonant trigrams and triads of words consist of three such chunks, the Murdock results make considerable sense from an intraunit interference point of view. Units containing one chunk of information would generate little intraunit interference and should be recalled better than units consisting of three chunks of information. In a subsequent experiment Melton (1963) investigated recall of units that

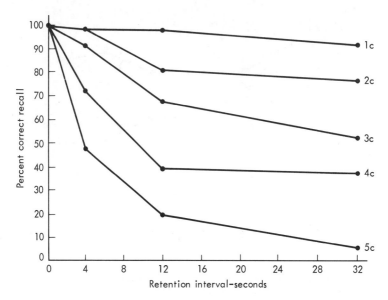

Figure 6.3   Percentage of correct recall of units of one to five consonants.
(After Melton, 1963.)

consisted of one to five consonant letters. The results of this study, which are shown in Figure 6.3, indicate that recall decreases over the retention interval as a function of the number of letters or chunks in the to-be-remembered units. These findings appear to support the view that interference effects are common to both STM and LTM. The validity of this interpretation, however, is open to question.

Underwood (1964) points out that it is likely that more learning takes place on one trial for a single-consonant *unit* than for a five-consonant *unit*. This is due to the greater opportunity to rehearse the single consonant. If this is the case, a simple interpretation may be made of Melton's findings in terms of differences in degree of learning. It should be noted that Melton's finding that the initial level of recall is nearly 100 percent for all unit sizes does not rule out the possibility of differences in degree of learning. For example, in studies of LTM, overlearning systematically improves retention, although this effect is not reflected in differences in performance on the last learning trial. Performance on the last trial is perfect both for groups given overlearning and groups that terminate training once the criterion of one errorless trial is reached. It may be that the retention functions for differing unit sizes shown in Figure 6.3 reflect differences in degree of original learning and not differences in intraunit interference.

Repetition and Dual Processing

One of the most reliable findings in the study of memory, which dates back at least to the studies conducted by Ebbinghaus (1885), is that the persistence of an item in memory is directly related to the number of repetitions of the item. The theoretical importance of simple repetition is also reflected in certain distinctions between STM and LTM. Experiments in LTM typically involve many repetitions of the materials; experiments in STM usually involve a single presentation. In part, this difference in procedure occurs because the materials used in STM experiments are subspan and can be perfectly recalled following a single presentation, whereas the materials employed in studies of LTM are supraspan and cannot be perfectly recalled after one presentation. This distinction closely follows Hebb's (1949) concept of STM for events experienced once and LTM for events experienced many times.

Since it is well established that probability of recall increases as a function of the number of repetitions, different theoretical positions will explain "Ebbinghaus's axiom" in different ways. Interference theory typically explains this empirical relationship between repetition and recall in terms of increases in the strength of stimulus-response associations. Habits established in one trial, however, are not considered to be intrinsically different from those established in multiple trials. The difference here is presumed to be quantitative (habit strength) and not qualitative (differences in storage systems). In contrast, trace versions of dual-process theory suggest that information gained in one trial is stored in a way that is qualitatively different from the way information obtained over many trials is stored. The general assumption is that immediate repetition "encourages" the transition from autonomously decaying STM traces to LTM structures, thereby providing for the stability of well-practiced memories. We have already touched on the argument that STM and LTM are subject to disruption from different sources. Presumably STM is affected by decay or overload but not by associative interference, whereas LTM is subject to interference factors but not to decay or overload. Now let us turn to the question of whether memories resulting from single-trial experiences are qualitatively different from those established over many trials.

One of the first challenges offered to Hebb's earlier assumption that more than a single presentation is required to establish an event in LTM came from an experiment by Hebb (1961) himself. In this experiment each trial consisted of the presentation of a nine-digit number followed by immediate serial recall. The digits were read aloud at a rate of one per second, and no digit was repeated within a given nine-digit series. A total of twenty-four trials was employed. Exactly the same sequence of digits was presented on every third trial, that is, on trials 3, 6, 9, 12, 15, 18, 21, and 24. On all other trials the digits were presented in different random orders with no sequence presented more than once. Figure 6.4 depicts the relationship between repetitions of the list and percentage of correct recalls.

The data in the figure show that there is a "learning" curve for repetitions of the critical list. This observation, in contrast to the absence of improvement for nonrepeated lists, indicated to Hebb that some form of structural trace results from a single presentation of the list. If a transient activity trace had been established with the first presentation of the critical list, as Hebb (1949) had previously believed, the trace would probably have faded away prior to list repetition and there would have been little or no effect of repetitions. The data, however, indicated an increasing effect of repetition over trials. This suggested to Hebb that the structural trace persists despite large amounts of retroactive interference from interpolated (nonrepeated) lists and that this trace cumulates with structural changes from subsequent repetitions.

The general effect of repetition reported by Hebb (1961) has been confirmed by other investigators (Melton, 1963; Bartz, 1969). In one of these studies, Melton (1963) replicated and extended Hebb's experiment. Melton used lists of nine-digit numbers but varied the number of inter-

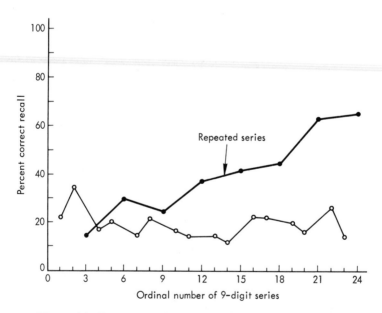

Figure 6.4   Percentage of correct recall of sequences of nine-digit numbers. For the "repeated series," the same nine-digit sequence occurred in the 3rd, 6th, 9th . . . 24th position in the series of tests.
(After Hebb, 1961.)

polated (nonrepeated) lists that occurred between repetitions of the critical list, instead of holding this number constant. Using the mean number of digits correctly recalled as the measure of performance, Melton observed the same effect of repetitions that was reported by Hebb. He also found an effect of nonspecific practice, or learning to learn. This effect, which is shown in Figure 6.5, is one of increasingly higher levels of recall across trials even when each successive digit list is new and different.

The observation of nonspecific practice effects, which is quite common in LTM studies, complicates the interpretation of repetition effects in studies of STM. These nonspecific practice effects increase over trials, and hence they are necessarily confounded with the effects of list repetition. That is, it is difficult to determine whether improvements in the recall of the critical list are due to repetition or to the effects of nonspecific practice. In Melton's experiment this confounding becomes more serious, since increases in the number of nonrepeated lists interpolated between repetitions of the critical list are accompanied by increases in the amount of nonspecific practice.

To get around these problems of interpretation, Melton used the

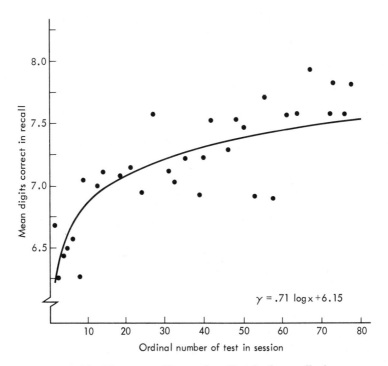

Figure 6.5 The nonspecific practice effect in the recall of new and different nine-digit numbers.
(After Melton, 1963.)

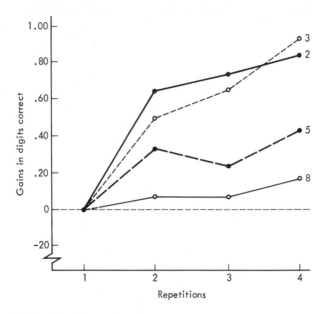

Figure 6.6 **Mean gains in number of digits correctly recalled when corrected for nonspecific practice effects. The four functions represent gains in digits recalled when 2, 3, 5, or 8 nonrepeated sequences are interpolated between repetitions.** *(After Melton, 1963.)*

empirical function shown in Figure 6.5 to correct for the effects of non-specific practice. Figure 6.6 shows the results of Melton's study once this correction has been made. It can be seen that repetition effects are obtained in all conditions of the experiment, and only when eight lists (seventy-two digits) are interpolated between repetitions of the critical list is the repetition effect substantially attenuated. Recall levels would of course be expected to decrease with increases in the number of interpolated lists because there is greater opportunity for retroactive interference.

Melton's (1963) findings seemed to confirm Hebb's (1961) conclusion that a stable structural trace, quite resistant to disruption from subsequent inputs of great similarity, may result from a single input. The data, however, do not directly indicate what it is that repetitions do to increase the probability of recall. Some ways in which repetition may influence the probability of recall include the possibility that repetition may affect the organization or reorganization of inputs in memory and the potential effects of repetition through rehearsal. Repetition may also influence storage and retrieval of events in memory.

Repetition and Reorganization. It will be recalled that Ebbinghaus found the number of nonsense syllables he could recall following a single presentation to be about seven. This observation by Ebbinghaus suggested some sort of fixed capacity for short-term or immediate memory. The notion that people have a fixed capacity in STM was developed more systematically in a now classic paper by George A. Miller (1956). After reviewing a great deal of information, Miller suggested that the limit of the human memory span was of the order of seven units or chunks of information.

Chunks are difficult to define precisely, but they refer to coding units in memory. Consider, for example, the observation that it is usually easier to recall common words than uncommon words following a single presentation. According to the notion of chunking, this occurs because the more meaningful materials can be reorganized and held together by *fewer* relationships or associations than the less meaningful materials. Thus it is the efficient use of fewer coding units that underlies the differences in recall favoring common words rather than meaningfulness per se. It should be clear that the absolute number of items recalled, as opposed to chunks, can be well beyond seven. The number recalled depends on the efficiency of the chunking operations. Efficiency here refers to the number of items coded or recorded into each chunk. One way of introducing organization into materials is by means of mnemonic devices that increase the number of items per chunk. According to the chunking hypothesis, however, there is still a limit placed on the number of coding units in immediate memory—seven, plus or minus two.

In considering the effects of repetition on recall, Melton (1963) suggested that repetition might lead to a reduction in the number of chunks contained in an experimental list. Thus an experimental list that exceeds the immediate memory span might be reduced to a subspan list through repetition. Presumably this would result from a reorganization of the inputs so that more information would be carried in each chunk. For example, in the nine-digit lists used by Hebb (1961) and Melton (1963), such a reorganization might result in three chunks containing three digits each. Although this is an interesting hypothesis, there is little evidence to support or deny its validity. This is largely because of the difficulty in providing any independent measure of chunk size. Until such measures are provided we can only speculate about the relationship between repetition and the size of coding units in memory.

Repetition and Rehearsal.   As previously noted, Ebbinghaus found that the usual number of nonsense syllables he could recall correctly following one presentation of the experimental list was about seven. Of course, with additional practice trials he was able to recall the entire list to a criterion of one perfect trial. Since Ebbinghaus's time a great deal of additional evidence has been accumulated which indicates that repetition improves both long-term and short-term retention (cf. Melton, 1963; Postman, 1962). Hellyer (1962) has shown that the effects of repetition for supraspan lists in studies of both LTM and STM can also be demonstrated in STM with subspan lists.

In Hellyer's experiment, consonant trigrams were presented one, two, four, or eight times before being tested over retention intervals of three, nine, eighteen, and twenty-seven seconds. Each presentation of a trigram was visual and lasted for one second. In other respects this experiment followed the procedures used by Peterson and Peterson (1959). For instance, a given trigram might be presented eight times in succession, after which the subject would engage in a counting task for a specified period of time before recall was attempted. In other conditions the trigrams would be presented from one to four times prior to the rehearsal preventing activity. The results shown in Figure 6.7 clearly demonstrate that a consonant trigram is better remembered following repetition even though it is completely and correctly perceived and encoded in one presentation. The theoretical importance of this finding, together with the known effects of repetition previously noted, is that it was most consistent with a continuous, single-process interpretation of memory (cf. Melton, 1963).

While evidence in support of a single-process view of memory was being derived from studies such as Hellyer's, proponents of dual-processing

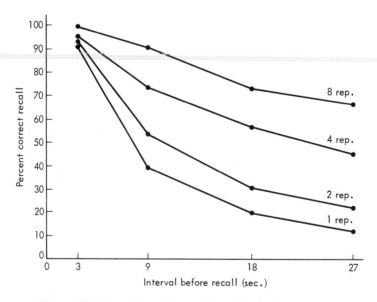

Figure 6.7 Percentage of correct recall of three-consonant trigrams as a function of number of repetitions (1, 2, 4, or 8) prior to beginning the retention interval.
(After Hellyer, 1962.)

theories were presenting evidence from experiments involving supraspan lists that seemed more consistent with the dual-process view. One such study, reported by Waugh and Norman (1965), involved the use of the probe-digit technique. In this experiment, lists of sixteen digits were employed in which no digit appeared more than twice in a row and in which the last digit was one that had occurred only one previous time. On its second appearance this probe-digit served as a cue to recall the digit that followed it on the initial presentation. For example, suppose a list consisted of the following digit sequence: 4, 9, 0, 4, 9, 8, 3, 8, 5, 2, 6, 3, 6, 2, 0, 5. In this case the probe-digit is 5, and the subject should recall the number 2.

The digits were presented auditorily at a rate of either one or four digits per second. The subject's task was to write down the digit that followed initial occurrence of the probe-digit, guessing if he did not know. In an attempt to control rehearsal (repetition) of groups of digits, the subjects were instructed to think only about the last digit presented and not about the earlier ones. The results of this experiment are summarized in Figure 6.8, which indicates probability of recall as a function of the number of digits presented *following* the to-be-recalled digit. With only one interfering item presented after the item to be recalled, performance is nearly perfect. As the number of interfering items increases, however,

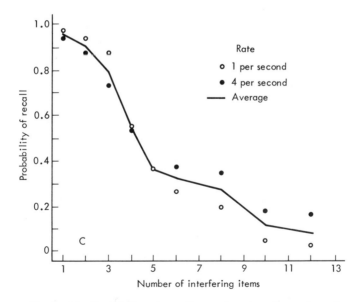

Figure 6.8 Probability of recall as a function of number of digits following the to-be-recalled digit.
(After Waugh and Norman, 1965.)

performance declines at a rapid rate. Although recall performance is slightly influenced by presentation rate, it is clear that the major source of forgetting in this experiment is retroactive interference from interpolated digits.

The Waugh and Norman experiment, like those of Hebb (1961) and Melton (1963), did little to support the contention that STM involves a transient trace mechanism. If this assumption had been correct, presentation rate should have had a major effect in forgetting. Notice, however, that recall of a digit followed by five other digits is the same under both rates of presentation. This occurs even though recall is required five seconds after presentation in the one-per-second condition but only one and one-fourth seconds following presentation in the four-per-second condition. Slight differences in recall as a function of presentation rate do occur in some cases, but they are not of sufficient magnitude to give much comfort to trace theorists.

Primary and Secondary Memory

Although Waugh and Norman do not accept the notion of a decaying trace in STM, they also reject the view that memory is a single-process system. Let us consider their theoretical views before examining the experimental evidence further. Waugh and Norman proposed a dual-process theory of memory consisting of a *primary memory* (PM) and a *secondary memory* (SM). As they use these terms, which were borrowed from William James (1890), PM is much like STM whereas SM is much like LTM. According to this theory, every item attended to first enters PM. The capacity of PM is seen as being sharply limited, with new items displacing old items. Items that are displaced are permanently lost. But when an item is rehearsed it remains in PM, and it may also enter into SM. Thus an item may be in PM and SM at the same time. Little is said about SM per se, but presumably it is virtually infinite in capacity and relatively permanent. Figure 6.9 illustrates Waugh and Norman's general scheme.

Perhaps the most critical aspect of this dual-memory model is the assumption that the two systems are not mutually exclusive. One consequence of this assumption is that experimental evidence indicating repetition effects in STM (e.g., Hebb, 1961; Hellyer, 1962; Melton, 1963) or proactive interference in STM (e.g., Keppel and Underwood, 1962) can no longer be considered as uniquely supportive of a single-process view of memory. If an item can be in STM and LTM at the same time, the processes characteristic of either memory system can be expected to influence retention. According to Waugh and Norman, even implicit repetition (i.e., rehearsal) of an item is sufficient to transfer the item into more permanent memory. Therefore, studies of STM can be expected to reveal processes thought to be characteristic of LTM, at least under certain circum-

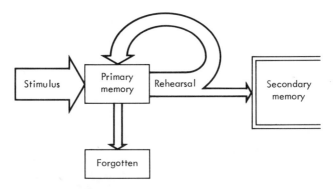

Figures 6.9 The primary and secondary memory system of Waugh and Norman. All verbal items enter primary memory, where they are either rehearsed or forgotten. Rehearsed items may enter secondary memory.
(After Waugh and Norman, 1965.)

stances. As a result, experiments whose outcomes were seen as supportive of single-process models are now seen as being equally consistent with a dual-process view of memory.

Since the work of Waugh and Norman, many psychologists have come to subscribe to a dual-process model of memory. It is not so much that the Waugh and Norman model or any other dual-process account is clearly supported by experimental evidence as it is that these stages of memory (STM and LTM) represent a convenient way for dealing with a variety of experimental evidence and theoretical speculation. Among other sets of experimental findings, a dual-process view of memory represents a convenient model for discussing serial position effects.

Serial Position Effects and Dual Processing

It will be recalled from our discussion of serial learning in Chapter 4 that the characteristic serial position curve shows a *primacy-recency* effect, with the items at the beginning of the list learned first (primacy), followed by the items at the end of the list (recency), and finally by the items in the middle of the list. A comparable outcome is also characteristic of serial recall following a single presentation of the list. In free recall, however, where the subjects are allowed to recall items in any order, the retention function following a single presentation is best described in terms of a *recency-primacy* effect. That is, items at the end of the list (most recent) are recalled best, items at the beginning of the list are recalled next best, and items in the middle of the list are most poorly recalled. The general shape of these functions is illustrated in Figure 6.10. The manner in which these retention functions are modified by the same variables has led

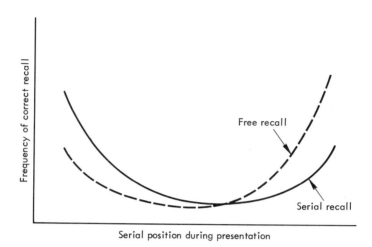

Fig. 6.10   Idealized serial position curves for serial and free recall.

to increased attention being given to the effects of one presentation on the formation of stable memories.

The results of several experiments have supported the view that at least two different recall mechanisms are involved in free recall. Murdock (1962) reported that the recency effect was not influenced by list length or rate of presentation, although both these factors did influence recall of earlier items in the list. Postman and Phillips (1965) demonstrated that recency effects in lists of ten, twenty, and thirty words were washed out when recall was delayed by thirty seconds while the subjects were engaged in activities assumed to prevent rehearsal. Recall of earlier items in the list was only slightly affected. These findings indicate that certain experimental variables influence retention for one part of the list while having little influence on another part. They also suggest the operation of at least two types of recall mechanism.

Glanzer and Cunitz (1966) also provide support for the notion of two recall mechanisms. In one experiment both duration of presentation and number of presentations per word were studied, since these variables were known to influence long-term retention. Lists of twenty words were presented at rates of three, six, or nine seconds per word. In addition to these three conditions in which presentation duration was varied, two other conditions were employed: in one, each word was presented twice in succession, with each presentation lasting three seconds; in the other, each word was presented three times in succession at the three-second rate. These conditions enabled Glanzer and Cunitz to compare the effects of duration of presentation with number of presentations held constant and number of presentations with duration of presentation held constant. In agreement with the previous findings of Murdock (1962), they found that duration of presentation influenced the primacy effect but not the recency effect. No clear influence was obtained for number of presentations (repetitions) beyond that attributable to longer presentation times. The authors suggested that this might be because the effect of repetition was offset by covert rehearsal of the nonrepeated items.

In a second experiment (Glanzer and Cunitz, 1966), a variable thought to influence short-term retention was studied. Fifteen-item lists were presented at a rate of one word per second and tested for recall following delays of either zero, ten, or thirty seconds. In the delay conditions the subjects performed a counting task to prevent rehearsal. The results of this experiment are shown in Figure 6.11. In agreement with the results of Postman and Phillips (1965), delay of recall was shown to attenuate the recency effect while having little influence on the remaining items in the list. With a ten-second delay the recency effect is greatly reduced, and after thirty seconds it is virtually eliminated.

The observation that different parts of the list were affected in differing ways by variations in presentation rate and delay of recall led Glanzer and Cunitz to suggest the operation of two distinct storage systems in free recall. Items from the earlier part of the list were seen as being in long-term storage, and items at the end of the list were thought to be in short-term

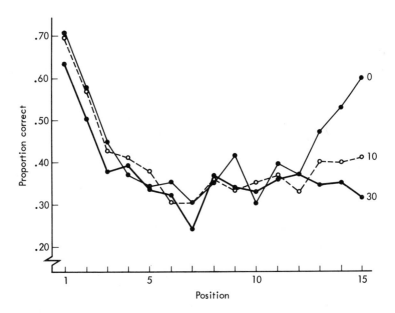

Figure 6.11 Serial position curves for 0, 10, and 30 seconds of delay prior to free recall.
(After Glanzer and Cunitz, 1966.)

storage. Presumably the opportunity for rehearsal of the earlier items allowed them to be placed in long-term storage, whereas the filled delay interval prevented rehearsal of the items from the end of the list or allowed memory traces of these items to decay.

The hypothesis advanced by Glanzer and Cunitz was based on the observations that different experimental operations had differential effects on the retention curve in free recall. Their data, however, do not necessarily implicate STM and LTM as the two processes involved. It should be noted that their hypothesis applied specifically to free-recall situations, although their reasons for selecting duration of presentation and delay of recall as critical variables are not so restricted.

These issues in free recall provided the motivation for a subsequent study in serial recall by Bartz (1969). He considered the findings reported by Hebb (1961) and Melton (1963), which indicated that a single input of digits might produce an effect that would persist and cumulate with additional inputs of the same string of digits, as being critical to dual-process theories. He suggested, however, that (1) serial recall, like free recall, involved both LTM (for initial items) and STM (for terminal items); and (2) repetition effects are only observed for items in LTM. As a test of this hypothesis, Bartz replicated Hebb's (1961) experiment, with the addition of delayed recall conditions. For example, the subject would hear a string of nine digits and would then be asked to recall them either immediately or following delays of up to thirty seconds. For some subjects the delay intervals were filled to prevent rehearsal, but for other subjects the delay intervals were unfilled.

Among the findings reported by Bartz is the observation that the recency effect was attenuated after a single presentation when the delay interval was filled to prevent rehearsal. This finding is comparable with that reported by Glanzer and Cunitz for free recall. Bartz also presented evidence suggesting that subjects were learning the serial list from beginning to end and that the effect of repeating a digit sequence was to gradually incorporate more items from beyond the primacy part of the list into LTM. He also cited an unpublished study by Schwartz and Bryden (1966) which indicated that replacement of terminal items from trial to trial did not decrease the effects of repetition on serial recall, but replacement of initial items obliterated the repetition effect. These observations are quite consistent with the hypothesis advanced by Bartz (1969).

In this section we have seen a great deal of evidence that is consistent with a dual-process theory of memory from studies of both free and serial recall. Bartz's findings appear to raise some important issues for theories of memory and also challenge Hebb's (1961) revision of his earlier dual-process model. These results suggest that items may be placed in either LTM or STM on a single presentation but that subsequent repetitions of the input list affect only those items in LTM. The results of another experiment (McHugh, Turnage, and Horton, 1973) suggest that all the items in a serial list may be in LTM following a single presentation but that the typically observed recency effect occurs because the terminal items may also be in STM.

Now that we have examined much of the evidence concerning single-process and dual-process views of memory, let us turn our attention to some other aspects of memory that have been investigated experimentally. The theoretical and experimental considerations raised previously will also contribute much to our subsequent discussion. In the following sections we will see more evidence of the complexity of memory and support for the view that memory is a multiprocess system. However, our main purpose is to review certain aspects of memory that have not been treated in previous sections. We begin with a general discussion of storage and retrieval processes.

STORAGE AND RETRIEVAL PROCESSES

Melton (1963) has defined the domain of memory in terms of two broad classes of problems—the storage of events in memory and the retrieval of events previously stored in memory. Our preceding discussion has focused on distinctions between STM and LTM as two types of storage system. Tulving (1968), however, has suggested that *all* input information may be stored in some unitary system and that the differences in recall, which appear to suggest STM and LTM as separate stores, instead reflect differences in item retrieval.

In a general review of memory, Tulving and Madigan (1970) suggested that the understanding of retrieval processes requires an appreciation of basic principles that were accepted by scholars of antiquity. These include the belief that failure of retrieval does not necessarily imply the loss of information from storage and that the very attempt to retrieve events from memory indicates there may be some recollection, albeit incomplete, of the events in question. Tulving and Madigan also suggest that information in storage remains there in one form or another, although sometimes it cannot be used for the desired purpose. In their view, what others have called STM is best described as active memory, operational memory, or even consciousness. Such an analysis of memory leads to a consideration of the factors that influence the loss of retrieval cues, rather than the loss of events from storage.

Repetition and Retrieval

Most of our previous discussion of repetition effects has been concerned with problems of storage. That is, we have focused on distinctions between STM and LTM as separate storage systems and on ways in which information is transferred from one to the other. The experimental evidence drawn upon, in this regard, derives largely from studies of recall. But when we shift focus to those factors that determine differences between two or more measures of retention, such as recognition and recall, we begin to enter the domain of retrieval problems.

Melton (1967, 1970) used the method of free recall in a series of experiments designed to investigate the effects of repetition on both recognition and recall. His subjects were presented with long lists of unrelated items, some containing as many as eighty words, in which repetition was manipulated by repeating some words once within the list. Distribution of input, or what Melton called *lag,* was manipulated by varying the number of other words that were presented between the initial occurrence of an item and the point at which it was repeated. To minimize primacy and recency effects inherent in such lists, the first eight and the last eight items were considered as buffer items and were ignored in analysis of the results. It was anticipated that repetition would improve recall, but the major focus here was on whether the occurrence of other unrelated items between repetitions of an item would also facilitate recall. That is, the experimental question was whether repetition of a word following several intervening words (distributed practice) would facilitate recall more than repetition of a word immediately following its first presentation (massed practice).

In an initial study, Melton (1967) investigated the relationship between recognition of the fact that a word had been repeated and subsequent recall of that word. As each word in the free-recall list was presented, the subject described it as either a *new* or an *old* word. An old word, of course, was one that occurred previously in the list and reflected the repetition of an event. A new word was one being presented for the first time. To illustrate the subject's task, imagine that letters of the alphabet represent words in the list and that the subject was shown a sequence such as *J, X, B, J, N, N,* and so on. In this case the correct responses would be "new," "new," "new," "old," "new," and "old." In this example it may be noted that when *J* was repeated the lag was two, since two other items intervened between the initial occurrence of *J* and its repetition. Similarly, the repetition of *N* reflects a lag of zero, since there were no intervening items. The items *B* and *X* represent nonrepeated items.

Once the list had been completely presented, the subject engaged in free recall of the experimental items. These procedures provided two important measures of retention—a measure of recognition of old items as a function of lag and a measure of recall as a function of lag. Figure 6.12 shows the results for three presentation rates, which are representative of the findings obtained by Melton for free recall. The ordinate in this figure indicates the frequency with which items are recalled, and the abscissa

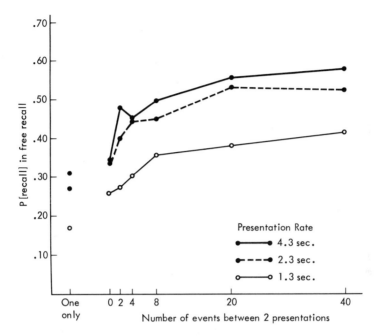

Figure 6.12 Probability of recall of words that occur once or twice, with varying numbers of events between the two presentations, when presented visually at rates of 1.3, 2.3, and 4.3 seconds per word.
(After Melton, 1970.)

indicates the number of times occurring between repetitions of an item (i.e., lag).

As can be seen in Figure 6.12, the probability of recall increases as a function of increasing lag. Melton (1967), however, reports that the occurrence of many intervening items between two presentations of the same word lowers the probability of recognizing that the second presentation of a given word constitutes a repetition. Yet this large lag increases the probability that the word will be remembered subsequently in free recall. These findings have been confirmed by other investigators for both recognition (Winograd and Raines, 1972) and recall (Glanzer, 1969; Madigan, 1969).

Melton's interpretation of these opposed observations is that distribution of practice provides the subject experience with a given word in two different contexts. The contexts consist of the other words that surround each presentation of a particular repeated word. This experience, in turn, provides the subject with opportunities for increasing the number of *retrieval tags* or *access routes* which may facilitate the subsequent free recall of the word in question. As the lag between presentations of a word increases, the contexts in which the word occurs become increasingly dissimilar and therefore the number of different retrieval tags is likely to increase. Although this increase facilitates retrieval of a word, it also lowers the probability that a word already in storage will be recognized as one that was presented previously. Thus repetition in the form of distribution of practice (lag effects) may, through resulting changes in the context in which an event occurs, have contrasting influences on storage and retrieval processes.

A related view of such context effects is that repetition of an event can increase the probability of *coding* the event in question in more than one way. When we speak of coding, we usually refer to the manner in which humans transform, tag, organize, or abstract stimulus events and store the results of the transformations in memory. This general definition is, of course, closely related to the theoretical problem of distinguishing between the nominal and the functional stimulus which we encountered in previous chapters. Let us now illustrate how repetition of an event in different contexts might provide the opportunity for coding, or representing, that event in more than one way in memory.

Coding Processes

Suppose the word *bat* is repeated in a serial list as follows: *ball,* bat, *glove, base, robin, hawk,* bat, *wren, hag, wife, shrew,* bat. It can be seen that the word *bat* may be coded in memory in at least three different ways: (1) as an item of sports equipment, (2) as a flying animal, and (3) as an onerous spouse. Correspondingly, changes in context that result from items repeated at long lags (cf. Melton, 1970) might also result in the items being coded in different ways. If so, such increases in the number of representations for items in storage should increase their probability of being recalled. On the other hand, if an item is coded differently on each presentation, it may not then be recognized as an "old" item. Whether or not this coding argument is valid with respect to lag effects, it does serve to lead us directly into the role of coding processes in memory experiments.

Coding and Short-Term Memory. Complex coding across semantic dimensions may occur automatically and rapidly, even in situations where a minimum of processing might be assumed. This argument has been convincingly made in a series of studies summarized by Wickens (1970) which involved a STM task similar to that employed by Peterson and Peterson (1959). In one experiment by Wickens and his associates, the stimulus materials consisted of word triads that had been scaled on the major meaning dimensions of the *semantic differential* (cf. Osgood, Suci, and Tannenbaum, 1957). On the first four trials, the experimental subjects were tested with triads that fell at one end of a given scale (e.g., *religious, success, nice,* from the positive end of the evaluative dimension). Then, on the fifth trial, they were shifted to triads that fell at the opposite end of the same scale (e.g., *kill, danger, worry,* from the negative end of the evaluative dimension). Control subjects were not shifted on the fifth trial but continued to recall the same type of triads they had been given on the first four trials. The general results of the study are illustrated in Figure 6.13.

As can be seen in the figure, there is a systematic decrease in level of recall over the first four trials for both experimental and control subjects. Within the context of interference theory, this decrease is presumed to reflect a "buildup" of proactive interference on successive tests. On the fifth trial, however, performance improved substantially for the experimental subjects. This improvement in recall, or "release from proactive interference," must have resulted from the shift in meaning of the stimulus materials on the fifth trial. Apparently the subjects were rapidly encoding the triads on some semantic basis.

Wickens (1970) has also reported evidence from several experiments which indicates the general importance of various factors, including mean-

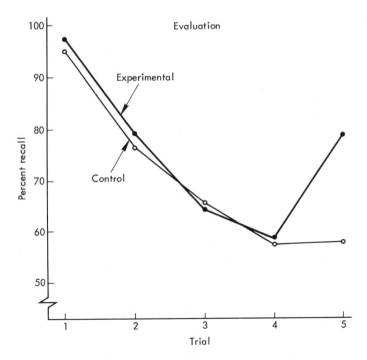

Figure 6.13   The effect of shifting from one end of the evaluation dimension to the other end.
(After Wickens, 1970.)

ing, in the coding process. Among the changes in material shown to result in a "release from proactive interference" are (1) input modality (e.g., auditory to visual), (2) taxonomic class (e.g., birds to trees), (3) sense impressions (e.g., "round" nouns such as *barrel, knob, doughnut* to "white" nouns such as *chalk, lint, soap*), (4) word frequency (e.g., high- to low-frequency nouns), and (5) number of phonemes (e.g., one or two per word to four or five per word). The magnitude of "release" observed in these cases varies with the stimulus characteristics, and not all changes (e.g., a shift in grammatical class) produce the effect. The subjects in these experiments are frequently unaware of differences in the materials, although they still show the "release effect." In general, these observations indicate that the coding process involved is rapid, complex, and automatic and that it is carried out at low levels of consciousness. They also indicate that some coding cues are more salient than others in the STM situation. Of particular interest here is the evidence relating to the role of auditory codes in immediate memory.

Auditory Coding in Memory. Considerable evidence indicates that when subjects are presented with visual stimuli, they code them auditorily and not in a visual form. Much of this evidence derives from the work of Conrad (1964), who was able to demonstrate a high correlation between the kinds of errors subjects make under both auditory and visual presentation. Conrad's visual task consisted of presenting six-letter consonant sequences to subjects and asking for immediate recall. These same letters were also used in an auditory task where the subjects attempted to identify them as they were spoken against a background of noise. The errors made in both tasks were quite similar, and they were largely of an acoustic nature. For example, the letters v and b, which we might expect to be confused in the auditory task, were also confused in visual presentation. Similar findings were obtained for other letters, such as f and s. These observations suggest that the memory code for items in immediate memory is related to the spoken representation, even when the items are presented visually.

Conrad was attempting to illustrate that errors in immediate memory reflected a systematic relationship to the original stimulus, as some trace decay models might predict. As a trace decays, whatever aspects of it remain at the time of the recall would be expected to influence recall. Recall errors would not be random but should reflect the remaining aspects of the trace. In fact, this is just what Conrad observed. Although the letter v was a likely substitute for b, it was almost never substituted for x. This finding poses particular problems for trace models that assume that once the trace has decayed to some critical level, *any* alternative response might interfere with it.

At least two issues have been raised by findings such as Conrad's.

One of these concerns the difference between acoustic and articulatory representation, that is, whether the stored representation of the letters is more closely related to their acoustic form or to the movements used to speak them. Although this issue is not resolved as yet (cf. Hintzman, 1967; Murray, 1968), it has important implications for theories of speech perception. A second issue raised by Conrad's data concerns the STM–LTM distinction. That is, although Conrad's findings suggest an auditory code for STM, it is well known that semantic codes are of major importance in LTM.

Auditory versus Semantic Coding. In a series of experiments Baddeley (1966a, 1966b) has shown that acoustic similarity of items is more likely to produce interference in short-term tasks, whereas semantic similarity leads to marked interference in long-term tasks. A similar interpretation can be made of the results reported by Kintsch and Buschke (1969). In this experiment the subjects were presented with lists of sixteen items immediately followed by a probe item. The probe item was an item from the list, and when it was presented again the subject's task was to recall the item that had followed it previously. The lists consisted of eight pairs of words that sounded alike (homophones), or eight pairs of words with the same meaning (synonyms), or a control list of sixteen unrelated words. The results indicated superior recall of items in the early part of the synonym list, in comparison with the control list, with no difference for terminal items. On the other hand, recall of items from the homophone list indicated superior recall of terminal items and no difference on initial items. These findings suggest differential coding of initial and terminal items which, according to some accounts, are stored in LTM and STM, respectively.

Although these studies suggest selective auditory coding in STM and selective semantic coding in LTM, the issue is far from settled. We have already noted the finding of a "release from proactive interference" as a function of shifts in meaning (cf. Wickens, 1970). In addition, Shulman (1971, 1972) reports that semantic coding is readily demonstrated in STM tasks when the task requires such coding or when slow rates of incoming information are employed. Thus there is evidence for semantic coding in STM, or at least in experimental situations comparable with that of Peterson and Peterson (1959). When we turn from STM to LTM situations, there also appears to be evidence for both auditory and semantic coding there.

Bruce and Crowley (1970) used lists of thirty-two words in a study of free recall. Four acoustically similar words were massed early, massed late, or spaced evenly in the lists. Four semantically similar words and four unrelated control words were also massed or spaced in the same way in the lists. In an attempt to eliminate the STM component, free recall was delayed for thirty seconds following list presentation by having the subjects name visually presented geometric shapes. Both semantically and acoustically related items were recalled better than the unrelated (control) items when they were massed in either the early or late parts of the lists. When the items were evenly distributed in the list, however, recall of acoustically similar items was no better than than for control items. Semantically related items were still better recalled than the control items, but not as well as when they were massed in one part of the list. These findings indicate that acoustic and semantic factors are probably handled differently in memory, but the part of the list from which the items come does not necessarily determine how they are coded.

Although acoustic or semantic attributes of incoming information are probably important determinants of the coding process, both may be affected by demands of the task and characteristics of the subjects. Shulman (1972) has shown that semantic coding is readily demonstrated in short-term memory when the task requires the subjects to process semantic characteristics of the material. The linguistic background of the subject may also influence coding. For example, Turnage and McGinnies (1973) found that immediate serial recall for verbal items varying in meaning was facilitated with visual input for Chinese subjects, but with auditory input for American subjects. This finding appeared to be related to differential opportunities for visual as opposed to auditory confusions within a given language, rather than to primitive differences in immediate memory. To the extent that auditory codes are basic in STM and semantic codes are basic in LTM, it would have been expected that corresponding coding effects would be "culture free."

Studies with deaf subjects using sign language suggest that it is an individual's natural mode of communication that may determine the nature of encoding in immediate memory. It has been found that errors in STM are not attributable to either the acoustic form of the words indicated by particular signs or the meaning of these signs. Instead, errors are related to substitution of particular spatial and gestural features. For example, a sign may be reproduced with the correct shape and movement of the hand, but in an incorrect spatial location. This pattern of errors with the deaf is directly related to their primary mode of communication, just as acoustic errors are most common in hearing subjects (cf. Bellugi and Siple, 1973).

We have indicated a number of salient characteristics of stimulus events that may be important in the coding process. Among these are attributes such as meaning, acoustic representation, position in a stream of information (serial position), frequency in the language, and number of past occurrences. Underwood (1969) has suggested that a memory can be conceptualized as a collection of attributes that serve to differentiate one memory from another and to act as a basis for retrieving memories. Thus a memory is defined by its attributes.

Coding and Attributes of Memory.   In the context of attribute theory as used by Underwood (1969), coding refers to the process by which memory attributes become established. Two broad categories of attributes are distinguished by Underwood on the basis of their dependence on the nature of the event in question. The first category includes attributes that are assumed to be independent of the nature of the event. Examples include the temporal, spatial, frequency, and modality attributes. Such attributes serve to locate an event in time or space, to index its past frequency of occurrence, and to indicate the sensory modality through which an event has been experienced.

The second category includes attributes that are directly dependent on the nature of the event. This includes the orthographic, associative nonverbal, and associative verbal attributes. The orthographic attribute refers to the written form of a verbal event and may include such characteristics as the initial letter or the number of letters. Associative nonverbal attributes refer to such things as the acoustic spectrum produced by the event, a visual image to which an event may give rise, the affective response to an event, and information about the context in which an event occurred. When the event is verbal, the associative verbal attribute is also relevant. In essence, this attribute refers to other words that are not part of the event but may be elicited by the event implicitly.

According to Underwood, the nonassociative attributes serve primarily to provide a basis for discrimination between memories, whereas the associative attributes serve a retrieval function. Furthermore, the relative importance of various attributes may change with a person's age or the meaning of an event. In the young child some attributes, such as the acoustic and spatial attributes, may be dominant. These attributes may also be dominant in the case of an adult learning difficult and relatively meaningless material. Underwood, however, suggests that in the normal course of development the associative verbal attribute becomes increasingly important with age.

Underwood's attribute theory would be difficult to test, although he cites a great deal of evidence in support of the specific attributes proposed. One study that provides support for the validity of several attributes was reported by Brown and McNeill (1966). Their study was concerned with the "tip of the tongue" phenomenon. The subjects were read dictionary definitions of relatively uncommon words. Brown and McNeill were interested in those words the subjects felt they knew but could not produce. When a subject indicated that he was in this "state," he was asked questions about the word he was attempting to recall. The questions included asking for the initial letter of the word, the number of letters and syllables in the word, and words of similar sound. The results indicated that the subjects could answer such questions with considerable accuracy (e.g., 57 percent of the time subjects were correct about the initial letter), even though they could not recall the words. These observations suggest that attributes such as those proposed by Underwood are in some way involved in the coding process.

GENERAL THEORETICAL APPROACHES

Atkinson and Shiffrin.   One of the more comprehensive analyses of multiple processing in memory has been outlined in a series of papers by Atkinson and Shiffrin (cf. Atkinson and Shiffrin, 1968; Shiffrin and Atkinson, 1969). In their system, memory is represented in terms of three major storage systems: (1) a *sensory register,* (2) a *short-term store,* and (3) a *long-term store.* The general model, illustrated in Figure 6.14, indicates that incoming information enters the sensory register and may either be lost or be transferred into other storage systems. It should be noted that *transfer* does not mean the shifting of information from one store to another. Instead, transfer is an operation by which information in one store is "copied" into the next store without affecting its status in the original store.

According to Atkinson and Shiffrin, various "control processes" may be used to regulate the flow of information in the memory system. These "control processes" (see Figure 6.14) are transient phenomena under the control of an individual, and their use depends on such factors as task instructions and the past experiences of an individual. "Control processes" may be used to regulate such activities as rehearsal, memory search, and response output. These "control processes" may also be used to transfer information from one memory store to another and to regulate the rate at which such transfer takes place. For example, tasks like stenography require a rapid assimilation or transfer of information, with little emphasis on what the input means. Other tasks, such as studying for an examination, require assimilation of complex concepts and meanings. To deal with such diverse tasks efficiently, the rate of encoding, transfer, and retrieval of information must come under the conscious control of the information processor.

Our main concern in this chapter is with the short-term and long-term stores. In Chapter 7 we will discuss the notion of a sensory register, but for the present it is sufficient to note that information entering the sensory register decays and is no longer available after a brief period of time. Therefore, if information entering the sensory register is to be retained, it must be transferred to the short-term store.

Atkinson and Shiffrin assume that information entering the short-term store also decays and disappears completely over time but that the decay time is longer than it is in the sensory register. In addition, information may be maintained in short-term store by means of the control process of rehearsal. Rehearsal serves to regenerate the short-term memory

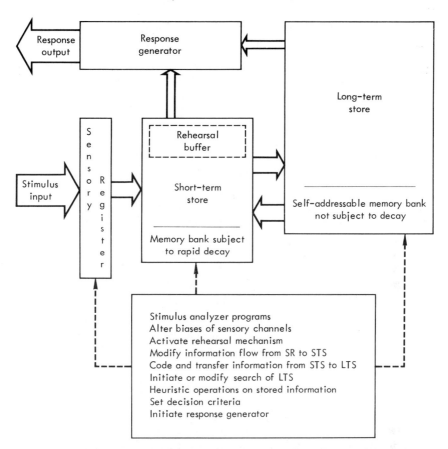

Figure 6.14   A flowchart of the memory system. Solid lines indicate paths of information transfer. Dashed lines indicate connections that permit comparison of information arrays residing in different parts of the system; they also indicate paths along which control signals may be sent to activate information transfer, rehearsal mechanisms, etc.
(From Shiffrin and Atkinson, 1969.)

trace in the so-called rehearsal buffer (see Figure 6.14). The rehearsal buffer is a limited capacity system which can only hold a few items of information at a time. When the buffer is filled, the entry of new items will cause items already in the buffer to be displaced, or "bumped out." For example, if new numbers enter the buffer while you are attempting to hold a telephone number in short-term storage, part of the telephone number may be displaced.

The rehearsal buffer turns out to be an essential component of the short-term storage system, since rehearsal provides one way by which information may be transferred from short-term to long-term memory. The probability that information will indeed be transferred into long-term storage depends on a number of factors. For example, the limited capacity of the buffer constrains the amount of information that can be rehearsed there. In addition, items in the buffer may be displaced, or "bumped out," by other items entering it. In general, the probability that a given item will be transferred from the buffer to the long-term store is a function of how long it has been in the buffer and how many other items have entered the buffer. As a practical illustration of this, imagine that you are attempting to memorize a string of digits that you have heard only once. As you rehearse, new digits are added to what is stored in long-term memory. Obviously you are likely to lose some of the original information (fail to transfer it to long-term storage) because you cannot maintain all the old and new information in the increasingly crowded short-term system. Some of the information from the short-term buffer system, however, is likely to be transferred to the long-term system.

The long-term store provides almost unlimited storage space for information entering from the short-term store. It may also be used to facilitate the *identification* of items in the sensory register so that meaningful representations of these items may be entered into the short-term store. For example, a brief succession of tones might be "identified" as part of a familiar melody and tagged or coded as such when the string is transferred from the sensory register to the short-term store. Thus, previously stored information may facilitate the entry of new information into store.

In general, items are directly retrievable from short-term store if they stay in the rehearsal buffer. If they have been transferred to long-term store, they may be "searched out" and retrieved on the basis of some psychological dimension or an available cue. Rehearsal per se, however, is not the only way information enters the long-term storage system. Coding operations involving selective alteration of or addition to the information being processed may occur in the short-term storage system. These coding operations are based on information retrieved from long-term storage by a search and retrieval process, and such coding operations serve to increase the *strength* of the stored information.

The important aspect of the process by which information is transferred from short-term to long-term store is that there is considerable variability in what can be accomplished by various control processes. When an individual is concentrating on rehearsal, the transferred information would be in a relatively weak state and easily subject to interference. When coding processes are employed, however, the strength of the stored information is increased and the transferred information is less subject to interference. For example, new information that is incorporated in some meaningful way with old information often appears easier to recall than when the same information is learned by rote through rehearsal. Thus it may be easier to remember that "Columbus set sail in 1492" by adding to this information the familiar fact that "blue" and "two" rhyme. In other words,

"Columbus sailed the ocean blue, in fourteen hundred and ninety two" codes the desired information in a very stable and highly accessible manner.

The assumption of three memory stores, as proposed by Atkinson and Shiffrin, does not require any particular assumption concerning the physiological locus of the stores. The theory is compatible both with the view that each memory store involves separate physiological structures and with the view that short-term memory involves a temporary activation of information permanently stored in long-term memory. Differences do of course appear in the coding, storage, and retrieval of information in various types of memory experiments, and a theory such as that proposed by Atkinson and Shiffrin is well equipped to deal with these differences.

The theory proposed by Atkinson and Shiffrin represents a multiprocess view of memory that is subscribed to by many contemporary psychologists. In addition, this theory provides the most comprehensive and detailed account of human memory that has been offered from the information-processing point of view. Shiffrin and Atkinson (1969) and Shiffrin (1970) have also proposed an analysis of storage and retrieval processes in long-term memory. Although we shall not review these considerations here, an examination of storage and retrieval in long-term memory is clearly necessary for any general theory of memory.

Craik and Lockhart.   Some of the objections to a multistore view of memory (cf. Melton, 1963; Murdock, 1972; Tulving and Madigan, 1970) have encouraged an alternative framework in terms of multiple levels of information processing. For example, the observation that material learned by rote may not be as well recalled as that put into a more meaningful context might be explained in terms of the degree of semantic or cognitive analysis involved. A good illustration of such a theoretical approach is provided by Craik and Lockhart (1972).

Craik and Lockhart propose a series or hierarchy of processing stages through which new information is passed. Processing begins at a preliminary level with inputs being analyzed in terms of physical or sensory features such as lines, angles, brightness, and pitch. Subsequent processing stages are more concerned with pattern recognition and the extraction of meaning. For example, once a word has been recognized it may lead to associations, images, or stories based on an individual's prior experiences with the word. According to this view, "depth of processing" implies a greater degree of semantic or cognitive analysis at "deeper" levels in the hierarchy.

Rather than placing a limit on the amount of storage capacity available at any given level in the hierarchy, Craik and Lockhart prefer the notion of a limited capacity central processor. At any point in time the capacity of this processor can be used to analyze information at progressively deeper levels. Although it is the capacity of the central processor that is limited, and not the available storage, the number of items that can be dealt with depends on the level in the hierarchy at which the processor is operating. For instance, at deeper levels greater use can be made of previously learned rules and prior knowledge, with the result that information can be handled more efficiently and more information can be retained.

As for retention of particular items, Craik and Lockhart suggest that stronger and more enduring memory traces are found at the deeper levels of analysis. They reason that since the extraction of meaning is usually of primary concern to the individual, it is of value to store the products of these deeper levels of analysis more permanently. In contrast, there is often little need to store the products of a preliminary analysis for more than a brief period of time. Thus retention is typically seen as being a function of the depth of analysis that is attained.

The limited capacity of the central processor can also be used to recirculate information at a particular level of analysis. When processing capacity is used in this way, to maintain information at a particular level, the phenomena characteristic of short-term memory will appear. Of course, the particular short-term memory effects to be observed will depend on the modality (i.e., visual, auditory, etc.) within which the processor is operating. The essential feature of this view of short-term memory is that material is still being attended to. In fact, Craik and Lockhart consider such descriptions as "rehearsal of items," "keeping items in consciousness," "holding items in short-term memory," or "attending to items" as references to maintaining information at one level of processing. Once attention is diverted from the items, however, information will be lost at a rate appropriate for the level in the hierarchy at which the processor had been operating. Information would therefore be lost more rapidly when the processor had been operating at preliminary levels than if it had been operating at deeper levels.

In the Craik and Lockhart model it is the depth of analysis that determines retention. In many situations this relationship would imply that total processing time should covary with degree of retention. Two qualifications must be introduced here. The first is that if processing capacity is used to recirculate information at a given level, there will be no relationship between total processing time and retention. The second qualification stems from the assumption that more meaningful inputs—with existing cognitive structures (e.g., pictures or sentences)—will be more rapidly processed to a deep level than will less meaningful inputs. Thus the total time allowed for processing does not necessarily predict degree of retention.

The theoretical approach offered by Craik and Lockhart is consistent with a variety of evidence concerning memory. Much the same is true of the Atkinson and Shiffrin model. Actually, the Craik and Lockhart approach is less a theory than it is a set of orienting attitudes concerning the memory process. But taken together these approaches are illustrative of general theories of memory (cf. Postman, 1975). Other theoretical views of a general type can be found in the work of Underwood (1969) and Wickens (1970, 1972), which were discussed previously.

CONCLUSION

In this chapter we have reviewed biological, clinical, and experimental evidence that seems to support a multiprocess view of human memory. Much of the early evidence suggested a dual-process model of memory in which STM and LTM served as the major components of memory. In general, STM was often characterized as transient, subject to overload (due to its limited capacity), and particularly affected by acoustic characteristics of incoming information. In contrast, LTM was often characterized as permanent, relatively unlimited in capacity, and organized in terms of the associational and semantic characteristics of stored information. Although the question of unique coding mechanisms in STM and LTM remains unresolved, both acoustic and semantic coding must be considered in any general theory of memory. We shall encounter evidence in the next chapter for a third storage system (a preperceptual system), in which information is held for very brief periods of time (on the order of 250 msec.). The processes of memory are undoubtedly varied and complex, both in storage systems and in coding processes.

Although the evidence in support of multiprocess theories of memory is substantial, the evidence in support of any particular theory has been decidedly mixed. We have cited evidence for interference effects, semantic coding, and auditory coding in both STM and LTM. Such evidence suggests a continuity of processes rather than discrete memory systems. The overall complexity of such coding and interference effects in memory has weakened the case for any single-process theory that presumes to be comprehensive. In addition, the relatively simple analysis of memory in terms of dual processing has given way to more complex multiprocess theories.

In reviewing the more general multiprocess theories of memory, it was noted that Atkinson and Shiffrin (1968) emphasize both multiple-storage systems and "control processes" or strategies which are employed to regulate the flow of information. These "control processes" may be used to determine which inputs are attended to, rehearsed, and transferred to more permanent storage systems. This approach might be compared with that of Craik and Lockhart (1972) where the role of attention and other cognitive factors is emphasized but where incoming information is processed to different levels of analysis instead of being transferred to different storage systems. Still a third approach is illustrated by the theories proposed by Underwood (1969) and Wickens (1970, 1972). These theories appear to have a less-focused cognitive emphasis but do deal with complex strategies that subjects adopt when they encode items in memory on the basis of attribute analysis or semantic characteristics.

The various multiprocess theories reviewed here are not necessarily mutually exclusive. In many respects Atkinson and Shiffrin's main contribution may lie in their emphasis on "control processes" to regulate the flow of information in the memory system. These "control processes" might well be included in theories such as those proposed by Craik and Lockhart or Underwood, where the emphasis seems to be on longer-term retention and retrieval. All of these models share the assumption that some version of multiprocess theory is preferable to a single-process model of memory. In addition, almost all of the multiprocess models assume, at least implicitly, that *attention* is an important factor in the processing, storage, and retrieval of information. We shall pursue this point directly in the next chapter.

7

Attention
and the Processing
of Information

In previous chapters our concern has been with ways in which humans store and retrieve information. We now turn to several other important aspects of human information processing. In Chapter 6 we considered the notion that there may be at least two kinds of memory, STM and LTM. Both of these supposed systems involve the storage and retrieval of information. At this point, however, we wish to contrast the storage and retrieval aspects of these memory systems with other factors involved in the processing of information. For example, stimulus inputs must be perceived before they can be encoded and stored. Presumably this requires that the organism must attend to those inputs.

At one time it was conventional to discuss the processing of information in terms of several stages. Such discussions typically began with sensory inputs which were then perceived, learned, and stored in memory. The role of attention was often seen as one of selecting those sensory inputs that would be perceived. It is no longer possible to talk about clear separation of stages. It now appears that information processing involves many factors, which interact in diverse ways. A variety of factors may become involved in the processing of information from the point at which information is presented to the organism to the point at which this information is encoded and stored. It should be noted that the topics considered in this chapter range from processing that may take place prior to the involvement of either STM or LTM to processing that involves these memory systems. We treat these topics in a separate chapter because, in a certain sense, they are less directly concerned with memory per se than they are with the ways information is processed into the memory system. We begin with a general discussion of attention.

Attention in Psychology

The scientific popularity of attention in psychology has waxed and waned over the last two centuries (cf. Trabasso and Bower, 1968). Apparently the early British empiricists, such as Hume and Locke, did not find much use for this concept because it did not fit well with the rather mechanical laws of association. Any systematic use of attention as an explanatory device is difficult to deal with in a mechanical model of learning and memory. The very term *attention* conjures up images of will, volition, and mental focusing. Such images seem to imply that the human mind is too capricious to be described by strict laws like those of associationism. With the advent of structuralism and functionalism in the late 1800s, however, attention became a factor of psychological interest. Since these schools of thought placed a great emphasis on the use of introspective analysis of mental activities, it was to be anticipated that the inward-turning eye of the introspectionists would perceive threads of attention that seemed to bind the web of human consciousness tightly together.

A major figure in bringing attention to the forefront of psychological thinking about this time was the philosopher-psychologist William James. He devoted an entire chapter to attention in his classic and very influential *Principles of Psychology* (1890). There he observed that past experience in itself was not enough to explain the organization and emphasis that results from the "raining down" of experience. As James saw it, millions of events are presented to the senses which never properly enter into one's experience. "Why? Because they have no *interest* for me. *My experience is what I agree to attend to.* Only those items which I notice shape my mind —without selective interest, experience is an utter chaos." To James, attention "is the taking possession by the mind, in clear and vivid form, of one out of what seem several simultaneously possible objects or trains of thought. Focalization, concentration, of consciousness are of its essence. It implies withdrawal from some things in order to deal effectively with others . . ." (James, 1890, pp. 402–4).

A number of the points made by James in his analysis of attention have a most contemporary ring:

1. Attention is deliberate and it is an active, not a passive, process.
2. Conscious selection of items for concentrated analysis or for incorporation into experience is another attribute of attention processes.
3. Attention has some sort of limit of capacity, or at least it involves the

need to ignore some things in order to deal more effectively with others.

4. Items in consciousness can, apparently, only be dealt with effectively one at a time, not simultaneously.

It would be well to keep these points in mind during our subsequent discussion, since much of what James suggested as the basic elements and restrictions of attention have formed the nuclei of many present-day analyses of attention.

Although James's defense of the importance of attention to psychology theory was most eloquent, interest in attention subsided with the domination of psychology by the behaviorists from 1920 to 1950. Attention was regarded as too vague, too mentalistic, and too dependent upon introspective evidence to be of systematic importance to the early behaviorists. In addition, as Berlyne (1960) notes, theorists who accepted the stimulus-response model placed a much greater emphasis on the particular response that would be selected by the organism than on a given stimulus input.

In many ways the failure or inability of the behaviorist to take attention into account may have turned out to be an Achilles' heel. Predictions about response selection often proved to be incorrect because of the tendency of subjects to "pay attention" to certain elements of the stimulus while ignoring others. We saw evidence of this tendency in our previous discussion of nominal and functional stimuli, and it seemed to characterize the behavior of both animal and human subjects. For example, work like that of Lawrence (1949, 1950) suggested that even the rat paid selective attention to familiar stimuli in various discrimination learning situations and responded differently as a consequence. Findings such as these forced theorists to introduce the concept of mediating reactions (unobservable responses) and orienting responses in order to float behaviorism out of troubled theoretical waters. Of course the behavioristic system could only remain internally consistent if attention could be dealt with in terms of unobservable responses that obeyed the same laws as observable responses. But once "unobservables" were introduced into stimulus-response theories, it became easier to substitute "attention" for "mediating responses" in describing some aspects of behavior.

The "decontamination" of attention was facilitated by the publication of D. O. Hebb's *Organization of Behavior* in 1949. The main thrust of Hebb's approach was to integrate important psychological and neurophysiological concepts available at the time. One point developed by Hebb was that psychologists needed to reject the assumption of *complete* sensory control of behavior which held "that behavior is a series of *reactions* (instead of actions), each of which is determined by the immediately preceding events in the sensory system" (Hebb, 1949, p. 3). As Hebb saw it, this assumption was not consistent with evidence indicating the existence of set, attitude, or attention and thus created an implicit inconsistency which was at the root of confusion in psychological theory at the time.

Our personal experiences can be used to illustrate the general suggestion that both *voluntary* and *involuntary* factors determine the ways in which we come to "pay attention." We often actively seek out, or focus on, items in the environment that become part of our field of attention. This is seen, for example, when we try to spot a songbird whistling a merry tune in a nearby tree. We would insist that this is voluntary attention on our part. We are choosing to pay attention. Involuntary focusing is also important, however, as illustrated by our typical response to a sudden loud noise in a heretofore quiet reading room. Our startle reaction is rather automatic and not consciously directed. That is, our attention is captured without conscious intent on our part, and our behavior, in some sense, is quite "stimulus bound" in this instance.

What factors determine the extent to which attention is dominated by sensory stimulation? In his analysis of the problem, Hebb (1949) suggested that two important determinants were involved. First, one must consider genetic factors that determine sensory-perceptual mechanisms in a given species. For example, higher organisms such as man inherit brains which permit the possibility of more complex, longer control of behavior by central mechanisms. This can be considered in terms of the proportion of association cortex relative to sensory cortex. Presumably association cortex involves neurological mechanisms that allow the organism to profit from past experience without being completely controlled by immediate stimulation, whereas the reverse would be more likely for sensory cortex. When the total amount of sensory cortex is large relative to the total amount of association cortex (as in the rat), the organism is likely to remain relatively "stimulus bound" and stereotyped in its behavior. But when the amount of association cortex is large relative to the amount of sensory cortex (as in the human), there is more opportunity for mechanisms deriving from learning and memory to exercise control. These mechanisms presumably include such cognitive processes as directed attention and set.

A second factor determining the degree to which the organism is controlled by immediate stimulation is the developmental history of the organism. Even when the opportunity is there, little central control is possible in the early stages of an organism's development. As the organism continues to interact with its environment, development of association areas takes place, with the result being greater potential for central control over behavior. Hebb called this period of development the stage of *primary learning*. Because of species differences, periods of primary learning are rather abbreviated in animals like the rat, whereas they are more prolonged and have greater psychological consequences in organisms like the human.

Even so, although the potential for "voluntary" behavior is greater for the human than it is for other organisms, the human also remains "stimulus bound" to some degree. An interesting example here is our inability to pursue an imaginary target by smooth movement of the eyes, no matter how hard we consciously try to do so. Instead, the eyes will move in fast jumps called *saccadic* movements. On the other hand, when a stimulus is actually moving "out there" in a smooth path, our eyes can easily track it in smooth, slow sweeps (cf. Kahneman, 1973).

It is difficult to determine the exact impact of Hebb's (1949) analysis on psychological theories of attention, but he undoubtedly helped liberate the skeleton of attention from its behavioristic closet. His arguments were to be given even greater weight by new discoveries in psychology and neurophysiology that took place over the next twenty years. As these discoveries became integrated into a broad picture, it became evident that not all stimulus input fed into the sensory system reaches the upper levels of the brain that involve consciousness and, hence, the process of *selective attention*. Relatively automatic neurophysiological mechanisms had to be involved in "filtering" stimulus information prior to the time it was dealt with on a conscious level. Let us consider some of these mechanisms that are believed to influence the further processing of information.

SOME BIOLOGICAL ASPECTS OF PROCESSING

It may be recalled from introductory courses in psychology that sensory receptors in *Mammalia* are composed of specialized cells that are sensitive to only certain forms of energy with which a particular stimulus may be characterized. Receptors in the eye are responsive to electromagnetic energy, although only a small segment of the entire electromagnetic spectrum is involved. Receptors in the ear associated with hearing are likely to be activated by pressure waves in the air, but this likelihood depends on the frequency of these waves being roughly between 20 and 20,000 cycles per second. Thus some stimulus selection in terms of what we can attend to in both audition and vision is determined at the receptor level.

Even when the stimulus energy is in the form and within the range necessary to generate receptor activity, further processing of the input may still be constrained in such a way that the information does not necessarily get to the higher levels presumed to be involved in consciousness. For example, there appear to be complex systems in the brain that act as traffic control centers for certain kinds of information, depending on the importance of that information to the perceiver at the moment. This traffic control system may act either to accentuate or to attenuate sensory input before it has an opportunity to enter consciousness.

Reticular Activation System. Intricately involved in such traffic control is the reticular activation system (RAS). This system functions as a sort of general filter system for stimulus inputs. The RAS is particularly likely to pass on information to upper cortical areas that reflect sudden changes in the environment, novel stimulation, or other kinds of events important to the survival of the organism (cf. Samuels, 1959). Unlike other control systems, such as the thalamus, the RAS is a relatively diffuse system that does not keep different sensory systems entirely separate from each other and seems to activate rather wide regions of the cerebral cortex.

Indirect evidence of the filtering effects of the RAS comes from a study by Hernández-Peón, Sherrer, and Jouvet (1956). They used a cat as a subject and employed three different stimuli to manipulate the animal's attention. The stimuli consisted of (1) two mice in a bottle (visual), (2) a click (auditory), and (3) fish odors (olfactory). The clicks were presented to the cat's ear, and electrophysiological recordings were taken of activity in the auditory pathway (dorsal cochlear nucleus). This "auditory activity" was substantially dampened when the cat's attention was diverted by the visual or the olfactory stimulus. In other words, when the cat "paid attention" to different inputs, as indicated by its behavior in watching the mice or sniffing the fish odors, there seemed to be selective exclusion of the incoming auditory signals. This suggests that there is a way of "filtering" out irrelevant information and "accentuating" relevant information at the physiological level. More direct evidence that the RAS is involved in such effects comes from a study by Fuster (1958). He found that direct stimulation of RAS areas improved the efficiency of rhesus monkeys in discrimination learning, presumably through subserving attentive behavior.

Although there is little direct evidence concerning the role of the RAS in human behavior, a study by Berlyne, Borsa, Hamacher, and Koenig (1966) provides some indirect evidence. These investigators studied the effects of RAS arousal in human subjects during paired-associate learning under white noise. The assumption involved in the use of white noise was that "all exteroceptive stimulation activates the reticular arousal system" (Berlyne et al., 1966, p. 1). The results of their study suggested that the presence of white noise during learning induced RAS arousal and led to better recall over a twenty-four-hour period.

Feature Detector Mechanisms. A second line of neurophysiological evidence that is directly relevant to theories of attention involves the investigation of automatic feature analysis. That is, there appear to be attributes of stimuli that are especially likely to engage attentional mechanisms because there are specialized receptors that respond to these attributes. Data from experiments with cats indicate that single nerve cells respond selectively to such stimulus features as *horizontal, vertical, angle, corner,* and *directional movement* (cf. Hubel and Wiesel, 1965). Such research has led to speculation that the human visual system may contain similar specialized mechanisms for responding selectively to features of incoming signals.

The notion of special "feature detectors" at the neurophysiological level has intriguing implications. Thompson (1969) speculates that even *concepts* may be coded in a single cell. That, indeed, would be specialization of the first order. Thompson also cites evidence—from studies of the cat— for single cells that code color, stimulus form, and even number. He reports finding what appeared to be a "number 7" cell in the association cortex of the cat. This particular cell had a higher probability of firing after the seventh input in a sequence of ten, and this observation suggested that the cell, in some sense, was capable of "counting to seven."

In a previous chapter we discussed evidence indicating that auditory stimuli may have some advantage over visual stimuli with respect to processing in short-term memory. This, in turn, might be related to some special feature detectors or special processors for auditory inputs in humans. There is evidence to support the hypothesis that man's unique biological heritage may have provided him with special ways of processing auditory signals when those signals are in the form of speech. Whether or not such specialized ways of processing speech signals accounts for the apparent prominence of auditory coding in short-term memory remains to be seen.

Thus far, our selected review of biological aspects of processing has suggested that theories of attention will have to deal with the possibility that there is more "filtering," "prewiring," and "involuntary selection" involved in processing stimulus inputs than was thought to be the case previously. Some aspects of these theoretical requirements were touched on by Hebb (1949) in his discussion of problems relating to perception and attention. He suggested the need to distinguish between basic neurophysiological processes and those mechanisms that derive from learning experiences and provide for other modes of perceptual organization. As a case in point, Hebb cites the work of Senden (1932).

Senden's monograph represents a compilation of published reports on the vision of congenitally blind individuals who subsequently recovered their sight through surgical operations. These individuals had no visual experiences until they recovered from the operation, and the early perceptual difficulties of these patients provided some insight into the distinctions between learned and unlearned modes of perceptual organization. For example, a typical patient presented with an object dangling from a string would be "aware" of the presence of the figure. That is, the patient could distinguish "figure" from "ground." But he could do little else in the visual mode. He could not discriminate among simple shapes as readily as normal adults, and he could not, without extensive practice, recognize visual figures as ones he had seen before. Of course the observation that practice led to improved performance in these tasks indicates that the deficiency was not permanent but could be modified through experience.

What might we conclude from Senden's reports? They certainly suggest that some aspects of perception, such as recognizing the presence of a figure against a background, are "built into" the organism and depend on basic neurophysiological processes. Hebb (1949) suggested that such innate processes underlay a visually inexperienced subject's perception of the *primitive unity* of a figure—allowed him to recognize that something was "out there." Such a subject, however, might fail to recognize that two circles were similar in that both are round or that a triangle viewed from different angles is still a triangle, since these perceptions of *identity* appeared to be dependent on prolonged experience. In other words, some aspects of our everyday perceptions of the world about us seem more dependent on learning; other aspects seem more dependent on the neural apparatus we have inherited. These innate and learned factors interact to produce perceptual units that may engage our attention.

PREPERCEPTUAL ANALYSIS

Much of the information that we obtain from the "external world" comes to us through the senses of vision and of audition. Visual and auditory stimuli impinge on specialized receptors, trigger complex responses in neural pathways, engage filter systems, and may eventuate in conscious perception. Sometimes this information pours into the nervous system but does not quite reach the level of consciousness. At other times this information may make only a fleeting contact with consciousness. If it does so, further analysis and elaboration of the significance of the input may take place through mechanisms of attention. At this point we begin to deal with information being held in a relatively "raw" form by what has been described as *preperceptual systems*.

Preperceptual Visual System

In the early 1960s evidence began to be reported concerning an extremely short-term visual storage system (Sperling, 1960). This system has some very interesting properties which led some psychologists to the notion that it may underlie various phenomena in visual cognition, such as perceptual set and span of apprehension (cf. Neisser, 1967). This system, however, is generally viewed as prememorial and preassociational in that it does not seem to directly engage either STM or LTM (cf. Melton, 1963). At least one reason for maintaining a distinction between this system and memory systems in general is that the preperceptual visual system does not appear to obey the same laws as STM and LTM.

The persistence of visual stimulation after the original stimulus has disappeared is a phenomenon that has been recognized in the laboratory at least since the middle of the nineteenth century. This same persistence can also be noted in our personal experiences, as when we experience an afterimage following intense visual stimulation. Such visual experiences do not necessarily suggest the opportunities that this lingering trace may provide for abstraction of complex information nor the rapidity with which this potential information can disappear. Nevertheless, it is precisely these factors that have been emphasized in experimental studies of the preperceptual visual system (cf. Sperling, 1960; Averbach and Coriell, 1961).

Sperling (1960) presented his subjects with an array of letters of the alphabet arranged in rows of, say, three each. The arrays were presented visually for very brief intervals of time (50 msec.). Since this presentation time was much faster than the time required for directed eye movement (about 200 msec.), there was little opportunity for the subject to search out characteristics in the original display *before* the stimulus disappeared. Two recall procedures were used in reporting information from the array after the stimulus had been terminated: *full report* and *partial report*.

With full report, the subjects were asked to report all the items they had seen. In such cases, they usually recalled a total of only four or five letters, even though they insisted that more letters had been presented than they could remember. This suggested that some very rapid forgetting was occurring in the short period of time involved. With partial report, the subjects were signaled to report only a *single* row of letters from the display. The signal indicating which row to report was a tone presented immediately after the array disappeared. With this procedure, the subjects showed almost perfect recall. Now, since the subjects did not know which of the rows they were to recall until after the array terminated, the partial report technique indicated to Sperling that *all* of the information in the array was registered. With the full report technique, however, only part of the total amount of information registered could be reported back, presumably because of the rapid decay of the aftereffects of the stimulus array. Neisser (1967) dubbed these aftereffects the *icon* and referred to the system involved as *iconic memory*.

Iconic Memory.   The basic characteristics of iconic memory of interest to memory theorists concern the rate at which the icon decays and the manner in which it may be obliterated or "erased." Let us consider the decay characteristic first. Sperling (1960) investigated rate of decay by varying the interval of time that elapsed between termination of the array and presentation of the tone. His results, some of which are given in Figure 7.1, indicate that accuracy of the report decreased when the tone was

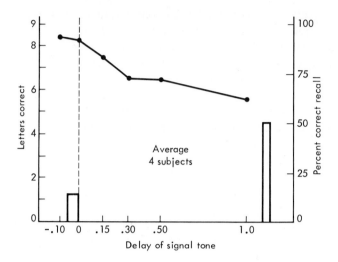

Figure 7.1 Percent correct recall over a one-second interval as assessed by partial report technique. The bar at the right indicates recall of full reports given immediately following stimulus presentation.
(After Sperling, 1960.)

presented with even a fraction of a second delay. With delays of one second, accuracy dropped to a level characteristic of full reports. In other studies the duration of the icon has been reported to be as short as one-fourth of a second (Averbach and Coriell, 1961), although it may last for somewhat longer when presentation conditions are optimum.

The question arises, If the icon decays in one second or less, how can the subject recall as many as four or five letters? Certainly the time necessary to report those letters is much greater than the duration of the icon. One way of explaining this discrepancy is to assume that the visual information represented in the icon is transformed into a somewhat more permanent form of storage through verbal coding. The observer "sees" the stimulus material for a short period of time, stores it, *selects* certain information for rehearsal, and then reports from short-term memory what he remembers of the rehearsed material (cf. Sperling, 1963).

If subjects tend to process visual information into some sort of verbal code which is then stored in STM, we should find that acoustic confusions are common in STM situations. As we saw in the last chapter, this is often the case. Subjects frequently confuse stimuli that are acoustically similar, such as *v* and *b,* whereas confusions based on visual similarity are less common. Such acoustic errors support both the notion of verbal coding of information from the icon and the proposition that coding in STM is auditory. But Neisser (1967) points out that this is probably not the only way visual information is preserved, since nonverbal children and animals also learn from visual experience.

A second characteristic of iconic memory is that the icon is subject to "erasure," or "masking." An early demonstration of erasure was reported by Averbach and Coriell (1961). In this experiment the subjects were shown a row of several letters very briefly after which they were asked to report one of them. A visual pointer appeared above the location where the to-be-reported letter had appeared. When the pointer appeared immediately following the row of letters, recall was very accurate. On some trials, however, a circle was presented surrounding the previous location of the letter to be recalled. When this was done, the circle served to "mask," or "erase," the letter from the icon. Several investigators have reported similar demonstrations of erasure, but the phenomenon is complex and not fully understood.

An interesting demonstration of the complexity of the erasure phenomenon was provided by Fehrer and Raab (1962). In this experiment the subject's principal task involved rapid motor response to presentation of the stimulus. Stimuli were presented either alone or followed by a masking stimulus. Although erasure was demonstrated, comparisons indicated that reaction time to a stimulus followed by a masking stimulus was no longer than reaction time to the stimulus presented alone. Similar findings were reported by Schiller and Smith (1966). These observations suggest that the visual processes that give rise to what Hebb called "primitive unity" are sufficient to activate the subject's response. Once the subject recognizes the presence of some stimulus the reaction is initiated, even though subsequent presentation of the masking stimulus erases the original stimulus from the icon before the subject can identify it.

These findings suggest that iconic memory can be characterized in several ways. Apparently the icon represents a form of preperceptual storage that decays in a very short time once the visual stimulus has been removed. The icon seems to have a restricted capacity, particularly in terms of the amount of information that can be extracted from it during its brief duration. Verbal coding may represent at least one way of transforming information from the icon to a somewhat more permanent form of storage. We also saw, in work such as that of Fehrer and Rabb (1962), that we can respond directly to gross characteristics of the icon (e.g., figure-ground relations) even before we can perceive (identify) the visual stimulus. In addition to these characteristics, the discovery of the icon for vision suggests the possibility of comparable systems for other sensory modalities. We can "feel" a tactual stimulus, such as the touch of a finger to our forearm, even after the finger is lifted from the skin. With the exception of vision and audition, however, little is known about preperceptual systems for other modes of information processing.

Preperceptual Auditory System

One basic difference between auditory and visual information concerns the manner in which the information is presented in time. In the visual situation much information is presented simultaneously, or in *parallel*. We see a great deal of the stimulus "all at once," as when we read written material. In contrast, in the auditory situation we get bits of the stimulus a little at a time, as when someone reads to us. Thus the information in an auditory stimulus is more spread out in time. As a result, we can only process auditory information as it arrives. If it takes too long to present the information in the required *serial* fashion, we may need some way of preserving information from the earlier part of the series until all of the information has been received. Some theorists have suggested that this extension over time is accomplished by some sort of redundancy in the auditory signal or by perseveration of an auditory trace that outlives the stimulus and permits further processing. In his discussion of this mechanism, Neisser (1967) introduces the term *echoic memory* to complement the *iconic memory* system for vision.

Echoic Memory.   Various estimates have been offered concerning the duration of the "echo" in the auditory preperceptual system. Broadbent (1958) postulated the existence of such a sensory store that holds information on the order of seconds. If attention is not directed toward the information during this period of time, it will be lost. Neisser (1967) cites evidence that suggests that the echo may last for as little as one second or less (Guttman and Julesz, 1963) or for as long as ten seconds (Eriksen and Johnson, 1964), depending on the difficulty of the experimental task. One issue here is that of reconciling reports showing substantial variations in the duration of the echo with reports showing consistent, very brief durations of the icon.

A pertinent experiment in this regard is one by Massaro (1972) suggesting an auditory store that is preperceptual and has a duration much closer to that found for the icon. The experimental procedure involved a masking technique in the auditory modality somewhat similar to that for the visual modality. Subjects were presented with one of two tones, which were described as "high" or "low," followed by a masking tone. The test tone was presented for 20 msec., and the interval between the test and the masking tone varied from 20 to 420 msec. After termination of the masking tone, the subjects reported whether the test tone was "high" or "low."

The results of this experiment indicated that performance in terms of correct recognition was close to the chance level of 50 percent correct when the intertone interval was 20 msec. This would suggest that the masking tone "erased" the test tone from the preperceptual store. As the interval between tones increased, however, the subject's recognition accuracy also increased until an asymptote was reached with an intertone interval of about 250 msec. At this point most subjects were performing around 95 percent correct in the recognition task.

Massaro interpreted these findings to be indicative of an auditory preperceptual store or echo with a duration of about 250 msec. This is the same duration reported for the icon by Averbach and Coriell (1961). To explain the apparent discrepancy between his findings and those of other investigators, Massaro proposed an intermediate stage between the preperceptual store and a more abstract short-term memory. He refers to this intermediate stage as *synthesized auditory memory*. Massaro suggests that the preperceptual store contains information about the acoustic characteristics of the stimulus which decays at a rapid rate. The process of recognizing a particular sound pattern, however, produces a percept that enters synthesized auditory memory. Thus the recognition process involves nothing more than transformation of preperceptual information into a synthesized percept. The information available in the synthesized percept is much like that which enables us to remember the sound quality of a tone or a speaker's voice. At this point meaning is derived from synthesized auditory memory and is placed in a more abstract memory.

It should be noted that Massaro's experimental findings do not require such a brief preperceptual auditory store, although they are consistent with that interpretation. Observing that the masking stimulus is no longer effective after 250 msec. only requires the interpretation that 250 msec. is sufficient for a synthesized percept. This does not necessarily mean that information is lost from the preperceptual store at this point, although Massaro does make that interpretation. Nevertheless, Massaro's model is capable of explaining a variety of otherwise discrepant findings, and later versions of his model (cf. Massaro, 1975) are likely to receive considerable attention.

Additional evidence pertinent to the concept of a preperceptual auditory store is provided by studies of the *stimulus suffix effect* (cf. Crowder and Morton, 1969; Morton, Crowder, and Prussin, 1971). In such studies, subjects are asked to recall serial lists of spoken items. If the last of the items in a series is followed by another spoken input, the additional input selectively interferes with the recall of the last two or three items in the list. The actual amount of interference that results depends on a number of factors. For example, disruption may occur with any suffix sound uttered in the same voice as the list of items being recalled whether the sound belongs to the same class of materials or not. Thus, recall of a string of digits followed by a meaningful word might be disrupted. In contrast, the disruptive effect is lessened when the suffix is not a speechlike sound (such as a tone) or is spoken in a different voice. As might be expected, if the suffix is a visual stimulus, disruptive effects are quite unlikely.

Morton and Crowder generally view such findings as evidence for what they term a *precategorical acoustic storage* (PAS) system (cf. Morton, 1970). The fact that a visual suffix does not produce disruptive effects suggests that the interference effects observed occur somewhere in the auditory system. The fact that a suffix that is a word may disrupt recall of digits indicates that the PAS system is precategorical. That is, there is no semantic analysis carried out in the system. Finally, the fact that disruptive effects are reduced when the suffix is spoken in a different voice, or comes from a different location, suggests that items that arrive and are treated as part of the same unit are stored in the same system.

Although the Morton-Crowder interpretation of the suffix effect in terms of a PAS system is convincing, it is still possible to question the preperceptual nature of the system they propose. The fact that interference occurs when the suffix is physically similar to the input material does not require an explanation in terms of preperceptual systems. And if the PAS system is truly preperceptual and precategorical, it is not clear why the spoken list of items must be followed by a spoken suffix—instead of by some arbitrary signal such as a tone—in order for interference effects to be enhanced. This result suggests that some analysis or "categorization" has occurred for items presumed to be in the PAS system. On the other hand, interference effects in the PAS do seem to be independent of semantic relations between the suffix items and the list items, as would be expected in a preperceptual system.

The assumption made by Morton and Crowder that the PAS is subject to "overwriting" and decay is also consistent with the assumption of a preperceptual system. The PAS, however, also is said to have a useful life (period of time during which information can be extracted) of about two seconds (cf. Morton, 1970). This is a considerable storage time for a preperceptual system. Crowder (1972) argues that this period of time is necessary for audition but not for vision because of the serial nature of auditory inputs in contrast to the parallel form of visual inputs. In any case, Morton and Crowder do view the PAS as a preperceptual system for auditory inputs and distinguish it from another storage system, the *response buffer*. The response buffer has characteristics that resemble many of those identified with short-term store in dual-processing theories of memory, as discussed in Chapter 6 (cf. Morton, 1970).

The preceding discussion has focused on a number of important dimensions of information processing. In the review of biological factors and in the discussion of preperceptual systems, we have seen that certain aspects of information processing can apparently take place without much aid from attention. As information is being processed through successive stages or levels, however, the necessity for attention is increased. This seems to be particularly true for information that is transformed into or maintained in what has been called short-term memory. At this point, then, let us return to the discussion of attention that opened this chapter.

FOUNDATIONS OF ATTENTION

There seems to be quite a bit of wisdom in the old saying that "familiarity breeds indifference" insofar as attention is concerned. *Novelty,* or lack of familiarity, appears to be one of the most powerful determinants of attention, and, as we shall see, the terms covers a great deal. In general, novelty is dependent on the extent of the organism's past experience with a particular stimulus, and therefore it varies with the developmental history of the organism.

In other words, an organism's past experience provides a common core of reference with respect to new and old information. The term *novel* refers to many psychological dimensions of experience, such as new or old, frequent or infrequent, recent or long past, predictable or unpredictable, and similar or dissimilar. All of these dimensions are directly relevant to attention processes.

Consider a sound that we hear for the first time in a particular context. It is likely to attract our attention because it is novel. If the sound occurs in a regular pattern, as with the ticking of a clock, we may habituate to it and pay less attention as a consequence. It is no longer novel and it is highly predictable. If the sound suddenly ceases, we may become attentive again because of the absence of the familiar ticking. We may also realize at this point that only recently have we stopped giving our full attention to the ticking. Such fluctuations in attention suggest that such factors as relatively automatic monitoring of inputs, voluntary focusing, and memory are all involved in the general process we call attention.

Developmental Factors

We have suggested that to a great extent events may be characterized as novel or familiar because of the learning history of the organism. Yet we see in the behavior of the developing infant that many aspects of attention also involve largely automatic reactions to rather simple characteristics. That is, the early responses of infants can be accounted for by assuming the infant is automatically "captured" by sensory input to a greater degree than is an older child or an adult. As the infant develops through childhood to adulthood, he seems to be less and less a "captive" of sensory stimulation and more and more a "capturer" of sensory input. This change appears to involve quite an orderly process of reflecting both "built-in" coding mechanisms and accumulating learning experiences (cf. Bond, 1972).

This developmental trend is consistent with Hebb's (1949) analysis of attention as involving central processing of information in a way that is not completely controlled by sensory input even though it is influenced by such input. This hypothesis assumes certain attention mechanisms are optimally responsive to certain kinds of stimulation. For instance, the infant's automatic responses seem largely due to such stimulus characteristics as contours, angles, and stimulus change (cf. Bond, 1972). This also means that there is much more organization in the infant's perceptual world than has been explicitly acknowledged in the past. Thus William James's (1890) observation that the world of the infant was probably "booming, buzzing, confusion" is likely to be an exaggeration. There appears to be considerable perceptual organization at birth, and many theories of learning and memory have failed to take this organization into account. This is not to say that perceptual experiences are completely organized at birth. Some learning is certainly involved. However, there appears to be much more organization "built in" the organism than previously suspected.

Extensive work with the neonate reported by Kagan and his associates (Kagan, 1967; Kagan, Henker, Hen-tov, and Lewis, 1966) indicates an early capacity for discriminating among various types of visual patterns. Such discriminative skill, of course, implies reasonably well organized perceptual capacity. Hershenson, Munsinger, and Kessen (1965) report that newborn infants show preference for geometrical figures of intermediate complexity, and Munsinger and Weir (1967) report that older children show preference for the most complex figures. It may be that this developmental shift in preference results from limitations in processing capacity in the immediate memory of the newborns. This would mean that the initial "built-in" capacities of the organism have much to do with "deciding" which stimulus inputs will be processed at higher psychological levels.

Research on visual attention in the infant also reveals some influence of experience on the infant's responses to old inputs. This work indicates that infants as young as three months of age can "remember" old inputs. Much of this research involves photographing the infant's eyes with respect to the image of some stimulus that is presented to him. The rationale behind this measure is that infants tend to look at (pay attention to) new or novel stimuli longer than to stimuli with which they have become familiar (Fagan, 1970). Thus, during the infant's early development, selective attention begins to involve a residue of past experience. With increasing experience learning and memory come to exert even greater influences on the attention process. As this happens, the infant becomes a "capturer" of stimulation and a maker of abstractions and transformations derived from stimulus inputs.

Limits inherent in the information-processing capacity of the human organism constrain the operation of attentional processes. This continues to be true no matter how much experience the organism has acquired. Most theories of attention consider at least three factors in this regard:

1. The human organism has a limited capacity for dealing with incoming information. This is illustrated by the need to *withdraw our attention from one object to pay attention to some other object.*
2. Filtering systems serve to keep our information-processing mechanisms from being overloaded. That is, our limited capacity for dealing with new information is balanced to some extent by controls which prevent a flood of information from entering the processing system.
3. Special storage systems, such as the preperceptual systems, serve to extend the amount of time available for extracting information from relatively short-lived inputs.

Since we have already considered some aspects of the third factor, let us now review the other two factors relating to limited capacity.

Limited Processing Capacity

In general, our ability to "pay attention" appears to be restricted by the fact that the "alerted brain" has a limited capacity for processing incoming information (cf. Mackworth, 1970). Psychological and neurophysiological mechanisms, however, serve to keep attention systems from being overloaded by a constant flood of stimulation. At the neurophysiological level, certain sensory gates, or filters, work to control the stream of stimulus input so that much potential information is never processed at the conscious level. At the psychological level, two major factors seem to be involved in the reduction of overload. The first involves shifting our attention to one aspect of a stimulus situation at the expense of some other aspect. Such shifts of attention may include both learned and unlearned processes. The second factor involves coding operations that tap into learning and memory more exclusively. As we have already noted, the familiar is easier to deal with than the unfamiliar. Unlike new events, old events seem to demand little attention, and some well-learned activities like walking may be primarily controlled by lower brain centers even though a number of decisions about particular turns need to be made on any given walk (cf. Mackworth, 1970). Past learning may also facilitate coding or the transformation of new stimulus information so that more information can be dealt with at any particular time (cf. Miller, 1956). But no matter how refined our coding techniques become, how familiar incoming information may be, or how facile we are in shifting attention, we still have a capacity limit in terms of our ability to process incoming information.

Miller (1956) considered this limitation on our processing capacity in terms of the "amount of information" contained in a message and how this information might be processed. Considering the information process-ing that goes on in terms of a general input-output model of communica-tion, we would expect some systematic relationship between input and output. The relationship need not be perfect, however. For example, as the amount of input information increases, the information processor is likely to show both an increase in output information and an increase in error rate. At some point the amount of output information should level off, and this should provide an index of the organism's processing ca-pacity—or what Miller referred to as his *channel capacity*.

A Bit of Information. Before we discuss channel capacity, we should say something about the measurement of information contained in stimulus inputs. A useful concept is that of a *bit* of information. The con-cept of bits arises out of *information theory* (Shannon and Weaver, 1949) and can be given a rigorous mathematical definition, but we need not concern ourselves with such definitions here. In brief, one bit of informa-tion reflects the amount of information needed to make a decision be-tween two equally likely alternatives. If a particular stimulus can only be "red" or "green," we need one bit of information to make a decision be-tween these two alternatives. Two bits of information are required to decide among four equally likely alternatives, three bits of information are needed for eight alternatives, and so on. The general rule is that each time the number of alternatives is increased by a factor of two, some additional bit of information is required to make a decision.[1]

The amount of information conveyed by a given stimulus cannot be determined from an examination of the stimulus alone. Amount of in-formation depends on the number of things that could have happened but did not. In a sense, the greater the number of alternatives, the greater the amount of information conveyed by a single bit of information. For exam-ple, suppose you are attempting to guess a whole number that someone else is thinking about. In terms of eliminating possible alternatives, notice how much information you receive when told that the number consists of only one digit. It should also be emphasized that the concept of a bit of information is mathematical and should not be confused with the psycho-logical concept of "meaning."

In his discussion of channel capacity, Miller (1956) focused on a common limit that appears to arise in a number of situations. For instance, when subjects are asked to make absolute judgments about stimuli that vary on a single dimension, they cannot deal with more than six or seven different stimuli without error. This is well illustrated in a study by Pollack (1952). Pollack asked listeners to identify tones that varied in frequency by assigning different numbers to them. As the tones were repeatedly sounded, the listener responded to each with a number and was then told

---

[1] The term *bit* is a contraction of *binary digit*.

whether or not the response was correct. When the listener had to deal with no more than four tones, errors in the identification of tones were rare. With five or more tones, however, the errors increased rapidly.

The data obtained in Pollack's experiment were quite consistent with the results of other experiments discussed by Miller (1956) involving unidimensional stimuli. In studies of loudness, taste, and position of a pointer on a line, channel capacity varied from about four to eight stimuli, or from two to three bits of information. The range finally decided upon by Miller as representative of the limits of channel capacity was "seven plus or minus two" stimulus events.

Of course the limits suggested by Miller applied only to unidimensional judgments. When stimuli are allowed to vary along several dimensions at the same time, the situation becomes more complex. Miller notes the ability of humans to identify a single face among hundreds or a single word among thousands. But he also raises the possibility that even with multidimensional stimuli there still are restrictions in terms of channel capacity. These limits might be reflected in "trade-off" functions between accuracy and the number of additional dimensions involved. In other words, rather fine judgments of a few simple characteristics may be possible, but when several things are involved simultaneously only relatively crude judgments can be made.

Span of Immediate Memory.   As we have seen, absolute judgments of unidimensional stimuli can only be made with high accuracy for seven plus or minus two stimuli. In terms of information measurement this means we can deal with stimuli conveying from around two to three or so bits of information. These findings suggest that the ability to make absolute judgments is determined by amount of information. A different picture is presented in studies of the span of immediate memory.

The immediate memory span refers to the number of sequentially presented items that a subject can recall following a single presentation. In studies involving recall of items such as digits or words, Miller (1956) reports the span to be "seven plus or minus two items." Although the number of items here is comparable with the number of stimuli we can deal with in making absolute judgments, the amount of information processed is quite different. For example, we can recall about seven single-digit numbers, each of which contains about 3.3 bits of information. This means a total recall of around 23 bits of information. On the other hand, Miller estimates that isolated English words convey about 10 bits each, and if the amount of information that can be processed is constant, we should only be able to recall two or three words instead of seven.

The observation that the immediate memory span is limited by the number of items and not by the amount of information led Miller to suggest the concept of a *chunk* of information. We considered this concept in a somewhat different context in the preceding chapter, but we could offer no precise definition. *Chunk,* unlike *bit,* is a psychological concept that is difficult to define. Nevertheless, the immediate memory span appears to be limited by the number of "chunks" (i.e., seven plus or minus two) in a way that is analogous to the limits placed on absolute judgments in terms of *bits.*

Recoding. The observation that the immediate memory span for isolated letters is comparable with the span for isolated words suggests that chunks are formed by some sort of *recoding* procedure. Since seven words of, say, five letters each contain many more letters than the number of isolated letters we can recall, it appears that the subject is recoding the letter inputs into another code (words) which involves fewer chunks with more information (bits) per chunk. Although there are probably many ways to recode, Miller suggests that the simplest may be to group the input events, apply a new name, and remember the new name instead of the original inputs.

Miller (1956) provides an illustration of recoding by grouping inputs and remembering the new names assigned to the groups. The subject is presented with a string of binary digits (e.g., 101000100111001110) which, in "raw" form, are well beyond the memory span. But if the subject recodes these binary digits as octal digits, the task becomes much easier. To illustrate, the subject must first group the digits in threes to get (101), (000), (100), (111), (001), and (110). Octal digits are then assigned to each group. In the octal system, or base-eight arithmetic, (000) is 0, (001) is 1, (010) is 2, (011) is 3, (100) is 4, (101) is 5, (110) is 6, and (111) is 7. Once octal digits are assigned to the groups of binary digits, the subject need only recall the sequence 504716, which is likely to be within the memory span. If the subject can recall these six digits and *decode* them successfully, he should be able to produce the original eighteen binary digits. Miller cautions that such accuracy should not be thought of as a mnemonic trick. Instead, one should consider that recoding in any form is an efficient way of dealing with large amounts of information without overloading the immediate memory system.

The concept of recoding has numerous potential applications for the processing of information. It seems entirely appropriate to speak of recoding information briefly carried in the preperceptual systems and storing the result in a more permanent memory. We can also invoke recoding when we talk about the transfer of information from STM to LTM. In fact, one way to view the processing of information is in terms of continuous recoding operations that take information in a "raw" form and move it through several stages until it is eventually stored in a more abstract form in permanent memory.

MENTAL SCAN AND THE LIMITS OF CONSCIOUSNESS

Sternberg (1969) notes that if we wish to distinguish between the content of immediate memory and the content of immediate consciousness, the former may be of the order of seven plus or minus two, but the latter is probably much closer to a *single* unit. This hypothesis stems from a series of studies dealing with high-speed mental scanning of items in consciousness. Sternberg's basic concern in these experiments was with the interaction of immediate inputs with information previously stored as well as the process of directed mental search and decision. Obviously, understanding such processes is fundamental to the understanding of the problem of attention to new stimulus inputs.

Sternberg points out that one of the oldest ideas in psychology is that there is a chain or series of stages between a stimulus input and a response output which are so arranged that one stage does not begin until the preceding stage has ended (cf. Donders, 1868). This so-called stage theory suggests that the reaction time (RT) to a stimulus can be partitioned in various ways to provide insight concerning the structure of mental operations. As an example, suppose a subject has been instructed to respond to a particular stimulus once it has been identified. The stimulus is presented and the experimenter measures the subject's reaction time. Let us refer to this as RT_1. Then the subject is told to respond directly to the onset of the stimulus without attempting to identify it (RT_2). Under the assumptions of stage theory the difference in reaction times ($RT_1 - RT_2$) could be used as an estimate of identification time. Sternberg has developed more sophisticated techniques with appropriate controls for analyzing such mental processing, but they are all based on the use of reaction time as an index of speed and mode of mental operation.

The flavor of Sternberg's approach is reflected in a series of experiments (cf. Sternberg, 1969) concerned with the retrieval of information when learning and retention are essentially perfect. The method used in these experiments involves presenting subjects with a list of items that is short enough to be within the span of immediate memory (e.g., the digits 0, 1, 4, and 9). Then the subjects are asked questions about the short lists, with instructions to respond as rapidly as possible. For example, the subject might be asked if the digit 0 was in the set just seen. If his answer was yes he would pull one lever, but if his answer was no he would pull another lever. In this situation it is the speed of reaction that is of major interest, since the subject is likely to perform without error. An additional requirement is that the subject must recall all the items from the list after he has responded. This requires him to retain the items in the order presented.

Type of Scan.   One question dealt with by Sternberg in these experiments is whether the subject scans the items in memory in a *serial* or in a *parallel* manner. When the test item is presented the subject might search his memory in a serial manner, examining one item at a time until he finds one that matches the test item. Alternatively, the subject might simultaneously compare the test item with the entire set of items in memory. This process of simultaneous comparison is known as *parallel scan,* in contrast to the *serial scan* involved when only one item at a time is considered.

If the scan is serial, the mental operations would require that only a small amount of the information be in immediate consciousness. If parallel scan is involved, however, the entire set of digits contained in immediate memory would be "attended to" at the same time. In addition, if the scan is serial, the subject might arrive at a positive response either by comparing the test item with each item in memory until a match is achieved or by comparing the test item with all items in memory before making a response. The former process would be described as a *self-terminating serial search;* the latter would be an *exhaustive serial search.* In *parallel scan* all items are considered simultaneously, so this distinction does not apply.

An exhaustive search requires more comparisons, on the average, than does a self-terminating search. Consider a case in which the test item occurs in the third position in the memorized list. If the scan or search is self-terminating, the total number of items in the list should make little difference in reaction time. In contrast, reaction time would be expected to increase as list length increases under an exhaustive search, even when the test item remains in the third position. This analysis indicates some general notions behind Sternberg's approach to mental scanning, although his techniques and the analysis of his results are more sophisticated and detailed. Nevertheless, our description is close enough to suggest the way in which he reached his conclusions concerning mental scanning.

When the subject's task is to judge the presence or the absence of a test item in a previously memorized set (i.e., memory search), the results typically obtained by Sternberg are shown in Figure 7.2. Notice that reaction time is related to the size of the memorized set in a linear manner. This indicates that it takes a constant amount of additional time to scan each additional item in the set. In these experiments using a varied set procedure, in which a new set is memorized on each trial, the slope of the function relating reaction time to set size indicates that it takes about 38 msec. to scan each item in memory. It should be noted that the findings are unchanged when a fixed set procedure is employed in which the subjects are given many trials (e.g., 60 practice trials and 120 test trials) with the same memorized set. In either case, the mental scan is carried out at a very rapid rate.

Sternberg interpreted the results of experiments such as those just described as being indicative of a high-speed exhaustive serial search. Two

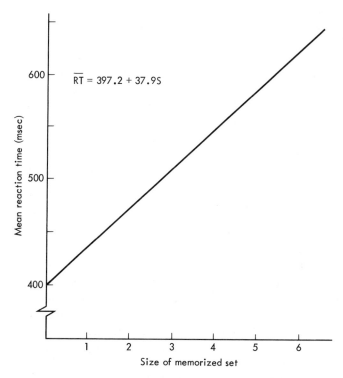

$$\overline{RT} = 397.2 + 37.9S$$

Figure 7.2 Illustrative findings for item recognition using a varied set procedure. The slope of the function relating set size (S) and mean reaction time ($\overline{RT}$), 37.9, is an estimate of the processing rate for each digit. The function shown represents a line fitted by least squares to actual means.
From Saul Sternberg, "Memory-Scanning: Mental Processes Revealed by Reaction-Time Experiments," in John S. Antrobus, COGNITION AND AFFECT, p. 19. Copyright © 1970 by Little, Brown and Company (Inc.). Redrawn by permission.

observations suggest that the scan is exhaustive rather than self-terminating. First, reaction time was not influenced by the position of an item in the memorized set. As we noted previously, this finding would be expected if the search was exhaustive but not if it was self-terminating. In addition, the functions relating reaction time to set size were parallel for *yes* responses and for *no* responses. This is also consistent with an exhaustive search, since all items would be scanned whether the response was yes or no. In contrast, the *RT* function for the no responses should increase at a faster rate than the function for the yes responses if the search were self-terminating. A self-terminating search would stop in the middle of the list, on the average, for a *yes* response but would continue through the entire list for a *no* response. Although these findings support the view that mental scan involves an exhaustive serial process, they are also consistent with certain models of parallel scanning in which all items are considered simultaneously (cf. Atkinson, Holmgren, and Juola, 1969).

Cavanaugh (1972), in comparing memory span size with rate of scanning, examined empirical data gathered in a number of studies. He concluded that the total time required to process a full memory load was constant (about one-quarter of a second) across a variety of materials. The materials sampled included digits, nonsense syllables, random forms, words, geometrical shapes, letters, and colors. Now, since the actual memory span (number of items) for these materials differs, Cavanaugh's analysis means that the greater the size of the memory span, the faster the processing rate for the particular materials involved. For example, he estimated 7.1 items as the memory span size for colors and 38 msec. as the scanning rate. The product of these two values gives 269.8 msec. (about one-quarter of a second) as an estimate of total processing time. In contrast, the corresponding values for geometric shapes were 5.3 items for span size and 50 msec. for scanning rate, which gives 265.0 msec. as an estimate of total processing time. Again, this is about one-quarter of a second.

Cavanaugh noted that a number of theories might predict this reciprocal relationship between storage capacity and processing rate, but the simplest theory appears to be what he termed the "size" hypothesis. In brief, this hypothesis assumes that short-term memory can hold only a limited number of features. Hence the greater the number of features per stimulus, the fewer the number of stimuli that will fit into short-term memory. An exhaustive serial search procedure in mental scanning of the sort suggested by Sternberg (1966, 1969) appears to be required by the "size" hypothesis. If the search were not exhaustive, total search times would differ for different kinds of material in contrast to the constant value noted by Cavanaugh. Of course, alternatives to the "size" hypothesis might not require the assumption of an exhaustive search.

Sternberg's findings suggest an exhaustive scan when the subject judges only the presence or the absence of an item in the memorized set. When the subject must find the location of an item in the list, a different process appears to be involved. In these experiments the test item always is contained in the set, but the subject's task is to report the item in the set that *followed* the test item. In this situation the scan appears to be one of self-terminating serial search. In addition, the scanning process is much slower—an average of about 250 msec. per item. Sternberg also notes that the process of locating the position of items appears to be independent of how well a list has been learned. Since mental scan appears to be exhaustive in this situation and self-terminating in the previous situation, Sternberg concludes that the mental scanning process is serial in nature.

Two other implications of Sternberg's findings should be mentioned. One of these concerns active or short-term memory. Sternberg suggests that although retention in short-term memory may involve rehearsal through covert speech, the subjects in his experiments used visual rather than auditory memory representations when making comparisons with the visually presented test item. This conclusion is based on the great speed involved in mental scanning. Scanning appears to take place at a faster rate than covert articulation could occur, although this does not rule out the possibility of some more abstract auditory representation. The second implication follows from Sternberg's conclusion that mental scanning involves a serial process. If he is correct, there is a decided implication that we can "think about" only one thing at a time. Therefore, the capacity of immediate consciousness may be even more restricted than was thought to be the case previously.[2] In the next section we shall consider this implication in a different experimental context.

SELECTIVE AND DIVIDED ATTENTION

In our previous discussion of the limits of our information-processing capacity, three ways to prevent overloading the processing system were suggested: (1) by extending the effective time that a brief input is available for analysis through storage in the preperceptual systems; (2) by "packing" more and more information into each chunk of memory by employing various recoding techniques; and (3) by using selective filtering systems that block or attenuate certain aspects of the input so that other aspects can be subjected to further analysis. Of course, selective filtering implies a distinction between information that is being directly attended to and information that is being "ignored," either for the moment or permanently. Since the first two alternatives have already been discussed, we now turn to a consideration of techniques used to investigate selective attention.

Shadowing Studies. One of the first modern studies of selective attention was reported by E. Colin Cherry (1953). He described the problem as "the cocktail party problem." At a cocktail party, we often find ourselves in a crowded room with sounds and conversations taking place all around us. If we attempt to participate in too many conversations at the same time, we are likely to experience an overload of our information-processing systems. In the more common situation, however, we selectively attend to one conversation while excluding other conversations. It was just this situation that was of interest to Cherry.

In his studies of selective attention, Cherry introduced an experimental procedure known as *shadowing*. In this task the subject is required to

[2] It should be noted, however, that Sternberg (1969) indicates that the high-speed scanning process does not have any obvious correlate in conscious experience. For example, subjects often say they used self-terminating search, or knew immediately without search, whether or not a test stimulus was in the memorized list.

repeat a spoken message aloud as it is presented, staying as "close behind" the speaker's voice as possible. At the same time, other auditory or visual inputs may also be presented to the subject. In Cherry's experiments two auditory messages were presented, and the subjects were instructed to shadow one message or the other. The messages sometimes were presented dichotically, with one message presented through a headphone to the subject's right ear and the other message presented through a different headphone to the left ear. At other times the messages were presented over separate loud speakers located at different places in the room.

Cherry reported that the subjects experienced no difficulty with the shadowing task. One characteristic of the subject's voice, however, was its monotony. The subject recognizes all the words on a literal level, since he is able to repeat them, but the repetition occurs with little of the emotional tone and stress contained in the shadowed message. In addition, the subject may remember very little of the shadowed message, even though he has recognized all the words. These observations suggest that shadowing can be a difficult task, but it can be made much easier under certain conditions, such as when the speaker does not talk too fast.

Although Cherry's observations concerning the shadowed message are important, his main point of interest concerned what the subjects could remember about the rejected message. When the rejected message was speech, the subjects always identified it as speech. But if the rejected message changed from English to German or to reversed English, the subjects did not notice the change. When the rejected signal was a nonspeech input such as a 400 Hz pure tone, the subjects always observed the tone and they could also identify a change in voice, as in going from a man's voice to a woman's voice. These observations suggest that shadowing is a powerful way of focusing attention on the required message. They also suggest that little of the information contained in the rejected message gets into the processing system.

Moray (1959) confirmed Cherry's observations concerning the limited amount of retained information from the rejected message. In this experiment he found that even when words in the rejected message were repeated as often as thirty-five times, the subjects showed no retention of them. Both Cherry and Moray used delay intervals of about thirty seconds between the end of shadowing and the retention test. It is possible that if these subjects had been tested immediately following the shadowing task, some trace of the rejected message would have remained. Just such evidence was reported by Norman (1969). He found a temporary memory for items in the rejected message, but no evidence of any lasting memory. These findings suggest that items from the rejected message may get into the preperceptual system, but if attention is not directed to them within a very short time after entry, no memory for the items will remain.

Treisman (1964a, 1964b) has presented evidence that also supports this interpretation. In her experiment both the shadowed message and the rejected message were the same. The subjects did not know this and were only told that the rejected message was a distraction they should ignore. Treisman investigated the time lag between the two messages. On the average the shadowed message was recognized as being identical to the rejected message when the shadowed message led by 4.5 seconds. When the rejected message led, the messages were recognized as identical when the lag averaged 1.4 seconds. These findings are consistent with a very brief preperceptual memory for items in the rejected message and a somewhat longer memory for items in the shadowed message.

The major conclusions to be drawn from these experiments are basically the same as those we have already noted. The general findings appear to indicate that little of the rejected message is noticed or remembered and that although the appropriate message can be shadowed accurately, little is retained of its informational content. These observations suggest a conclusion similar to that reached by Sternberg (1969) in his studies of high-speed mental scan: We can attend to only one thing at a time. In addition, the shadowing studies suggest that if attention cannot be given to particular inputs for a long enough period of time, retention of these inputs will be poor. This would explain why so little of the shadowed message is retained, even though all the words are recognized and repeated.

Listen and Report Studies. The experiments to be considered in this section differ from those we have just examined in a variety of ways. The most obvious difference is that in the listen and report studies the subjects hear the entire input or message before responding. No shadowing of messages as they are presented is involved. The inputs to the subjects are typically presented dichotically. But in contrast to the selective attention involved in shadowing studies, these listen and report experiments have been viewed as studies of *divided attention,* or "split-span." Nevertheless, many of the implications derived from listen and report experiments are in close agreement with those derived from studies of shadowing. A second difference in procedure is that the messages in shadowing studies are usually quite long, whereas the inputs in listen and report studies are typically within the immediate memory span.

The technique of dichotic listening was pioneered by Broadbent (1954). In his experiment the subjects were presented with three pairs of simultaneous digits to both ears. One member of each pair was presented to the left ear, while the other digit was presented to the right ear. The subject's task was to report the entire message. On some trials the subjects reported the message in any order; on other trials a specified order was required. The digit pairs were presented at rates that varied between one pair every one-half second to one pair every two seconds.

The results of this experiment were quite surprising in two ways. First, the subjects had difficulty recalling only four or five digits in contrast to the seven or so observed in studies of the memory span for digits. Second, the subjects preferred to organize their reports by ears rather than by pairs. For example, if the digits 2, 5, 9 were presented to one ear and the digits 8, 6, 3 were presented to the other ear, a typical subject might report the digits 2, 5, 9, 8, 6, in that order. Thus he would recall all the inputs to one ear before he would attempt to recall inputs to the other ear. Only when the rate of digit-pair presentation is relatively slow can the subjects report the order of arrival of the pairs (i.e., 2-8, 5-6, 9-3).

According to Moray (1970), Broadbent's findings are highly reliable, particularly with unpracticed subjects and comparable materials and presentation rates. Moray and Barnett (1965) reported essentially the same findings in a nondichotic situation. In this experiment the digit pairs were presented over a loudspeaker using a female voice to present one member of each digit pair and a male voice to present the other digit. However, there is evidence for efficient coding other than by ear of input when the incoming material contains features that facilitate coding in other ways (Gray and Wedderburn, 1960). For example, if the inputs are mixed strings, such as those shown below, recall is just as good phrase-by-phrase (i.e., 437, poor aunt Jane) as it is by ear:

| Left ear: | 4 | aunt | 7 |
| Right ear: | poor | 3 | Jane |

In this case, recall by ear is poorer than in Broadbent's experiment, and this suggests that a reduction in ear-by-ear coding is involved rather than an enhancement of an alternative coding strategy (cf. Moray, 1970).

Theories of Selective Attention

One of the first theories of selective attention was offered by Broadbent (1957, 1958). This theory was developed through a series of experiments, the best known of which was the dichotic listen and report experiment discussed in the preceding section. The approach taken by Broadbent focused on the notion that certain inputs are "passed on" for further processing while other inputs are rejected. The mechanism involved in selecting some inputs for further processing while rejecting other inputs has been called a *filter,* and the theoretical approach is often referred to as *filter theory.*

Filter Theory.   Broadbent (1957, 1958) assumed that when several messages reach the sense organs simultaneously, they are initially processed through a number of parallel sensory channels. In addition to the obvious channels associated with the various sense organs, other channels could involve such characteristics as the direction from which a message came or the quality of a speaker's voice. These channels were assumed to have distinct neural representation so that messages could be selected on the basis of pitch, loudness, position in space, and the like. Further processing of a message takes place only when it is attended to and consequently passed through the selective filter into the *limited capacity channel*.

According to Broadbent, information that has not passed the selective filter is held in a kind of preperceptual system, which he called the *S-system*. Information in the S-system becomes degraded very rapidly and has a duration of, at most, a few seconds. But once information passes the selective filter it enters the *P-system* where it may be retained for relatively long periods of time. The basic elements of this processing system are given in Figure 7.3.

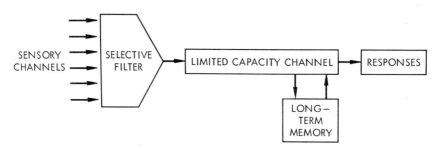

Figure 7.3 Information flow diagram for Broadbent's filter theory. *(After Broadbent, 1958.)*

Notice that the selective filter represents a kind of bottleneck—more information is processed through the parallel sensory channels than the limited capacity channel can handle. Therefore, the initial parallel processing of information is followed by serial processing in order to avoid an overload of the processing system. To accomplish this, Broadbent assumed that the selective filter could be "tuned" to any of the sensory channels over which information was being passed. Once information passed the filter it could interact with other information already held in long-term memory, and there was also provision for access to various output or response systems.

The results of Cherry's studies of selective attention are entirely compatible with a filter model. The few features of the rejected message that are noticed can be explained on the basis of rapid switching to the rejected channel to detect those characteristics that can be stored in the preperceptual system, such as voice quality. In a similar manner, the model is consistent with the results of Broadbent's dichotic listen and report experiment. Presumably, the subject attends selectively to the inputs to one ear and processes these inputs into the P-system as they arrive. This would explain the superior recall level noted for the ear reported first. Since this report takes time, the subject can only process and report some items from the inputs to the unattended ear before they have faded from the preperceptual system. Only when presentation rates are extremely slow can the subject switch attention from one ear to the other and report the order of arrival of the digits in pairs.

Problems with Filter Theory.   Although Broadbent's filter model successfully explains a number of important findings reported in studies of selective attention, it does not handle some other findings nearly so well. Many of the difficulties stem from the assumption that the filter operates on an all-or-none basis. This assumption implies that meaningful content in an unattended message would make no impression and would go unnoticed. Several investigators have shown that this does not appear to be true.

In studies of shadowing, Moray (1959) reports that information presented to the unattended ear may be noticed by a subject if it is preceded by the subject's own name. Although this finding could be explained by assuming that an individual is always "set" to respond to his own name, a number of other findings cannot be explained so easily. In a series of experiments Treisman (1960, 1964a, 1964b) has reported a number of such findings. We have already noted that subjects can detect the identity of two messages under appropriate delay conditions. This occurs even when the two messages which are exactly the same are read by two different speakers. Therefore the detection of identity does not depend on simple acoustic cues.

In one experiment Treisman played a message in English to one ear and a translation of that message to the other ear. Her bilingual subjects had no difficulty shadowing the message in English, and about half of them realized the two messages had the same meaning. Treisman has also reported that words from the rejected message are noticed when they are highly probable in the context of the shadowed message. For example, consider a situation in which subjects are instructed to shadow the inputs to a particular ear rather than the content of a given message. At a certain time the messages reaching the two ears are switched. Under these conditions subjects often give a word or two from the continuation of the originally shadowed message even after that message has been switched to the unshadowed ear.

Results from shadowing experiments are not the only ones that are difficult to account for by filter theory. In listen and report studies, Bryden (1971) reports a time course for the unattended message that is longer than one would have predicted from Broadbent's model. In these experiments, subjects are told to attend to a particular ear after which the inputs to both ears are to be reported. Half of the subjects are instructed to report the attended inputs first while the other half report the unattended inputs first. The results indicated that recall of inputs to the attended ear suffers more from delay in reporting than does recall of inputs to the unattended ear. Although recall of attended inputs is superior to recall of unattended inputs, the findings concerning delay effects are not consistent with the assumption of a preperceptual system in which unattended inputs are held for only a very short time.

Other listen and report studies also raise questions about the preperceptual storage of unattended inputs. For example, both Achenbach (1966) and Bartz (1972) report that repetition increases the probability of recall of inputs to the ear reported second but not to the ear reported first. Since their subjects were instructed which ear to report first on each trial, it is assumed that the ear reported first was the attended channel. To the extent that this assumption is correct, these findings are just the opposite from those predicted by Broadbent's filter model. According to the filter model, repetition might influence recall of inputs processed into the limited capacity channel but should not influence recall of inputs held in the preperceptual system.

It could of course be argued that results from listen and report studies are not really relevant to theories of selective attention. Since the subjects in these experiments know they are to report the inputs to both channels, the situation is more of "divided" attention than of "selective" attention. Such an analysis would appear to explain the discrepancy between repetition effects in listen and report studies and shadowing. It will be recalled that Moray (1959) reported that even thirty-five repetitions of a word in the nonshadowed channel went unnoticed. But this analysis of listen and report studies does not appear to save a filter model that assumes that the filter operates on an all-or-none basis. If the filter only accepts inputs from one channel at a time "divided" attention would not be possible.

Attenuation Filter. An alternative to the all-or-none operation has been proposed by Treisman (1960, 1961, 1964a, 1964c). She suggests that the selective filter acts to "attenuate" rather than "block" the rejected message. According to her proposal, recognition of inputs is accomplished through a series or hierarchy of tests that lead to a unique outcome for each word or other linguistic unit. The first tests distinguish inputs on the basis of physical or sensory features, and subsequent tests provide for identification of words and meaning. The thresholds for deciding the outcome of particular tests could be raised or lowered on the basis of context or importance. Thresholds for highly significant stimuli, such as one's name, are permanently lowered. The threshold for a word made probable by context is lowered temporarily. Signals that have been attenuated by the filter would pass tests only if the relevant thresholds have been lowered. Because of threshold variation it is possible for an important or probable signal on a rejected channel to be perceived.

Treisman suggests that all incoming signals are analyzed to some degree. To account for recognition of the identical message in the rejected channel, she proposes that the test thresholds are lowered for a short period of time because of recent use. Recognition of words in the rejected message can be explained by assuming that the context of the shadowed message resulted in a lowering of the threshold for certain words. By assuming a close relationship between words in one language and their equivalents in another language, it is not difficult to explain the observation that bilinguals can detect the identity of messages in the accepted and rejected channels. Thus the notion of a filter that acts to attenuate signals can explain many of the observations not accounted for by an all-or-none filter.

Selective Perception or Selective Response?   When subjects are asked to shadow a particular message, they normally can report very little about the verbal content of an unattended message. Broadbent (1958) explained this in terms of a selective filter that rejects messages that might overload the information-processing system. Treisman (1964a) suggests that the filter may act to "attenuate" rather than "block" the unattended message. In both of these proposals the emphasis is upon selection of inputs. A contrasting proposal has been offered by Deutsch and Deutsch (1963). They argue that *all* incoming stimuli receive *full* analysis and that the selective aspects of attentive behavior arise only with respect to motor output, memory storage, and awareness. They suggest that

> a message will reach the same perceptual and discriminatory mechanisms whether attention is paid to it or not (p. 83).

According to this view the most important message at any given moment will inhibit responses to other inputs and prevent awareness or memory. This proposal is consistent with the finding that relevant or particularly meaningful inputs are sometimes detected in an otherwise unattended message and with the observation that sudden or novel inputs may override other potential inputs and impose their effects on behavior.

The main difficulty with the Deutsch and Deutsch proposal is that it does not account for the facts of selective attention that filter theory was designed to explain. That is, although their system allows for presetting in advance to recognize important stimuli (e.g., your name), it cannot be preset in advance for stimuli on a particular channel (e.g., right ear) unless the nature of the stimuli is known. Norman (1968) has reformulated the Deutsch and Deutsch proposal in an attempt to overcome this difficulty, but problems still exist with this approach (cf. Kahneman, 1973).

Still another approach to attention is provided by Neisser (1967). He sees most attentive behavior as the result of two processing stages. The first stage is preattentive, and during this stage detection of the stimulus occurs. For example, the presence of an object may be detected although the nature of the object is not recognized. The actual perception or recognition of the object takes place during the analysis by synthesis stage. Recognition of a spoken message takes place by covertly reproducing it. Thus, perception is an act of construction or synthesis. Although Neisser's theory provides an adequate account of selective attention, there are few predictions that differentiate it from Treisman's attenuation theory.

It would be difficult, at present, to determine which of these approaches is more acceptable. All appear to explain some aspects of the available evidence, and the main theoretical controversy concerns the level of processing at which selection takes place. Some evidence from studies of signal detection supports the notion of attenuation (cf. Broadbent and Gregory, 1963; Treisman and Geffen, 1967), but other evidence (cf. Moray and O'Brien, 1967) suggests an "on-off" switch rather than an attenuator. In fact, Moray (1970) holds that the listener is attending to and sampling from only one message at a time. In contrast to both of these views are the views of Deutsch and Deutsch (1963) and Norman (1968) that emphasize response selection. Still another alternative, proposed by Neisser (1967), emphasizes the constructive nature of perception and equates attentive behavior with the constructive process. This controversy in attention theory appears to reflect a continuing historical argument in psychology over whether or not selection of inputs and selection of responses can ever be disentangled.

CONCLUSION

The present chapter has focused on attention and the processing of information. The area is a complex one and difficult to describe in terms of attentional, perceptual, or memorial processes. The concept of attention has had a cyclic influence upon the development of theories of perception, learning, and memory. Early British empiricists, in discussing the rather mechanical laws of association, had little to say about attention, but the structuralists and functionalists found the concept of considerable psychological interest. With the rise of behaviorism at the beginning of the twentieth century, however, even the eloquence of William James was not enough to keep attention from being "swept under the rug" because it seemed too mentalistic and capricious to be understood in a rigorous scientific manner.

Toward the middle of the twentieth century, however, the role of attention was again being seriously considered by theorists. In part, this was because of the inability of stimulus-response theories to deal with certain important problems of response selection in experimental situations. The "decontamination" of attention was also facilitated by attempts to integrate neurophysiological and psychological facts into a general theoretical system. Such attempts made it clear to many psychologists that theories that ignored central influences like attention and set were likely to be limited in their explanatory powers. This conclusion was also strengthened by subsequent discoveries which suggested that there were rather specialized neurophysiological systems modulating the organism's attention mechanisms and filtering stimulus inputs before they reached higher cortical levels and, hence, engaged conscious psychological processes. There also appeared to be special receptor cells that were selectively sensitive to certain attributes of stimuli as abstract as "directional movement," which also pointed to the possibility of unique mechanisms for attention processes.

In the early 1960s investigators began to report evidence for highly specialized visual and auditory preperceptual systems in which "raw" unencoded information was stored for very brief periods of time. At times this information was subsequently processed and stored in more permanent memory systems; at other times it made only fleeting contact with consciousness; and at still other times it rapidly faded away without leaving any conscious impression at all. Naturally, the question arose as to what factors might determine these different possibilities, and it was obvious that one important factor was likely to be whether the information had been "attended to" or not. As theorists developed explanations of the flow and processing of information from preperceptual systems to more permanent storage systems, the complexity of the interactions of these systems with mechanisms of attention and memory became clearer. For example, attention and immediate memory both appeared to be restricted by capacity limitations. Only so much information could be attended to, and only so much of what was attended to at any given moment could be stored. Thus there was always the potential problem of the system's being overloaded with information. The problem of overload, however, was lessened by the preperceptual systems. That is, to the extent that such systems extended the time available for abstraction of information from earlier inputs, they increased the overall capability of the processing systems to analyze and store incoming information.

Further economies of information processing arose from the fact that people appeared to actively chunk and code information in a way that increased the capacity of short-term memory as well as the efficiency of coding and retrieval operations. Even so, there still appeared to be a limit of seven plus or minus two "chunks" of information that could be carried in active or short-term memory. In addition, it appeared that the limit of immediate consciousness was even more abbreviated, perhaps as small as one single item.

The role of attention in processing and storage of information was also demonstrated in shadowing and listen and report studies. In such tasks, subjects may focus on one message while paying little attention to another message. Experimental results from such studies suggested that even though the subjects were aware of many aspects of the unattended message, little of the information there was processed into more permanent storage systems. These findings were consistent with the concept of preperceptual systems in which potential information is briefly stored and from which information disappears rapidly unless it is attended to in some active manner.

General theories of attention discussed in this chapter can be divided into two general classes: *selective perception* and *selective response* theories. The most influential of the selective perception theories have emphasized the concepts of selective filters and limited capacity channels. For example, Broadbent (1957, 1958) proposed that certain inputs are "passed on" for further processing while other inputs are rejected or filtered out. This particular *filter theory* has been modified by Treisman (cf. Treisman, 1964a) to account for some findings not readily explained by Broadbent's original model. Her version of filter theory suggests that filters act to "attenuate" rather than "block" signals and that all incoming signals are analyzed to some degree. This can be thought of as a more-or-less rather than an all-or-none filter model of attention. Deutsch and Deutsch (1963) offer a contrasting proposal to filter theories in terms of a selective response theory of attention. In their view, *all* incoming stimuli are fully analyzed, and the selective aspects of attentive behavior involve such response factors as motor output, memory storage, and response inhibition. The capacity limitation is, in a sense, on the response side and not the stimulus side. Similar views were expressed by Norman (1968). In addition, Neisser's (1967) analysis by synthesis model equates attentive behavior with the constructive process of active synthesis. It remains to be seen which of these theoretical approaches will be the more viable.

The concept of attention, and its relationship to consciousness, is difficult to define. *Attention* will probably continue to be a viable concept in psychology until we can provide alternative ways of explaining experimental findings of the sort discussed in this chapter. In an important sense attention fits in well with the current *Zeitgeist* in human learning and memory. Man is no longer viewed as a passive sponge soaking up a flood of information. Instead, he is seen as an active seeker of information which he then filters, processes, encodes, and organizes into complex hierarchical schemes. We turn to a consideration of these organizational schemes in the next chapter.

8

Organization in Memory

THE TWO PRECEDING CHAPTERS examined various aspects of information processing ranging from the detection of stimulus events at the sensory level to the coding and storage of information about such events in memory. Little was said about one of the more obvious characteristics of human memory—that it is organized. Information about the events we experience is stored in memory in terms of complex organizational schemes and not as discrete, isolated units. In the sense intended here, organized memory refers to memory for material that significantly engages the contents of long-term storage. The organization may be revealed by asking subjects to recall material that has been in long-term storage for some time (e.g., recall all the states in the United States) or by investigating memory for material that is represented sufficiently well in long-term storage to provide some basis for organizing an otherwise unorganized input.

Traditional approaches to the study of organized memory have drawn heavily upon the work of Ebbinghaus and the subsequent speculations of behaviorists. These approaches emphasized associative connections as the sole basis for organization in memory. It will be recalled that Ebbinghaus invented the nonsense syllable for use as the basic unit in his investigations of learning and memory. For Ebbinghaus, each nonsense syllable was intended to represent an idea, and list learning consisted of associating the ideas represented by the nonsense syllables units. These nonsense syllables bore no relation to each other, nor to ideas outside of the experimental task. That is, the experimental materials were unrelated to information or knowledge in the subject's long-term memory. As a result the outcome of Ebbinghaus's experiments reflected the serial structure of his learning task and did little to contradict the associative hypotheses on which they were based.

Following the work of Ebbinghaus, most traditional views of organized memory emphasized associations as the basic units of both learning and memory. The organization of memory was seen as being unitary in form and depending most importantly upon the particular network of associations previously acquired by the individual. That is, output or retrieval from memory was seen as depending closely on input. Subsequent investigations of learning and memory that employed the paired-associate, rather than the serial task, only served to strengthen this belief—particularly when nonsense syllables were used. Meaningful words became more widely used as experimental materials when students of memory became more interested in verbal behavior and language. Although this shift in experimental materials did not produce a dramatic difference in the outcomes of most experiments, there were indications that the meaningfulness of the material to the subject did influence experimental findings.

We saw several illustrations of the effects of meaningfulness in Chapters 4 and 5. It will be recalled that early association theorists predicted positive transfer from serial to paired-associate learning on the basis of a presumed commonality of stimulus-response structure. However, the experimental evidence is that although positive transfer is obtained with nonsense materials, little or no facilitation is found with meaningful words (cf. Horton and Turnage, 1970). Findings such as these suggest that the validity of associative principles may well depend on the *context* in which they are evaluated.

It would be misleading to conclude that evidence for associative organization in memory is restricted to situations in which prior information from long-term storage plays little or no role. In fact, one of the oldest techniques employed to investigate the structure of memory is the word association test. This was developed by Galton to study associative relationships in long-term memory (cf. Galton, 1883). As the test is typically employed, a subject is presented with a list of words, one at a time, and is asked to report "the first word that comes to mind." When the subject is told to report "any word" that comes to mind, the procedure is called *free association*. But when the subject's response is constrained in some way, such as by instructions to report "opposites" or "synonyms," the task is known as *controlled association*.

The word association test has been used to determine both the type of response given and the strength of associative connections. In fact, numerous sets of word association norms collected over the years provide both types of information (cf. Postman and Keppel, 1970). In such norms each stimulus word is reported, together with a list of the responses given to each word by a group of subjects, and the relative frequency with which each response was given. The relative frequencies of occurrence have been interpreted as an index of the strength of associative connections. For instance, if 80 percent of the subjects in a particular population give the word *chair* as a response to the word *table,* this percentage provides an index of the associative strength between *table* and *chair* in that population. Of course, such percentages are considered to be relative, not absolute, indices of associative strength.

A second measure of associative strength is the associative reaction time, or the time required to produce a response to a given stimulus word. Obviously the more rapidly a response is made, the stronger the presumed connection between it and the stimulus word. Measures of associative strength based on reaction time agree quite closely with those based on relatively frequency of occurrence (Thumb and Marbe, 1901). This relationship has come to be known as *Marbe's law,* and, in general, it indicates that the reponses given most frequently in word association are also the responses given most rapidly (cf. Woodworth, 1938).

The basic assumption underlying the study of word association has been that the habits reflected in the norms mirror the prior experiences of the subjects and the organization of their memory. Certain evidence supports this point of view. As in the serial and paired-associate tasks, however, other evidence leads us to question the associationists' basic assumption that output directly reflects input. Many contemporary psychologists have rejected the proposition that the human organism is a passive receiver of inputs that are reacted to with automatic, stereotyped responses. The more contemporary view is that inputs are often translated and reorganized in such a way as to prevent straightforward relationships between input and output from being observed, except under rather limited circumstances.

The theoretical issues that arise in connection with the study of organized memory are quite complex, and in many instances the same experimental outcomes are seen as being supportive of very different points of view. Therefore we shall examine some of the experimental findings before considering alternative interpretations of these findings in any greater detail. We begin with a discussion of input-output relationships —a topic that is of importance both to associationists and to other theorists as well.

INPUT AS A PREDICTOR OF OUTPUT

Apart from an obvious relationship to predictions derived from association theory, there are many observations that lead us to expect that output is closely related to input. Perhaps one of the more obvious illustrations of this relationship is found when young children begin to use words from their native language. Young children do not learn languages to which they are not exposed, and the vocabularies they do acquire are those derived from their experiences with language. Other evidence of the relationship between input and output comes from observations of our daily conversations. Here we are likely to use a word like *house* rather than one like *dwelling,* even though both may have the same referent. At least in part, such behavior results from our having encountered the word *house* more often than the word *dwelling.* Therefore, there is a common pool of frequently encountered words which are quite likely to occur in our daily conversations. This notion is further strengthened by the observation that many different words may occur quite infrequently in our conversations, whereas a small core of words may occur over and over again. According to one estimate, the one hundred most frequently occurring words in the conversations of college students account for 63 percent of their total speech (cf. Osgood, 1953). Thus we are repetitious in our speech, and we appear to select words for output on the basis of certain statistical characteristics of input. Of course, such factors as what we intend to communicate and the grammatical structure of our language also influence the selection and organization of words.

Input Frequency and Output.   Some evidence suggests that the more often we encounter a word, the more likely it is to appear in subsequent output. When this proposition is examined in the context of a simple experimental situation, order of output seems to be related to input frequency. In Chapter 4 we noted that Underwood and Schulz (1960) have characterized this relationship in terms of the *spew hypothesis.* Their view was that the order of emission of verbal units is directly related to frequency of experience with those units, although they acknowledged that certain restrictions do apply in particular situations. Notice that this hypothesis does not say that associations between words are formed more rapidly as a function of input frequency. Instead, the spew hypothesis predicts that the more frequently experienced units are more likely to be given first in a free-responding situation and hence are more *available* to enter into associations.

An observation consistent with the spew hypothesis is that, generally speaking, the words given most often as responses to stimulus words in a word association test tend to be more common in the language (cf. Howes, 1957). The fact that free association responses tend to be common words also implies that associations are more likely to develop among familiar words than among unfamiliar words (cf. Deese, 1961). Since a common word is one to which we have had considerable exposure, we might speculate that frequency of input would be related both to "spew" in terms of availability and order of output as well as to the probability of a word occurring as an associate to some other word.

Underwood and Schulz cite a study by Mattocks which provides a partial test of the spew hypothesis. In this experiment one group of subjects learned a prescribed list of paired associates in which the stimulus and response terms were unrelated. A second group of subjects was asked to supply and remember their *own* responses to the same set of stimuli. As each stimulus was presented, the subject was to provide a response to it and remember on the next trial which response had been provided. This task would appear to be easy, but it turned out to be more difficult than learning the prescribed set of responses. Apparently the "most probable" responses, which presumably occur on the basis of spew, are not necessarily the "most easily associated" responses. It is not immediately clear why this should be the case here, but the experiment exemplifies situations in which frequency and recency of input do not predict "hookup" in straightforward ways.

Of course there are numerous exceptions to the proposition that there is a direct relationship between frequency of input and output. This is especially true of complex situations where the exceptions clearly constitute the rule. For instance, in recall of prose passages, we know that reproduction of the exact sequence of words is neither very likely nor very important. What counts in this situation is something we might describe as "paraphrase of essential ideas." However, noteworthy discrepancies between input and output are also common in more restricted situations. In the next section we shall consider some of the discrepancies common to *free recall*—an experimental task that has provided us with considerable information about organization in memory.

Input-Output Relations in Free Recall

The free-recall task usually involves presentation of a list of words in a random order which the subjects are then asked to recall in any order they choose. By comparing the degree of correspondence between the order of words during input and their order during output, it becomes possible to describe whatever discrepancies do arise. Tulving (1968) has characterized the input-output discrepancies most common to free recall in terms of *primary* and *secondary* organization.

Primary Organization. Certain discrepancies between input and output orders tend to occur in free recall irrespective of the meaning of the items in the list or the subject's past experience with the items. Tulving views such discrepancies as evidence of primary organization. In a sense, primary organization refers to what might be called the "raw" organizational structure inherent in the free-recall task. Perhaps the most stable characteristic of this structure is the so-called recency-primacy effect, which was introduced in Chapter 6. The effect is most clearly revealed in *single-trial free recall* of a once-presented list of unrelated items. Recall of these items shows that the terminal or most recently presented items are re-called first and recalled best. Initial items from the list are recalled next best (primacy), and the middle items are the most poorly recalled (cf. Murdock, 1962).

The form of the recency-primacy curve for free recall has been interpreted as being due to two different memory systems. It has been argued that following single input, initial items in the list are recalled from long-term storage and terminal items are recalled from short-term storage (cf. Glanzer and Cunitz, 1966). Tulving, however, prefers the view that *all* information is stored in a single unified system and that the recency-primacy curve reflects differences in accessibility of the items rather than different storage systems.

Tulving (1968) suggests that terminal items may be more accessible than earlier items because certain information is stored *with* these items that may no longer be available for items presented earlier in the series. Such information might include the acoustic trace of items the subject has seen recently and encoded acoustically. Presumably the acoustic traces from items presented earlier would have already decayed from the sensory store. In addition, Tulving suggests that temporal dating or serial position information may explain the superior recall of initial and terminal items over items from the middle of the list. Thus Tulving prefers to view primary organization, including the recency-primacy effect, in terms of retrieval processes, whereas others (e.g., Glanzer and Cunitz, 1966) have emphasized organization due to different storage systems.

The study of primary organization has interested many psychologists and has produced an extensive experimental literature. Some of these investigations have been reviewed in Chapter 6. The focus in this chapter, as noted at the outset, is on organized memory for materials that engage the contents of long-term storage in an important way. Since primary organization refers to organization that is independent of the meaning of items and the subject's past experience with them, it does not fall within the scope of the present chapter. Therefore, we now turn our attention to secondary organization.

Secondary Organization. Studies of primary organization typically involve single presentation of lists of relatively unrelated items. In contrast, studies of secondary organization typically involve either lists of related items or lists that are presented for several trials (i.e., *multitrial free recall*). Tulving (1968) distinguishes between two varieties of secondary organization, *clustering* and *subjective organization,* which, among other things, differ in terms of the presentation conditions.

Clustering refers to a situation in which a list of related items, ar-ranged in random order, is presented to one or more subjects for free recall. The list is usually presented only once, and clustering is revealed when the subjects group related items together in recall. For example, Jenkins and Russell (1952) have shown that randomly presented associates, as defined by word association norms, are readily clustered in recall. Similarly, Bousfield (1953) has demonstrated that lists of items that can be grouped into various semantic categories (e.g., professions, articles of clothing) will be clustered in recall even though they are widely separated during input. In both of these cases the discrepancies between input and output orders presumably result from the subject's prior familiarity with the items and knowledge of their meanings. This is not to imply that primary organization plays no role in recall, but rather that the clustering measure only reflects secondary organization.

In contrast to clustering, studies of subjective organization typically involve multiple presentation of a list of unrelated items. The subject attempts to recall the items after each presentation, and the list is presented in a new random order on each trial. Since the items are unrelated at the start, the experimenter has no prior knowledge of the way items may be grouped in recall. Therefore, the procedure used for determining subjective organization differs from that used for clustering. In subjective organization the output order provided by the subject on a given trial serves as the reference point for the following trial. If two or more items are grouped in essentially the same way on successive trials, the common grouping serves to indicate subjective organization. The closer the correspondence between orders of output on successive trials, the greater the degree of subjective organization.

Apart from differences in experimental procedures and measures of organization, other differences between clustering and subjective organization should be emphasized. For instance, since clustering is usually assessed following a single presentation of the list, it only serves to indicate whether or not the organization built into the list by the experimenter influenced the organization of recall. Therefore, the clustering task is mainly useful for confirming the importance of those aspects of organization previously identified on other grounds. In subjective organization, however, each subject may impose his own unique form of organization on the list of items. To the extent that subjects agree on the form of organization (cf. Tulving, 1962), the technique can be used to discover new principles of organization.

A further comment is in order concerning the way organization is defined in studies of clustering and subject organization. In clustering the experimenter defines which items must be grouped, whereas in subjective organization the subject's output order on each trial defines the item relations which are said to reflect organization on the following trial. Of course, it is the subject who ultimately defines the organization in either case. In clustering the organization reflected in recall must, in some sense, already exist within the subject. With only a single presentation of the items, little opportunity is provided for learning a novel organization. Of course this does not imply that all subjects will "discover" the organizing principle with equal speed or to the same degree. Nor does failure to find evidence of whatever organization was provided by the experimenter in clustering imply that the output was not organized. It only means that the expected form of organization was not in evidence.

Now that the main categories of secondary organization have been identified, let us examine some of the experimental findings and their theoretical implications in greater detail. We begin with a consideration of frequency effects and clustering, since these phenomena have been closely tied to associative theories. Following this we discuss subjective organization and some evidence for a more dynamic, cognitive view of organization in memory.

FREE RECALL AND ORGANIZATION

In the 1950s the free-recall task became one of the most widely used techniques for investigating associative factors in the organization of memory. A major advantage of the free-recall task over others popular at the time, such as the serial and paired-associate tasks, was that output order was free to vary. This meant that discrepancies between input and output orders could provide evidence concerning organizational processes in memory. In contrast, such discrepancies rarely occurred in the serial and paired-associate tasks, and when they did occur, they were of little theoretical significance.

Frequency Effects

In the preceding discussion we have seen several examples in which item frequency played a major role in determining order of output. Such observations were of particular importance to associationists, since frequency of prior occurrence was a major principle in association theory. In general, this principle held that items that occur often in the past history of an individual should also occur frequently, and rapidly, in a free-responding situation. Although this principle had been demonstrated in the context of word association tests, it was of some importance to demonstrate its generality to other situations as well.

Bousfield and his associates have reported several studies concerning frequency effects in a free-responding task similar to free recall. Bousfield and Barclay (1950) asked subjects to name as many members of restricted categories as they could. The categories included birds, carpenter tools, celestial bodies, and so forth. When output order was compared with frequency of recall, it was found that the category members recalled most often were also recalled first in the output sequence. In an earlier study Bousfield and Sedgewick (1944) reported that subjects asked to respond with category members such as "cities in the United States" first responded with nearby cities and then with others farther away. This tendency to order responses on the basis of geographical proximity is probably due to both frequency and secondary organization, although it would be difficult to specify which input conditions lead to such output sequences.

We previously noted that associative reaction time in the word association test is closely related to the frequency of occurrence of associative responses (i.e., Marbe's law). Bousfield, Cohen, and Silva (1956) have provided evidence that Marbe's law also holds in free recall. In this experiment the recall sequence produced by each subject was divided into tenths (deciles). Then a comparison was made between the average decile in which each word appeared (a measure of reaction time or latency) and the number of subjects that produced each response (relative frequency). The result was a significant negative relationship indicating that the most common responses were given earliest in the output sequence.

Clustering Effects

One of the more obvious ways of investigating the effects of associations on organization in memory is by means of the clustering technique. As noted previously, clustering refers to the occurrence of sequences of related responses in the recall of randomized word lists. More specifically, clustering is reflected in terms of a repetition during output where a repetition is defined as the contiguous occurrence of two or more words from the same experimenter-defined category. The greater the number of repetitions found in an output sequence, the greater the clustering effect.

Jenkins and Russell (1952) asked subjects to engage in free recall of lists composed of associated word pairs identified in free-association norms (e.g., table-chair, command-order). Since the elements of the pairs were never presented contiguously during input, any grouping of appropriate elements during output could be taken as evidence of *associative clustering*. In a later study Jenkins, Mink, and Russell (1958) investigated the effects of variations in associative strength on clustering. The materials used in this experiment consisted of word pairs varying in association strength according to free-association norms. As might be anticipated, their results indicated that associative clustering varied directly with the associative strength of the word pairs.

A second type of clustering, called *category clustering*, consists of the subject's being given a list of words that represent several semantic categories. In contrast to associative clustering, category clustering typically involves several items per category instead of only two. Because there are several items per category, the same item may appear in more than one repetition. For example, suppose a subject recalled the words *cat, dog, horse, carrot, pea, lawyer, cow,* and *doctor* from a list composed of names of animals, professions, and vegetables. Three repetitions can be identified in this sequence (*Cat-dog, dog-horse,* and *carrot-pea*), and *dog* appears in two of these repetitions. The maximum number of possible repetitions is equal to the number of words recalled minus one (seven in this example), since the first item in the sequence is not counted as a repetition.

Bousfield (1953) was one of the first investigators to study category clustering. In this experiment the subjects were shown a list of sixty words containing fifteen examples from each of four mutually exclusive categories (animals, names, professions, and vegetables). After the list was presented, the subjects were given ten minutes to recall as many words as they could. The results indicated a significant level of clustering during the initial part of the recall interval, after which clustering rose to a maximum and finally dropped off to a chance level. These findings are shown in Figure 8.1.

The low initial level of clustering observed by Bousfield (1953) is quite common when the single-trial free-recall procedure is employed. This result is usually due to primary organization in the form of a recency

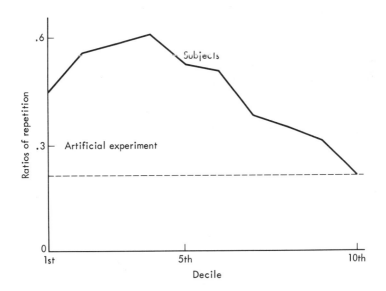

Figure 8.1 Ratios of repetitions (number of repetitions divided by number of words recalled minus one) in successive deciles of total items recalled. The dotted line indicates expected "clustering" if items were recalled in a random order. *(After Bousfield, 1953.)*

effect (cf. Tulving, 1968). It is less clear why clustering drops to chance levels later in the recall sequence. This could be due to a breakdown of organization, or it could be a natural consequence of having depleted the supply of words available for recall.

Although studies of clustering have usually been restricted to a single input-output sequence, Bousfield and Cohen (1953) have examined the effect of multiple input trials. Their task consisted of presenting a four-category, forty-item list from one to five times prior to free recall. The results indicated that both the number of words recalled and the degree of clustering increased as a function of number of presentations. Both of these outcomes were apparently due to an increase in cluster size during recall, since the number of nonclustered items recalled did not increase systematically with number of presentations.

Associative and Category Clustering. Demonstrations of clustering such as that provided by Jenkins and Russell (1952) have generally been seen as rather straightforward examples of associative organization in memory. The essential feature in these studies is that direct associative connections are "known" to exist between the elements of a word pair, and these connections are presumed to provide the theoretical basis for the clustering effect. Of course, a more neutral position could be taken by simply saying that whatever is responsible for the relationships noted in word association norms is also responsible for the clustering effect.

In contrast to the situation in associative clustering, category clustering has been interpreted in various ways. In his earlier studies Bousfield emphasized the role of superordinate structures in explaining clustering. His view was that the presentation of category members (subordinates) served to activate a superordinate structure (category label), and once the superordinate system was activated it would tend to facilitate recall of words belonging to the same category. In associational terms, such a superordinate system is similar to a mediational process in which the common element that mediates recall of category members is the category label.

Yet another interpretation of category clustering is based on the notion of a coding process (cf. Cofer, 1966; Gonzalez and Cofer, 1959). The basic idea here is that during input the subject recodes the list items into categories and stores the category labels in memory. At the time of recall the subject retrieves the category label and as many members of the category as he can. Some support for this interpretation comes from the observation that the number of words recalled per category is quite consistent over a fairly wide range of conditions (cf. Cohen, 1966; Tulving and Pearlstone, 1966).

Although associative and category clustering have been studied for many years, it is still not possible to conclude that any given theoretical interpretation is superior to any other interpretation. In part, this is because the alternative interpretations outlined above make very similar predictions about clustering. Support for associative explanations comes from numerous studies that show clustering to occur on the basis of various indices of word relatedness derived from free or controlled association norms (cf. Marshall and Cofer, 1963). Of course, as Tulving (1968) points out, these studies only show that similar processes may be involved in the word association and free-recall contexts. They do not necessarily reveal the nature of the underlying processes.

A more general demonstration of associative effects on organization in free recall has been discussed by Deese (1959, 1961). Deese has provided a measure of *direct* association within a list of words called *interitem associative strength* (IIAS). This measure is defined as the average percentage with which list members elicit each other as free associates. If no list item occurs as a direct associate to any other list item, IIAS is said to be zero. But the greater the frequency with which list items elicit one another, the greater the IIAS.

With a general measure of associative relatedness such as IIAS, it is difficult to identify associative clusters in terms of specific word pairs. Of course, other associative indices could be used for this purpose. Nevertheless, Deese has shown that lists high in IIAS tend to be well recalled, highly organized, and resistant to interference from extraneous sources in free-recall situations. This suggests that a great deal of organization is due to interitem associations that converge upon each other at the time of recall and systematically exclude extralist associations from intruding.

Although considerable evidence supports associative views of clustering, there also is evidence to indicate the importance of category labels in the organization of recall. For example, exhaustive category lists are recalled better than nonexhaustive category lists. An exhaustive category list is one in which the list items exhaust, or nearly exhaust, all of the members of the categories (e.g., *north, south, east, west*). On the other hand, nonexhaustive categories are only partially exhausted by list members (e.g., *dog, horse, lion, zebra*). Cohen (1963a, 1963b) has shown that more words are recalled from exhaustive categories than from nonexhaustive categories, although the number of categories from which at least one word is recalled does not differ in the two cases. In addition, interitem associative strength was shown to be related to recall of items within a category but not to recall of the categories themselves.

Cofer, Bruce, and Reicher (1966) report a study of category clustering that supports the importance of both category labels and associative relations. They confirmed the earlier finding of Bousfield, Cohen, and Whitmarsh (1958) which showed higher recall and greater clustering of words when list members are high-frequency associates to the category label than when they are low-frequency associates. This observation is equally consistent with the various theoretical interpretations mentioned previously.

These investigations also report that for high-frequency lists, greater clustering and recall of words is found when list items are presented in categorized
blocks than when they are arranged at random. This finding suggests a role
for coding or superordination but is also consistent with associative mediation and a direct associational explanation (cf. Cofer, 1965).

Organization in Storage or Retrieval?   It is well known that subjects
do not recall all list items presented for free recall. Older versions of association theory tended to interpret such failures of recall as evidence of
forgetting. The more contemporary view, however, emphasizes the role of
retrieval factors. Support for this notion comes from the observation that
presentation of retrieval cues at the time of recall (cf. Lloyd, 1964) leads
to improved retention. The interesting theoretical issue raised by such findings is whether the effectiveness of retrieval cues is attributable to factors
operative at the time of storage or at the time of retrieval.

Tulving and Pearlstone (1966) have shown that cued recall is superior to noncued recall when the cues match those presented at the time
of input. These investigators employed lists of words belonging to explicit
categories. The lists varied in length (twelve, twenty-four, or forty-eight
words) and in number of words per category (one, two, or four). Both
category labels and category instances were presented during input, but
the subjects were told that only the instances were to be recalled. For
half the subjects recall was tested in the presence of category labels and
for the other half recall was not cued.

Tulving and Pearlstone found that cued recall was superior to noncued recall, with the advantage for cued recall being greater with longer
lists and smaller category sizes. The main effect of cueing was to increase
the number of categories from which items were recalled and not the number of words recalled per category. In addition, although more categories
were recalled from longer lists, the number of items recalled per category
remained constant. These findings tend to support the view that recall of
categories and recall of category members are independent.

Tulving and Osler (1968) have confirmed and extended these findings. In a similar study they also found that cued recall was superior to
noncued recall when the cue words were presented during both input and
output. When retrieval cues were only presented during output, however,
there was no advantage for cued recall. Tulving and Osler concluded that
retrieval cues were only effective so long as they tap the organization established at the time of input. In other words, it is the way material is organized
at the time of input that determines whether specific retrieval cues will
facilitate recall. They suggest that the advantage often found for cued recall
results from the use of retrieval cues that tap into the organization employed
by the subject during input.

The implications of these studies of cued recall are decidedly contrary to the view that organization of recall takes place at the time of retrieval. Jenkins and Russell (1952) explicitly suggested that associative mediational mechanisms operate during recall to organize the output. This position is consistent with that taken by Deese (1959, 1961), and it holds that once a word is recalled, it acts as a stimulus to facilitate recall of other words on the list. In addition to the studies already cited, however, other investigations have challenged this interpretation. For instance, Hudson (1969) examined clustering in the recall of lists where the subjects were told either before or after input that the words could be categorized on some basis. The list words used in this study were selected from categories such as "round" (e.g., *globe, spool, button, balloon*) or "white" (e.g., *snow, ivory, napkin, linen*). In contrast to the performance of an unin-structured control group, his results indicated that only when the instructions were given prior to input was clustering enhanced. Such findings support the view that storage processes at the time of input play the major role in determining organization of output.

Context and Organization.   If organization of inputs for storage is of major significance in determining subsequent recall, then those factors that influence such organization may be expected to play an important role in subsequent recall. Among the more obvious factors that may influence organization of input are instructions to the subject and the experimental context in which the stimulus materials are presented.

Howes and Osgood (1954) have reported on two important context effects in word association. The subjects in their experiments were given precise instructions about the nature of free-association tasks. Examples of stimulus words and possible responses were presented, and the impor-tance of giving the first word that comes to mind was emphasized. The subjects were then told that on each trial of the experiment four words would be read aloud but that only the last word was the stimulus word. That is, the subjects were instructed to respond to only the last word in each series of four.

In one experiment the critical manipulation was the number of words in the experimental context that could be related to the stimulus word. For example, if the stimulus word was *dark,* the entire preceding context might be related to the stimulus word (e.g., *devil, fearful,* and *sinister*). In other cases only one word (e.g., *devil, eat,* and *basic*) or two words (e.g. *devil, fearful,* and *basic*) would be related to the stimulus word. There was also a control condition in which none of the words in the experimental context was related to the stimulus word.

The results of this experiment are shown in Figure 8.2. Here the probability of a response such as *hell* to the stimulus word *dark* is plotted as a function of the number of related words in the context. It should be noted that *hell* is a high-frequency associate to *devil* in the usual free-

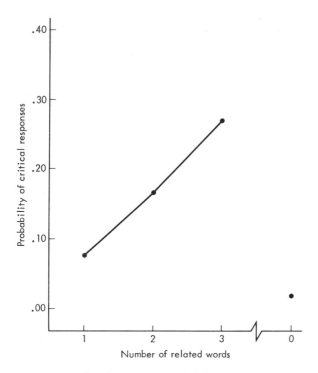

Figure 8.2 Probability of critical responses as a function of the number of context words strongly associated with the stimulus word.
(After Howes and Osgood, 1954.)

association task but a very low frequency response to *dark*. As the amount of related context increased, however, the probability of *hell* as a response to *dark* also increased. Correspondingly, the probability of *light* as a response to *dark*, which is a very high frequency associate in the usual task, decreased as the amount of related context increased.

In a second experiment only one of the context words was related in a specific way to the stimulus word, but its position in the series was varied. For example, consider the words *skin, wind,* and *mountain* as context for the stimulus word *rough*. In this situation Howes and Osgood demonstrated that the probability of a response such as *hands* depended on where *skin* was located in the series. In general, the closer *skin* was to *rough,* the greater was the probability of a response such as *hands*. In both this experiment and the one discussed previously, we see a major influence of context on the probability of occurrence of various responses. Depending on the situation, responses that normally occur with high frequency may occur less often, and very infrequent responses may occur with much greater frequency.

In the case of free recall, one of the more extensive demonstrations of context effects comes from a series of studies reported by Gonzalez and Cofer (1959). These investigators showed that clustering in free recall could be either augmented or virtually eliminated by appropriate manipulation of the experimental context. In one study forty unrelated adjectives were used to modify forty nouns representing four different semantic categories. The result was that clustering of the nouns by category was reduced to a chance level. In another study a list of unrelated nouns, which did not cluster when presented alone, was modified by a list of adjectives representing discrete categories. Recall of the nouns in this situation revealed significant clustering when scoring was on the basis of the adjective category used to modify each noun.

Gonzalez and Cofer also demonstrated facilitation and interference effects on clustering when both the stimulus words and the modifiers represented discrete categories. For example, when categorized adjectives were used to modify categorized nouns, both recall and clustering of the nouns were facilitated so long as the categories for paired adjectives and nouns were congruent. But when the category for a given noun was not congruent with that of the paired adjective, both recall and clustering were impaired. In a subsequent report Cofer (1960) points out that such outcomes can be predicted on the basis of changes in associative relationships introduced by the experimental context.

A second method for manipulating context effects in word association and free-recall tasks is to vary the instructions to the subject. One example of such an effect is revealed by comparing the responses given under free and under controlled association instructions. With the controlled association procedure the subject is told to restrict his response alternatives in some way (e.g., report synonyms), and the result is to alter the frequency and even the type of response given in comparison with those obtained in free association (cf. Woodworth and Schlosberg, 1954). Such effects are well documented, and although the results of both procedures are usually interpreted in associationistic terms, they may suggest additional aspects of organization in memory. If associative strength was developed strictly on a frequency basis, as classic theory predicts, it is difficult to see how instructions to limit responses to particular categories could have such major effects on the type of response given. The result seems to imply that category organization has already been established and that the organism *actively* sorts inputs in different ways and does not simply respond on a *passive* basis, as classical asociation theory predicted.

A subtle indication that individuals often "know" more than their free associations indicate comes from some investigations of *associative commonality*. Commonality of associations refers to the tendency to report the most frequent or culturally popular response to stimuli in a word association task. The more popular responses an individual gives, the higher his commonality score. Traditional association theory would seem to predict that commonality score should be a straightforward reflection of an individual's prior verbal experiences. Yet when subjects are asked to report the culturally popular response in a word association task, their average commonality score is substantially higher than it is when they are asked to free associate to the stimulus words (cf. Jenkins, 1959; Horton, Marlowe, and Crowne, 1963).

Another method used to investigate the effects of instructional context in free recall is known as *incidental learning*. Various procedures have been employed in studies of incidental learning (cf. Postman, 1964), but the basic ingredient in all of them is that the *incidental learner* is required to perform some *orienting task* that directs his attention away from those aspects of the stimulus materials that the intentional learner is concentrating upon. As might be expected, the performance of the incidental learner is often inferior to that of the intentional learner. In a review of the incidental learning literature, however, Postman (1964) concludes that both incidental and intentional learning appear to be governed by the same principles, and except for purposes of convenience in referring to experiments where instructions are manipulated, there is little or no reason to maintain a distinction between the two situations.

Postman, Adams, and Bohm (1956) reported an investigation of recall and clustering using the incidental learning paradigm. Their subjects were shown a randomly arranged list of high-frequency associates and were then asked for free recall. The intentional learners were told to remember the words because their recall would be tested. In contrast, the incidental learners were told to rate each stimulus word as it was presented for frequency of usage in English. On the subsequent recall test the incidental group showed poorer overall recall but about the same level of clustering as the intentional group.

Findings such as those reported by Postman, Adams, and Bohm (1956) raise several questions concerning the influence of orienting tasks on the level and organization of subsequent recall. Among these questions are those relating to the effect of intention to learn on recall and organization. In a series of investigations Jenkins and his colleagues have shown that the answer to this and other questions depends to a great extent on the nature of the orienting task and the influence of this task on the way subjects process the stimulus materials. These experiments closely followed the procedure employed by Postman, Adams, and Bohm.

In the first investigation (Hyde and Jenkins, 1969) subjects were presented with a list of strong associates, taken from word association norms, and subsequently tested for free recall. One group of subjects was given the usual free-recall instructions. Three additional groups of subjects were given different orienting tasks during input and were also asked for free recall of the stimulus words. In one orienting task the subjects were asked to indicate whether or not each stimulus word contained the letter

E as it was being read aloud. A second orienting task involved estimating
the number of letters in each word, and in the third task each word was
rated for "pleasant-unpleasant." Half of the subjects given each orienting
task were also told that the stimulus words were to be recalled later,
whereas the other half received only the appropriate instructions for the
orienting task.

The main results of this investigation are shown in Table 8.1. It can
be seen that levels of word recall and clustering are comparable for those

Table 8.1   Mean words recalled and percentage of clustering for various incidental
learning conditions and an intentional learning condition.

Conditions	Mean Words Recalled	Percentage of Clustering
Incidental Instructions		
Pleasantness rating	16.3	67.5
E checking	9.4	26.3
Number of letters	9.9	30.9
Incidental and Recall Instructions		
Pleasantness rating	16.6	71.5
E checking	10.4	41.7
Number of letters	12.4	40.3
Intentional Instructions	16.1	63.7

(AFTER HYDE AND JENKINS, 1969.)

subjects given standard intentional instructions and for those performing
the pleasantness rating. However, both total recall and clustering in these
groups were superior to the performance of subjects engaged in estimating
number of letters or *E* checking. In two other experiments, also reported by
Hyde and Jenkins (1969), essentially the same pattern of results was found.

The findings reported by Hyde and Jenkins support Postman's (1964)
contention that the incidental-intentional dimension is not of critical importance in determining learning and retention. What these findings also
suggest is that the semantic character of the orienting task is of major
importance. Subjects required to process each word they heard as an
orthographic object consisting of a string of letters showed poor recall and
little clustering. But when the orienting task requires the subject to process
the meaning of the stimulus word, as when rating each word for pleasantness, both recall and clustering are comparable with the performance of
intentional learners. Notice also that the addition of recall instructions,
when subjects are performing the semantic task, has little effect on recall
and clustering. This observation further strengthens the view that intention
to learn, by itself, accomplishes very little. Rather it is what the subject
does with the inputs that is of major importance. These findings also sup-

port the position that holds that organization of output depends mainly on the way materials are organized during input and not on retrieval processes active at the time of recall.

In subsequent experiments Jenkins and his colleagues (cf. Jenkins, 1974) have shown that various orienting tasks lead to levels of recall and clustering comparable with those of intentional learners. These tasks include writing relevant adjectives for noun stimuli and vice versa, estimating frequency of usage for words, and rating words on a dimension of activity versus passivity. Presumably these tasks all engage semantic processes in one way or another. Tasks that lead to lower recall and less clustering include writing words that rhyme with the stimulus words, counting the number of syllables in a word, indicating the part of speech (i.e., noun, verb, etc.), and indicating whether a word was produced by a male or a female voice. These tasks do not require subjects to process the semantic content of the stimulus words.

All of these investigations of clustering in free recall provide one source of information about organization in memory. A second source of such information comes from studies of subjective organization. Let us now examine these investigations and the theoretical issues that arise in the context of subjective organization.

Subjective Organization

Studies of clustering in free recall usually involve a single presentation of items related in known ways. As a result, clustering measures reflect only the organization being looked for by the experimenter and not alternative means of organization that may be imposed by the subject. In addition, the single-trial procedure characteristic of clustering studies limits their implications for learning as opposed to memory. This limitation occurs because the index of learning (number of items recalled) is the same as the index of memory.

One way of avoiding some of the limitations imposed by the typical clustering task involves presenting a list of unrelated items for many trials, with free recall of the items required following each presentation. Tulving (1962) adopted such a procedure for investigating the form of secondary organization which he termed subjective organization (SO). Actually the abbreviation *SO* refers to the technique Tulving developed for measuring the degree of organization imposed by a subject on a list of to-be-recalled items. Several other procedures have been developed for the assessment of these subjectively organized units as well (cf. Shuell, 1969).

Two of the more widely cited indices of subjective organization are the SO measure developed by Tulving and the measure of intertrial repetitions (ITR) introduced by Bousfield, Puff, and Cowan (1964). We need not go into the computational procedures involved in these measures beyond noting that both reflect consistency of output order across successive trials of free recall. The greater the consistency of output order on successive trials, the greater the degree of subjective organization. The result of a typical experiment showing the relationship between SO and number of trials is given in Figure 8.3.

Consistency of output orders in such experiments is usually measured in terms of pairs of items, although the measurement principles can easily be extended to larger groups of items (cf. Tulving, 1962). In addition, the use of the multitrial task also makes it possible to disentangle learning from memory. In this situation, *memory* refers to what is retained on a given trial, whereas *learning* refers to changes in recall over successive trials.

Units of Subjective Organization.   The measured units in clustering studies are those defined by the experimenter, and those assessed in studies of subjective organization are subject defined. Tulving (1968) refers to

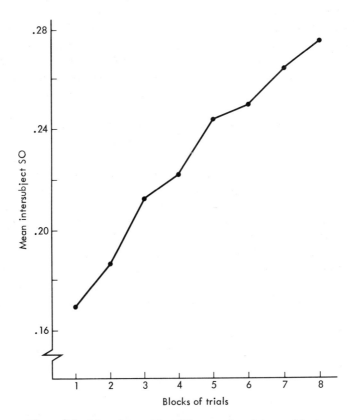

Figure 8.3   Mean intersubject SO scores for sixteen subjects on eight successive blocks of two trials.
(From Tulving, 1962.)

these units as E-units and S-units, respectively. His view is that S-units do not always correspond to E-units, although particular E-units are often perceived and remembered as parts of higher-order S-units. This distinction is quite similar to the one drawn between nominal and functional stimuli (Underwood, 1963).

Tulving defines an S-unit as a subset consisting of two or more items, each of which is more likely to be recalled adjacent to other items from that subset than adjacent to items from another subset. Even with lists of relatively unrelated items, subjects have little difficulty forming such S-units, although some make more sense, after the fact, than others. For instance, Tulving reports groupings such as *warship, massacre,* and *shrapnel* or *jewel* and *jelly* as illustrations of sensible S-units. Less sensible units are represented by groupings such as *conquest, ornament,* and *demand* or *spoon* and *chimney.*

Associative and Organizational Explanations. Performance over trials in free recall of unrelated words is characterized both by an increase in the number of items recalled and by an increase in SO. The theoretical question of interest here is how to explain these observations. Notice that the two performance measures are logically independent in the multitrial situation. In principle, an increase in items recalled *could* occur without an increase in organization, or we *could* have greater organization in the absence of increased recall.

Association theory would appear to offer quite straightforward explanations for both the increase in items recalled and the increase in organization. Recall of items should increase as a function of their frequency of occurrence. Such a prediction would follow from either of two associative principles. According to the spew hypothesis, the availability of an item should increase with increases in item frequency. As items become more available, they are more likely to be recalled. A second principle leading to the same prediction is that of the "contextual" association. Applied to the free-recall situation, the prediction is that increases in frequency of occurrence of list items serve to strengthen associative connections between the items and the general experimental context in which they occur. This too should lead to increased item recall as the same experimental context is reintroduced on successive trials.

When we turn to the question of increased organization over trials, the predictions derived from association theory are somewhat more complicated. Traditionally, association theory has emphasized the importance of contiguity of inputs. In the free-recall situation, however, input order is altered on each succeeding trial so that contiguity among particular items no longer exists. In more contemporary analyses, associative models have tended to emphasize the role of input contiguity in a more conceptual sense. This has led to an emphasis upon mediators where the critical contiguity relation is between observed events and implicit mediators. An explanation emphasizing just such a process has often been used to explain category clustering. In this case the category label, which is never presented, serves as the basis for organization. Another associative explanation for increased organization over trials comes from the work of Deese (1959, 1961). His position is that interitem associative strength develops over trials and serves to produce the organization observed in recall. Thus associative principles can be used to explain organized groupings among items even when input contiguity relations change from trial to trial (cf. Postman, 1971).

As an alternative to more strictly associative explanations, Tulving (1962, 1968) prefers to view the observed increases in item recall as a direct reflection of increased organization. His position is based on Miller's (1956) notion that information-processing capacity in immediate memory is decidedly limited. Tulving suggests that only a limited number of S-units can be recalled on each of the successive trials of free recall. Therefore the learning curve indicating increases in item recall over trials necessarily reflects increases in the size of S-units. The mechanism for increasing the size of S-units could well be in the form of interitem associations, as Tulving (1968) seems to imply. This explanation, however, places little emphasis on traditional associative principles such as frequency and contiguity. Instead, the emphasis is on a developing organization, however the organization comes about. Even intrusions of items not on the input list are seen as reflecting the organization. Tulving suggests that such intrusions at the time of recall represent responses made to list items at the time of storage. These intrusions admittedly fail to correspond to items on the experimenter's tally sheet, but they do represent "ideas" remembered from earlier parts of the experiment.

Effects of Input Frequency on Item Recall. Association theorists usually explain increases in item recall over trials in terms of either the spew hypothesis or the development of contextual associations. In contrast, Tulving's organizational explanation says that item recall increases as a function of increasing organization. Let us consider the results of several experiments that have a bearing on this issue.

Murdock and Babick (1961) measured the probability of recalling a single word on successive trials of free recall. The critical word, which was the same word on each trial, was always presented within the context of new words. Since the context changed on each trial, no interitem associations could be developed. However, the repeated occurrences of the critical item should lead to increased item availability in terms of "spew" and to a stronger association between the item and the general experimental context.

The results of this experiment, contrary to associative expectations, showed that the probability of recall of the repeated item remained constant over trials.

Studies reported by Mechanic (1964) and by Glanzer and Meinzer (1967) compared performance of subjects instructed to repeat items over and over again with performance of other subjects who were free to do what they wished during the interval between items. In both experiments recall was superior for subjects left to their own devices when trying to remember the items. Such observations seriously question the importance of item frequency per se and suggest that the critical factor is what subjects do with the inputs when they are trying to remember them. Whether or not semantic processing of the sort emphasized by Hyde and Jenkins (1969) is critical in this case is not clear. Some evidence suggests that repeating an item over and over again may alter its semantic interpretation (cf. Lambert and Jakobovitz, 1961).

Other evidence that is contrary to the usual frequency interpretation of increased item recall comes from an investigation reported by Battig, Allen, and Jensen (1965). In three experiments involving multitrial free recall, they report that newly learned items tend to be recalled earlier during output than items that were correctly recalled on previous trials. Some of their findings are shown in Figure 8.4. The investigators suggest that this observation may reflect an active "strategy" developed by the subjects which leads them to pay increased attention to previously unlearned items.

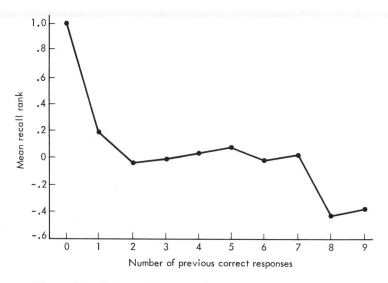

Figure 8.4   Mean recall rank for all items as a function of the number of previous correct recalls.
(After Battig, Allen, and Jensen, 1965.)

Alternative explanations are also possible, but the main implication is that input frequency does not automatically determine order of output.

Some evidence that suggests that organization is a more important determiner of output than is input frequency comes from work reported by Mandler (1967; Mandler and Pearlstone, 1966). The experimental situation, in this case, was not one involving multiple recalls. Instead, the subjects were asked to sort from fifty-two to one hundred "unrelated" words into categories of their own choice. The same words were sorted over and over again until the subjects achieved a criterion of two successive identical sorts. At this point most subjects were using from two to seven different categories. The subjects then were asked to recall as many of the words as they could.

The results of this investigation showed that amount recalled and degree of clustering (defined in terms of the subject-defined categories) increased as a function of the number of categories employed in sorting. Contrary to frequency predictions, these relationships were not affected by the number of sorting trials required to reach criterion. Tulving (1968) interpreted these findings as further evidence that recall is not determined by input frequency, but rather by the number of higher-order units into which the inputs have been organized.

Contiguity Effects and Item Recall. Association theory can be used to predict item recall and organization even when input contiguity relations among the items change from trial to trial. It is also clear, however, that when item contiguity is maintained over successive trials, both item recall and organization should be facilitated. This prediction was tested in a study by Waugh (1961). She compared multitrial free recall of words that were presented in either a fixed order or a variable order on successive trials. Her findings are given in Figure 8.5. The results show virtually identical performance in terms of item recall over successive trials for the two conditions. This observation suggests that immediate contiguity of input items is of little importance as a determiner of total recall in a free-learning situation. This does not mean that the contiguity relations did not influence item organization, only that they did not facilitate total recall.

Postman (1971) has reported a series of experiments that suggest that associative explanations of item organization may apply equally well to paired-associate and free-recall tasks. In one experiment subjects were asked to learn a free-recall list of twenty items followed by a paired-associate task consisting of the same twenty items (ten pairs). In another part of the experiment the order of the tasks was reversed, with the paired-associate task coming first.

When transfer from the free-recall to the paired-associate task was investigated, substantial negative transfer was observed. The opposite transfer effect was found when the task order was reversed. According to Post-

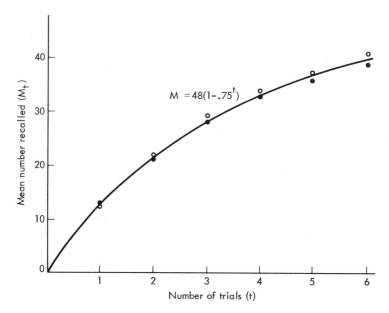

Figure 8.5 **Mean number of words recalled as a function of the number of trials under fixed order (open circles) and variable order (solid circles).**
(After Waugh, 1961.)

man, both outcomes are consistent with an associative view of organization. When the free-recall task comes first, it is unlikely that the organization of items will be the same as the organization required in paired-associate learning, and negative transfer will result. Alternatively, when the paired-associate task is first, the acquired pairwise associations can be expected to facilitate subsequent learning in free recall.

Although results such as those reported by Postman (1971) are consistent with associative expectations, the findings in other transfer studies are less supportive of association theory. Tulving (1966; Tulving and Osler, 1967) has reported studies in which subjects learn two lists in succession by the free-recall method. For some subjects the first list consisted of a subset of items from the second list; for other subjects the second list consisted of a subset from the first list. Compared with control subjects who learned two unrelated lists, both of these conditions produced negative transfer.

From an associative viewpoint it is not surprising to find negative transfer when going from the longer list to the shorter list. In this case, associations between items developed during first-list learning could easily disrupt second-list learning because some of the associates would no longer be on the list. When the shorter list is learned first, however, it is less clear why the associations strengthened during first-list learning would not lead to positive transfer. The implication, in both cases, seems to be that subjects actively adopt an organization for the whole list which is different from that for the sublist, and competition of some sort between the organizational schemes produces negative transfer for whichever list is learned second.

In the preceding sections we have considered several aspects of organization in memory. For the most part, our discussion has focused on the phenomena of clustering and subjective organization in free recall. In both situations some evidence for association models as well as more cognitive models of memory organization has been reported. The study of organization in memory, however, has not been restricted to the study of free recall or to the concepts developed in the free-recall situation. Therefore we now turn to a general consideration of memory codes, memory structures, and organization in memory which has been largely developed outside of the clustering and subjective organization tasks.

CODING AND ORGANIZATION

The concept of *coding,* as well as the concepts of recoding and encoding, generally refers to a process by which individuals transform stimulus inputs and store the results of the transformations in memory. During our discussion of secondary organization in free recall we frequently referred to coding in terms of the extraction of semantic information, and we noted that a subject's use of such semantic codes often facilitated both the learning and the retention of stimulus information. The concepts of code and coding can of course be employed in more diverse ways, and we shall examine some of these alternatives in the following sections.

The Nature of Codes

One of the more complex issues that arises in any discussion of coding is the specifying of what is meant by a memory code. As Deese and Hulse (1967) point out, one of the basic facts about human behavior is that it is inventive. Humans observe rules in nature, and they use rules in organizing what they know. Nowhere is this seen more clearly than in memory codes—both those employed by individuals in everyday situations and those developed by psychologists who study human memory.

The basis for much of the present interest in coding is to be found in Miller's (1956) work (see Chapters 6 and 7). It will be recalled that Miller was concerned with operations by which stimulus inputs could be coded or recoded to form higher-order units called *chunks.* The objective of these coding operations was to circumvent the capacity limitations otherwise imposed on the information-processing system. Although Miller's views provided a foundation for much of the subsequent theorizing about coding, he dealt with the nature of memory codes mostly by example.

In the period since Miller's work first appeared, many psychologists have invoked the concept of coding in discussions of memory. In Chapter 6 we examined several types of memory code ranging from acoustic codes, which seem to play an important role in short-term memory, to the semantic codes of long-term memory. Posner and Warren (1972) reviewed various studies concerned with coding, and they suggest that there is evidence for at least three different types of code which may result from perception of a single stimulus. Let us examine these types in some detail.

Consider a situation in which the stimulus input consists of a word such as *plant*. One type of code resulting from the perception of this word, presented either in an auditory or in a visual manner, is a memory trace that preserves the individual character of the experience. Posner and Warren refer to this trace as a *physical code*. The information contained in the physical code includes the particular acoustic or visual details of structure that characterized stimulus presentation. They also suggest that this system of codes underlies our limited ability to recognize and recreate the detailed structure of our own prior experiences.

When a world like *plant* has been presented, the physical code is rapidly followed by what Posner and Warren call the *name code*. This code consists of the name of the stimulus word and the names of related words. The name code is independent of the mode of stimulus presentation and of idiosyncrasies in form of presentation which are represented in the physical code. That is, the name code remains the same irrespective of differences in the physical code that result from variations in presentation, such as the use of different typefaces for visual stimuli or different voices for auditory stimuli.

Morton (1969) has suggested a similar type of code for word recognition. In his system the memory units related to recognition of a word are called *logogens*. The term is derived from *logos* ("word") and *genus* ("birth"). Logogen units may be thought of as concepts that can be activated by a variety of inputs that differ in physical character. Such concepts provide a system for storing the general character of past experience in memory. The nature of past experience serves to organize these logogens in such a way, for example, that different forms of the same word or different views of the same human face can be recognized despite differences in the physical code. In this way, logogens represent integrated concepts derived from prior experiences.

In their discussion of coding Posner and Warren (1972) take issue with the traditional assumption that we must consciously attend to an input before it comes in contact with information in long-term memory. This assumption implies that long-term memory structures are activated only through conscious effort. Their view is that information in long-term memory automatically imposes a structure upon stimulus inputs and determines, to an important degree, what will be perceived. In support of this view, Posner and Warren cite evidence to indicate that a word is perceived as a whole because it already exists as a unit in long-term memory (cf. Reicher, 1969; Krueger, 1970). These alternative viewpoints are illustrated in Figure 8.6.

The third type of memory code distinguished by Posner and Warren is based on *conscious constructions* on the part of the individual experiencing the stimulus input. Codes of this type result from active, conscious operations being performed upon stimulus inputs, and they are not the result of the automatic processes that give rise to physical codes or name codes. Examples of such conscious operations include those involved in rehearsal and the development of mediators. Codes resulting from conscious processing are seen as being more varied than those more closely dependent upon prior learning. Since codes of this type involve conscious processing, however, they are restricted by the limited capacity of the processing system. For example, when imposing a serial ordering code on a list of items, only a limited number of such items can be handled at one time. According to Posner and Warren, each conscious operation uses some portion of the available limited capacity. As a result, such coding operations are seen as being subject to rather strict time constraints.

Posner and Warren suggest that those three types of codes provide

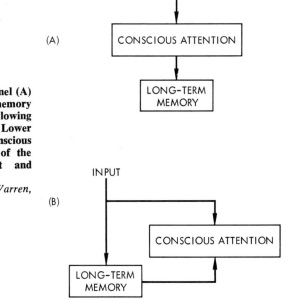

Figure 8.6 Upper panel (A) portrays long-term memory being activated following conscious attention. Lower panel (B) portrays conscious attention as a result of the interaction of input and long-term memory.
(After Posner and Warren, 1972.)

the basis for much of human memory. As they see it, each type of code corresponds to a memory system at a particular level. Codes at all three levels may result from the same stimulus input, although the development of codes at a given level does not obliterate those at other levels. Thus the coding system is seen as being essentially parallel.

This view of coding contrasts with those discussed in Chapter 6. For example, one view commonly held suggests that the physical code is only effective for a short time, as in short-term memory. After this period it is then replaced by some sort of semantic code that is relatively permanent. But some studies (cf. Posner, 1969) indicate that when a subject is shown a figure that looks like a particular letter(e.g., *A*), both the physical code and the name code remain in memory. Posner and Warren also note that if the physical code was only preserved for a short time, we should never be able to recognize such things as accent in speech. Such observations suggest that at least certain aspects of the physical code remain in memory for a long time.

Coding Operations

The view of coding offered by Posner and Warren (1972) suggests two general classes of coding operations. One class, which they identify with both physical and name codes, is relatively passive and automatic. Codes developed in this manner depend on the inherent organization of the information-processing system and on habits or sets acquired through past experience. The other class of coding operations is both active and conscious. Subject to capacity limitations, a variety of codes can be developed in this manner. Beyond these general considerations, Posner and Warren offer little in the way of specific comments about the operations used in coding.

Although psychologists have introduced a variety of coding operations (cf. Melton and Martin, 1972), most of these can be classified in terms of a limited number of categories. Bower (1972) has suggested four main types of coding operation: *stimulus selection, rewriting, componential description,* and *elaboration.* Let us consider each of these classes separately.

Coding by Stimulus Selection. This type of coding operation refers to the explicit selection by a subject of some component of a complex stimulus. The component selected is then used as the critical element of the complex. We saw several examples of this operation in our discussion of nominal and functional stimuli (see Chapter 4). Stimulus selection occurs in paired-associate learning when some aspect of the nominal stimulus, say the first letter of a trigram, is taken as the cue for responding. It also occurs in concept identification (see Chapter 12) when a particular stimulus dimension (e.g., color) or a given stimulus attribute (e.g., red) is selected for attention.

Coding by stimulus selection seems to occur in any of a variety of experimental situations so long as the stimuli presented to the subjects are capable of being fractionated into component parts. As the term is typically employed, stimulus selection implies a rather active, conscious decision on the part of the subject (cf. Richardson, 1972). According to Posner and Warren, this implies that the codes resulting from stimulus selection will be constrained by limitations on information-processing capacity. This might mean that the operation of stimulus selection would only be efficient when the number of nominal stimuli was quite limited.

Coding by Rewriting. According to Bower (1972), rewriting was the sense of coding used initially by Miller (1956) in his paper on the "Magical Number 7." The basic idea is that rewriting involves translating the input into another mode. The translation is then stored in memory and decoded at a later time to mediate recall of the original input. The example cited by Miller (1956) involved recoding binary digits into octal digits (see Chapter 7). A somewhat less obvious example, involving verbal codes for sequences of binary digits, was studied by Glanzer and Clark (1963). It was shown that a briefly presented binary sequence (e.g., 010101) was well remembered if it tended to arouse a short verbal description (e.g., "alternating zeros and ones").

As rewriting is discussed by Bower (1972), it also seems to involve an active, conscious operation on the part of the subject. As in stimulus selection, there is the implication of a capacity limit placed on codes produced in this way. Certainly the rewriting of binary digits into octal digits, which are subsequently decoded in binary form, cannot go on indefinitely. It should be noted, however, that rewriting systems have been suggested for natural language which apply quite generally, and seemingly without limit. We shall consider such systems in a subsequent chapter.

Coding by Componential Description. The essential nature of this coding operation is that the codes it produces consist of the attributes or features that characterize the stimulus inputs. According to this view, the set of features that constitutes a particular code results from a relatively complete analysis of the input. In the case of words, these features may be of both an acoustic and a semantic variety. Take the word *jam,* for example. Its semantic features may depend on whether the reference is to a traffic jam or strawberry jam and whether it is used as a noun or a verb. Its acoustic features may include the fact that it sounds like *ram, dam, ham,* and so on.

A number of psychologists have suggested forms of coding based on componential description. One of the earliest was an analysis of connotative meaning based on *semantic differential* ratings by Osgood, Suci, and Tannenbaum (1957). Their view was that the connotative meaning of inputs could be described in terms of their location on each of several dimensions, such as evaluation (good-bad), potency (strong-weak), and activity (fast-slow). The location of an input on each dimension constituted a feature, and the memory code consisted of the set of such features.

Similar views of coding have been offered by both Underwood (1969) and Wickens (1972). We considered the main characteristics of their views in Chapter 6. It will be recalled that Underwood suggested memory codes for verbal materials based on a collection of attributes. The attributes specified such things as location and modality of input, frequency of input, and relations among present and past inputs. Wickens's (1972) views are closely tied to his investigations of "release from proactive interference." He suggests a complete analysis of inputs with respect to a number of dimensions. If the memory codes for two items are similar, no "release from proactive interference" should occur. But if the memory codes are different, "release from proactive interference" should take place.

Contrary to the coding operations considered previously, coding by componential description seems to take place automatically. Of course it is at least partially dependent upon habits or sets developed through prior experience, but apparently there is no limit on the number of features that can be extracted from an input at a given time. Such an operation could be used to produce either the physical codes or the name codes discussed by Posner and Warren (1972).

Coding by Elaboration.   The fourth type of coding operation suggested by Bower (1972) is based on the assumption that inputs give rise to "associated operators" that transform the to-be-remembered units in a qualitative manner. For example, a nonsense item such as *pym* may be altered to make it into a word (e.g., payment). The idea here is that both the word and the transformation are stored in memory, and at the time of recall the word must be detransformed to recover the nonsense item (cf. Prytulak, 1971). A second illustration of elaboration coding is based on mental imagery. In this case the stimulus is replaced by a mental image which is then stored in memory. Presumably both the image and the stimulus have the same referent, so that decoding the image for recall is not difficult. This form of coding has been investigated by a number of individuals (cf. Paivio, 1969).

As Bower uses the term, elaboration coding is similar to coding by stimulus selection and rewriting in that it seems to require the use of active, conscious processes. This comes as no surprise, since coding by elaboration also involves the selection of a rewriting rule which must be stored in memory as part of the code. It may be the case, particularly with mental imagery, that the total process can become almost automatic with practice, but it still appears that the subject must in some sense decide to employ the imagery code. Thus, coding by elaboration appears to be constrained by the same capacity limitations that seem to apply to coding by stimulus selection and rewriting.

Types of Memory Code

We shall now consider three broad classes of memory code, each of which has stimulated both theoretical interest and experimental inquiry: *mental imagery, mnemonics,* and *relational structures.*

Mental Imagery. The concept of imagery has played an important role in accounts of memory for some time. Early Greek and Roman orators often used imagery to facilitate recall of memorized materials, and everyday experience suggests that imagery may be a powerful aid in recall. Professional memory experts also suggest elaborate forms of imagery as aids in recall (cf. Norman, 1969). Although early behaviorists such as Watson (1913) rejected imagery outright, the concept has been widely used in explaining various phenomena of memory. But only recently has imagery been subjected to serious experimental inquiry.

Paivio (1969) offered an explanation of the role of imagery in a number of associative tasks which he calls the *conceptual peg hypothesis.* Although the original use of this term did not refer to imagery (cf. Lambert and Paivio, 1956), it has been extended by Paivio to include imagery. The basic assumption is that the stimulus member of a to-be-associated pair serves as a "conceptual peg" for retrieval of a compound image consisting of images evoked by both the stimulus and response members of the pair. Once the compound image has been retrieved, recall of the response term follows in a fairly straightforward manner.

The conceptual peg hypothesis holds that the imagery value of both the stimulus and response terms contributes to the compound image. On test trials, however, when the stimulus term is presented alone, the image-arousing value of the stimulus becomes particularly important. Thus the hypothesis leads to the prediction that the imagery value of stimulus terms is more important than the imagery value of response terms. In the case of verbal materials, there is also the prediction that concrete words such as *house* will provide better conceptual pegs than abstract words such as *truth.* Concrete words are higher in image-arousing value, since they elicit images more readily.

Paivio (1965) tested these predictions in a paired-associate learning experiment. The task involved learning a list consisting of four pairs of each possible combination of concrete and abstract words. Ratings of imagery obtained from an independent group of subjects indicated that the concrete nouns used in the experiment (e.g., *house, pencil, woman*) elicited images more readily than the abstract nouns (e.g., *freedom, idea, truth*). Learning was limited to four trials to allow differences in pair difficulty to be revealed.

The results of this experiment are shown in Table 8.2. As the conceptual peg hypothesis predicted, learning was most rapid when both

Table 8.2 Average number of correct responses on four trials a function of concrete *(C)* or abstract *(A)* stimulus and response members.

CC	CA	AC	AA
11.41	10.01	7.36	6.05

(AFTER PAIVIO, 1965.)

members of a pair were concrete words and least rapid when they were abstract words. When the pairs consisted of one concrete and one abstract word, learning was best if the stimulus term was a concrete word. These findings support the notion that concrete words provide better conceptual pegs than do abstract words.

Paivio (1969) emphasizes that his concept of the effects of imagery as a memory code is based on nonverbal imagery. This is in contrast to verbal symbolic processes which may also be aroused by stimulus inputs and which also play a role in memory. In an effort to demonstrate the validity of his position, Paivio (1969) reviews a number of experiments in which the effects of *rated imagery* were compared with the effects of differences in the number of associates *(m)* given to an item. In general, the results of these studies suggest that imagery is the more important factor, although the importance of other verbal factors cannot be ruled out.

Bower (1970a) has also reported evidence indicating the importance of imagery in associative learning and has suggested that it is the relational structure of the entire image evoked by a pair, not the image of the stimulus alone, that is most critical. In one study (Bower, 1970b) subjects were asked to study word pairs according to one of three sets of instructions. One set of instructions emphasized learning by overt repetition of the pairs. Another set emphasized the use of separate images for each member of the pair, and the third set encouraged the subjects to imagine the objects denoted by the words interacting in some way. For example, an interactive image might consist of a "boat" shaped like a "shoe" as opposed to separate images of a "boat" and a "shoe."

The subjects in this experiment were given three lists of thirty pairs each for learning. Following each list, the thirty stimulus words were presented along with thirty distractors. The subject's task was to indicate whether or not each test word was from the list of pairs and, if he thought it was from the list, to recall the word paired with it. Accuracy in recognizing the prior stimulus words was high (85 percent) and did not differ with learning instructions. But correct recall of the response terms was much better for interaction instructions (53 percent) than it was for either overt repetition (30 percent) or separate image (27 percent) instructions. Bower suggests that these findings indicate the importance of relational organization in imagery, in contrast to stimulus coding. It is the relational structure of the total image, and not simply that both the stimulus and response terms are coded in the form of images, that seems to improve recall.

The experimental investigations of Paivio and Bower are representative of contemporary studies of mental imagery. They clearly reflect the renewed interest in imagery as a form of mental code. Further research will be needed to clarify the nature of images and their role as memory codes, but the study of imagery will undoubtedly continue to be important in considerations of both learning and memory.

Mnemonics.   Although experimental psychologists have only recently become interested in the study of mnemonics, the concept has long been linked to memory and to techniques for memorizing. Generally speaking, the term *mnemonics* refers to devices used in an attempt to relate material being learned to some previously learned organizational scheme. As Norman (1969) points out, early Greeks and Romans often used mnemonic devices as aids to memory. In modern times the closeness of the connection between mnemonics and memory can be seen in the observation that practicing memory experts are frequently called *mnemonists.*

Several well-known forms of mnemonic device are used by most of us. One of these is the rhyme mnemonic. Rhymes are effective memory devices when they are well constructed, because mistakes in the order of recall destroy the rhyme. Consider the rhyme many of us use to recall the number of days in each month of the year:

> Thirty days hath September, April, June, and November,
> All the rest have thirty-one, (etc.)

This rhyme establishes an organization that is easy to remember, even though recalling the days in certain months (e.g., December) is difficult without recalling the entire rhyme.

Rhyme mnemonics can be, and often are, combined with mental images to provide an aid to memory. Consider an attempt to memorize the order of a list of words beginning with *chair, boat, monkey,* and *snowman.* Here you might utilize a familiar pegword system such as one-bun, two-shoe, three-tree, and four-door. First, imagine a chair in a bun, a boat shaped like a shoe, a monkey swinging in a tree, and a glass door reflecting a snowman. Presumably you could then recall the list quite readily, with the number and its rhyme word providing an effective cue.

Norman (1969) attributes our ignorance of mnemonics to psychologists' tendency to regard such devices as clever uses of old knowledge, and not as sources of new information about memory. Mnemonics, however, are powerful retrieval schemes which provide a list of well-known cues and which often boost recall considerably. For this and other reasons, psychologists have become increasingly interested in mnemonic devices and the type of memory code they provide.

Among the mnemonic techniques found to be effective in memory are those based on grammatical relationships. Rohwer (1966) found that word pairs, in a paired-associate task, are better remembered when they are presented in the context of a linking sentence (e.g., the *cow* chased the *ball*) than when they are presented without the sentence context. Bobrow and Bower (1969) have extended this line of research to show that when the linking sentence is generated by the subject, recall is considerably better than when the experimenter provides the sentence context. These investigators suggest that the difference here arises because sentence comprehension is more reliable when the linking sentence is produced by the subjects. Presumably, when subjects are learning word pairs, they need not comprehend sentences presented to them in the same way as they comprehend sentences they produce themselves.

Several studies go into the reasons for the effectiveness of certain mnemonics. Bower and Bolton (1969) have shown that the effectiveness of rhymes in the paired-associate situation is due to the restriction in number of alternative responses from which the subject must choose the correct response. This was demonstrated in two ways. First, it was shown that rhymed pairs (e.g., *cat-hat*) were not easier to learn than pairs related through assonance rules (e.g., *bin-bit*). Second, it was found that when the number of response alternatives was equally restricted, through the use of multiple-choice tests, the advantage of rhymed pairs over unrhymed pairs disappeared.

Studies by both Earhard (1969) and Olton (1969) suggest that the effectiveness of mnemonics, at the time of retrieval, depends to a large extent on their use during storage. In the Earhard study, subjects were asked to use an alphabetic pegword system for recall of a list of words. It was found that the ability to use alphabetic cues as an aid to recall depended on whether instructions to use the alphabetic scheme were given before or after storage. The Olton study also showed poorer recall when mnemonic devices were only introduced after storage. These observations are consistent with others mentioned previously (cf. Tulving and Osler, 1968), which show that the effectiveness of retrieval cues at recall depends on their availability at the time of storage.

Relational Structures. A third class of memory codes is based on structural relations among input materials. The particular structural relations involved may be derived either from the past experience of individuals or from the nature of the input itself. This type of memory code was noted some years ago by Thorndike (1935) in his investigations of the principle of *belongingness.* He presented subjects with sentences like "John is a baker." "Bill is a plumber." "George is a doctor." Despite the temporal contiguity between words such as *baker-Bill* or *plumber-George,* he observed no tendency for contiguity to override the structural relations derived from the subject's prior knowledge of sentence organization.

Bower (1970c) discusses two investigations in which the critical structural relations are derived from the nature of the input organization. In one investigation (Bower and Winzenz, 1969) both recognition and recall of digits were studied. In the recognition experiment five-place numbers were read to the subject as digit groups. For example, a number like 17348 might be read as "seventeen, three hundred forty-eight" or as "one hundred seventy-three, forty-eight." Each five-place number occurred a second time either with the same grouping as in the first presentation or with a different grouping. The subject's task was to indicate whether or not the same sequence of digits (i.e., 17348) had occurred before. As the results in Figure 8.7 indicate, recognition was much poorer when the group

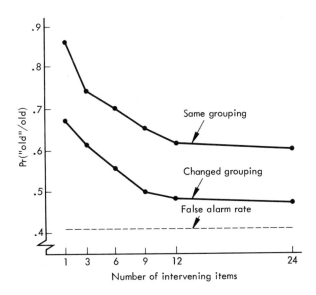

Figure 8.7 Recognition probability related to the number of intervening items for items repeated with the same or a different grouping.
(After Bower and Winzenz, 1969.)

structure changed. Similar findings were also obtained in a learning task where group structure of a digit sequence was either altered or unchanged across successive trials.

Bower, Lesgold, and Tieman (1969) have demonstrated similar disruptive effects of changing relational structures in free recall of words. In this experiment subjects were shown twenty-four unrelated nouns presented as six groups of four words. For example, on the first trial a given group might consist of the words *dog, bicycle, cigar,* and *hat.* The subjects were told to integrate the four words by imagining a scene in which the objects designated by the words were interacting. Bower (1970c) uses the illustration of a *dog* wearing a *hat,* and smoking a *cigar* while riding a *bicycle.* The critical manipulation occurred on the second and third trials of free recall where the word groupings either remained the same or were altered. The results indicated that changing the word grouping on successive trials appreciably lowered recall even though the same twenty-four words appeared on each trial.

An illustration of the influence of structural relations derived both from input relations and from prior knowledge of the subjects was provided by Bower, Clark, Winzenz, and Lesgold (1969). In one of their experiments, half of the subjects concurrently learned four 28-word conceptual hierarchies or trees of the kind shown in Figure 8.8. Each hierarchy was shown in a single presentation. As a control condition, the remaining subjects were shown four comparable 28-word spatial trees, but the words assigned to each tree were chosen randomly from the four conceptual

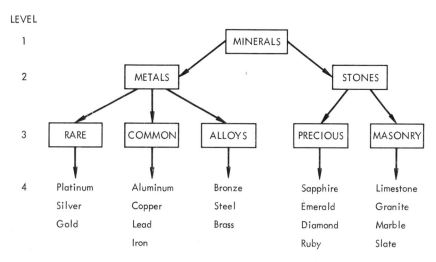

Figure 8.8   Example of a conceptual hierarchy of words.
(After Bower, Clark, Winzenz, and Lesgold, 1969.)

hierarchies. That is, although all subjects were shown the same 112 words, only the spatial trees presented to the experimental subjects made sense conceptually.

The results of this experiment, for four trials of free recall, are given in Figure 8.9. It is clear that recall is much better when the words are

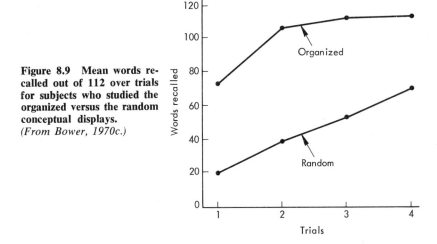

**Figure 8.9 Mean words re-
called out of 112 over trials
for subjects who studied the
organized versus the random
conceptual displays.**
(From Bower, 1970c.)

organized in the form of conceptual hierarchies. Examination of individual recall records also revealed some interesting observations. The recall of experimental subjects was entirely clustered in terms of conceptual hierarchies. In more than 90 percent of the cases where both a superordinate word and some of its subordinate words were recalled, the superordinate was recalled first. Thus, recall tended to be organized from the top to the bottom of each hierarchy. In addition, the probability of a given word's being recalled (e.g., *marble*) was much higher if its superordinate was recalled (e.g., *masonry*). When a given superordinate was not recalled, the words below it in the tree were not recalled. Relationships of this type were almost totally absent in the recall of control subjects.

Many aspects of coding evidently require some portion of the limited processing capacity available to the organism. This seemed to be the case for at least three of the four coding operations considered as well as for the memory codes based on imagery, mnemonics, and relational structure. Once an input has been coded, however, it is apparently stored in a memory system that is relatively free of capacity constraints. That is, once memory codes are established, they are stored in the long-term memory system which is characterized by a relatively unlimited capacity.

MEMORY STRUCTURE AND ORGANIZATION

When we turn to the question of how memory codes are organized, we find a number of suggested alternatives. Some of these alternatives were motivated mainly by a consideration of experimental findings; others have been directly influenced by developments in computer science and artificial intelligence. Among the latter we find computer models of such apparently diverse phenomena as information retrieval, understanding natural language, and problem solving (cf. Frijda, 1972).

Despite the considerable diversity of goals, the feature common to these models is that they include some reference to long-term semantic memory. These models all attempt to characterize certain aspects of memory organization in terms of semantic information which remains relatively stable over time. Models of this sort, particularly those involving computer programs, tend to be quite complex and often go well beyond existing sources of experimental evidence. We shall illustrate the general form of such models with two examples. Let us begin the discussion by examining various forms of hierarchical structure that are often found in models of organized memory.

Hierarchical Structures in Memory

The notion that memory can be organized in terms of hierarchies is not especially new in psychology. Hull (1934) suggested that alternative responses to a particular stimulus might be organized in the form of a *habit-family hierarchy*. In such a hierarchy, each response is ordered in terms of associative strength, with the strongest associate being most likely to occur, then the next strongest associate, and so on down the hierarchy. The concept of a habit-family hierarchy has been used to explain the observed rank order of responses found in word association norms and the difference in frequency with which category labels elicit category instances in a clustering situation. But such associationistic concepts, based as they are on the frequency of prior stimulus-response contiguities, have definite limitations in explaining many aspects of organization in memory.

In our discussion of category clustering, it was noted that Bousfield (1953) suggested a form of hierarchical organization that was not based on associative concepts. His view was that of a superordinate structure in which category instances (subordinates) were organized in terms of category labels (superordinates). Deese (1968) points out that Bousfield was correct in his rejection of contiguous associations as the basis for memory organization, even though the alternative he proposed was too elementary to describe the observed complexities of memory.

A hierarchical system that incorporates Bousfield's principle of organization, as well as Miller's (1956) notion of a limited processing capacity, has been proposed by Mandler (1968). The units of this system, at the theoretical level, are thought to be word equivalents similar to what Morton (1969) calls logogens. As can be seen in Figure 8.10, each level of the organization has a limit of five units.

Starting at the top of the diagram, we have a single superordinate category which serves as the name for the entire hierarchy. From this point we proceed down the hierarchy through the five categories at each level. The numbers shown on the right-hand side of the figure indicate that even such a simple schema as this can accommodate 3,125 units. In addition, there is no reason why units occurring in one hierarchical organization cannot also appear in other organizations. For example, the word *table* may appear in one organization as an item of furniture, in another as a way of presenting information, and in still another with reference to "tabling a motion."

The hierarchical concepts of memory organization proposed by both Bousfield and Mandler are closely tied to the types of organization seen in free recall. Alternative concepts of hierarchical organization, however, have been based on computer models such as Quillian's (1969) *Teachable Language Comprehender*. This model attempts to deal with a wide variety of human knowledge, including language, although we shall restrict our attention to memory for words and concepts. The basic elements of the model are *units, properties,* and *relations.* Each unit is stored in memory along with the set of properties that represents its meaning. Both units and properties are organized in a hierarchical structure that includes both subordinate and superordinate relations. These features of the model are illustrated in Figure 8.11.

It can be seen that a subordinate unit, such as *canary,* is stored below the superordinate *bird* but at the same level as *ostrich.* In turn, units like *bird* and *fish* are stored below the superordinate *animal.* Each unit in the hierarchy is represented as a node consisting of a set of properties. For example, *canary* is the name of a node with the properties "can sing" and "is yellow." Notice that properties characteristic of nodes that are above *canary,* such as *bird* or *animal,* need not be represented with *canary.* This notion of storing properties at a higher level in the hierarchy when they do not uniquely specify a particular concept has been called *cognitive economy* in memory storage. When a particular subordinate (e.g., *ostrich*) fails to manifest a property generally characteristic of its superordinate (e.g., "can fly"), this exception must be indicated at the subordinate level.

Collins and Quillian (1969) attempted to test the validity of this model in a human memory situation. The experimental task consisted of presenting a series of sentences that were to be judged as being true or false. As each sentence was presented, the subject pressed an appropriate

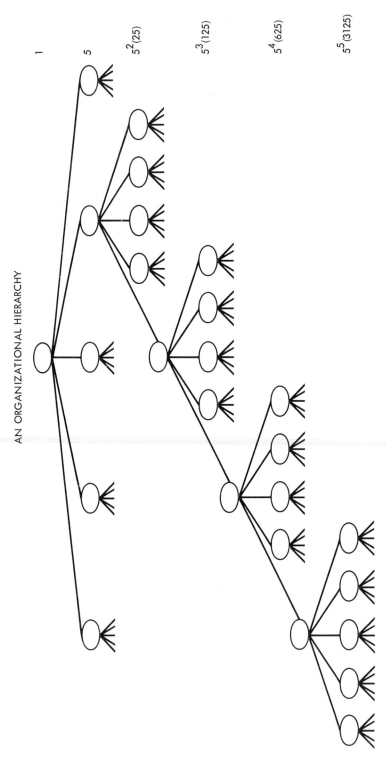

AN ORGANIZATIONAL HIERARCHY

1

5

5^2 (25)

5^3 (125)

5^4 (625)

5^5 (3125)

Figure 8.10 Schematic model of a single organizational hierarchy with five units per category, five categories per level, and five levels. (*After Mandler, 1968.*)

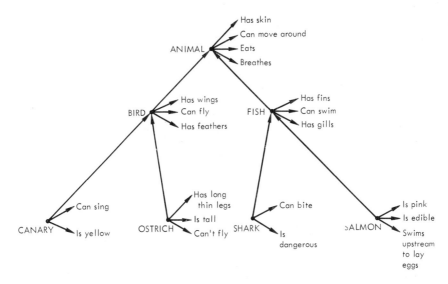

Figure 8.11 Illustration of the hypothetical memory structure for a three-level hierarchy.
(From Collins and Quillian, 1969.)

button to indicate truth or falsity, and reaction time was measured from sentence onset to button press. Each sentence was presented for two seconds followed by a blank interval of two seconds before the next sentence appeared.

To test the model, Collins and Quillian made several additional assumptions about memory search and retrieval. The most basic of these was that it takes time both to retrieve a property from a given node and to move from one node to another. But it takes no longer to retrieve properties stored at one node than it does to retrieve properties stored at any other node. Therefore the model predicts that differences in the time taken to evaluate the truth or falsity of various statements will be due to the time taken to move from one node to another. For example, it should take longer to decide that "a canary can fly" than it does to decide that "a canary can sing" because the information about flying is not stored at the *canary* node but at the superordinate node, *bird*. Similarly, it should take even longer to decide that "a canary has skin."

The results of the Collins and Quillian (1969) study are presented in Figure 8.12. As the model predicts, the time taken to respond to true sentences depends on the level in the hierarchy at which the properties are stored. That is, it does take longer to respond to "a canary can fly" than to "a canary can sing." In general, the results shown in Figure 8.12 are consistent with the view that the time required to move to each successive node in the hierarchy (e.g., P0, P1, P2) is a constant. Perfect confirmation

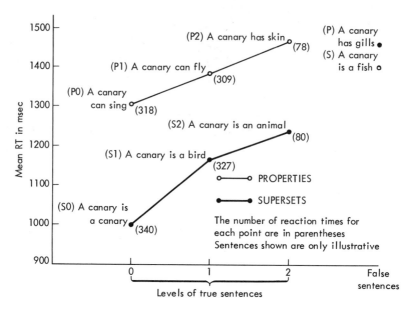

Figure 8.12   Average reaction times for different types of sentences in three experiments.
(From Collins and Quillian, 1969.)

of such a constant would require the two lines to be exactly parallel. Also notice that the distance between adjacent points along a particular line is generally smaller than the distance between lines. This observation suggests that it takes longer to retrieve a property from a particular node than it takes to go from that node to the next higher node. For example it takes about 200 msec. longer to respond to "a canary can fly" once the bird node (e.g., "a canary is a bird") has been reached (P1–S1), but it takes less than 100 msec. to move from the *bird* node (S1) to the *animal* node (S2).

The results for false sentences in the Collins and Quillian study are difficult to evaluate, and they have few implications concerning the basic form of organization. The problem here is to decide how search and retrieval works for false sentences and not whether information in memory is organized hierarchically. Collins and Quillian considered several alternative possibilities but found little support for any of them.

Collins and Quillian's findings that memory may be organized in a hierarchical manner have been confirmed in other investigations (cf. Collins and Quillian, 1970; Conrad, 1972). There does seem to be some question concerning their assumption of *cognitive economy* in memory storage. The issue here is whether properties that do not uniquely define a word or a concept are stored only at a higher level in the hierarchy (cf. Conrad,

1972). Further research will be needed to resolve this issue. Let us now turn to more general models of organized memory, many of which are based on hierarchical relations similar to those proposed by Collins and Quillian.

A Computer Simulation Approach

One approach to the study of organized memory involves trying to write a computer program to simulate relevant aspects of human behavior. Many such programs or models have been proposed (cf. Frijda, 1972), and we shall briefly examine some of the characteristics of one model in order to illustrate the approach. The model we have chosen is one proposed by Rumelhart, Lindsay, and Norman (1972). In many respects this model is more comprehensive than most others based on the computer simulation approach.

Basic Ideas. The name of Rumelhart, Lindsay, and Norman's program, *Elinor,* is derived from pronouncing the first letters of the authors' last names in the order LNR. The basic building blocks in this memory model are concepts and relations, as in the Quillian (1969) model. Concepts are represented as nodes in the system which are connected by *labeled relations.* For example, in (1) the nodes A and B are shown in relationship R:

$$(1) \quad B \xrightarrow{\quad R \quad} A$$

Note that the arrowhead only serves to define the direction in which the relation applies. If R indicates a *superset* relation (i.e., A is a superset of B), then R-inverse indicates that B is a *subset* of A. In addition, any number of relations can originate from or end at a single node.

Three classes of information are represented in *Elinor's* memory system: *concepts, events,* and *episodes.* Each class consists of nodes and relations that serve to interconnect the nodes. Concepts refer to particular ideas, and three types of functional relations are of primary importance here. One of these, the *isa* relation, defines set membership (e.g., *John isa person; dog isa animal*). That is, the *isa* relation indicates a class to which a concept belongs. In this way, hierarchical structures can be built up. To specify a subset or exemplar relation, the inverse of *isa* may be used (e.g., *animal isa-inverse dog*).

The other types of functional relations, indicated by *is* and *has,* are used to define property relations. The *has* relation is used for objects (e.g., *animal has feet*), and the *is* relation is used for qualities (e.g., *John is fat*). Although these three functional relations are not exhaustive, they do pro-

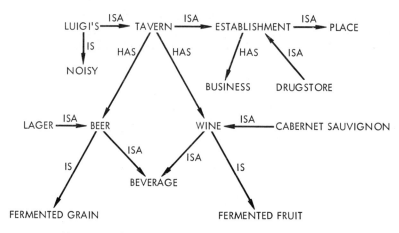

Figure 8.13 Illustration of the use of three types of functional relations.
(After Rumelhart et al., 1972.)

vide for much of the definitional information required by the memory system. Figure 8.13 illustrates the use of these functional relations.

In *Elinor*'s memory system an *event* is represented in terms of an action sequence centered around the verb node, with qualifying relationships connecting to other nodes. The representation for an event such as "The rock rolled down the mountain" is shown in Figure 8.14. "Roll" is

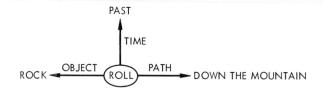

Figure 8.14 Illustration of an event.
(After Rumelhart et al., 1972.)

the action, "rock" is the object, "down the mountain" specifies the path of the action, and *time* is in the past. As we shall see in Chapter 11, this integrative character of memory may turn out to be very important.

Whereas an event is represented in *Elinor's* memory in terms of a single action, however complex, an *episode* represents a cluster of events or actions. Relations between events are indexed by connectives like *while* and *then*. The connective *then* indicates temporal order and *while* connects events with unspecified temporal order, although such events are more or less simultaneous in many instances. An illustration of the use of *while* and *then* in a memory representation of an episode is shown in Figure 8.15.

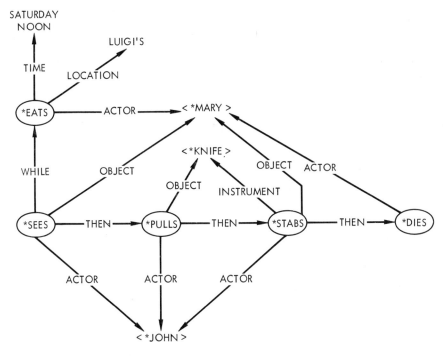

Figure 8.15   Illustration of an episode.
(After Rumelhart et al., 1972.)

Evaluation.   The model proposed by Rumelhart, Lindsay, and Norman represents an attempt to describe ways in which a wide range of
information might be stored in long-term memory. It should be clear,
even from the few basic features discussed here, that *Elinor* is capable of
coding input information into a variety of memory structures which would
be quite useful in many cognitive tasks. It seems likely that information
must be coded in ways similar to this for long-term memory to display
many of the characteristics we observe. *Elinor* accomplishes this complex
task with relatively few types of relations. That is, *Elinor* constitutes an
efficient memory system of considerable scope. Several major weaknesses
in *Elinor* are often characteristic of computer simulation models, however.

The major weakness of the *Elinor* system is the dearth of experimental
evidence to support the model, and in its present form, little evidence will
be forthcoming. The problem can be illustrated in two ways. First, the rules
of the model do not describe the psychological processes by which new
memory structures are acquired. There is no specification of which particular inputs serve to activate which particular rules. The result is that
Elinor provides a comprehensive and interesting picture of the structures

that *might* exist in memory but not of the way these structures come into existence.

The second difficulty concerns *Elinor*'s procedures for memory search and retrieval from memory. Some of these procedures would be required by any computer model in order to carry out the simulation, but most such procedures are not psychologically relevant. Therefore the model does not contain many of the psychologically important factors needed to predict experimental outcomes in any but the most general ways. Rumelhart et al. or others will undoubtedly provide these important factors in future models, but until this is accomplished it will be difficult to evaluate the real potential of the system. At this point we can only say that *Elinor* represents an interesting, and potentially valuable, characterization of organization in memory.

An Information-Processing Approach

A memory model that meets many of the objections concerning *Elinor* but with a decidedly reduced scope is one proposed by Anderson and Bower (1973), which they call *HAM* (Human Associative Memory). We have called it an information-processing model, even though the theoretical framework is not unlike that of *Elinor,* because the model proposes to account for outcomes of a variety of experiments dealing with the processing of information. For example, in their discussion Anderson and Bower relate the model to studies of list learning and retention, sentence learning, and the recognition process. It is much too soon to evaluate the potential of such a model. Our aim is simply to illustrate some aspects of memory organization in *HAM* and certain rules *HAM* uses for coding information in memory.

The basic unit of information in *HAM* is a proposition that corresponds to the kind of conceptualization contained in an assertion or statement. This does not imply that inputs to *HAM* can only be in statement form. Any sensory input may be represented in long-term memory. Propositions are represented in memory in the form of hierarchical structures called *trees,* which consist of nodes and connections between nodes. These structures are similar in form to those we have seen in other memory models and similar to the linguistic trees we shall encounter in Chapters 10 and 11. A simple tree illustrating the subject(S)–predicate(P) distinction in a proposition is shown in Figure 8.16.

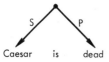
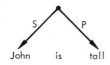

Figure 8.16 Examples of subject(S)–predicate(P) constructions for simple propositions.
(After Anderson and Bower, 1973.)

Trees containing much more complex information can also be found in *HAM*'s memory system. Two illustrations of such trees are given in Figure 8.17. Panel A illustrates the relation(R)–object(O) distinction. In this case we see that the subject(S) bears the relation(R) to the object(O). Panel B illustrates the context(C)–fact(F) distinction as well. The fact is

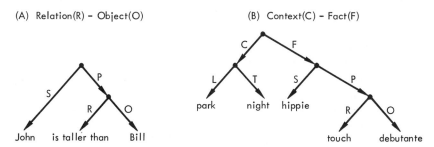

Figure 8.17   Illustrations of two distinctions in HAM's memory system. *(After Anderson and Bower, 1973.)*

represented as "hippie touch debutante" and the context indicates the important characteristics of time (*night*) and place (*park*). In many situations such references to context prevent overgeneralizations of factual statements.

The preceding examples only serve to illustrate a fragment of *HAM*'s memory system. It is from a basis such as this, however, that Anderson and Bower go on to construct a fairly elaborate memory system. Since their main concern is with accounting for experimental data, the model is primarily addressed to problems encountered in memory for lists and sentence memory experiments. It also deals with specific retrieval problems such as those encountered in studies of recognition memory. The major contribution here is that an attempt is made to define the mechanisms by which memory structures are constructed, stored, searched, recognized, and forgotten in particular memory tasks. Although psychology is a long way from solving these problems, the approaches represented by both *HAM* and *Elinor* may provide an important step toward our understanding of organized memory.

CONCLUSION

This chapter focused on organization in long-term memory and on the role of semantic factors in memory. We began by reviewing some of the more traditional assumptions that influenced the study of organization in memory. It was noted that both in Ebbinghaus's studies and in early studies of word association, the associative principles of contiguity and frequency were thought to be the major determinants of mental organization. Within this context, we proceeded to consider whether these characteristics of input experiences influenced output in expected ways. Whereas both contiguity of events and frequency of experience predicted characteristics of output in some situations, their influence was virtually eliminated in others. Such discrepancies between input and output were particularly common in free recall in the form of both primary and secondary organization.

A major part of the chapter considered organizational factors in free recall. The focus here was on the phenomena of clustering and subjective organization. In clustering it was noted that both degree of clustering and amount of material recalled tend to covary. That is, the greater the observed organization in output, the more items subjects tend to recall. In many situations this correlation seems to result from either an increase in the size of recalled clusters or an increase in the number of categories recalled. Increases in cluster size usually result when sets of items have strong interitem associations or when they are closely related to a category label. Increases in the number of categories recalled often result from experimental manipulations such as cueing at the time of recall. To be effective, however, it appears that such cues must tap into the organization imposed on the materials at the time of input or storage.

Both associative and category clustering in the free-recall situation can be predicted on the basis of either free or controlled association norms. Such predictions also extend to the occurrence of facilitative and interfering effects resulting from variations in the stimulus context. Although these observations are consistent with traditional association theory, they can also be seen as supportive of a more cognitive organization. What these observations necessarily demonstrate is that whatever factors influence performance in the word association situation also influence performance in clustering.

Correlations between word association indices and clustering indices are consistent with associative interpretations, but other aspects of the results found in clustering studies are quite contrary to what traditional associative models would seem to predict. For example, given a passive organism of the sort depicted by traditional associative theorists, it is difficult to see why cueing effects should be limited on the input side. Even as ingrained a tendency as that of alphabetizing inputs does not seem to be effective unless subjects are told the list can be organized in that way. Another difficulty for association theory arises from the observation that semantic processing seems to play such an important role in determining amount recalled and degree of clustering. Thus, although studies of clustering support some associative concepts, they suggest the importance of other factors that have little or no status in association theories.

When attention was shifted from clustering to studies of subjective organization, the validity of associative principles was also called into question. In this case the main observation to be explained is the increase in both item recall and degree of subjective organization that takes place across trials. There is little evidence to indicate that contiguity of inputs has an effect on these output measures, and even the supposedly basic frequency principle often fails to predict item recall. We did see evidence concerning the importance of subjectively organized categories, but it was not clear whether the organizational principles were associative in any fundamental way. To the extent that associations are established as a result of paired-associate learning, there was evidence of associative factors in subjective organization. This observation, however, is similar to the observed correlation between clustering and word association indices. It only suggests that the same factors are responsible for performance in both experimental situations.

In our discussion of memory codes and memory structure, we noted several levels at which inputs might be coded in memory. These range from codes at a more or less physical level to the name codes or codes resulting from conscious constructions which appear to be increasingly semantic. Although our discussion of memory codes was neutral with respect to major theoretical viewpoints, we noted that many aspects of coding apparently require that an active part be played by the organism. This seems particularly true for codes resulting from conscious constructions and for coding operations based on stimulus selection, some forms of rewriting, and elaboration. Active, conscious processes also seem to be important in coding by imagery, in the development of mnemonics as aids in retrieval, and in some aspects of coding by means of relational structures or grouping. Thus many aspects of coding suggest a viewpoint contrary to the associative concept of a passive organism that responds to inputs in a rather automatic and stereotyped way.

In contrast to the other sections of this chapter, the discussion of organizational structures in memory involved more theoretical speculation than experimental evidence. There was evidence to suggest that long-term memory codes may be organized in hierarchical ways. Other than this, however, little experimental evidence could be found to support concepts about the structure of memory. Two theoretical approaches were briefly illustrated and may suggest future trends, but at this point we can only say that these approaches have potential value.

As to the future of associative concepts, we can add little to what has already been said. Certainly the trend is to abandon the view that conceives of a passive organism responding automatically to inputs. Less emphasis is also placed on the traditional associative principles of contiguity and frequency, although no one would deny the importance of these principles in learning. Associative concepts are still widely used in a descriptive way to indicate a relation between two or more inputs or memory codes. In most cases, however, the theoretical status of "an association" is more like that of "a bridge" or "a pathway" and is not used in the older sense of an automatic, stimulus-response *bond* (Thorndike) or *habit* (Hull). In the future we will probably continue to see the concept of associations used in psychological thought, but in a way that is more descriptive and more theoretically neutral than in the past.

III

The Structural Analysis Approach

9

The Sounds
of Speech

IN THIS CHAPTER and in Chapters 10–12 we shall consider an approach to the study of human learning that emphasizes an analysis of structures, particularly those characterizing language. The main concern here is with spoken language as opposed to written language. The effort has been to develop descriptions of various aspects of language and to determine what these descriptions tell us about the language user. This is not to imply that any particular description of the structure of language is necessarily "real" in a psychological sense. For example, the rules of arithmetic describe the structure of that area of mathematics, but these rules do not necessarily tell us how a mathematician solves problems.

In the case of language separate descriptions can be offered for each of three components: the rules governing the sound system (phonology), including those that relate to syllable and word formation; the rules pertaining to word combination (syntax); and the rules determining the meanings of words and combinations of words (semantics). These descriptions frequently involve rather abstract concepts, which are far removed from the level of direct observation. We shall see illustrations of these abstract concepts in the present chapter, which considers the sound system and describes concepts not found in the acoustic signals which can be directly observed. Before we discuss such concepts, however, let us make some observations about speech sounds.

If you were to record utterances from numerous native speakers of some particular, but unfamiliar, language and subject these utterances to careful analysis, you would find that each utterance was physically distinct from every other utterance. In fact, each segment of your record would probably differ from every other segment in various ways. There are several reasons for these wide differences that are found among the sounds of speech even within a given language community. One of the most obvious is that the speech signal contains cues that serve to identify individual speakers. These cues are important to communication, although they do not convey information that is particularly relevant to the "linguistic content" of the message. For example, telephone systems can be degraded to the point where the cues for identification of the speaker are no longer transmitted even though the intelligibility of the message may still be high. Other sources of variation among speech sounds arise from the presence of cues that aid in identifying the age and sex of the speaker as well as the speaker's emotional state.

Apart from these personal sources of variation, however, there still remain very large differences among speech sounds. This variability may seem surprising, but what we ordinarily think of as single, physically identical, speech sounds are instead classes or categories of sound that are responded to in the same way by speakers of a particular language. Therefore, one of our major concerns in this chapter will be to examine the ways in which members of a given language community group sounds into these categories. Of course there are differences from one language community to another concerning which sound characteristics are of primary importance. But before elaborating on these variations in speech sounds and their implications for speech perception and production, it would be well to review some of the basic aspects of sound production.

Sound Production

Speech sounds begin when breath is forced from the lungs through the vocal folds at the top of the windpipe. The opening in the vocal folds is called the *glottis,* and the vocal folds themselves function rather like a pair of lips that can open or close over the glottis. To make a sound, the vocal folds move together and close the glottis while air pressure builds up. When the air pressure is sufficient, the vocal folds part briefly, and a puff of air is released. The folds then close again until sufficient air pressure is built up again. The opening and closing takes place one hundred or two hundred times per second to provide the sound that is our voice.

When the vocal folds are opened the passage of air sets them in vibration, and variations in air pressure and vocal fold tension produce sounds that vary in pitch or frequency as well as in loudness. These sounds are further modified during the course of transmission through the cavities of the throat, nose, and mouth. These cavities act as a set of filters to selectively emphasize certain aspects of the sound and to de-emphasize or eliminate certain others. Additional modification of the initial sound can be produced by the action of other articulators. These changes are produced when the mobile parts of the mouth such as the lips or tongue move to articulate with the fixed parts of the mouth such as the teeth, gum ridge, or hard and soft palates.

As everyone knows the sounds of speech can be roughly categorized as vowels and consonants, although the basis for this classification is extremely complicated and not complete. Vowel sounds are produced when the initial glottal sound is only modified by adjusting the size and shape of the cavities in the throat, nose, and mouth. Different vowel sounds may result, however, depending on the height to which the tongue is raised (three to seven levels have been suggested), the shape of the lips (rounded or unrounded), the part of the tongue that acts as a mobile articulator (front, middle, or back), the action of the very tip of the tongue, whether or not the vowel is nasalized (by dropping the nasal flap or velum), and so forth. Obviously, many physically different sounds are possible.

Consonant sounds are produced by combining the type or manner of articulation with the position or place of articulation. Examples of differences in the type or manner of articulation include the initial consonant in *ba* or *da* where the stream of air is completely stopped by closing the passage. These sounds are referred to as *stops*. When a narrow slit is formed for the air to pass through, as when producing the *th* in *thin* or the *sh* in *shine,* the sound is called a *fricative*. Position or place of articulation refers to various combinations of fixed with mobile articulators. Of course, not all combinations are possible; for example, the mobile lower lip does not make contact with the fixed hard palate.

Most classifications identify four types of articulation and eight positions of articulation, which combine to produce thirty-two consonants. These thirty-two combinations are not totally exhaustive, however. In fact, if the goal was to specify every unique sound, there would be no end to the linguistic analysis of speech sounds. Heights of the tongue, lip roundings, and regions of the tongue might be subdivided endlessly. In addition, there still remain the linguistically unimportant physical differences in speech sound which serve to identify just who is speaking as well as the significant prosodic features of the language, including variations of duration, pause pattern, rhythm, loudness, and pitch.

In view of the almost infinite variety of speech sounds that might be identified, linguists have typically described languages in terms of the sounds or classes of sound that make a systematic perceptual difference. Although specification of what constitutes a perceptual difference is quite variable and depends on the amount of linguistic training one has, in most cases the procedure has been adequate. The result is a classification of those speech sounds that can be combined to form the larger units (e.g., words) which provide the basis for grammatical and semantic analysis.

Phonetic and Phonemic Classification

The various speech sounds, or classes of speech sounds, that characterize a particular language are first classified phonetically. That is, sounds are classified on the basis of various acoustic and articulatory characteristics, and each different sound or class of sounds is assigned a particular phonetic symbol. In a given language, however, some of the differences between sounds that are assigned different phonetic symbols may turn out to be unimportant. For example, in some languages it may be of no consequence whether certain sounds are nasalized or not. In cases such as these, the phonetic differences may be ignored and the sounds are classified as instances of a single *phoneme*.[1] In English, the sound of the initial consonant in the word *pin* is phonetically different from its occurrence in *spin;* the first is said to be aspirated (accompanied by a strong puff of air), whereas the second is nonaspirated. In phonemic classification this phonetic difference is said to be unimportant, and both sounds are listed as instances of the phoneme /p/. A *phoneme* is typically defined as the smallest unit of sound that makes a difference to a native speaker of a given language. That is, a phoneme is the shortest segment of sound that makes a significant difference between utterances. The phoneme, however, has no meaning in itself.

Linguists have traditionally identified phoneme classes for particular languages on the basis of *acoustic similarity* of speech sounds, *articulatory similarity* in sound production, and *complementary distribution* of the phonetic elements. The exact procedures for this classification are rather complex—the essential problem is to determine which phonetic differences really make a difference and which do not. For example, consider two elements that are only somewhat similar in sound and articulation but never occur in exactly the same sound environments. Such elements may be said to be in complementary distribution and classified as instances of the same phoneme. This is the case with /p/ in the words *pin* and *spin* or with /t/ in *table* and *faultless*. By applying procedures such as these, linguists can reduce enormous differences in the physical characteristics of speech sounds to the point where relatively few categories are identified as being significant for a given language.

In recent years linguists have increasingly supported the view that the significant sound categories in all natural languages are based on a system of "distinctive features" (cf. Jakobson, Fant, and Halle, 1963; Chomsky and Halle, 1968). The features refer to various aspects of artic-

---

[1] Phonetic distinctions are ordinarily written in a special fine-grained "alphabet" of symbols which mark all the features of articulatory and acoustic variation that the trained phonetician can detect. All of the phonetic distinctions that can be classed together in the linguistic analysis are considered as belonging to the abstract class of a phoneme. Each phoneme is ordinarily written as a symbol between slashes (e.g., /p/ indicates the phoneme *p*).

ulation, and any given phoneme in a particular natural language is said to be characterized by a set or bundle of features. As many as fifteen to twenty features may characterize speech sounds in any given language, and for purposes of classification the features are considered to be binary. As a first approximation we may think of features as being present (plus) or absent (minus). For example, rounded sounds (+) are produced by a narrowing of the lip orifice, whereas nonrounded sounds (−) do not involve such a narrowing.

Phonemes in a language may differ in terms of one or more of these distinctive features. For instance, the English stop consonants /b/ and /p/ differ only in the feature of voicing, with /b/ being voiced and /p/ being unvoiced. Following Chomsky and Halle (1968), the term *unvoiced,* or *voiceless,* is restricted to sounds produced with a glottal opening that is so wide that it prevents vocal cord vibration if air flows through the opening. Thus, in voiced sounds, some narrowing of the glottis is implied. Lisker and Abramson (1964) have suggested that this feature might better be characterized as "voice onset time" rather than the more traditional "voiced"-"voiceless" distinction. The critical factor here is the onset time of vocal cord vibration in the following vowel relative to the moment of release of the stop closure.

Other distinctive features include those that refer to position of the tongue (e.g., high-low) or place of articulation (front-back). There is general agreement on a system of features as the underlying basis for phonetic categories, although it should be pointed out that there is much less agreement on just what constitutes a particular feature, as we saw in the case of voicing.

In English, as in most other written languages, the letters of the alphabet can be roughly translated into the vowels and consonants of spoken speech. The vowels and consonants of our alphabet do not exhaust the phonemes of our language, however. In fact, there are approximately forty phonemes in English. In addition to these phoneme classes, important differences may be signaled by variations in stress or intonation. The English word *permit* (pér-mit) with stress on the first syllable is not the same as *permit* (per-mít) with stress on the second syllable. Similarly, the utterance "John hit the ball" can be changed from a declarative statement to a question indicating surprise by merely altering the intonation contour. These and other differences are found in many languages, and we shall have occasion to return to a discussion of them later.

THE PERCEPTION OF SPEECH SOUNDS

Now that we have some understanding of the mechanisms for producing speech sounds and of the way physically distinct sounds are grouped into phoneme classes, let us consider the question of how speech sounds are perceived. At the phoneme level, the traditional assumption has been that there is a one-to-one correspondence between certain characteristics of the acoustic stimulus and the phoneme that is perceived. That is, it was assumed that for every different phoneme there existed a unique set of acoustic elements or cues. Of course, certain differences were known to exist among the instances of a given phoneme, such as the difference between aspirated and nonaspirated /p/, but it was assumed that after years of practice with these sounds the hearer simply learned to ignore these differences. From this beginning the perception of larger sound units, such as syllables and words, was thought to involve a simple process of stringing phonemes together in serial order, much as we string letters together in writing. In recent years, however, an increasing amount of evidence has shown that this simple view of speech perception is grossly in error. Before we examine this evidence let us turn our attention to the acoustic stimuli that make up speech sounds.

Spectrographic Analysis

First look at the sample *spectrograms* in Figure 9.1. These examples of visual speech are produced by a *speech spectrograph,* which through a series of filters produces a visible record of spoken speech on light-sensitive paper. The frequency of the sounds is represented on the vertical dimension with low frequencies at the bottom and high frequencies at the top. The time dimension (duration) is represented horizontally, and amplitude (loudness) is indicated by the degree of darkening. The dark bars indicate what are called *formants* of the sound, and they seem to convey the information most essential for speech perception. These formants are the result of filtering action produced by the place and manner of articulation as well as by the size and shape of the vocal cavities (throat, mouth, and nose). The lowest bar is called the first formant, the next bar is the second formant, and so forth. In general, three to four formants are used to distinguish natural speech sounds.

One characteristic of natural speech that should be noted in the spectrograms is the absence of distinct boundaries between individual phonemes or between syllables and words. This characteristic, which is so unlike the case in written language, may have important implications for the acquisition of spoken language. Much ground remains to be covered before we can turn to that question, however.

When the spectrogram was first invented, it was thought that the study of language and language learning would be greatly advanced. It seemed reasonable at the time that spectrographic records would provide a clear indication of the acoustic correlates of the various phonemes and that the study of language would proceed rapidly from that point. But after

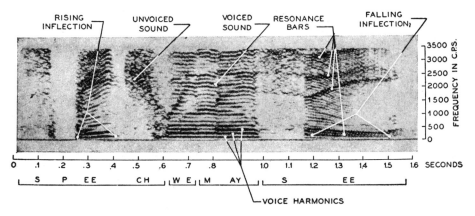

**Figure 9.1a Sound spectrogram for the words "Speech we may see,"
using a narrow-band analyzing filter to reveal the individual harmonics.**
(From Visible Speech *by Potter, Kopp and Green, 1947 by Litton Educational Publishing, Inc. Reprinted by permission of Van Nostrand Reinhold Company.)*

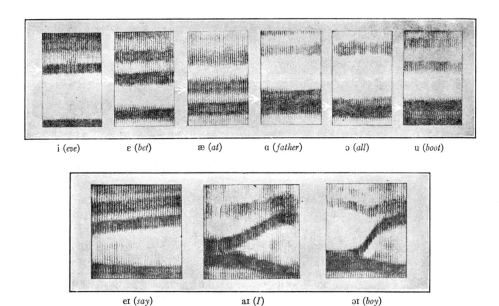

Figure 9.1b Dark bars indicate the formants of the different vowel sounds.
(From Visible Speech *by Potter, Kopp and Green, 1947 by Litton Educational Publishing, Inc. Reprinted by permission of Van Nostrand Reinhold Company.)*

more than twenty years of study, spectrographic records remain a puzzle. They are exceedingly difficult to interpret even if the reader has had many years of experience. In fact, few findings of importance to the study of language have been obtained through the analysis of spectrograms alone.

Despite the fact that spectrographic analysis was not the "magic key" some had supposed, the spectrogram has provided some important and useful information to speech scientists. The direction of this development is well illustrated by the work of scientists at Haskins laboratories (cf. Liberman, 1957). The group at Haskins began to study speech perception in the late 1940s. They first developed a device called the *pattern playback,* which was capable of translating the visual spectrogram back into sound. With this instrument available, these scientists experimented with the cues necessary for speech perception.

Beginning with spectrographic records, controlled changes were made in various aspects of the acoustic pattern and then evaluated in terms of the sound that was heard. Initially the experimentation involved the use of hand-painted spectrograms, although in recent years the emphasis has been on computer-generated signals for work on speech synthesis. Using these techniques, speech scientists have studied various aspects of the speech signal and have succeeded in identifying several cues that are critical in speech perception.

Speech Sounds and Percepts

Despite the traditional assumption that a one-to-one correspondence exists between the acoustic stimulus and what is perceived, recent evidence indicates that widely varying acoustic stimuli give rise to a *single* percept. For example, consider the simulated spectrographic patterns shown in Figure 9.2. These patterns contain two formants which when played on the *pattern playback* are sufficient to produce the consonants /d/ and /g/ before various vowels. This is not to imply that only the first and second formants carry linguistic information but rather that these two formants are sufficient in this case. It turns out, as we shall see, that higher-order formants, particularly the third formant, are critical for accurate perception in some other contexts. The patterns shown in Figure 9.2 are decidedly simplified forms in contrast to those presented in Figure 9.1, which are representative of natural speech. Regardless of the gross differences in appearance, however, both sets of patterns are easily identified as particular speech sounds when played on the *pattern playback*.

In Figure 9.2, look first at the patterns that characterize /d/ in various vowel contexts. Notice that there is significant variation among the second formants in terms of both frequency level and direction of the transition. Yet despite these gross differences in the acoustic signal, the consonant is always perceived as /d/. It is tempting to suggest that the

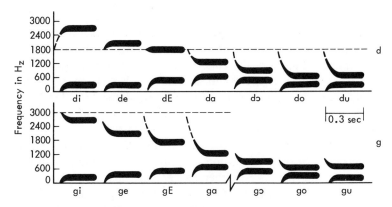

Figure 9.2 The spectrographic patterns that produce /d/ and /g/ before various vowels. (The dashed lines are extrapolations to the /d/ and /g/ loci.)
(*After Liberman, 1957.*)

underlying basis for the common percept lies in the first formant, which shows little variation across vowel environments. This temptation is quickly dismissed when we examine the first formant in the patterns for /g/. Here we see that for each vowel environment, the first formant in the /g/ pattern is identical to the first formant in the /d/ pattern. Thus, whereas the first formant could provide a basis for the common consonant perception of /d/ before various vowels, it cannot provide a basis for differentiating between /d/ and /g/ in any vowel environment.

Another possible cue for the perception of /d/ was suggested by the work of Delattre, Liberman, and Cooper (1955). These investigators paired a number of steady-state second formants with various first formants having a rising transition. Listening to these patterns indicated that an initial /d/ sound was heard most strongly when the second formant was at 1800 Hz. Stevens and House (1956) also have indicated that what is common to /d/ before these vowels is that the vocal tract is closed at almost the same point. Furthermore, they note that the resonant frequency of the vocal cavity at the moment of closure is about 1800 Hz. Of course, no sound is produced until the tract is opened somewhat, so that the locus frequency is not transmitted into sound. Nevertheless, this locus might serve as a common cue for the perception of the /d/ consonant.

Notice, before we go on, that a similar possibility will not hold for /g/. In Figure 9.2 we can see that the second-formant transitions for /g/ before /i/ through /g/ before /a/ all point toward a frequency of 3000 Hz and show progressively longer transitions. Between /a/ and the next vowel /ɔ/, however, a sudden shift takes place. Now the second-formant transition is short and there is no tendency for the transition to point toward the 3000 Hz frequency.

Delattre, Liberman, and Cooper (1955) evaluated the possibility of a specific "locus" for /d/ using synthetic patterns like those shown in Figure 9.3. First look at the second formants shown in part *A* of the figure. These formants all begin at the 1800 Hz frequency. Notice that the second-formant transitions are not identical, nor could they be superimposed. They only share the characteristic of originating at the 1800 Hz frequency. The basic question here was whether or not these second formants, when paired individually with the first formant shown at the bottom of the figure, would all be heard as /d/. The answer was that they were not. Taking the second formants in order, from top to bottom, the resulting patterns were heard first as /b/, then as /d/, then as /g/, and finally as /d/ again.

Now look at the second formants shown in part *B* of Figure 9.3. Notice that these formants do not originate at 1800 Hz, although they do "point" in that direction (also see Figure 9.2). This is more like natural speech where the locus frequency cannot be transmitted because the vocal tract is closed. Again, each pattern consisted of pairing one of the second formants with the first formant shown at the bottom in part *B* of the figure. When these patterns were presented the consonant was always perceived as /d/. Of course the consonant was always perceived as preceding a vowel.

The combined results for the patterns illustrated in Figure 9.3 suggest that the 1800 Hz frequency does not constitute a physical cue for the per-

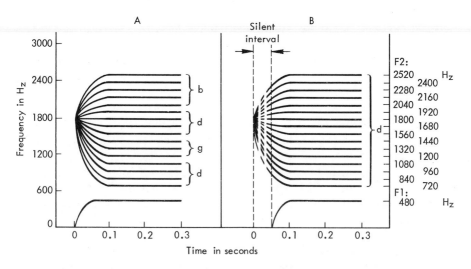

Figure 9.3   Part A shows second-formant transitions that start at the /d/ locus, and part B shows comparable transitions that merely "point" at it, as indicated by the dotted lines. Those of part A produce syllables beginning with /b/, /d/, or /g/, depending on the frequency level of the formant; those of part B produce only syllables beginning with /d/.
(After Delattre, Liberman, and Cooper, 1955.)

ception of /d/. When this acoustic cue is introduced, a variety of consonants are perceived. Only when the physical cue is removed are the patterns perceived as containing the /d/ consonant. Thus it appears that the 1800 Hz frequency is not part of the acoustic cue for perceiving /d/, nor can it be made a part of the signal without grossly altering the perception of the consonant (Delattre, Liberman, and Cooper, 1955).

We have just seen that widely varying acoustic stimuli may give rise to a single percept, but a single acoustic stimulus may also give rise to varying percepts. One of the earliest studies showing this effect was reported by Liberman, Delattre, and Cooper (1952). Using synthetic patterns these investigators demonstrated that the same brief burst of noise at 1440 Hz was perceived as /p/ before /i/, as /k/ before /a/, and as /p/ again before /u/. This finding has also been verified for real speech in a tape-splicing study by Carol Schatz (1954).

A related finding has been reported by Bastian, Eimas, and Liberman (1961). These investigators inserted silent intervals of varying lengths after the initial sound of /s/ in natural recordings of the word *slit*. For relatively short silent intervals the stimuli were perceived as the word *slit*, but for the longer intervals, around 100 msec., the stimuli were heard as the word *split*. But in another context, *sag*, similar variation in the length of the silent interval resulted in perception of either *sag* or *stag*. Thus we see that the same stimulus, a silent interval, is perceived differently in different contexts.

Context-Conditioned Variation

Findings such as those described above as well as those summarized in Figures 9.2 and 9.3 are broadly illustrative of what has been called *context-conditioned variation* (Liberman, Cooper, Shankweiler, and Studdert-Kennedy, 1967). That is to say, the way a particular acoustic signal will be perceived is highly dependent upon the context in which the signal appears. This observation is totally contrary to what would be expected according to traditional views. If each phoneme were represented by a unique aspect of sound, then speech perception should proceed by means of a simple alphabet. The phenomenon of context-conditioned variation suggests, however, that speech perception as well as speech production involves a complex code based on a *restructuring* of phonemes at the sound level. To more fully understand the nature of the restructuring, let us consider the synthetic patterns shown in Figure 9.4.

The patterns given in Figure 9.4, when converted into sound, will be heard as /di/ and /du/. They are examples of the highly simplified patterns that have been used for investigating complex acoustic signals. Each pattern consists of two formants, and each formant consists of a transition plus a steady-state signal. The steady-state portions have a duration of approximately 250 msec., and when the steady-state portions of both formants

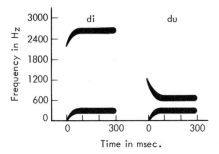

Figure 9.4   Spectrographic patterns sufficient for the synthesis of /d/ before /i/ and /u/.
(After Liberman et al., 1967.)

in each pattern are converted into sound, this is sufficient to produce the vowel sounds /i/ and /u/. But it is the rapid 50 msec. transitions that are of greatest interest here. The transition of the first or lowest formant which rises from a very low frequency level is the cue for the consonant class of voiced stops /b,d,g/. That is, this first formant transition would be the same in patterns that produce /bi/, /bu/ or /gi/, /gu/ as it is in the patterns of Figure 9.4. The transition is, generally speaking, a cue for the type or manner of articulation as well as the presence of voicing.

The transition of the second formant in the patterns of Figure 9.4 is the cue for distinguishing among the class of voiced stops and in this case for identifying the consonant as /d/. That is, if the sounds we wished to produce were /gi/, /bi/ instead of /di/ or /gu/, /bu/ instead of /du/ the transition of the second formant would be altered, although the first-formant transition and the steady-state portions would remain the same (see Figure 9.2). It should also be noted that the second-formant transition for /d/ is radically different in the two vowel contexts. In the case of /di/ the transition is ascending and rises from 2200 Hz to 2600 Hz. For /du/, however, the transition rapidly descends from 1200 Hz to 700 Hz. This illustrates the essence of context-conditioned variation.

The context in which the second-formant transition appears is critical to the perception of speech. If we take these transitions out of their context the transition for /di/ sounds like "chirps" rising in pitch, whereas the transition for /du/ sounds like "chirps" falling in pitch. That is, when removed from the speech context, these transitions are readily discriminable from each other and are *not* heard as speech sounds. In the speech context, however, they both are heard as the consonant /d/.

Categorical Perception

At this point we need to ask whether the various instances of a phoneme class such as /d/ actually sound just the same or whether they are merely treated the same as a result of our extensive experience in listening to speech. We just noted that the important cue for the consonant in /di/

and /du/ is the second-formant transition. We also saw that these transitions are perceived as being very different sounds when they are removed from the speech context. Therefore, a question arises about their similarity in the speech context. This question is also related to the notion of stimulus generalization. For example, consider the set of synthetic spectrographic patterns given in Figure 9.5.

As can be seen, the first-formant transitions and the steady-state portions of these patterns are the same. The differences lie in the direction and extent of the second-formant transitions, which are sufficient in this case to produce several instances of the consonants /b/, /d/, and /g/ in the context of the same vowel. In fact, when these patterns were presented to subjects one at a time in an irregular order, the identification functions for the consonants resembled those given in Figure 9.6, which were obtained from a typical subject.

The question we might ask about these results is whether the patterns heard as a single consonant are really perceptually identical. For example, for /d/ perhaps patterns 6 or 7 represents the "true" /d/, whereas the other patterns that produce /d/ are just too similar to perceive as being different in a natural setting. If this is the case it should be possible to show that subjects can differentiate the various /d/ sounds in a discrimination test.

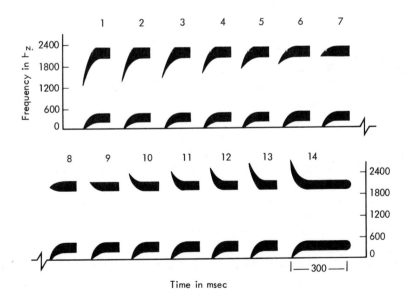

Figure 9.5 The spectrographic patterns, varying in the direction and extent of second-formant transition, that were converted into sound for identification as /b/, /d/, or /g/. *(After Liberman, Harris, Hoffman, and Griffith, 1957.)*

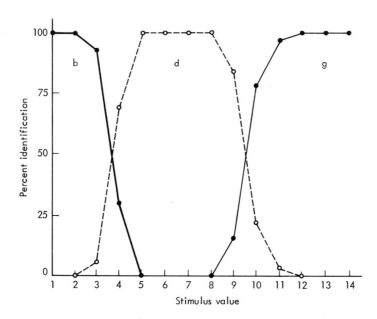

Figure 9.6 Identification of the consonants synthesized with the spectrographic patterns shown in Figure 9.5. Each point shows the relative frequency of the responses /b/, /d/, and /g/ in thirty-two presentations of each stimulus to one listener. *(After Liberman et al., 1957.)*

Suppose a subject is presented with the synthetic patterns of Figure 9.5 in a discrimination test. The procedure is to select any two patterns and present them in succession and then to repeat one of the patterns. The subject is told to indicate whether the first or second pattern was repeated. This is sometimes called the *ABX* procedure. The subject is presented with patterns *A, B,* and *X* in that order and is asked to indicate whether the sound of pattern *X* is the same as the sound of pattern *A* or *B*. Discrimination between phonemes is tested when the instances of *A* and *B* come from different phoneme classes, as determined by the identification functions for that subject.

On the basis of stimulus generalization we would expect the easiest discriminations to be between those patterns that differ most acoustically. For example, for the subject whose identification functions are shown in Figure 9.6, it should be easier to distinguish between patterns 5 and 8 than to distinguish between patterns 6 and 7. Similarly, it should be easier for this subject to distinguish between patterns 5 and 14 than to distinguish between patterns 8 and 11 or 9 and 10. Several experiments have been reported regarding this issue (cf. Liberman et al., 1967).

In general the results of these studies have been contrary to what would be expected on the basis of stimulus generalization. For several consonant distinctions, such as /b,d,g/, /d,t/, and /b,p/, the data indicate that discrimination is much better across the phoneme boundary than it is within the phoneme class. That is, any instance of one phoneme, say /b/, can be more readily differentiated from any instance of another phoneme, say /d/, than is the case for two instances of a particular phoneme irrespective of the acoustic separation. Using Figure 9.6, this means that patterns 3 and 4 or 9 and 10 which cross the phoneme boundaries are better differentiated than patterns 5 and 8 or 10 and 14 even though the acoustic difference is much greater in the latter cases (see Figure 9.5). Findings such as these have led various investigators to argue for *categorical perception* of phonemes. That is, you can perceive the phonemes, but you cannot *hear* the variations that occur within the phoneme class.

Certain evidence suggests that categorical perception is stronger for consonants than it is for vowels. Pisoni (1973) has shown that although the identification functions (see Fig. 9.6) are equally sharp for vowels and consonants, comparable results are not found in discrimination. Both consonants and vowels are most easily discriminated at phoneme boundaries, but subjects can make discriminations at well above chance levels within a vowel class and not within a consonant class.

Before turning to other issues we should consider the importance of the speech context in categorical perception. We have seen that synthetic spectrographic patterns such as those shown in Figure 9.5 yield sharp identification and discrimination functions for the consonants /b,d,g/. We also noted that the only difference in these patterns lies in the direction and extent of the second-formant transition. Therefore, we might ask whether or not these transitions are discriminated in the same way when they are presented in isolation, outside of the speech context.

In one study Mattingly, Liberman, Syrdal, and Halwes (1971) compared the discriminability of second-formant transitions both within the speech context and outside of it. Their synthetic patterns were generated by means of a computer and were similar to those of Figure 9.5. In the speech context the sounds were perceived as the consonants /b/, /d/, and /g/ accompanied by a common vowel. When the second-formant transitions were played in isolation, the sounds were perceived as birdlike chirps. The results of the discrimination test indicated categorical perception for sounds in the speech context. But when the second-formant transitions were removed from the speech context, they not only sounded like nonspeech sounds (chirps) but were much easier to discriminate. When heard as chirps, these second-formant transitions no longer fell into categories with sharp boundaries but instead were perceived much more in accordance with the continuous acoustic variations actually present in the signal.

We have seen that speech perception at the phoneme level is much more complex than it was once thought to be. For the most part, phoneme perception does not change just because the acoustic stimulus has been altered. It is only when the signal is changed in particular ways that a different phoneme is perceived. The changes required also seem to be more qualitative than quantitative. As we have seen in studies of categorical perception, very small changes in the physical characteristics of the acoustic stimulus may result in perception of a different phoneme but much larger changes may not. In addition, these required alterations in the acoustic signal are context dependent. What is required to perceive a particular speech sound depends on which other sounds occur in the same context, and these other sounds must be speech sounds as well. It is this relative aspect of speech perception that leads us to ask whether speech sounds appear as distinct and separate entities.

Parallel Transmission

In the preceding sections it was noted that the cues for identifying the class of voiced stops /b,d,g/, and for differentiating between the members of this class, are found in the form transitions. Yet when these transitions are removed from the accompanying steady-state portions of the formants, they are not perceived as speech sounds. That is, either we hear one of these consonants plus a vowel or we hear a nonspeech sound. There is no point at which we hear only the consonant. According to Liberman et al. (1967):

> This is so because the formant transition is, at every instant, providing information about two phonemes, the consonant and the vowel—that is, the phonemes are being transmitted in parallel (p. 436).

A better illustration of the kind of parallel transmission that occurs in speech is given in Figure 9.7. The synthetic spectrogram shown in the figure is sufficient to produce the syllable /b æ g/ ("bag") when converted

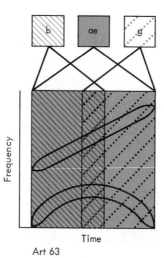

Figure 9.7 Parallel transmission of phonetic segments after encoding by the rules of speech to the level of sound.
(From Liberman, 1970.)

Art 63

to sound. The figure also indicates that information about the vowel is carried throughout the signal and information about the consonants extends through approximately two-thirds of the signal. That this is so can be demonstrated by attempting to alter the syllable. Changing the initial consonant so as to produce /g æ g/ ("gag") instead of /b æ g/ requires a change in the second formant that extends from the beginning of the signal to a point roughly two-thirds of the way along the formant. A change in the vowel from /b æ g/ to /big/ would require a change in the entire second formant. A similar change in the last two-thirds of the formant is required to alter the last consonant /g/.

We can see from this example that every part of the second formant is carrying information about at least two phonemes, much as the second-formant transition in /di/ or /du/ conveys information about both the consonant and the vowel simultaneously. In addition, the middle portion of the second formant in Figure 9.7 carries information about all three phonemes. The phonemes of this syllable are transmitted in parallel, and there is no simple stringing together of acoustic elements similar to what we find in handwriting. There is no simple correspondence between the phoneme and any particular segment of the syllable because several phonemes have been encoded into the same segment of the signal (cf. Liberman, Mattingly, and Turvey, 1972).

The Speech Code

In the preceding sections we have considered several aspects of speech perception that suggest that the speech signal may be a complex code rather than an alphabet. That is, instead of being an alphabetic sequence in which a particular segment of sound uniquely specifies a particular phonetic element, the speech signal constitutes a complex code based on a restructuring of phonetic elements at the sound level. This restructuring occurs in such a way that different sounds convey the same phonetic message in different sound environments, and the same sounds may simultaneously convey more than one phonetic message. It is this restructuring of elements that gives us the impression that phonemes occur as discrete, serially ordered sounds when, in fact, they do not.

The contrast between speech as a complex code and speech as an alphabetic sequence is illustrated in Figure 9.8. When speech is considered

Figure 9.8 Speech as an alphabet. Each segment is considered to lead a specific percept, irrespective of the speech context.

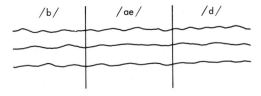

to be an alphabet, each segment is seen as leading to the perception of a particular speech sound. In addition, this relationship is thought to be constant across inputs. That is, whatever gives rise to the perception of a given speech sound in one context is thought to lead to the perception of that sound in every other context. We have seen, however, that the acoustic cues leading to perception of various speech sounds are highly dependent on the context. Furthermore, in our discussion of parallel transmission we saw that information about more than one speech sound is typically carried in every segment of the signal. Thus speech appears to be best characterized as a code rather than as an alphabet.

Several other aspects of speech perception also seem to indicate that speech is not an alphabet. For example, apparently no part of the frequency range is critical for accurate perception of human speech. Studies of selective filtering have shown that we can communicate perfectly well with only the frequencies above 1900 Hz. We can also communicate equally well with only those frequencies below 1900 Hz (cf. Miller, 1951). Thus no particular portion of the speech spectrum is crucial to discrimination of speech sounds.

The investigation of compressed speech also supports the view that speech could not be an alphabetic sequence. The various techniques employed for speech compression (cf. Foulke, 1971) have shown that speech can be followed, though with difficulty, at rates up to four hundred words per minute (Orr, Friedman, and Williams, 1965). Liberman et al. (1967) have suggested that if each English word is assumed to be four or five phonemes in length, on the average, this means that to understand rates as high as four hundred words per minute we would have to process thirty phonemes per second. However, these authors go on to indicate that research in auditory psychophysics shows that processing thirty discrete sounds per second would overreach the temporal resolving power of the ear. That is, the ear is not capable of discriminating between sounds transmitted at rates as high as thirty per second—at this rate discrete acoustic events would merge into an unanalyzable buzz. Even rates of fifteen phonemes per second, which are not uncommon in normal conversation, would appear to be more than the ear could handle if phonemes were transmitted as discrete acoustic units.

Fortunately, it appears that our ability to process speech is not dependent upon the assumption of an alphabetic sequence of sounds. We have seen that phonetic transmission is accomplished in parallel—that information relevant to the identification of two or more phonemes is transmitted at the same time. Thus the restructuring of phonemes that is accomplished at the sound level results in our being able to process speech at very high rates. Such rates would be impossible if each phoneme were signaled by discrete acoustic units.

Still another reason for believing that speech is a complex code and not an alphabet comes from the attempts to develop a sound alphabet. We are all generally familiar with the international Morse code. Morse code is an alphabet, as the term is defined here, based on a series of "dots" and "dashes." This alphabet can be used only very slowly in comparison with human speech, even by individuals who have had years of practice. Morse is not the only or even the best example of a sound alphabet from a psychological viewpoint. Several more interesting but less well known alphabets have been developed in connection with the attempt to build reading machines for the blind. In general these systems convert print into sound by substituting an acoustic alphabet for one that is visual. In the more than one-half century of this effort, however, no sound alphabet has been designed that will carry information efficiently. Even after very extensive practice with these acoustic alphabets, none has proved more efficient than Morse and all are decidedly less efficient, by a factor of about ten, than human speech (cf. Liberman et al., 1967).

Generality of the Speech Code

In this chapter we have emphasized the view that speech is a complex code and not an alphabet. However, the data we have presented thus far to illustrate various aspects of the code, such as context-conditioned variation, categorical perception, and parallel transmission, have been quite limited. Therefore it is appropriate to say a few more words about the generality of the code and the restructuring that characterizes the code.

Extensive research over more than two decades seems to indicate that most consonant sounds are encoded in the manner described previously. That is, even with slow articulation where the vowels may be represented by a fixed and unique acoustic signal, the consonants are highly restructured (Liberman, Mattingly, and Turvey, 1972). But in rapid articulation such as that which takes place in normal speech when vowels often occur between consonants, the vowels themselves may show considerable restructuring. In such a context the acoustic signal does not correspond to the vowel at any given instant but instead reflects the influence of the preceding or the following consonant. Thus we can say with some confidence that the speech code is quite general, and although exceptions do occur at times, considerable restructuring of phonetic elements takes place at the sound level.

The Motor Theory

In recent years as the evidence mounted to indicate that speech perception was not based on a simple acoustic alphabet, the search began for alternative theories of speech perception. One of the earliest theories to attract general interest maintained that "articulatory movements and their sensory effects mediate between the acoustic stimulus and the event we call perception" (Liberman, 1957, p. 122). This view has been referred to as the *motor theory of speech perception,* and the sequence of events to which it refers can be illustrated as follows:

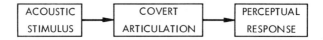

The theory says that the way you understand speech is to make the articulatory responses required to produce an acoustically comparable signal. Of course, to avoid confusion the hearer's responses are made covertly. In effect, then, the hearer knows what is being said because he has generated the responses required to produce the acoustic signal himself. The general procedure, referred to as *analysis by synthesis,* has been applied to many areas of cognition (cf. Neisser, 1967). In all such cases, the point is that one understands an externally produced event through a process of synthesizing an internal event that is comparable with it. In the present case the external event is an acoustic stimulus, and the synthesized event is a covert match produced through covert articulation.

The motor theory derived its initial support from the observation that the perceptions of the listener are more closely correlated with the patterns of articulation required to produce the speech signals than they are with the acoustic signals themselves. From this observation it was inferred that covert patterns of articulation actually mediate between the acoustic signals and the perception of the hearer. The earliest versions of this theory also assumed pretty much of a one-to-one correspondence between an articulatory response and phoneme perception. Such an assumption is not supported by the investigations of context-conditioned variation or parallel transmission. In addition, the movements of the articulators are far from being perfectly correlated with perception, and on the assumption of a one-to-one correspondence between articulation and phoneme perception, the movements are almost certainly too slow to account for the rate at which phonemes can be processed.

Where does this leave us with regard to the underlying basis for the speech code? At the present time neither an acoustic alphabet nor the simple version of the motor theory of speech perception is well supported by data, although other alternatives have been offered. One of these involves an extension of the motor theory that investigators at Haskins laboratories have been considering in one form or another for several years (Liberman, Cooper, Harris, and MacNeilage, 1963; Liberman et al., 1967).

Perhaps the best statement of this idea is offered by Liberman, Mattingly, and Turvey (1972). They begin with a very general description of the articulatory process for production of a syllable such as /b æ g/. Initially it is assumed that the phonetic elements of this syllable are represented in terms of its constituent features, such as place of production, manner of production, and condition of voicing. These features are represented as neural signals that can become commands to the articulatory muscles. Before the final commands to the muscles are made, however, these neural signals are organized in such a way that the greatest possible overlap in activity of the independent muscles is produced. In addition, some reorganization of the neural signals may take place to ensure cooperative activity of the various muscle groups, particularly when they act on the same organ (e.g., tongue). At this point the neural equivalents of the constituent features have been organized, although they still exist as largely independent entities. That is, they have not been thoroughly encoded.

The next stage in the production process, which Liberman et al. (1972) see as being relatively straightforward, involves the final commands to the muscles. In their view, however, it is not in these commands but in the remaining conversions from muscle contraction to vocal tract shape to sound that the output is radically restructured and where true encoding takes place. It is in this stage that the activity of the independent but overlapping muscle groups becomes merged, as reflected in the acoustic signal:

> In the case of /b ae g/, the movement of the lips that represents a feature of the initial consonant is overlapped with the shaping of the tongue appropriate for the next vowel segment. In the conversion to sound, the number of dimensions is reduced, with the result that the simultaneous activity of lips and tongue affect exactly the same parameter of the acoustic signal, for example, the second formant (p. 316).

Liberman, Mattingly, and Turvey (1972) point out that their description is only intended to show that a very crude model can account for the complexly encoded relation between the speech signal and the phonetic message. We should note, however, that this model also provides a basis for speech perception. Now the listener is required to decode the speech signal by reference to a "general model of the articulatory process," including the neural signals, and does not rely solely on a synthesis of the articulatory movements. Thus, in contrast to the earlier version of the motor theory, this description provides the listener with a general articulatory model as the basis for carrying out an analysis by synthesis. Decoding of heard speech can therefore be accomplished at the higher level of neural signals and need not be carried out solely at the level of articulatory movements. To the extent that the articulatory process is still involved in perception, it is appropriate to refer to this model as a motor theory of speech perception. Of course, a great deal of research must be carried out before this or any other theory of speech perception can be validated. The model proposed by Liberman et al. (1972), however, does have the advantage of providing an explanation of many of the complex aspects of speech perception, including context-conditioned variation and parallel transmission.

LOCALIZATION OF FUNCTION

At least implicit in our preceding discussion is the suggestion that speech is processed differently than other auditory inputs. For example, in examining categorical perception we saw that the same acoustic signals (second-formant transitions) are treated differently depending on whether or not they appear in a speech context. The notion that speech is processed in a special way that is different from other auditory inputs also suggests that there may be a special center for speech in the brain. Actually, the suggestion of a special center for speech is a very old one, dating back to Broca's (1861) hypothesis that the third frontal convolution of the left hemisphere contains a center for language. Penfield and Roberts (1959) have demonstrated the localization of some language mechanisms in both the frontal and temporoparietal areas of the left hemisphere. But much of their evidence, like Broca's, comes from clinical study of brain-injured patients, and it is only in recent years that experimental evidence on normal individuals has become available.

Dichotic Listening

The experimental investigation of localization of function for auditory stimuli has been greatly advanced by the application of a technique developed by Broadbent (1954) called *dichotic listening*. In this procedure separate stimuli are presented through earphones such that they arrive at the two ears at the same time. Doreen Kimura (1961a, 1961b) pioneered the use of this technique in studying the relative contribution of the two hemispheres in speech perception. She discovered that when groups of digits are presented to the ears at about the same time, subjects more accurately report the digits presented to the right ear than those presented to the left ear. Although the differences were small they were consistent across subjects. Since the right ear is more strongly connected to the left hemisphere than the left ear is, this finding suggests that the speech-processing centers are located in the left hemisphere.

It should be emphasized here that there are projections from each ear to both hemispheres. As we just noted, the projection to the opposite, or *contralateral*, hemisphere is dominant over the projection to the same side, or *ipsilateral*, hemisphere. This does not mean that the advantage of one ear over the other is very great. The inputs to a given ear still go to both hemispheres of the brain, and the advantage of one ear over the other is likely to be quite small. Based on past experience this should not surprise us. We know, for example, that in listening to a telephone message it makes no difference which ear we listen through. Thus, for individuals with intact nervous systems, it appears that dichotic presentation provides a unique situation for observing these laterality effects.

Speech versus Nonspeech Inputs

One of the more obvious questions to be explored concerns whether or not speech stimuli show a different laterality effect than nonspeech stimuli under dichotic presentation. This possibility was strongly suggested by Milner's work (1962) with the Seashore Measures of Musical Talents. She demonstrated that performance on the tonal pattern perception and timbre discrimination subtests of this well-known aptitude test is selectively impaired by right temporal lobectomy. This finding suggests that in musical patterns a left-ear advantage, contrary to the right-ear advantage for speech, may exist.

Kimura (1964) developed a melodies test in which different melodic fragments were presented to the two ears at the same time. After each pair of melodic fragments was presented, the subjects were presented with four melodies, one at a time. The subjects' task was to identify which two of the four melodies had been presented dichotically. The task was one of recognition, not naming, and Kimura found that the subjects performed significantly better on melodies presented to the left ear. When the same subjects were given the dichotic test with groups of digits, they were more accurate on digits presented to the right ear. The melodies and digits tasks used by Kimura have been presented to patients with localized lesions of the left or right temporal lobe. In two studies (Shankweiler, 1966; Kimura, 1967) it was shown that patients with lesions in the right temporal lobe were impaired on the melodies task but not on the digits task, whereas patients with lesions in the left temporal lobe were impaired on the digits task but not on the melodies task.

The combined results from the preceding studies seem to indicate that the dimension of speech stimuli versus nonspeech stimuli is the decisive factor in determining the direction of laterality effects. Studies employing a wider range of auditory inputs will obviously be required, but as of now it seems that speech stimuli have a right-ear, left-hemisphere advantage and nonspeech stimuli have a left-ear, right-hemisphere advantage. The direction of these differences is further supported by Curry (1967), who reports that common environmental noises are also better recognized in the left ear.

Lateralization of Speech Sounds

One characteristic of the studies we have just reviewed is that the speech stimuli were all spoken digits. That is, the speech stimuli were meaningful words. This raises the question as to whether the meanings of these stimuli had to be perceived for the observed laterality effects to be found. Of course it could be that nonmeaningful speech stimuli would show the same laterality effect. If all that is required is speech sounds, whether or not they are meaningful, this would have important implications concerning the possibility that speech perception relies on different mechanisms than those involved in perceiving other sound stimuli.

Investigators at Haskins laboratories have been studying the lateralization of nonmeaningful speech sounds for several years. The initial experiments in this series were carried out by Shankweiler and Studdert-Kennedy. In their first experiment the stimuli were produced synthetically by the *pattern playback*. The stimuli consisted of all combinations of the six stop consonants /b,d,g,p,t,k/ followed by the vowel /a/. Thus the stimuli differed from one another only at the beginning of the signal, about 50 msec. The stimuli were presented in pairs, with one member of the pair directed to each ear. The order of presentation was carefully counterbalanced so that each syllable pair (e.g., /ka-da/) was presented with /ka/ going to the right and left ears just as often as /da/. The subjects were told that two different stimuli would be presented on each trial. They were asked to write down both syllables they heard, reporting first the syllable they were most confident of having heard. To make certain that perception and not memory of the syllables was the critical factor, all syllables appeared at the top of the answer sheet. The subjects were required to write down two syllables on every trial, even if they had to guess.

The results indicated a highly significant advantage for the right ear, with fourteen of fifteen subjects obtaining better scores on those syllables presented to the right ear. The average right-ear advantage was 16 percent. On the basis of these findings Shankweiler and Studdert-Kennedy (1967) concluded that the special speech-processing center of the left hemisphere was engaged at the sound level and did not depend upon meaningful stimulus inputs. They also noted that since the laterality effect was observed with single pairs of syllables, thus not overloading memory, the effect probably has a genuine perceptual basis and is not due to memory. Other investigators (e.g., Kimura, 1962) had also reached a similar conclusion.

Shankweiler and Studdert-Kennedy also have performed experiments to investigate laterality effects with vowels and to compare laterality effects with both real and synthetic speech stimuli. The stimuli used in these studies were CVC syllables where the initial consonant was one of the six stop consonants. Six vowels /i, ɛ , æ, ɑ , ɔ, u/ were also used, and the final consonant was always /p/. The synthetic stimuli were synthesized as in the previous study, and the real speech stimuli were spoken by a trained phonetician experienced in making speech recordings. The stimuli were presented in pairs as in the earlier experiment, but on any given trial the syllables contrasted only in the initial consonant or only in the vowel, but not in both. The subjects were again asked to report both syllables.

Since trials on which both syllables are given either correctly or incorrectly contribute nothing to the assessment of laterality, the only trials scored were those on which a subject was correct on one syllable and wrong on the other syllable. The results are given in Figure 9.9. As the

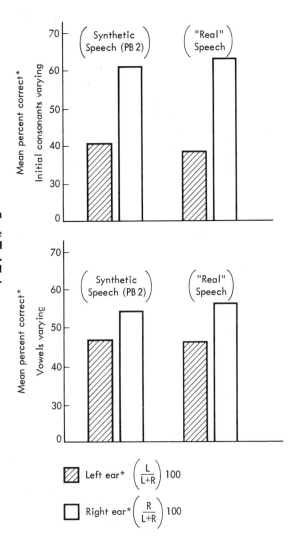

Figure 9.9 $\dfrac{R+L}{R-L}$ **(100) as a measure of the ear difference for dichotically presented syllables, synthetic and real. This tabulation includes all trials on which one error occurred.**
(From Shankweiler, 1971.)

data in the upper section of this figure indicate, there is a pronounced advantage for the right ear in consonant perception. There is also no difference between synthetic speech and real speech in terms of the laterality effect. However, the size of the laterality effect for consonants is appreciably greater than for vowels (see lower section of figure). This suggests that the special speech-processing mechanisms of the left hemisphere play a greater role in consonant perception than in vowel perception. This finding should not surprise us, since we know that consonants are more highly restructured than vowels. Of course the degree of restructuring is a relative matter, and although the consonants do show a pronounced laterality effect, the vowels also are lateralized to some extent.

In a recent study Darwin (1971) demonstrated a significant right-ear advantage for dichotically competing vowels when subjects were uncertain about the size of the vocal tract that produced them. Darwin used synthetic signals designed to reflect differences in vocal tract size and which contrasted in the vowel. The main difference produced by vocal tract size in this case was to alter the fundamental frequency or pitch of the vowel. For one group of subjects the dichotic pairs presented on a given trial contained sounds from (1) only the larger vocal tract, (2) only the smaller vocal tract, (3) the larger tract to the left ear and the smaller tract to the right ear, or (4) the larger tract to the right ear and the smaller tract to the left ear. Across trials these subjects were presented signals from all four categories. A second group of subjects was tested only with sounds for the smaller vocal tract being presented on each trial.

The results of this study indicated a significant right-ear advantage in the mixed condition. When subjects heard sounds appropriate for both vocal tract sizes, a right-ear advantage was found. Even on those trials when sounds from the same size vocal tract were presented to both ears, the right-ear advantage held up. But when subjects were only exposed to sounds from one vocal tract on every trial, no laterality effects were found. Thus, although the more highly encoded consonants show a fairly large and consistent right-ear advantage (cf. Liberman, Mattingly, and Turvey, 1972), this study indicates that the less-encoded vowels do engage the speech-processing mechanisms under certain conditions.

The Nature of Lateralization

Increasing evidence indicates that the contralateral pathway to the dominant hemisphere has an advantage over the ipsilateral pathway for the perception of speech. In most right-handed individuals the left hemisphere is dominant, and since most people are right-handed, they are typically selected as subjects in laterality studies. Left-handed individuals also may show a left-hemisphere dominance, but this is the case less consistently than with right-handed individuals. However, there is a great deal to be learned about the nature of the dominance, and research is just beginning to reveal some of the underlying factors.

Milner, Taylor, and Sperry (1968), using Kimura's dichotic-digits task, reported an investigation of patients with surgical disconnection of the cerebral hemispheres. The effect of the disconnection is to eliminate communication between the two hemispheres, although the connections from each ear to both hemispheres remain intact. These patients are equally accurate in reporting monaurally presented digits to either ear, but under dichotic presentation they cannot report left-ear inputs. In contrast, normal subjects showed only a slight, but significant, right-ear advantage. These findings indicate that the ipsilateral pathway can be utilized but that it is somehow suppressed in the presence of a competing stimulus from the contralateral ear when communication between the hemispheres is prevented. The results also support the dominance of contralateral over ipsilateral connections.

In recent years researchers have begun to exploit this dissociation of the hemispheres and its implications for both speech perception and production. For example, Wood, Goff, and Day (1971) have reported differential cortical-evoked potentials in the left hemisphere during perception of speech and nonspeech stimuli. No differences in these neural responses are obtained from the right hemisphere. On the production side, McAdam and Whitaker (1971) report similar differences in neural activity between the two hemispheres occurring up to one second before the pronunciation of polysyllabic words. No doubt future research in this area will provide considerable insight into the nature of neural functioning during speech.

Several recent studies suggest that the dominant hemisphere may provide a special decoding mechanism for phonetic features. In two experiments (Halwes, 1969; Studdert-Kennedy, and Shankweiler, 1970) it was found that perceptual errors often result from combining features from separate inputs to the two ears. For example, if a voiced stop such as /ba/ is presented to the left ear and an unvoiced stop such as /ka/ is presented to the right ear, the errors subjects make in reporting what is heard are most likely to be /pa/ and /ga/. In this case /pa/ takes the place feature (front of mouth) from the left ear and the voicing feature (unvoiced) from the right ear while /ga/ takes the voicing feature (voiced) from the left ear and the place feature (back of mouth) from the right ear. These errors are more likely than either /da/ or /ta/, which share only a single feature with one of the inputs. That is, /da/ and /ta/ are produced in the middle of the mouth and do not share the place feature with either input, although /da/ is voiced as is /ba/, and /ta/ is unvoiced as is /ka/.

These investigations suggest that the ear difference takes place at the level of phonetic analysis. More concrete support for this view has been reported by Studdert-Kennedy, Shankweiler, and Pisoni (1972). They synthesized eight CV syllables using the consonants /b,p,d,t/ and two vowels /i,u/. The four consonants yield six contrasting pairs with the pairs /b/,

/p/ or /d/, /t/ sharing a place feature; /b/, /d/ or /p/, /t/ sharing a voice feature; and /b/, /t/ or /d/, /p/ sharing neither feature. In addition, these consonant pairs could be presented with the members of the pair being followed by the same vowel or by different vowels. Table 9.1

Table 9.1 Paired combinations of four stop consonants according to features of voicing and place of articulation.

| | Place of articulation | |
	Front	*Middle*
Unvoiced	b	d
Voiced	p	t

| Pairs sharing | | |
Place alone	*Voicing alone*	*Neither feature*
b-p	b-d	b-t
d-t	p-t	d-p

AFTER STUDDERT-KENNEDY ET AL., 1972.

shows the paired consonants and the features they share, and Figure 9.10 gives schematic spectrograms of the CV syllables.

The experiment involved dichotic presentation of these contrasting pairs, and the subjects were instructed to identify both of the initial consonants from the set /b,p,d,t/. Figure 9.11 shows the findings for those trials on which both consonants were reported correctly. Notice that performance is clearly better on those pairs that have a feature in common. The question is whether the advantage for sharing a feature is auditory or phonetic. Studdert-Kennedy et al. reason that if the advantage due to sharing a feature has an auditory basis, then performance should be better when both a feature and a vowel are shared than when only the feature is shared. Presumably there is greater commonality among the auditory dimensions (pitch, loudness, timbre, duration) when both feature and vowel are shared. If the advantage has a phonetic basis, however, it should make no difference whether the vowels are the same or different. The data reported by Studdert-Kennedy et al. support a phonetic interpretation.

The results of this experiment were also examined for those trials on which one consonant was reported correctly and the other incorrectly. The data indicated a highly significant right-ear advantage for both the place and the voicing feature, although it made no difference whether the vowels were the same or different. These findings not only suggest that there is a

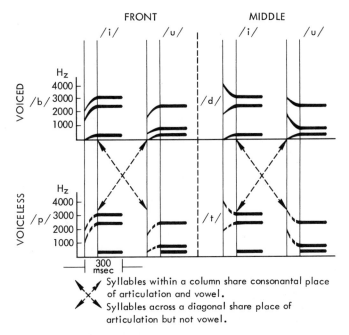

Figure 9.10   Schematic spectrograms of eight synthetic CV
syllables.
(After Studdert-Kennedy et al., 1972.)

special decoder for phonetic features but also suggest that the decoding
mechanisms are to be found in the left or dominant hemisphere.

The study of laterality effects has revealed several basic characteristics
of speech perception. In support of a very old hypothesis, there does appear to be a special processing center for speech which is usually found in
the left hemisphere of the brain. This is indicated by greater accuracy in
perceiving speech inputs presented to the right ear (left hemisphere) as
opposed to the left ear (right hemisphere). In contrast, the opposite relationship occurs when other auditory signals are employed.

The exact basis for the observed laterality effects is still open to
question, although meaningful inputs are not required to produce the effects. Lateralization occurs at the level of individual phonemes and is more
pronounced with consonants than with vowels. Laterality effects are also
found at the level of phonetic features. It appears that once these features
have been extracted from the context in which they were presented, they
can be combined as independent entities to account for some of the errors
observed in speech perception. Observations of this sort suggest that both
the restructuring of signals that is characteristic of the speech code and
the observed laterality effects may be due to the same processing mechanisms.

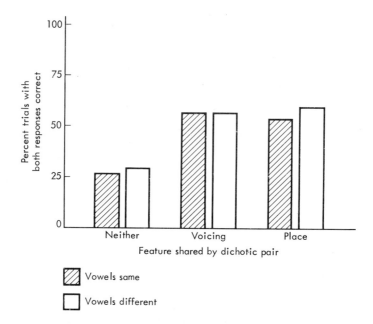

Figure 9.11   The percentage of trials on which both responses were correct as a function of the consonantal feature shared by dichotic CV pairs under two vowel conditions.
(From Studdert-Kennedy et al., 1972.)

UNITS OF SPEECH

One of the more puzzling facets of speech research has been the problem of segmentation. The critical issue here is to define the units that underlie both the production and the perception of speech. Several alternatives have been suggested, and there is support at the behavioral level for most of these. For example, an extensive analysis of errors in speech (Fromkin, 1970) shows that errors occur at the level of syllables (e.g., "butterpillar and catterfly"), phoneme-length segments (e.g., "the nipper is zarrow"), and phonetic features (e.g., "*te*bestrian" for "*pe*destrian"). In the last case the place of production of the two consonants is reversed.

Much of the work considered earlier in this chapter provides support for units at the phoneme or phonetic feature level. In fact, the studies of synthetic speech in which a "phoneme boundary" is observed can be viewed as providing support for either phonetic features or entire phonemes as units, since the segments on either side of the boundary differ in only one feature. For example, /ba/ and /da/ differ only in place of articulation.

Evidence for phonemes as units comes from a study reported by

Warren (1970). He began with tape-recorded sentences and removed from each sentence a single phoneme together with portions of the adjacent phonemes that might provide transition cues. The gap was either filled with an extraneous sound such as a cough or left unfilled. When the gap was unfilled, listeners had no difficulty detecting it and locating it correctly in the sentence. When the gap was filled, however, subjects believed they heard the missing phoneme and located the gap somewhere else in the sentence without interfering with the intelligibility of any phoneme. Warren points out that for listeners familiar with English these "phonemic restorations" are perhaps not so surprising, since no other phoneme could produce an English word. But this does not explain the listener's lack of awareness, the illusion that the sound was heard.

There is considerable support not only for phonetic features as basic units but also for feature units in studies of perceptual confusions and in multidimensional scaling (cf. Studdert-Kennedy, 1970). For example, it has been shown that the more features two segments have in common, the more likely they are to be confused (Miller and Nicely, 1955; Studdert-Kennedy and Shankweiler, 1970; Singh and Woods, 1970). Using a magnitude estimation technique, Greenberg and Jenkins (1964) showed that sounds differing on one feature were judged to be closer together than sounds differing on two features. There is even evidence from studies of short-term memory that both vowels and consonants may be encoded in terms of phonological features (Wickelgren, 1965, 1966, 1969).

The syllable has a somewhat different status than either the phoneme or the phonetic feature. Unlike the others, the syllable can be defined in articulatory and acoustic terms as well as linguistically. It is the unit of consonant-vowel coarticulation in that phonetic information is transmitted in parallel throughout the entire syllable. An experiment by Huggins (1964) also provides support for the syllable as a basic unit. He alternated incoming speech rapidly from one ear to the other and found that the rate most disruptive to speech perception was about 0.6 of a syllable. Of course, smaller, regularly recurring units could be involved.

A series of three experiments concerning the perceptual reality of phonemes and syllables was reported by Savin and Bever (1970). In a reaction time task the subjects were presented with a sequence of nonsense syllables. The syllables were recorded at the rate of one per second and presented to subjects in sequences that ranged from five to seventeen different syllables. There was one target to which the subject responded in each sequence. On half the trials for a given subject the target was a complete syllable (e.g., /b æ d/ or /s æ d/), and on the other half it was a particular phoneme from the same syllable (e.g., /b/ or /s/). In one experiment the target was always a word beginning with /b/. On "phoneme target" trials the subjects were told to respond to the first syllable beginning with /b/. On "syllable target" trials the target (/b æ d/) was presented in advance, and the subject was told to respond as soon as he heard the target in the subsequent series. In either case only one syllable beginning with /b/ occurred in each sequence, although the critical syllable changed from one sequence to the next.

The second experiment was identical to the first except that the target was always a syllable beginning with /s/, and in the third experiment the "phoneme target" was the medial vowel instead of the initial consonant. The conditions of the experiment were counterbalanced so that a given syllable (e.g., /s æ d/) was a "phoneme target" for half the subjects and a "syllable target" for the other half. The results of these experiments indicated that subjects responded more slowly to "phoneme targets" than they did to "syllable targets" containing the same phonemes. The difference in reaction time for "syllable targets" versus "phoneme targets" was 70 msec. for /b/, 40 msec. for /s/, and 250 msec. for the medial vowel /æ/. Savin and Bever conclude that "phonemes are perceived only by an analysis of already perceived syllables (or at least already perceived consonant-vowel pairs)" (p. 300). Similar findings and similar conclusions were reported by Warren (1971).

In view of the evidence concerning parallel transmission of phonemes, perhaps it should not surprise us to find that it takes longer to respond to phoneme targets than to syllable targets. If the information concerning the phoneme is distributed throughout the syllable, it is not unreasonable to suppose that it takes some time after the syllable has been presented to recover the information. Of course the findings of Savin and Bever (1970) and Warren (1971) certainly raise questions about the perceptual reality of the phoneme.

McNeill and Lindig (1973) have questioned the interpretation advanced by Savin and Bever. They asked subjects to monitor the appearance of targets that occurred in units at the same level or at different levels. For instance, phonemes might be targets when the stimuli presented were either phonemes or syllables. Similarly, syllables might be targets when the stimuli were either syllables or words. In a series of such comparisons, these investigators found that reaction time was always fastest when the level of the target and the level of the stimuli were the same. On the basis of these findings, McNeill and Lindig suggest that the Savin and Bever results are due to a mismatch between phoneme targets and syllable stimuli and are not a reflection of basic perceptual units.

The complexity of research on speech segmentation has been well illustrated in the investigations we have reviewed here. We have seen evidence to support the view that phonetic features, phonemes, or syllables may serve an important function and that all three may play an important role in either production or perception. Two other studies bear at least indirectly on the issues raised here and serve to further illustrate the complexity of speech processes.

Warren (1969) presented his subjects with four sounds consisting of a high tone, a hiss, a low tone, and a buzz, in that order. Each sound lasted 200 msec. and was followed immediately by the next sound. After the last sound (a buzz) the series was repeated immediately. The subjects knew the names of the sounds, which were readily discriminable, and could listen to repetitions of the series for as long as they wished. Nevertheless, these subjects performed no better than chance in identifying the order in which the sounds were presented. The important point to note here is that order information is not recovered in this situation even though each sound appears for a considerably longer duration (200 msec.) than does the average phoneme (70–80 msec.) in normal discourse. Warren does report that experienced listeners can accomplish this task when each sound has a duration of about 300 msec., which is roughly comparable with average syllable length. For accurate perception of speech, however, there appears to be some sense in which individual phonemes and their order also must be recovered. It is not clear whether Warren's results say anything about this, but his findings do imply that the special packaging of information that seems to characterize the speech code is particularly efficient for the recovery of order information as well as phoneme identification.

In our discussion of speech perception we have repeatedly noted that speech appears to be processed in a different way than other auditory inputs. We reviewed some of the results of studies in categorical perception that compared speech and nonspeech inputs in the form of identical second-formant transitions. These results suggest that the distinction between speech and nonspeech is not made at the acoustic or auditory level but instead may depend on whether the speech-processing mechanisms essential to the extraction of phonemes or phonetic features are engaged. A study by T. Rand (cited in Liberman, Mattingly, and Turvey, 1972) bears on this issue.

Rand used a dichotic listening task with different inputs to each ear. To one ear he presented a complete first formant together with steady-state portions of the second and third formants. Various patterns were used which, by themselves, all sounded vaguely like /da/. To the other ear he presented the 50 msec. second- and third-formant transitions, with the appropriate time relationships carefully preserved. As we have noted previously, these transitions by themselves sound like chirps. Depending on the particular pattern presented to each ear, however, the listeners clearly heard /ba/, /da/, or /ga/ in one ear and, simultaneously, nonspeech chirps in the other. Here we see that the same second- and third-formant transitions can be processed simultaneously as both speech and nonspeech. As Liberman et al. (1972) suggest, "the incoming signal goes indiscriminately to speech and nonspeech processors. If the speech processors succeed in extracting phonetic features, then the signal is speech; if they fail, then the signal is processed only as nonspeech" (pp. 323–24).

RHYTHMIC FACTORS IN SPEECH

Karl Lashley (1951), in a frequently cited paper dealing with the problem of serial order in behavior, discussed a number of difficulties with then prominent behavioristic accounts of serial ordering both in speech and in nonspeech activities. One of the topics mentioned was rhythmic action, and he even implied that rhythmic action might provide a natural link between the perception and the production of connected speech. Although Lashley's paper has been widely cited, his views on rhythmic action have rarely been considered in detail. One exception, until quite recently, has been Lenneberg (1967), who incorporated rhythm as a factor in his views on the motor organization of speech. Another potentially important paper dealing with rhythmic action was published by J. G. Martin (1972).

Martin suggested that Lashley's views on rhythm were among the most important in his paper. While acknowledging that Lashley was not quite clear on the nature of rhythmic action, Martin suggests that part of the reason for the neglect of rhythm is that several misconceptions about it are widely held. One common misconception is that rhythm implies periodic, relatively fixed, repetitive behavior, such as walking or breathing. Another is that rhythm necessarily means strict temporal regularities usually accompanied by complex, aesthetically motivated elaborations, such as those found in music. According to Martin, however, Lashley's views were not limited by either of these misconceptions.

Martin suggests that rhythm implies a patterning of events in time. The patterning occurs because sequences of natural movements produced by the motor system are constrained in various ways. For instance, some movements simply cannot be produced adjacent to other movements in natural sequences. Of particular importance in the case of speech are temporal constraints which are seen as playing a major role in determining the organization of speech sounds. For sequences of speech sounds, the nature of these temporal constraints is such that the concept of rhythm implies relative timing. This means that the temporal aspect of each sound element (e.g., syllable) bears a specific relationship to the temporal aspects of *all other* elements in a specific sequence. In addition, because of the pattern of relationships, some sound elements are accented or stressed more than others and therefore stand out to some degree.

The simplest rhythmic pattern is a binary one in which one element is accented or stressed more than the other. More complex patterns are organized hierarchically and consist of binary patterns occurring within other binary patterns. Figure 9.12 illustrates the structure of two- and four-element binary patterns.

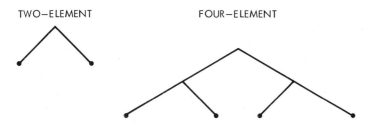

TWO—ELEMENT FOUR—ELEMENT

Figure 9.12 Structure of two-and four-elements patterns.
(After Martin, 1972.)

Martin (1972) proposes two rules based on these binary hierarchies to determine the accent level on each element in the sequence. The details of these rules are too complex to go into here, but one of the main implications of their application is that the more strongly accented elements are evenly spaced in time. For instance, in the four-element pattern of Figure 9.12, if the first element was given primary stress, then the third element would receive the next strongest accent. Although the number of elements in a particular rhythmic pattern may vary, the upper limit of such patterns is approximated by a short phrase or sentence. It should also be noted that whereas the accent on some elements may be perceived directly (particularly primary accent), most lower levels of accent are abstract and are only of theoretical importance. That is, there is generally no easy-to-define acoustic correlate of accent level.

The principle of relative timing has disinct implications for both the production and the perception of speech. In production, relative timing means that the temporal location of each sound element and its duration are related to the location of every other element in the pattern. This does not imply that the timing of a particular sequence of speech sounds is fixed. For example, say the words "John hit the ball" to yourself, emphasizing *John*. Now repeat those words, emphasizing *hit*. You can easily detect the difference in relative timing for the two versions. Actually, several other rhythmic patterns (e.g., emphasize *ball*) could be used to produce this sentence. The main point of Martin's position is that for any particular rhythmic pattern, the principle of relative timing holds. This means that given the accent levels of the elements in a pattern, relative timing is predictable. It also means that once we know both the primary accent and the relative timing, placement of the remaining accents is predictable by the rules Martin proposed.

Because of the rhythmic constraints placed on production, perceived speech sounds are temporally patterned. If speech sequences are rhythmically patterned, then some sound elements will be accented relative to other elements. The hierarchical organization of these sound patterns, however, suggests that main accents will fall on temporally predictable elements of the sound sequence.

Martin's theory suggests that the listener can anticipate the occurrence of accented elements on the basis of the rhythmic contours produced by the speaker. This implies that the *attention* of the listener will be focused, in an anticipatory manner, on the accented elements. The relationship between relative timing and accent levels is such that certain aspects of the spoken message become temporally predictable by the listener once he has "locked in" to the pattern. Since the listener's targets in perception are presumably the same as the speaker's targets in production (namely, the accented elements), it is possible for the listener to anticipate the onset of the more informative accented elements as part of the perceptual process. In contrast, an associative account of speech perception would seem to require continuous attention to the sound elements and would provide little opportunity for anticipation of later elements.

It is much too soon to evaluate the adequacy of Martin's contribution, but he provides a great deal of evidence in support of the general importance of rhythmic action in speech. He also presents some evidence for his model. For example, in one study (cf. Martin, 1972) fluent speakers of French, Italian, and Spanish were asked to identify the three most strongly accented syllables in tape-recorded excerpts from their native language. They were also asked to rank these three syllables in terms of relative accent level. The results indicated agreement among the fluent speakers as to the particular syllables that were accented (Martin, personal communication). In addition, those syllables on which fluent speakers were in agreement as to accent tended to be evenly spaced in time. Since accent levels beyond primary accent tend not to be revealed by acoustic cues, these findings provide considerable support for this theory.

Shields, McHugh, and Martin (1974) provide further support for this theory in an experiment involving a phoneme-monitoring task. In this experiment subjects responded to the phoneme /b/ which occurred in a nonsense word. The word was embedded in an otherwise coherent sentence, and the critical phoneme appeared in either the accented or the unaccented syllable (e.g., BIMfas or bimFAS). Reaction times to the sound of /b/ were faster when it occurred in an accented syllable. As the theory would predict, the subjects appeared to anticipate the accented syllable and hence attend more carefully to it on the basis of the rhythmic pattern of the earlier elements. This interpretation is supported by the observation that when the nonsense words are removed from the sentence context and presented in a string of other nonsense words produced separately, no reaction time differences appeared as a function of accented syllables.

If a model such as Martin's turns out to be correct, it will be of considerable importance to speech research. Not only does this model pertain to the sequencing of phonetic information but it may extend to morphology, syntax, and semantics as well. In addition, with the implications of the model for anticipating events in time, there may also be extensions to such topics as the focusing of attention and to memory in general.

ACQUIRING THE SOUNDS OF SPEECH

Not many years ago a popular conception of language acquisition held that speech sounds are learned according to traditional associationistic principles. This view assumed that all, or at least most, of the speech sounds that the human vocal system is capable of producing are produced by the human infant during the first year of life (cf. Staats and Staats, 1963). Presumably these sounds, including those of languages other than the infant's native language, occur during the babbling period when the infant is exploring the possibilities of his vocal mechanism. But only those sounds that the infant hears in his own language community, such as those produced by parents and older siblings, become selectively reinforced and learned. The sounds to which the infant is not exposed gradually disappear from his repertoire.

Once the initial sounds or basic building blocks are acquired, it was thought to be a simple matter to explain syllable and word formation through the process of successive approximations. That is, in the course of babbling the child might produce a sound that resembled a word in the language. Such occurrences would presumably be greeted by immediate reinforcement from observing adults, and according to the theory such sounds would be more likely to be produced in the future. On future occasions, however, reinforcement might be withheld until the child produced better and better approximations to the actual word. Through a succession of such approximations the child would gradually establish a vocabulary. Of course, not all words would have to be learned in this manner, for once syllabic units come under his control the child may quickly produce new words (Staats and Staats, 1963). Words occurring in this way also would be reinforced, and once the child had developed a sufficient vocabulary the application of similar procedures would lead to the formation of phrases and sentences.

This view of language acquisition was based on an extensive investigation of conditioning in both animals and humans, which appeared to indicate that reinforcement procedures played the major role in learning. Further support for this view was supposedly provided by studies dealing with the conditioning of verbal behavior. For example, it has been shown that certain vocal responses can be placed under the control of reinforcement in both adults and infants. Greenspoon (1955) reported that the frequency with which adults emit plural nouns can be increased through reinforcement, and Rheingold, Gewirtz, and Ross (1959) reported a similar finding for nonlanguage vocalizations of three-month-old infants. On the basis of such evidence, the point of view we are considering here seems to be as follows: If nonlanguage infant vocalizations can be controlled through the application of reinforcement procedures and these same procedures can be used to control the verbal responses of adults, then other infant or child vocalizations such as phonemes, syllables, and words could also be learned in this way.

Although this conception of the beginnings of language acquisition has a certain appeal, it contains many difficulties both at the rational and at the empirical level. To begin with, there is a certain inconsistency between the assumption that all or most speech sounds can be made initially by the infant and the traditional empiricist-associationist view that all learning is based on experience. A more serious problem for this theoretical position is the increasing evidence indicating that all speech sounds are not present in early life but are acquired gradually and in a systematic pattern.

McNeill (1970) reports that during the first year of life consonant sounds develop from the back of the mouth to the front, and vowel sounds develop from front to back. During the second year of life, however, the developmental pattern is just the opposite. The front consonants and back vowels of the second year are the first to appear as speech sounds, and the back consonants and front vowels of the prespeech period are among the last to be organized into a linguistic system. McNeill (1970) also points out that the combination of front consonants and back vowels serves as a starting point for speech irrespective of the language to which the children are exposed. Thus, although the language experiences of young children differ widely and the words they learn differ in accordance with their native languages, the particular speech sounds they use are common to all languages and are acquired in a similar order. English-speaking children say *tut* before *cut,* Swedish children say *tata* before *kata,* German children say *topf* before *kopf,* and Japanese children say *ta* before *ka* (Jakobson, 1941; McNeill, 1970).

Beyond the assumption that the infant can produce most speech sounds, there are other difficulties with the successive approximation point of view. One may seriously question the extent to which parents or other adults selectively reinforce the productions of young children in any systematic way. If adults exercised this type of control, we would expect greater differences across languages than those mentioned above. For example, Nakazima (1962), in a study of American and Japanese children, found little difference in the speech sounds used by the two groups even at the stage where words and phrases begin to appear. This is not to imply that children are not influenced by their language environment. Children do imitate the speech of adults and they do so a great deal (cf. McNeill, 1970). The fact of imitation, however, does not mean that language is acquired by imitation. Children also produce many forms that have no parallel in adult speech.

Menyuk (1971) suggests that the changing perceptual and productive capacities of the young child may have more to do with the development of speech than does the particular linguistic environment in which the child is raised. This notion is certainly consistent with Nakazima's findings. As further support for this position Menyuk cites a study by Preston and Yeni-Komshian (1967), which examined voice onset times for stop consonants in infants raised in different language environments (Arabic, English, and Hungarian). Although the pattern of voice onset times for stop consonants differs considerably among adult speakers of these languages, the patterns for children were quite similar and tended toward the middle of the range. This finding is quite unlike what would be expected according to a successive approximation view in which maximum similarity should exist within a language and not within an age group across languages.

Language Development

Little is known about the specifics of language development, and most of what we do know concerns the development of speech production and not speech perception. Most of the available evidence is derived from observations and clinical cases and is not experimental in nature. In addition, the observational data are subject to misinterpretation, since the adults listening to a child's vocalizations, or tape recordings of them, may interpret what they hear according to the classification system of their adult language. Nevertheless, what information is available suggests a much more complex system for language learning than that implied by the empiricist-associationist view we have been considering.

Apparently the first characteristic of speech to be discriminable in the babbling of children is the intonation contour or rhythm of the utterance. That is, children produce sound sequences that have no meaning and no definable phoneme structure but do have recognizable intonation contours, such as those that characterize questions or exclamations (Lenneberg, 1967). Only with further development does this whole become differentiated into its components to the extent that primitive phonemes appear in the infant's productions. Lenneberg (1967) suggests that this developmental pattern may result from the difficulty of controlling vocal tract adjustments. As the child begins to gain control over the vocal mechanism, the fine movements necessary for phoneme articulation become possible, but prior to that time the more general rhythmic characteristics reflected in the intonation contours are more noticeable.

When phonemes do begin to occur with some frequency, vowel sounds are most common. Not until around thirty months of age is the frequency of vowels and consonants sounds about equal (Irwin, 1946). This would appear to indicate an increasing frequency of consonant-vowel coarticulation in production. Beyond thirty months the frequency of consonants increases appreciably as words, phrases, and sentences become more prominent. We will leave these aspects of language development to the consideration of syntax and semantics in the next chapters.

Although the maturational aspects of motor development appear to play a role in phoneme production, the development of language is not dependent upon motor coordination. This is indicated by the observation that language comprehension precedes language production by several months, particularly between eighteen and thirty-six months of age (cf. Lenneberg, 1967). In addition, the developmental picture for speech and other motor activities is quite different. Most motor skills involve many years of training (e.g., piano playing), and individuals vary considerably in native ability. On the other hand, speech develops equally well in most individuals, with both the onset of speech and fluency occurring earlier than comparable mastery of other motor skills. Speech also develops with no particular training, as does walking. In fact, there is no evidence that any conscious or systematic teaching of language takes place at all (Lenneberg, 1967). Although it cannot be proved, there seems to be a maturational basis for the development of speech just as there is in walking.

Although there is considerable evidence for the lateralization of speech and the left hemisphere seems to play the dominant role in most individuals, evidence from the study of aphasia suggests that the left hemisphere may not be dominant initially. The term *aphasia* refers to a broad class of language disturbances in which there is a loss of the proper organization in either the expressive or the receptive process or both. Language in this sense is not lost, but there are disturbances in production or perception.

According to Lenneberg (1967), in children under two years of age brain lesions to the left hemisphere are no more likely to retard the onset of speech than are lesions to the right hemisphere. Apparently, at this age neither hemisphere is sufficiently specialized for language to prevent normal development. But once the child has reached the stage where language acquisition is possible, left-hemisphere dominance is indicated. Lenneberg (1967) states that left-hemisphere lesions result in speech disturbances in 85 percent of the cases, whereas right hemisphere lesions do so in only 45 percent of the cases. Thus it appears that the left hemisphere has greater potential for language development and that its dominance increases with age, although language can develop in the right hemisphere if there is damage on the left side.

Another interesting observation that comes from the study of aphasia concerns the recovery pattern in adults and children. Lenneberg (1967) indicates that the likelihood for total recovery for aphasia decreases with increasing age. He states that between age two and roughly age thirteen, recovery from aphasia is quite frequent, with the better prognosis associated with the earlier ages. After age thirteen, however, recovery is rarely complete; some trace of the aphasia is left behind.

These observations indicate that language can be developed in either hemisphere, but only for a certain period of time. Thus the normal course of development is one of increasing left-hemisphere dominance with increasing age, but if damage occurs to that hemisphere, the right hemisphere may take over if the individual is young enough. This is not to imply that second languages cannot be acquired after age thirteen, although the acquisition process may be somewhat altered. For example, it is commonly observed that speaking a language with a "foreign accent" is much more likely when the language is learned after the early teens.

Molfese (1972) has provided evidence that appears to contradict the view that the left hemisphere becomes increasingly dominant for speech with increasing age. He presented subjects with three classes of auditory stimuli and took recordings of averaged evoked potentials from both hemispheres during stimulus presentation. The stimuli consisted of syllables, words, and mechanically produced sounds such as a piano chord. The subjects were infants whose average age was 5.8 months, young children whose average age was 6 years, and adults whose average age was 25.9 years. The results indicated greater activity in the right hemisphere when mechanically produced sounds were presented and greater activity in the left hemisphere for speech sounds. With mechanically produced sounds the infants showed greater right-hemisphere dominance than either the young children or the adults. With speech sounds, however, both the infants and the young children showed greater left-hemisphere dominance than the adults.

These findings suggest that specialization of the two hemispheres for speech and nonspeech sounds is present as early as the first year of life. Both hemispheres still have some ability to respond to both types of stimuli. Although the observations suggest an early left-hemisphere dominance for speech, they do not necessarily imply that lesions in the left hemisphere will be more likely to retard the onset of speech than lesions in the right hemisphere.

A second implication of Molfese's findings is that the asymmetry for both speech and nonspeech sounds observed in the infants appears to decrease with age. This implication is exactly the opposite of Lenneberg's suggestion that left-hemisphere dominance for speech increases with age. Of course it is possible that the dominance of the left hemisphere does not decrease with age but merely becomes more difficult to detect because of increased development of the various commissures that interconnect the two hemispheres. Surgical disconnection of the two hemispheres results in a pronounced asymmetry during dichotic listening, even though the connections from the ears to the hemispheres remain intact (Milner, Taylor, and Sperry, 1968).

Language Acquisition and the Speech Code

As we noted previously, there is little in the way of experimental evidence concerning language acquisition at the sound level. Bakker (1968) has shown laterality effects for children from age nine to age thirteen, and the clinical evidence drawn from studies of aphasia suggests that lateralization of function begins at a very early age and becomes more pronounced with age. In addition, Molfese (1972) has shown that the left hemisphere may be dominant for speech as early as the first few months of life. Little is known about the specifics of the developmental process, however.

Some studies have shown that certain aspects of the speech code may be present in the perception of infants during the early months of life. These experiments have employed the habituation-dishabituation paradigm, with either heart rate or rate of nonnutritive conjugate sucking as the response measure. In either case the procedure is to repeatedly expose the infant to a given stimulus until the rate of response in question decelerates by some specified amount. Then a second stimulus is presented. If both stimuli are perceived as being the same, response rate should either remain the same or continue to decelerate. If the stimuli are perceived as being different, however, presentation of the second stimulus should result in an increase in response rate (i.e., dishabituation).

Using change in heart rate as the response measure, Moffitt (1971) has shown that five-month-old infants can discriminate between /ba/ and /ga/. This finding suggests that even very young infants are sensitive to the phonetic feature of place of articulation. That even younger infants may be sensitive to the feature of voicing or voice onset time has been shown in another study reported by Eimas, Siqueland, Jusczyk, and Vigorito (1971). These investigators used rate of nonnutritive conjugate sucking as the response measure and showed that infants of one and four months of age could discriminate the acoustic cue that underlies the adult distinction between the voiced stop /b/ and the unvoiced stop /p/.

Morse (1972) employed procedures that were very similar to those of Eimas et al. (1971) in a study of infants forty to fifty-four days of age. The results of this experiment indicated that these infants could discriminate according to place of articulation (/ba/ vs. /ga/) as well as a stimulus shift that consisted only of a change in the intonation contour (rising vs. falling). Taken together, these findings appear to suggest that categorical perception is accomplished by a process that may well be part of the organism's biological makeup and by a process that is operative at a surprisingly early age. If further research confirms these findings and extends them to other aspects of the speech code, the evidence against the empiricist-associationist view of speech development will be quite overwhelming.

CONCLUSION

Traditional explanations of speech perception have emphasized a close correspondence between specific speech sounds and specific percepts. Such accounts begin by assuming that some particular physical aspect of the acoustic signal is responsible for every percept. This assumption is equivalent to one we have encountered in previous chapters—namely, for each response (percept) there must be a particular stimulus. Explanations such as this also assume that speech constitutes an alphabetic sequence of sounds (stimuli), each of which gives rise to a particular response (percept). Thus, speech perception is viewed as being more or less like spelling a sequence of letters on a printed page.

It has also been traditional to consider speech sounds as being no different, in principle, from other auditory inputs. Speech perception was expected to conform to basic learning principles such as stimulus generalization. These learning principles were assumed to govern the acquisition of speech sounds and the combining of elementary sounds to produce more complex utterances. Although such concepts have been more or less accepted for a long time, an increasing amount of evidence indicates that these concepts are not correct.

In the present chapter we have emphasized the structure of speech at sound level. We began by considering whether or not the assumption of a one-to-one correspondence between speech sounds and percepts was valid. At least at the level of phonemes, studies of context-conditioned variation indicated that this assumption could not be supported. These studies indicated that what leads to the perception of most consonant sounds depends on the context in which the consonants occur. We saw that wide variations in the acoustic signal often lead to a single percept and that a single acoustic signal may lead to different percepts, depending on the context in which the signal appears.

The phenomena of categorical perception and parallel transmission are also inconsistent with traditional accounts. We noted in studies of categorical perception of consonants that very small acoustic changes could be discriminated with great accuracy when the changes involved crossing a phoneme boundary. Changes of the same magnitude, however, as well as greater changes, could not be discriminated within a single phoneme class. Although vowel sounds are not categorized so sharply in perception, the findings for consonants are clearly inconsistent with traditional learning principles such as stimulus generalization. Further evidence against traditional concepts is found in the observation of parallel transmission of phonemes. That is, instead of a one-to-one correspondence between the acoustic signal and phoneme perception, it appears that some information about two or more phonemes is carried simultaneously by the acoustic signal.

Speech sounds and nonspeech sounds are apparently not alike. The acoustic cues that are critical for perception of many consonants are not even perceived as speech sounds when they are removed from the speech context. Furthermore, the same acoustic cues that lead to categorical perception in the speech context will no longer do so when they are removed from that context and presented in isolation. Evidence also indicates that speech sounds are processed to a large extent in a different area of the brain (left hemisphere) than are nonspeech sounds (right hemisphere). These studies of localization of speech also suggest that speech perception depends on such abstract structures as phonemes and phonetic features which are not directly observable in the acoustic signal.

Extensive evidence contradicts traditional views concerning the nature of speech and the perception of speech, and it is therefore not surprising to find that traditional assumptions about the way language is acquired do not receive much support. As we have seen, language is acquired and it is acquired quite rapidly. Few traditional assumptions about the acquisition process are supported, however. Young children do not learn language in any significant way through training by imitation or reinforcement, at least not as those concepts have been traditionally interpreted. There is some evidence that language development follows a specific course, even across language communities. There is also some evidence that certain of the structures on which the adult depends for speech perception are present in the infant soon after birth. Findings such as these not only contradict traditional assumptions about the specifics of language learning but also suggest that language acquisition and use may depend in an important way on prewired connections in the brain.

10

Basic
Grammatical Theory
and Research

IN THE PRECEDING CHAPTER we considered those aspects of natural language that pertain to the perception and production of speech sounds. We now turn our attention to those aspects of natural language that pertain to the combining of words into sentences. Most of this chapter will focus on the structure of language at the level of syntax—the rules that relate the elements of a sentence to one another rather than the meaning of the individual elements. Following our discussion of grammatical theory, some of the experimental research dealing with syntax will be reviewed. Although semantic factors no doubt play a major role in these experiments, it should be remembered that the experiments were motivated mainly by the syntactic considerations which will be discussed in the earlier part of this chapter. In the next chapter we shall emphasize the issue of semantics and the interplay of semantic and syntactic processes.

According to most authorities, knowing a natural language means knowing a system of rules for producing and understanding sentences. This assumption appears necessary to account for one of the most important facts of natural language—its *creativity*. In the normal situation, speakers of a language produce and understand sentences they have never encountered before, and they can continue to do this without limit. This creativity is so characteristic of natural language that we often fail to take note of it. Because most of the sentences we hear do not contain new words, we might conclude that the stock of sentences could not be very large. With the exception of such utterances as customary greetings, direct quotations, and clichés, however, most sentences we encounter are novel in one way or another.

The creativity displayed in the production and understanding of sentences is similar in many ways to the creativity that a person exhibits when multiplying two numbers he has never multiplied before or never encountered before. An individual who knows how to "do" arithmetic is not limited to some particular set of problems whose solutions are well practiced. He can do any problem that he has the patience to undertake, no matter how new or complicated the numbers are. In the same way, a speaker of a natural language is not limited to those sentences that have been encountered before. In both situations the creativity involves the use of rules that abstractly represent an infinite number of *possible* constructions to produce one or another of the actual constructions that fall under those rules.

In the case of language, the rules we are talking about are not rules that can be explicitly stated by adult language users or explicitly taught to young children. In fact, the set of rules that applies to English or to any other natural language is far from being fully worked out. What we are saying is that a speaker of a natural language has the equivalent of a system of rules which enables him to behave as though he actually knew the rules. Of course, even though the rules of arithmetic can be stated explicitly, there is no certainty as to their use in solving problems. All that can be said about correct solution of arithmetic problems is that a person behaves as though he knows the rules of arithmetic and uses those rules to solve problems.

An attempt to characterize the rules of a particular natural language is called a grammar. Linguists write grammars for each natural language. Each grammar, unlike the "grammar" we encounter in school, represents an effort to describe the ways in which certain linguistic objects (sentences) are related to each other and to capture the linguistic skills of speaker-hearers. The rules of a grammar are in some ways analogous to the laws of a physical theory. They attempt to relate the various phonological, syntactic, and semantic events to observable speech. These grammars are *not* psychological theories, although they attempt to capture certain basic facts about the language behaviors of human beings. In addition, they relate only to particular aspects of language and not to all of language behavior.

Competence and Performance

According to Chomsky (1957), the grammars that linguists write for natural languages are theories of linguistic *competence*. These theories are primarily concerned with the ideal language user who not only knows his language perfectly but also is not affected by memory limitations, distractions, or shifts in attention or interest. As such, a grammar is an idealization in the same sense as any other scientific theory, and it is not a theory about *performance*. The rules of a grammar relate to *ideal* speakers under *ideal* conditions and not to the actual behavior of the language user. As Katz (1966) points out, it no more matters that some speakers fail to exhibit a distinction represented in the rules of a grammar than it matters in Newtonian mechanics that objects of certain shapes actually fall faster than objects of other shapes. The exceptions are to be explained as deviations due to factors that lie outside the domain of the theory.

Although linguists are not especially interested in the day-to-day use of language but instead are concerned with the underlying structures that make language possible, the psychologist or psycholinguist must be concerned with both. The psychologist must discover the "reality" of the linguistic rules as well as the factors that cause behavior to deviate from these rules. For example, limitations on the human memory span keep us from producing or understanding sentences beyond a certain length or level of complexity. Factors such as distractions or shifts in attention may also produce deviant linguistic behavior in the form of false starts or hesitations. Thus the psychologist is concerned with a theory of performance that relates the theory of competence to actual linguistic behavior.

LINGUISTIC SKILLS

Speakers of natural language exhibit a characteristic creativity in the production and understanding of sentences. These speakers, however, also display many other skills that reveal something about their knowledge of the languages they speak. It is useful for us to have information about this knowledge because it is just this knowledge that must be described by any acceptable theory of competence.

Degree of Grammaticality

One of the skills you have as a speaker of natural language is the ability to distinguish between grammatical and ungrammatical utterances. You can also make judgments of the degree of grammaticality of utterances. To use some examples provided by Chomsky (1961), you can see that the phrases in (1) are perfectly well formed English sentences but those in (2) and (3) are not:

(1) John plays golf.
    What did you do to the book, bite it?
(2) *golf plays John
    *What did you do to the book, understand it?
(3) *golf plays aggressive
    *What did you do to the book, justice it?

* Ungrammatical string.

Notice also that the phrases in (2) are not as extreme as those in (3) in terms of their violation of English grammatical rules and that you can interpret the deviant phrases in (2), whereas those in (3) can scarcely be interpreted at all.

The skill exhibited by speakers in making judgments of grammaticality, and in being able to interpret some ungrammatical strings but not others, is difficult to explain according to traditional associative views of language. Most traditional approaches have focused on the word rather than the sentence as the basic unit of analysis. One result of this approach is that differences between strings of words are typically seen as reflecting differences in associative strength between adjacent words in the strings or in terms of statistical approximations to the language in question.

If you selected words out of a dictionary totally at random you would have what is called a *zero-order approximation* to English. A first-order approximation to English would be obtained by selecting words at random but weighted according to their frequency of occurrence in the language. That is, words such as *the,* which occur frequently in the language, would be more likely to be selected than less-frequent words such as *innovate.* For the next degree of approximation you might provide individuals with one-word contexts and ask them to supply the next word. For each additional word of context, a high-order approximation is obtained. With one word of context you have a second-order approximation, with two words of context a third-order approximation, and so on for higher orders of approximation. Table 10.1 illustrates some of the strings that might be obtained with various orders of approximation to English.

Miller and Selfridge (1950) presented subjects with strings of ten to fifty words which varied in their order of approximation to English, including actual English text. The subjects heard the words read once and immediately attempted to recall them. As the data in Figure 10.1 indicate, recall increased as the order of approximation increased with words from a fifth-order approximation, or any higher-order approximation, being recalled as well as English text. Although these findings clearly demonstrate that increasing the predictability of a string of words leads to improved retention for the string, it is still difficult to see any relationship between the ability to make judgments of grammaticality and these variations in orders of approximation to English.

Consider, for example, the strings in (4) and (5). These strings, which are both meaningless, were provided by Chomsky (1957) to illustrate the concept of grammaticality:

(4) Colorless green ideas sleep furiously.
(5) Furiously sleep ideas green colorless.

Although neither string is semantically interpretable, any English speaker would realize that the string in (4) is more grammatical. No doubt the string in (4) would be easier to learn and recall. If you examine pairs of adjacent words in both (4) and (5), however, they appear to be equally improbable. That is, they appear to have about the same order of approx-

Table 10.1 Approximation to English.

Zero order—taken from dictionary randomly
    . . . provinciality Herat store sense Bursa energy high-priced ralliform talon watchband dialing boyant unceremoniously . . .

First order—taken from popular books
    . . . until this do grows he destiny the but the his same needs and profession in one before those there . . .

Second order—constructed by having the preceding word
    . . . have to take a part of their house is to make that here is nothing is close to twenty-two three blind man and then he . . .

Third order—constructed by having two preceding words
    . . . several more people than ever before he went to the cupboard is empty of milk and cream are good boys and girls go to the class is . . .

Sixth order—constructed by having five preceding words
    . . . Almost anyone can see that there is something beyond this world he knew there was sometimes something funny about the boy caught in the school was a teacher of children expected that they would come to our house every time that you looked you could see that he wanted to go . . .

(FROM DEMBER AND JENKINS, 1970.)

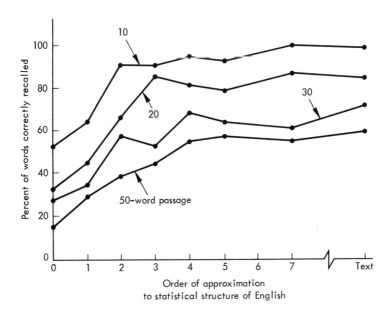

Figure 10.1 Accuracy of recall is plotted as a function of the order of approximation to English sentence structure. For all lengths of passages from 10 to 50 words, the recall was more accurate for high than for low orders of approximation.
(From Miller and Selfridge, 1950.)

imation to English, and they certainly do not appear in normal English discourse. Yet if you read these strings aloud Chomsky argues that you will find that (4) is read with a normal intonation pattern but (5) is not and that (4) "sounds like an English sentence" but (5) does not. Apparently the ability to produce and recognize grammatical utterances is not based entirely on statistical approximations to the language.

Two additional points need to be emphasized before we leave this topic. The first is that if you examine strings such as those in Table 10.1, which vary in order of approximation to English, you will notice that they also vary in their degree of grammaticality. Therefore, one may ask whether the improved retention of the higher orders of approximation is due to the grammaticalness of the string or to the order of approximation. It certainly seems likely that strings like (4) above would be recalled better than strings like (5) even though they do not appear to differ in their order of approximation to English.

The second point concerns the comparability of recall for fifth-order approximations and actual English text. Although this finding suggests that text is no easier to learn than a fifth-order approximation, the comparability in recall may be due to differences in what is learned. That is, one typically processes normal discourse by encoding the "gist" of what is said and not by keeping a verbatim record. Thus the subjects used by Miller and Selfridge (1950) may have recalled the essence of the text passage even though the number of words recalled that were identical to those in the message was no greater than it was for a fifth-order approximation.

Ambiguous Sentences

A second skill that is common to speakers of a natural language is the ability to detect ambiguity. A sentence is said to be ambiguous when the form in which it is actually presented, the *surface structure,* can be interpreted in two or more ways. A fairly trivial type is *lexical ambiguity,* which results when a particular word in a sentence has two or more meanings. For example, in sentence (6) the word "port" can refer either to the wine or to a geographical location. A more important type of ambiguity results when the surface structure of a sentence can be seen as having two or more meanings or interpretations. This is called *syntactic ambiguity* and is illustrated in sentences (7) and (8).

(6) The sailors liked the port.
(7) Flying planes can be dangerous.
(8) The shooting of the hunters was dreadful.

The ambiguity of sentence (7) is revealed by showing that it is related to two other sentences, (9) and 10).

(9) Flying planes is dangerous.

(10) Flying planes are dangerous.

Thus we can say that sentence (7) has one surface structure and two underlying structures. As shown in (9), one way of interpreting sentence (7) is to say that the act of flying a plane is dangerous whereas (10) illustrates the interpretation that flying planes themselves are dangerous. A similar ambiguity exists in (8), depending on whether the hunters did the shooting or the hunters were shot. Again a single surface structure can be related to either of two underlying structures.

More will be said about sentence ambiguity in later sections of this chapter. The important point to note at present is that the skill displayed by speakers in detecting syntactic ambiguity is difficult to account for according to any theory of language that treats a sentence as nothing more than a collection of words and their meanings. Notice that the meaning of the individual lexical items does not reveal the ambiguity in either (7) or (8). The ambiguity resides in the structure of the sentence itself, in the ways the various lexical items are related to each other. Most traditional association theories, which place the main emphasis on associative connections between individual words, would have considerable difficulty accounting for syntactic ambiguity. Yet an acceptable theory of language should be capable of explaining the skill exhibited by language users in detecting such ambiguities.

Sentence Structure

Speakers of a language are quite skillful in distinguishing between grammatical and ungrammatical utterances. They not only know what counts as a grammatical sentence, they can also determine a great deal about the internal structure of a sentence. Speakers can identify the subject and the object of a sentence, the way in which nouns and verbs are related, and considerably more.

Consider the sentences in (11):

(11) John is eager to please.
John is easy to please.

Notice how similar the surface structures are in these two sentences. They have the same sequence of form classes—that is, an initial noun followed by a verb which is followed by an adjective and so on. The words themselves are identical except for *eager* and *easy*. Yet as a speaker of English you know somehow that *John* is the logical subject in the first sentence but the logical object in the second sentence. You know that these sentences differ in their underlying structure, that the first sentence says John is eager to please *somebody* but the second says that it is easy for *somebody* to please *John*. This ability to go beneath the surface structure of sentences to discover their meanings is an important fact to be explained by any acceptable theory of language. Again, it should be noted that traditional association theories, or any other theories that treat sentences only as collections of words and their meanings, will not be able to explain these language skills.

This last point constitutes one of the more obvious weaknesses of associative theories of language and is a central point in contemporary linguistic grammars. Associative accounts typically treat sentences as a collection of words and their meanings, whereas most contemporary grammars make a distinction between the underlying structure and the surface structure of a sentence. Thus the associative theories deal with sentences at only one level, the surface structure, and usually in terms of a left-to-right sequence.

Even at the level of surface structure it is clear that more than a collection of words and their meanings is required. For example, consider the first sentence in (12):

(12) The boat sailed down the river.
      John was hit by Bill.
      John hit Bill.

Obviously, the first sentence is a perfectly clear, unambiguous sentence. If you were given the words of this sentence in random order and were asked to make up a sentence, you would have no trouble doing so. Now look at the other sentences in (12). You can see that the words themselves do not provide you with sufficient information to reconstruct the sentences. The words *Bill* and *John* could easily be interchanged. Notice, however, that even the additional requirement of word order does not provide sufficient information for complete sentence comprehension. The word *John* appears as the first word in two of the sentences in (12), but the role played by John is different in the two sentences. Apparently other structural information is required to interpret word order. As we noted in discussing ambiguous sentences, you must be able to determine the grammatical relations within a sentence to comprehend its meaning and to determine whether it is ambiguous. It is in these instances that the traditional explanations have not stood up well.

Relations Among Sentences

Still another linguistic skill common to speakers of a natural language is the ability to see grammatical relations among sentences. Consider the sentences in (13) and (14).

(13) John sold the car.
      The car was sold by John.
(14) Did John sell the car?
      John did not sell the car.

Any speaker of English knows that the active and passive sentences in (13) mean the same thing and that they are related to the sentences in (14). No doubt this skill is at least partially due to our ability to determine grammatical relations within a sentence. In the sentences in (13) and (14) this ability to determine grammatical relations tells us that the underlying structures of these sentences are quite similar even though the surface structures differ. This ability to perceive relations among sentences, to turn active sentences into passives, or to conjoin sentences is also a skill that should be accounted for by an acceptable grammatical theory. Unfortunately, most traditional theories of language, particularly associational approaches, have ignored such relations among sentences, tending for the most part to treat any differences in words or their arrangement as a different sentence.

MODELS OF GRAMMAR

A grammar for a natural language can be considered to be a theory of *linguistic competence.* Such a theory attempts to describe the ways in which sentences are related to each other and the linguistic skills common to language users. Some parts of this description may be common to all natural languages; other parts may be restricted to a particular language or language family. We can think of each natural language grammar as consisting of a part that is common to all languages, the set of *linguistic universals,* and a variable part that is peculiar to the particular language in question.

Models of grammar differ in their "generative capacity," or in what they will and will not account for. An acceptable grammar should account for the *four* types of linguistic skill previously described. That is, an acceptable grammar should capture the language user's ability to evaluate grammaticality, ambiguity, grammatical relations within a sentence, and relations among sentences. In addition to describing these four linguistic skills, one of the main criteria for a successful grammar is that it be capable of generating *all* and *only* the grammatical sentences of the language in question. If the grammar is too restrictive in generative capacity, it may not account for many types of grammatical sentences. But if the grammar is too powerful, it may generate all types of grammatical sentences in the language and describe many ungrammatical strings as sentences as well. This does not mean that language users utter only grammatical sentences.

The occurrence of ungrammatical utterances, however, is attributed by most theorists to failures in performance due to such factors as a lapse of attention or a shift of interest, and not to the user's linguistic competence. Of course this assumption, like any other theoretical assumption, is subject to empirical confirmation.

We shall consider three types of grammatical model. Each model is based on certain kinds of gramatical rules which specify the varieties of sentence structure that the model is capable of generating. For convenience, each of the models discussed is more powerful in generative capacity than the preceding model. That is, each successive model can generate all types of sentences generated by the preceding model and more besides. In addition, more powerful models accomplish this task with fewer grammatical rules. Our discussion of these models will provide a general theoretical framework within which particular grammatical theories can be evaluated. The desirable goal, of course, is to discover the simplest grammar that is capable of meeting the criteria mentioned above.

In the case of English or any other natural language, a particular grammatical model is considered to be inadequate if it can be shown that there are sentences in the language that the model cannot generate. For instance, the simplest type of grammatical model would be a *list* consisting of all sentences in a given natural language. Since the number of sentences in any natural language is presumably infinite, however, any finite list model would be inadequate. At any given point in a language user's experience, no sentence could be produced or understood unless it had previously been experienced. The important point to note here is that the grammatical model itself must be finite, although it must describe or be able to operate an infinite number of sentences.

Finite State Grammars

One way of attempting to represent the knowledge that language users have about their language is in terms of a *finite state grammar,* or *Markov process.* Such a model is typically represented as a left-to-right probabilistic process in which the occurrence of any given word is determined solely by the preceding word or series of words. Any finite state grammar can be represented in the form of a "state diagram" in which a word is produced by going from one state to another. Figure 10.2 shows a simple state diagram for a subset of English which was provided by Chomsky (1957).

The grammar shown in part *A* of the figure produces only two sentences—"The man comes" and "The men come." But as the grammar in part *B* indicates, several other sentences can be obtained with the addition of a single closed loop. The additional sentences include "The old man comes," "The old old man comes," "The old men come," and "The old old men come." In fact, the word "old" could be repeated several times,

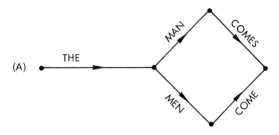

Figure 10.2 A finite state grammar.
(From Chomsky, 1957.)

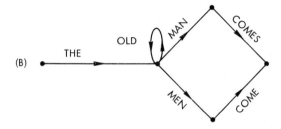

thereby producing many more sentences. By adding more states and more closed loops, it is possible to construct a grammar capable of producing an infinite number of sentences and sentences of infinite length. This appears to be an important property of a grammar, since, in principle, there is no limit to the length of a sentence and there are infinitely many sentences. To be sure, language users do not exhibit this skill, but they could undoubtedly do so if it were not for their limited memory and finite life span. It is for this reason that all grammars or theories of linguistic competence have such generative capacity.

All the stimulus-response association theories that we have discussed so far can be characterized as finite state models. This is well illustrated in our discussion of statistical approximations to English where each word in a series is determined only by the preceding word or words. We have also seen that these theories as grammars for English fail to meet several important criteria. They do not account for the speaker's skill in distinguishing between grammatical and ungrammatical utterances or his skill in identifying ambiguous sentences, grammatical relations within a sentence, and the relationship among various sentences. These skills exist independent of the sequential probabilities between the words of a sentence.

In addition to the shortcomings of stimulus-response association theories noted above, a deeper criticism applies to them and to any other finite state model as well. As Chomsky (1957) pointed out, these left-to-right probabilistic models cannot produce all types of grammatical sentences found in English, and it is very likely that they cannot do so for any other natural language either. The main problem for finite state models lies in the embedded structure of many English sentences. That is, one of the characteristics of English is the possibility of embedding sentences within other sentences.

Consider the following sentence based on Slobin (1971): "The man who said S is here." The symbol S represents another sentence, such as "Chomsky has very weak arguments." Therefore the first sentence could be rewritten as "The man who said Chomsky has very weak arguments is here." In this sentence the tenth word "is" is dependent upon the second word "man" and not upon the immediately preceding word "arguments." As Slobin points out, allowing each word in a probabilistic chain to be determined by all the words that precede it, rather than the immediately preceding word, does not get around the difficulty. The core of the problem for finite state probabilistic models here is that they have no way of identifying boundaries between phrases, clauses, or sentences. Unless these boundaries are marked, it is not possible to detect the dependency between the words "man" and "is" in the above sentence because "man" comes before the embedded sentence but "is" comes after it.

The whole matter of embedded sentences and the discontinuities among sentence elements which result from embedding is a complicated one. For example, the sentence we just discussed could be embedded with both an "if . . . then" and "either . . . or" construction to produce the following sentence, also taken from Slobin (1971): "If the man who said that Chomsky has very weak arguments is here then either he has to defend his point or he has to be open to criticism." Obviously the dependencies in such a sentence could never be specified by a grammar that does not provide for boundaries between phrases, clauses, and sentences.

A somewhat simpler, though more abstract, way of characterizing embedded sentences is found in Chomsky (1957). Although he discusses several embedded constructions, we shall limit our discussion to the *mirror-image* construction. Consider a language in which the total vocabulary consists of the letters *a* and *b*. Grammatical constructions in this language consist only of an arbitrary string of these letters followed by the mirror image of that string. Table 10.2 shows some grammatical and some ungrammatical strings for various sentence lengths in this language.

Several facts about the sentences in this language are apparent. First, there is no longest sentence. Sentences can be of unlimited length as is the case, at least in principle, in natural languages. Also there is no limit to the number of sentences that could be constructed. More important, however, is the nature of the dependencies. The last element of a string is always dependent upon the first, the second-to-last element is always dependent upon the second element, and so on until all elements are accounted for. Notice that the nature of these dependencies results from the way sentences are embedded in this language. The shortest sentences are "aa"

Table 10.2 Grammatical and ungrammatical strings for various sentence lengths in a mirror-image language.

Length	Grammatical Strings	Ungrammatical Strings
1		a or b
2	aa or bb	ab or ba
3		aba or bab
4	abba or aaaa	aaab or bbaa
5		aaaaa or aabbb
6	aabbaa or abbbba	ababab or bbaaab

and "bb." Four-element sentences are obtained by embedding another of these sentences between the elements of a two-element sentence to produce "aaaa," "bbbb," "abba," or "baab." Because of the embedding a finite state grammar cannot produce the mirror-image language.

To make the application of this example clear in the case of natural language, it is important to realize that the elements dependent upon one another are not necessarily the same. For instance, consider the English sentence "The man the dog bit died." This is an example of a mirror-image construction of the "abba" variety where the last element (died) is dependent upon the first element (the man), and the next to last element (bit) is dependent upon the second element (the dog). Thus the sentence construction captures the fact that the dog did the biting and it was the man who died. The process of embedding can of course be carried on indefinitely, and the result is always that any given element in the last half of a sentence is determined by a particular element in the first half of the sentence.

It is precisely because of the possibility of unlimited embeddings that finite state models fail to provide an adequate grammar for this language. Unlimited embeddings require an infinite number of states, with the result being that the grammar is no more efficient than a list of the infinitely many possible sentences. If only a finite number of states is allowed, then any novel sentence beyond the level of complexity provided by the grammar must be rejected as not being a sentence. It should be clear, however, that anyone who understands the mirror-image principle that underlies these sentences can continue to produce grammatical strings indefinitely.

The mirror-image language represents only one of several structures discussed by Chomsky (1957) that cannot be accounted for by finite state devices. These structures all involve discontinuous elements which result from embedding sentences within sentences. Such discontinuities are commonly found in natural language, and they pose particular problems for left-to-right probabilistic models in which each successive element is selected on the basis of the immediately preceding element. Any successful grammar of English will have to account for these discontinuities.

Phrase Structure Grammar

Most association models of language focus attention on the individual word as the basic unit of analysis and build up sentences piece by piece in chains. An alternative approach, which linguists have been using for some time, is to begin with the sentence and proceed to analyze the constituent structure of the sentence. Grammars based on a constituent analysis of sentences are called *phrase structure grammars.* These grammars are considerably more powerful than finite state grammars and do a better job of representing some of the skills exhibited by language users.

There are several ways of depicting the results of a constituent analysis. Let us begin with *box diagrams* such as those given in Figure 10.3

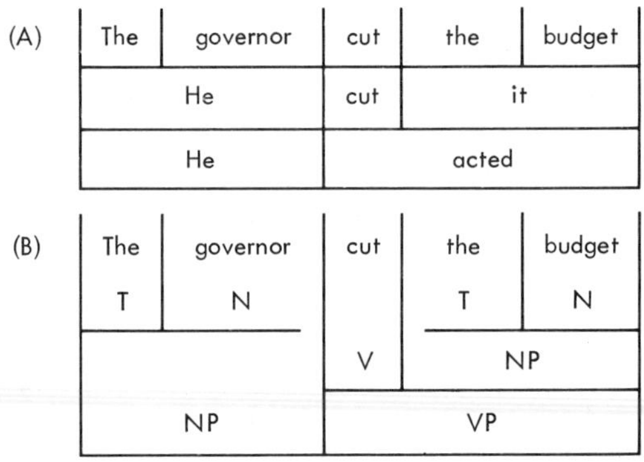

(A)

The	governor	cut	the	budget
He		cut	it	
He		acted		

(B)

The	governor	cut	the	budget
T	N		T	N
		V	NP	
NP		VP		

Figure 10.3 Constituent analysis for the sentence "The governor cut the budget."

for the sentence "The governor cut the budget." The diagrams are similar to those of Slobin (1971) and show the constituents of the sentence at each linguistic level. Notice that the analysis of constituents becomes finer and finer as you go from the bottom to the top of each diagram. The levels show which constituents are subordinate to which other constituents of the sentence. At the bottom or deepest level the sentence is divided into its two major constituents. In diagram *B* the major constituents are represented as a noun phrase (*NP*) plus a verb phrase (*VP*). At the next level the analysis of the *VP* into verb (*V*) plus another *NP* is shown. Finally, at the top level, the *NP*s are divided into article (*T*) plus noun (*N*), and the individual lexical items are given. Each diagram, taken as a whole, shows the constituent structure of the sentence. The top level represents the surface structure, and the lower levels reflect the underlying structure which determines the meaning of the sentence.

The importance of constituent analysis can readily be seen by considering an ambiguous sentence such as "They are flying planes." Instead of using box diagrams we shall represent the alternative constituent structures of this sentence with the *tree diagrams* given in Figure 10.4. The levels

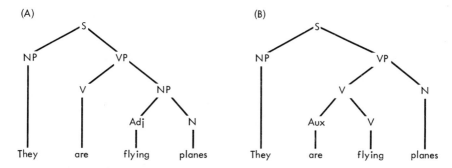

Figure 10.4   Constituent analysis for the sentence "They are flying planes."

in the tree diagram are analogous to the levels of the box diagrams except that the lowest level is represented at the top of the tree diagram. As you can see from the tree diagrams in *A* and *B,* the meaning of this sentence depends upon the structure of its constituents. If the structure is that of *A,* then it is clear that the planes are doing the flying. In *B,* however, the word *flying* is a verb that indicates that "they" are doing the flying. Since two structures underlie the surface structure of this sentence, we know the sentence is ambiguous.

Another method of representing constituent analysis is a labeled bracketing procedure. In the following example this procedure is used to show the same ambiguity reflected in the tree diagrams. As you can see, the bracketing procedure reveals the constituent structures just as clearly as either the box diagram or the tree diagram:

(A)   (They) ((are) (flying planes))
  NP   NP VP V V   NP   NP VP

(B)   (They) ((are flying) (planes))
  NP   NP VP V   V   NP   NP VP

We have characterized a grammar as a system of rules for describing the knowledge one must have in order to speak and understand a natural language. Each rule of the grammar reflects some aspect of this knowledge, and the rules of phrase structure grammar reflect the knowledge obtained through constituent analysis. Actually, several varieties of phrase structure grammar are possible. Figure 10.5 provides an illustration of some rewrite rules from a phrase structure grammar for one English sentence. Notice that the symbols introduced in Figure 10.3 are also used in these rules. In addition, the symbol *S* stands for "sentence" and the arrow (⟶) means that whatever appears to the left is *rewritten* as whatever appears to the right.

To generate a sentence with these rules, we begin with the symbol *S*.

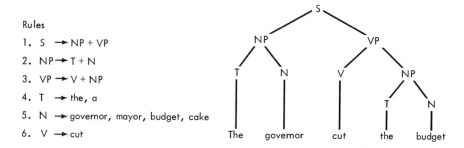

Rules

1. S → NP + VP
2. NP → T + N
3. VP → V + NP
4. T → the, a
5. N → governor, mayor, budget, cake
6. V → cut

Figure 10.5   Rewriting rules and tree diagram for the sentence "The governor cut the budget."

Only one element is rewritten at each step in the derivation, and all *non-terminal elements* are rewritten until only terminal elements remain. Terminal elements are those to which no rewriting rules apply. Thus, according to rule 1, we begin by rewriting *S* as *NP* + *VP*. Rule 2 tells us to rewrite *NP* as *T* + *N*. Following rule 3, *VP* is rewritten as *V* + *NP*. Applying rules 4, 5, and 6 gives us three terminal elements, "the," "governor," and "cut." Now we must go through the rules again to eliminate the remaining nonterminal elements. Rule 2 gives us *T* + *N* for *NP,* and we see that rule 3 no longer applies. Following rules 4 and 5 we can write the remaining nonterminal elements as "the" and "budget." Now we have what is called a *terminal string,* a string that consists only of terminal elements.

The example of phrase structure grammar presented here is highly simplified, but it shows that several sentences can be produced with these rules and the limited vocabulary provided. For example, either "the governor" or "a governor" can cut "the budget" or "the cake." With the addition of other rules and a larger vocabulary, phrase structure grammar can capture the creativity in sentence production and understanding that is so characteristic of natural language. It should be noted that the rules provided are not sufficient, however, since they allow for the generation of such ungrammatical strings as "The budget cut the cake." Additional restrictions must be introduced into the grammar to avoid the generation of such nonsentences.

It is important to emphasize at this point that the rules of phrase structure grammar represent linguistic structure. It is argued that they describe *tacit* knowledge, not necessarily knowledge that speakers are capable of stating. However, the rules are offered as an attempt to represent the knowledge of language users, and it should be clear, even from our simple example of English rules, that they do capture much of the information that underlies the linguistic skills of English speakers. Phrase structure grammar can deal not only with sentence ambiguity and grammatical relations within a sentence but also with embedded sentences. All that is required is the use of such rules as the following:

$$S \longrightarrow a(S)a$$
$$S \longrightarrow b(S)b$$

These rules are called *recursive* rules, since the symbol on the left recurs on the right. The parentheses are used to indicate that the S on the right is optional—it can be retained or deleted. Since phrase structure trees are constructed from top to bottom, not left to right, the use of recursive rules makes it possible to insert another sentence at selected points in the tree.

In contrast to the phrase structure rules illustrated in Figure 10.5, recursive rules have the property of applying to their own outputs. So long as the optional S is retained in the first application of the rule, it can in turn be rewritten by the same rule that produced it. The use of recursive rules to account for embedded sentences can be illustrated with the strings of the mirror-image language. The two-element grammatical strings, "aa" and "bb," can be produced by deleting the optional S in the above rules. If the optional S is retained, as in "aSa" or "bSb," it can be written as a two-element grammatical string between the existing elements. This would yield such strings as "abba," "baab," "bbbb," or "aaaa." Similarly, the optional S can be retained through successive steps of the derivation, the only requirement being that S cannot appear in a terminal string, since it is not a terminal element. Thus it is quite easy to account for mirror-image structures with phrase structure rules, although these same structures cannot be accounted for by finite state models.

Phrase structure grammars go a long way toward capturing the linguistic information that cannot be accounted for by finite state models. Phrase structure grammars also have their limitations, however. For example, the sentences within (15) and (16) are obviously related, but a phrase structure grammar does not capture this relationship:

(15) The governor cut the budget.
     What did the governor cut?
(16) Bill hit John.
     John was hit by Bill.

Thus one limitation of a phrase structure grammar is its inability to capture grammatical relationships among sentences.

A second limitation of phrase structure grammar is its inability to generate all and only the grammatical sentences of language. For the English language, this point can be illustrated in several ways. In the rules given in Figure 10.5, only one way of rewriting the element V was given

—namely, as "cut." Even with the root fixed, however, this element can assume other forms, such as *cuts, has cut, will cut, has been cut,* and *is being cut.* The role of these "auxiliary verbs" is not difficult to describe with a set of rules different from those found in phrase structure grammar. But by using phrase structure rules, auxiliary verbs can only be handled in a cumbersome and complex manner, if at all.

One of the most common ways of forming new sentences is by the process of sentence conjunction. This process, however, can only be described with difficulty, if at all, with phrase structure grammar. Consider the following examples from Chomsky (1957):

(17) a. the scene—of the movie—was in Chicago
      b. the scene—of the play—was in Chicago
      c. the scene—of the movie and of the play—was in Chicago

(18) a. the scene—of the movie—was in Chicago
      b. the scene—that I wrote—was in Chicago
      c. the scene—of the movie and that I wrote—was in Chicago

In (17) we can easily combine (a) and (b) to produce (c). But in (18) we cannot form (c) from (a) and (b). A fairly simple rule can be used to account for this process of conjunction. Take two sentences of the form $Z + X + W$ where X is a constitutent of each sentence (e.g., *NP* or *VP*) and Z, W are segments of the terminal string. These sentences can be conjoined as follows: $Z + X_1 +$ and $+ X_2 + W$. Sentences (a) and (b) of (17) fit this rule and can therefore be conjoined to produce (c). The problem with the sentences in (18) is that the two X constitutents in (a) and (b) are not of the same form and thus cannot be conjoined.

Although the rule for conjunction introduced here seems to be satisfactory for these sentences, it cannot be incorporated into phrase structure grammar. There is simply no way to incorporate a rule that makes reference to two distinct sentences in phrase structure grammar. The rules of phrase structure grammar allow only one element to appear to the left of the rewrite symbol, but this rule amounts to having two elements on the left, S_1 and S_2. The essential property of this rule for conjunction is that to form a new sentence it is necessary to know the constituent structures of the sentences to be conjoined as well as their derivational histories. Rules of this type require a different kind of grammar, a transformational grammar.

Transformational Grammars

Phrase structure grammar is capable of representing many important aspects of language. A transformational grammar does not ignore this capability but instead builds on it. Such a grammar contains both phrase structure rules and transformational rules. The products of the phrase structure rules are called *base phrase markers,* which can be represented by tree diagrams similar to those we have previously encountered. The application of a transformation rule to such a base phrase marker results in a *derived phrase marker,* and a derived phrase marker that describes the surface structure of a sentence is called a *final derived phrase marker.*

Several basic properties of a transformational grammar can be illustrated with the phrase marker in (19). Phrase structure rules are employed to generate such phrase markers, and these phrase markers represent underlying structures or *deep structures* in a transformational grammar. Notice, however, that the terminal string in (19) is not an actual English sentence, since it still contains a symbol that represents past tense. Base phrase markers generated by phrase structure rules do not have true sentences as their terminal strings. For example, if the tense indicated in (19) was present tense, a transformation to delete the tense symbol would still have to be applied to produce the sentence "Bill hit John."

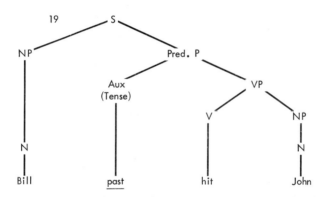

Chomsky states in *Syntactic Structures* that a transformation rule is defined by a structural description (SD) of the strings the rule applies to and the structural change (SC) that results. In our previous discussion of conjunction the structural description of each sentence was of the form $Z + X + W$. The structural change that resulted from conjoining the two sentences was $Z + X_1 +$ and $+ X_2 + W$. Notice here that the transformation rule is applied to the constituent elements of the two sentences and not to individual words in the terminal strings.

The appropriate transformation rule for the phrase marker in (19) is the passive transformation. This rule is given in (20), and it states that the passive transformation may be applied whenever an underlying structure consists of a noun phrase followed by an auxiliary which is in turn followed by a verb and, finally, by a second noun phrase.

(20) SD: $NP_1 - Aux - V - NP_2$
      SC: $NP_1 - Aux - V - NP_2 \rightarrow NP_2 - Aux + be + en -$
      $V - by + NP_1$

Notice that the transformation is accomplished by switching the positions of the *NPs*, attaching *be + en* for the past participle to the *Aux,* and placing *by* before the last noun phrase. Now let us return to the phrase marker in (19).

You can see that the phrase marker fits the structural description for applying the passive transformation and that it can be transformed into the string given in (21):

(21) John + *past* + be + en + hit + by + Bill

Of course, the string in (21) is not a sentence in English, and eventually *past + be + en* must be rewritten accordingly as *was.* Thus the terminal string "John was hit by Bill" is produced. Of course, more complex forms of the passive result when the *Aux* is expanded more fully (e.g., "John has been bit by Bill").

The preceding examples illustrate several important characteristics of a transformational grammar. We have seen that a transformational grammar adds another level of linguistic description to what is achieved with a phrase structure grammar. The phrase structure rules are still used to generate deep structures, but actual sentences result only when deep structures are modified by the application of transformational rules. The examples also indicate that transformation rules do not apply to terminal strings in the deep structure but rather to underlying abstract element sequences. As shown in (20), most transformations apply in this way.

The transformation rules of a grammar may be used to perform any of several operations. These operations include *deletion* of elements, *replacement* of elements by other elements, *addition* of elements, and *permutation* of elements. We have seen several of these operations illustrated in the preceding examples. In our illustration of the transformation for conjunction we saw examples of deletion, addition, and replacement. The example of the passive transformation illustrated permutation of elements in the switching of *NPs* and addition of elements in attaching *be + en* to the *Aux* and in placing *by* before the last *NP.* Most transformations involve several of these operations.

Although our discussion of transformation rules has been somewhat oversimplified, a grammar consisting of these rules, in addition to a phrase structure component, would obviously have a considerable advantage over finite state models for language. As we have seen, the rules of a transformational grammar account for part of the creativity that is found in natural language and describe knowledge that underlies linguistic skills or intuitions that speakers have about their language. Such a grammar is able to capture sentence ambiguity, grammatical relations within a sentence, and grammatical relations among sentences as well. Of course, we have yet to determine whether or not these rules adequately represent the tacit knowledge that English speakers have about their language. That question will be taken up in the following section.

In our discussion of transformational grammar the main focus has been on sentence structure, or syntax—the analysis of sentences into constituents, the specification of the relations among constituents, and the operations involved in reordering constituents or modifying them in other ways. Notice that a transformational grammar does not say anything about what we talk about or why we speak but instead attempts to represent the knowledge that makes sentence production and understanding possible.

PSYCHOLOGICAL STUDIES OF GRAMMAR

In the years since Chomsky's publication of *Syntactic Structures* (1957), considerable psychological research has been done concerning language. Much of this research has dealt with the extent to which the rules of a transformational grammar adequately describe the processes involved in producing, understanding, and remembering sentences. In other words, much of this research has been concerned with determining the "psychological reality" of the rules of the grammar. A transformational grammar appears to be quite adequate in representing the tacit knowledge that underlies various linguistic skills or intuitions about language that are exhibited by speakers. In fact, linguistic theorists such as Chomsky and his followers have relied quite heavily on these skills or intuitions in constructing the particular rules of their grammars. But the adequacy of these rules in describing the tacit knowledge that language users must have does not guarantee that the rules have a similar adequacy for describing the processes by which sentences are understood or produced. The point here is analogous to the fact that knowing the rules of mathematics does not necessarily tell us how mathematicians solve problems. It is important to realize that the particular form of grammatical rules, and the ways in which they relate to each other, constitute only one way of representing linguistic knowledge. No doubt the processes that underlie sentence production and understanding are intimately related to the rules of the grammar, but the actual degree of correspondence is open to question.

Let us begin by looking at some investigations of the way sentences are processed. In the initial sections we will focus on studies that deal with some of the major features of a transformational grammar. Of course, the results of these studies reflect upon the actual performance of language users and not only upon the linguistic competence that the grammar attempts to describe. The intrusion of performance factors, particularly subject strategies and general cognitive abilities, makes it difficult to evaluate some of the research outcomes. Nevertheless, the basic processes described by the grammar should be reflected in performance if grammatical rules are psychologically valid.

Sentence Structure

Most psycholinguistic research can be related in one way or another to the structure of sentences. In this section, however, our main concern will be with experiments whose results seem especially relevant to the influence of surface structure and deep structure relationships on sentence processing. Johnson (1965) reported a study that indicates a role for surface structure relations in learning. He had subjects learn an eight-pair PA list in which the stimuli were the digits one to eight and the responses were complete sentences. The subjects' performance on each trial was scored for *transitional error probability* (TEP) between words. The TEP is a conditional probability that indicates the probability that a given word is recalled incorrectly providing that the preceding word is recalled correctly. Johnson's results indicated that the largest TEPs occurred between major constituents of the surface structure. For example, in sentences such as "The house across the street burned down," the TEP was greatest for *across,* given that *house* was recalled correctly, and for *burned,* given that *street* was recalled correctly. Since these transitions mark the major constituent boundaries of the surface structure, the results suggest that sentences may be learned and remembered in units that correspond to major constituents or phrases.

A study by Mehler and Carey (1967) examined the role of both surface and deep structure in the perception of sentences. The subjects in this experiment saw ten sentences of the same structure followed by a test sentence which had either the same or a different structure. For example, surface structure relations were tested with sentences like those given in (22) and (23):

    (22) They are forecasting cyclones.
    (23) They are conflicting desires.

In (22) we know that forecasting cyclones is not a unit, whereas *conflicting desires* is a unit in (23). The subjects listened to each sentence and then wrote it down immediately. The results for the critical eleventh sentence indicated that it was much more readily perceived when the preceding sentences were of the same surface structure as the test sentence. The results for sentences differing in deep structure relations tended to support a similar interpretation but were not nearly as conclusive.

A series of experiments initiated by Fodor and Bever (1965) has been cited frequently as an indication of the influence of constituent structure. In the first study subjects listened to a series of sentences and clicks presented dichotically. Sentences were presented in one ear, and sometime during the presentation of each sentence a click was heard in the other ear. The subject's task was to listen to each sentence, then write it down, and finally, to indicate where the click occurred. Nine recordings were made of twenty-five different sentences. Each recording had the click in a different location, although any given subject heard only one recording of a particular sentence. To illustrate, consider the example in (24) which shows a sentence divided into its two major constituents and a distribution of click positions about the major constituent boundary.

(24) (That he was happy) (was evident from the way he smiled)

△   △   △   △   △   △   △   △   △

For each sentence, one recording had a click placed at the major boundary, and in remaining recordings the clicks were located at progressively farther distances on either side of the boundary. The results of this experiment showed a strong tendency for subjects to judge click locations as being closer to the boundary than they actually were. Fodor and Bever interpreted their results in terms of the constituent structure of the sentences. They suggested that the systematic errors in click location were due to the active use of constituent structure to segregate perceptual units of speech. This appears to imply that subjects shift click location to those points that correspond to perceptual units in speech. In the present case such a point presumably is found at the major constituent or clause boundary.

A possible objection raised to the Fodor and Bever (1965) study is that click displacements may be due to some acoustic factor in the signal and not to the active processing of the signal into its constituents. An experiment by Garrett, Bever, and Fodor (1966) rules out this alternative. They used pairs of sentences that contained a substring of identical words. For example, the last seven words in (25) and (26) are identical, but the constituent structure of the two sentences is different:

(25) (In her hope of marrying) (Anna was surely impractical)
(26) (Your hope of marrying Anna) (was surely impractical)

In this case two recordings of (25) might be made, but for one of the recordings the words *in her* would be replaced with the word *your* by means of tape splicing. Thus the last seven words in both sentences would be acoustically identical. The clicks were placed in identical locations in the two sentences, and the results indicated that judgments of click positions shifted toward the appropriate constituent boundary in both sentences. This finding clearly shows that the effect is not due to some acoustic cue in the sentence.

The findings of the two preceding experiments can be attributed to factors other than those involved in perception. Since the subjects hear the entire sentence before making their response, the judgment of click location could be attributed either to memory failure or to some sort of response bias. Subjects may correctly perceive click location at the time of its occurrence but may incorrectly recall the location after the entire sentence has been presented. Assuming the subject recalls that the click occurred somewhere in the middle of the sentence, and not at the beginning or end, the judged location of clicks may reflect a response bias in which the subjects locate clicks near the major grammatical boundary within the sentence. This is not to imply that the listeners are responding to a physical cue, such as an acoustic pause, at the constituent boundary. Martin has demonstrated that the perception of pause location by listeners does not closely correspond to actual pause location in the speech signal (cf. Martin and Strange, 1968; Martin, 1971). Thus a response bias explanation is consistent with the assumption that major constituents within a sentence are psychologically real, although it is not consistent with the view that click location depends on a perceptual factor.

Two studies using a GSR response to electric shock (Bever, Kirk, and Lackner, 1969) and immediate reaction time to a click (Abrams and Bever, 1969) have attempted to clarify this situation. The results of these experiments are difficult to evaluate, however, perhaps because the unusual nature of the experimental task alters normal speech perception in some way. In any case, whether the results are due to perception, memory, or response bias on the part of the subject, the constituent structure of the sentence is apparently involved in judgments of click locations. The particular sentence relations thought to produce these effects were initially viewed as residing in the surface structure. More recently, however, the effects have been attributed to deep structure relations. The latter interpretation is at least partially supported by the observation that constituent breaks within clauses of the surface structure do not produce similar errors in judgment of click locations (cf. Bever, Lackner, and Kirk, 1969). It may of course be that both surface structure and deep structure relations which coincide at the major constituent breaks combine to produce the effect.

The role of deep structure relations in memory for sentences is indicated in studies by Blumenthal (1967) and Blumenthal and Boakes (1967). In the latter experiment subjects were asked to learn a set of sentences and then to recall each sentence when an appropriate prompt word from the sentence was provided. The sentences were either of the type shown in (27) or of the type shown in (28).

(27) John is eager to please.
(28) John is easy to please.

These sentences have the same surface structure but differ in deep structure. The prompt words included the initial noun (John) and the adjectives (eager or easy). As we saw earlier, however, *John* is the subject in (27) but the object in (28). In addition, the adjectives function in different ways. In (27) *eager* is a noun modifier, it is John who is eager. In (28) *easy* can be thought of as a sentence modifier, since it is not John who is easy. The most interesting result of this experiment was that noun prompts facilitated recall the most in sentences with the structure of (27), whereas adjective prompts were most effective with sentences like (28). Similar results were reported by Blumenthal (1967).

We have seen in several experiments that both surface and deep structure relations play a role in various aspects of sentence processing. It is often difficult to determine whether the surface structure or the deep structure is more important, but these critical features of a transformational grammar undoubtedly do influence performance. Of course this observation does not necessarily support particular rules of the grammar or their psychological reality, but it does suggest that certain aspects of the grammar are psychologically important.

Degree of Grammaticality

Fluent speakers of a language can make judgments concerning the grammaticalness of a string of words even if that string is without meaning. In an attempt to see if grammaticalness alone could influence the learning of strings, Epstein (1961) used a task in which subjects learned strings of nonsense syllables that varied in grammatical structure. An example of the most grammatical string used by Epstein is given in (29). The least grammatical strings consisted of rearranging the items in strings like (29) so that the order would be ungrammatical.

(29) A vapy koobs desaked the citar molently um glox nerfs

Intermediate between these were strings like (29) with the bound morphemes *y, ed, ly,* and *s* removed. Epstein's results showed that recall of strings like (29) was superior to recall of the other two types and that recall of the intermediate type was superior to recall of the ungrammatical type.

Several other studies concerning the effect of variations in grammaticalness have been reported. Coleman (1965) constructed sets of sentences at four levels of grammaticalness. Subjects ranked these sentences for grammaticality, and the rankings were in agreement with predictions.

Learning of the sentences was also related to grammaticality. Comparisons have been reported between grammatical, anomalous, and ungrammatical strings in both perception (Miller and Isard, 1963) and learning (Marks and Miller, 1964). Examples of these sentence types, taken from Miller and Isard, follow:

> Grammatical: A witness signed the official legal document.
>
> Anomalous: A witness appraised the shocking company dragon.
>
> Ungrammatical: A legal glittering the exposed picnic knight.

In both studies subjects performed best with the meaningful grammatical sentences, next best with the grammatical but anomalous sentences, and poorest with the ungrammatical string. Both of these studies as well as others reported subsequently (e.g., Martin, 1968; Danks, 1969) revealed an influence of both syntactic and semantic factors in processing.

According to linguistic theory (cf. Chomsky, 1965), a sentence is grammatical if at least one structural description can be assigned to it. All other sentences are ungrammatical. This does not mean that an ungrammatical sentence cannot be interpreted semantically. Chomsky (1961) and Katz (1964) have suggested that the hearer, upon presentation of an otherwise ungrammatical string, assigns the "closest" structural description to it in order to provide a semantic interpretation. According to this view, the degree of grammaticalness of an utterance would presumably depend upon the type of syntactic rule that was violated. The more general the rule, the more ungrammatical the string

Downey and Hakes (1968) provided a careful test of the preceding view of grammaticality. They used fully grammatical sentences that were all of the same form as the example in (30). For each grammatical sentence, they constructed three additional sentences by violating one of three syntactic rules.

> (30) The woman may endure grief.

The string in (31) is an example of violating a phrase structure rule by substituting an adjective for the verb. In (32) a subcategorization rule is violated by using an intransitive verb instead of a transitive verb. In (33) a selection rule is violated by substituting an inappropriately marked transitive verb.

> (31) The woman may petty grief.
>
> (32) The woman may arrive grief.
>
> (33) The woman may escort grief.

For example, if the object is marked human, the verb would be marked abstract, or vice versa. Subjects rated these sentences for grammaticality on a four-point scale ranging from "completely acceptable" to "completely unacceptable." Of course, each subject rated only one string of a related set, such as the strings given in (30) through (33). According to linguistic theory, violation of a phrase structure rule should have the most severe effect and violation of a selection rule should have the least severe effect. The results were as predicted, with strings such as (30) rated most acceptable followed by strings such as (33), (32), and (31), in that order.

Downey and Hakes (1968) also used these same sentences in a learning task. Each subject was given ten sentences for five trials of free-recall learning. As in the rating task, performance was best on strings such as (30) which are grammatical and poorest on strings such as (31) which involve a phrase structure violation. Performance on the other two types, however, were just the opposite from the predictions. A factor of possible importance in explaining this reversal may be that the rule violations in (32) and (33) are not purely syntactic but instead involve a major semantic component. The attempt to separate semantic and syntactic processes has caused severe problems for psycholinguistic theory.

Degrees of grammaticality, therefore, appear to be related to performance in a variety of situations. Of course there are deviations from predictions, as we saw in the learning task of Downey and Hakes (1968). More importantly, however, it should be noted that we cannot be sure what is being tapped by variations in grammaticality or how these variations may be related to semantic factors and subject strategies. Nevertheless it does seem that the linguistic concept of grammaticality is related to the performance of subjects in certain situations.

Ambiguous Sentences

Various types of ambiguity can be found in sentences, ranging from simple ambiguity of the lexical type to ambiguities involving deep structure relations. Psychologists are interested in these forms of ambiguity for two reasons. The first is the common observation that people do not tend to notice ambiguities in ordinary discourse even though the ambiguities are readily understood once they are pointed out. The second reason for the interest in sentence ambiguity is in terms of what the ease of detecting various types of ambiguity may reveal about linguistic structure. MacKay and Bever (1967) presented subjects with sentences that varied in ambiguity. Their data indicated that deep structure ambiguities (e.g., "The idea of the natives was dreadful") are the most difficult to resolve, with surface structure ambiguities (e.g., "The old men and women did not cooperate") and lexical ambiguities (e.g., "The office of the president is vacant") being progressively easier. They also showed that sentences with more than one ambiguity were more difficult than sentences with a single ambiguity.

A study of ambiguity based on a sentence completion task was reported by MacKay (1966). He used incomplete strings of various types which subjects were asked to complete. The strings themselves either were unambiguous or had ambiguities at the lexical, surface structure, or deep structure level. In addition, some strings had more than one ambiguity. For each ambiguous string, a corresponding unambiguous string was constructed. For example, the strings in (34) are ambiguous, but the corresponding strings in (35) are not:

(34) Although he was continually bothered by the cold, . . .
      Although he mentioned the problems with the bishop, . . .
(35) Although he was continually bothered by the headache, . . .
      Although he mentioned the problems to the bishop, . . .

MacKay's first observation was that even though subjects are often unaware of the ambiguity, they take more time to complete ambiguous strings than they do unambiguous strings. Among the ambiguous strings, the time required for completion was least for lexical ambiguity, with progressively longer times required to complete surface structure and deep structure ambiguities. Adjusting for differences in complexity of the to-be-completed strings, the median completion times for all sentence fragments are given in Figure 10.6. The findings suggest that ambiguity somehow interferes with the process of extracting a single meaning for the string and that this difficulty depends upon the number of ambiguities present and the linguistic level of the ambiguity.

The results of these studies of sentence ambiguity have two major implications. The first is that the levels of description contained in linguistic theories do have psychological importance. The importance is revealed by the differences in time taken to either detect an ambiguity or complete an ambiguous string. It could even be argued that these time differences suggest the order in which various linguistic levels are reached in processing unambiguous sentences.

The second implication is that subjects do more processing of ambiguous sentences than of unambiguous sentences even when the ambiguity is not detected. This conclusion is suggested by MacKay's finding that it takes longer to complete ambiguous strings even when the ambiguity is not detected. Therefore, even though ambiguities are seldom recognized in ordinary discourse, there is evidence of linguistic processing of ambiguous sentences beyond that required for unambiguous sentences.

Relations Among Sentences

The ability to capture grammatical relationships among sentences is one of the central features of a transformational grammar. Consequently, a great deal of psycholinguistic research has been devoted to this topic. In this section we shall discuss work dealing mainly with similarity relation-

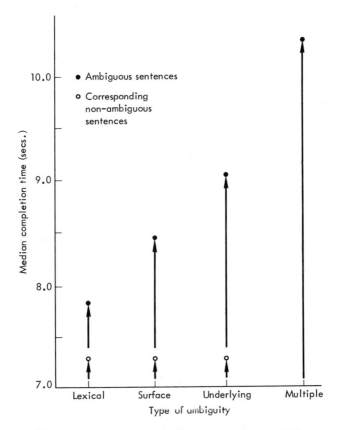

Figure 10.6 The median completion time for multiple ambiguous sentence fragments, for the three types of ambiguous sentence fragments, and their corresponding non-ambiguous fragments.
(From MacKay, 1966.)

ships. Much of the other research will be considered in the next chapter.

A comprehensive investigation of similarity relationships among certain English sentences was undertaken by Clifton and Odom (1966). They conducted a series of experiments using two basic procedures. In their first experiment subjects were asked to rank the similarity of the members of a set of sentences. The sentences used were taken from what they call the *P, N, Q* families. For example, take a simple, active, affirmative, declarative sentence (*SAAD*) such as "John hit the ball." Add to that sentence its passive (*P*) form, its negative (*N*), its question (*Q*), and the combinations *PN, PQ, NQ,* and *PNQ.* This provides the eight sentences of the *P, N, Q* family. For each sentence set, one sentence was selected as a reference point and the remaining seven sentences were ranked for similarity

to the reference sentence. The other experiments used a recognition procedure in which subjects were shown a few sentences and were then asked
to identify those sentences in a longer list of sentences.

The results of these experiments, together with a reanalysis of an
earlier experiment by Mehler (1963), were combined to provide an overall
picture of sentence relationships in a "similarity space." These relationships are represented in Figure 10.7. As can be seen in the figure, the

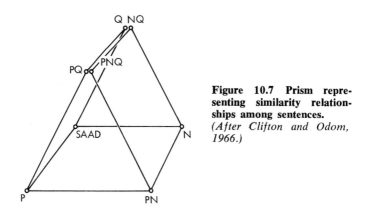

**Figure 10.7 Prism repre-
senting similarity relationships among sentences.**
*(After Clifton and Odom,
1966.)*

SAAD, N, P, and *PN* constructions form the base of the prism and are all
widely separated. However, the pairs *Q-NQ* and *PQ-PNQ* at the top are
close together. According to Clifton and Odom, the pattern represented here
is quite consistent with the pattern implied in the Katz and Postal (1964)
grammar. In their analysis Katz and Postal introduce differences between
question sentences and negative question sentences by means of phrase
structure rules rather than transformation rules. Thus the results of the
Clifton and Odom study provide support for both phrase structure grammar and transformational grammar. These authors carefully point out,
however, that a number of qualifications to this interpretation must be
considered. For example, the effect of semantic similarity in these experiments is difficult to evaluate, as are the effects of phonetic and orthographic
similarity. These and other factors may contribute to produce some of the
observed relationships.

Two investigations reported by Gough (1965, 1966) used a sentence
verification task to examine sentence relationships. In both studies subjects
were presented with sentences and were asked to state whether the sentence
was true or false on the basis of a picture that was presented at the end of
the sentence. The sentences consisted of eight *SAAD*s plus the corresponding *N, P,* and *NP* transformations. The results of these experiments are
shown in Table 10.3. It can be seen that verification times were faster for
actives than for passives, and faster for affirmatives than for negatives.

Table 10.3 Mean verification time (sec) as a function of sentence type and truth value.

| | Affirmative | | Negative | |
	True	False	True	False
Active	.87 (.92)	.96 (1.06)	1.18 (1.30)	1.18 (1.28)
Passive	.96 (1.01)	1.12 (1.20)	1.23 (1.35)	1.34 (1.36)

(FROM GOUGH, 1966, WITH COMPARABLE DATA FROM GOUGH, 1965, IN PARENTHESES.)

In addition, true sentences were verified faster than false sentences, but the advantage for true sentences was considerably reduced when the sentence was in the negative form. Although most of these results could be explained syntactically, the differential times for judging truth and falsity across affirmative and negative sentences clearly point to a semantic component. The true-false distinction is clearly semantic, and if the data were to be explained solely on the basis of syntax, any difference in the time required for true versus false judgments should be the same for all sentence types.

CONCLUSION

This chapter has focused on the grammatical structure of language and the extent to which descriptions of this structure capture aspects of language that are important psychologically. In the early part of the chapter we discussed the nature of language and various linguistic skills manifested by users of natural languages. It was noted in this context that many aspects of these linguistic skills are not adequately explained by traditional associative theories.

An important concept described in the early part of the chapter was that of a *grammar* of a natural language. It was noted that a grammar is a linguistic theory of *competence* and not a theory about actual language use or *performance*. The objective of a grammar is to provide a description of the various types of sentence structure that can occur in a language and the ways these sentence structures are related to each other. An acceptable grammar should also describe the linguistic relations that underlie the grammatical skills or intuitions manifested by language users.

The next section of the chapter dealt with three alternative models for a grammar of a natural language. The first, a finite state model, includes the theoretical approach followed by traditional theories. This type of grammar was shown to be inadequate for two reasons: it did not adequately explain certain linguistic skills manifested by language users, and it was not capable of producing many of the sentence types or structures found in English and in other natural languages.

The second model discussed, phrase structure grammar, begins with sentences and proceeds to analyze them into constituent elements. In contrast, finite state grammars usually begin with individual words and attempt to string them together to form sentences. It was noted that phrase structure grammars adequately describe more of the skills displayed by language users than do finite state grammars. Phrase structure grammars also produce more sentence types than do finite state grammars. Phrase structure grammars, however, fail to adequately describe certain linguistic skills, and they fail to produce some of the sentence structures found in natural languages.

The third model discussed, transformational grammar, has two basic elements: a phrase structure component to produce the deep structure of a sentence and a transformational component to relate deep structures to the surface structure form of actual sentences. From a purely grammatical point of view, transformational grammars were seen as being more adequate than either of the other models discussed. They capture more of the syntactic information necessary to describe the linguistic skills manifested by language users, and they do a better job of producing and relating the grammatical structures characteristic of natural language.

The last part of the chapter dealt with experimental investigations of sentence processing. The major question in this research was whether the linguistic descriptions contained in transformational grammar are psychologically important. The results of these experiments suggest that such basic linguistic concepts as surface structure, deep structure, and grammatical transformations are in some way "real" psychologically and are not simply linguistic fictions. For the most part, however, these studies do not reveal the specific mechanisms by which sentences are comprehended and remembered. We also saw that subject strategies, semantic considerations, and other cognitive factors played a role in the outcome of many experiments. We can therefore conclude that many linguistic factors are important psychologically, but we cannot say that a linguistic theory of competence is an adequate psychological theory of language use. In the next chapter we shall take up this issue more directly.

11

*Acquisition
and Use of Syntax
and Semantics*

IN THE PRECEDING CHAPTER we introduced some basic concepts of grammatical theory and reviewed some of the evidence that suggests the relevance of these concepts to a psychological understanding of language. The present chapter deals more directly with the role of syntax and semantics in the acquisition and use of language. Thus the present chapter emphasizes linguistic performance, whereas the preceding chapter emphasized linguistic competence. First we shall consider some aspects of language development in the young child from the standpoint of syntactic and semantic processes as well as the role of linguistic experience. Following this we shall consider language use in the adult. Here the major focus will be on the syntactic and semantic processes related to sentence memory and sentence comprehension.

LANGUAGE DEVELOPMENT

In most children, and in all natural languages studied thus far, the earliest evidence of meaningful speech consists of one-word utterances, which many writers have referred to as "holophrastic speech." The utterances themselves consist mostly of nouns and adjectives, with verbs only appearing much later in the developmental sequence. No doubt this predominance of nouns and adjectives reinforced the belief of association theorists that these utterances consisted mainly of attempts to name aspects of the child's environment. But to many students of language development, both past (e.g., de Laguna, 1927; Leopold, 1949; McCarthy, 1954) and present (e.g., McNeill, 1970), the holophrastic stage has been considered to be a period in which single-word utterances have been employed to express relatively complex ideas.

According to this view, an utterance of a word such as "ball" does not refer merely to a spherical object of a particular size but rather to the fact that the child "wants the ball" or that the child wants someone "to look at the ball." McNeill (1970) describes the view of de Laguna (1927) as one in which the single-word utterances of children are seen as comments made about a situation in which a child finds himself. Thus the holophrastic word serves as a comment about the extralinguistic context that is the topic of that comment. Together, the word and the context form a rudimentary kind of proposition which conceptually amounts to a full sentence. As McNeill points out, there are many cogent reasons for subscribing to just such a view of the holophrastic period. It must be obvious, however, that one cannot begin to study either syntactic development or a child's active grammar until the child begins to combine words to make primitive sentences. Let us now turn to this stage of development to see what these observations tell us about early syntax.

The earliest development in speech that is visibly grammatical comes about when two words are combined. According to many authorities, this occurs around eighteen months of age. Several investigators (cf. Braine, 1963a; Brown and Fraser, 1963; Miller and Ervin, 1964) have examined this early period in child language, and their results appear to be quite similar. In addition, there is a similarity between the structure of language described in these investigations and the language of children about the same age in a variety of linguistic environments other than English. The main focus in these investigations, however, has almost exclusively been on the role of syntax. Little attention was paid to what the child was attempting to communicate, and this neglect of meaning or semantics has been shown to constitute a serious oversight. But before we consider the issue of semantics, let us first examine the results of these investigations of the beginnings of syntactic development.

The growth in the number of two-word utterances appears to be slow at first, but it accelerates rapidly. For instance, the cumulative number of different two-word combinations recorded from the speech of one child in successive months was 14, 24, 25, 89, 350, 1,400, 2,500+ (Braine, 1963a). This indicates a significant increase in the number of new combinations within a relatively short time. When the individual words that make up these utterances were examined in terms of their distribution of occurrences, it became clear that the child was not simply combining words in an unstructured manner. Instead, it appeared to Braine (1963a, 1963b) and others that two relatively distinct classes of words were revealed.

Although this analysis is no longer considered to be satisfactory (cf. Brown, 1973), it is of some interest to examine the proposed classification.

According to Braine (1963a), one class contains a small number of words that occur quite frequently. This has been referred to as the "pivot" class. The other class contains a large number of words that occur less frequently, and Braine calls this the "open" class. Words from the pivot class typically appear in combination with words from the open class. They almost never occur alone or with each other. In contrast, words from the open class may appear together or alone. Words from the pivot class also have fixed positions in two-word utterances. They may appear in either the first or the second position, but any given pivot word tends to appear in only one of these positions. Not only is the size of the pivot class small but it tends to increase quite slowly. The open class, however, quickly adds new vocabulary. A sample of part of the *pivot-open grammar* for one child is given in Table 11.1. The nine words on the left constitute the entire set

Table 11.1 Fragment of pivot-open grammar of one child.

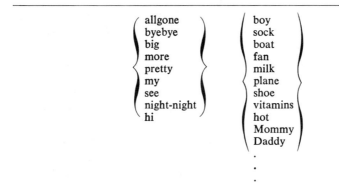

REPRINTED FROM *The Genesis of Language* BY FRANK SMITH AND GEORGE A. MILLER BY PERMISSION OF THE M.I.T. PRESS, CAMBRIDGE, MASSACHUSETTS. COPYRIGHT © 1966 BY THE MASSACHUSETTS INSTITUTE OF TECHNOLOGY. (FROM MCNEILL, 1966.)

of first-position pivot words; those on the right represent a small sample of the open class.

The words in Table 11.1 seem to indicate that the child has developed a system of his own that is not a direct copy of the adult system to which he was exposed. Notice that although the child has only two classes of words, both are quite heterogeneous in terms of an adult's classification of parts of speech. Furthermore, child utterances such as "allgone shoe" or "byebye plane" do not appear to be reduced imitations of adult speech, nor is it likely that adults speak to their children in this way. What seems more likely is that the child has already developed a limited linguistic system for creating utterances which is at least crudely described by this two-class grammar.

The assumption is made in this grammar that the child has categorized his vocabulary into classes and generates utterances by selecting words from one or both classes. For single-word utterances, the item is selected from the open class; and for two-word utterances, items are selected from either the open class (open, open) or from both classes (pivot, open). In this simple two-class grammar the structural description of an utterance is determined by its surface form. A major difficulty with this assumption is that it appears to require the child to classify individual words into fixed classes before the functional relationships that are expressed in any particular utterance have been considered.

The problem that arises in this case is that words occurring in utterances are most meaningfully classified in terms of the role they play in those utterances. The role may be that of subject, predicate, or object, according to the situation. An expression such as *me truck* could have a declarative character as in, "That is my truck," or a demand character as in "Give me my truck." But according to a pivot-open grammar, the structural description of an utterance, and hence the functional relationship expressed, depends only on the surface form of the utterance. A particular utterance must always have the same meaning.

This difficulty with a pivot-open grammar is well illustrated by some observations reported by Bloom (1970). Her research involved an extensive analysis of the speech of three English-speaking children. The speech of these children was recorded together with a careful notation of the context in which each utterance occurred. Although many of the recorded utterances were superficially similar in form to pivot-open constructions, the use of particular words appeared to be motivated primarily by their semantic function. For example, certain words met all the distributional requirements for pivot words but were clearly not instances of that class. A common example was the word "Mommy," which occurred frequently and in a relatively fixed position. Different utterances including the word "Mommy" meant different things, however. The utterance "Mommy sock" was used by one child both in the context of the child picking up her mother's sock and in the context of the mother putting the child's sock on the child. The semantic intent of the child is obviously quite different in these two instances, but both instances would be assigned the same structural description in a pivot-open grammar because the surface form of each is the same.

Bloom (1970) reports numerous other observations of early child speech which point out this same problem in a pivot-open grammar. These observations all suggest that a pivot-open grammar describes the early speech of children only in a very superficial way. As an alternative, Bloom suggests an explanation of early grammatical development that places emphasis on underlying semantics or cognitive factors. According to this view, the early speech of children is seen as a way of talking about known events in the world about them. Thus their utterances reflect considerable knowledge of the way in which these events are related, and this knowledge is reflected in the functional relationships between words that are expressed in their utterances. The important point concerning the development of grammar to be noted here is that the child does not appear to rely on a relatively simple syntactic frame such as pivot and open. Instead, the child talks about something, and syntax is learned by the child in his attempts to express conceptual relationships. Of course the processes that underlie this development are likely to be quite complex.

Development of Phrase Structure

As children mature, the average length of their utterances increases. One consequence of this increase in number of words per utterance is that greater complexity must be introduced in the grammar used to describe these utterances. McNeill (1970) gives three rules for summarizing the performance of a twenty-eight-month-old child, Adam, who was studied by Brown and some of his colleagues (Brown and Fraser, 1963; Brown and Bellugi, 1964; Brown, Cazden, and Bellugi, 1968). These rules describe the relationships between three classes of words, which can be roughly characterized as nouns (N), verbs (V), and pivots (P):

$$S \longrightarrow NP \text{ and/or } VP$$
$$NP \longrightarrow (P)N \text{ or } NN$$
$$VP \longrightarrow (V)NP$$

The rules describe sentences one to four words in length, depending on the options used. The first rule says that S must be rewritten as NP or VP or both. The second rule allows the NP to be rewritten as N, PN, or NN, since the parentheses around P indicate that this element is optional. In the same way the third rule allows VP to be rewritten as VNP or NP. Taken together these rules constitute a primitive phrase structure grammar.

According to this grammar, various "sentences" are possible. When the symbol S is rewritten as NP only, the first two rules lead to utterances such as *ball* (N), *that ball* (PN), or *Adam ball* (NN). All three rules combine to yield expressions like *Adam want ball* or *Adam mommy pencil*. The first of these expressions results when the initial NP is rewritten as N (Adam) and the VP becomes V (want) plus N (ball). For *Adam mommy pencil* the initial NP again becomes N (Adam), but the VP is rewritten only as NP which, in turn, becomes N (mommy) plus N (pencil).

McNeill (1966) reports the actual frequency of occurrence in Adam's speech of all two-word and three-word combinations permitted by these rules. Notice that the frequencies, given in Table 11.2, indicate that Adam

Table 11.2 Sentence patterns that correspond to basic grammatical relations.

Child's Speech		
Pattern	Frequency	Corresponding Grammatical Relations
P + N	23	modifier, head noun
N + N	115	modifier, head noun, subject, predicate
V + N	162	main verb, object
N + V	49	subject, predicate
Total	349	
P + N + N	3	modifier, head noun
N + P + N	1	subject, predicate, modifier, head noun
V + P + N	3	main verb, object, modifier, head noun
V + N + N	29	main verb, object, modifier, head noun
P + N + V	1	subject, predicate, modifier, head noun
N + N + V	1	subject, predicate, modifier, head noun
N + V + N	4	main verb, object, subject, predicate
N + N + N	7	subject, predicate, modifier, head noun
Total	49	

(FROM MCNEILL, 1966.)

uses all classes of the permitted combinations. According to McNeill (1968), no combinations appeared that were not permitted by these rules. This observation is quite surprising from a purely associative point of view.

As McNeill (1968) points out, if words from any class could be combined with words from any other class, it would be possible to have nine (3 × 3) classes of two-word combinations and twenty-seven (3 × 3 × 3) classes of three-word combinations. Of these, Adam uses only the four classes of two-word combinations and eight classes of three-word combinations permitted by the rules. An example of an admissible two-word combination is N + N (Adam ball), and an inadmissible combination might be P + P (my that). More interesting from an associative point of view are permitted patterns such as V + N + N (change Adam diaper), which do occur in Adam's speech, whereas patterns such as V + V + N (come eat pablum), which sound like reduced imitations of adult speech, do not occur. Adam has evidently developed a tightly structured system that cannot be viewed as a reduced copy of the adult system.

Acquisition of Transformations

Although three phrase structure rules are sufficient to describe Adam's performance at twenty-eight months of age, only eight months later a much more complicated grammar is required. Brown, Cazden, and Bellugi (1968) report that by thirty-six months of age, fourteen phrase structure rules are required instead of three, and instead of no transformational rules there now are two dozen. All this change occurs despite only a slight increase in the average length of utterance.

At the earliest stage in the development of transformations, utterances that convey the meaning of declaration, imperative, question, and negation are all being produced. According to Menyuk (1971), these utterances also display a characteristic form that changes in a regular manner as development proceeds. Examples of these forms, taken from Menyuk (1971), are given in Table 11.3. Notice, in the case of the negative, that

Table 11.3 Stages in the development of declarative, negative, question, and imperative sentences.

	A *Early*	B *In between*	C *Later*
Declarative	That box Big boat Rick go	That's box That big boat Rick going	That's a box That's a big boat Rick is going
Negative	No play No a book No fall down	I no play That not book (a) I not falling down (b) I'm not falling down	I won't play That's not a book I'm not falling down
Question	See shoe? Truck here? Where baby?	Mommy see shoe? Truck's here? (a) Where baby is? (b) Where's baby is?	Do you see the shoe? Is the truck here? Where's the baby?
Imperative	Want baby! No touch! Have it!		I want the baby or Give me the baby! Don't touch it! Give it to me!

(From Menyuk, 1971.)

the earliest form appears to involve tacking a negative word (*no* or *not*) onto an otherwise affirmative statement. Only later does the negative word become incorporated into the sentence itself. There is some controversy (cf. McNeill, 1970) as to whether the earliest forms are true negatives or conjunctions in which the word *no* is one utterance and the remainder of the sentence is another utterance. For example, in response to an adult question, "Do you want the ball?" a child might respond with "No, a book." However this issue may be resolved, it is clear that very shortly after this early stage true negation is introduced into the utterances of young children.

Much more could be said about the development of transformations.

This is a difficult area, however, and it seems likely that the entire development of early child grammar will have to be reexamined to include semantics in view of empirical investigations such as that of Bloom (1970) and theoretical considerations raised by others (cf. Macnamara, 1972; Brown, 1973). Before saying more about this issue, let us turn to another topic raised at the beginning of this chapter.

We have noted that syntactic development proceeds in a manner consistent with the view that the child is acquiring a transformational grammar. We have also noted that many facts associated with this developmental process are surprising from the point of view held by association theorists. Yet children do learn the languages they are exposed to and not others, so let us now consider more directly the role of linguistic experience, which according to associative theories is the major determiner of learning.

The Role of Linguistic Experience

Traditional behavioral theories such as those offered by Skinner (1957) or Staats and Staats (1963) state that language acquisition depends most importantly upon practice or repetition by the child, the child's imitations of adult vocalizations, and reinforcement of child vocalizations by the adult. There is little evidence to support these conclusions and little reason to believe that adults actively engage in language training. It is useful, however, to examine the evidence that does exist concerning the role of these factors.

Perhaps the most plausible factor of importance in language acquisition is *imitation*. There can be no question that children imitate the speech of adults a great deal. Although solid data are not easy to come by, McNeill (1970) reports that at least 10 percent of the speech of children at twenty-eight to thirty-five months of age is imitative in the records collected by Brown. In a very general sense imitation must provide the basis for introduction of vocabulary, and therefore this factor explains why children speak the language of their parents. But the fact that children imitate the speech of adults does not mean tnat language is acquired by imitation. This seems to be particularly the case with respect to grammatical constructions.

Ervin-Tripp (1964) has compared the structure of imitative and nonimitative constructions in the speech of children. The basic question here was whether or not the two categories of speech differed in complexity. That is, if imitation was used in acquiring new grammatical structures, then one might expect that the structure of imitations would be more complex than the structure of nonimitative, spontaneously produced utterances. Her data indicated no difference in the complexity of imitative and nonimitative utterances. In some cases children imitated constructions that were only produced spontaneously at a later time; in other cases they spontaneously produced constructions that were only imitated at a later time. Overall there were no differences in the complexity of imitative and nonimitative utterances. A similar pattern of results was obtained in an extensive analysis of the speech of one child reported by Slobin and Welsh (1971).

The question of the role of imitation is complex, and we are far from having a clear picture of it. Children do imitate the speech of adults, but, as we have seen, they also produce forms (e.g., "allgone shoe") for which there are no models in adult speech. These observations together with the evidence supplied by Ervin-Tripp (1964) and others do not suggest the major role for imitation that is implied by most associative explanations. This is not to deny any role for imitation but rather to suggest that the role of imitation is less obvious and direct than associative theory would imply.

A second factor of major theoretical importance in behavioristic theories of language acquisition and development is *reinforcement*. We saw that reinforcement has been used to influence the frequency of occurrence of various classes of sounds in the verbal conditioning situation. This is a long way from demonstrating that reinforcement can be or is used to influence the development of grammar. From what we already know about the complexity of grammatical constructions, it is difficult to see how reinforcement could be employed to influence language development. But perhaps more to the point, there also is evidence to support the observation that parents pay little attention to the grammatical correctness of what their children say.

Brown, Cazden, and Bellugi (1968) report that correction of children's speech by parents occurs mainly on nonlinguistic grounds. Utterances such as "He a girl" or "Her curl my hair" might be accepted by the parent, but others such as "The animal farmhouse" or "Walt Disney comes on, on Tuesday" might be rejected because the building was a lighthouse and because Walt Disney comes on some other day. Parents appear to be most interested in the content of what the child says and not in the grammatical form he uses.

One aspect of child speech that has several significant implications concerning language development is the overregularization of inflections. It is well known by parents and teachers that children persist in saying words like "comed," "goed," "doed" well into the elementary grades. That is, they take the inflection for past tense (-ed) which is appropriate for the class of regular or weak verbs and attach it to irregular or strong verbs. We might expect, on the basis of associative theory, that this merely involves overgeneralization. Children learn the correct inflection for some regular verbs and simply extend the inflection to all verbs. Ervin-Tripp (1964) has shown that the situation is much more complex. Her data indicate that children correctly inflect irregular verbs before the past tense inflection for regular verbs even appears. But as soon as the child learns even a few regular past tense forms (e.g., helped, walked), he immediately overregularizes the irregular verbs. This means the child says "he did" and then changes to the regular but incorrect "he doed" just as he changes the correct "he came" to "he comed."

It is not surprising that inflections for strong or irregular verbs are acquired first. These verbs are very frequent in both child and adult speech. Despite the extensive practice with these irregular inflections, however, they are swept away once the regular inflection appears. Contrary to what an associative theory would predict, this pattern indicates that highly practiced forms can rapidly disappear and that overt practice is not essential for less practiced forms to replace highly practiced, correct forms.

The evidence we have reviewed here is not extensive, and there is not a great deal more evidence that we could draw upon. The evidence that is available, however, does not provide much comfort for those who support associative explanations of language development. There appears to be little support for the view that practice, imitation, and reinforcement play the central role in language development that is predicted by associative theories. It seems much more likely that the grammatical developments in child speech represent a creative process based on some partial analysis of the language to which the child has been exposed. We shall now consider what may underlie this process.

Overview of Language Acquisition

Contemporary theories of language acquisition and language development have emphasized the importance of innate, biologically determined processes. A major motivation for such an assumption is the enormous complexity of the task facing the child. As we saw in Chapter 9, the child is faced with learning to use a complex sound system in which the acoustic information that corresponds to each phoneme varies with context and in which information about several phonemes may be transmitted at the same time. But even after this problem has been solved, the child must then proceed to the complex problem of discovering the underlying structures and meanings of sentences. Traditional association theory, with its reliance on the development of associations between stimuli and responses, is simply not equipped to deal with complexities of this magnitude. What the child learns is not a collection of associations but a system of rules. He is never exposed to the rules themselves, however, but only to utterances derived from these rules. How, then, is the child to discover the underlying system of rules?

One way to explain how the child is able to overcome these complexities is to suggest that the child's mind is "prewired" in some way to process the information that is received in a predetermined way. We saw some evidence of this view in Chapter 9 where the study of aphasia appears to suggest a biologically determined "critical period" for first language learning in childhood. In fact, Lenneberg (1967) has argued that the human brain probably has special structures, which are absent in all other animal brains, that perform these language functions. This is not to say that the grammar of a child's native language is innate but rather to suggest that the child has innately determined ways of discovering this grammar. Of course, even if this is the case the relative importance of syntactic and cognitive-semantic factors in the discovery process must still be determined.

In considering language acquisition from a syntactic point of view, it is useful to introduce the abstract Language Acquisition Device (LAD) [1] described by Chomsky (1965). Imagine if you will, that LAD is a machine that receives as input a *corpus* of speech. That is, the input consists of a set of utterances, some of which are grammatical and some of which are not. Following McNeill (1968), let us assume that the machine receives the number of utterances overheard by a typical two-year-old child. Based on these utterances, LAD formulates a grammar for the corpus. That is, LAD formulates a set of rules which function as a theory about the regularities found in the set of utterances. The grammar is formulated by passing the corpus through some kind of internal structure, and it is that structure that processes the corpus and extracts the grammatically relevant information. This process can be depicted as follows:

$$Corpus \longrightarrow \boxed{LAD} \longrightarrow Grammar$$

The nature of LAD's internal structure is far from clear. According to McNeill (1968), it consists of at least two components. One component can be thought of as a set of procedures for analysis of the corpus, although little is known about these procedures at the present time. The second component is thought to consist of various kinds of linguistic information. Several writers (Chomsky, 1965; Katz, 1966; McNeill, 1968) conceive of this information as specifying the general form of natural language. That is, the information amounts to a *universal linguistic theory* that is equally correct for all natural languages. Thus LAD should find all languages equally easy to acquire because it contains only information that is linguistically universal and no information that is unique to a particular language (McNeill, 1968).

This way of characterizing LAD constitutes a theory about the way children acquire language. McNeill (1968, 1970) makes several suggestions about the components of this theory while clearly indicating that the theory is still vague and speculative. Since all languages appear to be describable by some form of transformation grammar, one suggestion is that LAD may contain information about the form of such a grammar.

[1] The term LAD is from McNeill, 1966.

This would presumably include information about the general form of a transformation, but not the specific transformations that appear in each language. For example, the transformation relating underlying and surface structures of auxiliary verbs in English also appears in French, but it does not appear to be universal. Such transformations are not represented in LAD and must therefore be discovered.

McNeill also suggests that most universal features of language appear in the underlying structure of linguistic theory. These include basic grammatical concepts and relations such as the concept of a sentence, the concepts of and the relation between subject and predicate, and the notions of main verb and object of a verb phrase. If these suggestions are correct, the important aspects of deep structure relations are universal, and it could be said that children begin speaking deep structures directly. The specific transformations characteristic of any particular language, however, must be learned on the basis of information about the general form of transformational rules.

It is much too soon to evaluate this theory of language acquisition. The details of transformational grammar, and hence the way universal features are to be described, are in too great a state of flux. An alternative to this purely syntactic view of language acquisition is suggested by Bloom's (1970) findings. It will be recalled that Bloom's observations indicated the importance of cognitive-semantic factors in language acquisition. This general point of view has been endorsed by Macnamara (1972).

Macnamara's thesis is that very young children, including infants, use nonlinguistically based meaning as a clue to the linguistic code. That is, the child's task is to detect various syntactic structures and relate them to the semantic structures he has already acquired. In the case of infants, Macnamara finds support for this assumption in the work of Piaget (1963) and others, who provide evidence that the development of thought is initially independent of language. The main claim is that around the age of one year, when an infant begins to understand language, he has already learned much about himself and the world about him. Semantic or cognitive activity is proceeding at an advanced rate when language is only beginning.

Macnamara suggests that children begin language learning by attending to the main vocabulary items—particularly nouns, verbs, and adjectives. The child takes these main vocabulary items, determines what they refer to, and then uses his knowledge of the referents to decide which semantic structures are intended by the speaker. Once the child has determined the intended semantic structures, the final task is to see which syntactic factors (e.g., word order, prepositions) are correlated with the semantic structures. Macnamara argues that the child uses independently attained meaning to discover certain syntactic structures which are of basic importance. For example, consider the sentences in (1) through (4).

(1) Give the book to me.

(2) Give me the book.

(3) Give me a kiss.

(4) Kiss me.

If the child were to begin with the hypothesis that a single semantic relationship would always be expressed by a single syntactic structure, he would be quite confused by these sentences. Note that (1) and (2) express the same message, although the two surface structures differ. In (3) and (4) a similar relationship is found, and there is even a change in the syntactic category to which the word *kiss* belongs. Thus, without access to meaning, independent of syntax, language learning would prove to be exceedingly difficult.

Perhaps a better illustration of this point can be made with sentences (5) and (6), which are also from Macnamara (1972):

(5) The boy struck the girl.

(6) The girl struck the boy.

The issue here is, How would a child determine that these sentences are not stylistic variants such as those in (1) and (2) or (3) and (4)? Macnamara suggests that there is no way to decide this unless the child has independent access to meaning, probably by observing what is happening when sentences such as (5) and (6) are uttered.

The decision to treat (1) and (2) as equivalent sentences is based on the child's nonlinguistic knowledge that books can be given to people but people cannot be given to books. It must be noted that Macnamara does not claim that all syntactic structures are discovered through the use of semantic structures. He points out that gender in Indo-European languages does not correlate with any nonlinguistic classification. Also, the singular-plural rule that determines the ending for the verb in English on the basis of the number of the surface structure subject (e.g., he runs, they run) is a purely syntactic rule. Therefore, Macnamara argues for a view of language acquisition in which syntactic structures are acquired on the basis of both linguistic and nonlinguistic information. But it is clear in his discussion that the role of nonlinguistic information is the more important, at least in the early phases of language learning.

Views of language acquisition such as those proposed by Bloom (1970) and Macnamara (1972) also raise the issue of the overall relationship between language development and cognitive development. This general topic has been discussed by several writers (cf. Brown, 1973; Slobin, 1973). The basic question here is the extent to which it may be possible to trace out the course of linguistic development on the basis of what is known about patterns of cognitive development. An attempt to answer this question would be premature, although limited evidence is available. As Slobin (1973) points out, the earliest grammatical structures to appear in child speech are often those that studies of cognitive development suggest are available to the child mind at that particular time. The general pattern is far from clear, however, and whereas certain aspects of language acquisition can be discussed in terms of cognitive complexity, there is a point at which linguistic complexity also plays a role (Slobin, 1973).

In this section we have examined the role of both syntactic and semantic factors in language acquisition, as well as some of the more traditional associative principles. The available evidence is too limited and the problems to be solved are too numerous to allow much in the way of definite conclusions at this time. Stimulus-response association theories of the traditional variety seem to play a limited role in explaining the acquisition of a natural language. Syntactic theories do a much better job. These theories, however, will need to be supplemented by a consideration of various semantic and cognitive factors. This is not likely to be an easy task, but it certainly appears to be an essential one. Let us now turn to the use of language in the adult human.

SENTENCE COMPREHENSION
AND SENTENCE MEMORY

Perhaps the most extensive area of research concerning the role of grammatical rules is that which deals with sentence comprehension and sentence memory. A basic assumption in these experiments is that an individual must first comprehend an input sentence and store a representation of it in memory. In contrast to more traditional views, contemporary psycholinguists generally conceive of this stored representation as being abstract and not as being a verbatim copy of the sentence. Another way of putting this is to say that one stores the "gist" of the sentence and not the sentence itself.

Among the questions asked in this area of research are those dealing with what role grammatical factors play in extracting the gist of sentences and the nature or form of the abstract representation. When sentence memory is particularly at issue, there is also the question of the nature of the reconstruction process and what the role of grammatical factors might be in reconstructing a sentence from its abstract representation. Although several issues here can be considered separately, they were not clearly differentiated in the early period of psycholinguistic research. Therefore, sentence comprehension and sentence memory will initially be discussed as if they were more or less part of the same process and will then be considered separately. Semantic factors may play a major role in both sentence comprehension and sentence memory, but for the moment our main concern will be with grammatical considerations.

According to linguistic theory, the process of sentence generation is characterized as proceeding from top to bottom, or from deep structure to surface structure. One of the earliest views of sentence comprehension simply reversed this process. That is, the process of sentence comprehension or extracting the gist of a sentence was thought to involve recovery of deep structure relations by detransforming the surface structure of a sentence. A frequently cited adjunct to this view of sentence comprehension was that the complexity of a sentence and hence the speed with which it could be processed is related to the number of transformational steps involved in going from the surface structure to the deep structure. Several forms of this hypothesis have been put forward, and it will be convenient to discuss them separately. The experimental evidence cited is at least indirectly relevant to all of the alternatives, since they all follow the general characterization outlined above.

The Kernel Hypothesis

This hypothesis derives from the grammatical considerations provided by Chomsky in *Syntactic Structures* (1957). In this monograph Chomsky proposed that simple, active, affirmative, declarative sentences (*SAAD*) were derived from underlying strings by applying the minimum number of transformations required to produce an actual sentence. Chomsky referred to such sentences as "kernel sentences." Since only the minimum number of transformations was applied to generate kernel sentences, many psycholinguists concluded that the additional transformations required to generate other types of sentences were applied directly to kernel sentences rather than to their underlying strings. This conclusion turned out to be a misinterpretation of Chomsky's grammar, but it did lead to what has been called the *kernel hypothesis*.

According to this hypothesis, the memory representation of a sentence consists of the *SAAD* form plus a set of "tags" indicating the optional transformations involved. The larger the number of tags, the more complex the sentence and the greater the time involved in sentence comprehension. For instance, the memory representation for a passive sentence consists of the *SAAD* form plus a tag for the passive transformation, whereas a negative passive sentence requires two transformational tags. Both of these sentences are more complex than the active affirmative, since the memory representation of this sentence consists only of the *SAAD* form. In this case the tags refer only to transformations applied to the *SAAD* form in order to derive the actual sentence and not to the transformations required to produce the *SAAD* form itself.

The earliest evidence concerning the kernel hypothesis came from the work of G. A. Miller and his associates (cf. Miller, 1962). Their general approach was to present sentences to subjects and ask them to find corresponding sentences in a larger set. The subjects were told what transformations to apply to each sentence in order to find the corresponding sentence. For example, a passive sentence (*P*) such as "The ball was hit by the boy" might be presented with instructions to find its corresponding *SAAD*, "The boy hit the ball," in a larger list of sentences.

In one study (Miller and McKean, 1964) a sentence was presented briefly, and when the subject had performed the required transformation or transformations, he pressed a button which presented a search list. The time taken from presentation of the initial sentence to the pressing of the button was interpreted as being an index of processing time. The advantage of this procedure over those employed in earlier studies was that it separated processing time from the time required to search for the corresponding sentence. As was predicted, the results indicated that more processing time was required for sentences involving two transformations than for sentences requiring only a single transformation.

An investigation of sentence memory that is relevant to the kernel hypothesis was reported by Mehler (1963). He employed several sets of sentences from *P, N, Q* families in a learning task. A subject was shown eight sentences for five trials using a modified free-recall procedure. At the end of each trial the subject attempted to recall the eight sentences. The subject was also provided with a prompt word from each sentence. Of course, only one sentence from a given family was presented to any one subject. Mehler's results showed that the *SAAD* form is learned more rapidly than any other sentence type and that errors in recall tend to be in the direction of the simpler *SAAD* form, although the meaning of the sentence was usually unchanged. This latter finding suggests that subjects may be forgetting one or more of the transformational tags which, according to the kernel hypothesis, are stored in memory along with the *SAAD* form. More rapid learning of *SAAD* sentences would be expected, since no additional tags have to be stored in memory.

Mehler suggests these findings are consistent with the hypothesis that subjects tend to analyze sentences into a semantic component plus syntactic corrections when the sentences are learned and that this separation is one reason why the general meaning of the sentence is easier to recall than its syntactic form. A point that has continued to plague psycholinguistic theory concerns the relative importance of syntactic and semantic processes in sentence memory. It is clear that linguistic theory has emphasized the role of syntax. It could easily be argued, however, as Mehler appears to suggest, that sentence memory is based heavily on semantic processes, with syntactic processes coming into play only to ensure that whatever is remembered is stated in *some* appropriate grammatical form.

A significant but controversial study of sentence memory was reported by Savin and Perchonock (1965). Their study was based on the assumption that the greater the transformational complexity of a sentence, the greater the demands that are placed on memory. To test this hypothesis, subjects were presented with a series of sentences, each of which was followed by a different set of eight isolated words. For each sentence, the subject's task was to recall the sentence and as many of the eight words as he could remember. The number of words recalled correctly was the measure used to indicate the storage requirements for a particular sentence type. That is, assuming a fixed capacity in short-term memory, if a sentence is recalled correctly then the number of additional words recalled would indicate the storage requirements for the sentence. The greater the complexity of a sentence, the greater the number of transformational tags that must be stored in memory, and the fewer the number of additional words that should be recalled. It is important to remember that the number of words recalled is counted only when the sentence is correctly recalled. Otherwise there would be no basis for assuming differential storage requirements across sentence types.

The results of the Savin and Perchonock study are give in Table 11.4. In general these data support the basic hypothesis—the *SAAD* form yields the highest level of recall, and sentences requiring one transformation generally show higher recall than sentences requiring two transformations. Of course the difficulty of particular transformations is largely an empirical matter, but there appears to be some consistency in the combinations. For example, the passive question yields higher recall than the

Table 11.4 Mean number of words recalled after each of the sentence types.

Sentence type	Example	Mean number of words recalled
ACTIVE DECLARATIVE	The boy has hit the girl.	5.27
WH-QUESTION	What has the boy hit?	4.78
QUESTION	Has the boy hit the girl?	4.67
PASSIVE	The girl has been hit by the boy.	4.55
NEGATIVE	The boy has not hit the girl.	4.44
NEGATIVE QUESTION	Has the boy not hit the girl?	4.39
EMPHATIC	The boy *has* hit the girl.	4.30
NEGATIVE PASSIVE	The girl has not been hit by the boy.	3.48
PASSIVE QUESTION	Has the girl been hit by the boy?	4.02
NEGATIVE PASSIVE QUESTION	Has the girl not been hit by the boy?	3.85
EMPHATIC PASSIVE	The girl *has* been hit by the boy.	3.74

negative passive, which is consistent with the finding of better recall for the question than for the negative. Also note that these results are not due to sentence length. For instance, the *SAAD* example in Table 11.4 has six words, but the WH-question has only five. However, the WH-question is more complex, since it requires additional transformations. Similarly, the *SAAD* is less complex than the emphatic even though the same words and word order are involved in both examples. The emphatic form presumably requires special stress on the first auxiliary (i.e., *has* in the example), and this additional information must also be stored in memory.

Although such findings provide general support for the kernel hypothesis, in recent years this account has been discarded in favor of alternative hypotheses. There are several reasons for this change. One of these has to do with the misunderstanding that led to the kernel hypothesis in the first place. The result of the misunderstanding, as we saw before, was that primary emphasis was placed on the *SAAD* form and not on the deep structure strings underlying it. Of course, if the empirical evidence had more closely supported the kernel hypothesis, the kernel hypothesis would probably have survived.

Among the empirical difficulties are the repeated failures to satisfactorily replicate the findings of Savin and Perchonock. Matthews (1968) failed to reproduce their findings at all, and Glucksberg and Danks (1969) offered only a weak approximation of these results. Only Epstein (1969) obtained similar results using the experimental conditions employed by Savin and Perchonock. But when he asked subjects to recall the words prior to recalling the sentence, the effects of transformational complexity almost disappeared.

Other empirical evidence damaging to the kernel hypothesis has emerged. As but one example, consider the differences in recall of active and passive sentences which have been widely reported. According to the kernel hypothesis, an active sentence is stored in its *SAAD* form with no additional tags. The passive is stored in the same way with the addition of one transformational tag. Thus the active sentence in (7) would be stored as just that sentence, whereas the passive sentence in (8) would be stored in the exact same way plus a transformational tag:

(7) The boy hit the ball.
(8) The ball was hit by the boy.

According to this account, there is no way to explain the rather common observation that *boy* is recalled better than *ball* in the active sentence, whereas the opposite is true for the passive sentence (cf. Anderson, 1963; Coleman, 1964; Horowitz and Prytukak, 1969). Findings such as these together with the theoretical misunderstanding noted previously have led most investigators to consider alternative concepts to the kernel hypothesis.

The Deep Structure Hypothesis

The basic difference between this hypothesis and the kernel hypothesis lies in the linguistic description of the sentence. The kernel hypothesis considers sentence memory to consist of the *SAAD* form plus appropriate tags; the deep structure hypothesis considers the memory representation to consist of the deep structure plus appropriate transformational tags. Of course, with the deep structure hypothesis, all transformations would be tagged and not just those that apply to *SAAD* forms. The particular details of this hypothesis naturally vary with the linguistic theory on which it is based. Most investigators have relied on the theory offered by Chomsky (1965) or a similar version offered by Katz and Postal (1964).

Both the kernel and deep structure hypotheses are based mainly on syntactic considerations. This does not imply that the sentences presented to subjects, or the words they contain, are not interpreted semantically. Obviously, the meaning of the words and sentences is understood. But the critical factors that determine how an input sentence will be understood and remembered involve syntactic considerations. Both hypotheses assume that once the syntactic structure of a sentence has been appropriately determined, understanding the meaning of the sentence is a straightforward proposition. Furthermore, both hypotheses hold that it is the results of this syntactic analysis that are stored in memory.

We have already seen support for the deep structure hypothesis. In a previous section we reported studies by Blumenthal (1967) and Blumenthal and Boakes (1967) that showed differential effects of prompt words in sentences. The sentences differed in deep structure, but they had identical surface structures. The studies by Mehler (1963) as well as those by Savin and Perchonock (1965) can also be considered as generally supportive of this hypothesis. Of course the difficulties seen in attempts to replicate Savin and Perchonock are also relevant here and we shall return to this problem shortly.

Several other lines of research provide support for the deep structure hypothesis. Rohrman (1968) compared recall of subject nominalizations such as *growling lions* and object nominalizations such as *raising flowers* in sentences such as "Growling lions are unpleasant" and "Raising flowers is difficult." These strings have identical surface structure but differ in deep structure (e.g., Lions growl; Someone raises flowers). His subjects recalled subject nominalizations better, which he attributed to the greater complexity in the deep structure for object nominalizations. Rohrman also obtained evidence that deep structure complexity may be more important than transformational complexity in the recall of nominalizations. His suggestion was that more complex deep structures, where complexity is expressed as number of nodes in the deep structure tree, place greater demands on memory.

Another way of discussing complexity in the deep structure of sentences is in terms of the number of propositions represented in the deep structure that may be expressed in a single surface structure. Common examples of such complexity can be seen in embedded or conjoined sentences as opposed to simple sentences. In one study Perfetti (1969) reports an inverse relationship between the number of deep structure propositions underlying a given sentence and its probability of being recalled. Even with the length of sentences held constant in number of words, the more complex sentences in terms of the deep structure were more difficult to recall. Wanner (1968) has also shown that the effectiveness of a particular noun as a cue in recall is directly related to the number of propositions in the deep structure that contain this noun.

Despite support for the deep structure hypothesis, several questions arise. One of these questions concerns the relationship between deep structure and meaning. It has been commonly observed that we can remember the general meaning or gist of a sentence long after the point where we can no longer repeat it in the same words. This observation has been taken to imply that the deep structure, rather than the surface structure, of the sentence determines the way it is stored in memory. But as we noted in connection with the study reported by Mehler (1963), this observation does not reveal whether syntactic or semantic processes are more important in sentence memory.

An experiment that bears directly on this issue has been reported by Sachs (1967). Her subjects listened to passages of connected discourse (paragraphs), and after each paragraph a sentence recognition task was presented. Following each paragraph a test sentence was presented which was either a sentence from the passage or one that was altered. The altered sentences involved a change in semantic content (subject-object reversal), a change in syntactic form (active to passive voice), or a formal change (rearrangement of words or phrases). Depending on where in the passage the original sentence occurred, there were varying intervals of time between presentation of the original and corresponding test sentence. The test sentence was presented either immediately following the original sentence (zero delay) or after delays of 80 syllables (about twenty-seven seconds) or 160 syllables (about forty-six seconds).

With no delay between the original and the test sentence, subjects were able to recognize all changes with close to 90 percent accuracy. But although the ability to recognize *semantic* changes remained high in the delay conditions, syntactic changes and formal changes were not detected much better than chance after delays of 80 or 160 syllables. The observation that syntactic changes from passive to active voice were poorly detected following delays suggests that what is in memory does not correspond exactly to deep structure either. At least according to grammars such as Katz and Postal's (1964), passivity is supposed to be represented in the deep structure.

These findings led Sachs to argue for a processing model in which the original form of the sentence is retained for only the short amount of time required for sentence comprehension. Once the meaning of the sentence has been abstracted, the original sentence is rapidly forgotten. Although the subjects in her experiment did retain some information about sentence form after delay, Sachs points out that they expected to be questioned about the sentence materials, so that these results only indicate some upper limit on the ability to retain sentence form information following a delay. In fact, Wanner (1968) has shown that when subjects do not expect to be tested, their memory for sentence form is at a chance level even though they continue to recognize semantic changes most of the time. Thus it appears that very shortly after a sentence is heard little of its syntactic form is retained, only its general meaning or gist.

The implications of the findings reported by Sachs (1967) and Wanner (1968) are somewhat at odds with findings we discussed previously which appeared to support the deep structure hypothesis for sentence memory. Part of the problem lies with the current state of linguistic theory, which, as yet, has not fully come to grips with semantics. The effect of this problem can be seen in studies such as those mentioned above. Generally speaking, changes introduced in the deep structure of sentences result in changes in meaning as well. Therefore one cannot decide whether the representation of a sentence in memory is best described from a semantic or a syntactic point of view or from both. The resolution of this problem will not be easy, although some beginning steps have been suggested which we will consider in a subsequent section.

A second major question concerning the deep structure hypothesis involves the issue of transformational complexity. We have seen evidence that transformational tags are not retained over even fairly short intervals, particularly in situations such as those employed by Sachs (1967) where the stimulus object is an entire passage and not an isolated sentence. This does not necessarily imply that transformational complexity has no effect in terms of speed or ease of processing during that brief interval between hearing an utterance and the extraction of its gist. In the following two sections we shall consider some of the work that has been reported concerning both of these issues.

GRAMMATICAL FACTORS
IN SENTENCE COMPREHENSION

Sentence comprehension refers to those processes by which sentences are understood. Presumably such processes are engaged for only short periods of time, and once a sentence is understood sentence comprehension is said to be complete. According to accounts such as those embodied in the deep structure hypothesis, syntactic features play a major role in sentence comprehension processes. That is, the deep structure hypothesis states that in order to understand a sentence you must detransform the surface structure to recover the deep structure. This hypothesis suggests that both surface structure and deep structure relations as well as the number of transformational steps involved in going from one to the other should all play a role in sentence comprehension. As we have already seen, there is evidence to support the role of these factors in the perception and learning of sentences. In fact, not long ago it appeared quite reasonable to conceive of a sentence comprehension model that consisted of a device to determine surface structure relations, a transformational component to convert surface structures to deep structures, and a semantic component to provide an interpretation of the deep structures.

Despite its initial success the preceding view of sentence comprehension has been severely criticized in a series of papers by Fodor, Garrett, and Bever. The main focus of their attack is the hypothesis that states that the perceptual complexity of a sentence is determined by the number of grammatical rules employed in the derivation of that sentence. They term this hypothesis the *derivational theory of complexity* (DTC).

In reviewing studies that appear to support DTC, Fodor and Garrett (1966) point out that the materials used in these experiments involve few grammatical structures and even fewer transformational rules. Thus doubt is cast on the generality of the hypothesis. They also note that many predictions based on DTC are the same ones that might be offered on the basis of sentence length or meaning. For example, in the studies by Gough cited previously, we saw that active sentences were verified faster than passive sentences and affirmative sentences were verified faster than negative sentences. Although these findings are predicted by DTC, passive sentences are obviously longer than active sentences, and as Gough's results suggest, negative sentences may be more complex than affirmative sentences simply because they are negatives.

A further difficulty with DTC, pointed out by Fodor and Garrett (1967), is that the hypothesis appears to make predictions that do not seem plausible. For example, according to linguistic theory, truncated passives such as (9) are transformationally derived from full passives such as (10):

(9) The budget was cut.
(10) The budget was cut by someone.

This relationship appears to require the prediction, according to DTC, that (9) is more complex than (10). A similar situation exists for phrases like (11), which are tranformationally derived from phrases like (12):

(11) The red house.
(12) The house which is red.

Fodor and Garrett argue that these are not just isolated instances in which predictions based on DTC do not seem plausible. Instead they reveal a general difficulty with this hypothesis. Bever (1970) also came to this conclusion.

These considerations led Fodor, Garrett, and Bever to reexamine the relationship between sentence comprehension and models of linguistic competence. In essential agreement with the deep structure hypothesis, they concluded that in order for a sentence to be understood it would be necessary to recover the deep structure. This assumption appeared necessary to account for the various linguistic skills exhibited by speakers and listeners that were discussed earlier. But they rejected the view expressed in DTC that grammatical transformations are directly involved in the recovery of deep structures. Their alternative to DTC (Fodor and Garrett, 1967; Fodor, Garrett, and Bever, 1968) has been termed the *verb complexity hypothesis* (VCH).

This hypothesis consists of two components which may be thought of as perceptual strategies. The first component takes input sentences and projects the possible deep structure configurations that could underlie them. This is accomplished with reference to the verb. Specifically, it is hypothesized that verbs may be classified in terms of the types of deep structure configurations they can enter into or accept. For example, if the verb is a pure transitive which only takes a direct object, the deep structure would have the general form shown in (13):

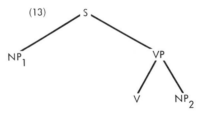

The governor discussed the budget.

Verbs may accept various types of complement, however. Although a pure transitive such as *discuss* can only enter into configurations like (13), other verbs, such as *believe,* can accept not only the deep structure configuration of (13) as in "John believed Bill" but also those represented in (14) and (15). Thus, depending on the nature of the *main* verb, one or more deep structure configurations are identified as possible.

The second component of VCH is used to choose among alternative deep structures by reference to explicit markers in the surface structure of the sentence. For example, the lexical items "that" in (14) and "to" in (15) presumably indicate the appropriate deep structure configuration for the verb "believed." In (13) it is the absence of such markers that identi-

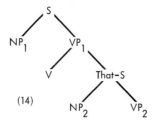

(14)

John believed that Bill came.

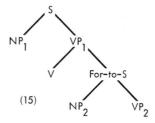

(15)

John believed Bill to be an idiot.

fies the configuration if the verb "believed" is introduced. In a general sense the information employed in this component is thought to derive from the transformational component of the grammar, although the transformational rules are not used directly in the recovery of deep structures. It is as if the information contained in a transformational grammar were used to construct a comprehension device which would in turn eliminate the need to refer to the grammar directly. In this way VCH emphasizes the importance of the transformational grammar and the linguistic skills that the grammar accounts for while avoiding the necessity of following grammatical rules explicitly in sentence comprehension.

Fodor and Garrett (1967) were the first to provide experimental evidence concerning VCH. This investigation involved the use of sentences with two embeddings, such as those shown in (16) and (17). The sentences were presented either with or without the relative pronouns indicated by parentheses.

(16) The pen (which) the author (whom) the editor liked used was new.
(17) The tiger (which) the lion (that) the gorilla chased killed was ferocious.

The basic idea to be tested was that once verb classification had indicated the alternative deep structure configurations possible, the relative pronouns would make it easier to decide among the alternatives. Thus it was predicted that these sentences would be comprehended more rapidly and accurately when the pronouns were included. An easier example to follow is given in (18) where the relative pronoun indicates a deep structure configuration in which the second NP is the subject of a transitive verb and the first NP is the object of that verb.

(18) The man whom the dog bit died.

The subject's task in this investigation was to paraphrase each sentence immediately following its presentation. Accuracy of paraphrase was scored in terms of the number of subject-object relations correctly reported. For example, in (16) this would require knowing that "the pen was new" or "the editor liked the author" or "the author used the pen." The number of subject-object relations correctly reported was then divided by the time taken to form the paraphrase. This yielded a score that Fodor and Garrett view as indicating the number of grammatical relations recovered per unit of response time. The results of their experiments consistently supported VCH. Subjects hearing sentences containing relative pronouns performed better than subjects not receiving the pronouns. This finding held for both visual and auditory presentations, and it was also shown to be independent of the number of steps involved in the derivation of the sentence, which is contrary to the prediction based on DTC.

A test of the verb component of VCH was reported in two experiments by Fodor, Garrett, and Bever (1968). The procedure of their first experiment closely followed that of Fodor and Garrett (1967). The sentences used contained two embeddings. Two versions of each sentence were recorded, which differed only in that one contained a verb that accepted complement structures where the other contained a transitive verb. The results indicated that sentences with simple verbs were paraphrased more accurately than sentences with complex verbs, although only a slight advantage was found in terms of response times. The second experiment showed that anagrams of sentences containing simple verbs were solved more readily than anagrams of sentences containing complex verbs. It is not clear how solutions in the anagram task are to be related to the processes involved in sentence comprehension, but the results of these two experiments taken together appear to provide some support for VCH.

Despite the initial support for VCH it is not possible at this time to decide whether VCH is superior to DTC or whether either hypothesis provides a particularly sound basis for a model of sentence comprehension. In a review of this issue Gough (1971) points out several weaknesses in VCH. At the experimental level he notes that the facilitation of paraphrase by the presence of relative pronouns in self-embedded sentences is predicted by both VCH and DTC. Thus this finding reported by Fodor and Garrett (1967) does not provide a basis for choosing between these hypotheses. In addition, Hakes (1971) has shown that verb complexity does not always yield the effects for paraphrase predicted by VCH. In only one of two studies does Hakes report more accurate paraphrase for simple as opposed to complex verbs.

Gough also points out that VCH has not been formulated with sufficient precision to allow for a rigorous evaluation. For example, VCH begins by assuming that an input sentence is marked at least crudely for segmentation, including identification of the main verb. There is no indication in VCH of how this is achieved, however; it is simply taken as a given, and processing continues from this point. Such considerations led Gough to conclude that the issue cannot be decided on the basis of present evidence and theoretical formulations. Although arguments against DTC offered by Fodor, Garrett, and Bever carry substantial weight, there is not sufficient support for VCH or any other alternative to allow for a reasoned choice among the alternatives.

Before we return to the discussion of sentence memory, let us briefly raise a methodological consideration concerning the process of sentence comprehension. In his review Gough (1971) points out that the traditional methods used to investigate sentence comprehension, including sentence verification, paraphrase, and recall, have in common the fact that they assess comprehension after it is complete. He suggests that we may learn more about sentence comprehension by investigating comprehension while it is going on rather than after it is complete. In this regard, a technique developed by Foss (1969) may hold some promise.

Phoneme Monitoring

Foss's technique consists of asking a subject to comprehend a sentence and at the same time to listen for the occurrence of a particular phoneme. When the phoneme is heard, the subject is to make a designated response as quickly as possible. The reaction time between the onset of the phoneme and the subject's response serves as the measure of performance. The task is called *phoneme monitoring* and the response measure is the phoneme-monitoring latency (PML).

The rationale for this technique begins with the assumption that only a limited amount of information can be processed at any given moment If the subject is engaged in one kind of processing, his performance on another task can be expected to suffer. For example, when sentence comprehension is demanding the subject's attention, his ability to perceive or respond to the critical phoneme will be reduced. An increase in PML can be presumed to indicate a momentary increase in difficulty of comprehension.

Foss and Lynch (1969) provided the first demonstration of the validity of this technique in a study that compared PML in right-branching and self-embedded sentences. It is well known that right-branching sentences such as (19) are easier to understand than self-embedded sentences such as (20):

(19) The store sold the whiskey that intoxicated the rioter that broke the window.

(20) The rioter that the whiskey the store sold intoxicated broke the window.

It should be clear that the difference in difficulty is due to the surface structure syntax and not to the difficulty of the words or the meanings conveyed. Foss and Lynch presented their subjects with sentences of each type, along with instructions to monitor the occurrence of the phoneme /b/. More specifically, the subjects were told to push a button whenever they heard a word starting with a /b/. Ten sentences of each type had the critical phoneme occur early in the sentence, ten additional sentences of each type had the critical phoneme occur late, and ten more sentences of each type had no words starting with /b/.

The results of this study were in accord with the rationale discussed previously. Response latency was reliably longer when the critical word appeared in the more difficult self-embedded sentences. Foss and Lynch also reported longer latencies when the critical word appeared late in the sentence, although this finding has not always been replicated in other investigations (cf. Shields, McHugh, and Martin, 1974).

Several other studies contribute to the view that PML is sensitive to processes involved in sentence comprehension. Foss (1969) reports that during sentence processing, PML is greater following relatively rare words than it is following more common words. Cairns and Foss (1971), however, report the rather perplexing finding that this effect holds for adjectives but not for nouns or verbs. Just why this should be so is far from clear. Foss (1970) has also shown that PML is greater during processing of ambiguous sentences than it is during processing of unambiguous sentences. This investigation also revealed that when subjects are instructed to classify the sentences for ambiguity immediately after hearing them, the longer PMLs occur only for sentences perceived as being ambiguous whether or not they are in fact ambiguous.

Two investigations have compared paraphrase and phoneme-monitoring techniques in a situation designed to indicate the effect of including relative pronouns in doubly self-embedded sentences. Hakes and Cairns (1970) confirmed the findings of Fodor and Garrett (1967) that the inclusion of relative pronouns increases accuracy in the paraphrase task. They also report that PML is less when the relative pronouns are included. Hakes and Foss (1970) have confirmed both of these findings, with some indication that phoneme monitoring may be a more sensitive measure of sentence comprehension than is the case for paraphrase.

Since this effect of relative pronouns appears to be predictable from both VCH and DTC, these findings do not appear to help resolve the theoretical issue for sentence comprehension. Unfortunately, the same comment can be made about another aspect of VCH. Hakes (1971) reports two experiments that compare the effects of simple and complex verbs. Unlike Fodor, Garrett, and Bever (1968), he did not use doubly self-embedded sentences, although the sentences were structurally complex. As we noted before, Hakes found that the paraphrase task yielded results predicted by VCH in one experiment but not in the other. Quite surprisingly, in view of the sensitivity of phoneme monitoring noted above, PML did not differ for simple and complex verbs.

Despite the ambiguous results reported by Hakes (1971), the phoneme-monitoring task provides a reasonable alternative to other tasks as a measure of sentence comprehension processes. In addition to the evidence cited here, it should be recalled that phoneme monitoring has been shown to be sensitive to rhythmic structure, as we noted in Chapter 9. It seems quite likely that rhythmic structure would have its greatest effect during, and not after, comprehension. Of course a great deal of additional research must be done before any definite conclusion can be drawn concerning just what PMLs do reflect.

We shall also have to await further research to reveal the role that models of linguistic competence may play in accounts of sentence comprehension and to determine whether linguistic competence as specified by a transformational grammar is directly reflected in comprehension, as suggested by DTC, or more indirectly related to comprehension, as suggested by VCH. These questions are now entirely open, and we will need to know much more about sentence comprehension in order to answer them.

SEMANTIC FACTORS IN SENTENCE MEMORY

A major weakness of the deep structure hypothesis as a model for sentence memory apparently results from the fact that it is derived from a linguistic theory in which semantic considerations play a very minor role. In recent years alternative approaches to linguistic theory, such as the "case grammar" of Fillmore (1968) or the semantically based deep structure of McCawley (1968), have moved away from the almost exclusive concern with syntax that characterized earlier linguistic theory. Although these approaches may have promise as psychological models, as yet there is not sufficient research against which to evaluate them. Clark (1969a, 1969b), however, has offered a psycholinguistic model of sentence memory that is based on semantic considerations and has proved to be quite effective in explaining a wide range of psychological evidence.

Clark's theory begins with the basic assumption that the process of sentence comprehension involves recovery of basic relations in the deep structure of a sentence. In one paper, Clark (1969a) describes these as functional relations that constitute the primitive or irreducible conceptual relations out of which sentences are constructed. For example, in both of the following sentences a listener knows that the lexical items *Mary, watched,* and *ballgame* are in the relation of subject, verb, and object. That is, Mary did the watching and it was the ballgame that she watched:

(21) Mary watched the ballgame.
(22) The ballgame was watched by Mary.

According to Clark, it is this type of information that is stored in memory immediately after comprehension, and this information is stored in a manner that is more readily available for retrieval than less basic kinds of information. In contrast, and in terms of information about the theme of the sentence, it is clear that sentence (21) is about Mary and sentence (22) is about the ballgame. Such information is of a different sort and is not to be found in the functional relations that underlie a sentence.

Once the basic functional relations of the deep structure have been extracted, Clark maintains that the memory representation of a sentence is more semantic than syntactic. The semantic representation is thought to consist of a complex of *semantic features*. Each feature designates the presence or absence of a particular property or a relational attribute of a lexical item in the sentence. For example, the word *father* might be coded as having the properties of being *human* and *male* in addition to the relational attribute of being the *parent of someone*.

Semantic features also may code information expressed in the organization of the sentence itself. For example, in (23) the distinction between the main and subordinate events must be coded. The main event, *signing*, is fixed in time; and the subordinate event, *eating*, must be located relative to the main event (in this case, after it):

(23) Before he ate his lunch he signed the bill into law.

This is a subtle distinction, but it must be assigned a semantic code just as the lexical items are assigned codes to designate properties and relational attributes.

In many situations an important part of Clark's model is the *principle of lexical marking*. With this principle Clark tries to specify some properties of semantic features and to suggest that some properties may be more complex and more readily forgotten than others. The central idea expressed in this principle is the distinction between *marked* and *unmarked* forms. In many pairs of antonymous adjectives, such as *good-bad* or *tall-short,* one member of the pair is considered to be unmarked while the other is marked. Unmarked adjectives such as *good* or *tall* can be used in two ways. One way is relatively neutral, what Clark refers to as the "nominal" sense of the word. Thus, unmarked adjectives can be used in noncommital questions like "How good?" or "How tall?" On the other hand, marked adjectives when used in this way imply a prior belief about the answer, as in "How bad?"

A second difference between marked and unmarked forms is that the unmarked adjective can refer to either the full scale (e.g., "How tall is he?") or just to part of it (e.g., "He is tall"), whereas marked adjectives refer to only part of the scale in either case (e.g., "How short is he?" or

"He is short"). According to Clark, this difference derives from the contrastive sense of these words where unmarked forms refer to much of the underlying dimension and marked forms refer to only part of the underlying dimension.

The importance of the principle of lexical marking can be seen from other aspects of Clark's theory. First, he assumes that semantic features are stored and can be forgotten independently. Second, he assumes that certain features are more easily forgotten than others. For example, he predicts that a particular semantic distinction is more likely to be remembered than whether that distinction was marked or unmarked. Third, he assumes that the marked form contains one more semantic feature than the unmarked form. The rationale for this assumption can be illustrated for the adjective pair *good-bad*. Presumably the use of either of these adjectives in a sentence would result in a semantic feature code for evaluation because both imply an evaluative meaning. However, *bad* would always require an additional feature to indicate that only the poorer end of the evaluative dimension was intended, whereas *good* might or might not require an additional feature depending upon whether the full or the restricted scale sense of the word was communicated. In conjunction with the preceding assumption, this difference leads to the general prediction that an individual is more likely to recall a marked form as unmarked than the other way around. Notice that forgetting the additional feature for *bad* or the restricted sense of *good* will bias recall in the direction of the unmarked form (i.e., good).

A third principle of Clark's model is what he calls the *principle of congruence*. This principle states that information stored in memory can only be retrieved when it is congruent, at the level of functional relations, with the information required by the task at hand. For example, suppose an individual is presented with a sentence and, at a later time, is asked a question about that sentence. According to the principle of congruence, the functional relations stored in memory must be in agreement with those extracted from the question if the question is to be answered. If the functional relations from the two sources are not congruent they must be made congruent, and the operations by which this is accomplished take time. Thus, fewer errors and shorter response latencies should be found when the functional relations are in agreement than when they are not. Of course it should be clear that the principle of congruence deals mainly with the way memory is searched for previously stored information, whereas the preceding principles specify what is stored in memory.

Clark's model for sentence memory has been quite successful in accounting for various experimental findings. Basic predictions derived from the model have been confirmed in situations ranging from word association to deductive reasoning and sentence memory. Clark and Card (1969) have reported that subjects tend to reconstruct unmarked adjectives from marked adjectives and that they more generally show error patterns in sentence recall that are more consistent with loss of semantic features than with an influence of surface structure or syntactic features. In those situations where comparisons are appropriate, Clark's model appears to provide a more adequate account of the data than does the deep structure hypothesis.

Clark's semantic feature approach therefore has two main advantages over the deep structure hypothesis as a model for sentence memory: it is able to account for findings not predictable from the deep structure hypothesis, and it attempts to specify at least some characteristics of the vague term *meaning* and to suggest an explicit role for meaning in sentence memory. Despite these advantages, however, there is reason to question the generality of Clark's model.

Sentences as Objects

The semantic feature model developed by Clark as well as the models of sentence memory based on the kernel and deep structure hypotheses follow the tradition of syntactic theory in that they all take the sentence as the basic unit of analysis. They all begin with the assumption that each sentence can be viewed as an isolated linguistic object and proceed from there to consider the memory representation of a sentence as being fully specified by a complete linguistic analysis of the sentence. Although this focus on the sentence as an isolated linguistic object may be adequate for a model of sentence comprehension, it may be of limited value when the information content of the incoming sentence has to be integrated with existing knowledge. Notice that the experimental evidence concerning sentence memory that we have previously reviewed typically involves a situation in which subjects are presented with unrelated sentences and are instructed to recall them verbatim. A complete model of sentence memory, however, must also specify how the information contained in the sentence is integrated with the information that is otherwise available to the listener either in memory or in the context of the situation.

Bransford and Franks (1971) report a series of experiments dealing with the acquisition and retention of complex ideas. First they constructed complex sentences called *fours* because each contained four propositions that could be expressed as simple declarative sentences called *ones*. An example of a *four* is given in (24), and the *ones* contained in this complex sentence are given in (25):

(24) The rock which rolled down the mountain crushed the tiny hut at the edge of the woods.

(25) The rock rolled down the mountain.
The rock crushed the hut.

The hut was tiny.
The hut was at the edge of the woods.

The *ones* could also be combined to generate *twos* and *threes* such as those given in (26) and (27), respectively:

(26) The tiny hut was at the edge of the woods.
(27) The rock which rolled down the mountain crushed the tiny hut.

From each reference sentence Bransford and Franks constructed four *ones*, four *twos*, three *threes*, and one *four*. From the four reference sentences used, a total of forty-eight sentences were possible.

The experiments consisted of an acquisition and a recognition task. The sentences presented in acquisition consisted of two *ones*, two *twos*, and two *threes* derived from each of the four reference sentences. These twenty-four sentences were chosen such that all four simple propositions contained in each reference sentence were presented at least once. During acquisition each sentence was read aloud to a group of subjects. To make sure that the subjects would have to hold the sentence in memory for a short time, the subjects engaged in about four seconds of color naming after presentation of each sentence. Following color naming, the subjects were asked an elliptical question about the previously presented sentence. For example, if the sentence was (28) the question might have been (29):

(28) The rock rolled down the mountain.
(29) Did what?

The subjects wrote down their answers to the question after which the experimenter read the next sentence. This procedure continued until all twenty-four acquisition sentences had been presented.

The recognition task following acquisition consisted of having the experimenter read numerous sentences to the subjects. Most of these sentences were derived from the four reference sentences, and some had been presented in acquisition (old) but others had not (new). In addition, several *noncase* sentences were presented, which involved changing the relationships across idea sets. For example, if one reference sentence was (24) and another was about "ants eating jelly in the kitchen," a *noncase* sentence might be (30):

(30) The rock which rolled down the mountain crushed the ants eating jelly in the kitchen.

In recognition the task was to indicate with a *yes* or a *no* response whether each sentence read had been presented during acquisition or not. Subjects were also asked to indicate their confidence in each response on a five-point scale ranging from "very low" if they were unsure to "very high" if they were certain that the sentence either had or had not been presented in acquisition. The confidence ratings were converted to yield a ten-point scale by assigning plus for a *yes* response and minus for a *no* response.

The results of these experiments revealed two basic findings. One finding indicated essentially no ability to discriminate between old and new sentences. The results are given in Figure 11.1. Thus it appears that once the full set of ideas becomes integrated in the mind of the listener, there no longer exists any discriminability between sentences actually presented and those that were not. The other major finding is shown in Figure 11.2. The data in this figure give the results for the first and second recognition trials. Subjects are apparently most confident that they have seen the *fours*, even though no *fours* were actually presented. Furthermore, the closer a given sentence comes to expressing the full set of propositions, the more confident subjects are that the sentence was presented previously. Notice that the subjects have little confidence, one way or the other, about the *ones*. They are quite certain, however, they have not seen any of the *noncase* sentences before. Findings such as these are difficult to account for with any model that considers a sentence to be an isolated linguistic object.

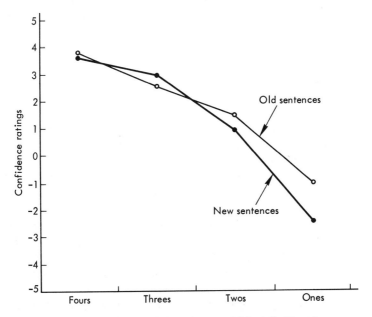

Figure 11.1 Confidence ratings for recognition of old and new sentences as a function of the number of propositions in the sentence.
(After Bransford and Franks, 1971.)

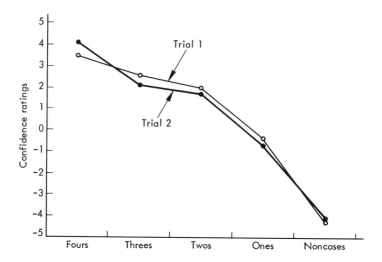

Figure 11.2 **Confidence ratings for recognition of all sentences on the first and second recognition trials.**
(After Bransford and Franks, 1971.)

A far more powerful demonstration of an individual's integrative and inferential skills in language comprehension was provided by Bransford, Barclay, and Franks (1972). Their task was comparable with that used by Bransford and Franks (1971), but the sentence materials were quite different. During acquisition, sentences such as those given in either (31) or (32) were presented:

(31) Three turtles rested *on* a log and a fish swam under *it*.
(32) Three turtles rested *beside* a log and a fish swam under *it*.

Notice that these sentences differ only in the use of the words *on* and *beside*. From these sentences two others were constructed by changing the final pronoun to *them*.

If the sentence given in (31) were presented during acquisition, the same sentence differing in the use of *them* as the final pronoun could be logically inferred from it. But if the acquisition sentence was (32), no other sentence in this set could be inferred from it. In the recognition test that contained sentences of both types as well as old and new sentences, subjects were unable to discriminate between old and new sentences that could be logically inferred from each other. That is, they were equally confident that these sentences had been presented previously. With sentences that did not necessarily follow from one another, however, subjects were confident that olds had been presented and that news had not been presented.

In a subsequent experiment that tested for cued recall following acquisition, similar outcomes were found. If sentences like (31) were presented during acquisition, subjects were much more likely to substitute *them* for *it* in recall than they were when sentences like (32) were presented during acquisition. It is clear that these results are not predictable from any existing linguistic theory, including semantic feature theory. The problem is that the structural descriptions for (31) and the equivalent sentence ending with *them* must differ in the same way as the two versions of (32) ending in *it* or *them*. Therefore the differences in performance that reflect differences in memory representation cannot be attributed to differences in the linguistic analysis.

The implications of the preceding studies are not immediately obvious. It may be that these results, in contrast to other findings, reflect differences in the task or object. That is, when the object is an isolated sentence, then its linguistic description becomes critical; but when the object involves a set of relations, some of which may be implicit, then the linguistic description becomes irrelevant. What appears to be required in the latter case, as Bransford, Barclay, and Franks (1972) point out, is a model in which the sentence is viewed as "a source of information which the listener assimilates to his existing cognitive knowledge" (p. 206). As Gough (1971) suggests, "This problem is, in the end, little short of the psychological problem of knowledge, and psycholinguistics is not ready for it" (p. 282).

It is also not clear whether results such as these have implications for sentence comprehension as well. Obviously, if the product of comprehension serves as the memory representation, then no theory that restricts this representation to linguistically expressed information and ignores the implications of that information is going to be adequate. But there is some indication (cf. Gough, 1971) that inferences occur beyond the stage of sentence comprehension. If this is true, linguistic analysis may still play an important role in comprehension and in situations where the sentence is, in fact, an isolated linguistic object. Beyond these situations, however, a more general cognitive machine, perhaps patterned along the lines of semantic models of memory, may well be required. In view of our discussion of syntactic and semantic factors in language acquisition, this conclusion is not surprising.

CONCLUSION

In Chapter 10 we considered a transformational grammar as a theory of linguistic competence, and we noted that such a grammar captures syntactic relations that are psychologically important in sentence processing. In the present chapter our main focus was whether the syntactic considerations provided by a transformational grammar would serve as an adequate model of language acquisition and use. That is, could a transformational grammar serve as a theory of performance?

The first part of the chapter was devoted to language development in the child. Here we saw evidence that the components of a transformational grammar, including phrase structure and transformational rules, do capture certain aspects of language development quite well. We also saw that the components of such a grammar are more closely related to language acquisition than is the case for associative concepts like practice, imitation, and reinforcement. As a theory of language acquisition, however, transformational grammar encounters difficulties because of the heavy reliance on syntactic considerations. Although the evidence is not definite as yet, future accounts of language acquisition will apparently have to include semantic and cognitive factors to a greater extent than has been the case in transformational grammar. This is not to imply that the grammar does not capture important aspects of language development but rather that the syntactic considerations provided by the grammar are not likely to be sufficient by themselves.

Most of this chapter was devoted to sentence comprehension and sentence memory in the adult language user. First we considered two general models of sentence processing derived from transformational grammar —the kernel hypothesis and the deep structure hypothesis. Both of these views hold that sentences are understood and remembered by recovering aspects of the underlying structure of sentences and noting the transformational steps involved in the recovery process. We saw some evidence in support of both of these hypotheses, although the evidence was decidedly mixed. Overall, the deep structure hypothesis appeared to be supported better than the kernel hypothesis. A major problem for both hypotheses is that syntactic aspects of input sentences do not seem to be remembered for more than a brief time after a sentence is processed, whereas semantic changes can be detected over much longer intervals. Such observations suggest certain inadequacies in transformational grammar as a psychological theory, and the appropriateness of considering accounts of sentence comprehension and sentence memory separately.

When sentence comprehension is at issue, the concern is with those processes that are engaged only until the sentence is understood. Here two hypotheses were considered—the derivational theory of complexity (DTC) and the verb complexity hypothesis (VCH). Both theories derive from the deep structure hypothesis in that both assume that sentence comprehension involves recovery of the deep structure. They differ in that DTC says that deep structures are recovered by detransforming surface structures, whereas VCH says that deep structures are recovered by means of a comprehension device derived from the grammar but not one that involves grammatical rules per se. Support for both theories was noted in studies of sentence verification, paraphrase, and recall as well as in studies of phoneme monitoring. This suggests that models of linguistic competence do capture some of the information that is relevant to the immediate comprehension of sentences. The evidence available, however, is not sufficient to support one point of view over the other or to conclude that grammatically based theories of sentence comprehension are likely to be sufficient by themselves in the long run.

It is in the area of sentence memory that theories based on transformational grammar have the greatest difficulty in accounting for performance. In general, semantic factors seem to be much more important than syntactic factors when sentence memory is at issue. The type of theory that seems to work best for sentence memory is one that considers both semantics and syntax. But even theories of this type seem to face major difficulties when the sentences to be processed are related to other input sentences or to information that is already in memory. Once the processes involved in integration, deduction, and reasoning become engaged, most current theories of sentence memory do not stand up well.

Psychological theories derived from syntactically based transformational grammars have many strengths and many weaknesses. On the positive side we can say that such theories provide better explanations of language acquisition and language use than those based on associative accounts of learning. Several complex aspects of both language development and sentence processing seem to be handled quite nicely by theories based on grammatical considerations. All such theories, however, seem to encounter difficulties when other cognitive information or knowledge comes into play. In language development this can be seen in the child's use of independently attained meaning to discover the significance of certain syntactic structures. In the adult, problems arise most obviously when sentences are not isolated objects but instead relate to previously acquired information. Thus it seems that grammatically based theories are likely to be most useful in accounting for the form of sentence production and the immediate comprehension of sentences. More complex cognitive models which rely heavily on semantic considerations will probably be required in other situations. In the next chapter we shall discuss some of the approaches that have been followed in an attempt to understand the acquisition and structure of cognitive concepts.

12

Concepts and Rules

ALTHOUGH THIS CHAPTER is about *concepts* and *rules,* neither of these terms is well defined in psychology. The word *concepts* is often used to refer to almost anything in which the writer is interested. Psychological investigations of concepts, however, have typically been restricted to those concepts that can be explicitly defined in terms of specifiable stimulus characteristics. The word *rules* is not so widely applicable, but it too can be used to refer to many different relationships.

Concepts and rules are not mutually exclusive categories. Whereas a concept can be viewed as a regular relation between a set of events and a rule can be said to define the particular regularity involved, it is often difficult to separate the concept from the rule in terms of what is learned. We have seen numerous examples of this confounding in the two preceding chapters. Many concepts, such as those of sentence, declarative sentence, passive sentence, or question, are defined in terms of particular sets of grammatical rules. Thus it seems just as appropriate to say that speakers of a language acquire the rule for the passive transformation as it is to say that they have acquired the concept of a passive sentence.

In a very meaningful sense we can speak of most human behavior as being based on the learning of concepts and rules which are then used to perform those acts required of us such as speaking, thinking, and problem solving. Of course, in many cases, such as language, the concepts and rules we use may only exist in an implicit sense, and they may not be specifiable in the explicit manner that has characterized most psychological studies of conceptual behavior. We shall return to this and related matters, but first let us consider the more common approaches to the study of conceptual behavior in psychology.

CONCEPTUAL BEHAVIOR: BASIC PROCEDURES

Types of Concept

Most investigations of concepts in psychology have been restricted to concepts that are defined in terms of specifiable stimulus characteristics. Much of the reason for this emphasis is attributable to the historical dominance of stimulus-response accounts of learning. Concept learning was seen by S-R theorists as being comparable to any other type of learning. Therefore the favored approach was to analyze the structure of concepts in terms of the specifiable stimulus characteristics to which responses could be associated. In addition, the concepts chosen for experimentation tended to be those having a relatively straightforward and clearly defined structure.

As theorists began to challenge stimulus-response accounts of concept learning, the alternative theories were tested mainly with concepts comparable in structure with those employed by S-R theorists. This has resulted in a considerable body of theory and evidence concerning a particular type of concept and the way such concepts are learned. Most of this chapter is devoted to this body of theory and evidence. Therefore, let us consider a concrete example of the type of concepts used in these investigations.

Imagine, if you will, a set of stimulus events that specify an object of a given color (red or blue), shape (circle or square), size (large or small), and texture (rough or smooth). In this case the stimulus *dimensions* are color, shape, size, and texture, and the stimulus *attributes* are the values on these dimensions. Thus, red and blue are the attributes on the color dimension, and circle and square are the attributes on the shape dimension. Any given stimulus event would consist of one attribute from each dimension, such as a large, rough, red square.

In a typical experiment the subject is told the nature of the task, including the names of the stimulus dimensions and the attribute values on those dimensions. Then a stimulus event is presented, to which the subject makes a response. This is followed by some indication from the experimenter of whether the response was correct or incorrect. Typically, this procedure is repeated on each trial until the subject is able either to state the concept verbally or to reach some specified criterion of correct responses in succession.

Suppose the conceptual problem were one of *single attribute identification* in which the correct attribute was redness. In this case all stimulus events containing the color red, irrespective of shape, size, or texture, would be classified as *positive instances* of that concept. Thus a positive instance of a concept is any stimulus event that exemplifies the concept. All other stimulus events are called *negative instances,* since they fail to exemplify the concept in one way or another.

Concepts of greater complexity can also be illustrated with the set of stimulus attributes described above. These more complex concepts are often referred to in terms of the rules, or connections between the attributes, that define the concepts. For example, consider an attribute identification problem involving *conjunction* in which the correct attributes are red and square. Positive instances would include all stimulus events containing a red square, irrespective of size or texture. All other stimulus events would be negative instances of the concept even though some would include the color red (i.e., red circle) and others would include the property of square-ness (i.e., blue square). Since the stimulus dimensions of size and texture play no role in the definition of this concept, it has been traditional to refer to them as *irrelevant dimensions* and their attribute values (large, small, rough, smooth) as *irrelevant attributes.* Therefore the *relevant dimensions* in this illustration are color and shape, and the *relevant attributes* are red-ness and squareness.

Another type of rule commonly used in the study of conceptual be-havior involves *disjunction.* Again, let us suppose that the correct attributes are red and square. In the case of conjunction, where the logical operator is *and,* the clear implication is that both relevant attributes must be present. In disjunction, however, the logical operator is *or,* and this implies that the presence of either relevant attribute is sufficient. Thus the stimulus events that are positive instances of this disjunctive concept consist of those containing a red square (positive instances of the conjunctive con-cept) as well as those containing red, irrespective of shape, size, or texture, and those containing a square, irrespective of color, size, or texture. The negative instances of this disjunctive concept include only those stimulus events that do not include either redness or squareness. The set of negative instances for a disjunctive concept constitutes the set of positive instances for another conceptual rule called *joint denial.* In joint denial the positive instances consist only of those stimulus events that are not red *and* not square.

The preceding discussion shows that many other and much more complex procedures for defining concepts can be considered. For example, conjunctive and disjunctive rules can be combined in various ways. A *conditional* concept can be introduced such that what counts as a relevant attribute on one dimension depends on the presence of another attribute on another dimension. If the stimulus event contains the color red, a positive instance is only realized if the shape is square, but for the color blue any shape is a positive instance. This example of a conditional concept as well as examples of the concepts discussed previously is given in Figure 12.1. Notice that the "plus" symbol in the figure indicates positive instances.

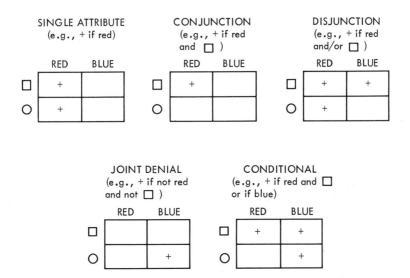

Figure 12.1 Illustrations of five conceptual rules for a two-dimension, two-attribute problem.

Types of Conceptual Behavior

In the preceding discussion we classified the conceptual problems involved as problems of *attribute identification.* In terms of typical experimental procedure this would mean that the subject not only knows the stimulus dimensions and their attribute values but also knows whether the concept is based on a single attribute, a conjunction of attributes, or a disjunction of attributes. In other words, the subject is told the nature of the conceptual rule used to define the concept, and his task is one of determining the relevant attributes. Of course, not all investigations of conceptual behavior are of this type. In many experiments the task is one of *rule identification.* Here the subject typically knows the stimulus dimensions, the attribute values, and even the relevant attributes. The task is one of determining which rule describes the concept.

Attribute identification and rule identification are the most common types of investigation of conceptual behavior in the adult subject. Of course, it is possible to talk about other kinds of conceptual activity. For example, *attribute learning* generally involves a situation that requires the subject to acquire new information about the set of stimulus events and their properties. This would include paying attention to a new dimension or attribute never previously noted or discriminated. *Rule learning,* on the other hand, requires the discovery of a new relationship among known stimulus events.

Although both attribute learning and rule learning may be important during development, it is obvious that most adults have extensive experience with both the attributes and the rules involved in these experiments.

For this reason many investigators prefer the concepts of *attribute identification* and *rule identification* in contrast to terms that emphasize learning. These labels seem particularly appropriate in the experimental situations most frequently used to investigate conceptual behavior, since both the attribute dimensions and the types of conceptual rules are explicitly made available to the subject.

One other type of conceptual behavior should be mentioned. In addition to the learning or identification of concepts, the utilization of concepts that have been acquired previously is also important. No doubt much of our everyday behavior requires the utilization of previously learned concepts. We are constantly using known attributes and rules to determine such things as the time required to travel given distances and other aspects of our daily routine. Thus, concept *utilization* is also an important aspect of our conceptual behavior.

Types of Task

In any investigation of conceptual behavior, the type of task presented to the subject and what the subject is told about the task are of considerable importance. For example, in attribute identification it is important to make sure that the task is clearly one in which only the attributes and not the rule or principle relating the attributes must be identified. Obviously, the instructions given to the subject can go a long way toward ensuring that his attention is directed toward the critical aspects of the problem.

In their discussion of conceptual behavior Bourne, Ekstrand, and Dominowski (1971) outline the main topics covered in instructions given to the subjects. Typically the instructions provide a general definition of concepts and a description of the entire population of stimulus events, including the stimulus dimensions and the attribute values to be employed. Also included is a description of how the stimulus events will be presented, how responses are to be made, and what feedback will be given following a response. Further instructions appropriate for the particular purpose of the investigation would also be given. For example, if the experiment involved rule identification or rule learning, the subject might be given the names of the relevant attributes.

According to Bourne et al. (1971), the most commonly used procedure in conceptual behavior studies involves the subject's making a response to a single stimulus selected by the experimenter on each trial. The subject's task is to label each stimulus event as either a positive or a negative instance of the concept, and the experimenter then indicates whether the response was correct. This is called the *reception paradigm*. One variation on this procedure involves presentation of two or more stimulus events on each trial with the requirement that the subject point out all of the positive instances. Another variation involves presenting all stimulus events simultaneously. In this case the subject may be asked to respond to each event in a specific order, but he always has the entire set of stimulus events available.

A somewhat different procedure, in which the subject chooses the stimulus he will respond to on each trial, is called the *selection paradigm*. On each trial the subject selects one stimulus from the known population of events which the experimenter then designates as a positive or a negative instance. This procedure continues across trials until the subject can state the general solution. Numerous variations on this procedure are also possible, depending on the objectives of the particular experiment. As with the reception paradigm, the subject deals with only one stimulus at a time, although he still determines which stimulus is presented on each trial.

An Illustrative Example

A series of experiments reported by Haygood and Bourne (1965) illustrate many of the procedures involved in studies of conceptual behavior. We shall describe their first experiment in some detail. In this experiment the subjects were presented with five problems in succession. The solution to all problems involved two relevant attributes selected from four stimulus dimensions. Each stimulus dimension was represented by three attribute values. The dimensions and their values were number of figures (one, two, and three), size (large, medium, and small), shape (square, triangle, and hexagon), and color (red, yellow, and blue). The experiment consisted of twelve conditions, each of which involved a particular set of instructions and a particular rule.

Three instructional conditions were employed: attribute identification, rule learning, and complete learning. In attribute identification the rule and all stimulus dimensions were described and illustrated, but the subject had to discover the two relevant attributes. In rule learning the stimulus dimensions and the two relevant attributes were explained, but the subject had to discover the rule. In complete learning the stimulus dimensions were described, but the subject had to discover both the relevant attributes and the correct rule.

Haygood and Bourne (1965) employed four different rules. The five successive problems presented to any given subject, however, always involved the same rule and the same set of instructions. Let us represent one of the relevant attributes as R (e.g., red) and the other as S (e.g., square). Now we can define the four rules employed as follows:

> Rule 1: Conjunction—all stimulus events that are both R and S (e.g., red and square).
>
> Rule 2: Disjunction—all stimulus events that are either R or S (e.g., red or square or both).

Rule 3: Joint Denial—all stimulus events that are neither *R* nor *S* (e.g., not red and not square).

Rule 4: Conditional—if a stimulus event is *R* then it must also be *S,* but if it is not *R* it is also a positive instance (e.g., a red square or any stimulus that is not red).

The problems were presented to the subjects using the reception paradigm with one stimulus event presented on each trial. The subject was required to say yes or no to indicate whether the stimulus was a positive instance or not. The experimenter then told him whether he was correct or incorrect. The subjects worked on each problem until they reached a criterion of sixteen successive correct responses. As the subject solved each problem he was given a new one until all five problems were completed. All problems were self-paced, and the instructions stressed acccuracy rather than speed.

The major results of this experiment are shown in Figure 12.2. Apparently both rule learning and attribute identification problems are solved faster than complete learning problems. Thus the partial information given

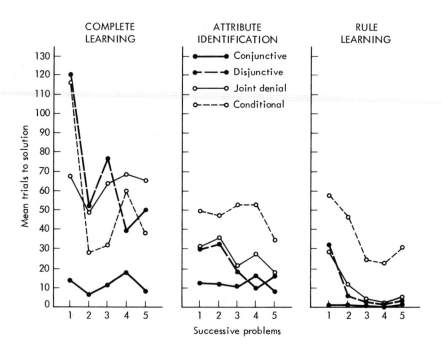

Figure 12.2   Mean trials to solution of problems based upon four different rules.
(After Bourne, 1967.)

to subjects in these conditions does lead to improved performance. In general, there is also an improvement in performance across successive problems. This is most clearly seen in rule learning. Improvement occurs with all rules except the conjunctive rule, which is very easy from the beginning. In all instructional conditions, particularly on the initial problems, the rules differ in difficulty. The conjunctive rule is the easiest, with the disjunctive and joint denial rules being more difficult at first but showing considerable improvement over problems. In the rule-learning conditions these three rules are essentially equal in difficulty by the time of the fourth problem, and only the conditional rule remains more difficult. In subsequent work Bourne (1967) has shown that even the conditional can be reduced to a lower level of difficulty with more practice problems. Initial differences in rule difficulty can therefore be overcome with more practice in rule utilization.

Attribute identification takes longer than rule learning even after practice on several problems. This is to be expected, of course, since subjects in the rule-learning conditions are given the relevant attributes and do not require several trials to discover them. That is, many different attribute combinations are possible, but only a small number of rules. Other research has shown that the effect of irrelevant dimensions is to increase the difficulty of attribute identification, but rule learning is virtually unaffected (Haygood and Stevenson, 1967).

THEORIES OF CONCEPTUAL BEHAVIOR

Now that we have described the basic procedures employed, let us consider theoretical approaches to the analysis of conceptual behavior. Clearly the oldest and most traditional approach is *associationism,* although there are several contemporary variations in that approach. A somewhat more recent but equally popular account is provided in the several versions of *hypothesis-testing* theory. In general, these theories hold that the behavior of subjects is always guided by some hypothesis. In contrast to the association approach, hypothesis-testing theories generally hold to an all-or-none view of learning rather than an incremental view.

A still more recent position is taken by advocates of *information-processing* theories. These theories were originally conceived on the basis of an analogy between man and high-speed computers. The basic idea is that both operate as a system consisting of an input source, a variety of internal procedures for processing the information contained in the inputs, and an output mechanism. Theories in this class place much greater emphasis on rule learning than on attribute identification.

In the following sections we shall describe several versions of each theoretical approach and examine some of the evidence most relevant to each. Many of the theories to be considered, however, were developed within the context of a particular type of conceptual problem such as attribute identification, and they may not provide an adequate account of findings obtained in other conceptual problem situations. It should also be noted that most of the theories discussed here were developed to account for the learning of readily specifiable concepts, and they may not provide a satisfactory explanation of learning for more abstract concepts.

Association Theories

All associative explanations of conceptual behavior have developed rather directly from the classical generalization-discrimination model we considered in Chapter 2. These theories emphasize the development of associations between positive and negative instances of a concept and the responses required of the subject. These associations are said to develop as a result of contiguity between stimulus and response events and through reinforcement of correct responses. Association theories attribute little to the organism other than memory for prior experiences. The organism is more or less viewed as a passive recipient of information, with little or no internal machinery for selecting and organizing information. Although associative accounts of concept-learning experiments can be traced as far back as Hull (1920), we shall restrict our discussion to more contemporary approaches.

Direct S-R Theory.   One approach to concept learning derives quite directly from Restle's (1955) theory of discrimination learning. Bourne and Restle (1959) extended this theory to provide a mathematical account of concept identification. The theory assumes that each stimulus attribute gives rise to numerous abstract stimulus elements. These abstract elements are only hypothetical, and they are not identified directly with observable events. On any given trial the subject somehow samples from the stimulus elements available, and these sampled elements become associated with the correct response at the time of reinforcement.

The stimulus elements that are sampled and conditioned on each trial come from both the relevant and irrelevant attributes. Over several learning trials, however, it is assumed that more elements from the relevant attributes are sampled and become associated with the correct response. Since elements from the irrelevant attributes appear in both positive and negative instances, their influence is presumably adapted out over trials, through the process of extinction. Learning is said to be complete when all relevant stimulus elements have become associated with the appropriate response and all irrelevant stimulus elements are ineffective.

The main objective of the Bourne and Restle theory is to describe the course of attribute identification, and the basic parameter of the theory is the rate at which associations are formed and adapted out. Without going into the mathematics involved, it is sufficient to note that this rate is taken to be a function of the proportion of relevant stimulus elements in the entire population of elements (i.e., both relevant and irrelevant). On any given trial the probability of a correct response is determined by the proportion of unadapted stimulus elements that up to that point have been conditioned to the correct response.

Within a fairly limited range of experiments, this theory performs quite acceptably. It does lead to equations that describe the learning curves obtained in many attribute identification experiments, and it accounts reasonably well for the detrimental effects of increasing the number of irrelevant dimensions. The theory does not apply in a wide variety of situations because it simply does not deal with certain factors, such as the importance or salience of stimulus events. In addition, like most other associative or hypothesis-testing accounts, this theory makes no provision for distinguishing between attributes and rules. The theory simply does not deal with rule learning or rule identification. This omission severely limits the number of situations to which the theory applies.

S-R Mediational Theory.   Theories of associative mediation have played a prominent role in the history of psychology. Most such theories have developed from the work of Clark Hull in the 1930s (Hull, 1930, 1939), although the most explicit statement of this type of theory can be found in Osgood (1953). The defining characteristic of mediation theory derives from the Hullian concept of a "pure stimulus act." Such acts are viewed as internal responses whose sole function is to produce internal stimulation, which then serves as a cue for further overt behavior. Pure stimulus acts are thought of as reduced, internal fragments of previously acquired overt behavior. The overt behavior itself is acquired in the same way as any response is acquired in associative theory. But once the overt behavior is acquired, the detachable fragments referred to as pure stimulus acts can occur independently of the presence of the original stimulus conditions and, therefore, can serve to *mediate* new behavior.

According to associative mediation theory, conceptual behavior can be described in terms of acquiring an equivalence for a set of perceptibly different stimulus events. For example, according to this view, lettuce, watermelon, and spaghetti are all instances of the concept *food,* not because they share physical stimulus attributes but because they elicit common mediational responses such as anticipatory salivation or chewing. Following is a simple diagram in which the mediating process is identified as consisting of these reduced, internal responses (r_c) and their stimulus consequences (s_c).

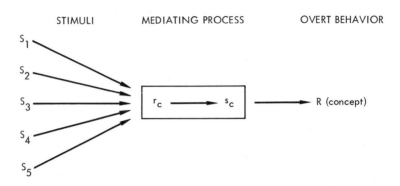

Associative mediation theories are rather direct extensions of non-mediated S-R theory. They see the subject's behavior as being determined by the frequency of previous behavior and by principles such as primary stimulus generalization. Even the addition of internal mediating processes does little to change the view of the organism as a passive recipient of information. Thus the predictions deriving from these two versions of association theory have much in common. The behavior accounted for by mediation theories, however, is more complicated, and in at least one significant area of research the two types of theories make different predictions. This is in the area of "solution shift," which is one form of concept utilization. Because concept utilization has been dealt with explicitly only within the framework of associative models, we shall consider solution shifts at this point and then continue with a discussion of hypothesis-testing models.

Solution Shifts.   The solution shift problems are basically of two types. In one, called *reversal shift,* or *intradimensional shift,* the subject first learns a particular solution for a conceptual problem and must then learn exactly the opposite solution for the same stimulus events. This is illustrated below for two dimensional stimuli where shape is represented as circle or square and color is represented as blue (B) or green (G). In the training problem all blue events are called R_1 and all green events are called R_2. But in the test problem the responses are reversed. Notice that shape is an irrelevant dimension in both problems, so that color remains the relevant dimension and it is only the response categories within the relevant dimension that are reversed.

The other solution shift problem is called *nonreversal shift,* or *extradimensional shift.* This is also illustrated using the same stimulus events. The training problem remains the same with all blue stimulus events called R_1 and all green stimulus events called R_2. The shift involved in the test problem, however, is a shift in relevant dimensions from color to shape. The result is that only half of the response category assignments are changed.

INTRADIMENSIONAL SHIFT

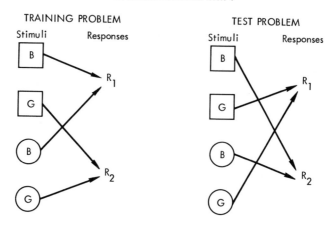

EXTRADIMENSIONAL SHIFT

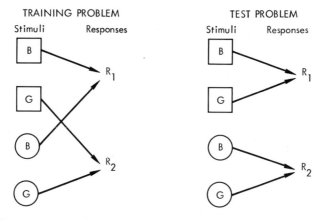

A direct association theory that views conceptual behavior as an automatic consequence of associating physical stimulus attributes to response categories would predict that the intradimensional shift is more difficult than the extradimensional shift. This prediction follows directly from the fact that only half of the stimulus events are assigned to a new response category in the extradimensional problem. On the other hand, the intradimensional problem requires that all associations established during training must be extinguished and new associations must be formed. Thus, on the basis of the differing numbers of new associations that must be formed, the extradimensional shift problem should take fewer trials to learn.

A mediational theory such as that of Kendler and Kendler (1962) makes just the opposite prediction. The situation depicted by this theory is shown in the following diagram. The idea is that during training the subject establishes mediators for the relevant color attributes. When the test problem in the case of intradimensional shift is presented, only the associations between the internal stimuli and the response categories must be changed. But when the test problem involves an extradimensional shift, and the relevant dimension is shape, the initial mediational process must be extinguished and replaced by a new one. According to mediational theory, this should make the extradimensional problem more difficult to solve.

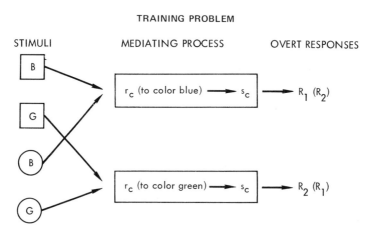

TRAINING PROBLEM

STIMULI   MEDIATING PROCESS   OVERT RESPONSES

B

r_c (to color blue) $\longrightarrow$ s_c $\longrightarrow$ R_1 (R_2)

G

B

r_c (to color green) $\longrightarrow$ s_c $\longrightarrow$ R_2 (R_1)

G

The results of experiments comparing performance on intradimensional and extradimensional shift problems are somewhat complicated. On the basis of several earlier experiments Kendler and Kendler (1962) concluded that extradimensional shifts are easier for young, verbally unskilled children, whereas intradimensional shifts are easier for older children and adults. This would imply that a direct S-R account is better for young children but a mediational account is more appropriate once verbal skills become well developed.

In attempting to explain these results, the Kendlers point out that the performance of young children is comparable with the performance of lower animals because young children and lower animals only gradually acquire an ability to respond to internal, response-produced cues. On the other hand, older children and adults automatically generate a mediating response that provides the basis for rapid reversal on intradimensional problems. The Kendlers conclude that the internal cues involve language and that the mediator is probably verbal.

Although the Kendlers' analysis seemed plausible, initially, subsequent research has challenged their conclusions. For example, children with normal hearing perform no better than deaf children on either type of problem (Youniss, 1964), and in certain situations younger subjects do not find extradimensional problems any easier than intradimensional problems (Cobb, 1965). Evidence also indicates that the relative ease of intradimensional problems for older subjects disappears when the irrelevant dimensions on the test problem in intradimensional shift are different from the irrelevant dimensions during training (Jeffrey, 1965).

In an extensive review of the literature, Wolff (1967) concluded that there was no compelling evidence to support the Kendlers' view that children are increasingly likely to mediate verbally as they grow older. Although verbal mechanisms are undoubtedly important in some reversal behavior, attentional and perceptual processes are also implicated. An experiment that suggests this and also provides the basis for a somewhat less complex account of solution shifts was reported by Johnson and White (1967).

These investigators tested six- and seven-year-old children to determine their knowledge of such simple stimulus dimensions as size and brightness. The tests required subjects to order objects properly along a particular dimension. The subjects were then given solution shift problems, with the relevant dimensions being those on which the subjects had been examined previously. The results indicated that the children who performed better on the dimensions test also found intradimensional problems easier than extradimensional problems. In contrast, the children who performed less well on the dimensions test did better on extradimensional than on intradimensional problems. Johnson and White took these results to mean that an intradimensional shift is only a reversal for subjects who "understand" the dimension in question. Those subjects who do not understand the dimension appear to learn mainly by assignment of independent stimulus events to response categories.

Hypothesis-Testing Theories

In contrast to associative mediation theories of conceptual activity, hypothesis-testing theories assume an "active" internal process on the part of the learner. In general, such theories assume that the subject's behavior is always guided by some hypothesis and that the learning process is characterized by the selection and testing of alternative hypotheses. One of the most influential treatments of conceptual behavior in terms of hypothesis-testing comes from the work of Bruner, Goodnow, and Austin (1956).

The approach suggested by these investigators is descriptive and analytic, although no precise theory of conceptual behavior is advanced. They suggest that the subject begins by selecting a hypothesis that is consistent with the stimulus input. For the most part Bruner et al. studied attribute identification so that the hypothesis could be stated as some combination of attributes. If the initial hypothesis was wrong, the subject had to decide how to change it. In their view, conceptual behavior is seen as a sequential decision-making process in which each decision is contingent upon all earlier decisions.

A second aspect of the Bruner et al. characterization of conceptual activity is the emphasis upon *strategies* that subjects use. One of the strategies outlined by Bruner et al. is called *conservative focusing*. This strategy is most useful with the selection paradigm, since it is assumed that the subject initially considers all hypotheses simultaneously and on each trial requests a stimulus event that differs from the last event in exactly one attribute. The name of this strategy derives from the fact that it guarantees some information on every trial.

Consider a situation in which the first stimulus event is a large blue square and the subject is told that it is a positive instance. The focusing strategy requires that the subject's initial hypothesis include all three of these attributes. Then he might select a small blue square as the next stimulus event. If this too is a positive instance, he knows that size is an irrelevant dimension. Next, he might select a large green square, since his current hypothesis is that blue square is the concept. If this is called a negative instance the next event selected would be a large blue circle, since he knows that color is a relevant dimension and size is not. If this event is a positive instance, he knows the concept is blue. The use of just such a strategy is revealed by the subject's selection of stimulus events and stated hypotheses.

A more reckless strategy which involves both greater risks and greater payoffs is called *focus gambling*. In our previous example the subject was first given a large blue square. If this subject had followed the strategy of focus gambling, he might have changed two attributes instead of only a single attribute. If the dimensions selected for change were size and shape, he would have asked for a small blue circle. Since this is a positive instance of the concept blue, he would have learned in one selection of a stimulus event what required three event selections according to the conservative focusing strategy. Of course other choices of dimensions to change would have led to much longer solution times. Consider how little information is provided by discovering that a small green square is a negative instance.

A third general strategy observed by Bruner et al. is called *scanning*. When using this strategy, subjects appear to adopt hypotheses about the solution that are consistent with but do not necessarily include all attributes present in the first or focal stimulus event. For example, in the previous case where a large blue square was the first event, one such hypothesis might be "all squares." The subject then proceeds to classify all subsequent events according to this hypothesis until proved wrong. Then he selects another hypothesis and proceeds accordingly. Scanning requires the subject to keep track of several stimulus events and various alternative hypotheses at the same time, and it is precisely because he does not do this effectively that this strategy is less efficient than focusing (Laughlin and Jordan, 1967).

Despite the richness of the Bruner et al. report, there still remain a number of problems in need of clarification. In the first place, subjects often do not report that they formulate and test hypotheses in the manner implied above. Frequently regularities can be detected in the subject's performance, although he may not be able to verbalize them. In addition, some subjects do not follow any strategy very closely and other subjects change strategies during the course of problem solution. Thus, many questions remain concerning the learning and utilization of strategies.

The Restle Model.   The earliest relatively precise formulation of hypothesis-testing models is due to the work of Restle (1962). In a manner somewhat reminiscent of Bruner's strategies, Restle considers alternative ways of testing hypotheses which range from testing one hypothesis at a time, to testing some subset of hypotheses, to simultaneous testing of all possible hypotheses defined by the task.

The theory assumes that the subject retains any hypothesis that is consistent with information provided on any given trial. In the one-hypothesis case this means that a subject stays with any hypothesis that leads to a correct response. Only on error trials does he elect another hypothesis. This assumption implies that an error trial always precedes selection of the correct hypothesis, and since the correct hypothesis always leads to correct responses, learning is seen as an all-or-none affair.

Another interesting feature of Restle's theory is that hypothesis sampling is done with replacement. That is, when an error leads the subject to discard a hypothesis, he selects another hypothesis but does not remember which one was discarded. Thus the theory contains the counterintuitive, and almost certainly incorrect, assumption that the subject has no memory of his previous experiences. Where more than one hypothesis is sampled on each trial, changes are expected to occur on both correct and error trials. Every trial leads the subject to retain those hypotheses consistent with the information presented on that trial and to reject all other hypotheses. Again, once a hypothesis has been discarded, there is no memory for that hypothesis or for the events that led to its being discarded.

Restle's various sampling procedures, ranging from considering one hypothesis at a time to considering all hypotheses at once, imply rather different psychological processes. The mathematical formulation of these models, however, reveals that they are mathematically equivalent. This implies that the performance of the subject is not influenced by the number of possible hypotheses being considered on any given trial. A note of caution should be introduced at this point. Since there is no necessary connection between the terms of the theory and events in the real world, the mathematical equivalence of these models does not necessarily mean that the implied psychological processes are identical.

The Bower-Trabasso Model. A model similar to Restle's in many ways has been proposed by Bower and Trabasso (1964). This model, which has gone through several revisions (Trabasso and Bower, 1964, 1966, 1968), is based on dimension sampling rather than on hypothesis sampling. That is, the subject is said to attend to one stimulus dimension at a time, and on each error trial another dimension is sampled at random. These assumptions are very similar to those found in Restle's "one hypothesis at a time" model. Bower and Trabasso differ from Restle in that they assume a limited memory on the part of the subjects. This memory is limited to the preceding trial, but it does mean that subjects can evaluate a sampled dimension with respect to information obtained both on the current trial and on the immediately preceding trial.

The Bower-Trabasso model is explicitly described as a theory of attribute identification. It is therefore designed for situations in which the stimulus dimensions are well known to the subjects and the attributes within dimensions are readily discriminable. As a result the main emphasis in the model is on dimension sampling. Since the relevant attributes are highly discriminable, once the relevant dimension is sampled, the conditioning of attributes to response categories is said to occur in a single trial. Like the Restle theory, this theory predicts an all-or-none learning process.

The Levine Model. A hypothesis-testing theory that differs from the preceding theories in several important ways has been proposed by Levine (1966, 1970). The main differences are that Levine proposes a subset sampling procedure, a substantial memory component, and assumes that learning takes place both on correct and on error trials. The picture of conceptual activity that emerges from his theory is as follows.

After the initial stimulus event has been classified as a positive or negative instance, the subject samples a subset of the possible hypotheses. One of these is designated as the *working hypothesis,* and only that hypothesis is used to classify the next stimulus event as a positive or negative instance. If the response on the next trial is correct, the working hypothesis is retained but other hypotheses in the subset are rejected. That is, even though the working hypothesis leads to a correct response, other hypotheses in the previously sampled subset may be inconsistent with the information provided on that trial. These hypotheses would then be discarded. But if feedback indicates that an incorrect response has been made, the working hypothesis is one of those discarded and a new working hypothesis is selected from those remaining in the subset. If all hypotheses in the subset have been discarded, then a new subset must be sampled and a new working hypothesis is chosen from this subset.

Levine's theory is similar in many respects to Restle's alternative of sampling several hypotheses at the same time. In both of these theories learning can be viewed as an incremental process, even though particular hypotheses are discarded on an all-or-none basis. That is, to the extent that hypotheses are gradually discarded over trials, there is a reduction in the number of hypotheses to be considered and this reduction can be viewed as a form of incremental learning.

Comparisons Among Association and Hypothesis-Testing Theories

The various association and hypothesis-testing theories outlined in the preceding sections all provide satisfactory accounts of at least some aspects of performance in concept-learning situations. In other situations, however, these theories all prove to be unsatisfactory. For example, neither direct S-R theories nor mediational theories deal with the distinction between attributes and rules, and this omission limits the applicability of such theories. But the same objection applies equally well to hypothesis-testing theories that fail to deal with rule learning or rule identification.

In our discussion of solution shifts it was noted that the empirical evidence failed to provide unequivocal support for either direct S-R or verbal mediation theories at any age level. Although this evidence somewhat weakens the case for both of these theoretical positions, hypothesis-testing theories do not address themselves to this problem at all. For the most part, hypothesis-testing theories simply fail to make any clear conceptual distinction between the learning of concepts and the utilization of concepts. These theories have little to say about performance in either reversal or nonreversal shift problems. We shall now consider other experimental evidence for which various theories offer contrasting predictions.

All-or-None Learning. Association theories generally assume that learning is a gradual process in which increments of associative strength are accumulated over trials. The same predictions apply to concept learning that apply to other types of learning. In contrast, most hypothesis-testing theories assume a discrete, all-or-none learning process in which the subject's performance is expected to shift from essentially a chance level to perfect performance on a single trial.

Bower and Trabasso (1964) reported an experiment that provides support for the all-or-none position. The stimulus event on each trial consisted of a series of five letters. In each of the five serial positions, one of two letters could appear. The critical position was the fourth. If one letter appeared in that position, response category 1 was reinforced; but if the other letter appeared, response category 2 was reinforced. Figure 12.3 shows the percentage of correct responses on each trial prior to the last error. As the model predicts, performance is essentially at a chance level

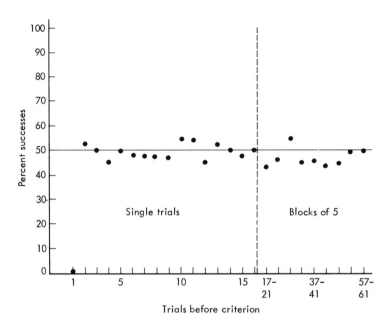

Figure 12.3   Backward learning curve: percentage of successes plotted over trials from last error.
Adapted from G. H. Bower and T. Trabasso, "Concept Identi-fication," Figure 2, p. 36 (data from Trabasso, 1961). In Studies in Mathematical Psychology, *ed. R. C. Atkinson (Stanford: Stanford University Press, 1964).*

across these trials. The Bower-Trabasso model also predicts that a correct response on any trial prior to the last error is no more likely to follow a correct response than an incorrect response. Their data also confirmed this prediction.

In a series of experiments Bower and Trabasso (1963, 1964; Trabasso and Bower, 1964, 1966) investigated the effects of changing correct response categories prior to solution. The rationale for these experiments was that according to their all-or-none model, presolution shifts should have no influence on trials taken to solution. They investigated the effect of changing solutions one or more times following error trials prior to the last error, and, in general, their results supported the all-or-none position. Levine (1962), however, has shown that randomly reinforcing both correct and incorrect responses in the early trials of a concept-learning task, which is similar to the procedure of changing the correct solution, significantly delays solution. These findings are difficult to reconcile with those of Bower and Trabasso or with the all-or-none assumption.

There is no clear resolution of the incremental versus the all-or-none issue, and a number of theoretical assumptions further complicate this question. One of these is the memory–no memory distinction. Findings such as those reported by Levine (1962) are at odds with hypothesis-testing theories that assume no memory for prior events. But Trabasso and Bower (1966) have shown that by allowing subjects to remember events on the last trial, as well as on the current trial, their model can account for both Levine's (1962) random reinforcement effect and their own findings concerning presolution shifts.

Another complication concerning the all-or-none issue is provided by subset sampling theories such as those of Restle (1962) and Levine (1966, 1970). In contrast to serial-processing accounts in which one hypothesis is considered at a time, these theories assume parallel processing. According to these parallel-processing accounts, incorrect hypotheses are gradually eliminated, although response probabilities may change in relatively discrete steps. Such theories hold that random reinforcement of both correct and incorrect responses during early trials would lower the rate at which incorrect hypotheses are eliminated and would delay problem solution even though specific hypotheses may be eliminated on an all-or-none basis. Thus there is no straightforward way to answer the question of whether or not learning takes place in an all-or-none fashion.

Learning on Error Trials. Several hypothesis-testing theories assume that subjects learn only on error trials. The behavior of the subject is assumed to be guided by some hypothesis, according to these theories, and only following error trials does the subject change his hypothesis. As we saw in Levine's (1966) model, however, not all hypothesis-testing theories make this assumption.

Levine (1966) reported a single-attribute identification experiment which has implications for several aspects of hypothesis-testing theories including the assumption that learning occurs only on error trials. His experimental task required subjects to choose one of two letters on each stimulus card. The letters differed in either of two ways on each of four stimulus dimensions. The dimensions and their attributes were color (black or white), form (X or T), position (left or right), and size (large or small). On the first trial of the experiment, a stimulus event was presented and the subject was told which of the two letters on the card was correct. This was followed by four more trials where the subject made a choice but where no feedback was given. The next trial was a feedback trial on which the subject was told whether he was correct or incorrect, and this trial was similarly followed by four trials without feedback. A third series involving one feedback trial followed by four trials without feedback concluded the experiment.

The purpose of the "no-feedback" trials was to reveal the working hypothesis being considered by the subject. Since no feedback occurred on these trials, it was assumed that the subject would respond according to the same working hypothesis on all four trials. Eight different hypotheses corresponding to the eight stimulus attributes were considered admissible. More complex hypotheses were ruled out in the instructions to the subjects.

The stimulus events presented in this study were designed in such a way that the experimenter could determine which hypothesis was being considered from the pattern of responses. The relation of each hypothesis to each response pattern is illustrated in Figure 12.4. For example, if a

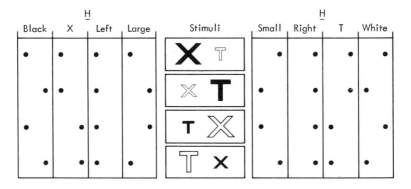

Figure 12.4   Eight patterns of choices corresponding to each of the eight hypotheses (H) when the four stimulus pairs are presented consecutively without outcomes.
(After Levine, 1966.)

subject held the hypothesis that "black" was correct, he would choose X on the first no-feedback trial followed by T on the second and third trials and X again on the fourth trial. Of course the subject could respond in a way that did not correspond to any hypothesis, such as choosing the left-hand stimulus on the first three trials and the right-hand stimulus on the fourth trial. Such a pattern might occur if the subject was not using any hypothesis or if the subject changed hypotheses during the no-feedback trials.

The data obtained in Levine's (1966) experiment clearly indicated that subjects do use hypotheses. One of the eight admissible hypotheses could be inferred from 92.4 percent of the response patterns obtained on the no-feedback trials. In those cases in which a hypothesis was inferred, the hypothesis correctly predicted the response following the four no-feedback trials (i.e., the next feedback trial) in 97.5 percent of the cases. The data also indicated that the subjects retained their hypothesis 95 percent of the time following a response that the experimenter called correct. After an incorrect response, however, the hypothesis was retained only 2 percent of the time. Of course this latter finding is equally consistent with Levine's views or the assumption that learning takes place only on error trials.

Let us consider Levine's (1970) interpretation in more detail. Levine assumes that the working hypothesis, on which the subject bases his response, is only changed on error trials. On correct trials, however, the subject should eliminate those hypotheses from the sampled subset that are inconsistent with the information provided on that trial. For example, suppose a stimulus event is presented which has a small black T on the left and a large white X on the right. Further suppose that the subject chooses the X and the experimenter indicates the response is correct. Now any hypothesis the subject has sampled from the subset including "small," "black," "left," or "T" should be discarded. Notice that it makes no difference whether the subject's choice was correct or incorrect. In either case the experimenter provides the same amount of information concerning incorrect hypotheses, and this information provides the basis, in this case, for discarding half of the possible hypotheses.

Levine has adopted the term *focusing* from Bruner, Goodnow, and Austin (1956) to characterize this process. A subject who focuses perfectly would sample all eight admissible hypotheses initially and would eliminate half of them on the first feedback trial. On the second feedback trial half of the remaining four hypotheses would be eliminated, and the third feedback trial would indicate which of the two remaining hypotheses was correct.

Levine (1966) was able to estimate the number of hypotheses his subjects were considering on each feedback trial. These estimates provided a comparison between the actual performance of his subjects and the expected performance of a perfect focusing subject. As the data in Figure 12.5 indicate, not all subjects are perfect focusers. These findings, however, do show that the subjects in this experiment perform more like perfect focusing subjects than like subjects who sample one hypothesis at a time and have no memory for which hypotheses have been sampled previously.

Levine's experiment supports the general class of hypothesis-testing theories in that it indicates that subjects do perform in accordance with particular hypotheses. This study, however, also supports the view that subjects learn, at least in the sense of eliminating incorrect hypotheses, both on correct and error trials. Therefore the assumption that learning occurs only on error trials is not supported. Levine's study also suggests that more than one hypothesis is considered at a time and that subjects do show evidence of memory for previous events.

Further support for the view that learning is not restricted to error trials alone comes from a study by Suppes and Schlag-Rey (1965). In this experiment each trial consisted of a stimulus event followed by a response and informative feedback as to whether the response was correct or in-

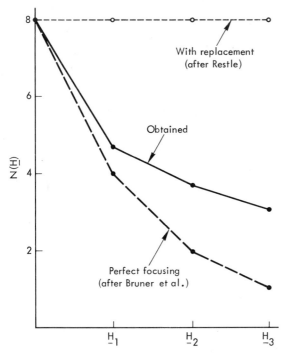

Figure 12.5 The size of the set of hypotheses, $N(H)$, from which the subject is sampling immediately following a "wrong" on trials 1, 2, and 3. (*After Levine, 1966.*)

correct. Following this sequence, the subjects were required to classify the entire stimulus population in one of two ways. These classification responses were equivalent to verbally stated hypotheses, and the purpose of the experiment was to examine changes in the classification responses on correct response and error trials. The results indicated that the proportion of changes in classification responses was nearly as high on correct response trials as it was on error trials. In addition, the proportion of changes was quite high (.65 in some cases) and the changes were not limited to particular subjects or to particular problems.

The No-Memory Assumption. As we have seen, Levine (1966) presented evidence to contradict the assumption found in some hypothesis-testing theories that subjects have no memory for prior events or for hypotheses sampled previously. This is not to say that memory for prior events is always good. For example, Trabasso and Bower (1964) presented six successive stimulus events to their subjects and classified each event as either a positive or a negative instance. The subjects then stated a general solution and attempted to recall each stimulus event and its classification. The main result was that subjects could recall only one of the six events correctly.

Erickson, Zajkowski, and Ehrmann (1966) used response latencies to study the use of memory in attribute identification. They argued that response latencies should decrease as the number of hypotheses being considered by the subject decreases. If this is the case, a theory such as Levine's (1966, 1970) would predict decreasing latencies until the solution to the problem was achieved. In contrast, a no-memory theory would predict that response latencies should be constant on trials prior to the last error and on trials after the last error. Of course, since such theories assume that problem solution occurs following the last error, the latencies before and after the last error should not be the same.

The results of the Erickson et al. study are shown in Figure 12.6. Notice that latencies following error trials are larger than those following correct response trials. This observation is consistent with either a memory

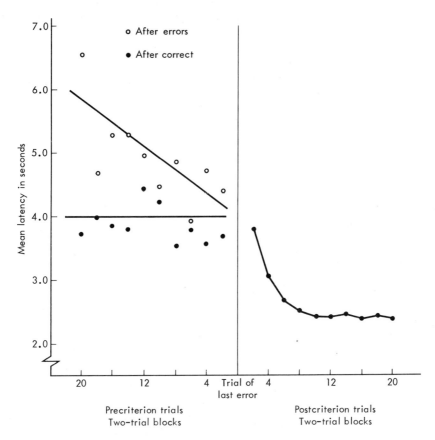

Figure 12.6 Mean latency on trials preceding the last error. The precriterion trials show latencies on trial n following errors (open circles) and following correct responses (closed circles) on trial n-1.
(After Erickson et al., 1966.)

or a no-memory assumption. A result that contradicts the no-memory assumption, however, is that latencies following error trials decrease considerably as the last error is approached. This observation suggests that hypotheses are being eliminated and that the subjects remember which hypotheses have been eliminated. Notice also that latencies continue to decrease for several trials following the last error. This could reflect increased confidence on the part of the subject, but it is also consistent with the view that other incorrect hypotheses are still being eliminated. If the latter interpretation is correct, this finding of decreased latencies following the last error supports the position that subjects learn on correct response trials as well as the view that more than one hypothesis is considered on each trial.

Levine (1969) has provided further evidence concerning latencies surrounding the last error. An additional feature of this experiment was that the subject was told to ring a bell once he knew the solution and to continue responding on subsequent trials. Levine's assumption was that latencies before and after the solution trial should yield two distinctly different functions. The basic findings are shown in Figure 12.7, and they are consistent with a memory theory that assumes that hypotheses are sampled in sets and eliminated over trials until the correct hypothesis is determined.

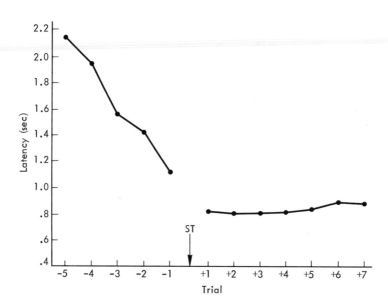

Figure 12.7 Mean latencies at successive trials before and after the solution trial (ST).
(From Levine, 1970.)

Latencies prior to solution should decrease over trials as the set of hypotheses being considered is reduced in size. Following problem solution, however, no further decrease in latency is expected. Levine has also shown that the two-part function appears irrespective of the number of trials that intervene between the trial of the last error and the solution trial. This suggests that the decrease in latency following the last error which was observed by Erickson et al. may be due to further elimination of incorrect hypotheses.

In the preceding sections we have considered several theories of concept learning of the associative and hypothesis-testing variety. Generally, these theories, and the experiments designed to test them, deal with attribute identification. None of them are concerned with rule learning or rule identification, and only the associational theories explicitly deal with the utilization of previously acquired behavior. Within these constraints both reason and evidence tend to favor the hypothesis-testing approach. There is considerable evidence that subjects do formulate and test hypotheses, and unless associative theories can be developed that deal more directly with this fact they are likely to prove unsatisfactory. Of course, hypothesis-testing theories must also deal with the problem of concept utilization.

The evidence concerning hypothesis-testing theories as a class seems to favor the subset-sampling assumption in which more than one hypothesis is considered at a time. Most hypothesis-testing theories, including that of Trabasso and Bower (1968), have adopted some version of this assumption. The evidence also appears to favor the view that learning *can* occur on both correct response and error trials. For the most part the no-memory assumption appears to be incorrect, although in situations such as that studied by Trabasso and Bower (1964), memory may be extremely limited. In fact, Erickson and Zajkowski (1967) have shown that if memory is overloaded, by requiring subjects to solve three concurrent problems, no evidence of memory is obtained. But in most of the situations considered, subjects do show at least some evidence of memory for both prior events and previously discarded hypotheses.

It was noted previously that hypothesis-testing theories make no provision for concept utilization. But they also say nothing about the initial source of hypotheses. That is, hypotheses are said to exist, but nothing is said about the way they come to exist. In the typical attribute identification experiment this omission presents no great problem, since subjects are usually told what the stimulus dimensions are as well as the particular values on these dimensions that will be employed. It is not difficult, however, to imagine a situation in which it is important to specify the principles governing hypothesis formation. Proponents of hypothesis-testing theories will no doubt have to come to grips with this issue as they extend their theories to explain a wider range of behavior phenomena.

INFORMATION-PROCESSING THEORIES

Historically speaking, the information-processing approach to concept learning has been largely based on analogies between man and computers. Both man and computers accept external inputs, operate on them in various ways, and produce some sort of response. Such theories, for the most part, are best characterized as extensions of hypothesis-testing theories in that they emphasize internal, cognitive activities. Not all the information-processing theories we shall review are closely tied to the computer analogy, but all place considerable emphasis on the selection and organization of information.

Hunt's Theory

One approach followed by some information-processing theorists is to write a computer program designed to simulate human conceptual behavior. The program, like any other theory, attempts to describe the processes by which conceptual problems are solved. The computer then solves problems of the same type as those presented to human subjects. If the computer simulation is similar to the subject's performance, there is evidence that the processes described by the program bear some relation to those employed by the subject. One must be cautious, however, in ascribing too great an importance to the closeness of the outcomes. A wide variety of programs or theories may account for performance equally well, and it is difficult to determine which of them best describes the underlying psychological processes. Nevertheless, the computer simulation approach has been of value in providing precise descriptions of presumed psychological processes. If a computer program is to be written employing a term like *strategy,* the investigator is forced into an explicit description of what is meant by a strategy.

As an illustration of the computer simulation approach, let us consider a program developed by Hunt (1962; see also Hunt, Marin, and Stone, 1966). This model involves a perceptual process, a process for storing stimulus attributes, and a process for constructing a decision rule. The perceptual process is the least well developed aspect of this model. The model simply assumes that the stimulus attributes are stored as they are presented and that positive and negative instances are stored separately. The critical part of the model involves construction of the decision rule. This aspect of the model employs a focusing principle not unlike that of Bruner, Goodnow, and Austin (1956). Positive and negative instances are scanned periodically to see if there are any stimulus attributes characteristic of the positive instances that are not found in the negative instances.

With the relatively simple single attribute or conjunctive problems, this procedure leads to a correct decision rule quite readily.

When more complex problems are presented, the focusing procedure become more complicated. For example, suppose the concept is based on a disjunctive rule such as *blue or circle.* Now, even after a long series of stimulus events, scanning reveals no single attribute common to only the positive or negative instances. At this point the program calls for selecting the attribute that occurs most frequently among previous positive instances and classifying subsequent stimulus events on the basis of the presence or absence of that attribute.

If the most frequent attribute among positive instances was *blue,* the class of stimulus events containing *blue* would all be positive instances and the remaining class of stimulus events would contain both positive and negative instances. Additional focusing within the latter class would eventually reveal the other attribute, *circle,* which combines with *blue* to form the disjunctive concept. A decision rule for this concept is illustrated in Figure 12.8.

Hunt's model of conceptual behavior is designed to deal with the learning or identification of either attributes or rules. Within this framework, rule learning consists of learning to ask questions in an hierarchically organized manner. Thus Figure 12.8 illustrates the organization of questions for the disjunctive decision rule. Each type of conceptual problem is defined by a particular set of ordered questions, and the difficulty of any decision rule is determined by the nature of the hierarchical organization of the questions. In general, the greater the number of questions asked, the more difficult the decision rule.

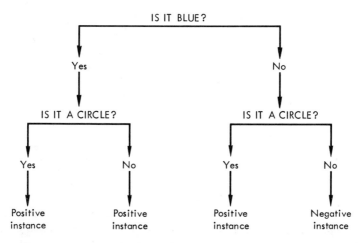

Figure 12.8   Illustration of a decision rule for the disjunctive concept *blue or circle.*

Although Hunt's model of human conceptual behavior does a fairly good job of predicting subject performance in some situations, in certain respects the model is more reminiscent of competence models such as those discussed in Chapter 10 than it is like a model of actual performance. For example, the model assumes both a perfect memory for numerous events and an error-free procedure for arriving at decision rules. Neither of these assumptions is consistent with empirical observations. The assumptions thus represent idealizations at best and cannot be viewed as descriptions of actual processes. A somewhat similar difficulty is encountered in the model's restriction to a single general strategy, focusing. As Bruner, Goodnow, and Austin (1956) have shown, there is considerable variability in the strategies that subjects employ to solve conceptual problems. It appears, then, that the use of focusing as a single general strategy also represents an idealization of sorts and not a description of all conceptual problem solvers.

Bourne's Truth-Table Approach

Bourne (1967, 1970) has developed an account of conceptual behavior based on a truth-table strategy. His view is that many aspects of conceptual problem solving can best be described by assuming that the subject has acquired an intuitive version of the logical truth table. This approach differs from the theories considered previously in at least two fundamental ways: (1) it is not a theory of conceptual behavior but rather a description of the development and use of a particular strategy; and (2) the truth-table approach is addressed exclusively to rule learning, whereas many of the theories considered previously were primarily theories of attribute identification. Thus the truth-table approach represents the description of a strategy for rule learning.

In describing the truth-table strategy, Bourne likens the presence or absence of *relevant* attributes to the truth (T) or falsity (F) of statements about the attributes. The presence of a given relevant attribute in a stimulus event is represented by the letter *T,* and the absence of that attribute is represented by the letter *F*. To illustrate the application of the truth-table strategy, let us consider a conceptual problem consisting of two relevant attributes, both of which are known to the subjects.

The set of stimulus events presented to the subjects can be classified in terms of whether they contain both relevant attributes (TT), one relevant attribute but not the other (TF or FT), or neither of the relevant attributes (FF). Once the subjects have learned which of these four patterns are associated with positive and negative instances, it is a relatively simple matter to determine the correct rule. For example, if the correct rule is conjunction, a positive instance occurs only when both relevant attributes are present (TT). For disjunction, however, a positive instance is realized if either (TF or FT) or both (TT) of the relevant attributes are present. Each of the rules commonly used in two-attribute problems is uniquely associated with the four patterns indicating presence or absence of the relevant attributes.

Bourne (1970) reports a study dealing with rule learning of these two-attribute problems. The subjects were required to solve a series of nine problems following the reception paradigm. For any given subject the rule remained constant for all nine problems, although different subjects used each of four different rules. Three of these rules—the conjunctive rule, the disjunctive rule, and the conditional rule—were described at the beginning of this chapter. The fourth rule is called the *biconditional rule*. For example, if the relevant attributes are *blue* and *circle*, positive instances under the biconditional rule are those that are both *blue and circle* as well as those that are *not blue and not circle*.

This experiment comprised four stimulus dimensions, and each dimension was represented by three attributes. The subjects were told what the two relevant attributes were on each of the nine problems. The first problem for any subject involved rule learning, and the remaining problems involved rule utilization. Table 12.1 gives the relationship between

Table 12.1 Relationship between truth-table values and each of four rules.

Truth-table values	Conjunctive rule	Disjunctive rule	Conditional rule	Biconditional rule
TT	+	+	+	+
TF	−	+	−	−
FT	−	+	+	−
FF	−	−	+	+

Note: + = positive instance, − = negative instance.
(ADAPTED FROM BOURNE, 1970.)

the truth-table values and each of the four rules. Notice that the location of positive instances in the truth-table is different for each rule.

The subject's task on each problem was to find the relationship between relevant attributes that would lead to errorless assignment of stimulus events as positive and negative instances. According to a simple S-R association account, the four rules should be of equal difficulty because subjects need to associate the appropriate response (positive or negative instance) to all possible stimulus events for each rule. The results of this experiment, given in Figure 12.9, indicate that substantial differences exist in the initial difficulty of the various rules, contrary to S-R predictions.

The results of this experiment also indicate that after a few problems, all subjects are using all rules with equal efficiency. Notice that beginning

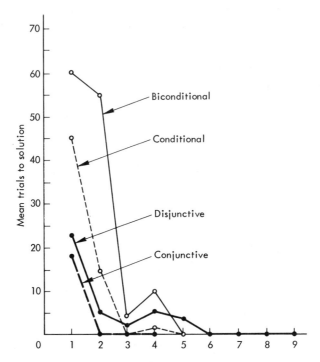

Figure 12.9 Mean trials to solution of nine successive rule-learning problems based on the four primary bidimensional rules—Experiment I.
(From Bourne, 1970.)

with the sixth problem only a single trial is required for solution. Bourne suggests that the ability of subjects to solve a particular problem following a single stimulus event is strong evidence for the truth-table solution. Remember that the same rule is correct for all problems presented to a given subject. Only the relevant attributes change from problem to problem. Assuming that each subject has learned the truth-table values for a given rule (see Table 12.1) by the sixth problem, it is not difficult to see why the remaining problems are solved so rapidly. Without such knowledge, however, rapid solutions would be difficult, if not impossible.

A second experiment reported by Bourne (1970) involved an investigation of interrule transfer. The subjects solved four series of three problems each. Each of the four rules noted above was used for one series. Following the twelve problems, one additional rule problem was presented in which the subjects had to discover which of the four rules was involved. As the data in Figure 12.10 indicate, interrule transfer was substantial. Performance improved on each problem using the same rule and on each series using different rules. On the last problem most subjects required only one stimulus event prior to solution.

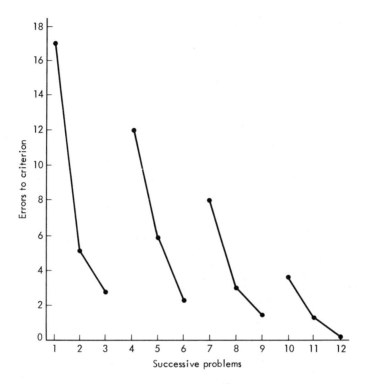

Figure 12.10 Mean errors to solution of twelve successive rule-learning problems. Problems are blocked into sets of three, each block being based on one of the four primary bidimensional rules—Experiment II.
(From Bourne, 1970.)

Evidence that the truth-table strategy was developing increased across each series of problems. On problem 1 no subject reached solution with only one instance of each of the four truth-table patterns. This suggests the truth-table strategy is not used initially. By problem 4, when the second rule was introduced, 13 percent of the subjects solved the problem with a single instance of each of the four patterns. This percentage increased to 25 on problem 7, when the third rule was introduced, and to 52 percent when the fourth rule was introduced on problem 10. Then, on problem 13, no more than one instance of each of the four patterns was required by 83 percent of the subjects. Thus it appears that once the subject has learned the way each rule is used to assign positive and negative instances to each pattern, the subject performs as the truth-table strategy would predict. According to previous experiments (Bourne and Guy, 1968; Dodd, 1967), subjects are more likely to manifest the truth-table strategy as the number of rules they learn increases.

In principle, at least, the truth-table strategy can be a powerful device for solving many types of problems. Since the strategy deals with rules, what the subject learns has considerably more applicability than what is learned in an attribute identification task. Learning a concept such as *blue* should allow an individual to recognize a variety of positive and negative instances of that concept. Learning a rule such as conjunction or disjunction, on the other hand, allows an individual to generate any number of instances of that rule using particular stimulus attributes.

In a certain sense a rule can be seen as a higher-order concept and the truth-table strategy as one that represents conceptual behavior as a hierarchical rule-following system. It should be recalled, however, that this strategy applies only to rule learning when the relevant attributes are known and not to attribute identification problems. In addition, although the strategy does apply to both rule learning and utilization, it does not explain the differential difficulty of the rules in any way like that accomplished by Hunt's hierarchical model. Nor is there any indication of how the truth-table strategy is acquired or why it is used. Little more can be said about Bourne's approach except to point out that it represents the beginnings of an attempt to deal with the generative nature of concepts.

An Inductive-Reasoning Approach

Trabasso, Rollins, and Shaughnessy (1971) have provided an analysis of concept learning that is based on an analog to inductive reasoning. The general idea is that when a subject is presented with a positive instance of a concept, he extracts features from it that form the basis for a hypothesis about the concept. This hypothesis is used to classify new stimulus events as positive or negative instances of the concept. When the hypothesis is supported, one gains greater confidence in its truth; but when the hypothesis is disconfirmed, an alternative hypothesis is selected on the basis of the available information.

The analysis provided by Trabasso et al. clearly involves a form of hypothesis testing. It also incorporates important aspects of Hunt's decision rules and Bourne's truth-table approach. Figure 12.11 gives the steps involved in constructing optimum decision rules for conjunctive and disjunctive concepts when the relevant attributes are known. To determine whether a given stimulus event is an instance of a conjunction such as red square, the subject first asks if one attribute is present, and if the answer is yes, he proceeds to ask about the presence of the second attribute. Of course, if the answer to either question is no, the conjunction is false. The same questions are asked for disjunction, although the critical answers are different.

A subject's use of such decision rules depends upon having prior

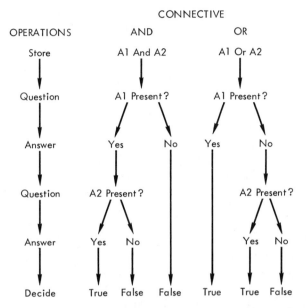

Figure 12.11 Optimal decision trees for processing conjunctive (AND) and inclusive disjunctive (OR) concepts. *(After Trabasso et al., 1971.)*

knowledge of these rules and the conditions under which their truth or falsity is demonstrated. In most concept-learning studies, however, this information cannot be assumed to be available. Trabasso et al. suggest that a two-stage learning process may be implied—in the first stage the appropriate truth values are acquired, and in the second stage decision rules are applied.

Trabasso et al. (1971) report a series of experiments designed to test their analysis of concept learning. In these experiments the main focus is on the way concepts are coded in memory and on the way they are verified. The typical procedure followed in these experiments was to present the subject with a statement of a concept (e.g., orange triangle and green circle) followed by presentation of a stimulus event that is either a positive or a negative instance of the concept. The subject's task was to determine whether the stimulus event contained an example of the concept. The time taken between presentation of the stimulus event and the subject's response was assumed to represent *concept verification* time. In some experiments the subject also controlled the amount of time in which the concept was presented. This was assumed to represent *concept storage* time. That is, the longer the subject chose to consider the concept before requesting that the stimulus event be displayed, the longer the concept storage time. Several types of conceptual rule were used, and concepts were presented in both affirmative (green circle) and negative (not a green circle) forms.

The results of this series of experiments provided support for the Trabasso et al. analysis of concept learning. The data generally supported the contention that once a concept is stored, subjects verify that concept using optimum decision trees. This also implies support for their assumption that once given the concept, the subject knows the truth-table entries for the conceptual rule. Only when the truth-table entries were known could the subject be expected to use optimum decision rules.

A second aspect of these experimental findings is also quite interesting. In some experimental conditions the attribute dimensions had only binary values. For instance, a given shape (e.g., triangle) had to be either orange or green. In such cases a concept defined as "not a green triangle and not a green circle" is equivalent to the concept "orange triangle and green circle." In general, the data indicated that for binary-valued dimensions, the subjects transformed negatives into affirmatives at the time of storage. This finding is illustrated in the data from the second experiment of Trabasso et al. (1971), which is presented in Figure 12.12.

For two dimensions with binary values, the number of negations involved in the presentation of the concept varied from zero to two. As the data show, concept storage time decreases considerably with practice, but the influence of negations continues to be substantial. Notice also that negatives do not influence concept verification time in this binary situation. The results concerning negation become more complex when the attribute dimensions contain more than two values. This would be expected, since the subjects cannot recode the stimuli in binary form. In this case it appears that the attribute value presented to the subject is stored along with a negative marker, and, as would be expected, the number of negations presented influences both storage and verification times.

The experiments reported by Trabasso et al. deal with those processes involved in the storage or coding of known concepts in memory and the subsequent verification of stimulus events as positive or negative instances of these concepts. If concept storage can be likened to the coding of hypotheses, then these experiments also provide evidence about situations where the relevant attributes and the conceptual rule are known. The general picture of conceptual behavior that results is one of formulating a hypothesis about some concept, knowing the truth-table entries for the corresponding conceptual rule, and applying optimum decision rules until the concept implied by the hypothesis is either verified or disconfirmed. Once a disconfirmation has occurred, a new hypothesis is selected on the basis of the available evidence and the entire process is repeated.

Trabasso et al. have shown that their analysis of conceptual behavior can be extended to explain the results of some experiments dealing with reasoning, psycholinguistics, problem solving, and arithmetic operations.

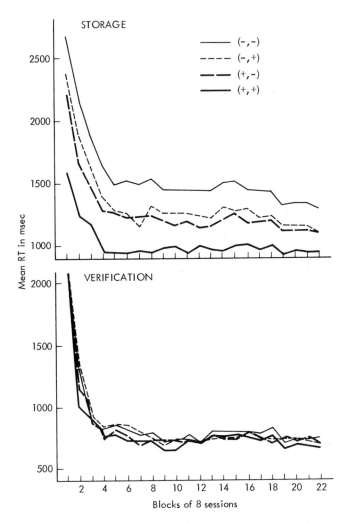

Figure 12.12 Reaction times to process concepts as a function of the number of negations of content during different stages of processing—Experiment II.
(From Trabasso et al., 1971.)

Although this is a particularly positive feature of their approach, a great deal of experimental evidence remains to be obtained concerning their model. In addition, their analysis says nothing specific about some of the major issues in concept learning. The memory–no memory issue is not addressed, although their discussion implies a limited memory at least. Similarly, the issue of sampling one or more hypotheses at the same time is not considered specifically. These issues will have to be addressed before the theoretical value of this approach can be adequately assessed. At this point the approach looks promising, and it draws together several of the most significant ideas from other theories.

EXTENDED CONCEPTS AND RULES

At the beginning of this chapter we noted that the terms *concept* and *rule* are frequently employed in a much broader sense than has been traditional in psychology. In the preceding sections of this chapter most references to the term *concept* or the term *rule* were based on specifiable stimulus events (attributes) and relations among these events (rules). As we have noted, this restriction to specifiable stimulus events derives historically from the associationists' definition of concepts either in terms of physical stimuli or the subject's response to those stimuli. Although contemporary psychologists are much less inclined toward such definitions, the tasks they have employed involve concepts that can be defined in the same way. As a result the theories and experiments we have been considering may only be relevant to conceptual behavior relating to particular types of concepts and particular kinds of rules. In the remainder of this chapter we shall consider a broader view of concepts and some experimental investigations that are relevant to a more extended view of concepts and rules.

In an important though little noticed paper, Jenkins (1966) explicitly argues that a concept is not a stimulus. Rather, he states, a concept is equivalent to a construct in scientific theory and is no more directly available than is typically the case with such constructs. For instance, consider the concept "an English word." No specific definition can be found for this concept, and although any English word is an example of the concept, no particular English word is equivalent to the concept itself. The same situation exists with respect to concepts that are much easier to specify in physical terms, such as the concept "blue triangle." This concept is represented by any blue triangle, but it is not identical with any one of them. The point to be made here is that concepts are not identical with particular instances of them but, instead, are defined in terms of an individual's knowledge of the concept. What you know about "English words" or "blue triangles" allows you to identify examples of them, but neither of these concepts is equivalent to any particular example of them.

Beginning with the view that a concept is a construct, Jenkins (1966) goes on to consider three broad classes of concepts. Concepts of the first class are dependent on shared characteristics of the physical stimulus. This type of concept learning, the first to be studied in psychology, dates back to the 1920s. Jenkins points out that concepts of this class can be quite complex, as in taxonomic zoology, or relatively simple, as in the traditional studies of attribute identification. The important point to note is that these concepts can be made explicit in the form of physical characteristics present in the stimulus display itself.

A second class of concepts began to be studied intensively in the 1930s and 1940s. These concepts are defined in terms of a common response or set of responses which the subject makes to different stimulus events. Thus the focus is shifted from characteristics of the stimulus display to characteristics of the subject's behavior. The behavior referred to here may be in the form of either directly observable or unobservable responses. The clearest case of such concepts is seen in mediation theory, and the simplest example is mediation through a naming or labeling response.

The third class of concepts, and the one Jenkins devotes the greatest attention to, is based on systematic relations. The concept is seen as having its existence in a body of rules, and the concept can be identified through testing procedures involving these rules even though no simple labels or common physical features can be identified. As an example of this class, Jenkins discusses the concept "English sentence."

Consider his three example strings shown below. It is readily agreed that the first two strings are sentences in English but the third string is not. It is difficult to say why this is so, but all speakers of English would agree that it is so.

(1) The boy hit the ball.
(2) Elephants trumpet at midnight.
(3) of Soldiers the street down march.

The problem cannot be solved by saying that the third string has a low probability of occurrence, because "odd" strings can be constructed such as (4), which we also agree are English sentences.

(4) The green cows on the cloud are eating pancakes.

Jenkins also notes that it is not fruitful to say the concept results from a common mediating response (e.g., "English sentence") which is made to these stimuli. There are an infinite number of English sentences, and there is no way to explain how the common mediating response comes to be made to all of them. While not denying the importance of the first two classes of concepts, Jenkins believes the third class is of considerable importance for psychological theory.

Linguistic Concepts and Meaningfulness

Defining a concept in terms of a set of rules led Jenkins and Greenberg to a series of experiments concerned with the meaningfulness of nonsense syllables. Their hypothesis was that variations in the meaningfulness of nonsense syllables could be due to variations in the degree to which the syllables departed from the rules of syllable formation in English. The set of rules for syllable formation has been established by linguists on the basis of phonemic sequences found to exist in the language. Therefore any given nonsense syllable can be evaluated in terms of how closely it conforms to these rules.

A sequence of phonemes such as *g v s u r s* would be called an impossible sequence in English. Among other considerations, it would be impossible "because all existent English syllables that begin with as many as three consonants (upper limit) have an initial s, a medial unvoiced stop (p, t, or k) and a final liquid or semivowel (r, l, w, or y)" (Jenkins, 1966, p. 72). The sequence *g v s u r s,* however, is not impossible in any universal sense. It is, in fact, a word in Georgian.

A second class of syllables might be termed possible but not actual sequences. This class would include sequences such as *s t r a b,* which conform to the rules of syllable formation noted above but are not actual English words. Variations occur among the sequences found in this class as well as among those that would be called impossible in English. For example, consider the sequence *s t w i p.* The initial consonant cluster in this case conforms to the rules, but this particular initial sequence does not occur in any English word. Thus *s t r a b* is more like an English word than *s t w i p,* and *s t w i p* is more like an English word than *g v s u r s.*

Using the linguistic rules for syllable construction in English, Greenberg developed a sixteen-step scale of "distance from English." His linguistic scale was based on a systematic use of sound substitution. At one end of the scale were sequences that actually occur in English, and at the other end were those that deviate most in terms of sounds and the order of sounds. Monosyllables were constructed to represent various points on the "distance from English" scale. These syllables were presented to subjects who rated them for distance from English.

Two rating procedures were employed, magnitude estimation and category rating scales. As the data in Figure 12.13 show, both rating procedures are closely related to the linguistic scale. The results from category rating correlated +.95 with the linguistic scale, and for magnitude estimation the correlation was +.94. The two rating procedures were also highly correlated, +.99 (Greenberg and Jenkins, 1964).

In a separate experiment reported by Jenkins (1966) the same syllables used by Greenberg and Jenkins were evaluated for meaningfulness.

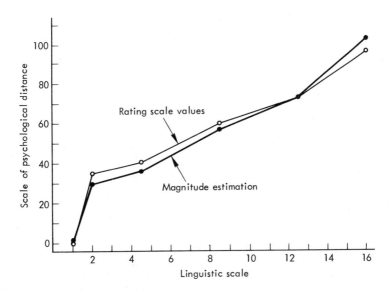

Figure 12.13 Relation between linguistic and psychological distance.
(From Jenkins, 1966.)

The procedure employed was similar to that of Noble (1952). The subjects were allowed fifteen seconds to write down associates to each syllable. Correlations were then computed between the median number of associates to each syllable and the values assigned to each syllable on the linguistic scale as well as the two rating procedures. The correlations were —.84 with both magnitude estimation and category rating, and —.75 with the linguistic scale. The syllables having the greatest number of associates were judged as being closest to English according to the two rating procedures and the linguistic scale. Jenkins (1966) states that these findings suggest that a typical index of meaningfulness of nonsense syllables, such as association value, may well constitute a "derived value that reflects how well a stimulus fits into the linguistic-conceptual-logical net which defines a syllable in English" (p. 74).

Since a question could be raised concerning the relatively few syllables employed in the previous studies, several additional comparisons were made which Jenkins (1966) also reported. In each case some characteristic of nonsense syllables, such as association value, was compared with measures of "distance from English" derived from the linguistic scale. Each of these comparisons showed a very close relationship between the two indices.

The evidence presented by Jenkins and his colleagues goes a long way toward suggesting that the meaningfulness of verbal stimuli is determined by the rules of the conceptual framework in which the stimuli are embedded, even though these rules are largely implicit. In the present case the rules are those for English syllable formation, and in this context the meaningfulness of nonsense syllables is seen as being determined by the linguistic deviation of the nonsense syllable from actual English forms. If this is so, then the various measures of nonsense syllables discussed in Chapter 4 (i.e., association value, frequency, pronunciability, m) can be seen mainly as consequences of the set of linguistic rules. Here the concept "syllable in English" is seen as having its existence in the body of rules for syllable formation. The concept can be tested with procedures involving these rules. Thus the meaningfulness of the verbal stimuli can be accounted for in terms of the concept, but the concept itself is not to be found in any simple way in the set of stimuli or the responses to them.

Conceptual Memory

Several investigations have attempted to develop Bartlett's (1932) notion of conceptual schema as a general characterization of memory structure. Among these investigations are a series of studies by Posner and his colleagues (cf. Posner, 1969; Posner and Keele, 1970) concerned with the learning of families of random dot patterns. Similar work concerning the learning of meaningful visual patterns has also been reported by Franks and Bransford (1971). Since the nature of the patterns used by Franks and Bransford makes it somewhat easier to specify the description of what may be stored in memory, we shall restrict our discussion to these experiments. In both the Posner and the Franks and Bransford studies, the concepts under investigation are less abstract than the linguistic concepts discussed by Jenkins (1966). In both cases, however, the concepts are based on systematic relations and are defined in terms of a set of rules.

The stimulus events employed by Franks and Bransford are illustrated in Figure 12.14. A prototypic configuration, called a *Base,* served to generate the other stimulus events. These other events were generated by applying various transformation rules to the Base configuration. As illustrated in Figure 12.14, pattern 2 is derived from the Base by reversal of the pair of elements on the left with those on the right. Pattern 3 is obtained by reversal of figure and ground relations for the elements on the left in the Base configuration, whereas in pattern 4 the figure-ground reversal is on the right. Pattern 5 is obtained by deleting the large square on the left, and pattern 6 results from substituting the hexagon for the square. Of course, more than one transformation can be applied to the Base configuration. This is illustrated in pattern 7 where three transformations have been applied in succession. First, the left and right sides of the Base are reversed, giving the second pattern shown in the figure. Next, a figure-ground reversal of the right-side elements results in a small square on a

ABSTRACTION OF VISUAL FORMS

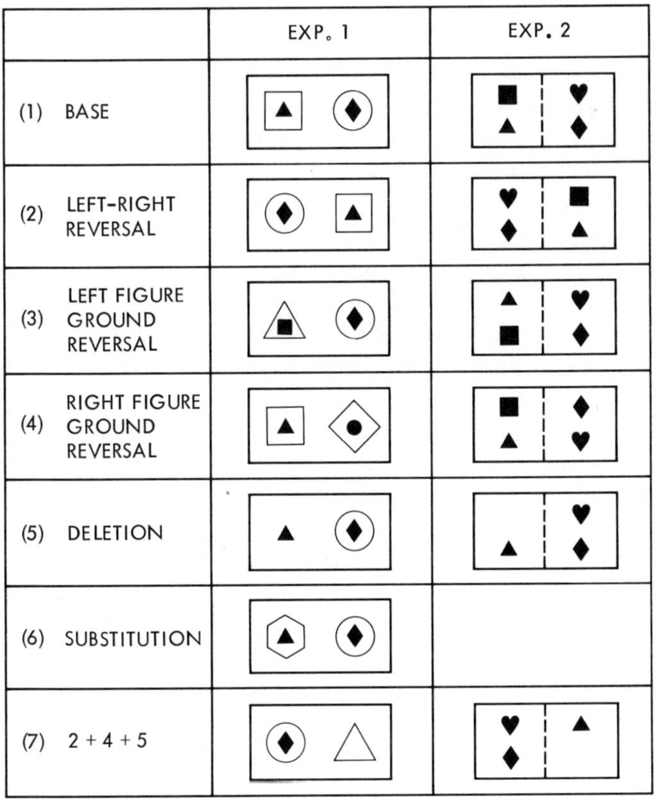

Figure 12.14 Examples of Bases and transformations.
(From Franks and Bransford, 1971.)

large triangle. Finally, by deletion the small square is removed giving the form of pattern 7.

In the acquisition phase of the first experiment, Franks and Bransford presented sixteen stimulus patterns to their subjects. The subjects were told that the experiment dealt with perceptual short-term memory and that their task would be to reproduce the patterns shown. Each pattern was exposed for five seconds after which the subjects counted to five aloud and in unison. Then the subjects attempted to reproduce the pattern they had just seen. The sixteen patterns were presented twice to each group of subjects. The patterns shown to the subjects included examples of each type of transformation and the possible combinations of transformations. The patterns also varied in the amount of deviation from the Base configuration, ranging from one transformation from the Base to five transformations from the Base. In all cases, however, the patterns were chosen so that the Base would be the prototype of the patterns presented in acquisition. That is, the Base was the pattern that was closest to the whole set of patterns in terms of transformational distance.

Following acquisition, the subjects were given a recognition test consisting of thirty-six patterns. As each pattern was presented, the subjects were asked to indicate whether that pattern had been presented during acquisition. They were also asked to indicate how confident they were about each answer. For example, if a subject responded yes to a given pattern, a confidence rating of 5 would indicate high confidence in the response, whereas a rating of 1 would show little confidence. The patterns presented in recognition consisted of the Base and thirty-five other patterns which varied from one to five transformations from the Base. None of these patterns, however, including the Base, had been presented during acquisition.

The recognition confidence ratings were converted to yield a ten-point scale by assigning plus for a *yes* response and minus for a *no* response. Using this procedure, an average recognition rating was obtained for all thirty-six patterns. The pattern that subjects were most confident they had seen in acquisition was the Base, which received a recognition rating of +4.04. The recognition ratings for the other patterns decreased, depending on their transformational distance from the Base. The average recognition ratings for patterns one to five transformations from the Base were 2.13, .33, −1.10, −2.60, and −3.13, respectively.

Franks and Bransford also report the results of comparing patterns having similar derivational histories. That is, two patterns, *A* and *B,* are said to have similar derivational histories if *A* and *B* resulted from application of the same transformations except that *B* has undergone one or more additional transformations. Following this rule, 152 comparisons were identified; in 144 of these the pattern that was transformationally closer to the Base had been given the higher recognition rating.

Franks and Bransford interpreted their findings as indicating that subjects abstract the prototypic configuration (i.e., the Base) as well as the rules of transformation during the acquisition phase and use this information to arrive at the ratings given to each pattern in recognition. This interpretation implies that there is little memory for specific patterns so long as the patterns are consistent with the prototype and rule information. Thus the subject is seen as acquiring general information about the set as a whole in which the abstracted Base serves as the central tendency or prototype, and other patterns are evaluated according to some notion of transformational distance from the prototype.

An alternative interpretation of these findings could be offered on the basis of a simple frequency explanation. According to this view, the subject is seen as storing information about the relative frequency of occurrence of the stimulus elements. The recognition ratings would then be a function of these frequencies of occurrence. Franks and Bransford point out that such an explanation would account for the results obtained in their first and second experiments. However, they go on to report two additional experiments in which the frequency explanation does not fare as well.

In their third experiment the patterns presented were selected in such a way that sixteen pairs of configurations directly contrasted the prototype-plus-transformations account with the frequency explanation. For the over-all averages, fourteen of these sixteen comparisons favored the prototype-plus-transformations model. These findings were replicated in the fourth experiment. Experiment four also contained patterns in recognition that were generated with the use of transformations not represented in acquisition. Even though the relative frequency of stimulus elements contained in these patterns was comparable with that of the other patterns tested, the recognition ratings were decidedly lower. Thus the prototype-plus-transformations model appears to offer a better account of the evidence than is possible with a simple frequency explanation.

We have considered two situations in which the concepts to be learned or employed by subjects were based upon systematic relations and not on common physical properties. That is, in contrast to the concepts used in most of the investigations discussed earlier in this chapter, those employed by Jenkins as well as by Franks and Bransford were seen as having their existence in a body of rules rather than in a set of physical stimulus characteristics. In both of these latter experiments, however, the subjects appeared capable of employing the concepts effectively, even though the rules on which the concepts were based were probably only known to the subjects in an implicit sense.

Unfortunately, our knowledge concerning concepts of this type is too limited at present to allow much to be said about the way these concepts are acquired. It does not appear that the theories considered previously have much to contribute toward the understanding of this form of conceptual behavior. Whether this is due to the limited types of conceptual problem solving these theories are intended to explain or to a more fundamental weakness in the theoretical mechanisms proposed cannot be determined at present. It seems likely that future investigators of conceptual behavior will be able to profit from a careful consideration of the studies reported by Jenkins (1966) as well as those reported by Franks and Bransford (1971). It also seems likely that the cognitive processes underlying the use of these types of concepts will be of great importance to the study of conceptual behavior.

CONCLUSION

We began this chapter by considering the types of concepts and the forms of conceptual behavior that have been most extensively investigated by psychologists. It was noted that most investigations have been restricted

to concepts that can be defined in terms of specifiable stimulus characteristics, even though the term *concept* is often used in a much broader sense.
Nevertheless, as the term has typically been employed, a *concept* is seen as
having two rather critical features: (1) the set of *relevant attributes* that
specify the stimulus characteristics of the concept, and (2) the *rule* that
defines the relationship between the relevant attributes. Together, the
relevant attributes and the rule serve to define the concept.

Most of the chapter focused on theories of conceptual behavior.
Three broad classes of theoretical approach were discussed. The most traditional approach is *associationism,* which holds that concepts are gradually
acquired as a result of a series of reinforced encounters with positive and
negative instances of the concept. For the most part such theories assert
nothing about the internal activities of the organism except for assuming
some form of memory trace for prior experience. That is, the organism
is viewed as a passive recipient of inputs, with no internal machinery for
selecting and organizing information. Concept learning is simply viewed
as an automatic consequence of associating attributes of the physical stimuli
to response categories. Although associative mediation theories supplement
these basic processes with the notion of internal responses and their stimulus
consequences, the fundamental view of learning is altered very little.

A second class of theories is that referred to as *hypothesis-testing
theory.* These theories hold that conceptual behavior is guided by some
hypothesis or set of hypotheses and that the learning process is characterized by the selection and testing of alternative hypotheses. In this way
hypothesis-testing theories emphasize a more active role for the learner
than do association theories. There is considerable variation within the set
of hypothesis-testing theories, however. Some theories hold to a serial
process in which only one hypothesis is tested at a time, and others emphasize a parallel approach with several hypotheses being tested at once.
In some theories little or no memory for prior events is attributed to the
subject, and learning is thought to take place only on trials on which errors
are made.

Experimental comparisons between association and hypothesis-testing
theories tend to favor the latter. Perhaps most clearly supportive of hypothesis-testing theory is the evidence indicating that subjects do formulate
and test hypotheses. This evidence not only suggests an active role for the
learner but tends to favor the view that several hypotheses are being tested
at the same time.

Within the class of hypothesis-testing theories, the experimental evidence tends to favor those holding the view that learning can take place
on both correct response and error trials. This observation also supports
the notion that several hypotheses may be tested at a time, with some of
them being eliminated on both correct and incorrect trials. The evidence
suggests at least some memory for prior events, although in certain cir-

cumstances memory may be quite limited. One issue that remains to be resolved here involves a distinction between memory for prior stimulus events and memory for the organization of prior information. Certainly the studies of Bransford and Franks, noted at the end of Chapter 11, suggest a good memory for prior organization and a rather poor memory for prior stimulus inputs.

Despite the apparent support for at least some forms of hypothesis-testing theory over association theories, several deficiencies should be noted. One is that hypothesis-testing theories make no provision for concept utilization, although it is not clear that association theories account for the consequences of solution shifts particularly well. Another problem is that hypothesis-testing theories say nothing about rule learning or rule identification. They also say nothing about the initial source of the hypotheses. Although such an omission causes little difficulty in the typical attribute identification situation, any complete theory of conceptual behavior will have to say something about the principles for hypothesis formation.

The third major class of theories we considered were those referred to as *information-processing theories*. Such theories are best characterized as extensions of hypothesis-testing theory in that they emphasize internal activities for selection and organization of information. In contrast to the hypothesis-testing theories considered previously, these theories place a greater emphasis on rule learning and on specific procedures for the development of hypotheses and decision rules. Although these characteristics represent an apparent improvement over alternative accounts, at present we cannot say that they do a better job of explaining the full range of experimental observations. It should also be noted that all of the theories discussed here have focused on the learning and utilization of concepts having readily specifiable structures in terms of concrete stimulus characteristics. It is simply not clear whether theories so formulated will be able to deal effectively with a broader range of conceptual situations.

In the final section of the chapter we considered some studies of conceptual behavior that were based on a much broader view of concepts than is usual. The class of concepts involved in these investigations was not based on common physical characteristics or on common responses. Instead, these concepts were based on systematic relations. That is, the concept was seen as having its existence in a body of rules. We saw that subjects could learn and employ such concepts even though no simple labels or common features could be identified. Everyday examples of such concepts include those of "word in English" or "sentence in English." We can all identify examples of these concepts, although no explicit definition for them can be provided. Investigations of conceptual behavior involving concepts of this type stand as a challenge to theorists in this area. It seems likely that the cognitive processes underlying the use of such concepts will be of considerable importance to our ultimate understanding of conceptual behavior.

Concluding
Remarks

13

Review
and Overview

IN THE PRECEDING CHAPTERS of this text we have examined major changes that have taken place in human learning with respect to theoretical orientation and the problems chosen for investigation. These changes have occurred over the past seven or eight decades. Of course, not every aspect of human learning could be considered. For the most part our focus has been on verbal behavior, since it is in the realm of verbal and linguistic skills that the behavior of man is most readily distinguished from the behavior of other organisms.

In each of the preceding chapters we have discussed various phenomena and theories of human learning. Only those theoretical details of greatest relevance to the main issues under consideration were emphasized. These chapters were organized around three main themes that can be generally described in terms of (1) learning (associationistic) approaches, (2) information-processing approaches, and (3) structural analysis approaches. These themes correspond to some of the differences in basic pretheoretical assumptions that have guided and characterized the development of theory and experimentation in the area of human learning. Therefore it seems appropriate to conclude this text with a resumé of those changes in theory and experimental strategy that appear to be of major significance in human learning. Let us begin by considering the status of theory around the middle of the twentieth century.

Association (S-R) Theory

Prior to the 1950s the study of human learning was mainly concerned with the problem of acquiring new habits or associations. The focus was on *what* was learned and *how* learning took place. The dominant theoretical position held that associations between stimulus (S) and response (R) events constituted the units of learning. These associations were thought to be acquired on the basis of the classic *law of contiguity*. This law held that associative strength increased as a direct function of the frequency with which contiguous events had been experienced.

The principle of contiguity has played a major role in theories of human learning since the days of British associationism. In its more contemporary form, the principle was characterized in terms of stimuli and responses, and additional behavioral principles were adduced to explain particular outcomes in behavior. For example, associations between contiguous stimulus-response events seemed to be more easily formed or to become stronger when these events were accompanied by reward, symbolic or otherwise. Hence the *law of effect* became an important focus of theoretical inquiry in human learning, especially in the very influential works of E. L. Thorndike (see Chapter 2).

Other major theorists such as E. C. Tolman, however, interpreted the effects of reward in terms of the more cognitive principles of motivation and emphasis, rather than in terms of automatic strengthening of associations. Despite these contrasting viewpoints, the most influential analyses of the effects of reward and punishment continued to be those cast in terms of behavioristic, stimulus-response models (e.g., Guthrie, 1940; Hull, 1943, 1951, 1952; Skinner, 1938).

Earlier stimulus-response analyses emphasized the direct effects of frequency and reward on habits. It soon became clear, however, that such primitive assumptions would not explain behavior in many common experimental situations. In many such situations an interpretation in terms of overt responses conditioned to covert mediating stimuli seemed appropriate. The theoretical derivation of such intermediate mechanisms was grounded on the basic principles of continuity, frequency, and reinforcement. Therefore, these basic principles were viewed as being quite general and applicable to *all* learning situations. In essence, complex behaviors were seen as resulting from the concatenation of simple stimulus-response associations acquired on the basis of general, elementary laws of association.

Although the emerging stimulus-response theories could trace many of their basic principles back to British associationism, these theories were also products of behaviorism. Hence, associative principles were translated with an emphasis on behavior. As a case in point, the venerable principle of contiguity was retained, but it was employed to explain associations between stimuli and responses, in contrast to the classical emphasis on association of mental events such as ideas. In addition, stimulus-response theorists accepted the empiricist assumption that man had little in the way of innate knowledge. This meant, of course, that virtually all knowledge, in the form of S-R associations, had to be acquired through experience. Man was seen as essentially a passive receiver of inputs, and learning was viewed as an automatic process that produced more or less faithful copies of man's experience.

The views of learning held by behavioristic theorists had decided implications for the kinds of experiments they performed. For example, investigations of learning were generally limited to a few carefully selected experimental situations in which precise control of stimulus presentation was presumed to exist. In the context of general S-R theory, this approach was quite appropriate. After all, if the laws of learning were completely general, they could be established in one learning situation just as readily as in another. Therefore, why not employ those learning tasks in which stimulus and response events *seemed* to be most easily defined. In the case of animal learning and certain forms of human learning, the tasks of choice were those defined by the classical and instrumental conditioning paradigms. In the case of verbal behavior in man, the serial and paired-associate tasks appeared to provide the maximum in experimental leverage.

The acquisition of associations was the principal matter of interest at this time. Memory was seen as being relatively uninteresting, since it could be viewed as a rather automatic consequence of learning. Perception and language were important, but it seemed that they could be readily accounted for on the basis of associative concepts as these concepts were developed within the favored conditioning and verbal learning tasks. Principles of organization in memory formed the basis for early debates between stimulus-response (interference) theorists and those who preferred to use trace concepts in explaining memory changes (e.g., the *Gestalt* psychologists). Such debates led to considerable interest in establishing the laws of forgetting.

The S-R psychologist proceeded with studies of basic learning processes with the conviction that these findings would generalize to other areas of psychological interest, including memory. Opposing viewpoints suggested that organization was an important factor in memory. The S-R theorist, however, replied that organization of memory depended on organization of experience, which was already the focus of theoretical inquiry. Therefore, even though a number of intriguing questions were being raised about organization in memory (cf. Bartlett, 1932; Koffka, 1935; Wulf, 1922), studies of the organization of memory were not popular among proponents of S-R theory.

Demise of S-R Theory.   In the preceding chapters we have discussed a number of specific issues that were difficult for S-R theory to resolve within a consistent theoretical framework. Research on a broad spectrum of topics—transposition, learning sets, the functional stimulus, learning without awareness—has highlighted the enormous difficulty of ever providing a clear-cut and unambiguous definition of the concept *stimulus*. Yet, for a theory that relied so heavily on explanatory concepts such as stimulus generalization and stimulus discrimination, such a definition was essential. For without a clearly defined stimulus, there could be little hope of predicting responses or dealing with a number of central issues that were critical to a general S-R theory of learning.

A related problem for S-R theory is illustrated by empirical findings that seem to challenge the assumption that there are completely general principles of learning. For example, the paired-associate situation has been compared to the classical conditioning paradigm. Such a comparison raises the following puzzle. Backward associations have been demonstrated in verbal learning, but it is difficult to demonstrate the supposedly analogous phenomenon of backward conditioning. We might also note that the evidence for spontaneous recovery in conditioning situations with animals or humans is much more convincing than it is in verbal learning situations with humans.

Such repeated discrepancies began to raise a number of disturbing questions about the generality of basic learning principles. Certainly this was not a completely impossible situation for S-R theory when the range of organisms and tasks varied enormously from classical conditioning in the dog to paired-associate learning in man. Such discrepancies, however, had much more theoretical impact when it became apparent, after many years of careful research, that the principles developed in the paired-associate situation did not always generalize directly to the serial learning context (cf. Battig, 1968; Young, 1968). Such problems, including those arising from inadequate definitions of the stimulus, reflected some critical difficulties faced by S-R theory. But these problems appear to us to be symptoms of, and not the primary reasons for, the theory's present theoretical eclipse. For that eclipse seems quite clear now in that S-R theory can apparently no longer provide an adequate or complete explanation of human behavior and learning.

Why then did S-R theory fail to maintain the theoretical prominence it had had for more than one-third of the twentieth century? The theory was not totally incorrect or wholly inadequate, since many of its principles remain viable today. The laws of contiguity, frequency, and reinforcement continue to be important, although they no longer play a central role in psychological thought. Few contemporary psychologists, however, would seriously consider S-R theory as a promising candidate for the future.

S-R theorists have sometimes been taken to task for their experimental zeal and rigor, as though their concern for objective experimental data somehow constituted a major weakness in their theoretical approach. This, of course, is not a valid objection. Proponents of the S-R approach themselves have often knowingly provided critical evidence against the theory on the basis of carefully collected objective information. In fact, the introduction of objective experimental procedures constitutes one of the major contributions of behavioristic psychology, and without access to such objective evidence no theory can be properly evaluated.

Perhaps the main reason for the eclipse of S-R theory is to be found in a number of pretheoretical assumptions contained in the behavioristic concept of man. There appear to be three aspects of this concept that have most seriously damaged S-R theory. First, the behaviorist has been characterized as subscribing to the traditional assumption of the empiricist that man has little in the way of innate knowledge or inborn ways of processing information. About the only innate structure attributed to man was the capability of forming S-R associations. Second, the behaviorist viewed man as a relatively static organism who processed inputs passively and responded to them in automatic, stereotyped ways. Third, there was the assumption that the principles by which man learned were completely general and applicable across all learning situations.

A major consequence of the behavioristic concept of man was that certain types of theoretical explanation and certain problems for experimentation were excluded at the outset. Acceptance of the empiricist assumption led the behaviorist to reject theoretical explanations in which innate knowledge or innate ways of processing information played a significant role. There was little interest in nativistic accounts of language acquisition. The possibility that specialized mechanisms might exist which respond selectively to inputs when they occur in one context (e.g., speech sounds) but not when they occur in other contexts (e.g., other auditory signals) was simply not considered or investigated by the behaviorists. In the entire field of perception there was little theoretical interest in anything other than a determination of the amount of physical energy required to perceive a stimulus and the change in stimulus energy required to detect a change.

Similar restrictions resulted from the behaviorist assumption that the laws of learning were completely general. Perception and language were largely ignored in behavioristic research. Much the same comment can be applied to many aspects of attention and memory. By relying so exclusively on the conditioning and verbal learning tasks, the behaviorist was prevented from observing many of the complexities revealed in recent investigations of preperceptual memory, selective attention, short-term memory, organization in memory, speech perception, and language learning.

In many ways the most damaging aspect of the behavioristic concept was the assumption that man is a passive receiver of inputs to which he responds in automatic and stereotyped ways. Throughout this text we have continually encountered evidence of man's active and creative nature. This nature is revealed in the active selection of functional stimuli from nominal stimuli, in the coding and recoding of information, in the extraction of semantic features to be stored in memory, in the recovery of deep structures from surface structures of sentences, and in the formulation of hypotheses to be tested in concept-learning situations. In fact, this very aspect of man's nature may be responsible, in large part, for the difficulties experienced by S-R theorists when attempting to define "the stimulus."

By assuming man to be a relatively passive organism, with little innate machinery for processing information, it was easy for the behaviorist to conclude that the meaning of stimulus events was to be found in the events themselves. Thus it came as some surprise to find that human subjects might locate stimuli along an underlying perceptual dimension even when the stimuli were not presented in any dimensional manner. Correspondingly, we have seen that human subjects quite readily engage in activities like integration, induction, and reasoning when appropriate stimuli are employed. When these processes are engaged, subjects often succeed in abstracting structures and discovering relations between inputs that were never contained in the stimuli presented to them.

Once the experimental and theoretical base for the study of human learning was sufficiently expanded, as it was by the 1960s, it became increasingly clear to psychologists that S-R theory was not going to be satisfactory. The theory rested on such a limited conception of man's nature and was developed within such a restricted set of experimental situations that its conceptual structure was not adequate to the task of explaining human learning. Studies of perception, memory, and language clearly indicated that man processed inputs in active, complex, and sometimes highly specialized ways. There also was evidence for innate processing mechanisms and perhaps even of innate knowledge. Thus S-R theory failed because it was not equipped with a sufficiently rich conception of man to develop the theoretical concepts required to account for the complex nature of learning and cognition in man.

The Rise of Cognitive Theory

As the problems with S-R theory emerged, psychologists became increasingly interested in alternative theoretical approaches. We have referred to these alternatives as cognitive theory because they focus on mental phenomena and cognitive activities in man. Two general types of cognitive theory have been proposed to account for various aspects of human learning. One of these is closely identified with the information-processing approach discussed in Part II of this text. The other is somewhat narrower in scope and has been identified with the study of language acquisition and use which was discussed in Part III. Let us briefly review these forms of cognitive theory.

Information-Processing Theory. In Chapter 1 it was noted that information-processing accounts of human behavior tend to focus on "the flow of information" in the organism. That is, the main emphasis here is on attempting to describe the passage of information in the organism from input to output. Historically speaking, this approach has been closely related to an analogy between man and computers, insofar as computers also accept inputs, process them in various ways, and produce outputs.

The development of information-processing theory has for the most part been rather closely identified with the experimental observations upon which the various theories were based. As a result theorists have remained relatively neutral with respect to many of the issues that led to the downfall of S-R theory. Although most theorists are committed to an active view of man as a processor of information, they remain rather neutral with respect to the empiricist assumption. Most seem willing to accommodate innate machinery for processing information, at least to a limited extent. But information-processing theorists remain quite cautious when it comes to the assumption of innate knowledge. In addition, the close relationship between data and theory that has characterized this approach has prevented hasty conclusions concerning the generality of the laws of learning.

Although the information-processing approach is concerned with man's cognitive activities in a general way, most of the theoretical efforts identified with it have been restricted to rather specific processing systems. Many of these theories have been discussed previously. Among them we find models dealing with various aspects of selective attention (e.g., Broadbent, 1958), preperceptual storage (e.g., Sperling, 1960; Massaro, 1972), short-term and long-term memory (e.g., Waugh and Norman, 1965), coding operations and memory codes (e.g., Morton, 1969; Posner and Warren, 1972), and conceptual behavior (e.g., Hunt, Marin, and Stone, 1966). In all of these models man is pictured as an active processor of inputs who selectively screens, codes, stores, and responds to incoming information in diverse ways.

Other forms of information-processing theory attempt to deal with learning and cognition somewhat more comprehensively. Craik and Lockhart (1972) have concentrated on a description of the processing stages involved in the acquisition of information. Atkinson and Shiffrin (1968) have emphasized the need for control processes or strategies that can be used to regulate the flow of information. In a different vein, Rumelhart,

Lindsay, and Norman (1972) have employed a computer simulation approach in attempting to provide a comprehensive description of the structure of permanent memory. All three of these approaches may point to future directions in theory and research.

Psycholinguistic Theory. Whereas the development of information-processing theory was closely tied to experimental observations, psycholinguistic theory was initially based on the emergence of theories of linguistic competence (cf. Chomsky, 1957, 1965). These theories of competence depend for their basic concepts on an analysis of the structures that characterize natural language. The main objectives of such theories have been to provide a description of the kinds of sentence structures that occur in natural language and the interrelationships of these structures. In addition, these theories attempt to describe the linguistic relations that underlie the grammatical skills manifested by language users. These skills include the ability of language users to judge grammaticality, to detect ambiguity, to evaluate relations within sentences, and to determine relations among sentences. In all these cases the initial theoretical emphasis was on a grammatical rather than a semantic analysis of sentence structure.

In contrast to S-R theory, psycholinguistic theory has been strongly committed to the nativist position. This is particularly clear in early theories of language acquisition which assumed that man was born with an innate conception of the character of natural language. This knowledge was of course assumed to be implicit and, therefore, not communicable from one individual to another. The argument was made that natural language was so complex that a considerable amount of innate information about it, or at least innate machinery for processing language in certain ways, would be necessary for language acquisition to take place.

Early psycholinguistic research indicated that many of the concepts represented in linguistic theory were important in a psychological sense. In fact, the early research was sufficiently encouraging that an initial effort was made to translate linguistic theory directly into a theory of psychological performance. The resulting psycholinguistic accounts were shown to have many advantages over S-R explanations of both language acquisition and use. Nevertheless, in many experimental situations predictions based on these psycholinguistic models simply could not be confirmed.

As the evidence from studies of language acquisition and language use began to accumulate, it became clear that one of the major weaknesses of linguistic theory was its almost exclusive emphasis on syntactic as opposed to semantic aspects of language. In study after study, the influence of semantic factors was seen to override the effects of syntactic considerations. In the face of such evidence both linguistic and psycholinguistic theory began to change. In linguistics an increasing regard for the importance of semantics has already been seen, although these changes in linguistic theory have yet to be evaluated in a psychological context. Nevertheless, psycholinguistic theory has begun to change as well.

More contemporary versions of psycholinguistic theory have moved away from an exclusive reliance on syntactic considerations. Although syntactic factors continue to be emphasized in accounts of sentence comprehension, semantic factors have assumed a major role when sentence memory is at issue. Only future research will tell us whether or not these changes will prove to be adequate as well as the extent to which psycholinguistic theory needs to be supplemented by a general model of cognition.

Theories of speech production and speech perception, like other language theories, are based on an analysis of the structure of language—in this case, the structure of speech sounds. The development of theories of speech production and perception, however, has been closely tied to experimental observations, and these theories rely much less on linguistic intuitions about the abstract nature of language. In this way, theories of speech production and perception more closely resemble theories of information processing.

Speech scientists share with other psycholinguists an acceptance of the nativist position. This belief has been strengthened by evidence for categorical perception and parallel processing of speech sounds as well as by indications that speech sounds are processed in a different way than other auditory inputs. Evidence for a special speech-processing center in the brain and the early segmentation of phonemes during infancy support this contention. Thus theories of speech production and perception have much in common with other forms of cognitive theory, although they cannot be strictly identified with either psycholinguistic theory or information-processing theory.

Rule-Governed Behavior

The use of rules as explanatory concepts is of relatively recent origin in the field of human learning. Yet throughout this text we have noted that a great deal of human behavior can be conceptualized in terms of rules that direct our speaking, thinking, and problem-solving activities. We have also seen situations in which explanations cast in terms of S-R theory appear forced, but when cast in terms of rules they appear to be relatively straightforward and simple. For example, transposition behavior in verbal children seems quite comprehensible in terms of a rule such as "Choose the larger one."

Strategies that subjects employ in learning various laboratory tasks can sometimes be described in terms of rules the subjects appear to follow during acquisition and transfer tasks. For example, if subjects employ a search strategy or rule in retrieving serial information, positive transfer might be expected from a serial to a paired-associate task. If they do not, little effective transfer might be expected. Theories of transfer that do not consider the possibility of such rules operating in the retrieval and utilization of stored information are often hard pushed to deal with the facts at hand.

The emergence of linguistic and psycholinguistic theories has been accompanied by an increasing concern with rule learning and rule-governed behavior. In early linguistic theory the reference was to grammatical rules thought to be part of man's tacit or implicit knowledge about language. This structural, or rule-governed, approach to the study of human language has led to a critical reexamination of some basic assumptions concerning the psychological nature of language. Conceptions about rule learning and rule-governed behavior, however, have not been restricted to language.

Jenkins (1966) suggests that certain important classes of concepts exist on the basis of some body of rules. For example, the meaningfulness of English nonsense syllables can be analyzed in terms of a conceptual framework based on the rules for syllable formation. Such concepts can be identified through testing procedures involving these rules even though no simple labels or common physical features can be identified. As in grammatical rules, then, these rules also seem to be implicit.

Other examples of rule-governed behavior previously discussed are worth noting here once again. Bourne (1970) speaks of rule learning as being an important aspect of conceptual behavior. Martin (1972), in his discussion of rhythmic action in speech, suggests that implicit rules may be employed to anticipate the occurrence of events in time. Contemporary theories of acquisition, storage, and retrieval also emphasize rules or strategies to regulate the flow of information (Atkinson and Shiffrin, 1968). Presumably, rules determine the nature of hierarchical memory structures. Rules also relate concepts within these structures, and still other rules determine the ways in which information is retrieved from memory.

The notion of rules and rule-governed behavior poses several problems for theorists and researchers. For example, is there a limited set of rules? Under what conditions does a given rule, or set of rules, operate? Are rules basically products of experience, or are they intrinsically involved in determining how our experiences are organized? Some of these questions have a long history in philosophy and psychology. Most of them will be difficult to answer, and they may require considerable time and effort. Nevertheless, they are questions that psychologists will have to try to answer, and the way in which they are approached will certainly have a major influence on broad, future developments in human learning. What might some of these future developments be?

Future Directions in Theory and Research

When we turn to the question of future developments, several trends seem probable. To begin with, the general theoretical orientation we have referred to as cognitive theory seems likely to be of importance for some time. This is because the conception of man subscribed to by most cognitive theorists is quite well supported and seems unlikely to change in the near future. Certainly there is no evidence to support a return to a strict behavioristic concept of man. If anything, future versions of cognitive theory are likely to contain an even greater emphasis on the active nature of information processing.

At the level of particular theories and topics for research, we suspect that there will be a continued interest in special processing mechanisms and innate structures believed to be involved in selective attention, speech perception, and coding operations. There are too many fascinating, unanswered questions in these areas to expect that interest in them will soon diminish. In the area of memory there will probably be an integrative trend, perhaps along lines similar to the approach suggested by Craik and Lockhart (1972). This may result in less concern with distinct memory systems, such as short-term and long-term memory, and a greater interest in describing the broad course of information processing. At the same time, we are likely to see a trend toward even more comprehensive theories that attempt to deal with much of cognitive activity. The development of such general theories has already been foreshadowed by the work of Anderson and Bower (1973).

Apart from such general trends, future developments in human learning will be influenced significantly by the way both researchers and theorists approach specific problems. Two issues appear to have implications for much of cognitive theory and research: *meaning* and *context*. These issues are by no means unrelated.

Meaning. The problem of meaning, or semantics, is one we have encountered throughout the preceding chapters, and it is a very old problem in human learning as well. The behaviorists were plagued by the difficulty of describing the meaning of stimulus events, and the classic associationists struggled unsuccessfully with the meaning of ideas. In contemporary work we have seen the difficulties encountered in attempting to explain language acquisition and language use without an adequate theory of semantics. It seems clear that future work in psycholinguistics will revolve about efforts to deal with this problem.

Language is by no means the only area of theory and research in which meaning is important. The problem of meaning has considerable significance in learning and memory. The influence of meaning can be seen in certain coding operations, including the extraction of semantic features. Meaning appears to play some role in short-term memory, and it is of obvious importance to descriptions of long-term memory. Theories of memory structure, such as that of Rumelhart, Lindsay, and Norman (1972), can be characterized as theories about the organization of meaning. The widespread significance of meaning in these areas indicates that the experimental and theoretical approaches to this problem will have important consequences for future developments in human learning.

Context. The problem of context is also a very old one in human learning, having been discussed off and on for more than three-quarters of a century. In many ways the problem arises because the role of context cannot be separated from that of meaning. That is, the meaning of an event, however the event is defined, depends on the context in which it occurs. Thus, meaning is a relative concept. Notice also that context here refers both to the external context of other events and the internal context that consists of an individual's prior knowledge of, or experience with, the same or similar events.

Numerous illustrations of context effects have been cited in the preceding chapters. For example, performance in the free-recall task is influenced by the context provided by the items in the to-be-remembered list. Performance in free recall is also influenced by the type of orienting task employed, even when the same items are presented to all subjects. In studies of sentence memory, accuracy in recognition depends on whether the various sentences presented to the subjects are related or not. These and other examples of context effects demonstrated the close relationship between context and meaning. Future research and theory in human learning will therefore certainly be influenced by the way these problems are treated.

Final Remarks

In this concluding chapter we have presented a brief review and overview of the changes in theory and experimentation that have characterized human learning in recent years. We have considered some of the reasons for the demise of S-R theory and the behavioristic movement in general. The theoretical orientations and experimental concerns that followed the behavioristic period were also reviewed. Finally, some of the trends and issues that appear likely to characterize human learning in the future were discussed.

References

The numbers in brackets at the end of each reference indicate the chapter(s) in which the reference appears.

ABRAMS, K. & BEVER, T. G. (1969) Syntactic structure modifies attention during speech perception and recognition. *Quarterly Journal of Experimental Psychology,* 21, 291-98 **[10]**.

ACHENBACH, K. E. (1966) *The effect of repetition on short-term storage in dichotic listening.* Unpublished doctoral dissertation, University of Florida **[7]**.

ANDERSON, B. F. (1963) *The short-term retention of active and passive sentences.* Unpublished doctoral dissertation, Johns Hopkins University **[11]**.

ANDERSON, J. R. & BOWER, G. H. (1973) *Human Associative Memory.* Washington, D.C.: V. H. Winston & Sons **[8, 13]**.

ARCHER, E. J. (1960) A re-evaluation of the meaningfulness of all possible CVC trigrams. *Psychological Monographs,* 74, No. 10 (Whole No. 497) **[4]**.

ASCH, S. E. (1968) The doctrinal tyranny of associationism. In T. R. Dixon & D. L. Horton (Eds.) *Verbal Behavior and General Behavior Theory.* Englewood Cliffs, N.J.: Prentice-Hall **[4]**.

ASCH, S. E. & EBENHOLTZ, S. M. (1962) The principle of associative symmetry. *Proceedings of the American Philosophical Society,* 106, 135-63 **[4]**.

ATKINSON, R. C. (1957) A stochastic model for rote serial learning. *Psychometrika,* 22, 87-96 **[4]**.

ATKINSON, R. C. (1974) Teaching children to read using a computer. *American Psychologist*, 29, 169-78 **[3]**.

ATKINSON, R. C., HOLMGREN, J. E., & JUOLA, J. F. (1969) Processing time as influenced by number of elements in a visual display. *Perception and Psychophysics*, 6, 321-26 **[7]**.

ATKINSON, R. C. & SHIFFRIN, R. M. (1968) Human memory: A proposed system and its control processes. In K. W. Spence & J. T. Spence (Eds.) *The Psychology of Learning and Motivation*, Vol. 2. New York: Academic Press **[6, 13]**.

AVERBACH, E. & CORIELL, A. S. (1961) Short-term memory in vision. *Bell System Technical Journal*, 40, 309-28 (Monograph 3756) **[7]**.

AYLLON, T. (1963) Intensive treatment of psychotic behavior by stimulus satiation and food reinforcement. *Behavior Research and Therapy*, 1, 53-61 **[3]**.

BADDELEY, A. D. (1966a) Short-term memory for word sequences as a function of acoustic, semantic, and formal similarity. *Quarterly Journal of Experimental Psychology*, 18, 362-65 **[6]**.

BADDELEY, A. D. (1966b) The influence of acoustic and semantic similarity on long-term memory for word sequences. *Quarterly Journal of Experimental Psychology*, 18, 302-9 **[6]**.

BAKKER, D. J. (1968) Ear-asymmetry with monaural stimulation. *Psychonomic Science*, 12, 62 **[9]**.

BARNES, J. M. & UNDERWOOD, B. J. (1959) "Fate" of first-list associations in transfer theory. *Journal of Experimental Psychology*, 58, 97-105 **[5]**

BARTLETT, F. C. (1932) *Remembering*. Cambridge: Cambridge University Press **[12, 13]**.

BARTZ, W. H. (1969) Repetition and the memory stores. *Journal of Experimental Psychology*, 80, 33-38 **[6]**.

BARTZ, W. H. (1972) Repetition effects in dichotic presentation. *Journal of Experimental Psychology*, 92, 220-24 **[7]**.

BASTIAN, J., EIMAS, P. D., & LIBERMAN, A. M. (1961) Identification and discrimination of a phonemic contrast induced by silent interval. *Journal of the Acoustical Society of America*, 33, 842 **[9]**.

BATTIG, W. F. (1962) Paired-associate learning under stimultaneous repetition and nonrepetition conditions. *Journal of Experimental Psychology*, 64, 87-93 **[4]**.

BATTIG, W. F. (1968) Paired-associate learning. In T. R. Dixon & D. L. Horton (Eds.) *Verbal Behavior and General Behavior Theory*. Englewood Cliffs, N.J.: Prentice-Hall **[4, 13]**.

BATTIG, W. F., ALLEN, M., & JENSEN, A. R. (1965) Priority of free recall of newly learned items. *Journal of Verbal Learning and Verbal Behavior*, 4, 175-79 **[8]**.

BATTIG, W. F. & BRACKETT, H. R. (1961) Comparison of anticipation and recall methods in paired-associate learning. *Psychological Reports*, 9, 59-65 **[4]**.

BATTIG, W. F., BROWN, S. C., & NELSON, D. (1963) Constant vs. varied serial order in paired-associate learning. *Psychological Reports,* 12, 695-721 **[4]**.

BATTIG, W. F., BROWN, S. C., & SCHILD, M. E. (1964) Serial positions and sequential associations in serial learning. *Journal of Experimental Psychology,* 67, 449-57 **[4]**.

BATTIG, W. F. & KOPPENAAL, R. J. (1965) Associative asymmetry in S-R vs. R-S recall of double-function lists. *Psychological Reports,* 16, 287-93 **[4]**.

BATTIG, W. F. & LAWRENCE, P. S. (1967) The greater sensitivity of the serial recall than anticipation procedure to variations in serial order. *Journal of Experimental Psychology,* 73, 172-78 **[4]**.

BELLUGI, U. & SIPLE, P. (1973) Remembering with and without words. In F. Bresson (Ed.) *Current Problems in Psycholinguistics.* Paris, France: Centre Nationale de la Recherche Scientifique, 1135-58 **[6]**.

BERLYNE, D. E. (1960) *Conflict, Arousal, and Curiosity.* New York: McGraw-Hill **[7]**

BERLYNE, D. E., BORSA, D. M., HAMACHER, J. H., & KOENIG, I. D. V. (1966) Paired-associate learning and the timing of arousal. *Journal of Experimental Psychology,* 72, 1-6 **[7]**.

BEVER, T. G. (1970) The cognitive basis for linguistic structures. In R. Hayes (Ed.) *Cognition and Language.* New York: Wiley **[11]**.

BEVER, T. G., KIRK, R., & LACKNER, J. (1969) An autonomic reflection of syntactic structure. *Neuropsychologia,* 7, 23-28 **[10]**.

BEVER, T. G., LACKNER, J. R., & KIRK, R. (1969) The underlying structures of sentences are the primary units in speech perception. *Perception and Psychophysics,* 5, 225-34 **[10]**.

BIJOU, S. W. & BAER, D. M. (Eds.) (1967) *Child Development: Readings in Experimental Analysis.* Englewood Cliffs, N.J.: Prentice-Hall **[3]**.

BIJOU, S. W., BIRNBRAUER, J. S., KIDDER, J. D., & TAGUE, C. (1966) Programmed instruction as an approach to teaching of reading, writing, and arithmetic to retarded children. *Psychological Record,* 16, 505-22 **[3]**.

BIRCH, H. G. (1945) The relation of previous experience to insightful problem solving. *Journal of Comparative Psychology,* 38, 367-83 **[2]**.

BLOOM, L. (1970) *Language Development: Form and Function in Emerging Grammars.* Cambridge: MIT Press **[11]**.

BLUMENTHAL, A. L. (1967) Prompted recall of sentences. *Journal of Verbal Learning and Verbal Behavior,* 6, 203-6 **[10, 11]**.

BLUMENTHAL, A. L. & BOAKES, R. (1967) Prompted recall of sentences, a further study. *Journal of Verbal Learning and Verbal Behavior,* 6, 674-76 **[10, 11]**.

BOBROW, S. A. & BOWER, G. H. (1969) Comprehension and recall of sentences. *Journal of Experimental Psychology,* 80, 455-61 **[8]**.

BOND, E. K. (1972) Perception of form by the human infant. *Psychological Bulletin,* 77, 225-45 **[7]**.

BORING, E. G. (1950) *A History of Experimental Psychology* (2nd ed.) Englewood Cliffs, N.J.: Prentice Hall **[1, 5]**.

BOURNE, L. E., JR. (1967) Learning and utilization of conceptual rules. In B. Kleinmuntz (Ed.) *Concepts and the Structure of Memory*. New York: Wiley **[12]**.

BOURNE, L. E., JR. (1970) Knowing and using concepts. *Psychological Review*, 77, 546-66 **[12, 13]**.

BOURNE, L. E., JR., EKSTRAND, B. R., & DOMINOWSKI, R. L. (1971) *The Psychology of Thinking*. Englewood Cliffs, N.J.: Prentice-Hall **[12]**.

BOURNE, L. E., JR. & GUY, D. E. (1968) Learning conceptual rules: I. Some interrule transfer effects. *Journal of Experimental Psychology*, 76, 423-29 **[12]**.

BOURNE, L. E., JR. & RESTLE, F. (1959) Mathematical theory of concept identification. *Psychological Review*, 66, 278-96 **[12]**.

BOUSFIELD, W. A. (1953) The occurrence of clustering in the recall of randomly arranged associates. *Journal of General Psycholoy*, 49, 229-40 **[8]**.

BOUSFIELD, W. A. & BARCLAY, W. D. (1950) The relationship between order and frequency of occurrence of restricted associative responses. *Journal of Experimental Psychology*, 40, 643-47 **[8]**.

BOUSFIELD, W. A. & COHEN, B. H. (1953) The effects of reinforcement on the occurrence of clustering in the recall of randomly arranged associates. *Journal of Psychology*, 36, 67-81 **[8]**.

BOUSFIELD, W. A., COHEN, B. H., & SILVA, J. G. (1956) The extension of Marbe's law to the recall of stimulus words. *American Journal of Psychology*, 69, 429-33 **[8]**.

BOUSFIELD, W. A., COHEN, B. H., & WHITMARSH, G. A. (1958) Associative clustering in the recall of words of different taxonomic frequencies of occurrence. *Psychological Reports*, 4, 39-44 **[8]**.

BOUSFIELD, W. A., PUFF, C. R., & COWAN, T. M. (1964) The development of constancies in sequential organization during repeated free recall. *Journal of Verbal Learning and Verbal Behavior*, 3, 489-95 **[8]**.

BOUSFIELD, W. A. & SEDGEWICK, C. H. W. (1944) An analysis of sequences of restricted associative responses. *Journal of General Psychology*, 30, 149-65 **[8]**.

BOWER, G. H. (1970a) Mental imagery in associative learning. In L. Gregg (Ed.) *Cognition in Learning and Memory*. New York: Wiley **[8]**.

BOWER, G. H. (1970b) Imagery as a relational organizer in associative learning. *Journal of Verbal Learning and Verbal Behavior*, 9, 529-33 **[8]**.

BOWER, G. H. (1970c) Organizational factors in memory. *Cognitive Psychology*, 1, 18-46 **[8]**.

BOWER, G. H. (1972) Stimulus-sampling theory of encoding variability. In A. W. Melton and E. Martin (Eds.) *Coding Processes and Human Memory*. Washington, D.C.: V. H. Winston & Sons **[8]**.

BOWER, G. H. & BOLTON, L. (1969) Why are rhymes easy to learn? *Journal of Experimental Psychology*, 82, 453-61 **[8]**.

BOWER, G. H., CLARK, M., WINZENZ, D., & LESGOLD, A. (1969) Hierarchical retrieval schemes in recall of categorized word lists. *Journal of Verbal Learning and Verbal Behavior*, 8, 323-43 **[8]**.

BOWER, G. H., LESGOLD, A., & TIEMAN, D. (1969) Grouping operations in free recall. *Journal of Verbal Learning and Verbal Behavior*, 4, 481-93 **[8]**.

BOWER, G. H. & TRABASSO, T. (1963) Reversals prior to solution in concept identification. *Journal of Experimental Psychology*, 66, 409-18 **[12]**.

BOWER, G. H. & TRABASSO, T. (1964) Concept identification. In R. C. Atkinson (Ed.) *Studies of Mathematical Psychology*. Stanford: Stanford University Press **[12]**.

BOWER, G. H. & WINZENZ, D. (1969) Group structure, coding, and memory for digit series. *Journal of Experimental Psychology Monographs*, 80, No. 2, Part 2, 1-17 **[8]**.

BOWER, T. G. R. (1966) Slant perception and shape constancy in infants. *Science*, 151, 832-34 **[1]**.

BRAINE, M. D. S. (1963a) The ontogeny of English phrase structure: The first phase. *Language*, 39, 1-13 **[11]**.

BRAINE, M. D. S. (1963b) On learning the grammatical order of words. *Psychological Review*, 70, 323-48 **[11]**.

BRANSFORD, J. D., BARCLAY, J. R., & FRANKS, J. J. (1972) Sentence memory: A constructive vs. interpretive approach. *Cognitive Psychology*, 3, 193-209 **[11]**.

BRANSFORD, J. D. & FRANKS, J. J. (1971) The abstraction of linguistic ideas. *Cognitive Psychology*, 2, 331-50 **[11]**.

BRELAND, K. & BRELAND, M. (1951) A field of applied animal psychology. *American Psychologist*, 6, 202-4 **[3]**.

BRELAND, K. & BRELAND, M. (1966) *Animal Behavior*. New York: Macmillan **[3]**.

BRIGGS, G. E. (1954) Acquisition, extinction, and recovery functions in retroactive inhibition. *Journal of Experimental Psychology*, 47, 285-93 **[5]**.

BROADBENT, D. E. (1954) The role of auditory localization in attention and memory. *Journal of Experimental Psychology*, 47, 191-96 **[7, 9]**.

BROADBENT, D. E. (1957) A mechanical model for human attention and immediate memory. *Psychological Review*, 64, 205-15 **[7]**.

BROADBENT, D. E. (1958) *Perception and Communication*. London: Pergamon Press **[7, 13]**.

BROADBENT, D. E. & GREGORY, M. (1963) Division of attention and the decision theory of signal detection. *Proceedings of the Royal Society* (London), Series B, 158, 222-31 **[7]**.

BROCA, P. (1861) Remarques sur le siége de la faculté du langage articulé suivies d'une observation d'aphémie. *Bulletin de la Societe Anatomique de Paris*, 36, 330-57 **[9]**.

BROWN, J. (1958) Some tests of the decay theory of immediate memory. *Quarterly Journal of Experimental Psychology*, 10, 12-21 **[6]**.

BROWN, J. (1959) Information, redundancy, and decay of the memory trace.

In *The Mechanization of Thought Processes*. London: H. M. Stationery Office [6].

BROWN, R. W. (1973) Development of the first language in the human species. *American Psychologist*, 28, 97-106 [11].

BROWN, R. W. & BELLUGI, U. (1964) Three processes in the child's acquisition of syntax. *Harvard Educational Review*, 34, 133-51 [11].

BROWN, R. W., CAZDEN, C., & BELLUGI, U. (1968) The child's grammar from I to III. In J. P. Hill (Ed.) *The 1967 Minnesota Symposium on Child Psychology*. Minneapolis: University of Minnesota Press [11].

BROWN, R. W. & FRASER, C. (1963) The acquisition of syntax. In C. N. Cofer and B. S. Musgrave (Eds.) *Verbal Behavior and Learning: Problems and Processes*. New York: McGraw-Hill [11].

BROWN, R. W. & MCNEIL, D. (1966) The "tip of the tongue" phenomenon. *Journal of Verbal Learning and Verbal Behavior*, 5, 325-37 [6].

BRUCE, D. & CROWLEY, J. J. (1970) Acoustic similarity effects on retrieval from secondary memory. *Journal of Verbal Learning and Verbal Behavior*, 9, 190-96 [6].

BRUNER, J. S., GOODNOW, J. J., & AUSTIN, G. A. (1956) *A Study of Thinking*. New York: Wiley [12].

BRYDEN, M. P. (1971) Attention strategies and short-term memory in dichotic listening. *Cognitive Psychology*, 2, 99-116 [7].

BUGELSKI, B. R. (1948) An attempt to reconcile unlearning and reproductive inhibition explanations of proactive inhibition. *Journal of Experimental Psychology*, 38, 670-82 [4].

CAIRNS, H. S. & FOSS, D. J. (1971) Falsification of the hypothesis that word frequency is a unified variable in sentence processing. *Journal of Verbal Learning and Verbal Behavior*, 10, 41-43 [11].

CATANIA, A. C. (Ed.) (1968) *Contemporary Research in Operant Behavior*. Glenview, Ill.: Scott, Foresman and Company [3].

CAVANAUGH, J. P. (1972) Relation between the immediate memory span and the memory search rate. *Psychological Review*, 79, 525-30 [7].

CHERRY, E. C. (1953) Some experiments on the recognition of speech with one and with two ears. *Journal of the Acoustical Society of America*, 25, 975-79 [7]

CHOMSKY, N. (1957) *Syntactic Structures*. The Hague: Mouton [1, 10, 11, 13].

CHOMSKY, N. (1961) Some methodological remarks on generative grammar. *Word*, 17, 219-39 [10].

CHOMSKY, N. (1965) *Aspects of the Theory of Syntax*. Cambridge: MIT Press [1, 10, 11, 13].

CHOMSKY, N. & HALLE, M. (1968) *The Sound Pattern of English*. New York: Harper and Row [9].

CIEUTAT, V. J., STOCKWELL, F. E., & NOBLE, C. E. (1958) The interaction of ability and amount of practice with stimulus and response meaningfulness (*m, m'*) in paired-associate learning. *Journal of Experimental Psychology*, 56, 193-202 [4].

CLARK, H. H. (1969a) Linguistic processes in deductive reasoning. *Psychological Review*, 76, 387-404 [11].

CLARK, H. H. (1969b) Influence of language on solving three-term series problems. *Journal of Experimental Psychology*, 82, 205-15 [11].

CLARK, H. H. & CARD, S. K. (1969) Role of sentences. *Journal of Experimental Psychology*, 82, 545-53 [11].

CLIFTON, C. & ODOM, P. (1966) Similarity relations among certain English sentence constructions. *Psychological Monographs*, 80, 5 (Whole No. 613) [10].

COBB, N. J. (1965) *Reversal and nonreversal shift learning in children as a function of two types of pretraining*. Ph.D. dissertation, University of Massachusetts [12].

COFER, C. N. (1960) An experimental analysis of the role of context in verbal behavior. *Transactions of the New York Academy of Sciences*, 22, 341-47 [8].

COFER, C. N. (1965) On some factors in the organizational characteristics of free recall. *American Psychologist*, 20, 261-72 [8].

COFER, C. N. (1966) Some evidence for coding processes derived from clustering in free recall. *Journal of Verbal Learning and Verbal Behavior*, 5, 188-92 [8].

COFER, C. N., BRUCE, D. R., & REICHER, G. M. (1966) Clustering in free recall as a function of certain methodological variations. *Journal of Experimental Psychology*, 71, 858-66 [8].

COFER, C. N. & FOLEY, J. P. (1942) Mediated generalization and the interpretation of verbal behavior: I. Prolegomena. *Psychological Review*, 49, 513-40 [2].

COHEN, B. H. (1963a) An investigation of recoding in free recall. *Journal of Experimental Psychology*, 65, 368-76 [8].

COHEN, B. H. (1963b) Recall of categorized word lists. *Journal of Experimental Psychology*, 66, 227-34 [8].

COHEN, B. H. (1966) Some-or-none characteristics of coding behavior. *Journal of Verbal Learning and Verbal Behavior*, 5, 182-87 [8].

COLEMAN, E. B. (1964) The comprehensibility of several grammatical transformations. *Journal of Applied Psychology*, 43, 186-90 [11].

COLEMAN, E. B. (1965) Responses to a scale of grammaticalness. *Journal of Verbal Learning and Verbal Behavior*, 4, 521-27 [10].

COLLINS, A. M. & QUILLIAN, M. R. (1969) Retrieval time from semantic memory. *Journal of Verbal Learning and Verbal Behavior*, 8, 240-47 [8].

COLLINS, A. M. & QUILLIAN, M. R. (1970) Does category size affect categorization time? *Journal of Verbal Learning and Verbal Behavior*, 9, 432-38 [8].

CONRAD, C. (1972) Cognitive economy in semantic memory. *Journal of Experimental Psychology*, 92, 149-54 [8].

CONRAD, R. (1964) Acoustic confusions in immediate memory. *British Journal of Psychology*, 55, 75-83 [6].

COONS, E. E. & MILLER, N. E. (1960) Conflict versus consolidation of memory to explain "retrograde amnesia" produced by ECS. *Journal of Comparative and Physiological Psychology,* 53, 524-31 **[6]**.

CRAIK, F. I. M. & LOCKHART, R. S. (1972) Levels of processing: A framework for memory research. *Journal of Verbal Learning and Verbal Behavior,* 11, 671-84 **[6, 13]**.

CROWDER, R. G. (1972) Visual and auditory memory. In J. F. Kavanaugh and I. G. Mattingly (Eds.) *Language by Ear and by Eye.* Cambridge: MIT Press **[7]**.

CROWDER, R. G. & MORTON, J. (1969) Precategorical acoustic storage (PAS). *Perception and Psychophysics,* 5, 365-73 **[7]**.

CURRY, F. K. W. (1967) A comparison of left-handed and right-handed subjects on verbal and non-verbal dichotic tasks. *Cortex,* 3, 343-52 **[9]**.

DANKS, J. H. (1969) Grammaticalness and meaningfulness in the comprehension of sentences. *Journal of Verbal Learning and Verbal Behavior,* 8, 687-96 **[10]**.

DARWIN, C. (1859) *On the Origin of the Species.* Reprinted. Cambridge: Harvard University Press (1964) **[2]**.

DARWIN, C. (1872) *The Expression of the Emotions in Man and Animals.* London: Murray **[2]**.

DARWIN, C. J. (1971) Ear differences in the recall of fricatives and vowels. *Quarterly Journal of Experimental Psychology,* 23, 46-62 **[9]**.

DAVIDSON, W. S. II (1974) Studies of aversive conditioning for alcoholics: A critical review of theory and research methodology. *Psychological Bulletin,* 81, 571-81 **[3]**.

DAVIDSON, W. S., II & SEIDMAN, E. (1974) Studies of behavior modification and juvenile delinquency: A review, methodological critique, and social perspective. *Psychological Bulletin,* 81, 998-1011 **[3]**.

DEESE, J. (1959) Influence of inter-item associative strength upon immediate free recall. *Psychological Reports,* 5, 305-12 **[8]**.

DEESE, J. (1961) From the isolated verbal unit to connected discourse. In C. N. Cofer (Ed.) *Verbal Learning and Verbal Behavior.* New York: McGraw-Hill **[8]**.

DEESE, J. (1968) Association and memory. In T. R. Dixon and D. L. Horton (Eds.) *Verbal Behavior and General Behavior Theory,* Englewood Cliffs, N.J.: Prentice-Hall **[8]**.

DEESE, J. & HULSE, S. (1967) *The Psychology of Learning* (3rd ed.) New York: McGraw-Hill **[4, 8]**.

DELATTRE, P. C., LIBERMAN, A. M., & COOPER, F. S. (1955) Acoustic loci and transitional cues for consonants. *Journal of the Acoustical Society of America,* 27, 769-73 **[9]**.

DEMBER, W. N. & JENKINS, J. J. (1970) *General Psychology: Modeling Behavior and Experience.* Englewood Cliffs, N.J.: Prentice-Hall **[10]**.

DESNOO, K. (1937) Das trinkende kind im uterus. *Monatschrift für Geburtsch und Gynak,* 105, 88 **[3]**.

DEUTSCH, J. A. (1960) *The Structural Basis of Behavior.* Chicago: University of Chicago Press [3].

DEUTSCH, J. A. & DEUTSCH, D. (1963) Attention: Some theoretical considerations. *Psychological Review,* 70, 80-90 [7].

DEWS, P. B. (1955) Modification by drugs of performance on simple schedules of positive reinforcement. *Annals of the New York Academy of Sciences,* 65, 266-81 [3].

DODD, D. H. (1967) Transfer effects from rule learning to logical problems. *Cognitive Processes Report* No. 105, University of Colorado: Mimeo [12].

DONDERS, F. C. (1868) Over de snelheid van psychische processen. Onderzoekingen gedaan in het Physiologisch Laboratorium der Utrechtsche Hoogeschool, 1868-1869, Tweede reeks 11, 92-120. Translated by W. G. Koster in W. G. Koster (Ed.) *Attention and Performance* II. Acta Psychologica, 1969, 30, 412-31 [7].

DOWNEY, R. G. & HAKES, D. T. (1968) Some psychological effects of violating linguistic rules. *Journal of Verbal Learning and Verbal Behavior,* 7, 158-61 [10].

DULANY, D. E. (1968) Awareness, rules, and propositional control: A confrontation with S-R behavior theory. In T. R. Dixon and D. L. Horton (Eds.) *Verbal Behavior and General Behavior Theory.* Englewood Cliffs, N.J.: Prentice-Hall [3].

EARHARD, M. (1969) Storage and retrieval of words encoded in memory. *Journal of Experimental Psychology,* 80, 412-18 [8].

EBBINGHAUS, H. (1885) *Memory.* Translated by H. A. Ruger and C. E. Bussenius. New York: Teachers College, 1913. Paperback edition, New York: Dover, 1964 [1, 2, 4, 5, 6].

EBENHOLTZ, S. M. (1963) Serial learning: Position learning and sequential associations. *Journal of Experimental Psychology,* 66, 353-62 [4].

EBENHOLTZ, S. M. (1966) The serial position effect of ordered stimulus dimensions in paired-associate learning. *Journal of Experimental Psychology,* 71, 132-37 [4].

EIMAS, P. D., SIQUELAND, E. R., JUSCZYK, P., & VIGORITO, J. (1971) Speech perception in early infancy. *Science,* 171, 303-6 [9].

EIMAS, P. & ZEAMAN, D. (1963) Response speed changes in an Estes' paired-associate "miniature" experiment. *Journal of Verbal Learning and Verbal Behavior,* 1, 384-88 [4].

EKSTRAND, B. (1966) Backward associations. *Psychological Bulletin,* 65, 50-64 [4].

ELLIS, H. C. (1965) *The Transfer of Learning.* New York: Macmillan [5].

EPSTEIN, W. (1961) The influence of syntactic structure on learning. *American Journal of Psychology,* 74, 80-85 [10].

EPSTEIN, W. (1969) Recall of word lists following learning of sentences and of anomalous and random strings. *Journal of Verbal Learning and Verbal Behavior,* 8, 20-25 [11].

ERICKSON, J. R. & ZAJKOWSKI, M. M. (1967) Learning several concept-identification problems concurrently: A test of the sampling-with-replacement assumption. *Journal of Experimental Psychology,* 74, 212-18 **[12]**.

ERICKSON, J. R., ZAJKOWSKI, M. M., & EHRMANN, E. D. (1966) All-or-none assumptions in concept identification: Analysis of latency data. *Journal of Experimental Psychology,* 72, 690-97 **[12]**.

ERIKSEN, C. W. & JOHNSON, H. J. (1964) Storage and decay characteristics of non-attended stimuli. *Journal of Experimental Psychology,* 68, 28-36 **[7]**.

ERVIN-TRIPP, S. (1964) Limitation and structural change in children's language. In E. H. Lenneberg (Ed.) *New Directions in the Study of Language.* Cambridge: MIT Press **[11]**.

ESTES, W. K. (1960) Learning theory and the new mental chemistry. *Psychological Review,* 67, 207-23 **[4]**.

ESTES, W. K., HOPKINS, B. L., & CROTHERS, E. J. (1960) All-or-none and conservation effects in the learning and retention of paired-associates. *Journal of Experimental Psychology,* 60, 329-39 **[4]**.

EYSENCK, H. J. (1961) The effects of psychotherapy. *Handbook of Abnormal Psychology.* New York: Basic Books **[3]**.

FAGAN, J. F., III (1970) Memory in the infant. *Journal of Experimental Child Psychology,* 9, 217-26 **[7]**.

FANTZ, R. L. (1963) Pattern vision in newborn infants. *Science,* 140, 296-97 **[3]**.

FECHNER, G. T. (1860) *Elemente der Psychophysik.* Leipzig: Breitkopf and Hartel **[1]**.

FEHRER, E. & RAAB, D. (1962) Reaction time to stimuli masked by metacontrast. *Journal of Experimental Psychology,* 63, 143-47 **[7]**.

FEIGENBAUM, E. A. & SIMON, H. A. (1962) A theory of the serial position effect. *British Journal of Psychology,* 53, 307-20 **[4]**.

FELDMAN, S. M. & UNDERWOOD, B. J. (1957) Stimulus recall following paired-associate learning. *Journal of Experimental Psychology,* 53, 11-15 **[4]**.

FERSTER, C. B., CULBERTSON, S., & BOREN, M. C. P. (1975) *Behavior Principles* (2nd ed.) Englewood Cliffs, N.J.: Prentice-Hall **[3]**.

FERSTER, C. B. & SIMMONS, J. (1966) Behavior therapy with children. *Psychological Record,* 16, 65-71 **[3]**.

FERSTER, C. B. & SKINNER, B. F. (1957) *Schedules of Reinforcement.* Englewood Cliffs, N.J.: Prentice-Hall **[2, 3]**.

FILLMORE, C. J. (1968) The case for case. In E. Bach and R. T. Harms (Eds.) *Universals in Linguistic Theory.* New York: Holt, Rinehart & Winston **[11]**.

FODOR, J. A. & BEVER, T. G. (1965) The psychological reality of linguistic segments. *Journal of Verbal Learning and Verbal Behavior,* 4, 414-20 **[10]**.

FODOR, J. A. & GARRETT, M. (1966) Some reflections on competence and performance. In J. Lyons and R. J .Wales (Eds.) *Psycholinguistics Papers.* Edinburgh: University of Edinburgh Press **[11]**.

FODOR, J. A. & GARRETT, M. (1967) Some syntactic determinants of sentential complexity. *Perception and Psychophysics,* 2, 289-96 **[11]**.

FODOR, J. A., GARRETT, M., & BEVER, T. G. (1968) Some syntactic determinants of sentential complexity, II: Verb structure. *Perception and Psychophysics,* 3, 453-61 **[11]**.

FOSS, D. J. (1969) Decision processes during sentence comprehension: Effects of lexical item difficulty and position upon decision times. *Journal of Verbal Learning and Verbal Behavior,* 8, 457-62 **[11]**.

FOSS, D. J. (1970) Some effects of ambiguity upon sentence comprehension. *Journal of Verbal Learning and Verbal Behavior,* 9, 699-706 **[11]**.

FOSS, D. J. & LYNCH, R. H., JR. (1969) Decision processes during sentence comprehension: Effects of surface structure on decision times. *Perception and Psychophysics,* 5, 145-48 **[11]**.

FOULKE, E. (1971) The perception of time compressed speech. In D. L. Horton and J. J. Jenkins (Eds.) *The Perception of Language.* Columbus, Ohio: Charles E. Merrill **[9]**.

FRANKS, J. J. & BRANSFORD, J. D. (1971) Abstraction of visual patterns. *Journal of Experimental Psychology,* 90, 65-74 **[12]**.

FREUD, S. (1938) *The Basic Writings of Sigmund Freud.* Translated and edited by A. A. Brill. New York: Modern Library **[2]**.

FRIJDA, N. H. (1972) The simulation of human memory. *Psychological Bulletin,* 77, 1-31 **[8]**.

FROMKIN, V. A. (1970) Tips of the slung or to err is human. University of California at Los Angeles: *Working Papers in Phonetics,* 14, 40-79 **[9]**.

FUSTER, J. M. (1958) Effects of stimulation of brain stem on tachistoscopic perception. *Science,* 127, 150 **[7]**.

GALTON, F. (1883) *Inquiries into Human Faculty and Its Development.* London: Macmillan **[8]**.

GARRETT, M., BEVER, T. G., & FODOR, J. A. (1966) The active use of grammar in speech perception. *Perception and Psychophysics,* 1, 30-32 **[10]**.

GERICKE, O. L. (1965) Practical use of operant conditioning procedures in a mental hospital. *Psychiatric Studies and Projects,* 3, 3-10 **[3]**.

GIBSON, E. J. (1940) A systematic application of the concepts of generalization and differentiation to verbal learning. *Psychological Review,* 47, 196-229 **[4]**.

GLANZER, M. (1969) Distance between related words in free recall: Trace of the STS. *Journal of Verbal Learning and Verbal Behavior,* 8, 105-11 **[6]**.

GLANZER, M. & CLARK, W. H. (1963) Accuracy of perceptual recall: An analysis of organization. *Journal of Verbal Learning and Verbal Behavior,* 1, 289-99 **[8]**.

GLANZER, M. & CUNITZ, A. R. (1966) Two storage mechanisms in free recall. *Journal of Verbal Learning and Verbal Behavior,* 5, 351-60 **[6, 8]**.

GLANZER, M. & DOLINSKY, R. (1965) The anchor for the serial position curve. *Journal of Verbal Learning and Verbal Behavior,* 4, 267-73 **[4]**.

GLANZER, M. & MEINZER, A. (1967) The effects of intralist activity on free recall. *Journal of Verbal Learning and Verbal Behavior*, 6, 928-35 **[8]**.

GLANZER, M. & PETERS, S. C. (1962) A re-examination of the serial position effect. *Journal of Experimental Psychology*, 64, 258-66 **[4]**.

GLAZE, J. A. (1928) The association value of nonsense syllables. *Journal of Genetic Psychology*, 35, 255-69 **[4]**.

GLUCKSBERG, S. & DANKS, J. H. (1969) Grammatical structure and recall: A function of the space in immediate memory or of recall delay. *Perception and Psychophysics*, 6, 113-17 **[11]**.

GONZALEZ, R. C. & COFER, C. N. (1959) Exploratory studies of verbal context by means of clustering in free recall. *Journal of Genetic Psychology*, 95, 293-320 **[8]**.

GOSS, A. E. (1965) Manifest strengthening of correct responses of paired-associates under post-criterion zero percent occurrence of response members. *Journal of General Psychology*, 72, 135-44 **[4]**.

GOUGH, P. B. (1965) Grammatical transformations and speed of understanding. *Journal of Verbal Learning and Verbal Behavior*, 4, 107-11 **[10]**.

GOUGH, P. B. (1966) The verification of sentences: The effects of delay of evidence and sentence length. *Journal of Verbal Learning and Verbal Behavior*, 5, 492-96 **[10]**.

GOUGH, P. B. (1971) Experimental psycholinguistics. In W. O. Dingwall (Ed.) *A Survey of Linguistic Science*. College Park: University of Maryland **[11]**.

GRAY, J. A. & WEDDERBURN, A. A. I. (1960) Grouping strategies with simultaneous stimuli. *Quarterly Journal of Experimental Psychology*, 12, 180-84 **[7]**.

GREENBERG, J. H. & JENKINS, J. J. (1964) Studies in the psychological correlates of the sound system of American English. *Word*, 20, 157-77 **[9, 12]**.

GREENSPOON, J. (1955) The reinforcing effect of two spoken sounds on the frequency of two responses. *American Journal of Psychology*, 68, 409-16 **[3, 9]**.

GRICE, G. R. & DAVIS, J. D. (1958) Mediated stimulus equivalence and distinctiveness in human conditioning. *Journal of Experimental Psychology*, 55, 565-71 **[2]**.

GUROWITZ, E. M. (1969) *The Molecular Basis of Memory*. Englewood Cliffs, N.J.: Prentice-Hall **[6]**.

GUTHRIE, E. R. (1935) *The Psychology of Learning*. New York: Harper & Row. **[4]**.

GUTHRIE, E. R. (1940) Association and the law of effect. *Psychological Review*, 47, 127-48 **[13]**.

GUTTMAN, N. & JULESZ, B. (1963) Lower limits of auditory periodicity analysis. *Journal of the Acoustical Society of America*, 35, 610 **[7]**.

GYNTHER, M. D. (1957) Differential eyelid conditioning as a function of stimulus similarity and strength of response to the CS. *Journal of Experimental Psychology*, 53, 408-16 **[2]**.

HAKES, D. T. (1971) Does verb structure affect sentence comprehension? *Perception and Psychophysics,* 10, 229-32 **[11]**.

HAKES, D. T. & CAIRNS, H. S. (1970) Sentence comprehension and relative pronouns. *Perception and Psychophysics,* 8, 5-8 **[11]**.

HAKES, D. T. & FOSS, D. J. (1970) Decision processes during sentence comprehension: Effects of surface structure reconsidered. *Perception and Psychophysics,* 8, 413-16 **[11]**.

HAKES, D. T., JAMES, C. T., & YOUNG, R. K. (1964) A reexamination of the Ebbinghaus derived list paradigm. *Journal of Experimental Psychology,* 68, 508-14 **[4]**.

HALWES, T. G. (1969) *Effects of Dichotic Fusion in the Perception of Speech.* Unpublished Ph. D. Thesis, University of Minnesota **[9]**.

HANSON, H. M. (1959) Effects of discrimination training on stimulus generalization. *Journal of Experimental Psychology,* 58, 321-34 **[2]**.

HARCUM, E. R. (1953) Verbal transfer of overlearned forward and backward associations. *American Journal of Psychology,* 66, 622-25 **[4]**.

HARLOW, H. F. (1949) The formation of learning sets. *Psychological Review,* 56, 51-65 **[2, 5]**.

HARLOW, H. F. & SUOMI, S. J. (1970) Nature of love—simplified. *American Psychologist,* 25, 161-68 **[3]**.

HAUGAN, G. M. (1970) The effects of reinforcement on conditioning of infant vocalizations. Unpublished doctoral dissertation, University of Maryland **[3]**.

HAYGOOD, R. C. & BOURNE, L. E., JR. (1965) Attribute- and rule-learning aspects of conceptual behavior. *Psychological Review,* 72, 175-95 **[12]**.

HAYGOOD, R. C. & STEVENSON, M. (1967) Effects of number of irrelevant dimensions in nonconjunctive concept learning. *Journal of Experimental Psychology,* 74, 302-4 **[12]**.

HEAPS, R. S., GREENE, W. A., & CHENEY, C. D. (1968) Transfer from serial to paired-associate learning with two paired-associate rates. *Journal of Verbal Learning and Verbal Behavior,* 7, 840-41 **[4]**.

HEBB, D. O. (1949) *The Organization of Behavior.* New York: Wiley **[5, 6, 7]**.

HEBB, D. O. (1961) Distinctive features of learning in the higher animal. In J. F. Delafresnaye (Ed.) *Brain Mechanisms and Learning.* London and New York: Oxford University Press, 37-46 **[6]**.

HECAEN, H. (1969) Clinico-anatomical and neurolinguistic aspects of aphasia. In G. A. Talland and N. C. Waugh (Eds.) *The Pathology of Memory.* New York: Academic Press, 9-28 **[6]**.

HELLYER, S. (1962) Supplementary report: Frequency of stimulus presentation and short-term decrement in recall. *Journal of Experimental Psychology,* 64, 650 **[6]**.

HERNÁNDEZ-PEÓN, R., SHERRER, H., & JOUVET, M. (1956) Modification of electrical activity in cochlear nucleus during "attention" in unanesthetized cats. *Science,* 123, 331-32 **[7]**.

HERRNSTEIN, R. J., & MORSE, W. H. (1956) Selective action of pentobarbital on component behaviors of a reinforcement schedule. *Science,* 124, 367-68 **[3]**.

HERSHENSON, M. (1964) Visual discrimination in the human newborn. *Journal of Comparative and Physiological Psychology,* 58, 270-76 **[1, 3]**.

HERSHENSON, M., MUNSINGER, H., & KESSEN, W. (1965) Preferences for shapes of intermediate variability in the newborn human. *Science,* 147, 630-31 **[7]**.

HILGARD, E. R. &. BOWER, G. H. (1966) *Theories of Learning* (3rd ed.) Englewood Cliffs, N.J.: Prentice-Hall **[1, 2]**.

HILGARD, E. R. & BOWER, G. H. (1975) *Theories of Learning* (4th ed.) Englewood Cliffs, N.J.: Prentice-Hall **[6, 13]**.

HINTZMAN, D. L. (1967) Articulatory coding in short-term memory. *Journal of Verbal Learning and Verbal Behavior,* 6, 312-16 **[6]**.

HOBBES, T. (1651) *Leviathan.* Reprinted. New York: Dutton, (1950) **[4]**.

HOROWITZ, L. M., BROWN, Z. M., & WEISSBLUTH, S. (1964) Availability and the direction of associations. *Journal of Experimental Psychology,* 68, 541-49 **[4]**.

HOROWITZ, L. M. & LARSEN, S. R. (1963) Response interference in paired-associate learning. *Journal of Experimental Psychology,* 65, 225-32 **[4]**.

HOROWITZ, L. M. & PRYTULAK, L. S. (1969) Redintegrative memory. *Psychological Review,* 76, 519-31 **[11]**.

HORTON, D. L. & KJELDERGAARD, P. M. (1961) An experimental analysis of associative factors in mediated generalization. *Psychological Monographs,* 75, 11, (Whole 515) **[2, 4, 5]**.

HORTON, D. L., MARLOWE, D., & CROWNE, D. P. (1963) The effect of instructional set and need for social approval on commonality of word association responses. *Journal of Abnormal and Social Psychology,* 66, 67-73 **[8]**.

HORTON, D. L. & TURNAGE, T. W. (1970) Serial to paired-associate learning: Utilization of serial information. *Journal of Experimental Psychology,* 84, 88-95 **[4, 8]**.

HOUSTON, J. P. (1964) Verbal transfer and interlist similarities. *Psychological Review,* 71, 412-16 **[4]**.

HOVLAND, C. I. (1937) The generalization of conditioned responses. I. The sensory generalization of conditioned responses with varying frequencies of tones. *Journal of General Psychology,* 17, 125-48 **[2]**.

HOWES, D. H. (1957) On the relation between probability of a word as an associate and in general linguistic contexts. *Journal of Abnormal and Social Psychology,* 54, 75-85 **[8]**.

HOWES, D. H. & OSGOOD, C. E. (1954) On the combination of associative probability in linguistic contexts. *American Journal of Psychology,* 67, 241-58 **[8]**.

HUBEL, D. H. & WIESEL, T. N. (1962) Receptor fields, binocular interaction, and functional architecture in the cat's visual cortex. *Journal of Physiology,* 160, 106-54 **[1]**.

HUBEL, D. H. & WIESEL, T. N. (1963) Shape and arrangement of columns in cat's striate cortex. *Journal of Physiology,* 165, 559-68 **[1]**.

HUBEL, D. H. & WIESEL, T. N. (1965) Receptive fields and functional architecture in two nonstriate visual areas (18 and 19) of the cat. *Journal of Neurophysiology,* 28, 229-89 **[7]**.

HUDSON, R. L. (1969) Category clustering for immediate and delayed recall as a function of recall cue dominance and response dominance variability. *Journal of Experimental Psychology,* 82, 575-77 **[8]**.

HUGGINS, A. W. F. (1964) Distortion of the temporal pattern of speech: Interruption and alternation. *Journal of the Acoustical Society of America,* 36, 1055-64 **[9]**.

HULL, C. L. (1920) Quantitative aspects of the evolution of concepts. *Psychological Monographs,* 28, (Whole No. 123) **[12]**.

HULL, C. L. (1930) Knowledge and purpose as habit mechanisms. *Psychological Review,* 57, 511-25 **[12]**.

HULL, C. L. (1933) The meaningfulness of 320 selected nonsense syllables. *American Journal of Psychology,* 45, 730-34 **[4]**.

HULL, C. L. (1934) The concept of the habit-family hierarchy and maze learning. *Psychological Review,* 41, 33-54; 134-52 **[8]**.

HULL, C. L. (1935) The conflicting psychologies of learning—a way out. *Psychological Review,* 42, 491-516 **[4]**.

HULL, C. L. (1939) The problem of stimulus equivalence in behavior theory. *Psychological Review,* 46, 9-30 **[2, 12]**.

HULL, C. L. (1943) *Principles of Behavior.* Englewood Cliffs, N.J.: Prentice-Hall **[4, 5, 13]**.

HULL, C. L. (1951) *Essentials of Behavior.* New Haven: Yale University Press **[13]**.

HULL, C. L. (1952) *A Behavior System.* New Haven: Yale University Press **[1, 4, 5, 13]**.

HUNT, E. B. (1962) *Concept Learning: An Information Processing Problem.* New York: Wiley **[12]**.

HUNT, E. B., MARIN, J. & STONE, P. J. (1966) *Experiments in Induction.* New York: Academic Press **[12, 13]**.

HUXLEY, A. L. (1946) *Brave New World.* New York: Harper **[3]**.

HYDE, T. S. & JENKINS, J. J. (1969) Differential effects of incidental tasks on the organization of recall of a list of highly associated words. *Journal of Experimental Psychology,* 82, 472-81 **[8]**.

HYDÉN, H. (1970) The question of a molecular basis for a memory trace. In K. H. Pribram and D. E. Broadbent (Eds.) *Biology of Memory.* New York: Academic Press **[6]**.

IRWIN, O. C. (1946) Infant speech: Equations for consonant-vowel ratios. *Journal of Speech Disorders,* 11, 177-80 **[9]**.

ISAACS, W., THOMAS, J., & GOLDIAMOND, I. (1960) Application of operant conditioning to reinstate verbal behavior in psychotics. *Journal of Speech and Hearing Disorders*, 25, 8-12 **[3]**.

JAKOBSON, R. (1941) *Kindersprache, Aphasie, und allgemeine Lautgesetze.* Uppsala: Almgvist and Wiksell, 1941. (English translation by A. Keiler, Child Language, Aphasia, and General Sound Laws. The Hague: Mouton, 1968) **[9]**.

JAKOBSON, R., FANT, G. & HALLE, M. (1963) *Preliminaries to Speech Analysis.* Massachusetts Institute of Technology Press: Cambridge, Massachusetts **[9]**.

JAMES, W. (1890) *The Principles of Psychology.* New York: Holt **[6, 7]**.

JEFFERY, W. E. (1965) Variables affecting reversal-shifts in young children. *American Journal of Psychology*, 78, 589-95 **[12]**.

JENKINS, J. G. & DALLENBACH, K. M. (1924) Obliviscence during sleep and waking. *American Journal of Psychology*, 35, 605-12 **[5]**.

JENKINS, J. J. (1959) Effects on word-association of the set to give popular responses. *Psychological Reports*, 5, 94 **[8]**.

JENKINS, J. J. (1963) Stimulus "fractionation" in paired-associate learning. *Psychological Reports*, 13, 409-10 **[4]**.

JENKINS, J. J. (1966) Meaningfulness and concepts; concepts and meaningfulness. In H. J. Klausmeier and C. W. Harris (Eds.) *Analyses of Concept Learning.* New York: Academic Press **[12, 13]**.

JENKINS, J. J. (1974) Can we have a theory of meaningful memory? In R. L. Solso (Ed.) *Theories in Cognitive Psychology: The Loyola Symposium.* New York: Lawrence Erlbaum Associates **[8]**.

JENKINS, J. J. & BAILEY, V. C. (1964) Cue selection and mediated transfer in paired-associate learning. *Journal of Experimental Psychology*, 67, 101-2 **[4]**.

JENKINS, J. J., MINK, W. D., & RUSSELL, W. A. (1958) Associative clustering as a function of verbal association strength. *Psychological Reports*, 4, 127-36 **[8]**.

JENKINS, J. J. & RUSSELL, W. A. (1952) Associative clustering during recall. *Journal of Abnormal and Social Psychology*, 47, 818-21 **[8]**.

JENNINGS, H. S. (1906) *Behavior in the Lower Organisms.* New York: Columbia University Press **[2]**.

JENSEN, A. R. (1962a) Temporal and spatial effects of serial position. *American Journal of Psychology*, 75, 390-400 **[4]**.

JENSEN, A. R., (1962b) Transfer between paired associate and serial learning. *Journal of Verbal Learning and Verbal Behavior*, 1, 269-80 **[4]**.

JOHNSON, N. F. (1965) The psychological reality of phrase-structure rules. *Journal of Verbal Learning and Verbal Behavior*, 4, 469-75 **[10]**.

JOHNSON, P. J. & WHITE, R. M., JR. (1967) Concept of dimensionality and reversal shift performance in children. *Journal of Experimental Child Psychology*, 5, 223-27 **[12]**.

KAGAN, J. (1967) The growth of the "face" schema: Theoretical significance and methodological issues. In J. Hellmuth (Ed.) *Exceptional Infant,* Vol 1. *The Normal Infant.* Seattle: Special Child Publications [7].

KAGAN, J., HENKER, B. A., HEN-TOV, A., & LEWIS, M. (1966) Infant's differential reactions to familiar and distorted faces. *Child Development,* 37, 519-32 [7].

KAHNEMAN, D. (1973) *Attention and Effort.* Englewood Cliffs, N.J.: Prentice-Hall [7].

KANFER, F. H. (1968) Verbal conditioning: A review of its current status. In T. R. Dixon and D. L. Horton (Eds.) *Verbal Behavior and General Behavior Theory.* Englewood Cliffs, N.J.: Prentice-Hall [3].

KATZ, J. J. (1964) Semi-sentences. In J. A. Fodor and J. J. Katz (Eds.) *The Structure of Language.* Englewood Cliffs, N.J.: Prentice-Hall [10].

KATZ, J. J. (1966) *The Philosophy of Language.* New York: Harper and Row [10, 11].

KATZ, J. J. & POSTAL, P. M. (1964) *An Integrated Theory of Linguistic Descriptions.* Cambridge: MIT Press [10, 11].

KENDLER, H. H. & KENDLER, T. S. (1962) Vertical and horizontal processes in problem-solving. *Psychological Review,* 69, 1-16 [12].

KENDLER, T. S. & KENDLER, H. H. (1959) Reversal and non-reversal shifts in kindergarten children. *Journal of Experimental Psychology,* 58, 56-60 [2].

KEPPEL, G. (1964) Retroactive inhibition of serial lists as a function of the presence or absence of positional cues. *Journal of Verbal Learning and Verbal Behavior,* 3, 511-17 [4].

KEPPEL, G. (1968) Retroactive and proactive inhibition. In T. R. Dixon and D. L. Horton (Eds.) *Verbal Behavior and General Behavior Theory.* Englewood Cliffs, N.J.: Prentice-Hall [5].

KEPPEL, G. & SAUFLEY, W. A., JR. (1964) Serial position as a stimulus in serial learning. *Journal of Verbal Learning and Verbal Behavior,* 3, 335-43 [4].

KEPPEL, G. & UNDERWOOD, B. J. (1962) Proactive inhibition in short-term retention of single items. *Journal of Verbal Learning and Verbal Behavior,* 1, 153-61 [6].

KIMBLE, G. A. (1961) *Hilgard and Marquis' Conditioning and Learning.* Englewood Cliffs, N.J.: Prentice-Hall [2, 3, 4].

KIMURA, D. (1961a) Cerebral dominance and the perception of verbal stimuli. *Canadian Journal of Psychology,* 15, 166-71 [9].

KIMURA, D. (1961b) Some effects of temporal-lobe damage on auditory perception. *Canadian Journal of Psychology,* 15, 156-65 [9].

KIMURA, D. (1962) Perceptual and memory functions of the left temporal lobe: A reply to Dr. Inglis. *Canadian Journal of Psychology,* 16, 18-22 [9].

KIMURA, D. (1964) Left-right differences in the perception of melodies. *Quarterly Journal of Experimental Psychology,* 14, 355-58 [9].

KIMURA, D. (1967) Functional asymmetry of the brain in dichotic listening. *Cortex,* 3, 163-78 [9].

KINTSCH, W. & BUSCHKE, H. (1969) Homophones and synonyms in short-term memory. *Journal of Experimental Psychology,* 80, 403-7 **[6]**.

KJELDERGAARD, P. M. (1968) Transfer and mediation in verbal learning. In T. R. Dixon and D. L. Horton (Eds.) *Verbal Behavior and General Behavior Theory.* Englewood Cliffs, N.J.: Prentice-Hall **[5]**.

KOFFKA, K. (1935) *Principles of Gestalt Psychology.* New York: Harcourt, Brace, and World **[13]**.

KÖHLER, W. (1925) *The Mentality of Apes.* (Translated by E. Winter) New York: Harcourt, Brace and World **[2]**.

KOPPENAAL, R. J. (1963) Time changes in strengths of A-B, A-C lists; spontaneous recovery? *Journal of Verbal Learning and Verbal Behavior,* 2, 310-19 **[5]**.

KRUEGER, L. (1970) Visual comparisons in a redundant display. *Cognitive Psychology,* 1, 341-57 **[8]**.

KRUEGER, W. C. R. (1934) The relative difficulty of nonsense syllables. *Journal of Experimental Psychology,* 17, 145-53 **[4]**.

KUENNE, M. R. (1946) Experimental investigation of the relation of language to transposition behavior in young children. *Journal of Experimental Psychology,* 36, 471-90 **[2]**.

KUHN, T. S. (1962) *The Structure of Scientific Revolutions.* Chicago: University of Chicago Press **[1]**.

KUSHNER, M. (1965) The reduction of a long-standing fetish by means of aversive conditioning. In L. P. Ullmann and L. Krasner (Eds.) *Case Studies in Behavior Modification.* New York: Holt, Rinehart and Winston **[3]**.

DELAGUNA, G. A. (1927) *Speech: Its Function and Development.* New Haven: Yale University Press **[11]**.

LAMBERT, W. & JAKOBOVITZ, L. (1960) Verbal satiation and changes in the intensity of meaning. *Journal of Experimental Psychology,* 60, 376-83 **[8]**.

LAMBERT, W. E. & PAIVIO, A. (1956) The influence of noun-adjective order on learning. *Canadian Journal of Psychology,* 10, 9-12 **[8]**.

LANDO, H. A. (1975) A comparison of excessive and rapid smoking in the modification of chronic smoking behavior. *Journal of Consulting and Clinical Psychology,* in press **[3]**.

LASHLEY, K. S. (1951) The problem of serial order in behavior. In L. A. Jeffress (Ed.) *Cerebral Mechanisms in Behavior.* New York: Wiley **[9]**.

LAUGHLIN, P. R. & JORDAN, R. M. (1967) Selection strategies in conjunctive, disjunctive, and biconditional concept attainment. *Journal of Experimental Psychology,* 75, 188-93 **[12]**.

LAWRENCE, D. H. (1949) Acquired distinctiveness of cues: I. Transfer between discriminations on the basis of familiarity with the stimulus. *Journal of Experimental Psychology,* 39, 770-84 **[7]**.

LAWRENCE, D. H. (1950) Acquired distinctiveness of cues: II. Selective association in a constant stimulus situation. *Journal of Experimental Psychology,* 40, 175-78 **[7]**.

LENNEBERG, E. H. (1967) *Biological Foundations of Language.* New York: Wiley **[3, 9, 11]**.

LEOPOLD, W. F. (1949) *Speech Development of a Bilingual Child: A Linguist's Record.* Vol. 3. *Grammar and General Problems in the First Two Years.* Evanston: Northwestern University Press **[11]**.

LEPLEY, W. M. (1934) Serial reactions considered as conditioned reactions. *Psychological Monographs,* 46, No. 205 **[4]**.

LEVINE, M. (1962) Cue neutralization: The effects of random reinforcements upon discrimination learning. *Journal of Experimental Psychology,* 63, 438-43 **[12]**.

LEVINE, M. (1966) Hypothesis behavior by humans during discrimination learning. *Journal of Experimental Psychology,* 71, 331-36 **[12]**.

LEVINE, M. (1969) The latency-choice discrepancy in concept learning. *Journal of Experimental Psychology,* 82, 1-3 **[12]**.

LEVINE, M. (1970) Human discrimination learning: The subset-sampling assumption. *Psychological Bulletin,* 74, 397-404 **[12]**.

LIBERMAN, A. M. (1957) Some results of research on speech perception. *Journal of the Acoustical Society of America,* 29, 117-23 **[9]**.

LIBERMAN, A. M. (1970) The grammars of speech and language. *Cognitive Psychology,* 1, 301-23 **[9]**.

LIBERMAN, A. M., COOPER, F. S., HARRIS, K. S., & MACNEILAGE, P. F. (1963) A motor theory of speech perception. *Proceedings of the Speech Communication Seminar.* Stockholm: Royal Institute of Technology, D3 **[9]**.

LIBERMAN, A. M., COOPER, F. S., SHANKWEILER, D., & STUDDERT-KENNEDY, M. (1967) Perception of the speech code. *Psychological Review,* 74, 431-61 **[9]**.

LIBERMAN, A. M., DELATTRE, P. C., & COOPER, F. S. (1952) The role of selected stimulus variables in the perception of the unvoiced stop consonants. *American Journal of Psychology,* 65, 497-516 **[9]**.

LIBERMAN, A. M., HARRIS, K. S., HOFFMAN, H. S., & GRIFFITH, B. C. (1957) The discrimination of speech sounds within and across phoneme boundaries. *Journal of Experimental Psychology,* 54, 358-68 **[9]**.

LIBERMAN, A. M., MATTINGLY, I. G., & TURVEY, M. T. (1972) Language codes and memory codes. In A. W. Melton and E. Martin (Eds.) *Coding Processes in Human Memory.* New York: V. H. Winston **[9]**.

LIPSITT, L. P. & KAYE, H. (1964) Conditioned sucking in the human newborn. *Psychonomic Science,* 1, 29-30 **[3]**.

LISKER, L. & ABRAMSON, A. S. (1964) A cross-language study of voicing in initial stops: Acoustical measurements. *Word,* 20, 384-422 **[9]**.

LLOYD, K. E. (1964) Short-term retention as a function of recall point coding. *Psychological Reports,* 14, 752-54 **[8]**.

LORENZ, K. Z. (1937) The companion in the bird's world. *Auk,* 54, 245-73 **[1]**.

LUH, C. W. (1922) The conditions of retention. *Psychological Monographs,* 31, No. 142 [5].

MCADAM, D. W. & WHITAKER, H. A. (1971) Language production: Electro-encephalographic localization in the normal human brain. *Science,* 172, 499-502 [9].

MCCARTHY, D. (1954) Language development in children. In L. Carmichael (Ed.) *Manual of Child Psychology.* New York: Wiley [11].

MCCAWLEY, J. D. (1968) The role of semantics in a grammar. In E. Bach and R. T. Harms (Eds.) *Universals in Linguistic Theory.* New York: Holt, Rinehart and Winston [11].

MCCRARY, J. W. & HUNTER, W. S. (1953) Serial position curves in verbal learning. *Science,* 117, 131-34 [4].

MCGEOCH, J. A. & IRION, A. L. (1952) *The Psychology of Human Learning* (2nd ed.) New York: Longmans [1, 4].

MCGOVERN, J. B. (1964) Extinction of associations in four transfer paradigms. *Psychological Monographs,* 78, No. 16 [5].

MCGUIRE, W. J. (1961) A multiprocess model for paired-associate learning. *Journal of Experimental Psychology,* 62, 335-47 [4].

MCHUGH, A., TURNAGE, T. W., & HORTON, D. L. (1973) Short-term recall as a function of similarity, serial position, and trials. *Journal of Experimental Psychology,* 97, 204-9 [6].

MACKAY, D. G. (1966) To end ambiguous sentences. *Perception and Psychophysics,* 1, 426-36 [10].

MACKAY, D. G. & BEVER, T. G. (1967) In search of ambiguity. *Perception and Psychophysics,* 2, 193-200 [10].

MACKWORTH, J. F. (1970) *Vigilance and Attention: A Signal Detection Approach.* Harmondsworth, Middlesex, England: Penguin Books [7].

MACNAMARA, J. (1972) Cognitive basis of language learning in infants. *Psychological Review,* 79, 1-13 [11].

MCNEILL, D. (1966) Developmental psycholinguistics. In F. Smith and G. A. Miller (Eds.) *The Genesis of Language: A Psycholinguistic Approach.* Cambridge: MIT Press [11].

MCNEILL, D. (1968) On theories of language acquisition. In T. R. Dixon and D. L. Horton (Eds.) *Verbal Behavior and General Behavior Theory.* Englewood Cliffs, N.J.: Prentice-Hall [11].

MCNEILL, D. (1970) *The Acquisition of Language: The Study of Developmental Psycholinguistics,* New York: Harper and Row [9, 11].

MCNEILL, D. & LINDIG, K. (1973) The perceptual reality of phonemes, syllables, words, and sentences. *Journal of Verbal Learning and Verbal Behavior,* 12, 419-30 [9].

MADIGAN, S. A. (1969) Intraserial repetition and coding processes in free recall. *Journal of Verbal Learning and Verbal Behavior,* 8, 828-35 [6].

MANDLER, G. (1967) Organization and memory. In K. W. Spence and J. T. Spence (Eds.) *The Psychology of Learning and Motivation,* Vol. 1. New York: Academic Press [8].

MANDLER, G. (1968) Association and organization: Facts, fancies, and theories. In T. R. Dixon and D. L. Horton (Eds.) *Verbal Behavior and General Behavior Theory,* Englewood Cliffs, N.J.: Prentice-Hall **[8]**.

MANDLER, G. & PEARLSTONE, Z. (1966) Free and constrained concept learning and subsequent recall. *Journal of Verbal Learning and Verbal Behavior,* 5, 126-31 **[8]**.

MARKS, L. E. & MILLER, G. A. (1964) The role of semantic and syntactic constraints in the memorization of English sentences. *Journal of Verbal Learning and Verbal Behavior,* 3, 1-5 **[10]**.

MARQUIS, D. P. (1941) Learning in the neonate: The modification of behavior under three feeding schedules. *Journal of Experimental Psychology,* 29, 263-82 **[3]**.

MARSHALL, G. R. & COFER, C. N. (1963) Associative indices as measures of word relatedness: A summary and comparison of ten methods. *Journal of Verbal Learning and Verbal Behavior,* 1, 408-21 **[8]**.

MARTIN, E. (1965) Transfer of verbal paired associates. *Psychological Review,* 72, 327-43 **[5]**.

MARTIN, J. G. (1968) A comparison of ordinary, anomalous, and scrambled strings. *Journal of Verbal Learning and Verbal Behavior,* 7, 390-95 **[10]**.

MARTIN, J. G. (1971) Some acoustic and grammatical features of spontaneous speech. In D. L. Horton and J. J. Jenkins (Eds.) *The Perception of Language.* Columbus, Ohio: Charles E. Merrill **[10]**.

MARTIN, J. G. (1972) Rhythmic (hierarchical) vs. serial structure in speech and other behavior. *Psychological Review,* 79, 487-509 **[9, 13]**.

MARTIN, J. G. & STRANGE, W. (1968) Determinants of hesitations in spontaneous speech. *Journal of Experimental Psychology,* 76, 474-79 **[10]**.

MASSARO, D. W. (1972) Perceptual and synthesized auditory storage. *Technical Report 72-1,* Wisconsin Mathematical Psychology Program, Madison, Wisconsin **[7, 13]**.

MASSARO, D. W. (1975) *Experimental Psychology and Information Processing.* Chicago: Rand McNally **[7]**.

MATTHEWS, W. A. (1968) Transformational complexity and short-term recall. *Language and Speech,* 11, 120-28 **[11]**.

MATTINGLY, I. G., LIBERMAN, A. M., SYRDAL, A. K., & HALWES, T. (1971) Discrimination in speech and nonspeech modes. *Cognitive Psychology,* 2, 131-57 **[9]**.

MECHANIC, A. (1964) The responses involved in rote learning of verbal materials. *Journal of Verbal Learning and Verbal Behavior,* 3, 30-36 **[8]**.

MEHLER, J. (1963) Some effects of grammatical transformations on the recall of English sentences. *Journal of Verbal Learning and Verbal Behavior,* 2, 346-51 **[10, 11]**.

MEHLER, J. & CAREY, P. (1967) Role of surface and base structure in the perception of sentences. *Journal of Verbal Learning and Verbal Behavior,* 6, 335-38 **[10]**.

MELTON, A. W. (1963) Implications of short-term memory for a general theory of memory. *Journal of Verbal Learning and Verbal Behavior*, 2, 1-21 **[5, 6, 7]**.

MELTON, A. W. (1967) Repetition and retrieval from memory. *Science*, 158, 532 **[6]**.

MELTON, A. W. (1970) The situation with respect to the spacing of repetitions and memory. *Journal of Verbal Learning and Verbal Behavior*, 9, 596-606 **[5, 6]**.

MELTON, A. W. & IRWIN, J. M. (1940) The influence of degree of interpolated learning on retroactive inhibition and the overt transfer of specific responses. *American Journal of Psychology*, 53, 173-203 **[5]**.

MELTON, A. W. & MARTIN, E. (Eds.) (1972) *Coding Processes in Human Memory*. Washington, D.C.: V. H. Winston & Sons **[8]**.

MENYUK, P. (1971) *The Acquisition and Development of Language*. Englewood Cliffs, N.J.: Prentice-Hall **[9, 11]**.

MILLER, G. A. (1951) *Language and Communication*. New York: McGraw-Hill **[9]**.

MILLER, G. A. (1956) The magical number seven, plus or minus two: Some limits on our capacity for processing information. *Psychological Review*, 63, 81-97 **[4, 5, 6, 7, 8]**.

MILLER, G. A. (1962) Some psychological studies of grammar. *American Psychologist*, 17, 748-62 **[11]**.

MILLER, G. A. (1963) Comments on Professor Postman's Paper. In C. N. Cofer and B. S. Musgrave (Eds.) *Verbal Behavior and Learning*. New York: McGraw-Hill **[4]**.

MILLER, G. A. & ISARD, S. (1963) Some perceptual consequences of linguistic rules. *Journal of Verbal Learning and Verbal Behavior*, 2, 217-28 **[10]**.

MILLER, G. A. & MCKEAN, K. O. (1964) A chronometric study of some relations between sentences. *Quarterly Journal of Experimental Psychology*, 16, 297-308 **[11]**.

MILLER, G. A. & NICELY, P. (1955) An analysis of some perceptual confusions among some English consonants. *Journal of the Acoustical Society of America*, 27, 338-52 **[9]**.

MILLER, G. A. & SELFRIDGE, J. A. (1950) Verbal context and the recall of meaningful material. *American Journal of Psychology*, 63, 176-85 **[10]**.

MILLER, W. & ERVIN, S. (1964) The development of grammar in child language In U. Bellugi and R. Brown (Eds.) *The Acquisition of Language*. Monograph of the Society for Research in Child Development, 29, (No. 92), 9-34 **[11]**.

MILNER, B. (1962) Laterality effects in audition. In V. B. Mountcastle (Ed.) *Interhemispheric Relations and Cerebral Dominance*. Baltimore: Johns Hopkins University Press **[9]**.

MILNER, B. (1970) Memory and the medial temporal regions of the brain. In K. H. Pribram and D. E. Broadbent (Eds.) *Biology of Memory*. New York: Academic Press **[6]**.

MILNER, B., TAYLOR, L., & SPERRY, R. W. (1968) Lateralized suppression of dichotically presented digits after commissural section in man. *Science,* 161, 184-85 **[9]**.

MOFFITT, A. (1971) Consonant cue perception by twenty- to twenty-four-week old infants. *Child Development,* 42, 717-31 **[9]**.

MOLFESE, D. L. (1972) *Cerebral asymmetry in infants, children and adults: Auditory evoked responses to speech and noise stimuli.* Ph. D. dissertation, Pennsylvania State University (modified version to appear in Brain and Language, 1975) **[9]**.

MORAY, N. (1959) Attention in dichotic listening: Affective cues and the influence of instructions. *Quarterly Journal of Experimental Psychology,* 11, 56-60 **[7]**.

MORAY, N. (1970) *Attention: Selective Processes in Vision and Audition.* New York: Academic Press **[7]**.

MORAY, N. & BARNETT, T. (1965) Stimulus presentation and methods of scoring in short term memory experiments. *Acta Psychologica,* 24, 253-63 **[7]**.

MORAY, N. & O'BRIEN, T. (1967) Signal detection theory applied to selective listening. *Journal of the Acoustical Society of America,* 42, 765-72 **[7]**.

MORSE, P. A. (1972) The discrimination of speech and nonspeech stimuli in early infancy. *Journal of Experimental Child Psychology,* 14, 477-92 **[9]**.

MORTON, J. (1969) Interaction of information in word recognition. *Psychological Review,* 76, 165-78 **[8, 13]**.

MORTON, J. (1970) A functional model for memory. In D. A. Norman (Ed.) *Models of Memory.* New York: Academic Press **[7]**.

MORTON, J., CROWDER, R. G., & PRUSSIN, H. A. (1971) Experiments with the stimulus suffix effect. *Journal of Experimental Psychology,* 91, 169-90 **[7]**.

MOWRER, O. H. (1960) *Learning Theory and the Symbolic Process.* New York: Wiley **[3]**.

MÜLLER, G. E. & PILZECKER, A. (1900) Experimentelle Beitrage zur lehre vom Gedächtnis. *Zeitschrift fur Psychologie, Ergbd.* 1, 1-300 **[5]**.

MUNSINGER, H. & WEIR, M. W. (1967) Infants' and young children's preference for complexity. *Journal of Experimental Child Psychology,* 5, 69-73 **[7]**.

MURDOCK, B. B., JR. (1958) Backward learning in transfer and learning. *Journal of Experimental Psychology,* 55, 111-14 **[4]**.

MURDOCK, B. B., JR. (1960) The distinctiveness of stimuli. *Psychological Review,* 67, 16-31 **[4]**.

MURDOCK, B. B., JR. (1961) The retention of individual items. *Journal of Experimental Psychology,* 62, 618-25 **[6]**.

MURDOCK, B. B., JR. (1962) The serial position effect of free recall. *Journal of Experimental Psychology,* 64, 482-88 **[6, 8]**.

MURDOCK, B. B., JR. (1972) Short-term memory. In G. H. Bower (Ed.) *Psychology of Learning and Motivation,* Vol. 5, New York: Academic Press **[6]**.

MURDOCK, B. B., JR. & BABICK, A. J. (1961) The effect of repetition on the retention of individual words. *American Journal of Psychology*, 74, 596-601 **[8]**.

MURRAY, D. J. (1968) Articulation and acoustic confusability in short-term memory. *Journal of Experimental Psychology*, 78, 679-84 **[6]**.

NAKAZIMA, S. (1962) A comparative study of the speech developments of Japanese and American English in childhood. *Studia Phonologica*, 2, 27-39 **[9]**.

NEISSER, U. (1967) *Cognitive Psychology*. Englewood Cliffs, N.J.: Prentice-Hall **[7, 9]**.

NEWMAN, S. E. & GRAY, C. W. (1964) S-R vs. R-S recall and R-term vs. S-term recall following paired-associate training. *American Journal of Psychology*, 77, 444-50 **[4]**.

NOBLE, C. E. (1952) An analysis of meaning. *Psychological Review*, 59, 421-30 **[12]**.

NOBLE, C. E. (1952) The role of stimulus meaning (*m*) in serial verbal learning. *Journal of Experimental Psychology*, 43, 437-46 **[4]**.

NOBLE, C. E. (1953) The meaning-familiarity relationship. *Psychological Review*, 60, 89-98 [4].

NOBLE, C. E. (1961) Measurements of association value (*a*), rated asociations (*a'*), and scaled meaningfulness (*m'*) for the 2100 CVC combinations of the English alphabet. *Psychological Reports*, 8, 487-521 **[5]**.

NOBLE, C. E. (1963) Meaningfulness and familiarity. In C. N. Cofer and B. S. Musgrave (Eds.) *Verbal Behavior and Learning*. New York: McGraw-Hill **[4]**.

NOBLE, C. E., STOCKWELL, F. E., & PRYOR, M. W. (1957) Meaningfulness (*m'*) and association value (*a*) in paired-associate syllable learning. *Psychological Reports*, 3, 441-52 **[4]**.

NORMAN, D. A. (1968) Toward a theory of memory and attention. *Psychological Review*, 75, 522-36 **[7]**.

NORMAN, D. A. (1969) *Memory and Attention*. New York: Wiley **[7, 8]**.

NORRIS, E. B. & GRANT D. A (1948) Eyelid conditioning as affected by verbally induced inhibitory set and counter reinforcement. *American Journal of Psychology*, 61, 37-49 **[3]**.

OLTON, R. M (1969) The effect of a mnemonic upon the retention of paired-associate verbal material. *Journal of Verbal Learning and Verbal Behavior*, 8, 43-48 **[8]**.

ORR, D. B., FRIEDMAN, H. L., & WILLIAMS, J. (1965) Trainability of listening comprehension of speeded discourse. *Journal of Educational Psychology*, 56, 148-56 **[9]**.

ORWELL, G. (1949) *Nineteen Eighty-four*. New York: Harcourt, Brace **[3]**.

OSGOOD, C. E. (1949) The similarity paradox in human learning: A resolution. *Psychology Review*, 56, 132-43 **[5]**.

OSGOOD, C. E. (1953) *Method and Theory in Experimental Psychology*. New York: Oxford University Press **[2, 4, 5, 8, 12]**.

OSGOOD, C. E., SUCI, G. J., & TANNENBAUM, P. H. (1957) *The Measurement of Meaning*. Urbana, Illinois: University of Illinois Press [6, 8].

PAIVIO, A. (1965) Abstractness, imagery, and meaningfulness in paired-associate learning. *Journal of Verbal Learning and Verbal Behavior*, 4, 32-38 [8].

PAIVIO, A. (1969) Mental imagery in associative learning and memory. *Psychological Review*, 76, 241-63 [8].

PAVLOV, I. P. (1927) *Conditioned Reflexes*. (Translated by G. V. Anrep) New York: Oxford [1, 2, 3, 5].

PENFIELD, W. & ROBERTS, L. (1959) *Speech and Brain Mechanisms*. Princeton, N. J.: Princeton University Press [9].

PERFETTI, C. A. (1969) Sentence retention and the depth hypothesis. *Journal of Verbal Learning and Verbal Behavior*, 8, 101-4 [11].

PETERSON, L. R. & PETERSON, M. J. (1959) Short-term retention of individual verbal items. *Journal of Experimental Psychology*, 58, 193-98 [6].

PIAGET, J. (1963) Le langage et les opérations intellectuelles. In *Problèmes de Psycho-linguistique* (Symposium de l'association de psychologie scientifique de langue francaise.) Paris: Presses Universitaires de France [11].

PISONI, D. B. (1973) Auditory and phonetic memory codes in the discrimination of consonants and vowels. *Perception and Psychophysics*, 13, 253-60 [9].

POLLACK, I. (1952) The information of elementary auditory displays. *Journal of the Acoustical Society of America*, 24, 745-49 [7].

POSNER, M. I. (1969) Abstraction and the process of recognition. In G. H. Bower and J. T. Spence (Eds.) *Psychology of Learning and Motivation*, Vol. 3. New York: Academic Press [8, 12].

POSNER, M. I. & KEELE, S. W. (1970) Retention of abstract ideas. *Journal of Experimental Psychology*, 83, 304-8 [12].

POSNER, M. I. & WARREN, R. E. (1972) Traces, concepts, and conscious constructions. In A. W. Melton and E. Martin (Eds.) *Coding Processes in Human Memory*. Washington, D.C.: V. H. Winston & Sons [8, 13].

POSTMAN, L. (1961) The present status of interference theory. In C. N. Cofer (Ed.) *Verbal Learning and Verbal Behavior*. New York: McGraw-Hill [5].

POSTMAN, L. (1962) Rewards and punishments in human learning. In L. Postman (Ed.) *Psychology in the Making*. New York: Knopf [2, 3].

POSTMAN, L. (1962) Retention as a function of degree of overlearning. *Science*, 135, 666-67 [6].

POSTMAN, L. (1962) Repetition and paired-associate learning. *American Journal of Psychology*, 75, 372-89 [4].

POSTMAN, L. (1963) One-trial learning. In C. N. Cofer and B. S. Musgrave (Eds.) *Verbal Behavior and Learning*. New York: McGraw-Hill [4].

POSTMAN, L. (1963) Does interference theory predict too much forgetting? *Journal of Verbal Learning and Verbal Behavior*, 2, 40-48 [5].

POSTMAN, L. (1964) Short-term memory and incidental learning. In A. W.

Melton (Ed.) *Categories of Human Learning.* New York: Academic Press **[8]**.

POSTMAN, L. (1971) Organization and interference. *Psychological Review,* 78, 290-302 **[8]**.

POSTMAN, L. (1975) Verbal learning and memory. *Annual Review of Psychology,* 26, 291-336 **[6]**.

POSTMAN, L., ADAMS, P. A., & BOHM, A. M. (1956) Studies in incidental learning: V. Recall for order and associative clustering. *Journal of Experimental Psychology,* 51, 334-42 **[8]**.

POSTMAN, L. & GREENBLOOM, R. (1967) Conditions of cue selection in the acquisition of paired-associate lists. *Journal of Experimental Psychology,* 73, 91-100 **[4]**.

POSTMAN, L. & KEPPEL, G. (Eds.) (1970) *Norms of Word Associations.* New York: Academic Press **[8]**.

POSTMAN, L. & PHILLIPS, L. W. (1965) Short-term temporal changes in free recall. *Quarterly Journal of Experimental Psychology,* 17, 132-38 **[6]**.

POSTMAN, L. & STARK, K. (1967) Studies of learning to learn. IV. Transfer from serial to paired-associate learning. *Journal of Verbal Learning and Verbal Behavior,* 6, 339-53 **[4]**.

POSTMAN, L. & STARK, K. (1969) Role of response availability in transfer and interference. *Journal of Experimental Psychology,* 79, 168-77 **[5]**.

POSTMAN, L., STARK, K., & FRASER, J. (1968) Temporal changes in interference. *Journal of Verbal Learning and Verbal Behavior,* 7, 672-94 **[5]**.

POTTER, R. K., KOPP, G. A., & GREEN, H. C. (1947) *Visible Speech.* New York: Van Nostrand **[9]**.

PRESTON, M. & YENI-KOMSHIAN, G. (1967) Studies of development of stop consonants in children. Haskins Laboratories, SR-11 **[9]**.

PRIMOFF, E. (1938) Backward and forward association as an organizing act in serial and in paired-associate learning. *Journal of Psychology,* 5, 375-95 **[4]**.

PRYTULAK, L. S. (1971) Natural language mediation. *Cognitive Psychology,* 2, 1-56 **[8]**.

QUILLIAN, M. R. (1969) The Teachable Language Comprehender. *Communications of the Association for Computing Machinery,* 12, 459-76 **[8]**.

RAYMOND, M. S. (1956) Case of fetishism treated by aversion therapy. *British Medical Journal,* 2, 854-57 **[3]**.

REICHER, G. M. (1969) Perceptual recognition as a function of meaningfulness of stimulus materials. *Journal of Experimental Psychology,* 81, 275-80 **[8]**.

RESTLE, F. (1955) A theory of discrimination learning. *Psychological Review,* 62, 11-19 **[12]**.

RESTLE, F. (1962) The selection of strategies in cue learning. *Psychological Review,* 69, 329-43 **[12]**.

RESTLE, F. (1965) Significance of all-or-none learning. *Psychological Bulletin,* 64, 313-25 **[4]**.

RESTORFF, H. VON (1933) Analyse von Vorgangen im Spurenfeld. I. Über die Wirkung von Bereichsbildungen im Spurenfeld. *Psychologie Forschung,* 18, 299-342 **[4]**.

RHEINGOLD, H. L., GEWIRTZ, J. L., & ROSS, H. W. (1959) Social conditioning of vocalizations in the infant. *Journal of Comparative and Physiological Psychology,* 52, 68-73 **[9]**.

RHEINGOLD, H. L., STANLEY, W. C., & COOLEY, J. A. (1962) Method for studying exploratory behavior in infants. *Science,* 136, 1054-55 **[3]**.

RIBBACK, A. & UNDERWOOD, B. J. (1950) An empirical explanation of the skewness of the bowed serial position curve. *Journal of Experimental Psychology,* 40, 329-35 **[4]**.

RIBOT, T. (1887) *Diseases of Memory: An Essay in the Positive Psychology.* Translated by W. H. Smith, New York: D. Appleton Co. **[6]**.

RICHARDSON, J. (1972) Encoding and stimulus selection in paired-associate verbal learning. In A. W. Melton and E. Martin (Eds.) *Coding Processes in Human Memory.* Washington, D.C.: V. H. Winston & Sons **[8]**.

RICKARD, H. O. & MUNDY, M. B. (1965) Direct manipulation of stuttering behavior: An experimental-clinical approach. In L. P. Ullman and L. Krasner (Eds.) *Case Studies in Behavior Modification.* New York: Holt, Rinehart & Winston **[3]**.

RILEY, D. A. (1958) The nature of the effective stimulus in animal discrimination learning: Transposition reconsidered. *Psychological Review,* 65, 1-7 **[2]**.

RILEY, D. A. (1962) Memory for form. In L. Postman (Ed.) *Psychology in the Making.* New York: Knopf **[5]**.

ROBINSON, E. S. (1927) The "similarity" factor in retroaction. *American Journal of Psychology,* 39, 297-312 **[5]**.

ROBINSON, E. S. (1932) *Association Theory Today.* New York: Appleton-Century-Crofts **[4]**.

ROCK, I. (1957) The role of repetition in associative learning. *American Journal of Psychology,* 70, 186-93 **[4]**.

ROCK, I. & HEIMER, W. (1959) Further evidence of one-trial associative learning. *American Journal of Psychology,* 72, 1-16 **[4]**.

ROHRMAN, N. L. (1968) The role of syntactic structure in the recall of English nominalizations. *Journal of Verbal Learning and Verbal Behavior,* 7, 904-12 **[11]**.

ROHWER, W. D. (1966) Constraint, syntax, and meaning. *Journal of Verbal Learning and Verbal Behavior,* 5, 541-47 **[8]**.

RUMELHART, D. E., LINDSAY, P. H., NORMAN, D. A. (1972) A process model for long-term memory. In E. Tulving and W. Donaldson (Eds.) *Organization and Memory.* New York: Academic Press **[8, 13]**.

RUSSELL, W. A. & STORMS, L. H. (1955) Implicit verbal chaining in paired-associate learning. *Journal of Experimental Psychology,* 49, 287-93 **[4]**.

RUSSELL, W. R. & NATHAN, P. W. (1946) Traumatic amnesia. *Brain,* 69, 280-300 **[6]**.

SABA, A. K. & TURNAGE, T. W. (1973) Unit-sequence interference in short-term memory. *Journal of Experimental Psychology*, 98, 328-34 **[5]**.

SACHS, J. S. (1967) Recognition memory for syntactic and semantic aspects of connected discourse. *Perception and Psychophysics*, 2, 437-42 **[11]**.

SAMUELS, I. (1959) Reticular mechanisms and behavior. *Psychological Bulletin*, 56, 1-25 **[7]**.

SAVIN, H. B. & BEVER, T. G. (1970) The non-perceptual reality of the phoneme. *Journal of Verbal Learning and Verbal Behavior*, 9, 295-302 **[9]**.

SAVIN, H. B. & PERCHONOCK, E. (1965) Grammatical structure and the immediate recall of English sentences. *Journal of Verbal Learning and Verbal Behavior*, 4, 348-53 **[11]**.

SCHATZ, C. (1954) The role of context in the perception of stops. *Language*, 30, 47-56 **[9]**.

SCHEIN, E. A. (1956) The Chinese indoctrination program for prisoners of war: A study of attempted "brainwashing." *Psychiatry*, 19, 149-72 **[3]**.

SCHILLER, P. H. & SMITH, M. C. (1966) Detection in metacontrast. *Journal of Experimental Psychology*, 71, 32-39 **[7]**.

SCHWARTZ, M. & BRYDEN, P. M. (1966) Retrieval and the effects of changing elements of a repeating sequence. Paper presented at the Canadian Psychological Association Convention **[6]**.

SCHWITZGEBEL, R. L. (1967) Short-term operant conditioning of adolescent offenders in socially relevant variables. *Journal of Abnormal Psychology*, 72, 134-42 **[3]**.

SENDEN, M. VON (1932) *Raum- und Gestaltauffasung bei Operierten Blindgeborenen Vor und Nach der Operation*. Leipzig: Barth **[7]**.

SHANKWEILER, D. (1966) Effects of temporal-lobe damage on perception of dichotically presented melodies. *Journal of Comparative and Physiological Psychology*, 62, 115-19 **[9]**.

SHANKWEILER, D. (1971) An analysis of laterality effects in speech perception. In D. L. Horton and J. J. Jenkins (Eds.) *The Perception of Language*. Columbus, Ohio: Charles E. Merrill **[9]**.

SHANKWEILER, D. & STUDDERT-KENNEDY, M. (1967) Identification of consonants and vowels presented to left and right ears. *Quarterly Journal of Experimental Psychology*, 19, 59-63 [9].

SHANNON, C. E. & WEAVER, W. (1949) The Mathematical Theory of Communication. Urbana: University of Illinois Press **[7]**.

SHIELDS, J. L., MCHUGH, A., & MARTIN, J. G. (1974) Reaction time to phoneme targets as a function of rhythmic cues in continuous speech. *Journal of Experimental Psychology*, 102, 250-55 **[9, 11]**.

SHIFFRIN, R. M. (1970) Memory search. In D. A. Norman (Ed.) *Models of Memory*. New York: Academic Press **[6]**.

SHIFFRIN, R. M. & ATKINSON, R. C. (1969) Storage and retrieval processes in long-term memory. *Psychological Review*, 76, 179-93 **[6]**.

SHUELL, T. J. (1969) Clustering and organization in free recall. *Psychological Bulletin*, 5, 353-74 **[8]**.

SHUELL, T. J. & KEPPEL, G. (1967) A further test of the chaining hypothesis of serial learning. *Journal of Verbal Learning and Verbal Behavior, 6,* 439-45 **[4]**.

SHULMAN, H. G. (1971) Similarity effects in short-term memory. *Psychological Bulletin,* 75, 399-415 **[6]**.

SHULMAN, H. G. (1972) Semantic confusion errors in short-term memory. *Journal of Verbal Learning and Verbal Behavior,* 11, 221-27 **[6]**.

SINGH, S. & WOODS, D. (1970) Multidimensional scaling of 12 American English vowels. *Journal of the Acoustical Society of America,* 48, 104 **[9]**.

SIQUELAND, E. R. & LIPSITT, L. P. (1966) Conditioned head-turning in human newborns. *Journal of Experimental Child Psychology,* 3, 356-76 **[3]**.

SKINNER, B. F. (1953) Teaching machines. *Science,* 128, 969-77 **[3]**.

SKINNER, B. F. (1957) *Verbal Behavior.* Englewood Cliffs, N.J.: Prentice-Hall **[11]**.

SKINNER, B. F. (1961) *Cumulative Record* (3rd ed.) Englewood Cliffs, N.J.: Prentice-Hall **[3]**.

SKINNER, B. F. (1938, 1966) *The Behavior of Organisms.* Englewood Cliffs, N.J.: Prentice-Hall **[2, 3, 4, 13]**.

SKINNER, B. F. (1971) *Beyond Freedom and Dignity.* New York: Knopf **[3]**.

SLAMECKA, N. J. (1964) An inquiry into the doctrine of remote associations. *Psychological Review,* 71, 61-76 **[4]**.

SLOBIN, D. I. (1971) *Psycholinguistics.* Glenview: Scott, Foresman, and Co. **[10]**.

SLOBIN, D. I. (1973) Cognitive prerequisites for the development of grammar. In C. A. Ferguson and D. I. Slobin (Eds.) *Studies of Child Language Development.* New York: Holt, Rinehart and Winston **[11]**.

SLOBIN, D. I. & WELSH, C. A. (1971) Elicited imitation as a research tool in development psycholinguistics. In C. S. Lauatelli (Ed.) *Language Training in Early Childhood Education.* Urbana: University of Illinois Press **[11]**.

SPELT, D. K. (1938) Conditioned responses in the human fetus *in utero. Psychological Bulletin,* 35, 712-13 **[3]**.

SPENCE, K. W. (1936) The nature of discrimination learning in animals. *Psychological Review,* 43, 427-49 **[2]**.

SPENCE, K. W. (1937) The differential response in animals to stimuli varying within a single dimension. *Psychological Review,* 44, 430-44 **[2]**.

SPERLING, G. A. (1960) The information available in brief visual presentations. *Psychological Monographs,* 74, Whole No. 498 **[7, 13]**.

SPERLING, G. A. (1963) A model for visual memory tasks. *Human Factors,* 5, 19-31 **[7]**.

STAATS, A. W. & STAATS, C. K. (1963) *Complex Human Behavior.* New York: Holt, Rinehart, and Winston **[9, 11]**.

STARK, K. (1968) Transfer from serial to paired-associate learning: A reappraisal. *Journal of Verbal Learning and Verbal Behavior,* 7, 20-30 **[4]**.

STERNBERG, S. (1966) High-speed scanning in human memory. *Science,* 153, 652-54 **[7]**.

STERNBERG, S. (1969) Memory-scanning: Mental processes revealed by reaction-time experiments. *American Scientist,* 57, 421-57. Also in J. S. Antrobus (Ed.) *Cognition and Affect.* Boston: Little, Brown (1970) **[7]**.

STEVENS, K. N. & HOUSE, K. S. (1956) Studies of formant transitions using a vocal tract analog. *Journal of the Acoustical Society of America,* 28, 578-85 **[9]**.

STEVENS, S. S. (1951) Mathematics, measurement, and psychophysics. In S. S. Stevens (Ed.) *Handbook of Experimental Psychology.* New York: Wiley **[2]**.

STUDDERT-KENNEDY, M. (1970) The perception of speech. *Status Report on Speech Research.* Haskins Laboratories, 23, 15-48 **[9]**.

STUDDERT-KENNEDY, M. & SHANKWEILER, D. (1970) Hemispheric specialization for speech perception. *Journal of the Acoustical Society of America,* 48, 579-94 **[9]**.

STUDDERT-KENNEDY, M., SHANKWEILER, D., & PISONI, D. (1972) Auditory and phonetic processes in speech perception: Evidence from a dichotic study. *Cognitive Psychology,* 3, 455-66 **[9]**.

SUPPES, P. & SCHLAG-REY, M. (1965) Observable changes in hypotheses under positive reinforcement. *Science,* 148, 661-62 **[12]**.

TAFFEL, C. (1955) Anxiety and the conditioning of verbal behavior. *Journal of Abnormal and Social Psychology,* 51, 496-501 **[3]**.

THOMPSON, R. F. (1969) Neurophysiology and thought: The neural substrates of thinking. In J. F. Voss (Ed.), *Approaches to Thought.* Columbus, Ohio: Charles E. Merrill **[7]**.

THORNDIKE, E. L. (1898) Animal intelligence: An experimental study of the associative processes in animals. *Psychological Review, Monograph Supplement,* 2, No. 8. **[1]**.

THORNDIKE, E. L. (1913) *The Psychology of Learning.* New York: Teachers College **[2, 4]**.

THORNDIKE, E. L. (1932) *The Fundamentals of Learning.* New York: Teachers College **[1, 2, 4]**.

THORNDIKE, E. L. (1933) An experimental study of rewards. *Teachers College Contributions to Education,* No. 580. New York: Teachers College, Columbia University **[2]**.

THORNDIKE, E. L. (1935) *The Psychology of Wants, Interests, and Attitudes.* New York: Appleton-Century-Crofts **[8]**.

THUMB, A. & MARBE, K. (1901) *Experimentelle Untersuchungen über die psychologischen Grundlagen der sprachlichen Analogiebildung.* Leipzig: W. Englemann **[8]**.

TRABASSO, T. R. & BOWER, G. H. (1964) Memory in concept identification. *Psychonomic Science,* 1, 133-34 **[12]**.

TRABASSO, T. R. & BOWER, G. H. (1966) Presolution dimensional shifts in concept identification: A test of the sampling with replacement axiom in all-or-none models. *Journal of Mathematical Psychology,* 3, 163-73 **[12]**.

TRABASSO, T. R. & BOWER, G. H. (1968) *Attention in Learning: Theory and Research.* New York: Wiley **[7, 12]**.

TRABASSO, T. R., ROLLINS, H., & SHAUGHNESSY, E. (1971) Storage and verification stages in processing concepts. *Cognitive Psychology,* 2, 239-89 **[12]**.

TREISMAN, A. M. (1960) Contextual cues in selective listening. *Quarterly Journal of Experimental Psychology,* 12, 242-48 **[7]**.

TREISMAN, A. M. (1961) *Attention and Speech.* Unpublished doctoral dissertation, University of Oxford **[7]**.

TREISMAN, A. M. (1964a) Monitoring and storage of irrelevant messages in selective attention. *Journal of Verbal Learning and Verbal Behavior,* 3, 449-59 **[7]**.

TREISMAN, A. M. (1964b) Selective attention in man. *British Medical Bulletin,* 20, 12-16 **[7]**.

TREISMAN, A. M. (1964c) The effect of irrelevant material on the efficiency of selective listening. *American Journal of Psychology,* 77, 533-46 **[7]**.

TREISMAN, A. M. & GEFFEN, G. (1967) Selective attention: Perception or response? *Quarterly Journal of Experimental Psychology,* 19, 1-17 **[7]**.

TULVING, E. (1962) Subjective organization in free recall of "unrelated" words. *Psychological Review,* 69, 344-54 **[8]**.

TULVING, E. (1966) Subjective organization and effects of repetition in multitrial free-recall learning. *Journal of Verbal Learning and Verbal Behavior,* 5, 193-97 **[8]**.

TULVING, E. (1968) Theoretical issues in free recall. In T. R. Dixon and D. L. Horton (Eds.) *Verbal Behavior and General Behavior Theory.* Englewood Cliffs, N.J.: Prentice-Hall **[6, 8]**.

TULVING, E. & MADIGAN, S. A. (1970) Memory and verbal learning. *Annual Review of Psychology,* 21, 437-84 **[5, 6]**.

TULVING, E. & OSLER, S. (1967) Transfer effects in whole/part free-recall learning. *Canadian Journal of Psychology,* 21, 253-62 **[8]**.

TULVING, E. & OSLER, S. (1968) Effectiveness of retrieval cues in memory for words. *Journal of Experimental Psychology,* 77, 593-601 **[8]**.

TULVING, E. & PEARLSTONE, Z. (1966) Availability versus accessibility of information in memory for words. *Journal of Verbal Learning and Verbal Behavior,* 5, 381-91 **[8]**.

TURNAGE, T. W. (1967) Unit-sequence interference in short-term memory. *Journal of Verbal Learning and Verbal Behavior,* 6, 61-65 **[5]**.

TURNAGE, T. W. & McCULLOUGH, T. A. (1968) Letter-sequence and unit-sequence effects during learning and retention. *Journal of Experimental Psychology,* 76, 141-46 **[5]**.

TURNAGE, T. W. & McGINNIES, E. (1973) A cross-cultural comparison of the effects of presentation mode and meaningfulness on short-term recall. *American Journal of Psychology,* 86, 369-81 **[6]**.

TURNAGE, T. W. & STEINMETZ, J. I. (1971) Unit-sequence interference and short-term recall. *American Journal of Psychology,* 84, 112-22 **[5]**.

UNDERWOOD, B. J. (1948) "Spontaneous recovery" of verbal associations. *Journal of Experimental Psychology,* 38, 429-39 **[5]**.

UNDERWOOD, B. J. (1957) Interference and forgetting. *Psychological Review,* 64, 49-60 **[5]**.

UNDERWOOD, B. J. (1961) An evaluation of the Gibson theory of verbal learning. In C. N. Cofer (Ed.) *Verbal Learning and Verbal Behavior.* New York: McGraw-Hill **[4]**.

UNDERWOOD, B. J. (1963) Stimulus selection in verbal learning. In C. N. Cofer and B. S. Musgrave (Eds.) *Verbal Behavior and Learning.* New York: McGraw-Hill **[4, 8]**.

UNDERWOOD, B. J. (1964) Degree of learning and the measurement of forgetting. *Journal of Verbal Learning and Verbal Behavior,* 3, 112-29 **[5, 6]**.

UNDERWOOD, B. J. (1966) *Experimental Psychology* (2nd ed.) Englewood Cliffs, N.J.: Prentice-Hall **[5]**.

UNDERWOOD, B. J. (1969) Attributes of memory. *Psychological Review,* 76, 559-73 **[5, 6, 8]**.

UNDERWOOD, B. J. (1972) Are we overloading memory? In A. W. Melton and E. Martin (Eds.) *Coding Processes In Human Memory.* Washington, D.C.: V. H. Winston and Sons **[6]**.

UNDERWOOD, B. J. & EKSTRAND, B. R. (1966) An analysis of some shortcomings in the interference theory of forgetting. *Psychological Review,* 73, 540-49 **[5]**.

UNDERWOOD, B. J. & FREUND, J. S. (1970) Relative frequency judgments and verbal discrimination learning. *Journal of Experimental Psychology,* 83, 279-85 **[5]**.

UNDERWOOD, B. J., HAM, M., & EKSTRAND, B. (1962) Cue selection in paired-associate learning. *Journal of Experimental Psychology,* 64, 405-9 **[4]**.

UNDERWOOD, B. J. & KEPPEL, G. (1962) One trial learning. *Journal of Verbal Learning and Verbal Behavior,* 1, 1-13 **[4]**.

UNDERWOOD, B. J. & KEPPEL, G. (1963) Retention as a function of degree of learning and letter-sequence interference. *Psychological Monographs,* 77, No. 4 **[5]**.

UNDERWOOD, B. J. & POSTMAN, L. (1960) Extraexperimental sources of interference in forgetting. *Psychological Review,* 67, 73-95 **[5]**.

UNDERWOOD, B. J., REHULA, R., & KEPPEL G. (1962) Item selection in paired-associate learning. *American Journal of Psychology,* 75, 353-71 **[4]**.

UNDERWOOD, B. J. & SCHULZ, R. W. (1960) *Meaningfulness and Verbal Learning.* New York: J. B. Lippincott **[4, 5, 8]**.

VERHAVE, T. (1966) The pigeon as a quality-control inspector. *American Psychologist,* 21, 109-15 **[3]**.

VERPLANCK, W. S. (1955) The control of the content of conversation: Reinforcement of statements of opinion. *Journal of Abnormal and Social Psychology,* 51, 668-76 **[3]**.

Voss, J. F. (1968) Serial acquisition as a function of successively occurring list items. *Journal of Experimental Psychology,* 78, 456-62 **[4]**.

Voss, J. F. (1969) Serial acquisition and stage of learning. *Journal of Experimental Psychology,* 79, 220-25 **[4]**.

WANNER, H. E. (1968) *On remembering, forgetting and understanding sentences: A study of the deep structure hypothesis.* Ph. D. dissertation, Harvard University **[11]**.

WARREN, R. M. (1969) Auditory sequence: Confusion of patterns other than speech or music. *Science,* 164, 586-87 **[9]**.

WARREN, R. M. (1970) Perceptual restoration of missing speech sounds. *Science,* 167, 392-93 **[9]**.

WARREN, R. M. (1971) Identification time for phonemic components of graded complexity and for spelling of speech. *Perception and Psychophysics,* 9, 345-47 **[9]**.

WATSON, E. H. & LOWREY, G. H. (1954) *Growth and Development of Children* (2nd ed.). Chicago: The Year Book Publishers **[3]**.

WATSON, J. B. (1913) Psychology as the behaviorist views it. *Psychological Review,* 20, 158-77 **[1, 8]**.

WATSON, J. B. & RAYNER, R. (1920) Conditioned emotional reactions. *Journal of Experimental Psychology,* 3, 1-14 **[3]**.

WAUGH, N. C. (1961) Free versus serial recall. *Journal of Experimental Psychology,* 62, 496-502 **[8]**.

WAUGH, N. C. & NORMAN, D. A. (1965) Primary memory. *Psychological Review,* 72, 89-104 **[6, 13]**.

WHITE, B. L. (1971) *Human Infants: Experience and Psychological Development.* Englewood Cliffs, N.J.: Prentice-Hall **[3]**.

WICKELGREN, W. A. (1965) Distinctive features and errors in short-term memory for English vowels. *Journal of the Acoustical Society of America,* 38, 583-88 **[9]**.

WICKELGREN, W. A. (1966) Short-term recognition memory for single letters and phonetic similarity of retroactive interference. *Quarterly Journal of Experimental Psychology,* 18, 55-62 **[9]**.

WICKELGREN, W. A. (1969) Auditory or articulatory coding in verbal short-term memory. *Psychological Review,* 76, 232-35 **[9]**.

WICKENS, D. D. (1970) Encoding categories of words: An empirical approach to meaning. *Psychological Review,* 77, 1-15 **[6]**.

WICKENS, D. D. (1972) Characteristics of word encoding. In A. W. Melton and E. Martin (Eds.) *Coding Processes in Human Memory.* Washington, D.C.: V. H. Winston & Sons **[6, 8]**.

WILLIAMS, M. (1969) Traumatic retrograde amnesia and normal forgetting. In G. A. Talland and N. C. Waugh (Eds.) *The Pathology of Memory.* New York: Academic Press **[6]**.

WINOGRAD, E. & RAINES, S. R. (1972) Semantic and temporal variation in recognition memory. *Journal of Verbal Learning and Verbal Behavior,* 11, 114-19 **[6]**.

WITMER, L. R. (1935) The association value of three-place consonant syllables. *Journal of Genetic Psychology,* 47, 337-60 **[4]**.

WOLFF, J. L. (1967) Concept-shift and discrimination-reversal in humans. *Psychological Bulletin,* 68, 369-408 **[12]**.

WOLPE, J. (1958) *Psychotherapy by reciprocal inhibition.* Stanford: Stanford University Press **[3]**.

WOLPE, J. (1962) The experimental foundations of some new psychotherapeutic methods. In A. J. Bachrach (Ed.) *Experimental Foundations of Clinical Psychology.* New York: Basic Books **[3]**.

WOLPE, J. & LAZARUS, A. (1968) *Behavioral Therapy Techniques.* New York: Pergamon Press **[3]**.

WOOD, C. C., GOFF, W. R., & DAY, R. S. (1971) Auditory evoked potentials during speech perception. *Science,* 173, 1248-51 **[9]**.

WOODWORTH, R. S. (1938) *Experimental Psychology.* New York: Holt, Rinehart, and Winston **[8]**.

WOODWORTH, R. S. & SCHLOSBERG, H. (1954) *Experimental Psychology* (Revised Edition). New York: Holt, Rinehart, and Winston **[6, 8]**.

WOODWORTH, R. S. & SHEEHAN, M. R. (1964) *Contemporary Schools of Psychology* (3rd ed.) New York: Ronald **[1]**.

WULF, F. (1922) Über die Veränderung von Vorstellungen (Gedäctnis und Gestalt). *Psychologische Forschung,* 1, 333-73 **[5, 13]**.

YOUNG, R. K. (1959) A comparison of two methods of learning serial associations. *American Journal of Psychology,* 72, 554-59 **[4]**.

YOUNG, R. K. (1961) The stimulus in serial verbal learning. *American Journal of Psychology,* 74, 517-28 **[4]**.

YOUNG, R. K. (1962) Tests of three hypotheses about the effective stimulus in serial learning. *Journal of Experimental Psychology,* 63, 307-13 **[4]**.

YOUNG, R. K. (1968) Serial Learning. In T. R. Dixon and D. L. Horton (Eds.) *Verbal Behavior and General Behavior Theory.* Englewood Cliffs, N.J.: Prentice-Hall **[4, 13]**.

YOUNG, R. K., HAKES, D. T., & HICKS, R. Y. (1965) Effect of list length in the Ebbinghaus derived-list paradigm. *Journal of Experimental Psychology,* 70, 338-41 **[4]**.

YOUNISS, J. (1964) Concept transfer as a function of shifts, age, and deafness. *Child Development,* 35, 695-700 **[12]**.

Name Index

Subject Index [1]

[1] Material referred to in the conclusion section of each chapter does not appear in the Subject Index.